PLA

FOOTBALL ANNUAL

2004–2005

57th edition

Editors: Glenda Rollin and
Jack Rollin

headline

Cover photographs Front and spine: Cristiano Ronaldo (Manchester U) –
Empics; back: Matthew Upson (Birmingham C) – *Sportsphoto*.

ISBN 0 7553 1312 7

Typeset by Wearset Ltd, Boldon, Tyne and Wear

Printed and bound in Great Britain by
Clays Ltd, St Ives plc

Headline's policy is to use papers that are natural, renewable and recyclable
products and made from wood grown in sustainable forests. The logging and
manufacturing processes are expected to conform to the environmental regulations
of the country of origin.

HEADLINE BOOK PUBLISHING
A division of Hodder Headline
338 Euston Road
London NW1 3BH

www.headline.co.uk
www.hodderheadline.com

CONTENTS

European and International Football

Other Football

Information and Records

EDITORIAL

Without doubt the performance of the England team in Euro 2004 dominated any reflection of the season as a whole. We made our not unaccustomed exit via the penalty spot and those who prefer to search for excuses rather than analyse the underlying problems which exist at this level and arguably in our game as a whole had plenty of scope for such discussion.

The first disappointment came through the injury to Wayne Rooney in the early stages of the quarter-final against host nation Portugal. The Everton striker had set the tournament alight with his goalscoring efforts. That was blow number one. Then came the next when Sol Campbell headed what appeared to be the winning goal in normal time. This was ruled out and though England came back to equalise in the extra period at 2-2, the penalty shoot-out again proved their undoing.

But though the euphoria which is now part of any national team in any sport in this country, is based on little more than hope, perhaps more diagnosis and fewer post-mortems would be of more constructive use.

Taking match by match, the French were lucky to survive only being a goal down. Indeed had David Beckham not had his penalty saved by Fabien Barthez, at 2-0 England surely would have gone on to win against a French team showing definite signs of being over the hill in footballing terms. In their case it was to be proved again and again before their own elimination.

A poorly defended free kick followed by a penalty and England on the brink had it stolen from them. Beckham having missed his last penalty against Turkey in a qualifying match, should not have taken the kick, especially against his former Manchester United colleague. Michael Owen was the player who should have been entrusted with the responsibility.

The Swiss proved tricky opponents and England might have been flattered against a ten-man team late on, though Rooney briefly made it as the youngest goalscorer ever in a European Championship final tournament. But a 3-0 win was encouraging and though the Croatian defence was dreadfully leaky, a 4-2 success shot England into the last eight.

Thus came the Portugal match. Owen scored first and it was not until late in the match that the home team levelled the score. Then came the disallowed goal. Campbell was able to take advantage of his central defensive colleague John Terry in climbing to head what appeared to be a goal, but Terry was clearly impeding the Portuguese goalkeeper, regardless of whether he would have reached the ball or not.

Long before the penalties arrived, our game plan seemed to have been destroyed with the disappearance of Rooney to the treatment room. Retreating seems to be a negative ingredient of the planning. Come the shoot-out and few would have risked a bet that it would not be Portugal to come out on top.

The next mistake was to allow Beckham to take the first attempt. A third time loser, the odds of him missing must have been short. Again Owen should have taken the first one, with Becks perhaps slotted in lower down the order. As far as David James was concerned at the other end of the lottery, which continues to be no way to decide any match whatever the level, he not only failed to seem likely to get in the way of any of them, he had the galling experience of being finally beaten by his opposing number. It was academic that Darius Vassell had had his effort stopped by the same Ricardo.

But these are cosmetic reasons for dismissal. The Portuguese were not at their most fluid, but certainly had the better of the play and given that this was a tournament of the underdog, England might have progressed further. Alas we are still far removed from the top flight and could be considered in the same straits as Germany, Spain, Italy and France who all seem to be passing through a decline.

Indeed it might be said that the emphasis on club football especially in the European arena is doing nothing for any of the top nations when it comes to international competition. The growth in stature of the Champions League and to a lesser degree the UEFA Cup has overshadowed national considerations. Our own Premier League continues to be regarded as the leading domestic competition in Europe and attracts outstanding players. Is this another excuse to be put forward to those seeking a scapegoat for a national team which still looks back to 1966 with misty eyes as the last time a trophy was lifted; in fact the only such occasion in the history of the game.

STOP PRESS

Summer transfers completed and pending: **Premier Division: Arsenal:** Robin Van Persie (Feyenoord) Undisclosed; **Aston Villa:** Martin Laursen (AC Milan) £3m; Peter Crouch (Aston Villa) £2m; **Birmingham C:** Mikael Forssell (Chelsea) Loan; Emile Heskey (Liverpool) £6,250,000; Muzzy Izzet (Leicester C) Free; Julian Gray (Crystal Palace) Free; Mario Melchiot (Chelsea) Free; **Blackburn R:** Paul Dickov (Leicester C) £150,000; Javier De Pedro (Real Sociedad) Undisclosed; Dominic Matteo (Leeds U) Free; **Bolton W:** Michael Bridges (Leeds U) Free; Les Ferdinand (Leicester C) Free; Radhi Jaidi (Esperance Tunis) Free; **Charlton Ath:** Stephan Andersen (AB Copenhagen) £721,000; Bryan Hughes (Birmingham C) Free; Dennis Rommedahl (PSV Eindhoven) £2m; Talal El Karkouri (Paris St. Germain) £1m; **Chelsea:** Peter Cech (Rennes) Undisclosed; Arjen Robben (PSV Eindhoven) £12m; Paulo Ferreira (Porto) £13.2m; **Crystal Palace:** Gabor Kiraly (Hertha Berlin) Free; Mark Hudson (Fulham) Undisclosed; **Everton:** Marcus Bent (Ipswich T) £450,000; Bjarni Vidarsson (Hafnarfjordur) Undisclosed; **Liverpool:** Djibril Cisse (Auxerre) £14m; Josemi (Malaga) Undisclosed; Djimi Traore (Laval) Undisclosed; **Leicester C:** Ben Thatcher (Leicester C) Undisclosed; **Manchester U:** Alan Smith (Leeds U) £7m; Gabriel Heinze (Paris St Germain) £6.9m; Liam Miller (Celtic) Free; Gerard Pique (Barcelona) Undisclosed; Giuseppe Rossi (Parma) Undisclosed; **Middlesbrough:** Michael Reiziger (Barcelona) Free; Mark Viduka (Leeds U) £4.5m; Jimmy Floyd Hasselbaink (Chelsea) Free; **Newcastle U:** James Milner (Leeds U) £5m; **Norwich C:** David Bentley (Arsenal) Loan; Paul Gallacher (Dundee U) Free; Youssef Safri (Coventry C) £500,000; **Portsmouth:** Andy Griffin (Newcastle U) Free; **Southampton:** Mikael Nilsson (Halmstad) Undisclosed; Jelle Van Damme (Ajax) Undisclosed; Peter Crouch (Aston Villa) £2m; **Tottenham H:** Rodrigo Defendi (Cruzeiro) £600,000; Marton Fulop (MTK) Undisclosed; Paul Robinson (Leeds U) £2m; Sean Davis (Fulham) Undisclosed; Pedro Mendes (Porto) £2m; Leigh Mills (Swindon) Undisclosed; **West Bromwich Albion:** Martin Albrechtsen (FC Copenhagen) £2.7m; Darren Purse (Birmingham C) £750,000; Riccardo Scimeca (Leicester C) Undisclosed.

Football League Championship: Burnley: Mike Duff (Cheltenham T) £30,000; **Coventry C:** Stephen Hughes (Charlton Ath) Free; Neil Wood (Manchester U) Free; **Gillingham:** Iwan Roberts (Norwich C) Free; **Leeds U:** Julian Joachim (Coventry C) Free; Matthew Spring (Luton T) Free; Paul Butler (Wolverhampton W) Free; **Leicester C:** Jason Wilcox (Leeds U) Free; Dion Dublin (Aston Villa) Free; **Nottingham F:** Kris Commons (Stoke C) Free; **Rotherham U:** Paolo Vernazza (Watford) Free; Phil Gilchrist (WBA) Free; **Stoke C:** Steve Simonsen (Everton) Free; **Sunderland:** Stephen Caldwell (Newcastle U) Free; **Watford:** Andy Ferrell (Newcastle U) Free; **Wigan Ath:** David Wright (Crewe Alex) Undisclosed.

Football League 1: Barnsley: Stephen McPhail (Leeds U) Free; Nick Colgan (Hibernian) Free; **Bristol C:** Bradley Orr (Newcastle U) Free; Paul Heffernan (Notts Co) £125,000; **Chesterfield:** Alex Bailey (Arsenal) Free; Shane Nicholson (Tranmere R) Free; **Colchester U:** Aidan Davison (Grimsby T) Free; **Doncaster R:** Nick Fenton (Notts Co) Free; **Huddersfield T:** Junior Mendes (Mansfield T) Free; Chris Brandon (Chesterfield) Free; **Hull C:** Roland Edge (Hibernian) Free; Junior Lewis (Leicester C) Free; Nick Barmby (Leeds U) Free; **Oldham Ath:** Rodney Jack (Rushden & D) Free; **Port Vale:** Dean Smith (Sheffield W) Free; **Sheffield W:** Steve MacLean (Rangers) Free; **Wrexham:** Dean Bennett (Kidderminster H) Free.

Football League 2: Bristol R: Paul Trollope (Northampton T) Free; **Cambridge U:** Abdu El Kholti (Yeovil T) Free; Ashley Nicholls (Darlington) Free; **Cheltenham T:** John Melligan (Wolverhampton W) £25,000; **Grimsby T:** Ashley Sestanovich (Sheffield U) Loan; **Lincoln C:** Dean West (Burnley) Free; **Macclesfield T:** Mark Bailey (Lincoln C) Free; **Northampton T:** David Rowson (Partick T) Free; **Notts Co:** Glynn Hurst (Chesterfield) Free; Chris Palmer (Derby Co) Free; **Oxford U:** David Woozley (Torquay U) Free; Leo Roget (Rushden & D) Free; Tommy Mooney (Swindon T) Free; **Southend U:** Lewis Hunt (Derby Co) Free; **Torquay U:** Gareth Owen (Stoke C) Free.

LEAGUE REVIEW AND CLUB SECTION

On Sunday 25 April at White Hart Lane, Arsenal finally clinched the FA Premier League title which had been predicted for months. But the important statistic at the time was that they had achieved the honour without losing a game in the competition. On top of this they then succeeded in the difficult task of remaining undefeated for their other four fixtures. The new Invincibles had arrived.

Certainly there were periods in matches in which they were unplayable and the overall standard was of the highest quality. Manager Arsene Wenger had made only minor changes to his squad for the season but swooped during the mid-winter transfer window to add the Spanish international striker Jose Antonio Reyes from Sevilla, to give the attack yet another option and dimension.

In fact Wenger was pretty consistent with his senior squad making judicious team changes when he felt it necessary, but overall using only 22 different players and one of these the young defender Justin Hoyte making a single appearance as a substitute.

There was only one ever present in the team, goalkeeper Jens Lehmann, the German recruited at the start of the season from Borussia Dortmund. Thierry Henry, arguably the jewel in the Wenger crown, missed only one match and was top scorer with 30 goals. He was both the PFA and Football Writers choice as Player of the Year. Kolo Toure who settled into a solid centre-back partnership with Sol Campbell, was absent only once but also made an outing from the bench.

Indeed injuries accounted for the fact that Fredrik Ljungberg and Patrick Vieira missed substantial chunks of the campaign. There were outstanding contributions from winger Robert Pires, second highest scorer with 14 goals, Edu the Brazilian midfield player who was used effectively as a replacement during games and England left-back Ashley Cole.

Having taken the title in that 2-2 draw at Tottenham, Arsenal continued to stack up the records. With two unbeaten games at the end of the 2002–03 season added on, Arsenal's run extended to 40 games. If they remain undefeated in the first three matches of the 2004–05 season they will set another top flight record currently held by Nottingham Forest from November 1977 to November 1978.

Chelsea were second 11 points behind the Gunners having overtaken Manchester United who had a disappointing end to the season. The crucial fourth place went to Liverpool who thus grabbed the other Champions League slot for the new season.

Of the promoted teams, Portsmouth did best with a useful start and finish which rescued them from possible relegation. They were 13th. Not so fortunate were Leicester City and Wolverhampton Wanderers who found the Premiership going too tough in the final analysis. Again the curse of going bottom at the turn of the year was proved correct for Wolves, though all three demoted teams finished on 33 points, Leeds United being sandwiched in between the other two. For Leeds in desperate financial straits, it meant their continued service in the Premier League was to end.

Official attendances were again at a new high with aggregate crowds numbering 13,303,133 for a healthy average of 35,008. The Football League, too, reported a seven per cent rise over the previous season.

Up from the First Division from automatic promotion were Norwich City and West Bromwich Albion. They were joined from the play-offs by Crystal Palace after an incredible rise from the depths of the division to beating West Ham United 1-0 in the final.

Walsall, Bradford City and Wimbledon, who found a new home at Milton Keynes were relegated to the Second Division, their places taken by Plymouth Argyle and Queens Park Rangers plus Brighton & Hove Albion through the play-offs.

The quartet demoted from the Second Division were Grimsby Town, Rushden & Diamonds, Notts County and Wycombe Wanderers. Doncaster Rovers, only a season from returning to the League won the Third Division and were accompanied by Hull City and Torquay United, while Huddersfield Town survived the penalty shoot-out in the play-offs.

Carlisle United after a valiant struggle to avoid the drop finally succumbed along with York City to go into the new Conference National, the newcomers being Shrewsbury Town after just one season out of the League, and Chester City the Conference champions, last in the Third Division in 1999–2000.

FA Barclaycard Premiership

		Home						Away						Total						
	P	W	D	L	F	A	W	D	L	F	A	W	D	L	F	A	Gd	Pts
1 Arsenal	38	15	4	0	40	14	11	8	0	33	12	26	12	0	73	26	47	90
2 Chelsea	38	12	4	3	34	13	12	3	4	33	17	24	7	7	67	30	37	79
3 Manchester U	38	12	4	3	37	15	11	2	6	27	20	23	6	9	64	35	29	75
4 Liverpool	38	10	4	5	29	15	6	8	5	26	22	16	12	10	55	37	18	60
5 Newcastle U	38	11	5	3	33	14	2	12	5	19	26	13	17	8	52	40	12	56
6 Aston Villa	38	9	6	4	24	19	6	5	8	24	25	15	11	12	48	44	4	56
7 Charlton Ath	38	7	6	6	29	29	7	5	7	22	22	14	11	13	51	51	0	53
8 Bolton W	38	6	8	5	24	21	8	3	8	24	35	14	11	13	48	56	-8	53
9 Fulham	38	9	4	6	29	21	5	6	8	23	25	14	10	14	52	46	6	52
10 Birmingham C	38	8	5	6	26	24	4	9	6	17	24	12	14	12	43	48	-5	50
11 Middlesbrough	38	8	4	7	25	23	5	5	9	19	29	13	9	16	44	52	-8	48
12 Southampton	38	8	6	5	24	17	4	5	10	20	28	12	11	15	44	45	-1	47
13 Portsmouth	38	10	4	5	35	19	2	5	12	12	35	12	9	17	47	54	-7	45
14 Tottenham H	38	9	4	6	33	27	4	2	13	14	30	13	6	19	47	57	-10	45
15 Blackburn R	38	5	4	10	25	31	7	4	8	26	28	12	8	18	51	59	-8	44
16 Manchester C	38	5	9	5	31	24	4	5	10	24	30	9	14	15	55	54	1	41
17 Everton	38	8	5	6	27	20	1	7	11	18	37	9	12	17	45	57	-12	39
18 Leicester C	38	3	10	6	19	28	3	5	11	29	37	6	15	17	48	65	-17	33
19 Leeds U	38	5	7	7	25	31	3	2	14	15	48	8	9	21	40	79	-39	33
20 Wolverhampton W	38	7	5	7	23	35	0	7	12	15	42	7	12	19	38	77	-39	33

LEADING GOALSCORERS 2003–04

FA BARCLAYCARD PREMIERSHIP

	League	Carling Cup	FA Cup	Other	Total
Thierry Henry (Arsenal)	30	0	3	6	39
Alan Shearer (Newcastle U)	22	0	0	6	28
Ruud Van Nistelrooy (Manchester U)	20	0	6	4	30
Louis Saha (Manchester U)	20	0	2	0	22
(including 13 League goals and 2 FA Cup goals for Fulham)					
Mikael Forssell (Birmingham C)	17	0	2	0	19
Nicolas Anelka (Manchester C)	16	0	4	4	24
Juan Pablo Angel (Aston Villa)	16	7	0	0	23
Michael Owen (Liverpool)	16	0	1	2	19
Ayegbeni Yakubu (Portsmouth)	16	2	1	0	19
Robert Pires (Arsenal)	14	0	1	4	19
James Beattie (Southampton)	14	3	0	0	17
Robbie Keane (Tottenham H)	14	1	1	0	16
Jimmy Floyd Hasselbaink (Chelsea)	12	2	1	2	17
Les Ferdinand (Leicester C)	12	0	1	0	13
Kevin Phillips (Southampton)	12	0	0	1	13
Mark Viduka (Leeds U)	11	0	1	0	12
Andy Cole (Blackburn R)	11	0	0	0	11

Other matches consist of European games, LDV Vans Trophy, Community Shield and Football League play-offs. Only goals scored in the respective divisions count in the table. Players listed in order of League goals total.

Nationwide Football League Division 1

				Home				Away					Total				
		P	W	D	L	F	A	W	D	L	F	A	W	D	L	F	A	Gd	Pts
1	Norwich C	46	18	3	2	44	15	10	7	6	35	24	28	10	8	79	39	40	94
2	WBA	46	14	5	4	34	16	11	6	6	30	26	25	11	10	64	42	22	86
3	Sunderland	46	13	8	2	33	15	9	5	9	29	30	22	13	11	62	45	17	79
4	West Ham U	46	12	7	4	42	20	7	10	6	25	25	19	17	10	67	45	22	74
5	Ipswich T	46	12	3	8	49	36	9	7	7	35	36	21	10	15	84	72	12	73
6	Crystal Palace	46	10	8	5	34	25	11	2	10	38	36	21	10	15	72	61	11	73
7	Wigan Ath	46	11	8	4	29	16	7	9	7	31	29	18	17	11	60	45	15	71
8	Sheffield U	46	11	6	6	37	25	9	5	9	28	31	20	11	15	65	56	9	71
9	Reading	46	11	6	6	29	25	9	4	10	26	32	20	10	16	55	57	-2	70
10	Millwall	46	11	8	4	28	15	7	7	9	27	33	18	15	13	55	48	7	69
11	Stoke C	46	11	7	5	35	24	7	5	11	23	31	18	12	16	58	55	3	66
12	Coventry C	46	9	9	5	34	22	8	5	10	33	32	17	14	15	67	54	13	65
13	Cardiff C	46	10	6	7	40	25	7	8	8	28	33	17	14	15	68	58	10	65
14	Nottingham F	46	8	9	6	33	25	7	6	10	28	33	15	15	16	61	58	3	60
15	Preston NE	46	11	7	5	43	29	4	7	12	26	42	15	14	17	69	71	-2	59
16	Watford	46	9	8	6	31	28	6	4	13	23	40	15	12	19	54	68	-14	57
17	Rotherham U	46	8	8	7	31	27	5	7	11	22	34	13	15	18	53	61	-8	54
18	Crewe Alex	46	11	3	9	33	26	3	8	12	24	40	14	11	21	57	66	-9	53
19	Burnley	46	9	6	8	37	32	4	8	11	23	45	13	14	19	60	77	-17	53
20	Derby Co	46	11	5	7	39	33	2	8	13	14	34	13	13	20	53	67	-14	52
21	Gillingham	46	10	1	12	28	34	4	8	11	20	33	14	9	23	48	67	-19	51
22	Walsall	46	8	7	8	29	31	5	5	13	16	34	13	12	21	45	65	-20	51
23	Bradford C	46	6	3	14	23	35	4	3	16	15	34	10	6	30	38	69	-31	36
24	Wimbledon	46	3	4	16	21	40	5	1	17	20	49	8	5	33	41	89	-48	29

NATIONWIDE DIVISION 1

	League	Carling Cup	FA Cup	Other	Total
Andy Johnson (Crystal Palace)	27	4	0	1	32
Marlon Harewood (West Ham U)	25	0	1	0	26
(including 12 League goals for Nottingham F)					
Robert Earnshaw (Cardiff C)	21	5	0	0	26
Robbie Blake (Burnley)	19	1	2	0	22
Dean Ashton (Crewe Alex)	19	1	0	0	20
Nathan Ellington (Wigan Ath)	18	1	0	0	19
Ricardo Fuller (Preston NE)	17	0	2	0	19
Darren Bent (Ipswich T)	16	0	0	1	17
Steve Jones (Crewe Alex)	15	1	0	0	16
Martin Butler (Rotherham U)	15	0	0	0	15
David Healy (Preston NE)	15	0	0	0	15
Marcus Stewart (Sunderland)	14	0	0	2	16
Darren Huckerby (Norwich C)	14	0	0	0	14
Dougie Freedman (Crystal Palace)	13	2	0	0	15
Patrick Agyemang (Gillingham)	13	0	0	0	13
(including 7 League goals for Wimbledon)					
Andy Reid (Nottingham F)	13	0	0	0	13
Peter Thorne (Cardiff C)	13	0	0	0	13

Nationwide Football League Division 2

			Home					Away					Total					
		P	W	D	L	F	A	W	D	L	F	A	W	D	L	F	A	Gd	Pts
1	Plymouth Arg	46	17	5	1	52	13	9	7	7	33	28	26	12	8	85	41	44	90
2	QPR	46	16	7	0	47	12	6	10	7	33	33	22	17	7	80	45	35	83
3	Bristol C	46	15	6	2	34	12	8	7	8	24	25	23	13	10	58	37	21	82
4	Brighton & HA	46	17	4	2	39	11	5	7	11	25	32	22	11	13	64	43	21	77
5	Swindon T	46	12	7	4	41	23	8	6	9	35	35	20	13	13	76	58	18	73
6	Hartlepool U	46	10	8	5	39	24	10	5	8	37	37	20	13	13	76	61	15	73
7	Port Vale	46	15	6	2	45	28	6	4	13	28	35	21	10	15	73	63	10	73
8	Tranmere R	46	13	7	3	36	18	4	9	10	23	38	17	16	13	59	56	3	67
9	Bournemouth	46	11	8	4	35	25	6	7	10	21	26	17	15	14	56	51	5	66
10	Luton T	46	14	6	3	44	27	3	9	11	25	39	17	15	14	69	66	3	66
11	Colchester U	46	11	8	4	33	23	6	5	12	19	33	17	13	16	52	56	-4	64
12	Barnsley	46	7	12	4	25	19	8	5	10	29	39	15	17	14	54	58	-4	62
13	Wrexham	46	9	6	8	27	21	8	3	12	23	39	17	9	20	50	60	-10	60
14	Blackpool	46	9	5	9	31	28	7	6	10	27	37	16	11	19	58	65	-7	59
15	Oldham Ath	46	9	8	6	37	25	3	13	7	29	35	12	21	13	66	60	6	57
16	Sheffield W	46	7	9	7	25	26	6	5	12	23	38	13	14	19	48	64	-16	53
17	Brentford	46	9	5	9	34	38	5	6	12	18	31	14	11	21	52	69	-17	53
18	Peterborough U	46	5	8	10	36	33	7	8	8	22	25	12	16	18	58	58	0	52
19	Stockport Co	46	6	8	9	31	36	5	11	7	31	34	11	19	16	62	70	-8	52
20	Chesterfield	46	9	7	7	34	31	3	8	12	15	40	12	15	19	49	71	-22	51
21	Grimsby T	46	10	5	8	36	26	3	6	14	19	55	13	11	22	55	81	-26	50
22	Rushden & D	46	9	5	9	37	34	4	4	15	23	40	13	9	24	60	74	-14	48
23	Notts Co	46	6	9	8	32	27	4	3	16	18	51	10	12	24	50	78	-28	42
24	Wycombe W	46	5	7	11	31	39	1	12	10	19	36	6	19	21	50	75	-25	37

NATIONWIDE DIVISION 2

	League	Carling Cup	FA Cup	Other	Total
Leon Knight (*Brighton & HA*)	25	0	0	2	27
Stephen McPhee (*Port Vale*)	25	0	1	1	27
Paul Heffernan (*Notts Co*)	20	0	1	0	21
Sam Parkin (*Swindon T*)	19	3	0	1	23
Tommy Mooney (*Swindon T*)	19	1	0	0	20
Kevin Gallen (*QPR*)	17	0	0	0	17
Scott Taylor (*Blackpool*)	16	3	6	2	27
Eugene Dadi (*Tranmere R*)	16	1	2	0	19
Paul Furlong (*QPR*)	16	0	0	0	16
Onandi Lowe (*Rushden & D*)	15	1	0	0	16
Lee Peacock (*Bristol C*)	14	2	0	0	16
David Friio (*Plymouth Arg*)	14	0	1	0	15
Steve Howard (*Luton T*)	14	1	0	0	15
James Hayter (*Bournemouth*)	14	0	0	0	14
Billy Paynter (*Port Vale*)	13	0	1	0	14
Eifion Williams (*Hartlepool U*)	13	0	0	1	14
Glynn Hurst (*Chesterfield*)	13	0	0	0	13

Nationwide Football League Division 3

			Home					Away					Total						
		P	W	D	L	F	A	W	D	L	F	A	W	D	L	F	A	Gd	Pts
1	Doncaster R	46	17	4	2	47	13	10	7	6	32	24	27	11	8	79	37	42	92
2	Hull C	46	16	4	3	50	21	9	9	5	32	23	25	13	8	82	44	38	88
3	Torquay U	46	15	6	2	44	18	8	6	9	24	26	23	12	11	68	44	24	81
4	Huddersfield T	46	16	4	3	42	18	7	8	8	26	34	23	12	11	68	52	16	81
5	Mansfield T	46	13	5	5	44	25	9	4	10	32	37	22	9	15	76	62	14	75
6	Northampton T	46	13	4	6	30	23	9	5	9	28	28	22	9	15	58	51	7	75
7	Lincoln C	46	9	11	3	36	23	10	6	7	32	24	19	17	10	68	47	21	74
8	Yeovil T	46	14	3	6	40	19	9	2	12	30	38	23	5	18	70	57	13	74
9	Oxford U	46	14	8	1	34	13	4	9	10	21	31	18	17	11	55	44	11	71
10	Swansea C	46	9	8	6	36	26	6	6	11	22	35	15	14	17	58	61	−3	59
11	Boston U	46	11	7	5	35	21	5	4	14	15	33	16	11	19	50	54	−4	59
12	Bury	46	10	7	6	29	26	5	4	14	25	38	15	11	20	54	64	−10	56
13	Cambridge U	46	6	7	10	26	32	8	7	8	29	35	14	14	18	55	67	−12	56
14	Cheltenham T	46	11	4	8	37	38	3	10	10	20	33	14	14	18	57	71	−14	56
15	Bristol R	46	9	7	7	29	26	5	6	12	21	35	14	13	19	50	61	−11	55
16	Kidderminster H	46	9	5	9	28	29	5	8	10	17	30	14	13	19	45	59	−14	55
17	Southend U	46	8	4	11	27	29	6	8	9	24	34	14	12	20	51	63	−12	54
18	Darlington	46	10	4	9	30	28	4	7	12	23	33	14	11	21	53	61	−8	53
19	Leyton Orient	46	8	9	6	28	27	5	5	13	20	38	13	14	19	48	65	−17	53
20	Macclesfield T	46	8	8	6	28	25	5	4	14	26	44	13	13	20	54	69	−15	52
21	Rochdale	46	7	8	8	28	26	5	6	12	21	32	12	14	20	49	58	−9	50
22	Scunthorpe U	46	7	10	6	36	27	4	6	13	33	45	11	16	19	69	72	−3	49
23	Carlisle U	46	8	5	10	23	27	4	4	15	23	42	12	9	25	46	69	−23	45
24	York C	46	7	6	10	22	29	3	8	12	13	37	10	14	22	35	66	−31	44

NATIONWIDE DIVISION 3

	League	Carling Cup	FA Cup	Other	Total
Steve MacLean (Scunthorpe U)	23	1	0	1	25
David Graham (Torquay U)	22	1	0	0	23
Leon Constantine (Southend U)	21	0	0	4	25
Liam Lawrence (Mansfield T)	18	0	3	0	21
Greg Blundell (Doncaster R)	18	2	0	0	20
Ben Burgess (Hull C)	18	0	0	0	18
Lee Trundle (Swansea C)	16	0	5	0	21
Matt Tipton (Macclesfield T)	16	0	3	0	19
Gary Fletcher (Lincoln C)	16	0	0	3	19
Jon Stead (Huddersfield T)	16	2	0	0	18
Gary Alexander (Leyton Orient)	15	0	1	0	16
Danny Allsopp (Hull C)	15	0	0	0	15
Steve Basham (Oxford U)	14	1	0	0	15
Barry Conlon (Darlington)	14	0	0	0	14
Stuart Elliott (Hull C)	14	0	0	0	14
Andy Booth (Huddersfield T)	13	1	0	0	14
Paul Tait (Bristol R)	12	0	·0	0	12

FA BARCLAYCARD PREMIERSHIP

HOME TEAM	Arsenal	Aston Villa	Birmingham C	Blackburn R	Bolton W	Charlton Ath	Chelsea	Everton	Fulham	Leeds U
Arsenal	—	2-0	0-0	1-0	2-1	2-1	2-1	2-1	0-0	5-0
Aston Villa	0-2	—	2-2	0-2	1-1	2-1	3-2	0-0	3-0	2-0
Birmingham C	0-3	0-0	—	0-4	2-0	1-2	0-0	3-0	2-2	4-1
Blackburn R	0-2	0-2	1-1	—	3-4	0-1	2-3	2-1	0-2	1-2
Bolton W	1-1	2-2	0-1	2-2	—	0-0	0-2	2-0	0-2	4-1
Charlton Ath	1-1	1-2	1-1	3-2	1-2	—	4-2	2-2	3-1	0-1
Chelsea	1-2	1-0	0-0	2-2	1-2	1-0	—	0-0	2-1	1-0
Everton	1-1	2-0	1-0	0-1	1-2	0-1	0-1	—	3-1	4-0
Fulham	0-1	1-2	0-0	3-4	2-1	2-0	0-1	2-1	—	2-0
Leeds U	1-4	0-0	0-2	2-1	0-2	3-3	1-1	1-1	3-2	—
Leicester C	1-1	0-5	0-2	2-0	1-1	1-1	0-4	1-1	0-2	4-0
Liverpool	1-2	1-0	3-1	4-0	3-1	0-1	1-2	0-0	0-0	3-1
Manchester C	1-2	4-1	0-0	1-1	6-2	1-1	0-1	5-1	0-0	1-1
Manchester U	0-0	4-0	3-0	2-1	4-0	2-0	1-1	3-2	1-3	1-1
Middlesbrough	0-4	1-2	5-3	0-1	2-0	0-0	1-2	1-0	2-1	2-3
Newcastle U	0-0	1-1	0-1	0-1	0-0	3-1	2-1	4-2	3-1	1-0
Portsmouth	1-1	2-1	3-1	1-2	4-0	1-2	0-2	1-2	1-1	6-1
Southampton	0-1	1-1	0-0	2-0	1-2	3-2	0-1	3-3	0-0	2-1
Tottenham H	2-2	2-1	4-1	1-0	0-1	0-1	0-1	3-0	0-3	2-1
Wolverhampton W	1-3	0-4	1-1	2-2	1-2	0-4	0-5	2-1	2-1	3-1

2003–2004 RESULTS

	Leicester C	Liverpool	Manchester C	Manchester U	Middlesbrough	Newcastle U	Portsmouth	Southampton	Tottenham H	Wolverhampton W
	2-1	4-2	2-1	1-1	4-1	3-2	1-1	2-0	2-1	3-0
	3-1	0-0	1-1	0-2	0-2	0-0	2-1	1-0	1-0	3-2
	0-1	0-3	2-1	1-2	3-1	1-1	2-0	2-1	1-0	2-2
	1-0	1-3	2-3	1-0	2-2	1-1	1-2	1-1	1-0	5-1
	2-2	2-2	1-3	1-2	2-0	1-0	1-0	0-0	2-0	1-1
	2-2	3-2	0-3	0-2	1-0	0-0	1-1	2-1	2-4	2-0
	2-1	0-1	1-0	1-0	0-0	5-0	3-0	4-0	4-2	5-2
	3-2	0-3	0-0	3-4	1-1	2-2	1-0	0-0	3-1	2-0
	2-0	1-2	2-2	1-1	3-2	2-3	2-0	2-0	2-1	0-0
	3-2	2-2	2-1	0-1	0-3	2-2	1-2	0-0	0-1	4-1
	—	0-0	1-1	1-4	0-0	1-1	3-1	2-2	1-2	0-0
	2-1	—	2-1	1-2	2-0	1-1	3-0	1-2	0-0	1-0
	0-3	2-2	—	4-1	0-1	1-0	1-1	1-3	0-0	3-3
	1-0	0-1	3-1	—	2-3	0-0	3-0	3-2	3-0	1-0
	3-3	0-0	2-1	0-1	—	0-1	0-0	3-1	1-0	2-0
	3-1	1-1	3-0	1-2	2-1	—	3-0	1-0	4-0	1-1
	0-2	1-0	4-2	1-0	5-1	1-1	—	1-0	2-0	0-0
	0-0	2-0	0-2	1-0	0-1	3-3	3-0	—	1-0	2-0
	4-4	2-1	1-1	1-2	0-0	1-0	4-3	1-3	—	5-2
	4-3	1-1	1-0	1-0	2-0	1-1	0-0	1-4	0-2	—

NATIONWIDE FOOTBALL LEAGUE

HOME TEAM	Bradford C	Burnley	Cardiff C	Coventry C	Crewe Alex	Crystal Palace	Derby Co	Gillingham	Ipswich T	Millwall
Bradford C	—	1-2	0-1	1-0	2-1	1-2	1-2	0-1	0-1	3-2
Burnley	4-0	—	1-1	1-2	1-0	2-3	1-0	1-0	4-2	1-1
Cardiff C	0-2	2-0	—	0-1	3-0	0-2	4-1	5-0	2-3	1-3
Coventry C	0-0	4-0	1-3	—	2-0	2-1	2-0	2-2	1-1	4-0
Crewe Alex	2-2	3-1	0-1	3-1	—	2-3	3-0	1-1	1-0	1-2
Crystal Palace	0-1	0-0	2-1	1-1	1-3	—	1-1	1-0	3-4	0-1
Derby Co	3-2	2-0	2-2	1-3	0-0	2-1	—	2-1	2-2	2-0
Gillingham	1-0	0-3	1-2	2-5	2-0	1-0	0-0	—	1-2	4-3
Ipswich T	3-1	6-1	1-1	1-1	6-4	1-3	2-1	3-4	—	1-3
Millwall	1-0	2-0	0-0	2-1	1-1	1-1	0-0	1-2	0-0	—
Norwich C	0-1	2-0	4-1	1-1	1-0	2-1	2-1	3-0	3-1	3-1
Nottingham F	2-1	1-1	1-2	0-1	2-0	3-2	1-1	0-0	1-1	2-2
Preston NE	1-0	5-3	2-2	4-2	0-0	4-1	3-0	0-0	1-1	1-2
Reading	2-2	2-2	2-1	1-2	1-1	0-3	3-1	2-1	1-1	1-0
Rotherham U	1-2	3-0	0-0	2-0	0-2	1-2	0-0	1-1	1-3	0-0
Sheffield U	2-0	1-0	5-3	2-1	2-0	0-3	1-1	0-0	1-1	2-1
Stoke C	1-0	1-2	2-3	1-0	1-1	0-1	2-1	0-0	2-0	0-0
Sunderland	3-0	1-1	0-0	0-0	1-1	2-1	2-1	2-1	3-2	0-1
Walsall	1-0	0-1	1-1	1-6	1-1	0-0	0-1	2-1	1-3	1-1
Watford	1-0	1-1	2-1	1-1	2-1	1-5	2-1	2-2	1-2	3-1
WBA	2-0	4-1	2-1	3-0	2-2	2-0	1-1	1-0	4-1	2-1
West Ham U	1-0	2-2	1-0	2-0	4-2	3-0	0-0	2-1	1-2	1-1
Wigan Ath	1-0	0-0	3-0	2-1	2-3	5-0	2-0	1-0	1-0	0-0
Wimbledon	2-1	2-2	0-1	0-3	3-1	1-3	1-0	1-2	1-2	0-1

DIVISION 1 2003–2004 RESULTS

Norwich C	Nottingham F	Preston NE	Reading	Rotherham U	Sheffield U	Stoke C	Sunderland	Walsall	Watford	WBA	West Ham U	Wigan Ath	Wimbledon
2-2	1-2	2-1	2-1	0-2	1-2	0-2	0-4	1-1	2-0	0-1	1-2	0-0	2-3
3-5	0-3	1-1	3-0	1-1	3-2	0-1	1-2	3-1	2-3	1-1	1-1	0-2	2-0
2-1	0-0	2-2	2-3	3-2	2-1	3-1	4-0	0-1	3-0	1-1	0-0	0-0	1-1
0-2	1-3	4-1	1-2	1-1	0-1	4-2	1-1	0-0	0-0	1-0	1-1	1-1	1-0
1-3	3-1	2-1	1-0	0-0	0-1	2-0	3-0	1-0	0-1	1-2	0-3	2-3	1-0
1-0	1-0	1-1	2-2	1-1	1-2	6-3	3-0	1-0	1-0	2-2	1-0	1-1	3-1
0-4	4-2	5-1	2-3	1-0	2-0	0-3	1-1	0-1	3-2	0-1	0-1	2-2	3-1
1-2	2-1	0-1	0-1	2-0	0-3	3-1	1-3	3-0	1-0	0-2	2-0	0-3	1-2
0-2	1-2	2-0	1-1	2-1	3-0	1-0	1-0	2-1	4-1	2-3	1-2	1-3	4-1
0-0	1-0	0-1	0-1	2-1	2-0	1-1	2-1	2-1	1-2	1-1	4-1	2-0	2-0
—	1-0	3-2	2-1	2-0	1-0	1-0	1-0	5-0	1-2	0-0	1-1	2-0	3-2
2-0	—	0-1	0-1	2-2	3-1	0-0	2-0	3-3	1-1	0-3	0-2	1-0	6-0
0-0	2-2	—	2-1	4-1	3-3	1-0	0-2	1-2	2-1	3-0	1-2	2-4	1-0
0-1	3-0	3-2	—	0-0	2-1	0-0	0-2	0-1	2-1	1-0	2-0	1-0	0-3
4-4	1-1	1-0	5-1	—	1-1	3-0	0-2	2-0	1-1	0-3	1-0	0-3	3-1
1-0	1-2	2-0	1-2	5-0	—	0-1	0-1	2-0	2-2	1-2	3-3	1-1	2-1
1-1	2-1	1-1	3-0	0-2	2-2	—	3-1	3-2	3-1	4-1	0-2	1-1	2-1
1-0	1-0	3-3	2-0	0-0	3-0	1-1	—	1-0	2-0	0-1	2-0	1-1	2-1
1-3	4-1	2-1	1-1	3-2	0-1	1-1	1-3	—	0-1	4-1	1-1	2-0	1-0
1-2	1-1	2-0	1-0	1-0	0-2	1-3	2-2	1-1	—	0-1	0-0	1-1	4-0
1-0	0-2	1-0	0-0	0-1	0-2	1-0	0-0	2-0	3-1	—	1-1	2-1	0-1
1-1	1-1	1-2	1-0	2-1	0-0	0-1	3-2	0-0	4-0	3-4	—	4-0	5-0
1-1	2-2	1-1	0-2	1-2	1-1	2-1	0-0	1-0	1-0	1-0	1-1	—	0-1
0-1	0-1	3-3	0-3	1-2	1-2	0-1	1-2	0-1	1-3	0-0	1-1	2-4	—

NATIONWIDE FOOTBALL LEAGUE

HOME TEAM	Barnsley	Blackpool	Bournemouth	Brentford	Brighton & HA	Bristol C	Chesterfield	Colchester U	Grimsby T	Hartlepool U
Barnsley	—	3-0	1-1	0-2	1-0	0-1	0-1	1-0	0-0	2-2
Blackpool	0-2	—	1-2	1-1	3-1	1-0	1-0	0-0	0-1	4-0
Bournemouth	2-2	1-2	—	1-0	1-0	0-0	2-2	1-1	0-0	2-2
Brentford	2-1	0-0	1-0	—	4-0	1-2	1-1	3-2	1-3	2-1
Brighton & HA	1-0	3-0	3-0	1-0	—	1-4	1-0	2-1	3-0	2-0
Bristol C	2-1	2-1	2-0	3-1	0-0	—	4-0	1-0	1-0	1-1
Chesterfield	0-2	1-0	1-1	1-2	0-2	1-1	—	1-2	4-4	1-2
Colchester U	1-1	1-1	1-0	1-1	1-0	2-1	1-0	—	2-0	1-2
Grimsby T	6-1	0-2	1-1	1-0	2-1	1-2	4-0	2-0	—	0-2
Hartlepool U	1-2	1-1	2-1	1-2	0-0	1-2	2-0	0-0	8-1	—
Luton T	0-1	3-2	1-1	4-1	2-0	3-2	1-0	1-0	1-2	3-2
Notts Co	1-1	4-1	0-1	2-0	1-2	1-2	1-1	3-0	3-1	1-0
Oldham Ath	1-1	2-3	1-1	1-1	1-3	1-1	2-0	0-0	6-0	0-2
Peterborough U	2-3	0-1	0-1	0-0	2-2	0-1	0-2	1-2	0-0	3-4
Plymouth Arg	2-0	1-0	0-0	2-0	3-3	0-1	7-0	2-0	2-2	2-0
Port Vale	3-1	2-1	2-1	1-0	1-1	2-1	1-1	4-3	5-1	2-5
QPR	4-0	5-0	1-0	1-0	2-1	1-1	3-0	2-0	3-0	4-1
Rushden & D	2-3	0-0	0-3	0-1	1-3	1-1	2-1	4-0	3-1	0-2
Sheffield W	2-1	0-1	0-2	1-1	2-1	1-0	0-0	0-1	0-0	1-0
Stockport Co	2-3	1-3	3-2	1-1	1-1	2-0	0-0	1-3	2-1	1-2
Swindon T	1-1	2-2	2-1	2-1	2-1	1-1	2-0	2-0	2-0	1-1
Tranmere R	2-0	1-1	1-1	4-1	1-0	1-0	2-3	1-1	2-1	0-0
Wrexham	1-0	4-2	0-1	1-0	0-2	0-0	0-0	0-1	3-0	1-2
Wycombe W	1-2	0-3	2-0	1-2	1-1	3-0	3-3	1-2	4-1	3-4

Luton T	Notts Co	Oldham Ath	Peterborough U	Plymouth Arg	Port Vale	QPR	Rushden & D	Sheffield W	Stockport Co	Swindon T	Tranmere R	Wrexham	Wycombe W
0-0	1-1	1-1	0-1	1-0	0-0	3-3	2-0	1-1	3-3	1-1	2-0	2-1	0-0
0-1	2-1	1-1	1-4	0-1	2-1	0-1	2-3	4-1	1-1	2-2	2-1	0-1	3-2
6-3	1-0	1-0	1-2	0-2	2-1	1-0	2-1	1-0	0-0	2-2	1-5	6-0	1-0
4-2	2-3	2-1	0-3	1-3	3-2	1-1	3-2	0-3	0-2	0-2	2-2	0-1	1-1
2-0	1-0	0-0	1-0	2-1	1-1	2-1	0-0	2-0	0-1	2-2	3-0	2-0	4-0
1-1	5-0	0-2	1-1	1-0	0-1	1-0	1-0	1-1	1-0	2-1	2-0	1-0	1-1
1-0	0-1	1-1	2-1	1-1	1-0	4-2	2-0	3-1	0-3	3-0	2-2	2-1	2-2
1-1	4-1	2-1	0-0	0-2	1-4	2-2	2-0	3-1	2-1	0-1	1-1	3-1	1-1
3-2	2-0	3-3	1-1	0-0	1-2	0-1	1-0	2-0	1-1	1-2	0-1	1-3	3-1
4-3	4-0	0-0	1-0	1-3	2-0	1-4	2-1	1-1	2-2	2-0	0-0	2-0	1-1
—	2-0	1-1	1-1	1-1	2-0	1-1	3-1	3-2	2-2	0-3	3-1	3-2	3-1
1-1	—	1-1	0-1	0-0	1-2	3-3	1-3	0-0	4-1	1-2	2-2	0-1	1-1
3-0	0-1	—	1-1	4-1	2-1	2-1	3-2	1-0	2-0	0-1	1-1	1-1	2-3
1-2	5-2	2-2	—	2-2	3-1	0-0	3-1	0-1	1-2	4-2	0-0	6-1	1-1
2-1	3-0	2-2	2-0	—	2-1	2-0	3-0	2-0	3-1	2-1	6-0	0-0	2-1
1-0	1-0	1-0	3-0	1-5	—	2-0	1-1	3-0	2-2	3-3	2-1	1-0	1-1
1-1	3-2	1-1	1-1	3-0	3-2	—	1-0	3-0	1-1	1-0	1-1	2-0	0-0
2-2	2-1	4-1	0-1	2-1	0-2	3-3	—	1-2	2-2	2-0	2-1	2-3	2-0
0-0	2-1	2-2	2-0	1-3	2-3	1-3	0-0	—	2-2	1-1	2-0	2-3	1-1
1-2	2-2	1-1	2-2	0-2	2-2	1-2	2-1	1-0	—	2-4	1-1	0-1	2-0
2-2	4-0	1-2	2-0	2-3	0-0	1-1	4-2	2-3	1-2	—	2-0	1-0	2-0
1-0	4-0	2-1	0-0	3-0	1-0	0-0	1-2	2-2	3-2	1-0	—	1-2	2-1
2-1	0-1	4-0	2-0	2-2	2-1	0-2	1-1	1-2	0-0	3-2	0-1	—	0-0
0-0	1-1	2-5	1-2	0-0	2-1	2-2	0-2	1-2	1-0	0-3	1-2	1-1	—

NATIONWIDE FOOTBALL LEAGUE

HOME TEAM	Boston U	Bristol R	Bury	Cambridge U	Carlisle U	Cheltenham T	Darlington	Doncaster R	Huddersfield T	Hull C
Boston U	—	1-0	1-0	1-2	1-0	3-1	1-0	0-0	2-2	1-2
Bristol R	2-0	—	1-2	0-2	1-0	2-0	0-3	1-2	1-1	2-1
Bury	1-3	0-0	—	1-0	1-3	1-1	1-1	1-3	2-1	0-0
Cambridge U	0-1	3-1	1-2	—	2-2	2-1	1-0	3-3	1-2	0-2
Carlisle U	2-1	0-2	2-1	0-0	—	1-1	1-1	0-1	1-0	1-1
Cheltenham T	1-0	1-2	1-2	0-3	2-1	—	2-1	1-3	1-1	0-2
Darlington	3-0	0-4	1-3	3-4	2-0	2-1	—	2-1	0-1	0-1
Doncaster R	3-0	5-1	3-1	2-0	1-0	1-1	1-1	—	1-1	0-0
Huddersfield T	2-0	2-1	1-0	2-2	2-1	0-0	0-2	3-1	—	3-1
Hull C	2-1	3-0	2-0	2-0	2-1	3-3	4-1	3-1	0-0	—
Kidderminster H	2-0	1-0	0-2	2-2	2-1	0-0	1-1	0-2	2-1	1-1
Leyton Orient	1-3	1-1	2-0	0-1	1-1	1-4	1-0	1-3	1-1	1-1
Lincoln C	1-1	3-1	2-1	2-2	2-0	0-0	1-1	0-0	3-1	2-0
Macclesfield T	0-0	2-1	1-0	0-1	1-1	1-2	0-1	1-3	4-0	1-1
Mansfield T	2-1	0-0	5-3	1-1	2-3	4-0	3-1	1-2	3-3	1-0
Northampton T	2-0	0-0	3-2	1-2	2-0	1-0	1-0	1-0	0-1	1-5
Oxford U	0-0	0-0	1-1	2-2	2-1	1-0	3-1	0-0	0-1	2-1
Rochdale	1-0	2-2	0-0	2-2	2-0	0-0	4-2	1-1	1-1	0-2
Scunthorpe U	0-1	1-2	0-0	4-0	2-3	5-2	0-1	2-2	6-2	1-1
Southend U	0-2	0-1	1-0	1-0	2-2	2-0	3-2	0-2	1-2	2-2
Swansea C	3-0	0-0	4-2	0-2	1-2	0-0	1-0	1-1	2-0	2-3
Torquay U	2-0	2-1	3-1	3-0	4-1	3-1	2-2	1-0	0-1	1-1
Yeovil T	2-0	4-0	2-1	4-1	3-0	0-0	1-0	1-0	2-1	1-2
York C	1-1	2-1	1-1	2-0	2-0	0-2	1-1	1-0	0-2	0-2

DIVISION 3 2003–2004 RESULTS

Kidderminster H	Leyton Orient	Lincoln C	Macclesfield T	Mansfield T	Northampton T	Oxford U	Rochdale	Scunthorpe U	Southend U	Swansea C	Torquay U	Yeovil T	York C
2-2	3-0	0-1	3-1	1-2	1-1	1-1	2-0	1-1	0-2	1-1	4-0	3-2	2-0
1-0	1-1	3-1	2-2	1-3	1-2	1-1	0-0	1-0	1-1	2-1	2-2	0-1	3-0
0-0	1-1	2-1	2-0	3-0	1-0	0-4	1-2	2-3	1-1	2-0	2-1	2-1	2-0
0-0	1-4	0-0	3-1	1-2	0-1	1-1	0-0	3-2	0-1	0-1	1-1	1-4	2-0
1-0	0-1	0-2	0-1	0-2	1-1	2-0	3-2	1-4	1-2	1-2	2-0	2-0	1-2
2-1	1-0	3-2	3-2	4-2	4-3	0-0	0-2	2-1	1-1	3-4	1-3	3-1	1-1
0-2	2-1	0-0	0-1	1-0	1-2	2-0	1-0	2-2	0-0	1-2	1-1	3-2	3-0
5-0	5-0	0-2	1-0	4-2	1-0	2-0	2-1	1-0	2-0	3-1	1-0	0-1	3-1
1-0	3-0	2-1	4-0	1-3	3-0	1-1	1-1	3-2	1-0	3-0	1-0	3-1	0-1
6-1	3-0	3-0	2-2	0-1	2-3	4-2	1-0	2-1	3-2	1-0	0-1	0-0	2-1
—	2-1	1-2	1-4	2-1	2-1	1-1	0-1	0-2	1-2	2-0	1-2	0-1	4-1
1-1	—	0-2	2-0	3-1	1-1	1-0	2-1	1-1	2-1	1-2	0-0	2-0	2-2
1-1	0-0	—	3-2	4-1	0-0	0-1	1-1	1-1	2-2	2-1	1-3	2-3	3-0
1-1	1-0	0-0	—	1-1	0-4	2-1	2-1	2-2	1-2	2-1	1-1	4-1	0-0
1-0	1-1	1-2	3-2	—	1-2	3-1	1-0	5-0	1-0	1-1	2-1	0-1	2-0
0-1	1-0	1-1	0-0	0-3	—	2-1	3-1	1-1	2-2	2-1	0-1	2-0	2-1
2-1	2-1	0-0	3-1	1-1	3-0	—	2-0	3-2	2-0	3-0	1-0	1-0	0-0
0-1	3-0	0-3	1-2	3-0	1-1	1-2	—	2-0	1-1	0-1	1-0	1-3	1-2
0-2	1-1	1-3	1-0	0-0	1-0	1-1	2-2	—	1-1	2-2	2-1	3-0	0-0
3-0	1-2	0-2	1-0	0-3	0-1	0-1	4-0	4-2	—	1-1	1-2	0-2	0-0
0-0	2-1	2-2	3-0	4-1	0-2	0-0	1-1	4-2	2-3	—	1-2	3-2	0-0
1-1	2-1	1-0	4-1	1-0	3-1	3-0	1-3	1-0	3-0	0-0	—	2-2	1-1
1-2	1-2	3-1	2-2	1-1	0-2	1-0	1-0	2-1	4-0	2-0	0-2	—	3-0
1-0	1-2	1-4	0-2	1-2	1-0	2-2	1-2	1-3	2-0	0-0	0-0	1-2	—

ARSENAL   FA PREMIERSHIP

Player	Ht	Wt	Birthplace	D.O.B.	Source
Aliadiere Jeremie (F)	6 0	11 00	Rambouillet	30 3 83	Scholar
Bentley David (F)	5 10	11 02	Peterborough	27 8 84	Scholar
Bergkamp Dennis (F)	6 0	12 10	Amsterdam	18 5 69	Internazionale
Birchall Adam (F)	5 7	11 08	Maidstone	2 12 84	Trainee
Campbell Sol (D)	6 2	15 07	Newham	18 9 74	Tottenham H
Clichy Gael (D)	5 9	10 04	Toulouse	26 7 85	
Cole Ashley (D)	5 8	10 05	Stepney	20 12 80	Trainee
Cregg Patrick (M)	5 9	10 04	Dublin	21 2 86	Trainee
Cygan Pascal (D)	6 4	13 12	Lens	19 4 74	Lille
Edu (M)	6 1	12 06	Sao Paulo	15 5 78	Corinthians
Fabregas Francesc (M)	5 9	10 09	Arenys de Mar	4 5 87	Barcelona
Fowler Jordan (M)	5 9	11 00	Barking	1 10 84	Trainee
Garry Ryan (D)	6 2	13 00	Hornchurch	29 9 83	Scholar
Henry Thierry (F)	6 2	13 05	Paris	17 8 77	Juventus
Hojsted Ingi (M)	5 9	9 10	Torshavn	12 12 85	Trainee
Hoyte Justin (D)	5 11	11 00	Waltham Forest	20 11 84	Scholar
Jeffers Francis (F)	5 10	11 02	Liverpool	25 1 81	Everton
Jordan Michael (G)	6 2	13 02	Enfield	7 4 86	Scholar
Karbassiyon Daniel (F)	5 8	11 07	Virginia	10 8 84	
Larsson Sebastian (M)	5 10	11 00	Eskiltuna	6 6 85	Trainee
Lauren Etame-Mayer (D)	5 11	11 07	Londi Kribi	19 1 77	Mallorca
Lehmann Jens (G)	6 4	13 05	Essen	10 11 69	Borussia Dortmund
Ljungberg Frederik (M)	5 9	11 00	Vittsjo	16 4 77	Halmstad
O'Donnell Steven (M)	5 9	11 02	Galway	15 1 86	Trainee
Owusu-Abeyie Quincy (F)	5 11	11 10	Amsterdam	15 4 86	
Parlour Ray (M)	5 10	12 13	Romford	7 3 73	Trainee
Pennant Jermaine (M)	5 9	10 06	Nottingham	15 1 83	
Pires Robert (M)	6 1	12 09	Reims	29 10 73	Marseille
Reyes Jose Antonio (F)	5 9	12 01	Utrera	1 9 83	Sevilla
Senderos Philippe (D)	6 1	13 10	Geneva	14 2 85	Servette
Shiels Dean (F)	5 11	9 10	Magherfelt	1 2 85	Trainee
Silva Gilberto (M)	6 3	12 04	Lagoa da Prata	7 10 76	Atletico Mineiro
Simek Franklin (D)	6 0	11 06	St Louis	13 10 84	Trainee
Skulason Olafur-Ingi (M)	6 0	12 04	Reykjavik	1 4 83	Fylkir
Spicer John (M)	5 11	11 08	Romford	13 9 83	Scholar
Stack Graham (G)	6 2	13 02	Hampstead	26 9 81	Scholar
Svard Sebastian (M)	6 0	12 06	Hvidovre	15 1 83	
Tavlaridis Efstathios (D)	6 2	12 11	Serres	25 1 80	Iraklis
Taylor Stuart (G)	6 5	14 03	Romford	28 11 80	Trainee
Toure Kolo (D)	5 10	13 08	Ivory Coast	19 3 81	ASEC Mimosas
Van Bronckhorst Giovanni (M)	5 9	11 03	Rotterdam	5 2 75	Rangers
Vieira Patrick (M)	6 4	13 09	Dakar	23 6 76	AC Milan

League Appearances: Aliadiere, J. 3(7); Bentley, D. 1; Bergkamp, D. 21(7); Campbell, S. 35; Clichy, G. 7(5); Cole, A. 32; Cygan, P. 10(8); Edu 13(17); Henry, T. 37; Hoyte, J. (1); Kanu, N. 3(7); Keown, M. 3(7); Lauren, E. 30(2); Lehmann, J. 38; Ljungberg, F. 27(3); Parlour, R. 16(9); Pires, R. 33(3); Reyes, J. 7(6); Silva, G. 29(3); Toure, K. 36(1); Vieira, P. 29; Wiltord, S. 8(4).

Goals – League (73): Henry 30 (7 pens), Pires 14, Bergkamp 4, Ljungberg 4, Silva 4, Vieira 3, Wiltord 3, Edu 2, Reyes 2, Campbell 1, Kanu 1, Toure 1, own goals 4.
Carling Cup (9): Aladiere 4, Kanu 2, Edu 1, Fabregas Soler 1, Wiltord 1.
FA Cup (15): Ljungberg 4, Henry 3, Reyes 2, Toure 2, Bentley 1, Bergkamp 1, Edu 1, Pires 1.
Community Shield (1): Henry 1.
Champions League (16): Henry 5, Pires 4, Edu 3, Ljungberg 2, Cole 1, Reyes 1.
Ground: Arsenal Stadium, Highbury, London N5 1BU. Telephone (020) 7704 4000.
Record Attendance: 73,295 v Sunderland, Div 1, 9 March 1935. **Capacity:** 38,500.
Manager: Arsène Wenger.
Secretary: David Miles.
Most League Goals: 127, Division 1, 1930–31.
Highest League Scorer in Season: Ted Drake, 42, 1934–35.
Most League Goals in Total Aggregate: Cliff Bastin, 150, 1930–47.
Most Capped Player: Kenny Sansom, 77 (86), England, 1981–1988.
Most League Appearances: David O'Leary, 558, 1975–93.
Honours – FA Premier League: Champions – 1997–98, 2001–02, 2003–04. **Football League:** Division 1 Champions – 1930–31, 1932–33, 1933–34, 1934–35, 1937–38, 1947–48, 1952–53, 1970–71, 1988–89, 1990–91. **FA Cup winners** 1929–30, 1935–36, 1949–50, 1970–71, 1978–79, 1992–93, 1997–98, 2001–02, 2002–03. **Football League Cup winners** 1986–87, 1992–93. **European Competitions: European Cup-Winners' Cup winners:** 1993–94. **Fairs Cup winners:** 1969–70.
Colours: Red shirts with white sleeves, white shorts, red stockings with yellow trim.

ASTON VILLA   FA PREMIERSHIP

Aaritalo Mika (F)	6 1	12 13	Taivassalo	25	7 85	TPS Turku
Allback Marcus (F)	5 9	12 00	Stockholm	5	7 73	Heerenveen
Angel Juan Pablo (F)	6 0	12 10	Medellin	24 10 75		River Plate
Barry Gareth (D)	5 11	12 06	Hastings	23	2 81	Trainee
Brazil Alan (M)	5 7	12 02	Edinburgh	5	7 85	Trainee
Bridges Stuart (D)	5 9	11 09	Oxford	6	1 86	Trainee
Cahill Gary (D)	6 2	12 06	Sheffield	19 12 85		Trainee
Cooke Stephen (M)	5 7	9 00	Walsall	15	2 83	
Crouch Peter (F)	6 7	11 12	Macclesfield	30	1 81	Portsmouth
Davis Steven (M)	5 7	9 07	Ballymena	1	1 85	Scholar
De la Cruz Ulises (D)	5 8	12 10	Bolivar	8	2 74	Hibernian
Delaney Mark (D)	6 1	11 07	Haverfordwest	13	5 76	Carmarthen T
Edwards Rob (D)	6 1	11 10	Telford	25 12 82		Trainee
Foley-Sheridan Steven (M)	5 4	9 02	Dublin	10	2 86	Trainee
Grant Lee (M)	6 2	12 02	York	31 12 85		Trainee
Henderson Wayne (G)	5 11	12 02	Dublin	16	9 83	Scholar
Hendrie Lee (M)	5 10	11 00	Birmingham	18	5 77	Trainee
Hitzlsperger Thomas (M)	6 0	11 12	Germany	5	4 82	Bayern Munich
Kouman Amadou (F)	5 9	11 00	Marcory	14	4 86	Trainee
Masalin Jon (G)	6 2	14 06	Helsinki	29	1 86	
McCann Gavin (M)	5 11	11 00	Blackpool	10	1 78	Sunderland
Mellberg Olof (D)	6 1	12 10	Amncharad	3	9 77	Santander
Moore Luke (F)	5 11	11 13	Birmingham	13	2 86	Trainee
Moore Stefan (F)	5 10	10 12	Birmingham	28	9 83	Scholar
Mulcahy Kevin (D)	5 10	11 00	Cork	2	3 86	Trainee

21

Nix Kyle (F)	5 6	9 10	Sydney	21 1 86	Manchester U
O'Connor James (D)	5 10	12 05	Birmingham	20 11 84	Scholar
Postma Stefan (G)	6 4	15 04	Utrecht	6 10 76	De Graafschap
Ridgewell Liam (D)	5 10	10 03	London	21 7 84	Scholar
Samuel J Lloyd (D)	5 11	11 04	Trinidad	29 3 81	Charlton Ath
Solano Nolberto (M)	5 9	11 06	Callao	12 12 74	Newcastle U
Sorensen Thomas (G)	6 4	13 10	Fredericia	12 6 76	Sunderland
Vassell Darius (F)	5 7	12 00	Birmingham	13 6 80	Trainee
Ward Jamie (M)	5 5	9 04	Birmingham	12 5 86	Scholar
Whittingham Peter (D)	5 10	9 13	Nuneaton	8 9 84	Trainee

League Appearances: Allback, M. 7(8); Alpay, O. 4(2); Angel, J. 33; Barry, G. 36; Crouch, P. 6(10); De la Cruz, U. 20(8); Delaney, M. 23(2); Dublin, D. 12(11); Hadji, M. (1); Hendrie, L. 32; Hitzlsperger, T. 22(10); Johnsen, R. 21(2); Kinsella, M. 2; McCann, G. 28; Mellberg, O. 33; Moore, L. (7); Moore, S. 2(6); Postma, S. (2); Ridgewell, L. 5(6); Samuel, J. 38; Solano, N. 10; Sorensen, T. 38; Vassell, D. 26(6); Whittingham, P. 20(12).

Goals – League (48): Angel 16 (2 pens), Vassell 9 (1 pen), Crouch 4, Barry 3 (1 pen), Dublin 3, Hitzlsperger 3, Hendrie 2, Samuel 2, Allback 1, Alpay 1, Johnsen 1, Mellberg 1, Moore S 1, own goal 1.

Carling Cup (15): Angel 7 (1 pen), Hitzlsperger 2, McCann 2, Samuel 1, Vassell 1 (pen), Whittingham 1, own goal 1.

FA Cup (1): Barry 1.

Ground: Villa Park, Trinity Road, Birmingham B6 6HE. Telephone (0121) 327 2299.

Record Attendance: 76,588 v Derby Co, FA Cup 6th rd, 2 March 1946.

Capacity: 42,573.

Manager: David O'Leary.

Secretary: Steven Stride.

Most League Goals: 128, Division 1, 1930–31.

Highest League Scorer in Season: 'Pongo' Waring, 49, Division 1, 1930–31.

Most League Goals in Total Aggregate: Harry Hampton, 215, 1904–15.

Most Capped Player: Steve Staunton 64 (102), Republic of Ireland.

Most League Appearances: Charlie Aitken, 561, 1961–76.

Honours – Football League: Division 1 Champions – 1893–94, 1895–96, 1896–97, 1898–99, 1899–1900, 1909–10, 1980–81. Division 2 Champions – 1937–38, 1959–60. Division 3 Champions – 1971–72. **FA Cup:** Winners 1887, 1895, 1897, 1905, 1913, 1920, 1957. **Football League Cup:** Winners 1961, 1975, 1977, 1994, 1996. **European Competitions: European Cup winners:** 1981–82. **European Super Cup winners:** 1982–83. **Intertoto Cup winners:** 2001.

Colours: Claret and blue shirts, white shorts, sky blue stockings.

BARNSLEY   FL CHAMPIONSHIP 1

Austin Neil (D)	5 11	11 09	Barnsley	26 4 83	Trainee
Beresford Marlon (G)	6 1	13 01	Lincoln	2 9 69	Luton T
Betsy Kevin (M)	6 1	12 00	Seychelles	20 3 78	Fulham
Boulding Mick (F)	5 8	11 05	Sheffield	8 2 76	Grimsby T
Kay Antony (M)	5 11	11 08	Barnsley	21 10 82	Trainee
Lumsdon Chris (M)	5 11	10 03	Newcastle	15 12 79	Sunderland
Shuker Chris (M)	5 5	9 03	Liverpool	9 5 82	Manchester C
Stallard Mark (F)	6 0	13 09	Derby	24 10 74	Notts Co

League Appearances: Alcock, D. (1); Atkinson, R. (1); Austin, N. 32(5); Baker, T. (1); Beresford, M. 14; Betsy, K. 42(3); Birch, G. 8; Boulding, M. 5(1); Burns, J. 16(6); Caig, T. 3; Carson, S. 9(2); Crooks, L. 20(3); Davies, A. 1(3); Fallon, R. 12(4); Gallimore, T. 20; Gibbs, P. (3); Gorre, D. 16(3); Handyside, P. 28; Hayward, S. 24(8); Ilic, S. 25; Ireland, C. 43; Kay, A. 39(4); Lumsdon, C. 17(11); Monk, G. 14(3); Mulligan, D. 2(2); Murphy, D. 10; Nardiello, D. 14(2); Neil, A. 17(14); O'Callaghan, B. 25(4); Rankin, I. 9(11); Rocastle, C. 4(1); Shuker, C. 9; Stallard, M. 10; Tonge, D. (1); Turnbull, R. 3; Walters, J. 7(1); Ward, G. 1; Warhurst, P. 3(1); Williams, R. 3(1); Wroe, N. 1(1).
Goals – League (54): Betsy 10 (1 pen), Gorre 7 (2 pens), Nardiello 7 (1 pen), Rankin 5, Fallon 4, Ireland 3, Kay 3, Lumsdon 3, Birch 2, Murphy 2, Neil 2, Burns 1, Carson 1, Hayward 1, Stallard 1, Williams 1 (pen), Wroe 1.
Carling Cup (1): Gorre 1 (pen).
FA Cup (4): Betsy 1, Kay 1, Monk 1, Rankin 1.
Ground: Oakwell Ground, Grove St, Barnsley S71 1ET. Telephone (01226) 211211.
Record Attendance: 40,255 v Stoke C, FA Cup 5th rd, 15 February 1936. **Capacity:** 23,009.
Manager: Paul Hart.
Secretary: Chris Patzelt.
Most League Goals: 118, Division 3 (N), 1933–34.
Highest League Scorer in Season: Cecil McCormack, 33, Division 2, 1950–51.
Most League Goals in Total Aggregate: Ernest Hine, 123, 1921–26 and 1934–38.
Most Capped Player: Gerry Taggart, 35 (50), Northern Ireland.
Most League Appearances: Barry Murphy, 514, 1962–78.
Honours – Football League: Division 3 (N) Champions – 1933–34, 1938–39, 1954–55. **FA Cup:** Winners 1912.
Colours: Red shirts, white shorts, red stockings.

BIRMINGHAM CITY   FA PREMIERSHIP

Barrowman Andrew (F)	5 11	11 06	Wishaw	27 11 84	Scholar
Bennett Ian (G)	6 0	13 01	Worksop	10 10 71	Peterborough U
Carter Darren (M)	6 2	12 11	Solihull	18 12 83	Scholar
Cisse Aliou (M)	5 9	12 02	Zinguichor	24 3 76	Montpellier
Clapham Jamie (M)	5 9	11 09	Lincoln	7 12 75	Ipswich T
Clemence Stephen (M)	6 0	12 09	Liverpool	31 3 78	Tottenham H
Cunningham Kenny (D)	5 11	12 07	Dublin	28 6 71	Wimbledon
Dunn David (M)	5 9	12 03	Blackburn	27 12 79	Blackburn R
Figueroa Luciano (F)	6 0	12 02	Argentina	19 5 81	Rosario Central
Grainger Martin (D)	5 10	12 11	Enfield	23 8 72	Brentford
John Stern (F)	6 0	12 11	Trinidad	30 10 76	Nottingham F
Johnson Damien (M)	5 9	11 09	Lisburn	18 11 78	Blackburn R
Kilkenny Neil (M)	5 8	10 08	Middlesex	19 12 85	Arsenal
Lazaridis Stan (M)	5 9	11 12	Perth	16 8 72	West Ham U
Morrison Clinton (F)	6 1	11 13	Tooting	14 5 79	Crystal Palace
Oji Samuel (D)			Westminster	9 10 85	
Purse Darren (D)	6 2	13 01	Stepney	14 2 76	Oxford U
Sadler Matthew (D)	5 11	11 08	Birmingham	26 2 85	Scholar
Savage Robbie (M)	5 11	11 00	Wrexham	18 10 74	Leicester C
Taylor Maik (G)	6 4	14 02	Hildeshein	4 9 71	Fulham
Taylor Martin (D)	6 4	15 00	Ashington	9 11 79	Blackburn R

Tebily Oliver (D)	6 0	13 05	Abidjan	19 12 75	Celtic
Upson Matthew (D)	6 1	11 04	Hartismere	18 4 79	Arsenal
Vaesen Nico (G)	6 3	12 13	Hasselt	28 9 69	Huddersfield T

League Appearances: Barrowman, A. (1); Bennett, I. 4(2); Carter, D. 1(4); Cisse, A. 5(10); Clapham, J. 22(3); Clemence, S. 32(3); Cunningham, K. 36; Devlin, P. (2); Dugarry, C. 12(2); Dunn, D. 20(1); Figueroa, L. (1); Forssell, M. 32; Grainger, M. 3(1); Horsfield, G. 2(1); Hughes, B. 17(9); John, S. 7(22); Johnson, D. 35; Kenna, J. 14(3); Kirovski, J. (6); Lazaridis, S. 25(5); Morrison, C. 19(13); Purse, D. 9; Savage, R. 31; Taylor, Maik 34; Taylor, Martin 11(1); Tebily, O. 17(10); Upson, M. 30.
Goals – League (43): Forssell 17 (1 pen). John 4, Morrison 4, Hughes 3, Savage 3 (2 pens), Clemence 2, Dunn 2 (1 pen), Kenna 2, Lazaridis 2, Dugarry 1, Grainger 1, Johnson D 1, Taylor Martin 1.
Carling Cup (0).
FA Cup (6): Forssell 2, Hughes 2, Clemence 1, Morrison 1.
Ground: St Andrews, Birmingham B9 4NH. Telephone (0121) 772 0101.
Record Attendance: 66,844 v Everton, FA Cup 5th rd,11 February 1939. **Capacity:** 29,949.
Manager: Steve Bruce.
Secretary: Julia Shelton.
Most League Goals: 103, Division 2, 1893–94 (only 28 games).
Highest League Scorer in Season: Joe Bradford, 29, Division 1, 1927–28.
Most League Goals in Total Aggregate: Joe Bradford, 249, 1920–35.
Most Capped Player: Malcolm Page, 28, Wales.
Most League Appearances: Frank Womack, 491, 1908–28.
Honours – Football League: Division 2 Champions – 1892–93, 1920–21, 1947–48, 1954–55, 1994–95. **Football League Cup:** Winners 1963. **Leyland Daf Cup:** Winners 1991. **Auto Windscreens Shield:** Winners 1995.
Colours: Blue shirts, white shorts, blue stockings.

BLACKBURN ROVERS   FA PREMIERSHIP

Amoruso Lorenzo (D)	6 2	13 10	Palese	28 6 71	Rangers
Black Ian (M)			Edinburgh	14 3 85	Trainee
Bruce Alex (D)			Norwich	28 9 84	Trainee
Cole Andy (F)	5 11	12 02	Nottingham	15 10 71	Manchester U
Danns Neil (M)	5 9	11 02	Liverpool	23 11 82	Blackpool
Derbyshire Matt (F)			Blackburn	14 4 86	Great Harwood T
Donnelly Ciaran (M)			Blackpool	2 4 84	Scholar
Douglas Jonathan (M)	6 0	12 07	Clones	22 11 81	Blackpool
Drench Steven (G)			Salford	11 9 85	Trainee
Emerton Brett (M)	6 1	13 05	Bankstown	22 2 79	Feyenoord
Enckelman Peter (G)	6 2	12 05	Turku	10 3 77	Aston Villa
Ferguson Barry (M)	5 7	9 10	Glasgow	2 2 78	Rangers
Fitzgerald John (D)			Dublin	2 10 84	Scholar
Flitcroft Garry (M)	6 0	11 08	Bolton	6 11 72	Manchester C
Friedel Brad (G)	6 3	14 00	Lakewood	18 5 71	Liverpool
Gallagher Paul (F)	6 1	12 00	Glasgow	9 8 84	Trainee
Gray Michael (D)	5 9	10 07	Sunderland	3 8 74	Sunderland
Gresko Vratislav (M)	6 0	11 05	Bratislava	24 7 77	Parma
Harkins Gary (M)	6 2	12 10	Greenock	2 1 85	Trainee
Jansen Matt (F)	5 11	11 03	Carlisle	20 10 77	Crystal Palace

Name			Birthplace				Previous club
Johansson Nils-Eric (D)	6 2	13 03	Stockholm	13	1	80	Nuremberg
Johnson Jemal (F)			New Jersey	3	5	84	
McEveley James (D)	6 1	12 11	Liverpool	11	2	85	Trainee
Morgan Alan (M)	6 0	12 06	Edinburgh	27	11	83	Scholar
Neill Lucas (M)	6 0	12 03	Sydney	9	3	78	Millwall
Peers Gavin (D)			Dublin	10	11	85	Trainee
Reid Andrew (M)			Kilmarnock	26	9	85	
Reid Steven (M)	6 0	12 07	Kingston	10	3	81	Millwall
Sakali Abdeltareck (F)			Torcy	25	4	86	Trainee
Short Craig (D)	6 3	14 06	Bridlington	25	6	68	Everton
Stead Jon (M)	6 3	12 02	Huddersfield	7	4	83	Huddersfield T
Thompson David (M)	5 7	10 00	Birkenhead	12	9	77	Coventry C
Todd Andy (D)	5 11	13 04	Derby	21	9	74	Charlton Ath
Tugay Kerimoglu (M)	5 9	11 00	Istanbul	24	8	70	Rangers
Watt Jerome (M)			Preston	20	10	84	Scholar
Weaver Paul (M)			Irvine	27	2	86	Trainee
Yelldell David (G)			Stuttgart	1	10	81	
Yorke Dwight (F)	5 10	12 04	Canaan	3	11	71	Manchester U

League Appearances: Amoruso, L. 11(1); Andresen, M. 11; Babbel, M. 23(2); Baggio, D. (9); Cole, A. 27(7); Danns, N. (1); Douglas, J. 14; Emerton, B. 31(6); Enckelman, P. 2; Ferguson, B. 14(1); Flitcroft, G. 29(2); Friedel, B. 36; Gallagher, P. 12(14); Grabbi, C. (5); Gray, M. 14; Gresko, V. 22(2); Jansen, M. 9(10); Johansson, N. 7(7); Mahon, A. 1(2); Neill, L. 30(2); Reid, S. 9(7); Short, C. 19; Stead, J. 13; Taylor, Martin.
Goals – League (51): Cole 11, Stead 6, Yorke 4, Amoruso 3, Babbel 3, Flitcroft 3, Gallagher 3, Emerton 2, Jansen 2, Neill 2, Baggio 1, Douglas 1, Ferguson 1, Friedel 1, Gresko 1, Short 1, Thompson 1, Tugay 1, own goals 4.
Carling Cup (3): Yorke 2, Ferguson 1.
FA Cup (0).
UEFA Cup (2): Emerton 1, Jansen 1.
Ground: Ewood Park, Blackburn BB2 4JF. Telephone (08701) 113232.
Record Attendance: 61,783 v Bolton W, FA Cup 6th rd, 2 March, 1929. **Capacity:** 31,367.
Manager: Graeme Souness.
Secretary: Tom Finn.
Most League Goals: 114, Division 2, 1954–55.
Highest League Scorer in Season: Ted Harper, 43, Division 1, 1925–26.
Most League Goals in Total Aggregate: Simon Garner, 168, 1978–92.
Most Capped Player: Henning Berg, 58 (100), Norway.
Most League Appearances: Derek Fazackerley, 596, 1970–86.
Honours – FA Premier League: Champions – 1994–95. Football League: Division 1 Champions – 1911–12, 1913–14. Division 2 Champions – 1938–39. Division 3 Champions – 1974–75. **FA Cup:** Winners 1884, 1885, 1886, 1890, 1891, 1928. **Football League Cup:** Winners 2002. **Full Members' Cup:** Winners 1986–87.
Colours: Blue and white halved shirts, white shorts with navy blue strip, white stockings with navy blue trim.

Blinkhorn Matthew (F)	6 0	10 10	Blackpool	2 3 85	Scholar
Bullock Martin (M)	5 5	10 07	Derby	5 3 75	Barnsley
Burns Jamie (M)	5 9	10 11	Blackpool	6 3 84	Scholar
Coid Danny (D)	5 11	11 07	Liverpool	3 10 81	Trainee
Davis Steve (D)	6 2	14 07	Hexham	30 10 68	Burnley
Evans Gareth (D)	6 0	11 11	Leeds	15 2 81	Huddersfield T
Flynn Mike (D)	6 0	11 00	Oldham	23 2 69	Barnsley
Herzig Denny (M)			Pobneck	13 11 84	Wimbledon
Jones Lee (G)	6 3	14 04	Pontypridd	9 8 70	Stockport Co
McMahon Steve (M)	5 9	10 05	Southport	31 7 84	Scholar
Murphy John (F)	6 2	14 00	Whiston	18 10 76	Chester C
Richardson Leam (D)	5 7	11 04	Leeds	19 11 79	Bolton W
Southern Keith (M)	5 10	12 06	Gateshead	24 4 81	Everton
Taylor Scott (F)	5 10	11 04	Chertsey	5 5 76	Stockport Co
Wellens Richard (M)	5 9	11 06	Manchester	26 3 80	Manchester U
Wiles Simon (M)	5 11	11 04	Preston	22 4 85	Scholar

League Appearances: Barnes, P. 19; Blinkhorn, M. 4(8); Bullock, M. 33(11); Burns, J. 3(8); Clancy, S. 1(1); Clarke, C. 11(7); Coid, D. 30(5); Danns, N. 12; Davis, S. 22(7); Dinning, T. 10; Doherty, S. (1); Donnelly, C. 8(1); Douglas, J. 15(1); Edge, L. 1; Elliott, S. 28; Evans, G. 21(2); Flynn, M. 29(1); Grayson, S. 28(5); Hessey, S. 4(2); Hilton, K. 12(2); Jaszczun, T. 5(2); Johnson, S. 3(1); Jones, B. 5; Jones, L. 21; Mangan, A. (2); Matias, P. 7; McMahon, S. 7(5); Murphy, J. 27(3); Richardson, L. 24(4); Sheron, M. 28(10); Southern, K. 15(13); Taylor, S. 30(1); Walker, R. 3(6); Wellens, R. 40(1); Wiles, S. (4).
Goals – League (58): Taylor 16 (1 pen), Murphy 9, Sheron 8, Coid 3, Dinning 3 (2 pens), Douglas 3, Wellens 3, Danns 2, Southern 2 (1 pen), Blinkhorn 1, Bullock 1, Clarke C 1, Davis 1, Flynn 1, Grayson 1, Hilton 1, Johnson 1, Matias 1.
Carling Cup (4): Taylor 3, Southern 1.
FA Cup (10): Taylor 6, Burns 1, Coid 1, Richardson 1, Southern 1.
LDV Vans Trophy (13): Murphy 4, Sheron 3, Coid 2, Taylor 2, Blinkhorn 1, Southern 1.
Ground: Bloomfield Road Ground, Blackpool FY1 6JJ. Telephone (0870) 443 1953.
Record Attendance: 38,098 v Wolverhampton W, Division 1, 17 September 1955.
Capacity: 9,500.
Manager: Colin Hendry.
Secretary: Peter Collins.
Most League Goals: 98, Division 2, 1929–30.
Highest League Scorer in Season: Jimmy Hampson, 45, Division 2, 1929–30.
Most League Goals in Total Aggregate: Jimmy Hampson, 246, 1927–38.
Most Capped Player: Jimmy Armfield, 43, England.
Most League Appearances: Jimmy Armfield, 568, 1952–71.
Honours – Football League: Division 2 Champions – 1929–30. **FA Cup:** Winners 1953. **Anglo-Italian Cup:** Winners 1971. **LDV Vans Trophy:** Winners 2002, 2004.
Colours: Tangerine shirts, white shorts, tangerine stockings.

BOLTON WANDERERS   FA PREMIERSHIP

Barness Anthony (D)	5 10	12 11	Lewisham	25	2 73	Charlton Ath
Campo Ivan (D)	6 1	12 12	San Sebastian	21	2 74	Real Madrid
Charlton Simon (D)	5 8	11 04	Huddersfield	25 10 71		Birmingham C
Davies Kevin (F)	6 1	13 11	Sheffield	26	3 77	Southampton
Gardner Ricardo (M)	5 9	11 00	St Andrews	25	9 78	Harbour View
Giannakopoulos	5 8	11 00	Athens	12	7 74	Olympiakos
Stelios (F)						
Hunt Nicky (D)	6 0	11 00	Westhoughton	3	9 83	Scholar
Jaaskelainen Jussi (G)	6 4	12 10	Mikkeli	19	4 75	VPS
Jardel Mario (F)	6 2	13 03	Fortaleza	18	9 73	Sporting Lisbon
Laville Florent (D)	6 2	13 12	Valence	7	8 83	Lyon
Livesey Danny (D)	6 3	12 10	Salford	31 12 84		Trainee
N'Gotty Bruno (D)	6 2	13 05	Lyon	10	6 71	Marseille
Nolan Kevin (M)	6 0	14 00	Liverpool	24	6 82	Scholar
Pedersen Henrik (F)	6 0	12 05	Jutland	10	6 75	Silkeborg
Ricketts Donovan (G)	6 1	11 05	St James	6	7 77	Village U
Thach Duong (F)			Minh Hai	9 12 85		Trainee

League Appearances: Ba, I. (9); Barness, A. 11(4); Campo, I. 37(1); Charlton, S. 28(3); Davies, K. 38; Djorkaeff, Y. 24(3); Emerson 25(1); Facey, D. (1); Frandsen, P. 22(11); Gardner, R. 20(2); Giannakopoulos, S. 17(14); Howey, S. 2(1); Hunt, N. 28(3); Jaaskelainen, J. 38; Jardel, M. (7); Javi Moreno 1(7); Laville, F. 5; Little, G. (4); N'Gotty, B. 32(1); Nolan, K. 37; Okocha, J. 33(2); Otsemobor, J. 1; Pedersen, H. 19(14); Vaz Te, R. (1).
Goals – League (48): Davies 9, Nolan 9, Djorkaeff 8 (1 pen), Pedersen 7, Campo 4, Giannakopoulos 2, N'Gotty 2, own goals 5.
Carling Cup (15): Jardel 3, Okocha 3, Giannakopoulos 2, Nolan 2, Pedersen 2, Davies 1, Djorkjaeff 1 (pen), N'Gotty 1.
FA Cup (2): Nolan 1, Shakes 1.
Ground: Reebok Stadium, Burnden Way, Lostock, Bolton BL6 6JW. Telephone Bolton (01204) 673673.
Record Attendance: 69,912 v Manchester C, FA Cup 5th rd, 18 February 1933.
Capacity: 27,879.
Manager: Sam Allardyce.
Secretary: Simon Marland.
Most League Goals: 100, Division 1, 1996–97.
Highest League Scorer in Season: Joe Smith, 38, Division 1, 1920–21.
Most League Goals in Total Aggregate: Nat Lofthouse, 255, 1946–61.
Most Capped Player: Mark Fish, 34 (62), South Africa.
Most League Appearances: Eddie Hopkinson, 519, 1956–70.
Honours – Football League: Division 1 Champions – 1996–97. Division 2 Champions – 1908–09, 1977–78. Division 3 Champions – 1972–73. **FA Cup winners** 1923, 1926, 1929, 1958. **Sherpa Van Trophy:** Winners 1989.
Colours: All white.

Beevers Lee (D)	6 1	13 00	Doncaster	4 12 83	Ipswich T
Clarke Ryan (D)	5 11	12 04	Sutton Coldfield	22 1 84	
Holland Chris (M)	5 9	12 13	Clitheroe	11 9 75	Huddersfield T
Hurst Kevan (F)	6 0	11 07	Chesterfield	27 8 85	Sheffield U
Melton Steve (M)	5 11	12 03	Lincoln	3 10 78	Hull C
Noble David (M)	6 0	12 04	Hitchin	2 2 82	West Ham U
Rusk Simon (M)	5 11	12 08	Peterborough	17 12 81	Peterborough U
Strong Greg (D)	6 2	11 12	Bolton	5 9 75	Hull C
Thomas Danny (F)	5 7	10 10	Leamington Spa	1 5 81	Bournemouth
Thompson Lee (M)	5 7	10 10	Sheffield	25 3 83	Sheffield U

League Appearances: Akinfenwa, A. 2(1); Angel, M. 12(11); Balmer, S. 25(1); Bastock, P. 46; Beevers, L. 40; Bennett, T. 35; Boyd, A. 14; Brown, J. 3(2); Chapman, B. 33(4); Clarke, R. 1(3); Cropper, D. 4(1); Douglas, S. 14(15); Duffield, P. 12(17); Ellender, P. 42; Greaves, M. 34(3); Hocking, M. 16(6); Hogg, C. 10; Holland, C. 3(2); Hurst, K. 3(4); Jones, G. 31(2); Logan, R. 4(4); Melton, S. 9; Morrow, S. (2); Noble, D. 14; Potter, G. 11(1); Redfearn, N. 19(4); Rusk, S. 16(3); Sabin, E. 2; Sutch, D. 6; Thomas, D. 8; Thompson, L. 20(15); Weatherstone, S. 14(3); White, A. 3(3).

Goals – League (50): Jones 6, Redfearn 6, Duffield 5, Thompson L 5, Boyd 4, Ellender 4, Weatherstone 4, Balmer 3, Thomas 3, Beevers 2, Noble 2, Angel 1, Bennett 1, Cropper 1, Douglas 1, Hurst 1, Melton 1.

Carling Cup (1): Redfearn 1 (pen).

FA Cup (0).

LDV Vans Trophy (3): Akinfenwa 1, Beevers 1, Duffield 1.

Ground: York Street, Boston, Lincolnshire PE21 6HJ. Telephone (01205) 364406.

Record Attendance: 10,086 v Corby Town, Friendly, 1955.

Capacity: 6639.

Manager: Steve Evans.

Secretary: John Blackwell.

Honours – Nationwide Conference: Champions 2001–02. **Dr. Martens:** Champions – 1999–2000. Runners-up – 1998–99. **Unibond League:** Runners-up – 1995–96, 1997–98. **Unibond Challenge Cup:** Runners-up – 1996–97. **FA Trophy:** Runners-up – 1984–85. **Northern Premier League:** Champions – 1972–73, 1973–74, 1976–77, 1977–78. **Northern Premier League Cup:** Winners – 1974, 1976. **Northern Premier League Challenge Shield:** Winners – 1974, 1975, 1977, 1978. **Lincolnshire Senior Cup:** Winners – 1935, 1937, 1938, 1946, 1950, 1955, 1956, 1960, 1977, 1979, 1986, 1988, 1989. **Non-League Champions of Champions Cup:** Winners – 1973, 1977. **East Anglian Cup:** – Winners 1961. **Central Alliance League:** Champions – 1961–62. **United Counties League:** Champions – 1965–66. **West Midlands League:** Champions – 1966–67, 1967–68. **Eastern Professional Floodlit Cup:** Winners – 1972.

Colours: Amber and black striped shirts, black shorts with amber stripe, black stockings with yellow top.

AFC BOURNEMOUTH   FL CHAMPIONSHIP 1

Browning Marcus (M)	6 1	12 12	Bristol	22 4 71	Gillingham
Connell Alan (F)	6 0	10 10	London	5 2 83	Ipswich T
Cummings Warren (D)	5 9	11 08	Aberdeen	15 10 80	Chelsea
Feeney Warren (F)	5 10	11 05	Belfast	17 1 81	Leeds U
Fletcher Carl (M)	5 10	11 07	Camberley	7 4 80	Trainee
Holmes Derek (F)	6 2	13 07	Lanark	18 10 78	Ross Co
Moss Neil (G)	6 2	13 10	New Milton	10 5 75	Southampton
Stewart Gareth (G)	6 0	12 08	Preston	3 2 80	Blackburn R
Stock Brian (M)	5 11	11 02	Winchester	24 12 81	Trainee
Tindall Jason (M)	6 1	12 13	Stepney	15 11 77	Charlton Ath

League Appearances: Broadhurst, K. 36(3); Browning, M. 41(1); Buxton, L. 24(2); Connell, A. 1(6); Cooke, S. 3; Cummings, W. 42; Elliott, W. 23(16); Feeney, W. 34(6); Fletcher, C. 40; Fletcher, S. 40(1); Hayter, J. 37(7); Holmes, D. 10(16); Jorgensen, C. 16(1); Maher, S. 23(6); Moss, N. 46; O'Connor, G. 28(9); Purches, S. 42; Stock, B. 11(8); Thomas, D. 2(8); Tindall, J. 2(17); Williams, G. (1); Young, N. 5(5).

Goals – League (56): Hayter 14, Feeney 12, Fletcher S 9, Elliott 3, Purches S 3, Stock 3, Cummings 2, Fletcher C 2, Holmes 2, O'Connor 2 (1 pen), Broadhurst 1, Maher 1, own goals 2.

Carling Cup (0).

FA Cup (2): Browning 1, Elliott 1.

LDV Vans Trophy (0).

Ground: The Fitness First Stadium at Dean Court, Bournemouth BH7 7AF. Telephone (01202) 726300.

Record Attendance: 28,799 v Manchester U, FA Cup 6th rd, 2 March 1957.

Capacity: 9600 rising to 12,000.

Manager: Sean O'Driscoll.

Secretary: K. R. J. MacAlister.

Most League Goals: 88, Division 3 (S), 1956–57.

Highest League Scorer in Season: Ted MacDougall, 42, 1970–71.

Most League Goals in Total Aggregate: Ron Eyre, 202, 1924–33.

Most Capped Player: Gerry Peyton, 7 (33), Republic of Ireland.

Most League Appearances: Sean O'Driscoll, 423, 1984–95.

Honours – Football League: Division 3 Champions – 1986–87. **Associate Members' Cup:** Winners 1984.

Colours: Red with black panel shirts, black shorts, black stockings.

BRADFORD CITY   FL CHAMPIONSHIP 1

Atherton Peter (D)	5 11	13 12	Wigan	6 4 70	Sheffield W
Bower Mark (D)	5 10	11 00	Bradford	23 1 80	Trainee
Branch Michael (F)	5 10	11 07	Liverpool	18 10 78	Wolverhampton W
Cadamarteri Danny (F)	5 9	12 10	Bradford	12 10 79	Everton
Combe Alan (G)	6 1	12 05	Edinburgh	3 4 74	Dundee U
Cornwall Luke (F)	5 10	12 01	Lambeth	23 7 80	Fulham
Edds Gareth (D)	5 11	11 01	Sydney	3 2 81	Swindon T
Emanuel Lewis (D)	5 8	12 01	Bradford	14 10 83	Scholar
Folkes Peter (D)	5 11	12 08	Birmingham	16 11 84	Bristol C

Forrest Danny (M)	5 10	11 07	Keighley	23 10 84	Trainee
Gavin Jason (D)	6 0	11 13	Dublin	14 3 80	Middlesbrough
Heckingbottom Paul (D)	6 0	12 05	Barnsley	17 7 77	Norwich C
Jacobs Wayne (D)	5 9	11 02	Sheffield	3 2 69	Rotherham U
Kearney Tom (M)	5 11	10 08	Liverpool	7 10 81	Everton
Paston Mark (G)	6 5	14 03	Hastings, NZ	13 12 76	Napier City R
Standing Michael (M)	5 10	10 05	Shoreham	20 3 81	Aston Villa
Summerbee Nicky (M)	5 11	12 08	Altrincham	26 8 71	Leicester C
Wetherall David (D)	6 3	13 12	Sheffield	14 3 71	Leeds U
Windass Dean (F)	5 10	12 03	North Ferriby	1 4 69	Sheffield U
Wolleaston Robert (F)	5 11	11 09	Perivale	21 12 79	Chelsea

League Appearances: Armstrong, A. 6; Atherton, P. 27; Beresford, M. 5; Bower, M. 11(3); Branch, M. 29(4); Cadamarteri, D. 14(4); Combe, A. 21; Cornwall, L. 2(1); Davies, C. 1(1); Edds, G. 19(4); Emanuel, L. 18(10); Evans, P. 20(3); Farrelly, G. 14; Forrest, D. 2(11); Francis, S. 25(5); Gavin, J. 37(1); Gray, A. 33; Heckingbottom, P. 43; Jacobs, W. 11(2); Kearney, T. 13(4); McHugh, F. 3; Muirhead, B. 12(16); Paston, M. 13; Penford, T. 3(1); Sanasy, K. 2(3); Standing, M. 2(4); Summerbee, N. 33(2); Vaesen, N. 6; Wallwork, R. 7; Wetherall, D. 34; Windass, D. 34(2); Wolleaston, R. 6(8).

Goals – League (38): Branch 6, Windass 6, Gray 5, Wallwork 4, Cadamarteri 3, Evans 3, Atherton 2, Emanuel 2, Muirhead 2, Armstrong 1, Sanasy 1, Summerbee 1, Wetherall 1, Wolleaston 1.

Carling Cup (0).

FA Cup (1): Gray 1 (pen).

Ground: Valley Parade, Bradford BD8 7DY. Telephone (01274) 773355.

Record Attendance: 39,146 v Burnley, FA Cup 4th rd, 11 March 1911. **Capacity:** 25,136.

Manager: Colin Todd.

Secretary: Jon Pollard.

Most League Goals: 128, Division 3 (N), 1928–29.

Highest League Scorer in Season: David Layne, 34, Division 4, 1961–62.

Most League Goals in Total Aggregate: Bobby Campbell, 121, 1981–84, 1984–86.

Most Capped Player: Jamie Lawrence, Jamaica.

Most League Appearances: Cec Podd, 502, 1970–84.

Honours – Football League: Division 2 Champions – 1907–08. Division 3 Champions – 1984–85. Division 3 (N) Champions – 1928–29. **FA Cup:** Winners 1911.

Colours: Claret and amber shirts, white shorts with claret and amber trim, claret stockings with amber and black trim.

BRENTFORD   FL CHAMPIONSHIP 1

Dobson Michael (D)	5 11	12 04	Isleworth	9 4 81	Trainee
Harrold Matt (F)	6 1	11 10	Leyton	24 7 84	Trainee
Hunt Steve (M)	5 7	12 06	Port Laoise	1 8 80	Crystal Palace
Hutchinson Eddie (M)	6 1	12 07	Kingston	23 2 82	Sutton U
Julian Alan (G)	6 2	13 07	Ashford	11 3 83	Trainee
Nelson Stuart (G)	6 1	12 12	Stroud	17 9 81	Doncaster R, Hucknall
O'Connor Kevin (F)	5 11	12 00	Blackburn	24 2 82	Trainee
Rhodes Alex (F)	5 9	10 04	Cambridge	23 1 82	Newmarket T
Smith Jay (M)	5 11	11 07	Hammersmith	29 12 81	Trainee

Somner Matt (D)	6 0	13 00	Isleworth	8 12 82	Trainee	
Sonko Ibrahima (D)	6 3	13 07	Bignola	22 1 81		
Tabb Jay (M)	5 5	9 07	Tooting	21 2 84	Trainee	
Talbot Stuart (M)	6 0	13 12	Birmingham	14 6 73	Rotherham U	

League Appearances: Beadle, P. 1; Blackman, L. (3); Bull, R. 20; Dobson, M. 42; Evans, S. 14(11); Fieldwick, L. 4(1); Fitzgerald, S. 9; Frampton, A. 10(6); Harrold, M. 5(8); Hughes, S. 1(8); Hunt. S. 38(2); Hutchinson, E. 36; Julian, A. 13; Kitamirike, J. 21(1); May, B. 38(3); Nelson, S. 9; O'Connor, K. 36(7); Olugbodi, J. (2); Peters, M. 2(7); Rhodes, A. (3); Roget, L. 15; Rougier, T. 29(2); Smith, J. 12(5); Smith, P. 24; Somner, M. 30(9); Sonko, I. 42(1); Tabb, J. 22(14); Talbot, S. 15; Wells, D. (1); Wright, T. 18(7).
Goals – League (52): Hunt 11 (5 pens), Tabb 9, May 7, Hutchinson 5, Rougier 4, Sonko 3, Wright 3, Evans 2, Harrold 2, Talbot 2, Dobson 1, O'Connor 1, Rhodes 1, own goal 1.
Carling Cup (0).
FA Cup (7): Harrold 3, Frampton 1, O'Connor 1, Rougier 1, own goal 1.
LDV Vans Trophy (5): Hunt 2 (2 pens), Tabb 2, Dobson 1.
Ground: Griffin Park, Braemar Road, Brentford, Middlesex TW8 0NT. Telephone (0870) 900 9229.
Record Attendance: 39,626 v Preston NE, FA Cup 6th rd, 5 March 1938. **Capacity:** 12,500.
Manager: Martin Allen.
Secretary: Lisa Hall.
Most League Goals: 98, Division 4, 1962–63.
Highest League Scorer in Season: Jack Holliday, 38, Division 3 (S), 1932–33.
Most League Goals in Total Aggregate: Jim Towers, 153, 1954–61.
Most Capped Player: John Buttigieg, 22 (98), Malta.
Most League Appearances: Ken Coote, 514, 1949–64.
Honours – Football League: Division 2 Champions – 1934–35. Division 3 Champions – 1991–92, 1998–99. Division 3 (S) Champions – 1932–33. Division 4 Champions – 1962–63.
Colours: Red and white vertical striped shirts, black shorts, black stockings.

BRIGHTON & HOVE ALBION   FL CHAMPIONSHIP

Beck Dan (F)	5 10	10 06	Worthing	14 11 83	Scholar
Carpenter Richard (M)	6 0	13 03	Sheppey	30 9 72	Cardiff C
Cullip Danny (D)	6 0	12 12	Ascot	17 9 76	Brentford
El-Abd Adam (D)	5 10	13 05	Brighton	11 9 84	Scholar
Hammond Dean (M)	6 1	11 02	Hastings	7 3 83	Scholar
Harding Daniel (D)	6 0	11 11	Gloucester	23 12 83	Scholar
Hart Gary (F)	5 9	12 07	Harlow	21 9 76	Stansted
Hinshelwood Adam (D)	5 11	13 00	Oxford	8 1 84	Scholar
Jones Stuart (G)					
Knight Leon (F)	5 5	10 02	Hackney	16 9 82	Chelsea
Kuipers Michels (G)	6 2	15 00	Amsterdam	26 6 74	Bristol R
Mayo Kerry (D)	5 9	13 10	Cuckfield	21 9 77	Trainee
McArthur Duncan (M)	5 9	12 06	Brighton	6 5 81	Trainee
McPhee Christopher (F)	6 0	11 11	Eastbourne	20 3 83	Scholar
Roberts Ben (G)	6 2	13 05	Bishop Auckland	22 6 75	Charlton Ath
Robinson Jake (F)	5 7	10 10	Brighton	23 10 86	Scholar

| Virgo Adam (D) | 6 2 | 13 12 | Brighton | 25 1 83 | |
| Watson Paul (D) | 5 8 | 11 04 | Hastings | 4 1 75 | Brentford |

League Appearances: Beck, D. (1); Benjamin, T. 10; Butters, G. 43; Carpenter, R. 40(2); Cullip, D. 40; El-Abd, A. 6(5); Flitney, R. 3; Harding, D. 17(6); Hart, G. 35(7); Henderson, D. 10; Hinshelwood, A. 16(1); Iwelumo, C. 10; Jones, N. 34(2); Jones, S. 2(1); Knight, L. 43(1); Kuipers, M. 9(1); Lee, D. 1(3); Marney, D. (3); Mayo, K. 31(3); McPhee, C. 17(12); Oatway, C. 29(2); Pethick, R. 6(8); Piercy, J. 8(16); Rehman, Z. 9(2); Reid, P. 4(1); Roberts, B. 32; Robinson, J. 1(8); Rodger, S. 7; Virgo, A. 20(2); Watson, P. 14(1); Wilkinson, S. (2); Yeates, M. 9.

Goals – League (64): Knight 25 (7 pens), Benjamin 5, Carpenter 4, Iwelumo 4, McPhee 4, Piercy 4, Butters 3, Hart 3, Henderson 2 (2 pens), Rehman 2, Cullip 1, Oatway 1, Virgo 1, own goals 5.

Carling Cup (1): McPhee 1.

FA Cup (1): McPhee 1.

LDV Vans Trophy (6): McPhee 3 (1 pen), Carpenter 1, Knight 1, Robinson 1.

Play-Offs (3): Carpenter 1, Knight 1 (pen), Virgo 1.

Ground: Withdean Stadium, Tongdean Lane, Brighton. East Sussex BN1 5JD. Telephone (01273) 695400

Record Attendance: 36,747 v Fulham, Division 2, 27 December 1958 (at Goldstone Ground).

Capacity: 6973 (all seated).

Manager: Mark McGhee.

Secretary: Derek Allan.

Most League Goals: 112, Division 3 (S), 1955–56.

Highest League Scorer in Season: Peter Ward, 32, Division 3, 1976–77.

Most League Goals in Total Aggregate: Tommy Cook, 114, 1922–29.

Most Capped Player: Steve Penney, 17, Northern Ireland.

Most League Appearances: 'Tug' Wilson, 509, 1922–36.

Honours – Football League: Division 2 Champions – 2001–02. Division 3 Champions – 2000–01. Division 3 (S) Champions – 1957–58. Division 4 Champions – 1964–65.

Colours: Blue and white striped shirts, white shorts, white stockings.

BRISTOL CITY   FL CHAMPIONSHIP 1

Amankwaah Kevin (D)	6 0	12 12	London	19 5 82	Scholar
Anyinsah Joseph (M)			Bristol	8 10 84	Scholar
Brown Aaron (M)	5 11	12 13	Bristol	14 3 80	Trainee
Burnell Joe (D)	5 8	12 00	Bristol	10 10 80	Trainee
Butler Tony (D)	6 1	13 07	Stockport	28 9 72	WBA
Coles Daniel (D)	6 0	13 05	Bristol	31 10 81	Scholar
Doherty Tom (M)	5 7	11 12	Bristol	17 3 79	Trainee
Fortune Clayton (D)	6 0	14 04	Forest Gate	10 11 82	Tottenham H
Goodfellow Marc (F)	5 10	11 00	Swadlincote	20 9 81	Stoke C
Hawkins Darren (M)	5 10	11 09	Bristol	25 4 84	Scholar
Hill Matt (D)	5 7	11 13	Bristol	26 3 81	Trainee
Lita Leroy (F)	5 7	11 12	Congo	28 12 84	Scholar
Loxton Craig (M)			Bath	14 9 84	Scholar
Miller Lee (F)	6 2	11 07	Lanark	15 3 83	Falkirk
Murray Scott (M)	5 7	11 02	Aberdeen	26 5 74	Reading

Phillips Steve (G)	6 0	13 06	Bath	6 5 78	Paulton R
Simpson Sekani (M)	5 10	11 10	Bristol	11 3 84	Scholar
Tinnion Brian (M)	6 0	13 05	Stanley	23 3 68	Bradford C
Wilkshire Luke (M)	5 10	11 00	Wollongong	2 10 81	Middlesbrough
Woodman Craig (D)	5 8	11 00	Tiverton	22 12 82	Trainee

League Appearances: Amankwaah, K. 4(1); Bell, M. 20(7); Brown, A. 29(1); Brown, M. 1(1); Burnell, J. 14(3); Butler, T. 37(1); Carey, L. 41; Clist, S. 1; Coles, D. 45; Doherty, T. 28(5); Fortune, C. 1(5); Goodfellow, M. 7(8); Hill, M. 40(2); Lita, L. 2(24); Matthews, L. 1(7); Miller, L. 32(10); Murray, S. 4(2); Peacock, L. 39(2); Phillips, S. 46; Roberts, C. 24(14); Rougier, T. 5(1); Tinnion, B. 36(9); Wilkshire, L. 35(2); Woodman, C. 14(7).

Goals – League (58): Peacock 14, Miller 8, Roberts 6, Brown A 5, Lita 5, Goodfellow 4, Coles 2, Doherty 2, Hill 2, Matthews 2, Tinnion 2, Wilkshire 2, Burnell 1, Butler 1, Carey 1, Rougier 1.

Carling Cup (5): Peacock 2, Bell 1 (pen), Coles 1, Miller 1.

FA Cup (6): Amankwaah 2, Matthews 1, Roberts 1, Wilkshire 1, own goal 1.

LDV Vans Trophy (0).

Play-Offs (3): Goodfellow 1, Roberts 1, Rougier 1.

Ground: Ashton Gate, Bristol BS3 2EJ. Telephone (0117) 9630630.

Record Attendance: 43,335 v Preston NE, FA Cup 5th rd, 16 February 1935.

Capacity: 21,479.

Manager: Brian Tinnion.

Secretary: Michelle McDonald.

Most League Goals: 104, Division 3 (S), 1926–27.

Highest League Scorer in Season: Don Clark, 36, Division 3 (S), 1946–47.

Most League Goals in Total Aggregate: John Atyeo, 314, 1951–66.

Most Capped Player: Billy Wedlock, 26, England.

Most League Appearances: John Atyeo, 597, 1951–66.

Honours – Football League: Division 2 Champions – 1905–06. Division 3 (S) Champions – 1922–23, 1926–27, 1954–55. **Welsh Cup winners** 1934. **Anglo-Scottish Cup:** Winners 1977–78. **Freight Rover Trophy winners** 1985–86. **LDV Vans Trophy winners** 2002–03.

Colours: Red shirts, red shorts, red stockings.

BRISTOL ROVERS FL CHAMPIONSHIP 2

Agogo Junior (F)	5 10	11 07	Accra	1 8 79	Barnet
Anderson Ijah (D)	5 8	10 06	Hackney	30 12 75	Brentford
Anderson John (D)	6 2	12 02	Greenock	2 10 72	Hull C
Austin Kevin (D)	6 0	14 00	Hackney	12 2 73	Cambridge U
Bryant Simon (M)	5 11	13 04	Bristol	22 11 82	Scholar
Clarke Ryan (G)	6 3	13 00	Bristol	30 4 82	
Edwards Christian (D)	6 2	12 08	Caerphilly	23 11 75	Nottingham F
Gibb Ali (M)	5 9	11 07	Salisbury	17 2 76	Stockport Co
Haldane Lewis (F)	6 0	11 03	Trowbridge	13 3 85	Scholar
Miller Kevin (G)	6 1	13 00	Falmouth	15 3 69	Exeter C
Parker Sonny (D)	5 11	11 11	Middlesbrough	28 2 83	Birmingham C
Savage David (M)	6 2	12 07	Dublin	30 7 73	Oxford U
Thorpe Lee (F)	6 1	12 07	Wolverhampton	14 12 75	Leyton Orient
Williams Ryan (M)	5 5	11 04	Sutton-in-Ashfield	31 8 78	Hull C

League Appearances: Agogo, J. 28(10); Anderson, I. 37(2); Anderson, J. 8; Arndale, N. 1(2); Austin, K. 21(2); Barrett, A. 45; Boxall, D. 23(1); Bryant, S. 7(5); Carlisle, W. 22(3); Clarke, R. 2; Edwards, C. 40(2); Gibb, A. 8; Gilroy, D. 1(3); Haldane, L. 16(11); Henriksen, B. 1(3); Hobbs, S. (2); Hodges, L. 5(8); Hyde, G. 33(4); Lescott, A. 8; Matthews, L. 9; Miller, K. 44; Parker, S. 13(2); Quinn, R. 23(12); Rammell, A. 1(4); Savage, D. 37(1); Street, K. 8(5); Tait, P. 28(5); Thorpe, L. 8(2); Twigg, G. 7(1); U'ddin, A. 1; Williams, D. 6; Williams, R. 15(4); Willock, C. (5).

Goals – League (50): Tait 12 (1 pen), Carlisle 7 (4 pens), Agogo 6, Haldane 5, Barrett 4, Hodges 2, Hyde 2, Rammell 2, Savage 2, Gibb 1, Parker 1, Quinn 1, Street 1, Thorpe 1, Williams D 1, Williams R 1, own goal 1.

Carling Cup (0).

FA Cup (0).

LDV Vans Trophy (1): Haldane 1.

Ground: The Memorial Ground, Filton Avenue, Horfield, Bristol BS7 0BF. Telephone (0117) 9096648

Record Attendance: 9464 v Liverpool, FA Cup 4th rd, 8 February 1992 (Twerton Park). 38,472 v Preston NE, FA Cup 4th rd, 30 January 1960 (Eastville). 11,433 v Sunderland, League Cup 3rd rd, 31 October 2000 (Memorial Ground).

Capacity: 11,679.

Manager: Ian Atkins.

Secretary: Rod Wesson.

Most League Goals: 92, Division 3 (S), 1952–53.

Highest League Scorer in Season: Geoff Bradford, 33, Division 3 (S), 1952–53.

Most League Goals in Total Aggregate: Geoff Bradford, 242, 1949–64.

Most Capped Player: Vitalijs Astafjevs, 31 (105), Latvia.

Most League Appearances: Stuart Taylor, 546, 1966–80.

Honours – Football League: Division 3 (S) Champions – 1952–53. Division 3 Champions – 1989–90.

Colours: Blue and white quartered shirts, white shorts, blue stockings.

BURNLEY

FL CHAMPIONSHIP

Blake Robbie (F)	5 9	11 00	Middlesbrough	4 3 76	Bradford C
Branch Graham (D)	6 2	12 02	Liverpool	12 2 72	Stockport Co
Camara Mo (D)	5 11	11 09	Conakry	25 6 75	Wolverhampton W
Chaplow Richard (M)	5 9	9 0	Accrington	2 2 85	Scholar
Grant Tony (M)	5 11	10 10	Liverpool	14 11 74	Manchester C
Jensen Brian (G)	6 4	12 04	Copenhagen	8 6 75	WBA
Johnrose Lenny (M)	5 10	12 06	Preston	29 11 69	Swansea C
Moore Ian (F)	5 11	12 02	Birkenhead	26 8 76	Stockport Co
O'Neill Matt (F)	5 11	10 00	Accrington	25 6 84	Scholar
Pilkington Joel (M)	5 8	10 04	Accrington	1 8 84	Scholar
Roche Lee (D)	5 10	10 11	Bolton	28 10 80	Manchester U

League Appearances: Adebola, D. (3); Blake, R. 44(1); Branch, G. 30(8); Camara, M. 45; Chadwick, L. 23(13); Chaplow, R. 30(9); Facey, D. 12(2); Farrelly, G. 9(3); Gnohere, A. 12(2); Grant, T. 34(3); Jensen, B. 46; Johnrose, L. 4(3); Little, G. 33(1); May, D. 34(1); McEveley, J. (4); McGregor, M. 20(3); Moore, A. 5(8); Moore, I. 38(2); O'Neill, M. (4); Orr, B. 1(3); Pilkington, J. (1); Roche, L. 21(4); Scott, P. (2); Todd, A. 7; Townsend, R. (1); Weller, P. 25(8); West, D. 25(7); Wood, N. 8(2).

Goals – League (60): Blake 19 (4 pens), Moore I 9, Chadwick 5, Chaplow 5, Facey

5, May 4, Branch 3, Little 3, Adebola 1, Gnohere 1, McGregor 1, Roche 1, West 1, Wood 1, own goal 1.

Carling Cup (3): Blake 1, Chadwick 1, Moore I 1.

FA Cup (5): Moore I 3, Blake 2.

Ground: Turf Moor, Burnley BB10 4BX. Telephone (0870) 4431882.

Record Attendance: 54,775 v Huddersfield T, FA Cup 3rd rd, 23 February 1924.

Capacity: 22,500.

Manager: Steve Cotterill.

Secretary: Cathy Pickup.

Most League Goals: 102, Division 1, 1960–61.

Highest League Scorer in Season: George Beel, 35, Division 1, 1927–28.

Most League Goals in Total Aggregate: George Beel, 178, 1923–32.

Most Capped Player: Jimmy McIlroy, 51 (55), Northern Ireland.

Most League Appearances: Jerry Dawson, 522, 1907–28.

Honours – Football League: Division 1 Champions – 1920–21, 1959–60. Division 2 Champions – 1897–98, 1972–73. Division 3 Champions – 1981–82. Division 4 Champions – 1991–92. **FA Cup winners** 1913–14. **Anglo-Scottish Cup:** Winners 1978–79.

Colours: Claret and blue shirts, white shorts, white stockings.

BURY   FL CHAMPIONSHIP 2

Dunfield Terry (M)	5 11	12 04	Vancouver	20 2 82	Manchester C
Duxbury Lee (M)	5 10	10 09	Keighley	7 10 69	Oldham Ath
Garner Glyn (G)	6 2	13 04	Pontypool	9 12 76	Llanelli
Kennedy Tom (D)	5 10	11 01	Bury	24 6 85	Scholar
Nugent Dave (F)	5 11	12 00	Liverpool	2 5 85	Scholar
Porter Chris (F)	6 1	12 06	Wigan	12 12 83	
Swailes Danny (D)	6 3	13 03	Bolton	1 4 79	Trainee
Whaley Simon (F)	5 10	11 11	Bolton	7 6 85	Scholar

League Appearances: Barrass, M. 19(3); Cartledge, J. 7(4); Challinor, D. 15; Charnock, P. 3; Clegg, G. 4(2); Connell, L. 23(5); Daly, J. 7; Dunfield, T. 28(2); Duxbury, L. 36(1); Flitcroft, D. 17; Garner, G. 46; Gulliver, P. 10; Gunby, S. 1(4); Kennedy, T. 22(5); Nugent, D. 20(6); O'Neill, J. 10(13); O'Shaughnessy, P. 21(6); Porter, C. 19(18); Preece, A. 10(4); Seddon, G. 28(12); Singh, H. 20(8); Strong, G. 10; Swailes, D. 42; Thompson, J. 1; Thornley, B. 5; Unsworth, L. 27; Whaley, S. 3(7); Whelan, G. 13; Woodthorpe, C. 39.

Goals – League (54): Seddon 11, Porter 9 (1 pen), Connell 6, Preece 5 (3 pens), Swailes 5 (2 pens), Nugent 3, O'Neill 3, Dunfield 2, Singh 2, Unsworth 2, Barrass 1, Cartledge 1, Daly 1, O'Shaughnessy 1, Whaley 1, own goal 1.

Carling Cup (0).

FA Cup (1): Porter 1.

LDV Vans Trophy (2): Preece 1, Thompson 1.

Ground: Gigg Lane, Bury BL9 9HR. Telephone (0161) 764 4881.

Record Attendance: 35,000 v Bolton W, FA Cup 3rd rd, 9 January 1960. **Capacity:** 11,669.

Manager: Graham Barrow.

Secretary: Jill Neville.

Most League Goals: 108, Division 3, 1960–61.

Highest League Scorer in Season: Craig Madden, 35, Division 4, 1981–82.

Most League Goals in Total Aggregate: Craig Madden, 129, 1978–86.

Most Capped Player: Bill Gorman, 11 (13), Republic of Ireland and (4), Northern Ireland.
Most League Appearances: Norman Bullock, 506, 1920–35.
Honours – Football League: Division 2 Champions – 1894–95, 1996–97. Division 3 Champions – 1960–61. **FA Cup winners** 1900, 1903. **Auto Windscreens Shield winners** 1997.
Colours: White shirts, royal blue shorts, white stockings.

CAMBRIDGE UNITED   FL CHAMPIONSHIP 2

Angus Stevland (D)	6 0	12 00	Essex	16 9 80	West Ham U
Bimson Stuart (D)	5 11	11 12	Liverpool	29 9 69	Lincoln C
Brennan Martin (G)	6 1	12 00	Whipps Cross	14 9 82	Charlton Ath
Bridges David (M)	6 0	12 00	Huntingdon	22 9 82	Scholar
Chillingworth Daniel (F)	6 0	12 06	Cambridge	13 9 81	Scholar
Gleeson Dan (M)	6 3	13 02	Cambridge	17 2 85	Scholar
Guttridge Luke (M)	5 5	8 06	Barnstaple	27 3 82	Torquay U
Marshall Shaun (G)	6 1	13 03	Fakenham	3 10 78	Trainee
Murray Fred (D)	5 10	11 12	Tipperary	22 5 82	Blackburn R
Nacca Franco (D)	5 6	10 00	Venezuela	9 11 82	Scholar
Tann Adam (D)	6 0	11 05	Fakenham	12 5 82	Scholar
Tudor Shane (M)	5 7	11 00	Wolverhampton	10 2 82	Wolverhampton W
Turner John (F)	5 10	11 00	Harrow	12 2 86	Scholar
Webb Daniel (F)	6 1	11 08	Poole	2 7 83	Hull C

League Appearances: Angus, S. 39(1); Bimson, S. 21(3); Bridges, D. 11(10); Chillingworth, D. 10(3); Clarke, C. (1); Daniels, D. (1); Duncan, A. 37; Dutton, B. (3); Easter, J. 10(5); Fleming, T. 17(1); Fuller, A. (1); Gleeson, D. 3(4); Goodhind, W. 25(1); Guttridge, L. 46; Kitson, D. 17; Lockett, R. 1(1); Marshall, S. 45; McCafferty, N. 5(1); Murray, F. 34(4); Nacca, F. 2(7); Nicholls, A. 15(1); Opara, L. 1(7); Peat, N. 3(3); Quinton, D. (1); Revell, A. 10(10); Robinson, M. 1(2); Ruddy, J. 1; Smith, S. 1(1); Tann, A. 31(3); Taylor, J. 6(3); Tudor, S. 30(6); Turner, J. 17(19); Venus, M. 21; Walker, J. 23; Webb, D. 19(2); Williams, G. 4.
Goals – League (55): Guttridge 11 (2 pens), Kitson 10, Chillingworth 7, Revell 3, Tudor 3 (1 pen), Turner 3, Webb 3, Bridges 2, Duncan 2, Easter 2, Tann 2, Angus 1, Fleming 1, Nicholls 1, Opara 1, Walker 1, Williams 1, own goal 1.
Carling Cup (1): Walker 1.
FA Cup (5): Turner 2, Guttridge 1, Kitson 1, Tann 1.
LDV Vans Trophy (0).
Ground: Abbey Stadium, Newmarket Road, Cambridge CB5 8LN. Telephone (01223) 566500. **Capacity:** 9217.
Record Attendance: 14,000 v Chelsea, Friendly, 1 May 1970.
Manager: Herve Renard.
Secretary: Andrew Pincher.
Most League Goals: 87, Division 4, 1976–77.
Highest League Scorer in Season: David Crown, 24, Division 4, 1985–86.
Most League Goals in Total Aggregate: John Taylor, 86, 1988–92; 1996–01.
Most Capped Player: Tom Finney, 7 (15), Northern Ireland.
Most League Appearances: Steve Spriggs, 416, 1975–87.
Honours – Football League: Division 3 Champions – 1990–91. Division 4 Champions – 1976–77.
Colours: Amber shirts, black shorts, amber stockings.

Name			Birthplace			Previous Club
Alexander Neil (G)	6 1	11 07	Edinburgh	10	3 78	Livingston
Anthony Byron (D)	6 1	11 00	Newport	20	9 84	Scholar
Barker Chris (D)	6 2	11 08	Sheffield	2	3 80	Barnsley
Boland Willie (M)	5 9	11 02	Ennis	6	8 75	Coventry C
Campbell Andy (F)	5 11	11 07	Middlesbrough	18	4 79	Middlesbrough
Collins James (D)	6 2	13 00	Newport	23	8 83	Scholar
Earnshaw Robert (F)	5 6	9 09	Zambia	6	4 81	Trainee
Fish Nicky (M)	5 10	11 04	Cardiff	15	9 84	Scholar
Fleetwood Stuart (F)	5 10	11 08	Gloucester	23	4 86	Scholar
Gabbidon Daniel (D)	6 0	11 02	Cwmbran	8	8 79	WBA
Huggins Kirk (D)	5 11	11 03	Cardiff	4	6 85	Scholar
Ingram Richard (F)	5 9	10 08	Merthyr	15	2 85	Scholar
Kavanagh Graham (M)	5 10	12 08	Dublin	2	12 73	Stoke C
Langley Richard (M)	5 10	11 04	Harlesden	27	12 79	QPR
Lee-Barrett Arran (G)	6 2	12 00	Ipswich	28	2 84	Norwich C
Lee Alan (F)	6 2	13 09	Galway	21	8 78	Rotherham U
Parkins Michael (M)	5 8	11 02	Cardiff	12	1 85	Scholar
Parry Paul (M)	5 11	11 12	Newport	19	8 80	Hereford U
Robinson John (M)	5 10	11 07	Bulawayo	29	8 71	Charlton Ath
Thomas Danny (F)	5 5	10 10	Caerphilly	13	5 85	Scholar
Thorne Peter (F)	6 0	12 10	Manchester	21	6 73	Stoke C
Vidmar Tony (D)	6 1	12 10	Adelaide	15	4 69	Middlesbrough
Weston Rhys (D)	6 1	12 03	Kingston	27	10 80	Arsenal
Whalley Gareth (M)	5 10	11 00	Manchester	19	12 73	Bradford C

League Appearances: Alexander, N. 24(1); Barker, C. 33(6); Boland, W. 33(4); Bonner, M. 14(6); Bowen, J. (2); Bullock, L. 4(7); Campbell, A. 6(19); Collins, J. 15(5); Croft, G. 23(4); Earnshaw, R. 44(2); Fleetwood, S. (2); Gabbidon, D. 41; Gordon, G. 7(8); Gray, J. 5(4); Kavanagh, G. 27; Langley, R. 39(5); Lee, A. 17(6); Lee-Barrett, A. ; Margetson, M. 22; Maxwell, L. (1); Parry, P. 14(3); Prior, S. 4(3); Robinson, J. 31(3); Thorne, P. 19(4); Vidmar, T. 45; Weston, R. 23(1); Whalley, G. 16(6).

Goals – League (68): Earnshaw 21 (4 pens), Thorne 13, Kavanagh 7 (1 pen), Langley 6 (1 pen), Bullock 3, Gabbidon 3, Lee 3, Campbell 2, Robinson 2, Whalley 2, Collins 1, Croft 1, Gordon 1, Parry 1, Vidmar 1, own goal 1.

Carling Cup (6): Earnshaw 5, Campbell 1.

FA Cup (0).

Ground: Ninian Park, Cardiff CF11 8SX. Telephone (029) 2022 1001.

Record Attendance: 61,566, Wales v England, 14 October 1961. **Capacity:** 21,508.

Manager: Lennie Lawrence

Secretary: Jason Turner.

Most League Goals: 95, Division 3, 2000–01.

Highest League Scorer in Season: Robert Earnshaw, 31, Division 2, 2002–03.

Most League Goals in Total Aggregate: Len Davies, 128, 1920–31.

Most Capped Player: Alf Sherwood, 39 (41), Wales.

Most League Appearances: Phil Dwyer, 471, 1972–85.

Honours – Football League: Division 3 (S) Champions – 1946–47. **FA Cup winners** 1926–27 (only occasion the Cup has been won by a club outside England). **Welsh Cup winners** 22 times.

Colours: Blue shirts, blue shorts, blue stockings.

Andrews Lee (D)	5 11	12 00	Carlisle	23	4 83	Scholar
Arnison Paul (D)	5 9	10 12	Hartlepool	18	9 77	Hartlepool U
Billy Chris (M)	6 0	12 13	Huddersfield	2	1 73	Bury
Cowan Tom (D)	5 6	11 10	Bellshill	28	8 69	York C
Farrell Craig (F)	6 0	12 06	Middlesbrough	5	12 82	Leeds U
Glennon Matty (G)	6 2	14 08	Stockport	8	10 78	Hull C
Gray Kevin (D)	6 0	13 00	Sheffield	7	1 72	Tranmere R
Jack Michael (M)	5 10	11 08	Carlisle	2	10 82	Trainee
Keen Peter (G)	6 0	13 00	Middlesbrough	16	11 76	Newcastle U
Kelly Darren (D)	6 0	13 00	Derry	30	6 79	Derry C
McDonagh Will (M)	6 0	12 06	Dublin	14	3 83	Bohemians
McGill Brendan (M)	5 7	11 00	Dublin	22	3 81	Sunderland
Murphy Peter (D)	5 11	12 06	Dublin	27	10 80	Blackburn R
Raven Paul (D)	6 1	13 02	Salisbury	28	7 70	Grimsby T
Rundle Adam (M)	5 8	11 00	Durham	8	7 84	Darlington
Shelley Brian (D)	6 0	13 00	Dublin	15	11 81	Bohemians
Summerbell Mark (M)	5 9	11 06	Durham	30	10 76	Middlesbrough

League Appearances: Andrews, L. 33(4); Arnison, P. 20(6); Baldacchino, R. (1); Billy, C. 39; Birch, M. 2; Boyd, M. 9; Byrne, D. 9(2); Cowan, T. 20; Duffield, P. 10; Farrell, C. 21(9); Foran, R. 20(3); Fryatt, M. 9(1); Glennon, M. 44; Gray, K. 25; Henderson, K. 10(9); Jack, M. (3); Keen, P. 2(1); Kelly, D. 9(1); Langmead, K. 3(8); Livingstone, S. 6; Maddison, L. 2; McDonagh, W. 23(4); McGill, B. 42(2); Molloy, D. 3(4); Murphy, P. 33(2); Preece, A. 23(2); Raven, P. 13; Rundle, A. 6(17); Russell, C. 3(3); Schumacher, S. 4; Shelley, B. 28(3); Simpson, P. 25; Smith, S. 4; Summerbell, M. 4(2); Wake, B. 2(13); Warhurst, P. (1).

Goals – League (46): Farrell 7 (1 pen), McGill 7, Simpson 6, Foran 4 (2 pens), Duffield 3, Gray 3, Preece 3, Henderson 2, Arnison 1, Billy 1, Boyd 1, Cowan 1, Fryatt 1, Kelly 1, Langmead 1, McDonagh 1, Murphy 1, Raven 1, own goal 1.

Carling Cup (1): Russell 1.

FA Cup (0).

LDV Vans Trophy (4): Wake 2, Rundle 1, Schumacher 1.

Ground: Brunton Park, Carlisle CA1 1LL. Telephone (01228) 526237.

Record Attendance: 27,500 v Birmingham C, FA Cup 3rd rd, 5 January 1957 and v Middlesbrough, FA Cup 5th rd, 7 February 1970. **Capacity:** 14,496.

Manager: Paul Simpson.

Secretary: Sarah McKnight.

Most League Goals: 113, Division 4, 1963–64.

Highest League Scorer in Season: Jimmy McConnell, 42, Division 3 (N), 1928–29.

Most League Goals in Total Aggregate: Jimmy McConnell, 126, 1928–32.

Most Capped Player: Eric Welsh, 4, Northern Ireland.

Most League Appearances: Allan Ross, 466, 1963–79.

Honours – Football League: Division 3 Champions – 1964–65, 1994–95. **Auto Windscreens Shield winners:** 1997

Colours: Blue shirts, white shorts, blue stockings.

CHARLTON ATHLETIC   FA PREMIERSHIP

Bartlett Shaun (F)	6 0	12 06	Cape Town	31 10 72	Zurich
Campbell-Ryce Jamal (F)	5 7	11 10	Lambeth	6 4 83	Scholar
Euell Jason (F)	5 11	11 13	Lambeth	6 2 77	Wimbledon
Fish Mark (D)	6 4	12 11	Cape Town	14 3 74	Bolton W
Fortune Jon (D)	6 2	12 12	Islington	23 8 80	Trainee
Holland Matt (M)	5 10	12 03	Bury	11 4 74	Ipswich T
Hreidarsson Hermann (D)	6 3	12 12	Reykjavik	11 7 74	Ipswich T
Jensen Claus (M)	5 11	12 00	Nykobing	29 4 77	Bolton W
Johansson Jonatan (F)	6 2	12 08	Stockholm	16 8 75	Rangers
Kiely Dean (G)	6 1	13 10	Salford	10 10 70	Bury
Kishishev Radostin (D)	5 11	12 03	Bourgas	30 7 74	Litets Lovech
Konchesky Paul (D)	5 10	11 07	Barking	15 5 81	Trainee
Lisbie Kevin (F)	5 10	11 06	Hackney	17 10 78	Trainee
Long Stacy (M)	5 8	10 00	Bromley	11 1 85	Scholar
McCafferty Neil (M)	5 7	10 00	Derry	19 7 84	Scholar
Perry Chris (D)	5 8	10 12	Carshalton	26 4 73	Tottenham H
Powell Chris (D)	5 8	11 12	Lambeth	8 9 69	Derby Co
Rachubka Paul (G)	6 1	13 01	San Luis Opispo	21 5 81	Manchester U
Rowett Gary (D)	6 0	13 00	Bromsgrove	6 3 74	Leicester C
Royce Simon (G)	6 1	13 09	Forest Gate	9 9 71	Leicester C
Rufus Richard (D)	6 1	12 12	Lewisham	12 1 75	Trainee
Sam Lloyd (F)	5 8	10 00	Leeds	27 9 84	
Sankofa Osei (D)	6 0	12 04	London	19 3 85	Scholar
Stuart Graham (M)	5 9	12 01	Tooting	24 10 70	Sheffield U
Thomas Jerome (M)	5 10	11 10	Brent	23 3 83	Arsenal
Turner Michael (D)	6 4	12 06	Lewisham	9 11 83	Scholar
Varney Alex (F)			Farnborough	27 12 84	Trainee
Young Luke (D)	6 0	12 04	Harlow	19 7 79	Tottenham H

League Appearances: Bartlett, S. 13(6); Campbell-Ryce, J. (2); Cole, C. 8(13); Di Canio, P. 23(8); Euell, J. 24(7); Fish, M. 23; Fortune, J. 21(7); Holland, M. 38; Hreidarsson, H. 33; Jensen, C. 27(4); Johansson, J. 16(10); Kiely, D. 37; Kishishev, R. 30(3); Konchesky, P. 17(4); Lisbie, K. 5(4); Parker, S. 20; Perry, C. 25(4); Powell, C. 11(5); Rowett, G. 1; Royce, S. 1; Stuart, G. 23(5); Svensson, M. 1(2); Thomas, J. (1); Young, L. 21(3).
Goals – League (51): Euell 10 (3 pens), Holland 6, Bartlett 5, Cole 4, Di Canio 4 (3 pens), Jensen 4, Johansson 4, Lisbie 4, Stuart 3, Fortune 2, Hreidarsson 2, Parker 2, Perry 1.
Carling Cup (4): Di Canio 1, Jensen 1, Lisbie 1, Parker 1.
FA Cup (2): Cole 1, own goal 1.
Ground: The Valley, Floyd Road, Charlton, London SE7 8BL. Telephone (020) 8333 4000.
Record Attendance: 75,031 v Aston Villa, FA Cup 5th rd, 12 February 1938 (at The Valley). **Capacity:** 26,875.
Manager: Alan Curbishley.
Secretary: Chris Parkes.
Most League Goals: 107, Division 2, 1957–58.
Highest League Scorer in Season: Ralph Allen, 32, Division 3 (S), 1934–35.
Most League Goals in Total Aggregate: Stuart Leary, 153, 1953–62.

Most Capped Player: Mark Kinsella, 33 (48), Republic of Ireland.
Most League Appearances: Sam Bartram, 583, 1934–56.
Honours – Football League: Division 1 Champions – 1999–2000. Division 3 (S) Champions – 1928–29, 1934–35. **FA Cup winners** 1947.
Colours: Red shirts, white shorts, red stockings.

CHELSEA   FA PREMIERSHIP

Name	Ht		Birthplace	DOB	Previous club
Ambrosio Marco (G)	6 1	13 04	Brescia	30 5 73	Chievo
Babayaro Celestine (D)	5 9	12 01	Kaduna	29 8 78	Anderlecht
Bridge Wayne (D)	5 10	12 08	Southampton	5 8 80	Southampton
Cole Carlton (F)	6 3	13 10	Croydon	12 10 83	Scholar
Cole Joe (M)	5 9	11 13	Islington	8 11 81	West Ham U
Crespo Hernan (F)	6 0	12 13	Florida	5 7 75	Internazionale
Cudicini Carlo (G)	6 1	12 06	Milan	6 9 73	Castel di Sangro
Desailly Marcel (D)	6 0	13 05	Accra	7 9 68	AC Milan
Di Cesare Valerio (D)	6 0	12 11	Rome	23 5 83	
Duff Damien (F)	5 9	12 02	Ballyboden	2 3 79	Blackburn R
Forssell Mikael (F)	6 0	13 08	Steinfurt	15 3 81	Moenchengladbach loan
Gallaccio Michele (F)	5 9	10 12	Rome	3 3 86	Lazio
Gallas William (D)	6 0	12 02	Asnieres	17 8 77	Marseille
Geremi(M)	5 9	13 03	Bafoussam	20 12 78	Middlesbrough
Gronkjaer Jesper (M)	6 2	12 11	Nuuk	12 8 77	Ajax
Gudjohnsen Eidur (F)	6 1	14 01	Reykjavik	15 9 78	Bolton W
Hasselbaink Jimmy Floyd (F)	5 10	13 11	Paramaribo	27 3 72	Atletico Madrid
Hollands Danny (M)	6 0	10 02	Ashford	6 11 85	Trainee
Huth Robert (D)	6 3	13 12	Berlin	18 8 84	
Johnson Glen (D)	5 11	12 11	Greenwich	23 8 84	West Ham U
Keenan Joe (M)	5 8	10 03	Southampton	14 10 82	Trainee
Kneissl Sebastian (F)	6 0	13 03	Lindelfels	13 1 83	
Lampard Frank (M)	6 0	13 12	Romford	20 6 78	West Ham U
Macho Jurgen (G)	6 3	13 05	Vienna	24 8 77	Sunderland
Makalambay Yves (G)	6 5	14 09	Brussels	31 1 86	PSV Eindhoven
Makelele Claude (M)	5 7	10 08	Kinshasa	18 2 73	Real Madrid
McKinlay Kevin (F)	5 11	11 01	Stirling	28 2 86	Trainee
Morais Filipe (M)	5 8	11 07	Lisbon	21 11 85	Trainee
Mutu Adrian (F)	5 11	11 11	Calinesti	8 1 79	Parma
Nicolas Alexis (M)	5 8	9 13	Westminster	13 2 83	Aston Villa
Oliveira Filipe (F)	5 10	11 11	Braga	27 5 84	
Parker Scott (M)	5 9	10 10	Lambeth	13 10 80	Charlton Ath
Pidgeley Lenny (G)	6 3	13 05	Isleworth	7 2 84	Scholar
Rocastle Craig (M)	6 1	12 13	Lewisham	17 8 81	Kingstonian
Smertin Alexei (M)	5 9	10 08	Barnaul	1 5 75	Bordeaux
Smith Dean (D)	5 10	9 11	Islington	13 8 86	Trainee
Stanic Mario (M)	6 2	13 11	Sarajevo	10 4 72	Parma
Sullivan Neil (G)	6 3	15 04	Sutton	24 2 70	Tottenham H
Terry John (D)	6 1	13 12	Barking	7 12 80	Trainee
Tillen Sam (D)	5 9	10 12	Reading	16 4 85	Trainee
Veron Juan Sebastian (F)	5 11	12 04	La Plata	9 3 75	Manchester U
Watt Steven (D)	6 3	13 12	Aberdeen	1 5 85	Trainee

Woodards Danny (F) 5 11 11 01 Forest Gate   7 10 83 Trainee
Zenden Boudewijn (M) 5 8 11 11 Maastricht   15 8 76 Barcelona

League Appearances: Ambrosio, M. 8; Babayaro, C. 5(1); Bridge, W. 33; Cole, J. 18(17); Crespo, H. 13(6); Cudicini, C. 26; Desailly, M. 15; Duff, D. 17(6); Gallas, W. 23(6); Geremi 19(6); Gronkjaer, J. 19(12); Gudjohnsen, E. 17(9); Hasselbaink, J. 22(8); Huth, R. 8(8); Johnson, G. 17(2); Lampard, F. 38; Makelele, C. 26(4); Melchiot, M. 20(3); Mutu, A. 21(4); Nicolas, A. 1(1); Oliveira, F. (1); Parker, S. 7(4); Petit, E. 3(1); Stanic, M. (2); Sullivan, N. 4; Terry, J. 33; Veron, J. 5(2).
Goals – League: (67): Hasselbaink 12 (2 pens), Crespo 10, Lampard 10 (2 pens), Gudjohnsen 6, Mutu 6, Duff 5, Johnson 3, Gronkjaer 2, Melchiot 2, Terry 2, Babayaro 1, Bridge 1, Cole J 1, Geremi 1, Parker 1, Veron 1, own goals 3.
Carling Cup (6): Cole J 2, Gudjohnsen 2 (1 pen), Hasselbaink 2.
FA Cup (8): Mutu 3, Gudjohnsen 2 (1 pen), Hasselbaink 1, Lampard 1, Terry 1.
Champions League (21): Lampard 4, Gudjohnsen 3, Bridge 2, Crespo 2, Hasselbaink 2, Duff 1, Gallas 1, Gronkjaer 1, Huth 1, Johnson 1, Mutu 1, own goals 2.
Ground: Stamford Bridge, London SW6 1HS. Telephone (020) 7385 5545.
Record Attendance: 82,905 v Arsenal, Division 1, 12 October 1935.
Capacity: 42,449.
Manager: Jose Mourinho.
Secretary: David Barnard.
Most League Goals: 98, Division 1, 1960–61.
Highest League Scorer in Season: Jimmy Greaves, 41, 1960–61.
Most League Goals in Total Aggregate: Bobby Tambling, 164, 1958–70.
Most Capped Player: Marcel Desailly, 67 (116), France.
Most League Appearances: Ron Harris, 655, 1962–80.
Honours – Football League: Division 1 Champions – 1954–55. **FA Cup winners** 1970, 1997, 2000. **Football League Cup winners** 1964–65, 1997–98. **Full Members' Cup winners** 1985–86. **Zenith Data Systems Cup winners** 1989–90. **European Cup-Winners' Cup winners** 1970–71, 1997–98. **Super Cup Winners:** 1999.
Colours: Royal blue shirts and shorts, white stockings.

CHELTENHAM TOWN   FL CHAMPIONSHIP 2

Bird David (M)   5 9 12 00 Gloucester   26 12 84 Cinderford T
Corbett Luke (F)   6 0 11 06 Worcester   10 8 84
Devaney Martin (M) 5 11 12 00 Cheltenham   1 6 80 Coventry C
Duff Michael (D)   6 1 12 05 Belfast   11 1 78 Trainee
Duff Shane (D)   6 1 12 10 Wroughton   2 4 82
Finnigan John (M)   5 8 10 09 Wakefield   29 3 76 Lincoln C
Fyfe Graham (D)   5 6 10 06 Dundee   7 12 82 Raith R
Higgs Shane (G)   6 3 14 06 Oxford   13 5 77 Bristol R
McCann Grant (M) 5 10 11 00 Belfast   14 4 80 West Ham U
Odejayi Kayode (F) 6 2 12 02 Ibadon   21 2 82 Bristol C
Spencer Damien (F) 6 1 14 00 Ascot   19 9 81 Bristol C
Victory Jamie (M)   5 10 12 13 Hackney   14 11 75 Bournemouth
Wilson Brian (D)   5 10 11 00 Manchester   9 5 83 Stoke C

League Appearances: Amankwaah, K. 11(1); Bird, D. 18(6); Book, S. 4(1); Brayson, P. 20(11); Brough, J. 23(3); Cleverley, B. 2(6); Corbett, L. (1); Cozic, B. 7; Devaney, M. 32(8); Dobson, C. (2); Duff, M. 42; Duff, S. 13(2); Finnigan, J. 32(1); Forsyth, R. 16(11); Fyfe, G. 15(5); Gill, J. 5(2); Griffin, A. 10(5); Henry, K. 8(1);

Higgs, S. 42; Howells, L. 7(2); Hynes, P. 2(2); Jones, D. 14; McCann, G. 43; Odejayi, K. 14(16); Spencer, D. 29(7); Taylor, B. 19(9); Victory, J. 44; Wilson, B. 14; Yates, M. 20(1).

Goals – League (57): Spencer 9, McCann 8 (2 pens), Brayson 7 (1 pen), Taylor 7, Devaney 5, Odejayi 5, Brough 2, Forsyth 2 (2 pens), Victory 2, Yates 2, Cozic 1, Duff S 1, Finnigan 1, Henry 1, Jones D 1, own goals 3.

Carling Cup (1): McCann 1.

FA Cup (7): McCann 3 (1 pen), Brayson 1, Spencer 1, Taylor 1, Yates 1.

LDV Vans Trophy (1): Devaney 1.

Ground: Whaddon Road, Cheltenham, Gloucester GL52 5NA. Telephone (01242) 573558.

Record Attendance: at Whaddon Road: 8326 v Reading, FA Cup 1st rd, 17 November 1956; at Cheltenham Athletic Ground: 10,389 v Blackpool, FA Cup 3rd rd, 13 January 1934.

Capacity: 7289.

Manager: John Ward.

Secretary: Paul Godfrey.

Most League Goals: 115, Southern League, 1957–58.

Highest League Scorer in Season: Dave Lewis, 33 (53 in all competitions), Southern League Division 1, 1974–75.

Most League Goals in Total Aggregate: Dave Lewis, 205 (290 in all competitions), 1970–83.

Most League Appearances: Roger Thorndale, 523 (702 in all competitions), 1958–76.

Most Capped Player: Grant McCann, 4 (9), Northern Ireland.

Football Conference: Champions – 1998–99. **FA Trophy winners** 1997–98.

Colours: Red and white striped shirts, black shorts, black stockings.

CHESTER CITY   FL CHAMPIONSHIP 2

Name	ft	in	wt	Birthplace	Date	Previous Club
Mark Beesley (F)	5 11	11 00		Burscough	10 11 81	Preston NE
Phil Bolland (D)	6 4	13 12		Liverpool	26 8 76	Oxford U
Jon Brady (M)	5 8	11 01		Newcastle (Aus)	14 1 75	Woking
Steve Brodie (M)	5 7	10 06		Sunderland	14 1 73	Swansea C
Wayne Brown (G)	6 0	11 12		Southampton	14 1 77	Weston S Mare
Paul Carden (M)				Liverpool	29 3 79	Doncaster R
Shaun Carey (M)	5 9	11 01		Kettering	13 5 76	Rushden & D
Daryl Clare (F)	5 9	12 05		Jersey	1 8 78	Boston U
Danny Collins (D)	6 0	12 00		Chester	6 8 80	Buckley T
Ben Davies (M)	5 6	10 07		Birmingham	27 05 81	Kidderminster H
Ian Foster (F)	5 7	11 00		Liverpool	11 11 76	Kidderminster H
Scott Guyett (D)	6 2	12 09		Ascot	20 1 76	Oxford U
Andy Harris (M)	5 11	12 05		Springs (S Africa)	26 2 77	Leyton Orient
Jamie Heard (M)				Sheffield	11 8 83	Hull C
Chris Lane (D)				Liverpool	25 5 79	Leigh RMI
Ian McCaldon (G)	6 5	16 00		Liverpool	14 9 74	Oxford U
Kevin McIntyre (D)				Liverpool	23 12 77	Doncaster R
Kevin Rapley (F)	5 10	12 02		Reading	21 9 77	Colchester U
Carl Ruffer (D)				Chester	20 12 74	Runcorn
Alex Smith (M)	5 9	10 06		Liverpool	15 2 76	Reading
Darryn Stamp (F)	6 2	12 00		Beverley	21 9 78	Northampton T
Michael Twiss (M)	5 11	13 03		Salford	26 12 77	Leigh RMI

Andy Woods (M) Colchester 15 1 76 Northwich Vic

Ground: Deva Stadium, Bumpers Lane, Chester CH1 4LT.
Record Attendance: 20,500 v Chelsea, FA Cup 3rd rd (replay), 16 January 1952 (at Sealand Rd)
Capacity: 6000.
Manager: Mark Wright.
Secretary: Tony Allan.
Most League Goals: 119, Division 4, 1964–65.
Highest League Scorer in Season: Dick Yates, 36, Division 3 (N), 1946–47.
Most League Goals in Total Aggregate: Stuart Rimmer, 135, 1985–88, 1991–98.
Most Capped Player: Bill Lewis, 13 (27), Wales.
Most League Appearances: Ray Gill, 406, 1951–62.
Honours – Conference: Champions – 2003–04. **Welsh Cup winners:** 1908, 1933, 1947.
Colours: Blue and white striped shirts, blue shorts, blue stockings.

CHESTERFIELD FL CHAMPIONSHIP 1

Davies Gareth (M)	6 0	12 05	Chesterfield	4	2 83	
Dawson Kevin (D)	5 11	13 00	Northallerton	18	6 81	Nottingham F
De Bolla Mark (F)	5 7	11 09	London	1	1 83	Charlton Ath
Evatt Ian (M)	6 3	14 00	Coventry	19	11 81	Derby Co
Folan Caleb (F)	6 2	14 00	Leeds	26	10 82	Leeds U
Hudson Mark (M)	5 11	11 08	Bishop Auckland	24	10 80	Middlesbrough
N'Toya Tcham (F)	5 10	12 10	Kinshasa	3	11 83	
Niven Derek (M)	6 1	11 02	Falkirk	12	12 83	Bolton W
O'Hare Alan (D)	6 1	12 04	Drogheda	31	7 82	Bolton W
Richmond Andy (G)	6 3	12 10	Chesterfield	9	1 83	Scholar
Robinson Marvin (F)	6 0	13 05	Crewe	11	4 80	Derby Co
Warne Stephen (M)	5 10	12 00	Sutton-in-Ashfield	27	2 84	Scholar

League Appearances: Allott, M. 35(5); Blatherwick, S. 36; Brandon, C. 39(4); Burt, J. (1); Cade, J. 9(1); Davies, G. 18(10); Dawson, K. 22(2); De Bolla, M. 3(5); Evatt, I. 43; Folan, C. 4(3); Fullarton, J. (1); Howson, S. 6(3); Hudson, M. 32(3); Hurst, G. 28(1); Innes, M. 17(5); McMaster, J. 4(2); Muggleton, C. 46; N'Toya, T. 3(3); Niven, D. 22; O'Halloran, M. 1(2); O'Hare, A. 40; Payne, S. 20; Reeves, D. 18(13); Robinson, M. 17(15); Rushbury, A. (5); Searle, D. 4(1); Smith, A. (3); Uhlenbeek, G. 36(1); Warhurst, P. 3(1).
Goals – League (49): Hurst 13, Robinson 6, Evatt 5, Brandon 4, Reeves 4 (3 pens), Allott 2, Blatherwick 2, Cade 2, Hudson 2, McMaster 2, De Bolla 1, Niven 1, O'Hare 1, Payne 1 (pen), Rushbury 1, own goals 2.
Carling Cup (0).
FA Cup (2): Davies 1, Evatt 1.
LDV Vans Trophy (5): Brandon 2, Cade 1, Robinson 1, Warhurst 1.
Ground: Recreation Ground, Chesterfield S40 4SX. Telephone (01246) 209765.
Record Attendance: 30,968 v Newcastle U, Division 2, 7 April 1939. **Capacity:** 8509.
Manager: Roy McFarland.
Secretary: Alan Walters.
Most League Goals: 102, Division 3 (N), 1930–31.
Highest League Scorer in Season: Jimmy Cookson, 44, Division 3 (N), 1925–26.

Most League Goals in Total Aggregate: Ernie Moss, 161, 1969–76, 1979–81 and 1984–86.
Most Capped Player: Walter McMillen, 4 (7), Northern Ireland; Mark Williams, 4 (30), Northern Ireland.
Most League Appearances: Dave Blakey, 613, 1948–67.
Honours – Football League: Division 3 (N) Champions – 1930–31, 1935–36. Division 4 Champions – 1969–70, 1984–85. **Anglo-Scottish Cup winners** 1980–81.
Colours: Blue shirts, blue shorts, white stockings.

COLCHESTER UNITED   FL CHAMPIONSHIP 1

Andrews Wayne (F)	5 10	11 02	Paddington	25 11 77	Oldham Ath
Baldwin Pat (D)	6 2	11 07	London	12 11 82	Chelsea
Cade Jamie (F)	5 8	10 10	Durham	15 1 84	Middlesbrough
Duguid Karl (M)	5 11	11 06	Hitchin	21 3 78	Trainee
Fagan Craig (F)	5 11	11 08	Birmingham	11 12 82	Birmingham C
Halford Greg (D)	6 3	13 10	Chelmsford	8 12 84	Scholar
Izzet Kem (M)	5 8	10 05	Mile End	29 9 80	Charlton Ath
Keith Joe (D)	5 7	10 06	London	1 10 78	West Ham U
Parkinson Phil (M)	6 0	12 09	Chorley	1 12 67	Reading

League Appearances: Andrews, W. 32(9); Baldwin, P. 1(3); Bowry, B. 18(6); Brown, S. 40; Brown, W. 16; Cade, J. 6(9); Chilvers, L. 29(3); Duguid, K. 30; Fagan, C. 30(7); Fitzgerald, S. 22(1); Gerken, D. 1; Hadland, P. (1); Halford, G. 15(3); Izzet, K. 43(1); Johnson, G. 14(4); Keith, J. 16(12); McGleish, S. 25(9); McKinney, R. 5; Myers, A. 21; Pinault, T. 31(9); Stockley, S. 44; Tierney, P. 2; Vine, R. 30(5); White, A. 30(3); Williams, A. 5(2).
Goals – League (52): Andrews 12, McGleish 10 (3 pens), Fagan 9 (1 pen), Vine 6, Halford 4, Izzet 3, Duguid 2, Keith 2, Williams 2, Johnson 1, White 1.
Carling Cup (2): Fagan 1, Pinault 1.
FA Cup (8): Vine 4, Keith 2, McGleish 1, own goal 1.
LDV Vans Trophy (14): McGleish 6, Andrews 2, Vine 2, Brown J 1, Izzet 1, Keith 1, Pinault 1.
Ground: Layer Road Ground, Colchester CO2 7JJ. Telephone (0845) 330 2975.
Record Attendance: 19,072 v Reading, FA Cup 1st rd, 27 Nov, 1948. **Capacity:** 6180.
Manager: Phil Parkinson.
Secretary: Andy Gardner.
Most League Goals: 104, Division 4, 1961–62.
Highest League Scorer in Season: Bobby Hunt, 38, Division 4, 1961–62.
Most League Goals in Total Aggregate: Martyn King, 130, 1956–64.
Most Capped Player: None.
Most League Appearances: Micky Cook, 613, 1969–84.
Honours – GM Vauxhall Conference winners 1991–92. **FA Trophy winners** 1991–92.
Colours: Blue and white striped shirts, navy shorts, white stockings.

COVENTRY CITY   FL CHAMPIONSHIP

Adebola Dele (F)	6 3	15 00	Lagos	23 6 75	Crystal Palace
Barrett Graham (F)	5 10	11 07	Dublin	6 10 81	Arsenal
Bates Tom (M)	5 10	12 00	Coventry	31 10 85	
Brush Richard (G)	6 1	12 00	Birmingham	26 11 84	Scholar

Cooney Sean (D)	6 3	13 00	Perth	31 10 83	Scholar
Davenport Calum (D)	6 4	14 00	Bedford	1 1 83	Trainee
Deloumeaux Eric (D)	5 10	11 13	Montbeliard	12 5 73	Aberdeen
Doyle Micky (M)	5 8	11 00	Dublin	8 7 81	Celtic
Jorgensen Claus (M)	5 11	11 00	Holstebro	27 4 76	Bradford C
McSheffrey Gary (F)	5 8	10 06	Coventry	13 8 82	Trainee
Morrell Andy (F)	5 11	11 06	Doncaster	28 9 74	Wrexham
Munn Stephen (D)	5 10	12 00	Belfast	28 4 86	Scholar
O'Donovan Roy (F)	5 10	11 07	Cork	10 8 85	Scholar
Osbourne Isaac (M)	5 9	11 11	Birmingham	22 6 86	Scholar
Pead Craig (M)	5 9	11 06	Bromsgrove	15 9 81	Trainee
Safri Youseff (M)	5 8	10 12	Casablanca	13 1 77	Raja
Shearer Scott (G)	6 3	14 08	Glasgow	15 2 81	Albion R
Staunton Steve (D)	6 0	12 12	Dundalk	19 1 69	Aston Villa
Suffo Patrick (F)	5 9	13 05	Ebolowa	17 1 78	Sheffield U
Thornton Kevin (M)	5 7	11 00	Drogheda	9 7 86	Scholar
Tuffey Jonathan (G)			Newry	20 1 87	Scholar
Whing Andrew (D)	6 0	12 00	Birmingham	20 9 84	Scholar

League Appearances: Adebola, D. 15(13); Arphexad, P. 5; Barrett, G. 20(11); Clarke, P. 5; Davenport, C. 31(2); Deloumeaux, E. 19; Doyle, M. 38(2); Giddings, S. (1); Gordon, D. 3(2); Grainger, M. 7; Gudjonsson, B. 17(1); Jackson, J. 2(3); Joachim, J. 27(2); Jorgensen, C. 4(4); Kerr, B. 5(4); Konjic, M. 36(6); Lowe, O. 1(1); Mansouri, Y. 9(5); McAllister, G. 14; McSheffrey, G. 16(3); Morrell, A. 19(11); O'Neill, K. (1); Olszar, S. 1(4); Pead, C. 6(11); Pitt, C. 1; Safri, Y. 31; Shaw, R. 11(8); Shearer, S. 29(1); Staunton, S. 34(1); Suffo, P. 20(7); Ward, G. 12; Warnock, S. 42(2); Whing, A. 26(2).

Goals – League (67): McSheffrey 11 (3 pens), Morrell 9, Joachim 8, Suffo 7, Doyle 5, Gudjonsson 3, McAllister 3 (2 pens), Staunton 3 (2 pens), Warnock 3, Adebola 2, Barrett 2, Jackson 2, Konjic 2, Deloumeaux 1, Lowe 1, Pead 1, Shaw 1, Whing 1, own goals 2.

Carling Cup (2): Adebola 1, Barrett 1.

FA Cup (4): Joachim 3, McSheffrey 1.

Ground: Highfield Road Stadium, King Richard Street, Coventry CV2 4FW. Telephone (0870) 421 1987.

Record Attendance: 51,455 v Wolverhampton W, Division 2, 29 April 1967.

Capacity: 23,633.

Manager: Peter Reid.

Secretary: Graham Hover.

Most League Goals: 108, Division 3 (S), 1931–32.

Highest League Scorer in Season: Clarrie Bourton, 49, Division 3 (S), 1931–32.

Most League Goals in Total Aggregate: Clarrie Bourton, 171, 1931–37.

Most Capped Player: Magnus Hedman, 44 (56), Sweden.

Most League Appearances: Steve Ogrizovic, 507, 1984–2000.

Honours – Football League: Division 2 Champions – 1966–67. Division 3 Champions – 1963–64. Division 3 (S) Champions 1935–36. **FA Cup winners** 1986–87.

Colours: Sky blue body shirts and shorts with white and navy side panel, sky blue stockings with white and navy turnover and centre white strip.

Ashton Dean (F)	6 2	12 08	Crewe	24 11 83	Schoolboy
Bell Lee (M)	5 11	11 00	Crewe	26 1 83	Scholar
Cochrane Justin (M)	5 11	11 07	Hackney	26 1 82	QPR
Edwards Paul (F)	6 0	11 07	Derby	10 11 82	
Foster Stephen (D)	6 0	11 05	Warrington	10 9 80	Trainee
Higdon Michael (M)	6 1	11 05	Liverpool	2 9 83	School
Ince Clayton (G)	6 3	13 00	Trinidad	13 7 72	Defence Force
Jones Steve (F)	5 10	10 05	Derry	25 10 76	
Lunt Kenny (M)	5 10	10 05	Runcorn	20 11 79	Trainee
McCready Chris (D)	6 1	12 05	Chester	5 9 81	Scholar
Morris Alex (M)	6 0	11 08	Stoke	5 10 82	Scholar
Moses Adi (D)	5 11	13 01	Doncaster	4 5 75	Huddersfield T
Platt Matthew (F)	6 0	11 03	Crewe	15 10 83	Scholar
Rix Ben (M)	5 9	11 05	Wolverhampton	11 12 82	Scholar
Roberts Mark (D)	6 1	12 00	Northwich	16 10 83	Scholar
Robinson James (F)	5 10	11 03	Whiston	18 9 82	Scholar
Sorvel Neil (M)	6 0	12 03	Widnes	2 3 73	Macclesfield T
Tomlinson Stuart (G)	6 1	11 02	Chester	10 5 85	Scholar
Tonkin Anthony (D)	5 11	12 02	Cornwall	19 1 80	Stockport Co
Varney Luke (F)	5 11	11 00	Leicester	28 9 82	Quorn
Vaughan David (M)	5 7	11 00	St Asaph	18 2 83	Scholar
Walker Richard (D)	6 2	12 08	Stafford	17 9 80	Trainee
Wilson Kyle (F)	5 10	11 05	Wirrall	14 11 85	Scholar
Wright David (D)	5 11	11 00	Warrington	1 5 80	Trainee

League Appearances: Ashton, D. 43(1); Barrowman, A. 3(1); Bell, L. (3); Brammer, D. 16; Cochrane, J. 37(2); Edwards, P. 2(8); Foster, S. 45; Higdon, M. 7(3); Hignett, C. 11(4); Ince, C. 36; Jones, B. 23(4); Jones, S. 43(2); Lunt, K. 43(2); McCready, C. 15(7); Moses, A. 15(6); Rix, B. 18(8); Roberts, M. (2); Robinson, J. 1(8); Smart, A. (6); Sorvel, N. 26(5); Symes, M. 1(3); Tomlinson, S. (1); Tonkin, A. 20(6); Varney, L. 5(3); Vaughan, D. 29(2); Walker, R. 17(3); Williams, B. 10; Wright, D. 40.

Goals – League (57): Ashton 19 (5 pens), Jones S 15, Lunt 7, Foster 2, Rix 2, Barrowman 1, Brammer 1, Higdon 1, Jones B 1, Robinson 1, Symes 1, Varney 1, Walker 1, Wright 1, own goals 3.

Carling Cup (2): Ashton 1 (pen), Jones S 1.

FA Cup (0).

Ground: Football Ground, Gresty Road, Crewe CW2 6EB. Telephone (01270) 213014.

Record Attendance: 20,000 v Tottenham H, FA Cup 4th rd, 30 January 1960.

Capacity: 10,107.

Manager: Dario Gradi MBE.

Secretary: Andrew Blakemore.

Most League Goals: 95, Division 3 (N), 1931–32.

Highest League Scorer in Season: Terry Harkin, 35, Division 4, 1964–65.

Most League Goals in Total Aggregate: Bert Swindells, 126, 1928–37.

Most Capped Player: Clayton Ince, 34, Trinidad & Tobago.

Most League Appearances: Tommy Lowry, 436, 1966–78.

Honours – Welsh Cup: Winners 1936, 1937.

Colours: Red shirts, white shorts, red stockings.

CRYSTAL PALACE   FA PREMIERSHIP

Berthelin Cedric (G)	6 4	15 00	Courrieres	25 12 76	
Black Tommy (M)	5 7	11 10	Chigwell	26 11 79	Arsenal
Borrowdale Gary (D)	6 0	12 01	Sutton	16 7 85	Scholar
Butterfield Danny (D)	5 10	11 06	Boston	21 11 79	Grimsby T
Clarke Matt (G)	6 4	13 08	Sheffield	3 11 73	Bradford C
Cronin Lance (G)	6 1	13 04	Brighton	11 9 85	Scholar
Derry Shaun (M)	5 10	13 02	Nottingham	6 12 77	Portsmouth
Freedman Dougie (F)	5 9	12 05	Glasgow	21 1 74	Nottingham F
Granville Danny (D)	6 0	12 00	Islington	19 1 75	Manchester C
Johnson Andrew (F)	5 7	10 09	Bedford	10 2 81	Birmingham C
Leigertwood Mikele (D)	6 1	11 04	Enfield	12 11 82	Wimbledon
Powell Darren (D)	6 4	13 03	Hammersmith	10 3 76	Brentford
Routledge Wayne (F)	5 6	10 07	Eltham	7 1 85	Scholar
Shipperley Neil (F)	6 0	13 00	Chatham	30 10 74	Wimbledon
Williams Gareth (F)	5 10	11 13	Germiston	10 9 82	Scholar

League Appearances: Berthelin, C. 17; Black, T. 12(13); Borrowdale, G. 14(9); Butterfield, D. 45; Clarke, M. 4; Derry, S. 25(12); Edwards, R. 6(1); Fleming, C. 15(2); Freedman, D. 20(15); Granville, D. 21; Gray, J. 24; Heeroo, G. (1); Hudson, M. 14; Hughes, M. 34; Johnson, A. 40(2); Leigertwood, M. 7(5); Mullins, H. 10; Myhre, T. 15; Popovic, T. 34; Powell, D. 10; Riihilahti, A. 24(7); Routledge, W. 32(12); Shipperley, N. 40; Smith, J. 13(2); Soares, T. (3); Symons, K. 12(3); Vaesen, N. 10; Watson, B. 8(8).

Goals – League (72): Johnson 27 (6 pens), Freedman 13 (3 pens), Shipperley 9, Routledge 6, Butterfield 4, Granville 3, Hughes 3, Derry 2, Gray 2, Edwards 1, Popovic 1, Watson 1.

Carling Cup (6): Johnson 4 (2 pens), Freedman 2 (1 pen).

FA Cup (0).

Play-Offs (5): Shipperley 2, Johnson 1, Powell 1, own goal 1.

Ground: Selhurst Park, London SE25 6PU. Telephone (020) 8768 6000.

Record Attendance: 51,482 v Burnley, Division 2, 11 May 1979. **Capacity:** 26,500.

Manager: Iain Dowie.

Club Secretary:

Most League Goals: 110, Division 4, 1960–61.

Highest League Scorer in Season: Peter Simpson, 46, Division 3 (S), 1930–31.

Most League Goals in Total Aggregate: Peter Simpson, 153, 1930–36.

Most Capped Player: Aleksandrs Kolinko, 23 (51), Latvia.

Most League Appearances: Jim Cannon, 571, 1973–88.

Honours – Football League: Division 1 – Champions 1993–94. Division 2 Champions – 1978–79. Division 3 (S) 1920–21. **Zenith Data Systems Cup winners** 1991.

Colours: Red and blue vertical striped shirts, red shorts, red stockings.

DARLINGTON   FL CHAMPIONSHIP 2

Clarke Matthew (D)	6 3	13 00	Leeds	18 12 80	Halifax T
Close Brian (D)	5 10	12 00	Belfast	27 1 82	Middlesbrough
Convery Mark (M)	5 6	10 05	Newcastle	29 5 81	Sunderland
Hughes Chris (M)	5 11	10 10	Sunderland	5 3 84	Scholar
Hutchinson Jonathan (D)	5 11	11 11	Middlesbrough	2 4 82	Birmingham C

Keltie Clark (M)	5 11	11 08	Newcastle	31	8 83	Shildon
McGurk David (D)	6 0	11 10	Middlesbrough	30	9 82	Scholar
Nicholls Ashley (M)	5 11	11 11	Suffolk	30	10 81	Ipswich T
Price Mike (G)	6 3	13 10	Ashington	3	4 83	Leicester C
Valentine Ryan (D)	5 10	11 05	Wrexham	19	8 82	Everton

League Appearances: Alexander, J. (3); Bossy, F. 4(2); Clark, I. 20(14); Clarke, M. 44(1); Close, B. 8(4); Coghlan, M. (3); Collett, A. 9; Conlon, B. 38(1); Convery, M. 17(8); Graham, D. 7(2); Hughes, C. 24(6); Hutchinson, J. 38(1); James, C. 10; Keltie, C. 23(8); Liddle, C. 43; Maddison, N. 30(2); Mason, C. (1); Matthews, L. 6; McGurk, D. 22(5); Mellanby, D. 5(2); Morgan, A. 4(1); Nicholls, A. 25(1); Pearson, G. 11(7); Price, M. 36; Robson, G. 3(3); Russell, C. 6(6); Sheeran, M. (6); Teggart, N. 9(6); Turnbull, R. 1; Valentine, R. 33(7); Wainwright, N. 30(5).

Goals – League (53): Conlon 14, Wainwright 7, Clark 4 (1 pen), Clarke M 4, Liddle 4, McGurk 4, Convery 2, Graham 2, Hughes 2, Valentine 2 (1 pen), James 1, Keltie 1, Maddison 1, Matthews 1, Morgan 1, Pearson 1, Russell 1, own goal 1.

Carling Cup (0).
FA Cup (0).
LDV Vans Trophy (1): Sheeran 1.
Ground: New Stadium, Neasham Road, Hurworth Moor, Darlington DL2 1GR. Telephone (01325) 387000.
Record Attendance: 21,023 v Bolton W, League Cup 3rd rd, 14 November 1960.
Capacity: 25,000.
Manager: David Hodgson.
Secretary: Lisa Charlton.
Most League Goals: 108, Division 3 (N), 1929–30.
Highest League Scorer in Season: David Brown, 39, Division 3 (N), 1924–25.
Most League Goals in Total Aggregate: Alan Walsh, 90, 1978–84.
Most Capped Player: Jason Devos, 3 (46), Canada.
Most League Appearances: Ron Greener, 442, 1955–68.
Honours – Football League: Division 3 (N) Champions – 1924–25. Division 4 Champions – 1990–91.
Colours: Black and white shirts, black shorts, black stockings.

DERBY COUNTY   FL CHAMPIONSHIP

Boertien Paul (D)	5 11	11 11	Carlisle	21	1 79	Carlisle U
Bolder Adam (M)	6 3	11 13	Hull	25	10 80	Hull C
Camp Lee (G)	5 11	11 11	Derby	22	8 84	Scholar
Doyle Nathan (M)	5 11	11 11	Derby	12	1 87	Scholar
Grant Lee (G)	6 2	13 00	Watford	27	1 83	Scholar
Huddlestone Tom (D)	6 3	14 12	Nottingham	28	12 86	
Hunt Lewis (D)	5 11	12 08	Birmingham	25	8 82	Scholar
Johnson Michael (D)	5 11	12 08	Nottingham	4	7 73	Birmingham C
Kenna Jeff (D)	5 11	12 04	Dublin	27	8 70	Birmingham C
Konjic Muhamed (D)	6 3	13 00	Bosnia	14	5 70	Coventry C
Labarthe Gianfranco (F)	5 10	10 07	Lima	20	9 84	Sport Boys
McLeod Izale (F)	6 0	11 02	Perry Bar	15	10 84	Scholar
Mills Pablo (D)	6 0	11 06	Birmingham	27	5 84	Trainee
Oakes Andy (G)	6 3	12 04	Crewe	11	1 77	Hull C
Peschisolido Paul (F)	5 7	11 08	Canada	25	5 71	Sheffield U
Reich Marco (F)	6 0	11 13	Meiserheim	30	12 77	Werder Bremen

Tudgay Marcus (F)	5 10	12 02	Worthing	3	2 83	Trainee
Twigg Gary (F)	6 0	11 02	Glasgow	19	3 84	Scholar
Vincent Jamie (D)	5 10	11 09	London	18	6 75	Portsmouth
Walton David (D)	6 2	13 00	Bellingham	10	4 73	Crewe Alex
Weckstrom Kristoffer (F)	5 9	11 04	Helsinki	26	5 83	IFK Mariehamn
Zavagno Luciano (D)	5 11	11 07	Rosario	6	8 77	Troyes

League Appearances: Boertien, P. 10(8); Bolder, A. 11(13); Bradbury, L. 7; Caldwell, G. 6(3); Costa, C. 23(11); Dichio, D. 6; Doyle, N. 1(1); Edwards, R. 10(1); Elliott, S. 2(2); Grant, L. 36; Holmes, L. 17(6); Huddlestone, T. 42(1); Hunt, L. 1; Jackson, R. 34(2); Johnson, M. 39; Junior 6(6); Kenna, J. 9; Kennedy, P. 5; Labarthe, G. (3); Manel 12(4); Mawene, Y. 30; McLeod, I. 4(6); Mills, P. 13(6); Morris, L. 21(2); Oakes, A. 10; Osman, L. 17; Peschisolido, P. 11; Reich, M. 9(4); Svensson, M. 9(1); Taylor, I. 42; Tudgay, M. 20(9); Valakari, S. 14(6); Vincent, J. 7; Walton, D. 3(2); Whelan, N. 3(5); Zavagno, L. 16(1).

Goals – League (53): Taylor 11 (6 pens), Tudgay 6, Morris 5, Junior 4 (1 pen), Peschisolido 4, Manel 3, Osman 3, Svensson 3, Holmes 2, Bolder 1, Costa 1, Dichio 1, Edwards 1, Johnson 1, Kennedy 1, McLeod 1, Reich 1, Vincent 1, Zavagno 1, own goals 2.

Carling Cup (1): Taylor 1.

FA Cup (0).

Ground: Pride Park Stadium, Derby DE24 8XL. Telephone (01332) 202202.

Record Attendance: 41,826 v Tottenham H, Division 1, 20 September 1969.

Capacity: 33,597.

Manager: George Burley.

Secretary: Keith Pearson ACIS.

Most League Goals: 111, Division 3 (N), 1956–57.

Highest League Scorer in Season: Jack Bowers, 37, Division 1, 1930–31; Ray Straw, 37 Division 3 (N), 1956–57.

Most League Goals in Total Aggregate: Steve Bloomer, 292, 1892–1906 and 1910–14.

Most Capped Players: Deon Burton, 41 (48), Jamaica and Mart Poom, 41 (98), Estonia.

Most League Appearances: Kevin Hector, 486, 1966–78 and 1980–82.

Honours – Football League: Division 1 Champions – 1971–72, 1974–75. Division 2 Champions – 1911–12, 1914–15, 1968–69, 1986–87. Division 3 (N) 1956–57. **FA Cup winners** 1945–46.

Colours: White shirts with black piping, black shorts, white stockings.

DONCASTER ROVERS   FL CHAMPIONSHIP 1

Albrighton Mark (D)	6 1	12 07	Nuneaton	6	3 76	
Beech Chris (D)	5 10	11 12	Congleton	5 11 75		Rotherham U
Blundell Greg (F)	5 9	12 02	Liverpool	1	1 76	
Doolan John (M)	6 1	13 00	Liverpool	7	5 74	Barnet
Fortune-West Leo (F)	6 3	13 10	Stratford	9	4 71	Cardiff C
Foster Steve (D)	6 1	12 00	Mansfield	3 12 74		Bristol R
Gill Robert (F)	5 11	11 00	Nottingham	10	2 82	
Green Paul (M)	5 10	11 07	Pontefract	10	4 83	
Jackson Ben (M)				0	0	
Maloney Jon (M)	6 0	11 12	Leeds	3	3 85	
Marples Simon (D)	5 10	11 00	Sheffield	30	7 75	

McGrath John (M)	5 10	10 04	Limerick	27	3 80	Aston Villa
McIndoe Michael (M)	5 8	11 00	Edinburgh	2 12 79		Luton T
Morley Dave (D)	6 2	12 07	St Helens	25 9 77		Oxford U
Mulligan David (D)	5 8	9 13	Fazakerley	24 3 82		Barnsley
Price Jamie (D)	5 9	11 00	Normanton	27 10 81		Trainee
Ravenhill Ricky (M)	5 10	11 03	Doncaster	16 1 81		
Rigoglioso Adriano (M)	6 1	12 07	Liverpool	28 5 79		
Ryan Tim (D)	5 10	11 00	Stockport	10 12 74		Scunthorpe U
Tierney Fran (M)	5 10	12 07	Liverpool	10 9 75		Exeter C
Warrington Andy (G)	6 3	12 13	Sheffield	10 6 76		York C

League Appearances: Akinfenwa, A. 4(5); Albrighton, M. 27(1); Barnes, P. 2(5); Beech, C. 11; Black, C. 1; Blundell, G. 41(3); Brown, C. 17(5); Burton, S. 1(5); Doolan, J. 36(3); Fortune-West, L. 28(11); Foster, S. 44; Gill, R. (1); Green, P. 38(5); Hynes, P. (5); Maloney, J. (1); Marples, S. 16; McGrath, J. 4(7); McIndoe, M. 45; Melligan, J. 21; Morley, D. 15(6); Mulligan, D. 14; O'Brien, R. 1; Paterson, J. 7(1); Price, J. 17(2); Ravenhill, R. 14(22); Rigoglioso, A. 5(12); Ryan, T. 41(1); Tierney, F. 10(3); Warrington, A. 46.

Goals – League (79): Blundell 18, Fortune-West 11, Brown 10, McIndoe 10 (6 pens), Green 8, Akinfenwa 4, Albrighton 3, Ravenhill 3, Tierney 3, Melligan 2, Ryan 2, Foster 1, Hynes 1, Morley 1, Mulligan 1, Paterson 1 (pen).

Carling Cup (4): Blundell 2, Barnes 1 (pen), Fortune-West 1.

FA Cup (0).

LDV Vans Trophy (1): Tierney 1.

Ground: The Earth Stadium, Belle Vue, Doncaster DN4 5HT. Telephone (01302) 539441.

Record Attendance: 37,149 v Hull C, Division 3 (N), 2 October 1948. **Capacity:** 9975.

Manager: Dave Penney.

Secretary: Mrs Joan Oldale.

Most League Goals: 123, Division 3 (N), 1946–47.

Highest League Scorer in Season: Clarrie Jordan, 42, Division 3 (N) 1946–47.

Most League Goals in Total Aggregate: Tom Keetley, 180, 1923–29.

Most Capped Player: Len Graham, 14, Northern Ireland.

Most League Appearances: Fred Emery, 417, 1925–36.

Honours – Football League: Division 3 Champions – 2003–04. Division 3 (N) Champions – 1934–35, 1946–47, 1949–50. Division 4 Champions – 1965–66, 1968–69. **Football Conference:** Champions 2002–03.

Colours: Red and white hooped shirts, red shorts and stockings.

EVERTON   FA PREMIERSHIP

Campbell Kevin (F)	6 0	13 13	Lambeth	4	2 70	Trabzonspor
Carsley Lee (M)	5 10	12 04	Birmingham	28	2 74	Coventry C
Chadwick Nick (F)	5 11	10 09	Stoke	26 10 82		
Clarke Peter (D)	6 0	12 00	Southport	3 1 82		Trainee
Ferguson Duncan (F)	6 4	13 07	Stirling	27 12 71		Newcastle U
Gravesen Thomas (M)	5 9	13 06	Vejle	11 3 76		Hamburg
Hibbert Tony (D)	5 9	11 05	Liverpool	20 2 81		Trainee
Kilbane Kevin (M)	6 1	13 05	Preston	1 2 77		Sunderland
Li Tie(M)	6 0	11 10	China	18 9 77		Lianing Bodao
Linderoth Tobias (M)	5 10	11 08	Marseille	21 4 79		Stabaek
Martyn Nigel (G)	6 1	15 11	St Austell	11 8 66		Leeds U

McFadden James (M)	6 0	12 11	Glasgow	14 4 83	Motherwell
Naysmith Gary (D)	5 9	12 01	Edinburgh	16 11 78	Hearts
Nyarko Alex (M)	6 0	13 00	Accra	15 10 73	Paris St Germain
Osman Leon (F)	5 8	10 09	Billinge	17 5 81	Trainee
Pascucci Patrizio (F)	5 9	12 04	L'Aquila	25 11 85	
Pistone Alessandro (D)	5 11	11 08	Milan	27 7 75	Newcastle U
Radzinski Tomasz (F)	5 7	11 10	Poznan	14 12 73	Anderlecht
Rooney Wayne (F)	5 10	12 04	Liverpool	24 10 85	Scholar
Stubbs Alan (D)	6 2	13 12	Kirkby	6 10 71	Celtic
Turner Iain (G)	6 3	12 10	Stirling	26 1 84	Trainee
Unsworth Dave (D)	6 1	15 02	Chorley	16 10 73	Aston Villa
Watson Steve (D)	6 0	12 07	North Shields	1 4 74	Aston Villa
Weir David (D)	6 5	14 03	Falkirk	10 5 70	Hearts
Wright Richard (G)	6 2	14 04	Ipswich	5 11 77	Arsenal
Yobo Joseph (D)	6 1	13 00	Kano	6 9 80	Marseille

League Appearances: Campbell, K. 8(9); Carsley, L. 15(6); Chadwick, N. 1(2); Clarke, P. 1; Ferguson, D. 13(7); Gravesen, T. 29(1); Hibbert, T. 24(1); Jeffers, F. 5(13); Kilbane, K. 26(4); Li Tie 4(1); Linderoth, T. 23(4); Martyn, N. 33(1); McFadden, J. 11(12); Naysmith, G. 27(2); Nyarko, A. 7(4); Osman, L. 3(1); Pembridge, M. 4; Pistone, A. 20(1); Radzinski, T. 28(6); Rooney, W. 26(8); Simonsen, S. 1; Stubbs, A. 25(2); Unsworth, D. 22(4); Watson, S. 22(2); Weir, D. 9(1); Wright, R. 4; Yobo, J. 27(1).

Goals – League (45): Rooney 9, Radzinski 8, Ferguson 5 (1 pen), Watson 5, Kilbane 3, Unsworth 3, Carsley 2, Gravesen 2, Naysmith 2, Yobo 2, Campbell 1, Osman 1, own goals 2.

Carling Cup (4): Ferguson 2 (1 pen), Chadwick 1, Linderoth 1.

FA Cup (5): Ferguson 2 (2 pens), Jeffers 2, Kilbane 1.

Ground: Goodison Park, Liverpool L4 4EL. Telephone (0151) 330 2200.

Record Attendance: 78,299 v Liverpool, Division 1, 18 September 1948. **Capacity:** 40,170.

Manager: David Moyes.

Secretary: David Harrison.

Most League Goals: 121, Division 2, 1930–31.

Highest League Scorer in Season: William Ralph 'Dixie' Dean, 60, Division 1, 1927–28 (All-time League record).

Most League Goals in Total Aggregate: William Ralph 'Dixie' Dean, 349, 1925–37.

Most Capped Player: Neville Southall, 92, Wales.

Most League Appearances: Neville Southall, 578, 1981–98.

Honours – Football League: Division 1 Champions – 1890–91, 1914–15, 1927–28, 1931–32, 1938–39, 1962–63, 1969–70, 1984–85, 1986–87. Division 2 Champions – 1930–31. **FA Cup:** Winners 1906, 1933, 1966, 1984, 1995. **European Competitions: European Cup-Winners' Cup winners:** 1984–85.

Colours: Royal blue shirts, white shorts, white stockings.

FULHAM   FA PREMIERSHIP

Baker Nicholas (G)			London	18 12 84	
Boa Morte Luis (F)	5 10	11 10	Lisbon	4 8 77	Southampton
Bocanegra Carlos (D)	6 0	12 04	Alta Loma	25 5 79	Chicago Fire
Bonnissel Jerome (D)	5 8	11 11	Montpellier	16 4 73	Rangers
Buari Malik (M)	5 11	11 11	Accra	21 1 84	Trainee

Name			Birthplace		Club/Status
Clark Lee (M)	5 8	11 10	Wallsend	27 10 72	Sunderland
Collins Matthew (M)			Merthyr	31 3 86	Trainee
Crossley Mark (G)	6 0	15 09	Barnsley	16 6 69	Middlesbrough
Davis Sean (M)	5 9	12 09	Clapham	20 9 79	Trainee
Flitney Ross (G)	6 1	11 11	Hitchin	1 6 84	Scholar
Fontaine Liam (D)			Beckenham	7 1 86	Trainee
Goma Alain (D)	6 0	13 05	Sault	15 10 72	Newcastle U
Green Adam (D)	5 9	10 11	Hillingdon	12 1 84	Scholar
Hammond Elvis (F)	5 10	11 06	Accra	6 10 80	Trainee
Harley Jon (D)	5 9	11 05	Maidstone	26 9 79	Chelsea
Herrera Martin (G)	6 0	12 06	Argentina	13 9 70	Alaves
Hudson Mark (D)	6 3	12 06	Guildford	30 3 82	Trainee
John Collins (F)	6 0	12 11	Zwandru	17 10 85	Twente
Knight Zat (D)	6 6	14 06	Solihull	2 5 80	
Lawless Alex (F)			Llwynupion	26 3 85	
Leacock Dean (D)	6 2	12 04	Croydon	10 6 84	Trainee
Legwinski Sylvain (M)	6 1	11 10	Clermont-Ferrand	6 10 73	Bordeaux
Malbranque Steed (M)	5 8	11 10	Mouscron	6 1 80	Lyon
Marlet Steve (F)	5 11	11 10	Pithiviers	10 1 74	Lyon
McBride Brian (F)	6 1	12 06	USA	17 8 72	Columbus Crew
McDermott Neale (M)	5 9	10 11	Newcastle	8 3 85	Newcastle U
Noble Stuart (F)	6 0	12 09	Edinburgh	14 10 83	Trainee
Ouaddou Abdes (D)	6 4	12 03	Ksar-Askour	1 11 78	Nancy
Pearce Ian (D)	6 3	14 04	Bury St Edmunds	7 5 74	West Ham U
Pembridge Mark (M)	5 7	11 09	Merthyr	29 11 70	Everton
Pratley Darren (F)	6 0	10 13	Barking	22 4 85	Scholar
Rehman Zesh (M)	6 2	12 09	Birmingham	14 10 83	Scholar
Rosenior Liam (M)	5 9	11 05	Wandsworth	9 7 84	Bristol C
Sava Facundo (F)	6 1	13 03	Ituzaingo	7 3 74	Gimnasia
Timlin Michael (M)			London	19 3 85	Trainee
Van der Sar Edwin (G)	6 5	14 08	Voorhout	29 10 70	Juventus
Volz Moritz (D)	5 10	12 06	Siegen	21 1 83	Arsenal
Watkins Robert (D)			Carshalton	14 10 85	Trainee

League Appearances: Boa Morte, L. 32(1); Bocanegra, C. 15; Bonnissel, J. 16; Buari, M. 1(2); Clark, L. 25; Crossley, M. 1; Davis, S. 22(2); Djetou, M. 19(7); Goma, A. 23; Green, A. 4; Harley, J. 3(1); Hayles, B. 10(16); Inamoto, J. 15(7); John, C. 3(5); Knight, Z. 30(1); Leacock, D. 3(1); Legwinski, S. 30(2); Malbranque, S. 38; Marlet, S. 1; McBride, B. 5(11); Melville, A. 9; Pearce, I. 12(1); Pembridge, M. 9(3); Petta, B. 3(6); Pratley, D. (1); Rehman, Z. (1); Saha, L. 20(1); Sava, F. (6); Van der Sar, E. 37; Volz, M. 32(1).

Goals – League (52): Saha 13 (2 pens), Boa Morte 9, Malbranque 6 (2 pens), Davis 5, Hayles 4, John 4, McBride 4, Clark 2, Inamoto 2, Marlet 1, Pembridge 1, Sava 1.

Carling Cup (0).

FA Cup (9): Malbranque 2 (1 pen), Saha 2, Boa Morte 1, Davis 1, Hayles 1, Inamoto 1, McBride 1.

Ground: Craven Cottage, Stevenage Road, London SW6 6HH. Telephone: (0870) 442 1222.

Record Attendance: 49,335 v Millwall, Division 2, 8 October 1938. **Capacity:** 22,400.

Manager: Chris Coleman.

Secretary: Lee Hoos.

Most League Goals: 111, Division 3 (S), 1931–32.

Highest League Scorer in Season: Frank Newton, 43, Division 3 (S), 1931–32.

Most League Goals in Total Aggregate: Gordon Davies, 159, 1978–84, 1986–91.
Most Capped Player: Johnny Haynes, 56, England.
Most League Appearances: Johnny Haynes, 594, 1952–70.
Honours – Football League: Division 1 Champions – 2000–01. Division 2
Champions – 1948–49, 1998–99. Division 3 (S) Champions – 1931–32. European
Competitions: Intertoto Cup winners: 2002.
Colours: White shirts, black shorts, white stockings.

GILLINGHAM   FL CHAMPIONSHIP

Name	Ht		Birthplace			Previous Club
Agyemang Patrick (F)	6 1	12 00	Walthamstow	20	9 80	Wimbledon
Ashby Barry (D)	6 2	14 05	Park Royal	2 11 70		Brentford
Awuah Jones (F)	5 11	11 06	Ghana	10	7 83	Scholar
Banks Steve (G)	6 0	13 12	Hillingdon	9	2 72	Wimbledon
Beckwith Dean (D)	6 3	13 04	Southwark	18	9 83	Scholar
Bossu Bertrand (G)	6 7	14 00	Calais	14 10 80		Barnet
Brown Jason (G)	6 0	15 12	Southwark	18	5 82	Charlton Ath
Cox Ian (D)	6 1	12 07	Croydon	25	3 71	Burnley
Crofts Andrew (F)	5 10	11 08	Chatham	29	5 84	Trainee
Henderson Darius (F)	6 2	13 02	Doncaster	7	9 81	Reading
Hessenthaler Andy (M)	5 8	11 05	Gravesend	17	6 65	Watford
Hills John (D)	5 8	12 04	St Annes-on-Sea	21	4 78	Blackpool
Hope Chris (D)	6 1	12 11	Sheffield	14 11 72		Scunthorpe U
Johnson Leon (D)	6 1	12 10	London	10	5 81	Southend U
Johnson Tommy (F)	6 0	13 01	Newcastle	15	1 71	Sheffield W
Nosworthy Nayron (D)	6 1	13 00	Brixton	11 10 80		Trainee
Pouton Alan (M)	6 0	12 10	Newcastle	1	2 77	Grimsby T
Rose Richard (D)	6 2	11 10	Pembury	8	9 82	Trainee
Saunders Mark (M)	6 1	13 02	Reading	23	7 71	Plymouth Arg
Sidibe Mamady (F)	6 4	14 03	Mali	18 12 79		CA Paris
Smith Paul (M)	6 0	13 13	East Ham	18	9 71	Brentford
Southall Nicky (M)	5 11	12 07	Stockton	28	1 72	Bolton W
Spiller Danny (M)	5 9	10 12	Maidstone	10 10 81		Trainee

League Appearances: Agyemang, P. 20; Ashby, B. 22(1); Banks, S. 13; Bartram, V.
1; Benjamin, T. 1(3); Bossu, B. 3(1); Brown, J. 22; Brown, W. 4; Cox, I. 32(1);
Crofts, A. 1(7); Henderson, D. 4; Hessenthaler, A. 27(9); Hills, J. 27(2); Hirschfeld,
L. 2; Hope, C. 37; James, K. 12(5); Jarvis, M. 2(8); Johnson, L. 18(2); Johnson, T.
6(9); King, M. 9(2); Nosworthy, N. 26(1); Perpetuini, D. 14(6); Pouton, A. 14(5);
Rose, R. 12(5); Saunders, M. 8(13); Shaw, P. 20(1); Sidibe, M. 34(7); Smith, P. 31(2);
Southall, N. 34(1); Spiller, D. 32(7); Vaesen, N. 5; Wales, G. 3(3); Wallace, R. 10(4).
Goals – League (48): Agyemang 6, Shaw 6, Spiller 6, Sidibe 5, King 4, Hope 3,
Johnson T 3, Hessenthaler 2, Hills 2 (2 pens), Nosworthy 2, Perpetuini 2, Ashby 1,
Benjamin 1, Brown 1 (pen), James 1, Saunders 1, Wales 1, Wallace 1.
Carling Cup (4): Hills 1, King 1, Nosworthy 1, Saunders 1.
FA Cup (4): Henderson 1, Johnson T 1, Sidibie 1, Smith 1.
Ground: Priestfield Stadium, Gillingham ME7 4DD. Telephone (01634) 300000.
Record Attendance: 23,002 v QPR, FA Cup 3rd rd 10 January 1948. Capacity: 11,400.
Player-Manager: Andy Hessenthaler.
Secretary: Mrs G. E. Poynter.
Most League Goals: 90, Division 4, 1973–74.
Highest League Scorer in Season: Ernie Morgan, 31, Division 3 (S), 1954–55; Brian

Yeo, 31, Division 4, 1973–74.
Most League Goals in Total Aggregate: Brian Yeo, 135, 1963–75.
Most Capped Player: Mamady Sidibe 7, Mali.
Most League Appearances: John Simpson, 571, 1957–72.
Honours – Football League: Division 4 Champions – 1963–64.
Colours: All blue.

GRIMSBY TOWN   FL CHAMPIONSHIP 2

Anderson Iain (M)	5 8	9 07	Glasgow	23	7 77	Preston NE
Antoine-Curier Mickael (F)	6 0	12 00	Orsay	5	3 83	Notts Co
Coldicott Stacy (M)	5 8	12 08	Worcester	29	4 74	WBA
Crane Tony (D)	6 5	12 05	Liverpool	8	9 82	Sheffield W
Crowe Jason (D)	5 9	10 09	Sidcup	30	9 78	Portsmouth
Davison Aidan (G)	6 1	13 12	Sedgefield	11	5 68	Bradford C
Hockless Graham (M)	5 7	10 02	Hull	20	10 82	
Mansaram Darren (F)	6 1	11 02	Doncaster	25	6 84	Scholar
McDermott John (D)	5 7	10 13	Middlesbrough	3	2 69	Trainee
Wheeler Kirk (D)	6 0	12 01	Grimsby	13	6 84	
Young Greg (D)	6 2	12 05	Doncaster	25	4 83	

League Appearances: Anderson, I. 24(5); Antoine-Curier, M. 3(2); Armstrong, C. 9; Barnard, D. 34; Bolder, C. 6(1); Boulding, M. 27; Campbell, S. 39; Cas, M. 13(7); Coldicott, S. 13(1); Crane, T. 37; Crowe, J. 27(5); Davison, A. 32; Daws, N. 17; Edwards, M. 32(1); Fettis, A. 11; Ford, S. 21(5); Groves, P. 7(4); Hamilton, D. 20(7); Hockless, G. 4(9); Jevons, P. 21(8); Lawrence, J. 5; Mansaram, D. 11(20); McDermott, J. 21; Nimmo, L. (2); Onuora, I. 18(1); Parker, W. (4); Pettinger, A. 3; Pouton, A. 5; Rankin, I. 12; Rowan, J. 9(5); Soames, D. (10); Ten Heuvel, L. 3(1); Thorpe, L. 5(1); Thorrington, J. 2(1); Warhurst, P. 5(2); Young, G. 10(7).
Goals – League (55): Boulding 12, Jevons 12 (3 pens), Anderson 5 (1 pen), Rankin 4, Crane 3, Mansaram 3, Onuora 3, Barnard 2, Cas 2, Hockless 2, Rowan 2, Armstrong 1, Campbell 1, Edwards 1, Ford 1, Lawrence 1.
Carling Cup (2): Anderson 1 (pen), Campbell 1.
FA Cup (3): Boulding 1, Cas 1, Jevons 1.
LDV Vans Trophy (1): Mansaram 1.
Ground: Blundell Park, Cleethorpes, North-East Lincolnshire DN35 7PY. Telephone (01472) 605050.
Record Attendance: 31,651 v Wolverhampton W, FA Cup 5th rd, 20 February 1937. **Capacity:** 10,033.
Manager: Russell Slade.
Secretary: Ian Fleming.
Most League Goals: 103, Division 2, 1933–34.
Highest League Scorer in Season: Pat Glover, 42, Division 2, 1933–34.
Most League Goals in Total Aggregate: Pat Glover, 180, 1930–39.
Most Capped Player: Pat Glover, 7, Wales.
Most League Appearances: John McDermott, 553, 1987–.
Honours – Football League: Division 2 Champions – 1900–01, 1933–34. Division 3 (N) Champions – 1925–26, 1955–56. Division 3 Champions – 1979–80. Division 4 Champions – 1971-72. **League Group Cup:** Winners 1981–82. **Auto Windscreens Shield:** Winners 1997–98.
Colours: Black and white striped shirts, black shorts, black stockings.

Name	Height	DOB	Birthplace		Previous club
Barron Micky (D)	5 11	11 10	Lumley	22 12 74	Middlesbrough
Boyd Adam (F)	5 9	10 12	Hartlepool	25 5 82	Scholar
Brackstone John (D)	5 11	10 08	Hartlepool	9 2 85	Scholar
Carson Stephen (M)	5 10	12 00	Ballymoney	6 10 80	Barnsley
Humphreys Richie (M)	5 11	12 07	Sheffield	30 11 77	Cambridge U
Jordan Andy (D)	6 2	13 05	Manchester	14 12 79	Cardiff C
Konstantopoulos Dimitrios (G)	6 4	14 02	Salonika	29 11 78	
McCann Ryan (M)	5 8	11 03	Bellshill	15 9 82	St Johnstone
Nelson Michael (D)	6 2	13 03	Gateshead	3 3 82	Bury
Porter Joel (F)	5 9	11 13	Adelaide	25 12 78	Sydney Olympic
Provett Jim (G)	6 0	13 04	Stockton	22 12 82	Trainee
Robertson Hugh (D)	5 9	13 11	Aberdeen	19 3 75	Ross Co
Robson Matty (D)	5 9	11 02	Durham	23 1 85	Scholar
Strachan Gavin (M)	5 10	11 07	Aberdeen	23 12 78	Southend U
Sweeney Anthony (M)	6 0	11 07	Stockton	5 9 83	Scholar
Tinkler Mark (M)	6 2	12 00	Bishop Auckland	24 10 74	Southend U
Westwood Chris (D)	5 11	12 10	Dudley	13 2 77	Wolverhampton W
Williams Eifion (F)	5 11	11 02	Bangor	15 11 75	Torquay U

League Appearances: Arnison, P. 2(2); Barron, M. 32; Boyd, A. 10(8); Brackstone, J. 5(1); Byrne, D. 2; Carson, S. 1(2); Clarke, D. 23(10); Craddock, D. 9(1); Danns, N. 8(1); Easter, J. (3); Foley, D. (1); Gabbiadini, M. 9(6); Henderson, K. 1(2); Humphreys, R. 46; Istead, S. 1(30); Jordan, A. 4(1); McCann, R. (4); Nelson, M. 38(2); Porter, J. 18(9); Provett, J. 45; Richardson, M. 3; Robertson, H. 18; Robinson, M. 4; Robinson, P. 19(12); Robson, M. 17(6); Shuker, C. 14; Strachan, G. 34(2); Sweeney, A. 8(3); Tinkler, M. 43(1); Walker, S. 5(1); Westwood, C. 45; Wilkinson, J. 2(2); Williams, A. 1; Williams, E. 39(2).
Goals – League (76): Williams E 13, Boyd 12 (1 pen), Robinson P 7 (2 pens), Tinkler 6 (1 pen), Clarke 5, Gabbiadini 5 (1 pen), Strachan 5 (2 pens), Robertson 4, Humphreys 3, Nelson 3, Porter 3, Wilkinson 2, Barron 1, Danns 1, Istead 1, Robson 1, Shuker 1, Sweeney 1, own goals 2.
Carling Cup (3): Robinson P 2 (2 pens), Istead 1.
FA Cup (5): Gabbiadini 2, Brackstone 1, Humphreys 1, Porter 1.
LDV Vans Trophy (3): Clarke 2, Williams E 1.
Play-Offs (2): Porter 1, Sweeney 1.
Ground: Victoria Park, Clarence Road, Hartlepool TS24 8BZ. Telephone (01429) 272584.
Record Attendance: 17,426 v Manchester U, FA Cup 3rd rd, 5 January 1957.
Capacity: 7629.
Manager: Neale Cooper.
Secretary: Maureen Smith.
Most League Goals: 90, Division 3 (N), 1956–57.
Highest League Scorer in Season: William Robinson, 28, Division 3 (N), 1927–28; Joe Allon, 28, Division 4, 1990–91.
Most League Goals in Total Aggregate: Ken Johnson, 98, 1949–64.
Most Capped Player: Ambrose Fogarty, 1 (11), Republic of Ireland.
Most League Appearances: Wattie Moore, 447, 1948–64.
Honours – Nil.
Colours: White shirts with royal blue pinstripe, blue shorts, white stockings.

HUDDERSFIELD TOWN   FL CHAMPIONSHIP 1

Abbott Pawel (F)	5 7	11 07	York	5 5 82	Preston NE
Ahmed Adnan (M)	5 10	11 12	Burnley	7 6 84	Scholar
Booth Andy (F)	6 1	13 00	Huddersfield	6 12 73	Sheffield W
Brown Nat (F)	6 2	12 05	Sheffield	15 6 81	Trainee
Carss Tony (M)	5 11	11 13	Alnwick	31 3 76	Oldham Ath
Clarke Nathan (D)	6 2	12 00	Halifax	30 11 83	Scholar
Fowler Lee (M)	5 7	10 00	Cardiff	10 6 83	Coventry C
Gray Ian (G)	6 2	13 13	Manchester	25 2 75	Rotherham U
Holdsworth Andy (D)	5 9	11 02	Pontefract	29 1 84	Scholar
Lloyd Anthony (D)	5 7	11 00	Taunton	14 3 84	Scholar
Mirfin David (M)	6 2	14 05	Sheffield	18 4 85	Scholar
Newby Jon (F)	5 11	11 00	Warrington	28 11 78	Bury
Schofield Danny (F)	5 11	12 00	Doncaster	10 4 80	Brodsworth
Senior Philip (G)	5 11	11 00	Huddersfield	30 10 82	Trainee
Sodje Efe (D)	6 1	12 00	Greenwich	5 10 72	Crewe Alex
Thompson Tyrone (F)	5 10	11 00	Sheffield	8 5 82	Sheffield U
Worthington Jon (M)	5 9	11 05	Dewsbury	16 4 83	Scholar
Yates Steve (D)	5 11	12 00	Bristol	29 1 70	Sheffield U

League Appearances: Abbott, P. 12(1); Ahmed, A. (1); Booth, A. 36(1); Booty, M. 3(1); Brown, N. 13(8); Carss, T. 35(1); Clarke, N. 25(1); Edwards, R. 11(6); Fowler, L. 27(2); Gray, I. 17; Harkins, G. 1(2); Holdsworth, A. 31(5); Holland, C. (3); Hughes, I. 12(1); Lloyd, A. 30(1); Mattis, D. 2(3); McAliskey, J. 5(3); Mirfin, D. 15(6); Newby, J. 10(4); Onibuje, F. (2); Onuora, I. (3); Rachubka, P. 13; Schofield, D. 38(2); Scott, P. 16(3); Senior, P. 16; Sodje, E. 37(2); Stead, J. 26; Thompson, T. 1(1); Thorrington, J. 3(2); Worthington, J. 36(3); Yates, S. 35.
Goals – League (68): Stead 16 (1 pen), Booth 13, Schofield 8, Abbott 5, McAliskey 4, Sodje 4, Lloyd 3, Worthington 3, Carss 2 (1 pen), Mirfin 2, Scott 2, Clarke N 1, Edwards 1, Hughes 1, Yates 1, own goals 2.
Carling Cup (6): Stead 2, Booth 1, Carss 1, Holdsworth 1, Thorrington 1.
FA Cup (0).
LDV Vans Trophy (0).
Play-Offs (4): Edwards 1, Mirfin 1, Onuora 1, Schofield 1 (pen).
Ground: The Alfred McAlpine Stadium, Leeds Road, Huddersfield HD1 6PX. Telephone (01484) 484100.
Record Attendance: 67,037 v Arsenal, FA Cup 6th rd, 27 February 1932.
Capacity: 25,000.
Manager: Peter Jackson.
Secretary: Ann Hough.
Most League Goals: 101, Division 4, 1979–80.
Highest League Scorer in Season: Sam Taylor, 35, Division 2, 1919–20; George Brown, 35, Division 1, 1925–26.
Most League Goals in Total Aggregate: George Brown, 142, 1921–29; Jimmy Glazzard, 142, 1946–56.
Most Capped Player: Jimmy Nicholson, 31 (41), Northern Ireland.
Most League Appearances: Billy Smith, 520, 1914–34.
Honours – Football League: Division 1 Champions – 1923–24, 1924–25, 1925–26. Division 2 Champions – 1969–70. Division 4 Champions – 1969–70. **FA Cup winners** 1922.
Colours: Blue and white striped shirts, white shorts, white stockings with blue trim.

Allsopp Danny (F)	6 1	14 00	Melbourne	10 8 78	Notts Co
Ashbee Ian (M)	6 1	13 07	Birmingham	6 9 76	Cambridge U
Burgess Ben (F)	6 3	14 13	Buxton	9 11 81	Stockport Co
Dawson Andy (D)	5 9	11 12	Northallerton	20 10 78	Scunthorpe U
Delaney Damien (D)	6 3	13 10	Cork	20 7 81	Leicester C
Donaldson Clayton (F)	6 1	11 07	Bradford	7 2 84	Scholar
Elliott Stuart (M)	5 10	11 09	Belfast	23 7 78	Motherwell
Fettis Alan (G)	6 1	11 04	Newtownards	1 2 71	York C
Forrester Jamie (F)	5 6	11 00	Bradford	1 11 74	Northampton T
France Ryan (M)	5 11	11 11	Sheffield	13 12 80	Alfreton T
Fry Russell (M)	6 0	11 13	Hull	4 12 85	Scholar
Green Stuart (M)	5 10	11 00	Carlisle	15 6 81	Newcastle U
Hinds Richard (D)	6 2	12 02	Sheffield	22 8 80	Tranmere R
Joseph Marc (D)	6 2	10 07	Leicester	10 11 76	Peterborough U
Myhill Boaz (G)	6 3	14 06	California	9 11 82	Aston Villa
Peat Nathan (D)	5 9	10 09	Hull	19 9 82	Scholar
Price Jason (M)	6 2	11 05	Pontypridd	12 4 77	Tranmere R
Thelwell Alton (D)	5 10	12 02	Holloway	5 9 80	Tottenham H
Walters Jonathan (F)	6 0	12 06	Wirral	20 9 83	Crewe Alex
Wiseman Scott (M)	6 0	11 06	Hull	9 10 85	Scholar

League Appearances: Allsopp, D. 31(5); Ashbee, I. 39; Burgess, B. 44; Dawson, A. 32(1); Delaney, D. 46; Elliott, S. 42; Fettis, A. 3; Forrester, J. 6(15); France, R. 7(21); Green, S. 38(4); Hinds, R. 34(5); Holt, A. 6(19); Joseph, M. 32; Keates, D. 9(5); Kuipers, M. 3; Lewis, J. 13; Marshall, L. 10(1); Melton, S. (5); Musselwhite, P. 17(1); Myhill, B. 23; Peat, N. 1; Price, J. 29(4); Thelwell, A. 22(4); Walters, J. 5(11); Webb, D. (4); Whittle, J. 15(3); Wiseman, S. (2).

Goals – League (82): Burgess 18, Allsopp 15, Elliott 14, Price J 9, Green 6 (1 pen), Forrester 4 (1 pen), Dawson 3, Ashbee 2, Delaney 2, France 2, Hinds 1, Holt 1, Joseph 1, Lewis 1, Thelwell 1, Walters 1, own goal 1.

Carling Cup (0).

FA Cup (1): Price 1.

LDV Vans Trophy (4): Forrester 1, France 1, Webb 1, Williams 1.

Ground: KC Stadium, The Circle, Walton Street, Hull HU3 6HU. Telephone (0870) 8370003.

Record Attendance: 55,019 v Manchester U, FA Cup 6th rd, 26 February 1949; 23,495 v Huddersfield T, Division 3, 24 April 2004 at KC Stadium.

Capacity: 25,400.

Manager: Peter Taylor.

Secretary: Phil Hough.

Most League Goals: 109, Division 3, 1965–66.

Highest League Scorer in Season: Bill McNaughton, 39, Division 3 (N), 1932–33.

Most League Goals in Total Aggregate: Chris Chilton, 195, 1960–71.

Most Capped Player: Theo Whitmore, Jamaica.

Most League Appearances: Andy Davidson, 520, 1952–67.

Honours – Football League: Division 3 (N) Champions – 1932–33, 1948–49. Division 3 Champions – 1965–66.

Colours: Black, amber and white shirts, black shorts, black stockings.

Bent Darren (F)	5 11	11 07	Tooting	6 2 84	Scholar
Bent Marcus (F)	6 2	12 04	Hammersmith	19 5 78	Blackburn R
Bowditch Dean (F)	5 11	10 08	Hertfordshire	15 6 86	Trainee
Collins Aidan (D)	6 3	13 09	Harlow	18 10 86	
Counago Pablo (F)	5 11	11 06	Pontevedra	9 8 79	Celta Vigo
Davis Kelvin (G)	6 1	14 00	Bedford	29 9 76	Wimbledon
Diallo Drissa (D)	6 0	11 08	Nouadhibou	4 1 73	
Hogg Chris (D)	6 0	12 07	Middlesbrough	12 3 85	Trainee
Kuqi Shefki (F)	6 2	13 10	Kosovo	10 11 76	Sheffield W
Miller Tommy (M)	6 1	11 12	Shotton Colliery	8 1 79	Hartlepool U
Mitchell Scott (M)	5 11	12 00	Ely	2 9 85	Scholar
Murray Antonio (M)	5 9	11 00	Cambridge	15 9 84	Scholar
Nash Gerard (D)	6 1	11 08	Dublin	11 7 86	Scholar
Patten Ben (D)	6 1	12 00	London	16 2 86	Ford U
Price Lewis (G)	6 3	13 06	Bournemouth	19 7 84	Academy
Reuser Martijn (M)	5 7	12 10	Amsterdam	1 2 75	Vitesse
Richards Matt (D)	5 8	10 10	Harlow	26 12 84	Scholar
Santos Georges (M)	6 3	14 00	Marseille	15 8 70	Grimsby T
Sobers Jerome (D)	6 2	13 05	London	18 4 86	Ford U
Westlake Ian (M)	5 11	11 00	Clacton	10 11 83	Scholar

League Appearances: Armstrong, A. 5(2); Bart-Williams, C. 23(3); Bent, D. 32(5); Bent, M. 4; Bowditch, D. 7(9); Counago, P. 18(11); Davis, K. 45; Diallo, D. 16(3); Elliott, M. 10; Kuqi, S. 29(7); Magilton, J. 46; Mahon, A. 7(4); Makin, C. 5; McGreal, J. 18; Miller, T. 27(7); Mitchell, S. (2); Nash, G. (1); Naylor, R. 28(11); Price, L. 1; Reuser, M. 3(14); Richards, M. 41(3); Santos, G. 28(6); Westlake, I. 30(9); Wilnis, F. 41; Wright, J. 42(3).

Goals – League (84): Bent D 16, Counago 11 (4 pens), Kuqi 11 (1 pen), Miller T 11 (5 pens), Westlake 6, Naylor 5, Wright 5, Bowditch 4, Reuser 3, Armstrong 2 (1 pen), Bart-Williams 2, Bent M 1, Magilton 1, Mahon 1, McGreal 1, Richards 1, Santos 1, own goals 2.

Carling Cup (2): Bowditch 1, Counago 1 (pen).

FA Cup (4): Kuqi 1, Miller 1, Naylor 1, Reuser 1.

Play-Offs (1): Bent D 1.

Ground: Portman Road, Ipswich, Suffolk IP1 2DA. Telephone (01473) 400500.

Record Attendance: 38,010 v Leeds U, FA Cup 6th rd, 8 March 1975.

Capacity: 30,311.

Manager: Joe Royle.

Secretary: David C. Rose.

Most League Goals: 106, Division 3 (S), 1955–56.

Highest League Scorer in Season: Ted Phillips, 41, Division 3 (S), 1956–57.

Most League Goals in Total Aggregate: Ray Crawford, 203, 1958–63 and 1966–69.

Most Capped Player: Allan Hunter, 47 (53), Northern Ireland.

Most League Appearances: Mick Mills, 591, 1966–82.

Honours – Football League: Division 1 Champions – 1961–62. Division 2 Champions – 1960–61, 1967–68, 1991–92. Division 3 (S) Champions – 1953–54, 1956–57. **FA Cup:** Winners 1977–78. **European Competitions: UEFA Cup winners:** 1980–81.

Colours: Blue shirts, white shorts, blue stockings.

KIDDERMINSTER HARRIERS   FL CHAMPIONSHIP 2

Burton Steven (D)	6 1	11 05	Hull	10 10 82	Hull C	
Christiansen Jesper (F)	6 3	13 06	Denmark	18 6 80	Odense	
Danby John (G)	6 2	14 06	Stoke	20 9 83		
Hatswell Wayne (D)	6 0	13 10	Swindon	8 2 75	Oxford U	
Jenkins Lee (M)	5 9	11 00	Pontypool	28 6 79	Swansea C	
Keates Dean (M)	5 6	10 10	Walsall	30 6 78	Hull C	
McHale Chris (D)	6 0	12 00	Birmingham	4 11 82		
Murray Adam (M)	5 9	11 11	Birmingham	30 9 81	Notts Co	
Rickards Scott (F)	5 9	12 00	Birmingham	3 11 81	Tamworth	

League Appearances: Antoine-Curier, M. (1); Bennett, D. 34(4); Betts, R. 8(1); Bishop, A. 8(3); Brock, S. 37; Brown, S. 8; Burton, S. 10(2); Christiansen, J. 11(10); Clarke, L. 3(1); Coleman, K. 10; Danby, J. 9; Dyer, L. 5(2); Flynn, S. 4(2); Foster, I. 10(1); Gadsby, M. 23(9); Hatswell, W. 32; Henriksen, B. 14(8); Hinton, C. 41(1); Jenkins, L. 5(2); Keates, D. 8; Lewis, M. 1(3); McHale, C. (1); Melligan, J. 5; Murray, A. 19(3); Parrish, S. 16(11); Rickards, S. 5(8); Sall, A. 6(1); Shilton, S. 9(5); Smith, A. 19(3); Stamps, S. 34(1); Viveash, A. 7; Ward, G. 17(4); White, A. 6(1); Williams, D. 28; Williams, J. 28(16); Willis, A. 12; Yates, M. 14.

Goals – League (45): Williams D 5, Williams J 4, Bennett 3, Foster 3 (1 pen), Murray 3, Parrish 3, Bishop 2, Brown 2, Gadsby 2, Hatswell 2, Henriksen 2 (1 pen), Keates 2, Yates 2 (1 pen), Christiansen 1, Dyer 1, Hinton 1 (pen), Melligan 1, Rickards 1, White 1, Willis 1, own goals 3.

Carling Cup (0).

FA Cup (6): Bennett 4, Burton 1, Williams J 1.

LDV Vans Trophy (0).

Ground: Aggborough Stadium, Hoo Road, Kidderminster DY10 1NB. Telephone (01562) 823 931.

Record Attendance: 9,155 v Hereford U, 27 November 1948.

Capacity: 6419.

Manager: Jan Molby.

Football Secretary: Roger Barlow.

Honours – Conference: Champions 1993–94, 1999–2000; Runners-up 1996–97. **FA Trophy:** 1986–87 (winners); 1990–91 (runners-up), 1994–95 (runners-up). **League Cup:** 1996–97 (winners). **Welsh FA Cup:** 1985–86 (runners-up), 1988–89 (runners-up). **Southern League Cup:** 1979–80 (winners). **Worcester Senior Cup:** (21). **Birmingham Senior Cup:** (7). **Staffordshire Senior Cup:** (4). **West Midland League Champions:** (6), Runners-up (3). **Southern Premier:** Runners-up (1). **West Midland League Cup:** Winners (7). **Keys Cup:** Winners (7). **Border Counties Floodlit League Champions:** (3). **Camkin Floodlit Cup:** Winners (3). **Bass County Vase:** Winners (1). **Conference Fair Play Trophy:** (5)

Colours: Red shirts with white flash, white shorts, red stockings with white trim.

LEEDS UNITED   FL CHAMPIONSHIP

Bakke Eirik (M)	6 2	13 03	Sogndal	13 9 77	Sogndal
Barmby Nick (M)	5 7	10 09	Hull	11 2 74	Liverpool
Bowler Justin (F)	5 8	11 02	Leeds	26 6 86	Trainee
Carson Scott (G)	6 3	13 09	Whitehaven	3 9 85	Scholar
Constable Robert (D)	6 0	11 13	Pontefract	26 1 86	Trainee

Corr Barry (F)	6 4	12 05	Co Wicklow	2 4 85	Scholar
Cousins Andrew (M)	5 8	11 02	Dublin	30 1 85	Scholar
Coyles William (G)	6 0	11 12	Co Antrim	20 12 84	Scholar
Cronin Kevin (D)	6 0	11 11	Dublin	18 5 85	Scholar
Duberry Michael (D)	6 1	14 09	Enfield	14 10 75	Chelsea
Edwards Stewart (D)	6 0	12 01	Swansea	1 1 84	Scholar
Gray Nicholas (M)	6 0	10 06	Harrogate	17 10 85	Trainee
Harte Ian (D)	5 11	12 06	Drogheda	31 8 77	Trainee
Johnson Seth (M)	5 10	12 06	Birmingham	12 3 79	Derby Co
Johnson Simon (F)	5 10	12 06	West Bromwich	9 3 83	Scholar
Jones Chris (M)	5 8	8 11	Bangor	9 10 85	Trainee
Keegan Paul (M)	5 11	12 00	Dublin	5 7 84	Scholar
Kelly Gary (D)	5 10	11 06	Drogheda	9 7 74	Home Farm
Keogh Andrew (F)	6 0	11 07	Dublin	16 5 86	Scholar
Keyes Edward (D)	5 9	10 10	Dublin	2 5 85	Scholar
Kilgallon Matthew (D)	6 1	12 02	York	8 1 84	Scholar
Leister Brenton (D)	5 11	11 12	Leeds	3 9 85	Scholar
Matteo Dominic (D)	6 1	13 08	Dumfries	28 4 74	Liverpool
McDaid Sean (D)	5 8	10 07	Harrogate	6 3 86	Trainee
McMaster Jamie (M)	5 11	12 00	Sydney	29 11 82	NSW Academy
McPhail Stephen (M)	5 9	12 02	London	9 12 79	Trainee
McStay Henry (D)	6 0	11 11	Co Armagh	6 3 85	Scholar
Mills Danny (D)	5 11	12 06	Norwich	18 5 77	Charlton Ath
Milner James (F)	5 9	11 00	Leeds	4 1 86	Trainee
Radebe Lucas (D)	6 0	11 10	Johannesburg	12 4 69	Kaiser Chiefs
Reeves Damian (F)	5 9	11 09	Doncaster	18 12 85	Trainee
Richardson Frazer (D)	5 11	11 08	Rotherham	29 10 82	Trainee
Shields Robbie (M)	5 6	9 13	Dublin	1 5 84	Scholar
Singh Harpal (F)	5 7	10 02	Bradford	15 9 81	Trainee
Smith Alan (F)	5 10	12 01	Leeds	28 10 80	Trainee
Tyrrell Derek (D)	6 1	12 00	Dublin	14 4 85	Scholar
Viduka Mark (F)	6 2	15 05	Melbourne	9 10 75	Celtic
Winter Jamie (M)	5 10	11 11	Dundee	4 8 85	Scholar
Woods Martin (M)	5 11	11 11	Bellshill	1 1 86	Trainee

League Appearances: Bakke, E. 8(2); Barmby, N. 1(5); Batty, D. 10(2); Bridges, M. 1(9); Caldwell, S. 13; Camara, Z. 13; Carson, S. 2(1); Chapuis, C. (1); Domi, D. 9(3); Duberry, M. 19; Harte, I. 21(2); Johnson, Seth 24(1); Johnson, Simon 1(4); Kelly, G. 37; Kilgallon, M. 7(1); Lennon, A. (11); Matteo, D. 33; McPhail, S. 8(4); Milner, J. 27(3); Morris, J. 11(1); Olembe, S. 8(4); Pennant, J. 34(2); Radebe, L. 11(3); Richardson, F. 2(2); Robinson, P. 36; Roque Junior, J. 5; Sakho, L. 9(8); Smith, A. 35; Viduka, M. 30; Wilcox, J. 3(3).

Goals – League (40): Viduka 11 (2 pens), Smith 9 (1 pen), Duberry 3, Milner 3, Johnson Seth 2, Kilgallon 2, Matteo 2, Pennant 2, Bakke 1, Caldwell 1, Camara 1, Harte 1 (pen), McPhail 1, Sakho 1.

Carling Cup (4): Roque Junior 2, Harte 1, Robinson 1.

FA Cup (1): Viduka 1.

Ground: Elland Road, Leeds LS11 0ES. Telephone (0113) 367 6000.

Record Attendance: 57,892 v Sunderland, FA Cup 5th rd (replay), 15 March 1967.

Capacity: 40,232.

Manager: Kevin Blackwell.

Secretary: Ian Silvester.

Most League Goals: 98, Division 2, 1927–28.

Highest League Scorer in Season: John Charles, 42, Division 2, 1953–54.
Most League Goals in Total Aggregate: Peter Lorimer, 168, 1965–79 and 1983–86.
Most Capped Player: Lucas Radebe, 58 (70), South Africa.
Most League Appearances: Jack Charlton, 629, 1953–73.
Honours – Football League: Division 1 Champions – 1968–69, 1973–74, 1991–92.
Division 2 Champions – 1923–24, 1963–64, 1989–90. **FA Cup:** Winners 1972.
Football League Cup: Winners 1967–68. **European Competitions: European Fairs
Cup winners:** 1967–68, 1970–71.
Colours: All white.

LEICESTER CITY   FL CHAMPIONSHIP

Benjamin Trevor (F)	6 2	14 04	Kettering	8 2 79	Cambridge U
Brooker Paul (M)	5 8	10 06	Hammersmith	25 11 76	Brighton & HA
Canero Peter (D)	5 9	11 04	Glasgow	18 1 81	Kilmarnock
Coyne Danny (G)	6 0	13 04	Prestatyn	27 8 73	Grimsby T
Dabizas Nikos (D)	6 1	12 07	Amindeo	3 8 73	Newcastle U
Dawson Stephen (M)	5 9	11 02	Dublin	4 12 85	Scholar
Dickov Paul (F)	5 6	10 06	Livingston	1 11 72	Manchester C
Elliott Matt (D)	6 3	14 12	Wandsworth	1 11 68	Oxford U
Gillespie Keith (M)	5 10	11 10	Larne	18 2 75	Blackburn R
Heath Matthew (D)	6 4	13 08	Leicester	1 11 81	Scholar
Hignett Craig (M)	5 9	12 06	Whiston	12 1 70	Blackburn R
Jones Matthew (M)	5 11	12 10	Llanelli	1 9 80	Leeds U
Logan Conrad (G)	6 0	14 04	Letterkenny	18 4 86	Scholar
McAnallen Conor (D)	5 11	9 13	Craigavon	3 1 86	Scholar
McGavigan Ryan (M)	5 9	11 02	County Donegal	31 3 86	Scholar
Morris Lee (F)	5 9	11 02	Driffield	30 4 80	Derby Co
Nalis Lilian (M)	6 1	13 03	Nogent sur Marne	29 9 71	Chievo
Pearmain Dominic (F)	5 9	10 03	Peterborough	2 9 84	Scholar
Petrescu Tomi (F)	5 9	10 05	Jyvaskyla	24 7 86	Scholar
Powell Liam (D)	5 10	12 06	Cardiff	18 9 85	Scholar
Scimeca Riccardo (M)	6 1	13 04	Leamington Spa	13 6 75	Nottingham F
Scowcroft James (F)	6 1	14 07	Bury St Edmunds	15 11 75	Ipswich T
Stewart Jordan (D)	5 11	12 06	Birmingham	3 3 82	Trainee
Thatcher Ben (D)	5 10	12 07	Swindon	30 11 75	Tottenham H
Walker Ian (G)	6 2	13 03	Watford	31 10 71	Tottenham H
Williamson Tom (M)	5 9	10 04	Leicester	24 12 84	Scholar
Wright Tommy (F)	6 0	12 02	Leicester	28 9 84	Scholar

League Appearances: Benjamin, T. 2(2); Bent, M. 28(5); Brooker, P. (3); Canero,
P. 2(5); Coyne, D. 1(3); Curtis, J. 14(1); Dabizas, N. 18; Davidson, C. 8(5); Deane,
B. (5); Dickov, P. 28(7); Elliott, M. 3(4); Ferdinand, L. 20(9); Freund, S. 13(1);
Gillespie, K. 7(5); Guppy, S. 9(6); Heath, M. 13; Hignett, C. 3(10); Howey, S. 13;
Impey, A. 11(2); Izzet, M. 30; McKinlay, B. 15(1); Nalis, L. 11(9); Rogers, A. 7(1);
Scimeca, R. 28(1); Scowcroft, J. 33(2); Sinclair, F. 11(3); Stewart, J. 16(9); Taggart,
G. 9; Thatcher, B. 28(1); Walker, I. 37.
Goals – League (48): Ferdinand 12, Dickov 11 (2 pens), Bent 9, Scowcroft 5, Izzet
2, Hignett 1, Howey 1, Nalis 1, Scimeca 1, Sinclair 1, Stewart 1, Thatcher 1, own
goals 2.
Carling Cup (1): Dickov 1 (pen).
FA Cup (3): Bent 1, Dickov 1, Ferdinand 1.

Ground: The Walkers Stadium, Filbert Way, Leicester LE2 7GL. Telephone (0870) 040 6000
Record Attendance: 47,298 v Tottenham H, FA Cup 5th rd, 18 February 1928.
Capacity: 32,500.
Manager: Micky Adams.
Secretary: Andrew Neville.
Most League Goals: 109, Division 2, 1956–57.
Highest League Scorer in Season: Arthur Rowley, 44, Division 2, 1956–57.
Most League Goals in Total Aggregate: Arthur Chandler, 259, 1923–35.
Most Capped Player: John O'Neill, 39, Northern Ireland.
Most League Appearances: Adam Black, 528, 1920–35.
Honours – Football League: Division 2 Champions – 1924–25, 1936–37, 1953–54, 1956–57, 1970–71, 1979–80. **Football League Cup:** Winners 1964, 1997, 2000.
Colours: Royal blue shirts, white shorts, blue stockings.

LEYTON ORIENT   FL CHAMPIONSHIP 2

Alexander Gary (F)	6 0	13 01	Lambeth	15 8 79	Hull C	
Barnard Donny (D)	5 10	11 05	Forest Gate	1 7 84		
Harrison Lee (G)	6 2	13 03	Billericay	12 9 71	Peterborough U	
Hunt David (D)	5 11	11 09	Dulwich	10 9 82	Scholar	
Ibehre Jabo (F)	6 2	13 00	Islington	28 1 83	Trainee	
Jones Billy (D)	6 1	11 04	Chatham	26 6 83	Trainee	
Lockwood Matt (D)	5 10	11 07	Rochford	17 10 76	Bristol R	
Mackie John (D)	6 1	13 00	London	5 7 76	Reading	
Miller Justin (D)	6 0	11 04	Johannesburg	16 12 80	Ipswich T	
Morris Glenn (G)	5 11	11 00	Woolwich	20 12 83	Scholar	
Newey Tom (D)	5 10	11 00	Sheffield	31 10 82	Leeds U	
Purser Wayne (F)	5 8	12 05	Basildon	13 4 80	Barnet	
Scott Andy (F)	6 1	12 04	Epsom	2 8 72	Oxford U	

League Appearances: Akinfenwa, A. (1); Alexander, G. 44; Barnard, D. 17(6); Brazier, M. 5; Cooper, S. 9; Downer, S. 1(2); Duncan, D. (1); Ebdon, M. 10(4); Forbes, B. (10); Hammond, D. 6(2); Harnwell, J. 1(2); Harrison, L. 19(1); Heald, G. 4; Hunt, D. 35(3); Hunt, W. 6; Ibehre, J. 17(18); Jones, B. 29(2); Joseph, M. 23(1); Lockwood, M. 24(1); Mackie, J. 20; McCormack, A. 8(2); McGhee, D. 10; Miller, J. 27(7); Morris, G. 27; Newey, T. 31(3); Peters, M. 39; Purser, W. 29(12); Saah, B. 4(2); Sam, L. 5(5); Scott, A. 8; Stephens, K. (1); Tate, C. 5(18); Thorpe, L. 15(2); Toner, C. 19(8); Zakuani, G. 9(1).
Goals – League (48): Alexander 15, Purser 5, Ibehre 4, Thorpe 4, Lockwood 2 (2 pens). Miller 2, Newey 2, Peters 2, Zakuani 2, Brazier 1, Hunt D 1, Mackie 1, McGhee 1, Scott 1, Tate 1, Toner 1, own goals 3.
Carling Cup (1): Ibehre 1.
FA Cup (3): Alexander 1, Lockwood 1, Purser 1.
LDV Vans Trophy (1): Lockwood 1 (pen).
Ground: Matchroom Stadium, Brisbane Road, Leyton, London E10 5NE. Telephone (020) 8926 1111.
Record Attendance: 34,345 v West Ham U, FA Cup 4th rd, 25 January 1964.
Capacity: 11,127.
Manager: Martin Ling.
Secretary: Lindsey Freeman.
Most League Goals: 106, Division 3 (S), 1955–56.

Highest League Scorer in Season: Tom Johnston, 35, Division 2, 1957–58.
Most League Goals in Total Aggregate: Tom Johnston, 121, 1956–58, 1959–61.
Most Capped Players: Tunji Banjo, 7 (7), Nigeria; John Chiedozie, 7 (9), Nigeria; Tony Grealish, 7 (45), Eire.
Most League Appearances: Peter Allen, 432, 1965–78.
Honours – Football League: Division 3 Champions – 1969–70. Division 3 (S) Champions – 1955–56.
Colours: Red shirts with black panel, red shorts, red stockings.

LINCOLN CITY   FL CHAMPIONSHIP 2

Butcher Richard (M)	6 0	12 12	Northampton	22	1 81	Kettering T
Fletcher Gary (F)	5 11	12 06	Liverpool	4	6 81	Leyton Orient
Futcher Ben (D)	6 7	12 05	Bradford	4	6 81	Oldham Ath
Gain Peter (M)	6 0	11 07	Hammersmith	2	11 76	Tottenham H
Green Francis (F)	5 9	11 04	Derby	23	4 80	Peterborough U
Logan Richard (D)	6 0	12 08	Barnsley	24	5 69	Scunthorpe U
Marriott Alan (G)	6 0	12 04	Bedford	3	9 78	Tottenham H
McCombe Jamie (D)	6 5	12 05	Pontefract	1	1 83	Scunthorpe U
Morgan Paul (D)	6 0	11 05	Belfast	23	10 78	Preston NE
Sandwith Kevin (D)	5 11	12 05	Workington	30	4 78	Carlisle U

League Appearances: Bailey, M. 34(1); Bloomer, M. 14(13); Butcher, R. 26(6); Carbon, M. 1; Cropper, D. 5(16); Ellison, K. 11; Fletcher, G. 42; Futcher, B. 43; Gain, P. 42; Green, F. 28(7); Liburd, R. 19(5); Marriott, A. 46; May, R. 1(4); Mayo, P. 31; McCombe, J. 8; McNamara, N. 2(8); Morgan, P. 41; Pearce, A. (3); Remy, E. (1); Richardson, M. 34(4); Rocastle, C. (2); Sandwith, K. 1(2); Sedgemore, B. 24(3); Wattley, D. 1(2); Weaver, S. 39; Wilford, A. (5); Willis, S. (3); Yeo, S. 13(28).
Goals – League (68): Fletcher 16, Yeo 11, Richardson 10 (1 pen), Gain 7, Green 7, Butcher 6, Mayo 6 (4 pens), Futcher 2, Bailey 1, Wilford 1, own goal 1.
Carling Cup (0).
FA Cup (3): Bloomer 1, Mayo 1 (pen), Yeo 1.
LDV Vans Trophy (7): Fletcher 2, Bailey 1, Green 1, Mayo 1 (pen), Richardson 1, Yeo 1.
Play-Offs (3): Bailey 1, Butcher 1, Fletcher 1.
Ground: Sincil Bank, Lincoln LN5 8LD. Telephone (01522) 880011.
Record Attendance: 23,196 v Derby Co, League Cup 4th rd, 15 November 1967.
Capacity: 9800.
Manager: Keith Alexander.
Secretary: F. J. Martin.
Most League Goals: 121, Division 3 (N), 1951–52.
Highest League Scorer in Season: Allan Hall, 41, Division 3 (N), 1931–32.
Most League Goals in Total Aggregate: Andy Graver, 144, 1950–55 and 1958–61.
Most Capped Player: David Pugh, 3 (7), Wales; George Moulson, 3, Republic of Ireland.
Most League Appearances: Grant Brown, 407, 1989–2002.
Honours – Football League: Division 3 (N) Champions – 1931–32, 1947–48, 1951–52. Division 4 Champions – 1975–76.
Colours: Red and white striped shirts, black shorts, red stockings.

LIVERPOOL   FA PREMIERSHIP

Babbel Markus (D)	6 0	13 03	Munich	8	9 72	Bayern Munich
Baros Milan (F)	6 0	13 02	Valasske Mezirici	28	10 81	Banik Ostrava
Biscan Igor (M)	6 3	12 08	Zagreb	4	5 78	Dynamo Zagreb
Carragher Jamie (D)	6 1	12 05	Liverpool	28	1 78	Trainee
Cheyrou Bruno (M)	6 1	13 03	Suresnes	10	5 78	Lille
Diao Salif (M)	6 1	13 03	Kedougou	10	2 77	Sedan
Diarra Alou (D)	6 2	12 07	Villepinte	15	7 81	
Diouf El Hadji (F)	5 9	12 03	Dakar	15	1 81	Lens
Dudek Jerzy (G)	6 2	12 08	Ribnek	23	3 73	Feyenoord
Finnan Steve (M)	6 0	12 09	Limerick	24	4 76	Fulham
Foy Robert (F)			Edinburgh	29	10 85	Trainee
Gerrard Steven (M)	6 1	12 03	Whiston	30	5 80	Trainee
Hamann Dietmar (M)	6 2	12 01	Waldasson	27	8 73	Newcastle U
Harrison Paul (G)			Liverpool	18	12 84	Scholar
Henchoz Stephane (D)	6 1	12 13	Billens	7	9 74	Blackburn R
Heskey Emile (F)	6 1	14 04	Leicester	11	1 78	Leicester C
Hyypia Sami (D)	6 4	13 11	Porvoo	7	10 73	Willem II
Kewell Harry (M)	5 11	13 00	Sydney	22	9 78	Leeds U
Kirkland Christopher (G)	6 6	14 12	Leicester	2	5 81	Coventry C
Le Tallec Anthony (M)	6 0	11 07	Hennebont	3	10 84	Le Havre
Luzi-Bernardi Patrice (G)	6 2	14 01	Ajaccio	8	7 80	
Mannix David (M)			Crewe	24	9 85	Trainee
Medjani Carl (D)	6 0	13 00	Lyon	15	5 85	
Mellor Neil (F)	6 0	13 07	Manchester	4	11 82	Scholar
Murphy Danny (M)	5 9	12 08	Chester	18	3 77	Crewe Alex
Otsemobor John (D)	5 10	12 07	Liverpool	23	3 83	Trainee
Owen Michael (F)	5 8	10 13	Chester	14	12 79	Trainee
Potter Darren (M)	6 1	11 05	Liverpool	21	12 84	Scholar
Raven David (D)			Wirral	10	3 85	Scholar
Riise John Arne (M)	6 1	12 08	Molde	24	9 80	Monaco
Sinama-Pongolle Florent (F)	5 7	12 02	Saint-Pierre	20	10 84	Le Havre
Smicer Vladimir (M)	5 10	12 02	Degin	24	5 73	Lens
Smyth Mark (M)			Liverpool	9	1 85	Scholar
Traore Djimi (D)	6 1	12 06	Saint-Ouen	1	3 80	Lens
Vignal Gregory (D)	5 11	12 03	Montpellier	19	7 81	Bastia
Warnock Stephen (M)	5 7	12 01	Ormskirk	12	12 81	Trainee
Welsh John (M)	5 7	11 06	Liverpool	10	1 84	Scholar
Whitbread Zak (D)	6 2	11 06	Houston	4	3 84	
Wilkie Ryan (M)			Glasgow	11	12 85	Trainee

League Appearances: Baros, M. 6(7); Biscan, I. 27(2); Carragher, J. 22; Cheyrou, B. 9(3); Diao, S. 2(1); Diouf, E. 20(6); Dudek, J. 30; Finnan, S. 19(3); Gerrard, S. 34; Hamann, D. 25; Henchoz, S. 15(3); Heskey, E. 25(10); Hyypia, S. 38; Jones, P. 2; Kewell, H. 36; Kirkland, C. 6; Le Tallec, A. 3(10); Luzi-Bernardi, P. (1); Murphy, D. 19(12); Otsemobor, J. 4; Owen, M. 29; Riise, J. 22(6); Sinama-Pongolle, F. 3(12); Smicer, V. 15(5); Traore, D. 7; Welsh, J. (1).

Goals – League (55): Owen 16 (4 pens), Heskey 7, Kewell 7, Murphy 5 (3 pens), Gerrard 4 (1 pen), Hyypia 4, Smicer 3, Cheyrou 2, Hamann 2, Sinama-Pongolle 2, Baros 1, own goals 2.

Carling Cup (6): Heskey 2, Murphy 2 (1 pen), Kewell 1, Smicer 1.
FA Cup (5): Cheyrou 2, Heskey 1, Murphy 1 (pen), Owen 1.
UEFA Cup (14): Kewell 3, Gerrard 2, Heskey 2, Owen 2, Baros 1, Hamann 1, Hyypia 1, Le Tallec 1, Traore 1.
Ground: Anfield Road, Liverpool L4 0TH. Telephone (0151) 263 2361.
Record Attendance: 61,905 v Wolverhampton W, FA Cup 4th rd, 2 February 1952.
Capacity: 45,362.
Manager: Rafael Benitez.
Secretary: Bryce Morrison.
Most League Goals: 106, Division 2, 1895–96.
Highest League Scorer in Season: Roger Hunt, 41, Division 2, 1961–62.
Most League Goals in Total Aggregate: Roger Hunt, 245, 1959–69.
Most Capped Player: Ian Rush, 67 (73), Wales.
Most League Appearances: Ian Callaghan, 640, 1960–78.
Honours – Football League: Division 1 – Champions 1900–01, 1905–06, 1921–22, 1922–23, 1946–47, 1963–64, 1965–66, 1972–73, 1975–76, 1976–77, 1978–79, 1979–80, 1981–82, 1982–83, 1983–84, 1985–86, 1987–88, 1989–90 (Liverpool have a record number of 18 League Championship wins). Division 2 Champions – 1893–94, 1895–96, 1904–05, 1961–62. **FA Cup:** Winners 1965, 1974, 1986, 1989, 1992, 2001. **League Cup:** Winners 1981, 1982, 1983, 1984, 1995, 2001, 2003. Super Cup: Winners 1985–86. **European Competitions: European Cup winners:** 1976–77, 1977–78, 1980–81, 1983–84. **UEFA Cup winners:** 1972–73, 1975–76, 2001. **Super Cup winners:** 1977.
Colours: All red.

LUTON TOWN   FL CHAMPIONSHIP 1

Bayliss Dave (D)	6 0	12 11	Liverpool	8 6 76	Rochdale
Davis Sol (D)	5 8	11 12	Cheltenham	4 9 79	Swindon T
Foley Kevin (M)	5 10	11 03	London	1 11 84	Scholar
Hillier Ian (D)	6 1	12 01	Neath	26 12 79	Tottenham H
Holmes Peter (M)	5 11	11 08	Bishop Auckland	18 11 80	Sheffield W
Howard Steve (F)	6 3	15 00	Durham	10 5 76	Northampton T
Leary Michael (M)	5 11	11 10	Ealing	17 4 83	Scholar
Mansell Lee (M)	5 9	11 00	Gloucester	28 10 82	Scholar
Neilson Alan (D)	5 11	12 12	Wegburg	26 9 72	Fulham
Nicholls Kevin (M)	5 10	12 04	Newham	2 1 79	Wigan Ath
Showunmi Enoch (F)	6 3	14 10	London	21 4 82	Willesden Constantin
Underwood Paul (M)	5 11	12 11	Wimbledon	16 8 73	Rushden & D

League Appearances: Bayliss, D. 6; Beckwith, R. 13; Beresford, M. 11; Boyce, E. 42; Brill, D. 4(1); Brkovic, A. 24(8); Coyne, C. 44; Crowe, D. (8); Davies, C. 4(2); Davis, S. 34(2); Foley, K. 32(1); Forbes, A. 21(6); Hillier, I. 8(3); Holmes, P. 11(5); Howard, S. 34; Hughes, P. 20(2); Hyldgaard, M. 18; Judge, M. (1); Keane, K. 14(1); Leary, M. 8(6); Mansell, L. 12(4); McSheffrey, G. 18; Neilson, A. 11(3); Nicholls, K. 21; O'Leary, S. 3(2); Perrett, R. 5(1); Pitt, C. 11(1); Robinson, S. 32(2); Showunmi, E. 18(8); Spring, M. 24; Thorpe, T. 2; Underwood, P. 1.
Goals – League (69): Howard 14, Forbes 9, McSheffrey 9 (1 pen), Showunmi 7, Boyce 4, Holmes 3, Coyne 2, Leary 2, Mansell 2, Nicholls 2 (2 pens), Perrett 2,

65

Robinson 2, Thorpe 2, Brkovic 1, Foley 1, Hughes 1, Keane 1, Neilson 1, O'Leary 1, Spring 1, own goals 2.
Carling Cup (8): Foley 2, Bayliss 1, Coyne 1, Howard 1, McSheffrey 1, Pitt 1, Thorpe 1.
FA Cup (8): Forbes 5 (1 pen), Boyce 1, Mansell 1, Robinson 1 (pen).
LDV Vans Trophy (3): Judge 1, Leary 1 (pen), Showunmi 1.
Ground: Kenilworth Road Stadium, 1 Maple Road, Luton, Beds. LU4 8AW. Telephone (01582) 411622.
Record Attendance: 30,069 v Blackpool, FA Cup 6th rd replay, 4 March 1959.
Capacity: 9975.
Manager: Mike Newell.
Secretary: Cherry Newbery.
Most League Goals: 103, Division 3 (S), 1936–37.
Highest League Scorer in Season: Joe Payne, 55, Division 3 (S), 1936–37.
Most League Goals in Total Aggregate: Gordon Turner, 243, 1949–64.
Most Capped Player: Mal Donaghy, 58 (91), Northern Ireland.
Most League Appearances: Bob Morton, 494, 1948–64.
Honours – Football League: Division 2 Champions – 1981–82. Division 4 Champions – 1967–68. Division 3 (S) Champions – 1936–37. **Football League Cup winners** 1987–88.
Colours: White shirts with orange and black trim, black shorts with orange and white trim, black stockings with two white hoops.

MACCLESFIELD TOWN   FL CHAMPIONSHIP 2

Name	Ht	Wt	Birthplace	Birthdate	Previous club
Brackenridge Steve (M)	5 10	10 08	Rochdale	31 7 84	Scholar
Carr Michael (D)	5 9	11 04	Crewe	6 12 83	Scholar
Carragher Matt (D)	5 9	10 07	Liverpool	14 1 76	Port Vale
Carruthers Martin (F)	5 11	11 10	Nottingham	7 8 72	Scunthorpe U
Miles John (F)	5 10	10 08	Fazackerley	28 9 81	Crewe Alex
Parkin Jonathan (F)	6 4	13 07	Barnsley	30 12 81	York C
Payne Steve (D)	5 11	12 00	Castleford	1 8 75	Chesterfield
Potter Graham (D)	6 1	11 12	Solihull	20 5 75	Boston U
Ross Neil (F)	6 1	12 02	West Bromwich	10 8 82	Stockport Co
Welch Michael (D)	6 3	11 13	Crewe	11 1 82	Barnsley
Whitaker Danny (M)	5 10	11 00	Manchester	14 11 80	
Wilson Steve (G)	5 10	10 07	Hull	24 4 74	Hull C

League Appearances: Abbey, G. 23(2); Adams, D. 27; Beresford, D. 5; Beswetherick, J. 3(1); Brackenridge, S. 2(5); Carr, M. 7; Carragher, M. 18; Carruthers, M. 30(9); Clark, S. 1(3); Flitcroft, D. 14(1); Haddrell, M. 4(6); Harsley, P. 16; Hitchen, S. 8(1); Jones, R. 1; Little, C. 18(6); Macauley, S. 16; Miles, J. 23(6); Munroe, K. 35(1); Myhill, B. 15; Olsen, J. (2); Parkin, J. 12; Payne, S. 13; Potter, G. 16; Priest, C. 26(3); Robinson, N. (1); Ross, N. 1(5); Smith, D. 7(3); Tipton, M. 34(4); Welch, M. 33(5); Whitaker, D. 33(3); Widdrington, T. 34(1); Wilson, S. 31(1).
Goals – League (54): Tipton 16 (4 pens), Carruthers 8, Miles 6, Little 5, Whitaker 5, Brackenridge 2, Harsley 2, Potter 2, Priest 2, Haddrell 1, Parkin 1, own goals 4.
Carling Cup (1): Whitaker 1.
FA Cup (7): Tipton 3 (1 pen), Carruthers 2, Little 1, Miles 1.
LDV Vans Trophy (1): Adams 1.
Ground: The Moss Rose Ground, London Road, Macclesfield, Cheshire SK11 7SP. Telephone (01625) 264686.

Record Attendance: 9008 v Winsford U, Cheshire Senior Cup 2nd rd, 4 February 1948. **Capacity:** 6208.
Manager: Brian Horton.
Secretary: Colin Garlick.
Most League Goals: 66, Division 3, 1999–2000.
Highest League Scorer in Season: Richard Barker, 16, Division 3, 1999–2000.
Most League Goals in Total Aggregate: John Askey, 31, 1997–.
Most Capped Player: George Abbey, 10, Nigeria.
Most League Appearances: Darren Tinson, 263, 1997–2003; Matt Tipton, 16, Division 3, 2003–04.
Honours – Nil.
Colours: Royal blue shirts, white shorts, blue stockings.

MANCHESTER CITY   FA PREMIERSHIP

Player			Birthplace		Previous club
Anelka Nicolas (F)	6 1	13 03	Versailles	14 3 79	Liverpool
Barton Joey (M)	5 11	11 09	Huyton	2 9 82	Scholar
Bennett Ian (M)			Rochdale	24 2 86	Trainee
Bermingham Karl (M)			Dublin	6 10 85	Scholar
Bischoff Mikkel (D)	6 3	13 11	Denmark	3 2 82	
Bosvelt Paul (M)	6 0	13 00	Doetinchem	26 3 70	Feyenoord
Croft Lee (F)		·	Wigan	21 6 85	Scholar
D'Laryea Jonathan (M)			Manchester	3 9 85	Trainee
D'Laryea Nathan (D)			Manchester	3 9 85	Trainee
Distin Sylvain (D)	6 3	14 08	Bagnolet	16 12 77	Newcastle U
Dunne Richard (D)	6 2	15 12	Dublin	21 9 79	Everton
Ellegaard Kevin Stuhr (G)	6 5	14 06	Charlottenlund	23 5 83	Farum
Elliott Stephen (F)	5 7	11 06	Dublin	6 1 84	School
Flood Willo (M)	5 6	9 11	Dublin	10 4 85	
Fowler Robbie (F)	5 10	12 05	Liverpool	9 4 75	Leeds U
James David (G)	6 5	14 02	Welwyn	1 8 70	West Ham U
Jihai Sun (D)	5 9	12 02	Dalian	30 9 77	Dalian Wanda
Jordan Stephen (D)	6 1	11 13	Warrington	6 3 82	Trainee
Laird Marc (M)			Edinburgh	23 1 86	Trainee
Macken Jon (F)	5 11	13 13	Manchester	7 9 77	Preston NE
Matthews James (M)			Dublin	2 2 85	Scholar
McCarthy Patrick (D)	6 2	13 07	Dublin	31 5 83	Scholar
McManaman Steve (M)	6 1	11 11	Liverpool	11 2 72	Real Madrid
Murphy Paul (D)			Wexford	12 4 85	Scholar
Negouai Christian (M)	6 4	14 01	Fort-de-France	20 1 75	Charleroi
Pearson Sean (M)			Manchester	7 3 85	
Proffitt Darrly (M)			Stoke	2 5 85	Scholar
Reyna Claudio (M)	5 9	11 08	New Jersey	20 7 73	Sunderland
Sibierski Antoine (M)	6 2	12 04	Lille	5 8 74	Lens
Sinclair Trevor (M)	5 9	13 05	Dulwich	2 3 73	West Ham U
Sommeil David (D)	5 10	12 12	Ponte-a-Pitre	10 8 74	Bordeaux
Tandy Jamie (M)			Manchester	1 9 84	Trainee
Timms Ashley (M)			Manchester	6 11 85	Scholar
Vuoso Vicente (D)	5 9	12 05	Mar del Plata	3 11 81	Independiente
Wanchope Paulo (F)	6 3	13 10	Heredia	31 7 76	West Ham U
Weaver Nick (G)	6 4	14 07	Sheffield	2 3 79	Mansfield T

Wright-Phillips   Lewisham   12 3 85   Scholar
   Bradley (M)
Wright-Phillips   5 5   9 12   London   25 10 81
   Shaun (M)

League Appearances: Anelka, N. 31(1); Barton, J. 24(4); Berkovic, E. 1(3); Bosvelt, P. 22(3); Distin, S. 38; Dunne, R. 28(1); Ellegaard, K. 2(2); Elliott, S. (2); Fowler, R. 23(8); James, D. 17; Jihai, S. 29(4); Jordan, S. (2); Macken, J. 7(8); McManaman, S. 20(2); Reyna, C. 19(4); Seaman, D. 19; Sibierski, A. 18(15); Sinclair, T. 20(9); Sommeil, D. 18; Tarnat, M. 32; Tiatto, D. 1(4); Van Buyten, D. 5; Wanchope, P. 12(10); Wright-Phillips, S. 32(2).
Goals – League (55): Anelka 16 (4 pens), Fowler 7, Wright-Phillips 7, Wanchope 6, Sibierski 5, Tarnat 3, Distin 2, Barton 1, Jihai 1, Macken 1, Reyna 1, Sinclair 1, Sommeil 1, own goals 3.
Carling Cup (4): Wright-Phillips 2, Fowler 1, Macken 1.
FA Cup (12): Anelka 4 (1 pen), Macken 2, Bosvelt 1, Distin 1, Fowler 1, Siberski 1, Tarnat 1, Wright-Phillips 1.
UEFA Cup (12): Anelka 4 (2 pens), Fowler 1, Huckerby 1, Jihai 1, Negouai 1, Siberski 1, Sinclair 1, Sommeil 1, Wright-Phillips 1.
Ground: City of Manchester Stadium, Sport City, Manchester M11 3FF. Telephone (0870) 062 1894
Record Attendance: (at Maine Road) 84,569 v Stoke C, FA Cup 6th rd, 3 March 1934 (British record for any game outside London or Glasgow). **Capacity:** 48,000.
Manager: Kevin Keegan.
General Secretary: J. B. Halford.
Most League Goals: 108, Division 2, 1926–27, 108, Division 1, 2001–02.
Highest League Scorer in Season: Tommy Johnson, 38, Division 1, 1928–29.
Most League Goals in Total Aggregate: Tommy Johnson, 158, 1919–30.
Most Capped Player: Colin Bell, 48, England.
Most League Appearances: Alan Oakes, 565, 1959–76.
Honours – Football League: Division 1 Champions – 1936–37, 1967–68, 2001–02. Division 2 Champions – 1898–99, 1902–03, 1909–10, 1927–28, 1946–47, 1965–66. **FA Cup winners** 1904, 1934, 1956, 1969. **Football League Cup winners** 1970, 1976.
European Competitions: European Cup-Winners' Cup winners: 1969–70.
Colours: Sky blue shirts, white shorts, sky blue stockings.

MANCHESTER UNITED   FA PREMIERSHIP

Bardsley Phillip (D)	5 11	11 08	Salford	28 6 85	Trainee
Barthez Fabien (G)	5 11	12 08	Lavelanet	28 6 71	Monaco
Bellion David (F)	6 0	11 09	Sevres	27 11 82	Sunderland
Brown Wes (D)	6 1	13 11	Manchester	13 10 79	Trainee
Butt Nicky (M)	5 10	11 11	Manchester	21 1 75	Trainee
Calliste Ramon (F)	5 10	11 06	Cardiff	16 12 85	Trainee
Carroll Roy (G)	6 2	13 12	Enniskillen	30 9 77	Wigan Ath
Chadwick Luke (M)	5 11	11 08	Cambridge	18 11 80	Trainee
Collett Ben (D)	5 8	10 00	Bury	11 9 84	Trainee
Cooper Kenny (F)	6 3	14 01	Baltimore	21 10 84	
Djemba-Djemba Eric (M)	5 9	11 13	Douala	4 5 81	Nantes
Djordjic Bojan (F)	5 10	11 01	Belgrade	6 2 82	
Eagles Chris (M)	6 0	10 08	Hemel Hempstead	19 11 85	Trainee
Ferdinand Rio (D)	6 2	13 12	Peckham	7 11 78	Leeds U

Fletcher Darren (M)	6 0	13 01	Edinburgh	1 2 84	Scholar
Forlan Diego (F)	5 8	11 11	Montevideo	19 5 79	Independiente
Fortune Quinton (F)	5 9	11 09	Cape Town	21 5 77	Atletico Madrid B
Fox David (M)	5 9	12 02	Stoke	13 12 83	Scholar
Giggs Ryan (F)	5 11	11 00	Cardiff	29 11 73	School
Heath Colin (F)	6 0	13 01	Chesterfield	31 12 83	Scholar
Heaton Tom (G)	6 1	13 06	Chester	15 4 86	Trainee
Howard Tim (G)	6 3	14 12	North Brunswick	6 3 79	NY/NJ MetroStars
Johnson Eddie (F)	5 10	13 05	Chester	20 9 84	Scholar
Jones David (M)	5 11	10 00	Southport	4 11 84	Trainee
Keane Roy (M)	5 11	11 10	Cork	10 8 71	Nottingham F
Kleberson Jose (M)	5 9	10 00	Urai	19 6 79	Atletico PR
Lawrence Lee (D)	5 7	9 02	Boston	1 12 84	Trainee
Lynch Mark (D)	5 11	11 03	Manchester	2 9 81	Trainee
McShane Paul (D)	5 11	11 05	Wicklow	6 1 86	Trainee
Nardiello Daniel (F)	5 11	11 06	Coventry	22 10 82	Trainee
Neumayr Marcus (M)	5 11	11 05	Aschaffenburg	26 3 86	Scholar
Neville Gary (D)	5 11	12 04	Bury	18 2 75	Trainee
Neville Phil (D)	5 11	12 00	Bury	21 1 77	Trainee
O'Shea John (D)	6 3	12 10	Waterford	30 4 81	Waterford
Poole David (F)	5 8	12 00	Manchester	12 11 84	Trainee
Port Graeme (M)	5 10	10 12	York	13 4 86	Trainee
Pugh Danny (D)	6 0	12 10	Manchester	19 10 82	Scholar
Ricardo(G)	6 2	13 12	Madrid	31 12 71	Valladolid
Richardson Kieran (M)	5 8	11 00	Greenwich	21 10 84	Scholar
Ronaldo Cristiano (F)	6 1	12 04	Funchal	5 2 85	
Saha Louis (F)	6 1	12 06	Paris	8 8 78	Fulham
Scholes Paul (M)	5 7	11 00	Salford	16 11 74	Trainee
Silvestre Mikael (D)	6 0	13 01	Chambray les Tours	9 8 77	Internazionale
Solskjaer Ole Gunnar (F)	5 10	11 11	Kristiansund	26 2 73	Molde
Spector Jonathan (D)	6 0	12 08	Arlington Heights	1 3 86	
Steele Luke (G)	6 2	12 00	Peterborough	24 9 84	Scholar
Stewart Michael (M)	5 11	11 11	Edinburgh	26 2 81	Trainee
Tierney Paul (D)	5 10	12 05	Salford	15 9 82	Scholar
Timm Mads (F)	5 9	12 10	Odense	31 10 84	Scholar
Van Nistelrooy Ruud (F)	6 2	12 13	Oss	1 7 76	PSV Eindhoven

League Appearances: Bellion, D. 4(10); Brown, W. 15(2); Butt, N. 12(9); Carroll, R. 6; Djemba-Djemba, E. 10(5); Ferdinand, R. 20; Fletcher, D. 17(5); Forlan, D. 10(14); Fortune, Q. 18(5); Giggs, R. 29(4); Howard, T. 32; Keane, R. 25(3); Kleberson, J. 10(2); Neville, G. 30; Neville, P. 29(2); O'Shea, J. 32(1); Ronaldo, C. 15(14); Saha, L. 9(3); Scholes, P. 24(4); Silvestre, M. 33(1); Solskjaer, O. 7(6); Van Nistelrooy, R. 31(1).

Goals – League (64): Van Nistelrooy 20 (1 pen), Scholes 9, Giggs 7, Saha 7, Forlan 4, Ronaldo 4, Keane 3, Bellion 2, Kleberson 2, Neville G 2, O'Shea 2, Butt 1, own goal 1.

Carling Cup (3): Bellion 1, Djemba-Djemba 1, Fowler 1.

FA Cup (15): Van Nistelrooy 6 (1 pen), Scholes 4, Ronaldo 2, Forlan 1, Silvestre 1, own goal 1.

Champions League (15): Van Nistelrooy 4 (1 pen), Forlan 2, Fortune 2, Butt 1, Djemba-Djemba 1, Giggs 1, Neville P 1, Scholes 1, Silvestre 1, Solskjaer 1.

Ground: Old Trafford, Sir Matt Busby Way, Manchester M16 0RA. Telephone (0161) 868 8000.

Record Attendance: 76,962 Wolverhampton W v Grimsby T, FA Cup semi-final. 25 March 1939. **Capacity:** 68,190.
Manager: Sir Alex Ferguson CBE.
Secretary: Kenneth Merrett.
Most League Goals: 103, Division 1, 1956–57 and 1958–59.
Highest League Scorer in Season: Dennis Viollet, 32, 1959–60.
Most League Goals in Total Aggregate: Bobby Charlton, 199, 1956–73.
Most Capped Player: Bobby Charlton, 106, England.
Most League Appearances: Bobby Charlton, 606, 1956–73.
Honours – FA Premier League: Champions – 1992–93, 1993–94, 1995–96, 1996–97, 1998–99, 1999–2000, 2000–01, 2002–03. **Football League:** Division 1 Champions – 1907–8, 1910–11, 1951–52, 1955–56, 1956–57, 1964–65, 1966–67. Division 2 Champions – 1935–36, 1974–75. **FA Cup winners** 1909, 1948, 1963, 1977, 1983, 1985, 1990, 1994, 1996, 1999, 2004. **Football League Cup winners** 1991–92. **European Competitions: European Cup winners:** 1967–68. **Champions League winners:** 1998–99. **European Cup-Winners' Cup winners:** 1990–91. **Super Cup winners:** 1991. **Inter-Continental Cup winners:** 1999.
Colours: Red shirts, white or black shorts, black or white stockings.

MANSFIELD TOWN   FL CHAMPIONSHIP 2

Artell Dave (D)	6 2	13 00	Rotherham	22 11 80	Rotherham U
Buxton Jake (D)	6 1	12 13	Sutton-in-Ashfield	4 3 85	Scholar
Corden Wayne (M)	5 10	11 08	Leek	1 11 75	Port Vale
Day Rhys (D)	6 2	12 08	Bridgend	31 8 82	Manchester C
Disley Craig (M)	5 10	11 00	Worksop	24 8 81	Trainee
John-Baptiste Alex (D)	5 11	11 07	Sutton-in-Ashfield	31 1 86	Scholar
Larkin Colin (F)	5 9	10 02	Dundalk	27 4 82	Wolverhampton W
Lawrence Liam (M)	5 10	11 03	Retford	14 12 81	Trainee
Pilkington Kevin (G)	6 2	12 10	Hitchin	8 3 74	Wigan Ath
White Jason (G)	6 2	12 01	Mansfield	28 1 83	Trainee
Williamson Lee (M)	5 10	10 04	Derby	7 6 82	Trainee

League Appearances: Artell, D. 24(2); Beardsley, C. 2(13); Buxton, J. 9; Christie, I. 24(3); Clarke, J. 11(1); Corden, W. 40(4); Curle, T. (1); Curtis, T. 34(4); D'Jaffo, L. 4(4); Day, R. 40(1); Dimech, L. 17(3); Disley, C. 18(16); Eaton, A. 3; Hassell, B. 33(1); John-Baptiste, A. 14(3); Larkin, C. 19(18); Lawrence, L. 41; MacKenzie, N. 25(7); Mendes, J. 36(3); Mitchell, C. (1); Mulligan, L. (1); Pacquette, R. 3(2); Pilkington, K. 46; Vaughan, T. 32; White, A. 2(12); Williamson, L. 29(6).
Goals – League (76): Lawrence 18 (10 pens), Mendes 11, Christie 8, Corden 8 (1 pen), Larkin 7, Day 6, Disley 5, Artell 3, MacKenzie 2, Vaughan 2, Beardsley 1, Buxton 1, D'Jaffo 1, Dimech 1, Pacquette 1, own goal 1.
Carling Cup (1): own goal 1.
FA Cup (10): Lawrence 3 (2 pens), MacKenzie 3, Christie 1, Curtis 1, Larkin 1, Mendes 1.
LDV Vans Trophy (1): Day 1.
Play-Offs (3): Curtis 1, Day 1, Mendes 1.
Ground: Field Mill Ground, Quarry Lane, Mansfield NG18 5DA. Telephone (0870) 756 3160.
Record Attendance: 24,467 v Nottingham F, FA Cup 3rd rd, 10 January 1953.
Capacity: 9899.
Manager: Keith Curle.

Secretary: Christine Reynolds.
Most League Goals: 108, Division 4, 1962–63.
Highest League Scorer in Season: Ted Harston, 55, Division 3 (N), 1936–37.
Most League Goals in Total Aggregate: Harry Johnson, 104, 1931–36.
Most Capped Player: John McClelland, 6 (53), Northern Ireland.
Most League Appearances: Rod Arnold, 440, 1970–83.
Honours – Football League: Division 3 Champions – 1976–77. Division 4
Champions – 1974–75. **Freight Rover Trophy winners** 1986–87.
Colours: Amber shirts, blue shorts, blue stockings.

MIDDLESBROUGH   FA PREMIERSHIP

Boateng George (M)	5 9	12 06	Nkawkaw	5	9 75	Aston Villa
Christie Malcolm (F)	6 0	12 06	Peterborough	11	4 79	Derby Co
Cooper Colin (D)	5 11	11 11	Sedgefield	28	2 67	Nottingham F
Davies Andrew (D)	6 3	14 08	Stockton	17	12 84	Scholar
Downing Stewart (M)	5 11	10 04	Middlesbrough	22	7 84	Scholar
Ehiogu Ugo (D)	6 2	14 10	Hackney	3	11 72	Aston Villa
Graham Danny (F)	5 11	12 05	Gateshead	12	8 85	Trainee
Greening Jonathan (M)	6 0	11 08	Scarborough	2	1 79	Manchester U
Job Joseph-Desire (F)	5 11	11 00	Venissieux	1	12 77	Lens
Jones Brad (G)	6 3	12 01	Armadale	19	3 82	Trainee
Juninho(F)	5 5	9 10	Sao Paulo	22	2 73	Vasco da Gama
Liddle Gary (M)			Middlesbrough	15	6 86	Trainee
Maccarone Massimo (F)	5 10	12 05	Galliate	6	9 79	Empoli
McMahon Anthony (D)	5 10	11 04	Bishop Auckland	24	3 86	Scholar
Morrison James (M)	5 10	10 06	Darlington	25	5 86	Trainee
Nash Carlo (G)	6 3	15 03	Bolton	13	9 73	Manchester C
Nemeth Szilard (F)	5 11	11 04	Komarno	8	7 77	Inter Bratislava
Parnaby Stuart (M)	5 11	11 00	Durham City	19	7 82	Trainee
Peacock Anthony (M)			Middlesbrough	6	9 85	Trainee
Queudrue Franck (D)	6 1	12 01	Paris	27	8 78	Lens
Ricketts Michael (F)	6 2	15 00	Birmingham	4	12 78	Bolton W
Riggott Chris (D)	6 2	13 09	Derby	1	9 80	Derby Co
Schwarzer Mark (G)	6 4	14 07	Sydney	6	10 72	Bradford C
Southgate Gareth (D)	6 0	12 03	Watford	3	9 70	Aston Villa
Stockdale Robbie (D)	6 0	12 03	Middlesbrough	30	11 79	Trainee
Taylor Andrew (D)	5 10	11 04	Hartlepool	1	8 86	Trainee
Turnbull Ross (G)	6 4	15 00	Bishop Auckland	4	1 85	Trainee
Wilson Mark (M)	5 10	12 07	Scunthorpe	9	2 79	Manchester U

League Appearances: Boateng, G. 35; Christie, M. 7(3); Cooper, C. 17(2); Davies,
A. 8(2); Doriva 19(2); Downing, S. 7(13); Ehiogu, U. 16; Greening, J. 17(8); Job, J.
19(5); Jones, B. 1; Juninho 26(5); Maccarone, M. 13(10); Marinelli, C. 1; Mendieta,
G. 30(1); Mills, D. 28; Morrison, J. (1); Nash, C. 1; Nemeth, S. 17(15); Parnaby, S.
8(5); Queudrue, F. 31; Ricketts, M. 7(16); Riggott, C. 14(3); Schwarzer, M. 36;
Southgate, G. 27; Stockdale, R. (2); Wright, A. 2; Zenden, B. 31.
Goals – League (44): Nemeth 9, Juninho 8, Maccarone 6 (1 pen), Job 5, Zenden 4,
Mendieta 2, Ricketts 2 (2 pens), Christie 1, Greening 1, Marinelli 1, Southgate 1,
own goals 4.
Carling Cup (9): Zenden 2 (1 pen), Christie 1, Job 1, Juninho 1, Maccarone 1,
Mendieta 1, Ricketts 1, own goal 1.

FA Cup (3): Job 1, Zenden 1, own goal 1.
Ground: Riverside Stadium, Middlesbrough, Cleveland TS3 6RS. Telephone (01642) 877700
Record Attendance: 53,596 v Newcastle U, Division 1, 27 December 1949 (at Ayresome Park) and 34,800 v Leeds U, Premier League, 26 February 2000.
Capacity: 35,120.
Manager: Steve McClaren.
Secretary: Karen Nelson.
Most League Goals: 122, Division 2, 1926–27.
Highest League Scorer in Season: George Camsell, 59, Division 2, 1926–27 (Second Division record).
Most League Goals in Total Aggregate: George Camsell, 325, 1925–39.
Most Capped Player: Wilf Mannion, 26, England.
Most League Appearances: Tim Williamson, 563, 1902–23.
Honours – Football League: Division 1 Champions 1994–95. Division 2 Champions 1926–27, 1928–29, 1973–74. **Football League Cup winners:** 2004. **Amateur Cup winners** 1895, 1898, **Anglo-Scottish Cup:** Winners 1975–76.
Colours: Red shirts with white chest band, red shorts, red stockings.

MILLWALL FL CHAMPIONSHIP

Name			Birthplace	Birthdate	Previous club
Braniff Kevin (F)	5 11	10 03	Belfast	4 3 83	Scholar
Cahill Tim (M)	5 10	10 12	Sydney	6 12 79	Sydney U
Clancy Tim (M)	5 11	10 11	Trim	8 6 84	
Cogan Barry (F)	5 9	9 0	Sligo	4 11 84	Scholar
Craig Tony (D)	6 0	10 03	Greenwich	20 4 85	Scholar
Dichio Danny (F)	6 4	13 10	Hammersmith	19 10 74	WBA
Dolan Joe (D)	6 3	13 02	Harrow	27 5 80	Chelsea
Donovan James (M)	6 2	13 12	Sidcup	11 9 84	Scholar
Dunne Alan (D)	5 10	10 13	Dublin	23 8 82	
Elliott Marvin (M)	6 0	12 02	Wandsworth	15 9 84	Scholar
Harris Neil (F)	5 11	12 01	Orsett	12 7 77	Cambridge C
Hearn Charley (M)	5 11	11 13	Ashford	5 11 83	School
Ifill Paul (M)	6 0	12 01	Brighton	20 10 79	Trainee
Lawrence Matthew (D)	6 0	12 07	Northampton	19 6 74	Wycombe W
Livermore David (M)	5 11	12 07	Edmonton	20 5 80	Trainee
Masterson Terence (G)	6 2	11 04	Dublin	5 6 86	Scholar
May Ben (F)	6 1	12 12	Gravesend	10 3 84	
McCammon Mark (F)	6 3	15 02	Barnet	7 8 78	Brentford
Muscat Kevin (D)	5 11	11 07	Crawley	7 8 73	Wolverhampton W
Peeters Bob (F)	6 5	13 12	Lier	28 1 72	Vitesse
Phillips Mark (D)	6 2	11 00	Lambeth	27 1 82	Scholar
Quigley Mark (M)	5 10	11 07	Dublin	27 10 85	Scholar
Rees Matt (D)	6 2	12 00	Swansea	2 9 82	Trainee
Roberts Andy (M)	5 11	14 05	Dartford	20 3 74	Wimbledon
Robinson Anton (M)			London	17 2 86	Scholar
Robinson Paul (D)	6 1	11 08	Barnet	7 1 82	Scholar
Robinson Trevor (M)	5 9	12 11	Jamaica	20 9 84	Scholar
Rose Jason (D)	6 1	10 13	Sidcup	28 1 85	Scholar
Sutton John (F)	6 0	14 02	Norwich	26 12 83	Swindon T
Sweeney Peter (F)	6 0	12 01	Glasgow	25 9 84	Scholar

Ward Darren (D)	6 4	11 04	Kenton	13 9 78	Watford
Weston Curtis (M)	5 11	11 09	Greenwich	24 1 87	Scholar
Wise Dennis (M)	5 6	10 10	Kensington	16 12 66	Leicester C

League Appearances: Braniff, K. 6(10); Cahill, T. 40; Chadwick, N. 11(4); Cogan, B. (3); Craig, T. 8(1); Dichio, D. 15; Dolan, J. (1); Dunne, A. 4(4); Elliott, M. 14(7); Fofana, A. 9(7); Gueret, W. 2; Harris, N. 26(12); Hearn, C. 3(4); Ifill, P. 29(4); Juan 2(1); Lawrence, M. 34(2); Livermore, D. 35(1); Marshall, A. 16; McCammon, M. 3(4); Muscat, K. 27; Nethercott, S. 11(3); Peeters, B. 16(4); Quigley, M. (1); Roberts, A. 29(4); Robinson, P. 7(2); Robinson, T. (1); Ryan, R. 28(2); Sadlier, R. (2); Sutton, J. 2(2); Sweeney, P. 21(8); Ward, D. 46; Warner, T. 28; Weston, C. (1); Whelan, N. 8(7); Wise, D. 26(5).

Goals – League (55): Cahill 9, Harris 9 (4 pens), Ifill 8, Dichio 7, Chadwick 4, Whelan 4, Peeters 3, Ward 3, Sweeney 2, Braniff 1, Livermore 1, Nethercott 1, Roberts 1, Wise 1, own goal 1.

Carling Cup (0).

FA Cup (8): Cahill 3, Braniff 1, Dichio 1, Harris 1, Ifill 1, Wise 1.

Ground: The Den, Zampa Road, Bermondsey SE16 3LN. Telephone (020) 7232 1222.

Record Attendance: 20,093 v Arsenal, FA Cup 3rd rd, 10 January 1994. **Capacity:** 20,146.

Manager: Dennis Wise.

Secretary: Yvonne Haines.

Most League Goals: 127, Division 3 (S), 1927–28.

Highest League Scorer in Season: Richard Parker, 37, Division 3 (S), 1926–27.

Most League Goals in Total Aggregate: Teddy Sheringham, 93, 1984–91.

Most Capped Player: Eamonn Dunphy, 22 (23), Republic of Ireland.

Most League Appearances: Barry Kitchener, 523, 1967–82.

Honours – Football League: Division 2 Champions – 1987–88, 2000–01. Division 3 (S) Champions – 1927–28, 1937–38. Division 4 Champions – 1961–62. **Football League Trophy winners** 1982–83.

Colours: Blue and white shirts, blue shorts, blue stockings.

NEWCASTLE UNITED   FA PREMIERSHIP

Ambrose Darren (M)	5 11	10 05	Harlow	29 2 84	Ipswich T
Ameobi Foluwashola (F)	6 3	12 03	Zaria	12 10 81	Trainee
Bellamy Craig (F)	5 10	11 00	Cardiff	13 7 79	Coventry C
Bernard Olivier (D)	5 7	10 11	Paris	14 10 79	
Bowyer Lee (M)	5 8	10 04	London	3 1 77	West Ham U
Bramble Titus (D)	6 2	14 10	Ipswich	31 7 81	Ipswich T
Brennan Stephen (D)	5 8	11 10	Dublin	26 3 83	
Brittain Martin (M)	5 8	10 07	Newcastle	29 12 84	Trainee
Caig Tony (G)	6 0	13 04	Whitehaven	11 4 74	Hibernian
Chopra Michael (F)	5 8	9 06	Newcastle	23 12 83	Scholar
Dyer Kieron (M)	5 7	9 07	Ipswich	29 12 78	Ipswich T
Elliott Robbie (D)	5 8	12 03	Gosforth	25 12 73	Bolton W
Gate Kris (D)	5 7	10 03	Newcastle	1 1 85	Trainee
Given Shay (G)	6 0	13 04	Lifford	20 4 76	Blackburn R
Guy Lewis (F)	5 10	10 08	Penrith	27 8 85	Trainee
Harper Steve (G)	6 2	13 00	Easington	14 3 75	Seaham Red Star

Hughes Aaron (D)	6 1	11 02	Cookstown	8 11 79	Trainee
Jenas Jermaine (M)	5 10	12 00	Nottingham	18 2 83	Nottingham F
Lua-Lua Lomano (F)	5 8	12 00	Kinshasa	28 12 80	Colchester U
McClen Jamie (M)	5 8	10 07	Newcastle	13 5 79	Trainee
O'Brien Alan (M)	5 9	11 00	Dublin	20 2 85	Scholar
O'Brien Andy (D)	6 1	11 05	Harrogate	29 6 79	Bradford C
Offiong Richard (F)	5 11	12 00	South Shields	17 12 83	Scholar
Ramage Peter (D)	6 1	11 13	Ashington	22 11 83	Trainee
Robert Laurent (M)	5 8	10 13	Saint-Benoit	21 5 75	Paris St Germain
Shearer Alan (F)	6 0	12 06	Newcastle	13 8 70	Blackburn R
Speed Gary (M)	5 10	10 12	Deeside	8 9 69	Everton
Taylor Steven (D)	6 1	13 00	Greenwich	23 1 86	Trainee
Viana Hugo (M)	5 9	11 09	Barcelos	15 1 83	Sporting Lisbon
Woodgate Jonathan (D)	6 2	12 06	Middlesbrough	22 1 80	Leeds U

League Appearances: Ambrose, D. 10(14); Ameobi, F. 18(8); Bellamy, C. 13(3); Bernard, O. 35; Bowyer, L. 17(7); Bramble, T. 27(2); Bridges, M. (6); Brittain, M. (1); Caldwell, S. 3(2); Chopra, M. 1(5); Dyer, K. 25; Given, S. 38; Griffin, A. 5; Hughes, A. 34; Jenas, J. 26(5); Lua-Lua, L. 2(5); O'Brien, A. 27(1); Robert, L. 31(4); Shearer, A. 37; Solano, N. 8(4); Speed, G. 37(1); Taylor, S. 1; Viana, H. 5(11); Woodgate, J. 18.

Goals – League (52): Shearer 22 (7 pens), Ameobi 7, Robert 6, Bellamy 4, Speed 3, Ambrose 2, Bowyer 2, Jenas 2, Bernard 1, Dyer 1, O'Brien 1, own goal 1.

Carling Cup (1): Robert 1.

FA Cup (4): Dyer 2, Robert 2.

Champions League (1): Solano 1.

UEFA Cup (24): Shearer 6, Bellamy 5, Ameobi 3, Bramble 3, Robert 3, Ambrose 1, Jenas 1, Speed 1, own goal 1.

Ground: St James' Park, Newcastle-upon-Tyne NE1 4ST. Telephone (0191) 201 8400.

Record Attendance: 68,386 v Chelsea, Division 1, 3 Sept 1930. **Capacity:** 52,193.

Manager: Sir Bobby Robson CBE.

Secretary: Russell Cushing.

Most League Goals: 98, Division 1, 1951–52.

Highest League Scorer in Season: Hughie Gallacher, 36, Division 1, 1926–27.

Most League Goals in Total Aggregate: Jackie Milburn, 177, 1946–57.

Most Capped Player: Shay Given, 51 (60), Republic of Ireland.

Most League Appearances: Jim Lawrence, 432, 1904–22.

Honours – Football League: Division 1 – Champions 1904–05, 1906–07, 1908–09, 1926–27, 1992–93. Division 2 Champions – 1964–65. **FA Cup winners** 1910, 1924, 1932, 1951, 1952, 1955. **Texaco Cup winners** 1973–74, 1974–75. **European Competitions: European Fairs Cup winners:** 1968–69. **Anglo-Italian Cup winners:** 1973.

Colours: Black and white striped shirts, black shorts, black stockings.

NORTHAMPTON TOWN   FL CHAMPIONSHIP 2

Amoo Ryan (M)	5 10	9 12	Leicester	11 10 83	Aston Villa
Asamoah Derek (F)	5 6	10 12	Ghana	1 5 81	Slough T
Carruthers Chris (D)	5 10	12 03	Kettering	19 8 83	Scholar
Chambers Luke (D)	6 1	11 13	Kettering	29 8 85	Scholar

Clark Peter (D)	6 1	12 01	Romford	10 12 79	Stockport Co
Low Josh (F)	6 2	14 03	Bristol	15 2 79	Oldham Ath
Morison Steven (F)	6 2	13 07	Enfield	29 8 83	Scholar
Reeves Martin (M)	6 0	12 01	Birmingham	7 9 81	Leicester C
Reid Paul (D)	6 2	12 05	Carlisle	18 2 82	Rangers
Richards Marc (F)	6 0	13 04	Wolverhampton	8 7 82	Blackburn R
Smith Martin (F)	5 11	12 07	Sunderland	13 11 74	Huddersfield T
Westwood Ashley (D)	6 0	12 09	Bridgnorth	31 8 76	Sheffield W
Willmott Chris (D)	6 2	13 08	Bedford	30 9 77	Wimbledon
Youngs Tom (F)	5 9	11 13	Bury St Edmunds	31 8 79	Cambridge U

League Appearances: Abidallah, N. (1); Amoo, R. (1); Asamoah, D. 4(27); Burgess, O. 3(6); Carruthers, C. 19(5); Chambers, L. 19(5); Clark, P. 6; Doig, C. 9; Dudfield, L. 12(7); Hargreaves, C. 41(1); Harper, L. 39; Harsley, P. 5(9); Lincoln, G. 4(3); Low, J. 28(5); Lyttle, D. 23(4); Morison, S. 2(3); Reeves, M. 9(5); Reid, P. 33; Richards, M. 27(14); Sabin, E. 9(2); Sadler, M. 7; Sampson, I. 35(2); Smith, M. 43(1); Taylor, J. 3(5); Thompson, G. 7(1); Trollope, P. 43; Ullathorne, R. 13; Vieira, M. 7(3); Walker, R. 11(1); Westwood, A. 8(1); Willmott, C. 35(1); Youngs, T. 2(10).

Goals – League (58): Smith M 11 (4 pens), Richards 8, Trollope 6, Sabin 5, Walker 4, Asamoah 3, Dudfield 3, Hargreaves 3, Low 3, Reid 2, Sampson 2, Vieira 2, Lincoln 1, Morison 1, Taylor 1, Ullathorne 1, Willmott 1, own goal 1.

Carling Cup (3): Dudfield 1, Hargreaves 1 (pen), Low 1.

FA Cup (10): Smith 3 (1 pen), Richards 2, Walker 2, Asamoah 1, Hargreaves 1, Low 1.

LDV Vans Trophy (5): Dudfield 2, Walker 2, Low 1.

Play-Offs (3): Hargreaves 1, Richards 1, Smith 1.

Ground: Sixfields Stadium, Upton Way, Northampton NN5 5QA. Telephone (01604) 757773.

Record Attendance: 24,523 v Fulham, Division 1, 23 April 1966. **Capacity:** 7653.

Manager: Colin Calderwood.

Secretary: Norman Howells.

Most League Goals: 109, Division 3, 1962–63 and Division 3 (S), 1952–53.

Highest League Scorer in Season: Cliff Holton, 36, Division 3, 1961–62.

Most League Goals in Total Aggregate: Jack English, 135, 1947–60.

Most Capped Player: E. Lloyd Davies, 12 (16), Wales.

Most League Appearances: Tommy Fowler, 521, 1946–61.

Honours – Football League: Division 3 Champions – 1962–63. Division 4 Champions – 1986–87.

Colours: Claret shirts, white shorts, claret stockings.

NORWICH CITY   FA PREMIERSHIP

Brennan Jim (D)	5 11	13 00	Toronto	8 5 77	Nottingham F
Briggs Keith (D)	6 0	11 02	Glossop	11 12 81	Stockport Co
Drury Adam (D)	5 10	11 07	Cottenham	29 8 78	Peterborough U
Edworthy Marc (D)	5 8	10 03	Barnstaple	24 12 72	Wolverhampton W
Fleming Craig (D)	5 11	12 06	Halifax	6 10 71	Oldham Ath
Francis Damien (M)	6 0	11 08	Wandsworth	27 2 79	Wimbledon
Green Robert (G)	6 3	13 01	Chertsey	18 1 80	Trainee

Henderson Ian (F)	5 9	10 12	Thetford	24 1 85	Scholar
Holt Gary (M)	6 0	12 00	Irvine	9 3 73	Kilmarnock
Huckerby Darren (F)	5 10	12 02	Nottingham	23 4 76	Manchester C
Jarvis Ryan (F)	6 0	11 04	Fakenham	11 7 86	Scholar
MacKay Malky (D)	6 3	13 02	Bellshill	19 2 72	Celtic
McKenzie Leon (F)	5 10	10 03	Croydon	17 5 78	Peterborough U
McVeigh Paul (F)	5 6	10 11	Belfast	6 12 77	Tottenham H
Mulryne Phil (M)	5 9	11 01	Belfast	1 1 78	Manchester U
Rivers Mark (F)	5 10	11 04	Crewe	26 11 75	Crewe Alex
Shackell Jason (D)	6 3	12 08	Hitchin	27 9 83	Scholar
Svensson Mathias (F)	6 1	12 08	Boras	24 9 74	Charlton Ath

League Appearances: Abbey, Z. 1(2); Brennan, J. 7(8); Briggs, K. 1(2); Cooper, K. 6(4); Crouch, P. 14(1); Drury, A. 42; Easton, C. 8(2); Edworthy, M. 42(1); Fleming, C. 46; Francis, D. 39(2); Green, R. 46; Hammond, E. (4); Harper, K. 9; Henderson, I. 14(5); Holt, G. 46; Huckerby, D. 36; Jarvis, R. (12); MacKay, M. 45; McKenzie, L. 12(6); McVeigh, P. 36(8); Mulryne, P. 14(20); Nielsen, D. 2; Notman, A. (1); Rivers, M. 7(5); Roberts, I. 13(28); Shackell, J. 4(2); Svensson, M. 16(4).
Goals – League (79): Huckerby 14 (2 pens), McKenzie 9 (1 pen), Roberts 8 (2 pens), Francis 7, Svensson 7, McVeigh 5, Crouch 4, Henderson 4, MacKay 4, Rivers 4 (2 pens), Fleming 3, Mulryne 3, Easton 2, Brennan 1, Holt 1, Jarvis 1, own goals 2.
Carling Cup (0).
FA Cup (1): Brennan 1.
Ground: Carrow Road, Norwich NR1 1JE. Telephone (01603) 760760.
Record Attendance: 43,984 v Leicester C, FA Cup 6th rd, 30 March 1963.
Capacity: 24,349.
Manager: Nigel Worthington.
Secretary: Kevan Platt.
Most League Goals: 99, Division 3 (S), 1952–53.
Highest League Scorer in Season: Ralph Hunt, 31, Division 3 (S), 1955–56.
Most League Goals in Total Aggregate: Johnny Gavin, 122, 1945–54, 1955–58.
Most Capped Player: Mark Bowen, 35 (41), Wales.
Most League Appearances: Ron Ashman, 592, 1947–64.
Honours – Football League: Division 1 Champions – 2003–04. Division 2 Champions – 1971–72, 1985–86. Division 3 (S) Champions – 1933–34. **Football League Cup:** Winners 1962, 1985.
Colours: Yellow shirts, green shorts, yellow stockings.

NOTTINGHAM FOREST   FL CHAMPIONSHIP

Beaumont James (M)	5 7	10 10	Stockton	11 11 84	Newcastle U
Biggins James (D)	5 9	11 13	Nottingham	6 6 85	Scholar
Bopp Eugene (M)	5 11	12 03	Kiev	5 9 83	Bayern Munich
Cash Brian (M)	5 9	11 01	Dublin	24 11 82	Trainee
Dawson Michael (D)	6 2	12 02	Northallerton	18 11 83	School
Doig Chris (D)	6 2	13 07	Dumfries	13 2 81	Trainee
Evans Paul (M)	5 8	12 06	Oswestry	1 9 74	Bradford C
Gardner Ross (M)	5 8	10 06	South Shields	15 12 85	Newcastle U
Hamilton Paul (D)			Belfast	28 10 86	Scholar
Johnson David (F)	5 6	12 00	Kingston, Jamaica	15 8 76	Ipswich T

King Marlon (F)	6 0	12 10	Dulwich	26 4 80	Gillingham
Kubilskis Alexis (F)			Berchem	10 12 86	Scholar
Louis-Jean Mathieu (D)	5 9	11 03	Mont-St-Aignan	22 2 76	Le Havre
Lukic John (G)			Enfield	25 4 86	Scholar
Morgan Wes (D)	6 2	14 00	Nottingham	21 1 84	Scholar
Perch James (D)			Mansfield	29 9 85	Scholar
Reid Andy (F)	5 8	11 02	Dublin	29 7 82	Trainee
Rigby Andrew (M)			Nottingham	19 1 87	
Roberts Justyn (D)			Lewisham	12 2 86	Scholar
Robertson Gregor (D)	6 0	12 04	Edinburgh	19 1 84	
Roche Barry (G)	6 5	14 00	Dublin	6 4 82	Trainee
Tarka David (D)			Perth	11 2 83	Perth Glory
Taylor Charlie (M)			Lewisham	28 12 85	
Taylor Gareth (F)	6 2	13 07	Weston-Super-Mare	25 2 73	Burnley
Thompson John (D)	6 0	12 01	Dublin	12 10 81	
Ward Darren (G)	6 0	13 02	Worksop	11 5 74	Notts Co
Weir-Daley Spencer (F)			Leicester	5 9 85	Scholar
Westcarr Craig (F)	5 11	11 04	Nottingham	29 1 85	Scholar
Williams Gareth (M)	6 1	12 03	Glasgow	16 12 81	Trainee
Wilmet Jonathan (F)			Ottegnies	7 1 86	

League Appearances: Barmby, N. 6; Bopp, E. 9(6); Cash, B. (1); Chopra, M. 3(2); Dawson, M. 30; Doig, C. 7(3); Evans, P. 8; Gardner, R. 1(1); Gerrard, P. 8; Gunnarsson, B. 9(4); Harewood, M. 19; Impey, A. 15(1); Jess, E. 21(13); Johnson, D. 10(7); King, M. 23(1); Louis-Jean, M. 37(1); McPhail, S. 13(1); Morgan, W. 30(2); Oyen, D. 4; Reid, A. 46; Robertson, G. 12(4); Roche, B. 6(2); Rogers, A. 12; Sonner, D. 19(9); Stewart, M. 11(2); Taylor, G. 28(6); Thompson, J. 26(6); Walker, D. 23(2); Ward, D. 32; Westcarr, C. (3); Williams, G. 38(1).

Goals – League (61): Reid 13, Harewood 12 (3 pens), Taylor 8, Johnson 7, Williams 6, King 5, Jess 2, Morgan 2, Barmby 1, Bopp 1, Dawson 1, Impey 1, Louis-Jean 1, Thompson 1.

Carling Cup (2): Bopp 2.

FA Cup (1): King 1 (pen).

Ground: City Ground, Nottingham NG2 5FJ. Telephone (0115) 9824444.

Record Attendance: 49,945 v Manchester U, Division 1, 28 October 1967.

Capacity: 30,602.

Manager: Joe Kinnear.

Secretary: Paul White.

Most League Goals: 110, Division 3 (S), 1950–51.

Highest League Scorer in Season: Wally Ardron, 36, Division 3 (S), 1950–51.

Most League Goals in Total Aggregate: Grenville Morris, 199, 1898–1913.

Most Capped Player: Stuart Pearce, 76 (78), England.

Most League Appearances: Bob McKinlay, 614, 1951–70.

Honours – Football League: Division 1 – Champions 1977–78, 1997–98. Division 2 Champions – 1906–07, 1921–22. Division 3 (S) Champions – 1950–51. **FA Cup:** Winners 1898, 1959. **Football League Cup:** Winners 1977–78, 1978–79, 1988–89, 1989–90. **Anglo-Scottish Cup:** Winners 1976–77. **Simod Cup:** Winners 1989. **Zenith Data Systems Cup:** Winners 1991–92. **European Competitions: European Cup winners:** 1978–79, 1979–80. **Super Cup winners:** 1979–80.

Colours: Red shirts, white shorts, red stockings.

Bewers Jon (D)	5 8	9 13	Kettering	10 9 82	Aston Villa
Bolland Paul (M)	5 11	12 05	Bradford	23 12 79	Bradford C
Briggs Mark (M)	6 0	11 07	Wolverhampton	16 2 82	WBA
Deeney Saul (G)	6 1	12 07	Londonderry	12 3 83	Scholar
Hackworth Tony (F)	6 1	13 03	Durham	19 5 80	Leeds U
Harrad Shaun (M)	5 10	12 04	Nottingham	11 12 84	Scholar
Heffernan Paul (F)	5 10	11 00	Dublin	29 12 81	Newton
McFaul Shane (M)	6 1	11 10	Dublin	23 5 86	Scholar
McHugh Frazer (M)	5 9	12 05	Nottingham	14 7 81	Bradford C
Mildenhall Steve (G)	6 5	15 01	Swindon	13 5 78	Swindon T
Oakes Stefan (M)	6 1	13 04	Leicester	6 9 78	Walsall
Pipe David (M)	5 9	12 01	Caerphilly	5 11 83	Coventry C
Richardson Ian (D)	5 10	11 01	Barking	22 10 70	Dagenham & Redbridge
Scoffham Steve (F)	5 11	11 04	Germany	12 7 83	Gedling
Williams Matthew (F)	5 8	9 11	St Asaph	5 11 82	Manchester U

League Appearances: Antoine-Curier, M. 4; Arphexad, P. 3; Baldry, S. 32(3); Baraclough, I. 30(4); Barras, T. 38(2); Bewers, J. (3); Boertien, P. 5; Bolland, P. 35(4); Brough, M. 5(5); Caskey, D. 29(4); Deeney, S. 3; Fenton, N. 42(1); Francis, W. (3); Garden, S. 12(1); Hackworth, T. 4(8); Harrad, S. (8); Heffernan, P. 31(7); Jenkins, S. 17; Livesey, D. 9(2); McFaul, S. 2(4); McGoldrick, D. 2(2); McHugh, F. 9(4); Mildenhall, S. 28; Murray, A. 1(2); Nicholson, K. 16(7); Oakes, S. 14; Parkinson, A. 10(4); Pipe, D. 18; Platt, C. 19; Rhodes, C. (1); Richardson, I. 40; Riley, P. 13(6); Scoffham, S. 4(11); Scully, T. 6(4); Stallard, M. 18(4); Williams, M. 5(2); Wilson, K. 2(1).

Goals – League (50): Heffernan 20 (4 pens), Stallard 4 (1 pen), Parkinson 3, Platt 3, Richardson 3, Riley 3, Scully 3, Barras 2, Caskey 2, Scoffham 2, Antoine-Curier 1, Baldry 1, Bolland 1, Fenton 1, own goal 1.

Carling Cup (4): Stallard 2 (1 pen), Baldry 1, Barras 1.

FA Cup (9): Platt 3, Fenton 2, Barras 1, Heffernan 1, Nicholson 1, Richardson 1.

LDV Vans Trophy (0).

Ground: County Ground, Meadow Lane, Nottingham NG2 3HJ. Telephone (0115) 952 9000.

Record Attendance: 47,310 v York C, FA Cup 6th rd, 12 March 1955. **Capacity:** 20,300.

Manager: Gary Mills.

Secretary: Tony Cuthbert.

Most League Goals: 107, Division 4, 1959–60.

Highest League Scorer in Season: Tom Keetley, 39, Division 3 (S), 1930–31.

Most League Goals in Total Aggregate: Les Bradd, 124, 1967–78.

Most Capped Player: Kevin Wilson, 15 (42), Northern Ireland.

Most League Appearances: Albert Iremonger, 564, 1904–26.

Honours – Football League: Division 2 Champions – 1896–97, 1913–14, 1922–23. Division 3 Champions – 1997–98. Division 3 (S) Champions – 1930–31, 1949–50. Division 4 Champions – 1970–71. **FA Cup:** Winners 1893–94. **Anglo-Italian Cup:** Winners 1995.

Colours: Black and white striped shirts, black shorts, white stockings.

OLDHAM ATHLETIC   FL CHAMPIONSHIP 1

Appleby Matty (M)	5 10	11 04	Middlesbrough	16	4 72	Barnsley
Beharall David (D)	6 0	11 06	Newcastle	8	3 79	Grimsby T
Boshell Danny (M)	5 11	11 08	Bradford	30	5 81	Trainee
Clegg Michael (D)	5 9	11 07	Ashton-under-Lyne	3	7 77	Manchester U
Cooksey Ernie (M)	5 9	11 04	Essex	17	9 78	Crawley T
Eyre John (M)	6 0	11 05	Hull	9	10 74	Hull C
Forde Danny (D)	5 10	11 07	Salford	26	10 87	Scholar
Griffin Adam (M)	5 7	10 03	Manchester	26	8 84	Scholar
Haining Will (D)	6 0	11 00	Glasgow	2	10 82	Scholar
Hall Danny (D)	6 0	12 01	Tameside	14	11 83	Scholar
Holden Dean (D)	6 1	12 05	Salford	15	9 79	Bolton W
Killen Chris (F)	6 0	11 05	Wellington	8	10 81	Manchester C
Tierney Marc (D)	5 11	11 02	Manchester	7	9 86	Trainee
Vernon Scott (F)	6 0	11 10	Manchester	8	7 84	Scholar
Wilkinson Wes (F)	5 10	11 01	Wythenshawe	1	5 84	Nantwich T

League Appearances: Antoine-Curier, M. 5(3); Barlow, M. (1); Beharall, D. 7; Bonner, M. 6(1); Boshell, D. 16(6); Clegg, M. 28(4); Cooksey, E. 22(14); Crowe, D. 2(3); Eyre, J. 42(1); Eyres, D. 22(7); Fleming, C. (1); Griffin, A. 25(1); Haining, W. 30(1); Hall, C. (1); Hall, D. 28(3); Holden, D. 37(2); Hudson, M. 15; Johnson, J. 18(2); Killen, C. 7(6); Lomax, K. (1); Murray, P. 41; Ndiwa, L. 3(1); O'Halloran, M. 2(11); Owen, G. 15; Pogliacomi, L. 46; Roca, C. (7); Sheridan, D. 18(9); Sheridan, J. 19(3); Tierney, M. (2); Vernon, S. 28(17); Walker, R. 1; Wilkinson, W. 2(3); Wolfenden, M. (1); Zola Makongo, C. 21(4).
Goals – League (66): Vernon 12, Murray 9, Eyre 6, Johnson 5, Sheridan J 5 (5 pens), Zola Makongo 5, Cooksey 4, Holden 4, Eyres 3, Antoine-Curier 2, Beharall 2, Haining 2, Killen 2 (1 pen), Crowe 1, Griffin 1, Hall D 1, O'Halloran 1, Owen 1.
Carling Cup (1): Antoine-Curier 1.
FA Cup (5): Cooksey 2, Eyre 1, Johnson 1, Zola 1.
LDV Vans Trophy (4): Vernon 2, Boshell 1, Zola 1.
Ground: Boundary Park, Oldham OL1 2PA. Telephone (0870) 753 2000.
Record Attendance: 46,471 v Sheffield W, FA Cup 4th rd. 25 January 1930.
Capacity: 13,595.
Manager: Brian Talbot.
Secretary: Alan Hardy.
Most League Goals: 95, Division 4, 1962–63.
Highest League Scorer in Season: Tom Davis, 33, Division 3 (N), 1936–37.
Most League Goals in Total Aggregate: Roger Palmer, 141, 1980–94.
Most Capped Player: Gunnar Halle, 24 (64), Norway.
Most League Appearances: Ian Wood, 525, 1966–80.
Honours – Football League: Division 2 Champions – 1990–91, Division 3 (N) Champions – 1952–53. Division 3 Champions – 1973–74.
Colours: Royal blue shirts with white piping, royal blue shorts, white stockings.

OXFORD UNITED   FL CHAMPIONSHIP 2

Alexis Michael (M)	6 2	12 02	Oxford	2	1 85	
Alsop Julian (F)	6 4	15 02	Nuneaton	28	5 73	Cheltenham T
Ashton Jon (D)	6 2	13 07	Nuneaton	4	10 82	Leicester C

Basham Steve (F)	5 11	12 01	Southampton	2 12 77	Preston NE
Brooks Jamie (M)	5 10	10 08	Oxford	12 8 83	Scholar
Brown Danny (M)	6 0	12 06	Bethnal Green	12 9 80	Barnet
Cox Simon (G)	6 1	11 00	Clapham	23 3 84	Scholar
Hackett Chris (M)	6 0	11 09	Oxford	1 3 83	Scholar
Louis Jefferson (F)	6 2	14 13	Harrow	22 2 79	Thame U
Rawle Mark (F)	5 11	12 02	Leicester	27 4 79	Southend U
Wanless Paul (M)	6 1	14 08	Banbury	14 12 73	Cambridge U
Whitehead Dean (M)	5 11	12 07	Oxford	12 1 82	Trainee
Winters Tom (M)	5 9	10 10	Banbury	11 12 85	Scholar

League Appearances: Alsop, J. 26(3); Ashton, J. 30(4); Basham, S. 38; Bound, M. 33(4); Brown, D. 12; Cox, S. 5; Crosby, A. 41(1); Foran, R. 3(1); Hackett, C. 6(16); Hunt, J. 36(5); Louis, J. 6(14); McCarthy, P. 28(1); McNiven, S. 41; Oldfield, D. 1(2); Omoyinmi, M. 1(2); Pitt, C. 5(3); Quinn, B. 5(1); Rawle, M. 10(21); Robinson, M. 40; Scott, A. 2(4); Steele, L. 3(13); Townsley, D. 9(2); Walker, R. 3(1); Wanless, P. 38; Waterman, D. 6(7); Whitehead, D. 37(7); Winters, T. (1); Woodman, A. 41.
Goals – League (55): Basham 14, Rawle 8, Whitehead 7, Alsop 5, Crosby 5 (5 pens), Wanless 5, Hunt 2, Louis 2, McCarthy 2, Bound 1, Hackett 1, Robinson 1, Steele 1, own goal 1.
Carling Cup (2): Basham 1, Louis 1.
FA Cup (0).
LDV Vans Trophy (0).
Ground: The Kassam Stadium, Grenoble Road, Oxford OX4 4XP. Telephone (01865) 337500.
Record Attendance: 22,750 (at Manor Ground) v Preston NE, FA Cup 6th rd, 29 February 1964. **Capacity:** 12,573.
Manager: Graham Rix.
Secretary: Mick Brown.
Most League Goals: 91, Division 3, 1983–84.
Highest League Scorer in Season: John Aldridge, 30, Division 2, 1984–85.
Most League Goals in Total Aggregate: Graham Atkinson, 77, 1962–73.
Most Capped Player: Jim Magilton, 18 (52), Northern Ireland.
Most League Appearances: John Shuker, 478, 1962–77.
Honours – Football League: Division 2 Champions – 1984–85. Division 3 Champions – 1967–68, 1983–84. **Football League Cup:** Winners 1985–86.
Colours: Yellow shirts, navy shorts and stockings.

PETERBOROUGH UNITED   FL CHAMPIONSHIP 1

Clarke Andy (F)	5 10	11 07	Islington	22 7 67	Wimbledon
Coulson Mark (M)			Huntingdon	11 2 86	Scholar
Day Jamie (M)	5 9	10 06	Wycombe	7 5 86	Scholar
Farrell Dave (M)	5 11	11 08	Birmingham	11 11 71	Wycombe W
Fotiadis Andrew (F)	6 0	12 13	Hitchin	6 9 77	Luton T
Gill Matthew (M)	5 11	11 07	Cambridge	8 11 80	Trainee
Jelleyman Gareth (D)	5 10	10 03	Holywell	14 11 80	Trainee
Jenkins Steve (D)	5 11	12 12	Merthyr	16 7 72	Notts Co
Kanu Chris (D)	5 8	11 04	Owerri	4 12 79	
Logan Richard (F)	6 0	12 05	Bury St Edmunds	4 1 82	Boston U
McShane Luke (G)	6 1	10 09	Peterborough	6 11 85	Scholar
Newton Adam (M)	5 10	11 00	Ascot	4 12 80	West Ham U

Nolan Matt (F)	6 0	12 00	Hitchin	25 2 82	Hitchin T
Platt Clive (F)	6 4	12 07	Wolverhampton	27 10 77	Notts Co
Pullen James (G)	6 2	14 00	Chelmsford	18 3 82	Ipswich T
Rea Simon (D)	6 1	13 00	Coventry	20 9 76	Birmingham C
Semple Ryan (M)	5 11	10 11	Belfast	4 7 85	Scholar
Showler Paul (M)	5 10	11 00	Doncaster	10 10 66	Luton T
St Ledger-Hall Sean (D)	6 0	11 09	Solihull	28 12 84	Scholar
Thomson Steve (M)	5 8	10 04	Glasgow	23 1 78	Crystal Palace
Tyler Mark (G)	5 11	12 00	Norwich	2 4 77	Trainee
Willock Calum (F)	6 0	12 09	London	29 10 81	Fulham
Woodhouse Curtis (M)	5 7	12 02	Driffield	17 4 80	Birmingham C

League Appearances: Arber, M. 43(1); Boucaud, A. 7(1); Branston, G. 14; Burton, S. 27(3); Clarke, A. 28(17); Farrell, D. 30(14); Fotiadis, A. (8); Gill, M. 27(6); Green, F. (3); Jelleyman, G. 13(4); Jenkins, S. 6(2); Kanu, C. 16(5); Legg, A. 38(4); Logan, R. 12(17); McKenzie, L. 19; Newton, A. 28(9); Nolan, M. (1); Pearce, D. 1(2); Platt, C. 17(1); Pullen, J. 3; Rea, S. 25(3); Semple, R. 1(1); Shields, T. 9; St Ledger-Hall, S. 1(1); Thomson, S. 28(7); Tyler, M. 43; Williams, T. 20(1); Willock, C. 22(7); Wood, N. 2(1); Woodhouse, C. 26(1).
Goals – League (58): Clarke 9, McKenzie 9, Willock 8, Logan 7, Woodhouse 7 (2 pens), Farrell 5, Arber 3 (2 pens), Newton 2, Platt 2, Boucaud 1, Burton 1, Rea 1, Thomson 1, Williams 1, Wood 1.
Carling Cup (0).
FA Cup (6): Clarke 2, Logan 1, Newton 1, Thomson 1, Willock 1.
LDV Vans Trophy (7): McKenzie 3, Burton 1 (pen), Clarke 1, Farrell 1, Logan 1.
Ground: London Road Ground, Peterborough PE2 8AL. Telephone (01733) 563 947
Record Attendance: 30,096 v Swansea T, FA Cup 5th rd, 20 February 1965.
Capacity: 15,314.
Manager: Barry Fry.
Secretary: Julie Etherington.
Most League Goals: 134, Division 4, 1960–61.
Highest League Scorer in Season: Terry Bly, 52, Division 4, 1960–61.
Most League Goals in Total Aggregate: Jim Hall, 122, 1967–75.
Most Capped Player: Tony Millington, 8 (21), Wales.
Most League Appearances: Tommy Robson, 482, 1968–81.
Honours – Football League: Division 4 Champions – 1960–61, 1973–74.
Colours: All blue.

PLYMOUTH ARGYLE   FL CHAMPIONSHIP

Adams Steve (M)	6 0	12 01	Plymouth	25 9 80	Trainee
Aljofree Hasney (D)	6 0	12 03	Manchester	11 7 78	Dundee U
Bastow Darren (M)	5 11	12 00	Torquay	22 12 81	Trainee
Capaldi Tony (M)	6 0	12 00	Porsgrunn	12 8 81	Birmingham C
Connolly Paul (D)	6 0	11 01	Liverpool	29 9 83	Scholar
Coughlan Graham (D)	6 2	13 04	Dublin	18 11 74	Livingston
Evans Micky (F)	6 0	13 04	Plymouth	1 1 73	Bristol R
Friio David (M)	6 0	11 05	Thionville	17 2 73	ASOA Valence
Gilbert Peter (D)	5 11	12 13	Newcastle	31 7 83	Birmingham C
Larrieu Romain (G)	6 2	13 00	Mont-de-Marsan	31 8 76	ASOA Valence
Lowndes Nathan (F)	5 10	12 06	Salford	2 6 77	Livingston
McCormick Luke (G)	6 0	13 12	Coventry	15 8 83	Scholar

Norris David (M)	5 7	11 06	Peterborough	22 2 81	Bolton W
Stonebridge Ian (F)	6 0	11 04	Lewisham	30 8 81	Tottenham H
Sturrock Blair (F)	6 0	11 01	Dundee	25 8 81	Dundee U
Villis Matt (D)			Bridgwater	13 4 84	
Worrell David (D)	5 11	11 08	Dublin	12 1 78	Dundee U
Wotton Paul (D)	5 11	11 01	Plymouth	17 8 77	Trainee

League Appearances: Adams, S. 25(11); Aljofree, H. 20(4); Bent, J. 13(5); Beresford, D. (1); Capaldi, T. 29(4); Connolly, P. 28(1); Coughlan, G. 46; Evans, M. 35(9); Friio, D. 35(1); Gilbert, P. 40; Hodges, L. 28(9); Keith, M. 28(12); Larrieu, R. 6; Lowndes, N. 18(15); McCormick, L. 40; Norris, D. 42(3); Phillips, M. 3(6); Stonebridge, I. 21(9); Sturrock, B. (24); Worrell, D. 18; Wotton, P. 31(7); Yetton, S. (1).

Goals – League (85): Friio 14, Evans 11, Keith 9, Wotton 9 (3 pens), Lowndes 8, Capaldi 7, Coughlan 7, Norris 5, Stonebridge 5, Hodges 3, Adams 2, Bent 1, Gilbert 1, Phillips 1, own goals 2.

Carling Cup (1): Evans 1.

FA Cup (2): Friio 1, Stonebridge 1.

LDV Vans Trophy (6): Lowndes 2, Coughlan 1, Evans 1, Gilbert 1, Keith 1.

Ground: Home Park, Plymouth, Devon PL2 3DQ. Telephone (01752) 562561.

Record Attendance: 43,596 v Aston Villa, Division 2, 10 October 1936.

Capacity: 20,134.

Manager: Bobby Williamson.

Secretary: Carole Rowntree.

Most League Goals: 107, Division 3 (S), 1925–26 and 1951–52.

Highest League Scorer in Season: Jack Cock, 32, Division 3 (S), 1926–27.

Most League Goals in Total Aggregate: Sammy Black, 180, 1924–38.

Most Capped Player: Moses Russell, 20 (23), Wales.

Most League Appearances: Kevin Hodges, 530, 1978–92.

Honours – Football League: Division 2 Champions – 2003–04. Division 3 (S) Champions – 1929–30, 1951–52. Division 3 Champions – 1958–59, 2001–02.

Colours: Green shirts, white shorts, green stockings.

PORTSMOUTH   FA PREMIERSHIP

Barrett Neil (M)	5 10	11 00	Tooting	24 12 81	Chelsea
Berger Patrik (M)	6 1	13 00	Prague	10 11 73	Liverpool
Berkovic Eyal (M)	5 9	10 13	Haifa	2 4 72	Manchester C
Burchill Mark (F)	5 8	11 09	Broxburn	18 8 80	Ipswich T
Buxton Lewis (D)	6 1	13 10	Newport (IW)	10 12 83	School
Clark Christopher (M)			Shoreham	9 6 84	Scholar
Cooper Shaun (D)	5 10	10 07	Isle of Wight	5 10 83	School
Curtis John (D)	5 10	11 07	Nuneaton	3 9 78	Leicester C
De Zeeuw Arjan (D)	6 0	13 06	Castricum	16 4 70	Wigan Ath
Duffy Richard (D)	5 10	9 05	Swansea	30 8 85	Swansea C
Faye Andy (M)	6 1	12 04	Dakar	12 3 77	Auxerre
Foxe Hayden (D)	6 3	13 05	Sydney	23 6 77	West Ham U
Harper Kevin (F)	5 6	12 00	Oldham	15 1 76	Derby Co
Hislop Shaka (G)	6 4	14 04	Hackney	22 2 69	West Ham U
Howe Eddie (D)	5 11	11 07	Amersham	29 11 77	Bournemouth
Hughes Richard (M)	6 0	13 03	Glasgow	25 6 79	Bournemouth
Mornar Ivica (F)	6 2	13 01	Split	12 1 74	Anderlecht

Name			Birthplace	DOB	Previous club
O'Neil Gary (M)	5 10	11 00	Beckenham	18 5 83	Trainee
Pericard Vincent de Paul (F)	6 1	13 08	Efko	3 10 82	Juventus
Primus Linvoy (D)	5 10	12 04	Forest Gate	14 9 73	Reading
Pulis Anthony (M)			Bristol	21 7 84	Scholar
Quashie Nigel (M)	5 9	12 08	Nunhead	20 7 78	Nottingham F
Robinson Carl (M)	5 10	12 10	Llandrindod Wells	13 10 76	Wolverhampton W
Schemmel Sebastian (D)	5 8	11 13	Nancy	2 6 75	West Ham U
Silk Gary (M)			Newport (IW)	13 9 84	Scholar
Stefanovic Dejan (D)	6 2	13 01	Belgrade	28 10 74	Vitesse
Stone Steve (F)	5 8	12 07	Gateshead	20 8 71	Aston Villa
Taylor Matthew (D)	5 11	12 03	Oxford	27 11 81	Luton T
Todorov Svetoslav (F)	6 0	12 02	Dobrich	30 8 78	West Ham U
Vine Rowan (F)	6 1	11 12	Basingstoke	21 9 82	Scholar
Wapenaar Harald (G)	6 1	13 01	Vlaardingen	10 4 70	Utrecht
Yakubu Ayegbeni (F)	6 0	13 01	Nigeria	22 11 82	Maccabi Haifa

League Appearances: Berger, P. 20; Berkovic, E. 10(1); Burton, D. (1); Curtis, J. 5(1); De Zeeuw, A. 36; Duffy, R. (1); Faye, A. 27; Foxe, H. 8(2); Harper, K. (7); Hislop, S. 30; Hughes, R. 8(3); Lua-Lua, L. 10(5); Mornar, I. 3(5); O'Neil, G. 3; Pasanen, P. 11(1); Pericard, V. (6); Primus, L. 19(2); Quashie, N. 17(4); Roberts, J. 4(6); Robinson, C. (1); Schemmel, S. 12(2); Sheringham, T. 25(7); Sherwood, T. 7(6); Smertin, A. 23(3); Srnicek, P. 3; Stefanovic, D. 32; Stone, S. 29(3); Taylor, M. 18(12); Todorov, S. 1; Wapenaar, H. 5; Yakubu, A. 35(2); Zivkovic, B. 17(1).

Goals – League (47): Yakubu 16 (2 pens), Sheringham 9 (1 pen), Berger 5, Lua-Lua 4, Stefanovic 3, O'Neil 2, Stone 2, Berkovic 1, De Zeeuw 1, Foxe 1, Mornar 1, Quashie 1, Roberts 1.

Carling Cup (9): Roberts 3, Sherwood 2, Yakubu 2, Taylor 1, own goal 1.

FA Cup (7): Taylor 3, Hughes 1, Schemmel 1, Sheringham 1, Yakubu 1.

Ground: Fratton Park, Frogmore Road, Portsmouth PO4 8RA. Telephone (023) 9273 1204.

Record Attendance: 51,385 v Derby Co, FA Cup 6th rd, 26 February 1949.

Capacity: 20,228.

Manager: Harry Redknapp.

Secretary: Paul Weld.

Most League Goals: 97, Division 1, 2002–03.

Highest League Scorer in Season: Guy Whittingham, 42, Division 1, 1992–93.

Most League Goals in Total Aggregate: Peter Harris, 194, 1946–60.

Most Capped Player: Jimmy Dickinson, 48, England.

Most League Appearances: Jimmy Dickinson, 764, 1946–65.

Honours – Football League: Division 1 Champions – 1948–49, 1949–50, 2002–03. Division 3 (S) Champions – 1923–24. Division 3 Champions – 1961–62, 1982–83.

FA Cup: Winners 1939.

Colours: Blue shirts, white shorts, red stockings.

PORT VALE   FL CHAMPIONSHIP 1

Name			Birthplace	DOB	Previous club
Armstrong Ian (M)	5 8	10 04	Liverpool	16 11 81	Liverpool
Birchall Chris (F)	5 9	13 02	Stafford	5 5 84	Scholar
Brain Jonny (G)	6 3	13 06	Carlisle	11 2 83	
Brooker Stephen (F)	5 11	13 10	Newport Pagnell	21 5 81	Watford
Brown Ryan (D)	5 9	11 04	Stoke	15 3 85	Scholar

Collins Sam (D)	6 3	13 12	Pontefract	5 6 77	Bury
Eldershaw Simon (F)	5 11	11 02	Stoke	2 12 83	Scholar
Goodlad Mark (G)	6 2	13 12	Barnsley	9 9 79	Nottingham F
James Craig (D)	6 2	12 10	Middlesbrough	15 11 82	Sunderland
Lipa Andreas (M)	6 2	12 04	Vienna	26 4 71	
McPhee Stephen (F)	5 8	12 02	Glasgow	5 6 81	Coventry C
Paynter Billy (F)	6 0	13 02	Liverpool	13 7 84	Schoolboy
Pilkington George (D)	5 11	12 07	Rugeley	7 11 81	Everton
Reid Levi (M)	5 6	11 12	Stafford	19 12 83	Scholar
Rowland Stephen (D)	5 10	12 00	Wrexham	2 11 81	Scholar

League Appearances: Armstrong, I. 4(16); Birchall, C. 1(9); Boyd, M. 20(2); Brain, J. 32; Bridge-Wilkinson, M. 27(5); Brightwell, I. 2; Brisco, N. 20(7); Brooker, S. 29(3); Brown, R. 17; Burns, L. 19(8); Collins, S. 43; Cummins, M. 42; Delany, D. 14; James, C. 8; Lipa, A. 27(3); Littlejohn, A. 24(12); McPhee, S. 46; Paynter, B. 42(2); Pilkington, G. 44; Reid, L. 7(4); Rowland, S. 26(3); Walsh, M. 12(1).
Goals – League (73): McPhee 25, Paynter 13, Brooker 8, Bridge-Wilkinson 7 (1 pen), Littlejohn 7, Collins 4, Cummins 4, Lipa 2, Armstrong 1, Pilkington 1, own goal 1.
Carling Cup (0).
FA Cup (4): Burns 1, McPhee 1, Paynter 1, own goal 1.
LDV Vans Trophy (1): McPhee 1.
Ground: Vale Park, Burslem, Stoke-on-Trent ST6 1AW. Telephone (01782) 655 800.
Record Attendance: 50,000 v Aston Villa, FA Cup 5th rd, 20 February 1960.
Capacity: 18,982
Manager: Martin Foyle.
Secretary: Fredrik W. Lodey.
Most League Goals: 110, Division 4, 1958–59.
Highest League Scorer in Season: Wilf Kirkham 38, Division 2, 1926–27.
Most League Goals in Total Aggregate: Wilf Kirkham, 154, 1923–29, 1931–33.
Most Capped Player: Tony Rougier, Trinidad and Tobago.
Most League Appearances: Roy Sproson, 761, 1950–72.
Honours – Football League: Division 3 (N) Champions – 1929–30, 1953–54. Division 4 Champions – 1958–59. **LDV Vans Trophy winners:** 2001
Colours: White shirts with black trim, black shorts, black stockings.

PRESTON NORTH END   FL CHAMPIONSHIP

Alexander Graham (D)	5 11	12 02	Coventry	10 10 71	Luton T
Cresswell Richard (F)	6 0	11 08	Bridlington	20 9 77	Leicester C
Davis Claude (D)	6 3	14 04	Jamaica	6 3 79	
Elebert David (D)			Dublin	21 3 86	Scholar
Etuhu Dixon (M)	6 2	13 00	Kano	8 6 82	Manchester C
Fuller Ricardo (F)	6 3	13 13	Kingston, Jamaica	31 10 79	Hearts
Gould Jonathan (G)	6 1	12 07	Paddington	18 7 68	Celtic
Healy David (F)	5 8	10 09	Downpatrick	5 8 79	Manchester U
Keane Michael (M)	5 4	13 07	Dublin	29 12 82	Scholar
Langmead Kelvin (F)	6 1	13 06	Coventry	23 3 85	Scholar
Lewis Eddie (M)	5 10	11 03	Cerritos	17 5 74	Fulham
Lonergan Andrew (G)	6 3	12 02	Preston	19 10 83	Scholar
Lucas David (G)	6 2	13 03	Preston	23 11 77	Trainee

Lucketti Chris (D)	6 0	13 06	Littleborough	28 9 71	Huddersfield T
Lynch Simon (F)	6 0	11 00	Montreal	19 5 82	Celtic
McCormack Alan (M)	5 8	11 05	Dublin	10 1 84	
McKenna Paul (M)	5 7	11 12	Eccleston	20 10 77	Trainee
Mears Tyrone (M)	5 10	11 09	Stockport	18 2 83	Manchester C
O'Neil Brian (D)	6 1	12 03	Paisley	6 9 72	Derby Co
O'Neil Joe (F)	6 0	10 05	Blackburn	28 10 82	Scholar
Skora Eric (M)	5 10	11 00	Metz	20 8 81	

League Appearances: Abbott, P. 2(7); Alexander, G. 45; Briscoe, L. 2; Broomes, M. 30; Burley, C. 1(3); Cartwright, L. 2(10); Cresswell, R. 41(4); Davis, C. 16(6); Edwards, R. 16(8); Etuhu, D. 23(8); Fuller, R. 37(1); Gemmill, S. 7; Gould, J. 37; Healy, D. 27(11); Jackson, Mark (1); Jackson, Michael 41(2); Keane, M. 21(9); Koumantarakis, G. 1(6); Lewis, E. 26(7); Lonergan, A. 8; Lucas, D. 1(1); Lucketti, C. 37; Lynch, S. 6(13); McCormack, A. 2(3); McKenna, P. 39; Mears, T. 11(1); O'Neil, B. 27(2); Skora, E. (2); Smith, J. (5).

Goals – League (69): Fuller 17, Healy 15, Alexander 9 (8 pens), Lewis 6, McKenna 6, Etuhu 3, Abbott 2, Cresswell 2, Davis 1, Gemmill 1, Keane 1, Koumantarakis 1, Lucketti 1, Lynch 1, Mears 1, O'Neil 1, own goal 1.

Carling Cup (0).

FA Cup (6): Fuller 2, Cresswell 1, Etuhu 1, Koumantarakis 1, O'Neil 1.

Ground: Deepdale, Sir Tom Finney Way, Preston PR1 6RU. Telephone (0870) 442 1964.

Record Attendance: 42,684 v Arsenal, Division 1, 23 April 1938. **Capacity:** 20,600.

Manager: Craig Brown.

Secretary: Janet Pam.

Most League Goals: 100, Division 2, 1927–28 and Division 1, 1957–58.

Highest League Scorer in Season: Ted Harper, 37, Division 2, 1932–33.

Most League Goals in Total Aggregate: Tom Finney, 187, 1946–60.

Most Capped Player: Tom Finney, 76, England.

Most League Appearances: Alan Kelly, 447, 1961–75.

Honours – Football League: Division 1 Champions – 1888–89 (first champions), 1889–90. Division 2 Champions – 1903–04, 1912–13, 1950–51, 1999–2000. Division 3 Champions – 1970–71, 1995–96. **FA Cup winners** 1889, 1938.

Colours: White shirts, navy shorts, white stockings.

QUEENS PARK RANGERS   FL CHAMPIONSHIP

Ainsworth Gareth (M)	5 10	12 05	Blackburn	10 5 73	Cardiff C
Bignot Marcus (D)	5 7	11 04	Birmingham	22 8 74	Rushden & D
Culkin Nick (G)	6 2	13 07	York	6 7 78	Manchester U
Cureton Jamie (F)	5 8	12 08	Bristol	28 8 75	Reading
Day Chris (G)	6 2	13 06	Whipps Cross	28 7 75	Watford
Gallen Kevin (F)	5 11	13 05	Hammersmith	21 9 75	Barnsley
Gnohere Arthur (D)	6 0	13 00	Yamoussoukro	20 11 78	Burnley
McLeod Kevin (M)	5 11	12 00	Liverpool	12 9 80	Everton
Padula Gino (D)	5 9	12 11	Buenos Aires	11 7 76	Wigan Ath
Perry Jack (M)			Islington	26 10 84	
Rowlands Martin (M)	5 9	10 10	Hammersmith	8 2 79	Brentford
Shittu Dan (D)	6 2	16 03	Lagos	2 9 80	Charlton Ath
Thorpe Tony (F)	5 9	12 01	Leicester	10 4 74	Luton T

League Appearances: Ainsworth, G. 21(8); Barton, W. 2(1); Bean, M. 23(8); Bignot, M. 6; Bircham, M. 36(2); Camp, L. 12; Carlisle, C. 32(1); Culkin, N. 5; Cureton, J. 2(11); Daly, W. (2); Day, C. 29; Edghill, R. 15(5); Forbes, T. 30; Furlong, P. 31(5); Gallen, K. 44(1); Gnohere, A. 17(1); Johnson, R. 10(1); Langley, R. 1; Marney, D. 1(1); McLeod, K. 26(9); Oli, D. (3); Pacquette, R. (2); Padula, G. 36; Palmer, S. 24(11); Rose, M. 15(5); Rowlands, M. 41(1); Sabin, E. 3(7); Shittu, D. 18(2); Thorpe, T. 22(9); Williams, T. 4(1).

Goals – League (80): Gallen 17 (1 pen), Furlong 16, Rowlands 10, Thorpe 10, Ainsworth 6, Palmer 4, McLeod 3, Padula 3, Bircham 2, Cureton 2, Bean 1, Carlisle 1, Langley 1, Sabin 1, own goals 3.

Carling Cup (4): Rowlands 2, Ainsworth 1, Langley 1.

FA Cup (0).

LDV Vans Trophy (6): Gnohere 1, Pacquette 1, Padula 1, Palmer 1, McLeod 1, Thorpe 1.

Ground: South Africa Road, W12 7PA. Telephone (020) 8743 0262.

Record Attendance: 35,353 v Leeds U, Division 1, 27 April 1974. **Capacity:** 19,091.

Manager: Ian Holloway.

Secretary: Sheila Marson.

Most League Goals: 111, Division 3, 1961–62.

Highest League Scorer in Season: George Goddard, 37, Division 3 (S), 1929–30.

Most League Goals in Total Aggregate: George Goddard, 172, 1926–34.

Most Capped Player: Alan McDonald, 52, Northern Ireland.

Most League Appearances: Tony Ingham, 519, 1950–63.

Honours – Football League: Division 2 Champions – 1982–83. Division 3 (S) Champions – 1947–48. Division 3 Champions – 1966–67. **Football League Cup winners** 1966–67.

Colours: Blue and white hooped shirts, white shorts, white stockings.

READING   FL CHAMPIONSHIP

Ashdown Jamie (G)	6 1	13 05	Reading	30 11 80	
Brown Steve (D)	6 1	13 10	Brighton	13 5 72	Charlton Ath
Campbell Darren (M)	5 5	10 00	Huntingdon	16 4 86	Scholar
Castle Peter (D)	6 0	12 02	Southampton	12 3 87	Scholar
Forster Nicky (F)	5 8	11 05	Caterham	8 9 73	Birmingham C
Goater Shaun (F)	6 1	11 10	Bermuda	25 2 70	Manchester C
Hahnemann Marcus (G)	6 3	16 04	Seattle	15 6 72	Fulham
Harper James (M)	5 10	11 02	Chelmsford	9 11 80	Arsenal
Hughes Andy (M)	5 11	12 01	Stockport	2 1 78	Notts Co
Ingimarsson Ivar (D)	6 0	12 07	Reykjavik	20 8 77	Wolverhampton W
Kitson Dave (F)	6 3	13 00	Hitchin	21 1 80	Cambridge U
Morgan Dean (F)	6 0	12 02	Enfield	3 10 83	Colchester U
Murty Graeme (D)	5 10	11 10	Saltburn	13 11 74	York C
Owusu Lloyd (F)	6 1	13 07	Slough	12 12 76	Sheffield W
Rifat Ahmet (D)	6 3	11 08	London	3 1 86	Scholar
Savage Bas (F)	6 4	13 08	London	7 1 82	Walton & Hersham
Shorey Nicky (D)	5 9	10 10	Romford	19 2 81	Leyton Orient
Sidwell Steven (M)	5 10	11 00	Wandsworth	14 12 82	Arsenal
Williams Adrian (D)	6 2	13 02	Reading	16 8 71	Wolverhampton W
Young Jamie (G)	5 11	13 01	Brisbane	25 8 85	Scholar

League Appearances: Ashdown, J. 10; Brooker, P. 5(6); Brown, S. 19; Butler, M.

(3); Daley, O. (6); Forster, N. 28(2); Goater, S. 30(4); Gordon, D. (3); Hahnemann, M. 36; Harper, J. 35(4); Henderson, D. (1); Hughes, A. 42(1); Ingimarsson, I. 24(1); Kitson, D. 10(7); Mackie, J. 7(2); Morgan, D. 3(10); Murray, S. 25(9); Murty, G. 37(1); Newman, R. 25(5); Owusu, L. 11(5); Salako, J. 32(5); Savage, B. 6(9); Shorey, N. 35; Sidwell, S. 43; Tyson, N. (8); Watson, K. 10(12); Williams, A. 33; Young, J. (1).

Goals – League (55): Goater 12 (3 pens), Sidwell 8, Forster 7, Kitson 5, Murray 5, Owusu 4, Hughes 3, Salako 3, Shorey 2, Harper 1, Ingimarsson 1, Mackie 1, Morgan 1, Williams 1, own goal 1.

Carling Cup (7): Forster 4, Harper 1, Salako 1, Sidwell 1.

FA Cup (4): Goater 2, own goals 2.

Ground: Madejski Stadium, Junction 11, M4, Reading, Berks RG2 0FL. Telephone (0118) 968 1100.

Record Attendance: 33,042 v Brentford, FA Cup 5th rd, 19 February 1927.

Capacity: 24,185.

Manager: Steve Coppell.

Secretary: Sue Hewett.

Most League Goals: 112, Division 3 (S), 1951–52.

Highest League Scorer in Season: Ronnie Blackman, 39, Division 3 (S), 1951–52.

Most League Goals in Total Aggregate: Ronnie Blackman, 158, 1947–54.

Most Capped Player: Jimmy Quinn, 17 (46), Northern Ireland.

Most League Appearances: Martin Hicks, 500, 1978–91.

Honours – Football League: Division 2 Champions – 1993–94. Division 3 Champions – 1985–86. Division 3 (S) Champions – 1925–26. Division 4 Champions – 1978–79. **Simod Cup winners** 1987–88.

Colours: Royal blue and white hooped shirts, blue or white shorts, white stockings with blue band.

ROCHDALE   FL CHAMPIONSHIP 2

Bertos Leo (M)	5 10	12 11	Wellington	20 12 81	Barnsley
Burgess Daryl (D)	6 0	13 05	Birmingham	24 1 71	Northampton T
Doughty Matt (D)	5 8	11 00	Warrington	2 11 81	Scholar
Gilks Matthew (G)	6 3	13 05	Rochdale	4 6 82	Scholar
Griffiths Gareth (D)	6 4	13 04	Winsford	10 4 70	Wigan Ath
Heald Greg (D)	6 1	12 10	Enfield	26 9 71	Leyton Orient
Holt Grant (M)	6 0	12 06	Carlisle	12 4 81	Sheffield W
McCourt Patrick (M)	6 0	11 13	Derry	16 12 83	Scholar
Simpkins Mike (D)	6 1	13 03	Sheffield	28 11 78	Cardiff C
Townson Kevin (F)	5 8	11 01	Kirby	19 4 83	
Warner Scott (M)	5 11	12 02	Rochdale	3 12 83	Scholar

League Appearances: Antoine-Curier, M. 5(3); Beech, C. 9(5); Bertos, L. 40; Betts, R. 4(1); Bishop, A. 8(2); Brannan, G. 11; Burgess, D. 33(2); Connor, P. 21(3); Donovan, K. 4(3); Doughty, M. 25(6); Edwards, N. 34; Evans, W. 45; Flood, W. 6; Gilks, M. 12; Grand, S. 11(6); Griffiths, G. 29(4); Heald, G. 10; Hill, S. 1; Holt, G. 14; Jones, G. 26; Livesey, D. 11(2); McClare, S. 33(5); McCourt, P. 6(18); McEvilly, L. 15(15); Ndiwa, L. (1); Patterson, R. 3(4); Pemberton, M. 1; Redfearn, N. 9; Shuker, C. 14; Simpkins, M. 25(2); Smith, J. 1; Smith, S. 13; Strachan, C. (1); Townson, K. 17(16); Warner, S. 10(4).

Goals – League (49): Townson 10 (2 pens), Bertos 9, McEvilly 6 (4 pens), Connor 5, Holt 4, Jones 4 (2 pens), Betts 2, McCourt 2, Antoine-Curier 1, Bishop 1, Brannan 1 (pen), Griffiths 1, Heald 1, Shuker 1, Warner 1.
Carling Cup (1): Townson 1.
FA Cup (2): Bertos 1, Townson 1.
LDV Vans Trophy (0).
Ground: Spotland, Sandy Lane, Rochdale OL11 5DS. Telephone (01706) 644648.
Record Attendance: 24,231 v Notts Co, FA Cup 2nd rd, 10 December 1949.
Capacity: 10,208.
Manager: Steve Parkin.
Secretary: Hilary Molyneux Dearden.
Most League Goals: 105, Division 3 (N), 1926–27.
Highest League Scorer in Season: Albert Whitehurst, 44, Division 3 (N), 1926–27.
Most League Goals in Total Aggregate: Reg Jenkins, 119, 1964–73.
Most Capped Players: Patrick McCourt, 1, Northern Ireland and Lee McEvilly, 1, Northern Ireland.
Most League Appearances: Graham Smith, 317, 1966–74.
Honours – Nil.
Colours: Blue shirts with white trim, blue shorts, blue stockings with white hoop on turnover.

ROTHERHAM UNITED   FL CHAMPIONSHIP

Barker Richard (F)	6 1	13 12	Sheffield	30 5 75	Macclesfield T
Barker Shaun (D)	6 2	12 10	Nottingham	19 9 82	Scholar
Butler Martin (F)	5 11	12 00	Wordsley	15 9 74	Reading
Garner Darren (M)	5 10	12 05	Plymouth	10 12 71	Plymouth Arg
Hurst Paul (D)	5 5	10 02	Sheffield	25 9 74	Trainee
McIntosh Martin (D)	6 2	13 00	East Kilbride	19 3 71	Hibernian
Monkhouse Andy (M)	6 2	12 12	Leeds	23 10 80	Trainee
Montgomery Gary (G)	6 1	14 01	Leamington Spa	8 10 82	Coventry C
Pollitt Mike (G)	6 4	15 01	Farnworth	29 2 72	Chesterfield
Proctor Michael (F)	6 0	11 08	Sunderland	3 10 80	Sunderland
Scott Rob (D)	6 1	12 08	Epsom	15 8 73	Fulham
Sedgwick Chris (M)	6 1	12 05	Sheffield	28 4 80	Trainee
Swailes Chris (D)	6 2	13 00	Gateshead	19 10 70	Bury
Warne Paul (F)	5 10	11 07	Norwich	8 5 73	Wigan Ath

League Appearances: Barker, R. 12(20); Barker, S. 36; Baudet, J. 8(3); Branston, G. 7(1); Butler, M. 36(1); Byfield, D. 26(2); Daws, N. 3(1); Garner, D. 10(3); Gilchrist, P. 10; Hoskins, W. (4); Hurst, P. 23(5); Lee, A. 1; McIntosh, M. 18; Minto, S. 28(4); Monkhouse, A. 17(10); Montgomery, G. 3(1); Morris, J. 9(1); Mullin, J. 35(3); Pollitt, M. 43; Proctor, M. 16(1); Robins, M. 2(7); Robinson, C. 14; Scott, R. 8(2); Sedgwick, C. 40; Stockdale, R. 16; Swailes, C. 43; Talbot, S. 19(4); Warne, P. 23(12).
Goals – League (53): Butler 15, Byfield 7 (3 pens), Proctor 6 (4 pens), Mullin 4, Monkhouse 3, Swailes 3, Barker S 2, Hoskins 2, McIntosh 2, Sedgwick 2, Barker R 1, Hurst 1, Morris 1, Stockdale 1, Talbot 1, Warne 1 (pen), own goal 1.
Carling Cup (4): Sedgwick 2, Byfield 1, Swailes 1.
FA Cup (2): Barker R 1, Hurst 1.
Ground: Millmoor Ground, Rotherham S60 1RH. Telephone (01709) 512434.
Record Attendance: 25,137 v Sheffield U, Division 2, 13 December 1952. **Capacity:** 11,499.

Manager: Ronnie Moore.
Most League Goals: 114, Division 3 (N), 1946–47.
Highest League Scorer in Season: Wally Ardron, 38, Division 3 (N), 1946–47.
Most League Goals in Total Aggregate: Gladstone Guest, 130, 1946–56.
Most Capped Player: Shaun Goater, 14 (19), Bermuda.
Most League Appearances: Danny Williams, 459, 1946–62.
Honours – Football League: Division 3 Champions – 1980–81. Division 3 (N) Champions – 1950–51. Division 4 Champions – 1988–89. **Auto Windscreens Shield:** Winners 1996
Colours: Red shirts with white trim, white shorts, red stockings.

RUSHDEN & DIAMONDS   FL CHAMPIONSHIP 2

Bell David (M)	5 10	12 01	Kettering	21 1 84	Trainee
Burgess Andy (M)	6 2	11 12	Bedford	10 8 81	
Dempster John (D)	6 0	12 05	Kettering	1 4 83	Trainee
Duffy Robert (F)	6 1	13 01	Swansea	2 12 82	
Gray Stuart (M)	5 10	13 07	Harrogate	18 12 73	Reading
Jack Rodney (F)	5 7	10 05	Kingston, Jamaica	28 9 72	Crewe Alex
Mills Gary (M)	5 9	11 11	Sheppey	20 5 81	
Sambrook Andrew (D)	5 10	11 09	Chatham	13 7 79	Gillingham
Talbot Daniel (M)	5 9	11 00	Enfield	30 1 84	
Turley Billy (G)	6 3	15 11	Wolverhampton	15 7 73	Northampton T

League Appearances: Ashdown, J. 19; Bell, D. 31(6); Benjamin, T. 5(1); Bignot, M. 35; Burgess, A. 32(5); Darby, D. 9(3); Dempster, J. 11(8); Duffy, R. 4(4); Edwards, A. 29; Evans, P. 2; Gray, S. 33(2); Hall, P. 28(5); Hanlon, R. 18(9); Hunter, B. 43; Jack, R. 44(1); Kelly, M. 4(4); Kitson, P. 18(10); Lowe, O. 24(2); Manangu, E. (1); Mills, G. 25(5); Okuonghae, M. (1); Quinn, B. 4; Roget, L. 16(1); Sambrook, A. 14(6); Story, O. (5); Talbot, D. 3(4); Turley, B. 25; Underwood, P. 30.
Goals – League (60): Lowe 15, Jack 12, Gray 5 (2 pens), Kitson 5, Burgess 4, Hunter 4, Edwards 3, Bignot 2, Darby 2, Hall 2, Bell 1, Benjamin 1, Hanlon 1, Mills 1, Talbot 1, own goal 1.
Carling Cup (1): Lowe 1.
FA Cup (0).
LDV Vans Trophy (2): Gray 1 (pen), Jack 1.
Ground: Nene Park, Diamond Way, Irthlingborough, Northants NN9 5QF. Telephone (01933) 652 000.
Record Attendance: 6431 v Leeds U, F.A. Cup 3rd rd, 2 January 1999.
Capacity: 6441
Manager: Ernie Tippett.
Secretary: David Joyce.
Most League Goals: 109, Southern League Midland Division, 1993–94.
Most capped player: Onandi Lowe, 9, Jamaica.
Honours – Football League: Division 3 Champions – 2002–03. **Conference:** Champions 2000–01. **Southern League Midland Division:** Champions 1993–94. **Premier Division:** Champions 1995–96. **FA Trophy:** Semi-finalists 1994. **Northants FA Hillier Senior Cup:** Winners 1993–94, 1998–99. **Maunsell Premier Cup:** Winners 1994–95, 1998–99.
Colours: White shirts with blue trim and red piping, blue shorts, white stockings.

SCUNTHORPE UNITED

FL CHAMPIONSHIP 2

Barwick Terry (M)	5 11	10 12	Doncaster	11 1 83	Scholar
Butler Andy (D)	6 0	13 06	Doncaster	4 11 83	Scholar
Byrne Cliff (D)	6 0	12 11	Dublin	27 4 82	Sunderland
Evans Tom (G)	6 1	13 11	Doncaster	31 12 76	Crystal Palace
Featherstone Lee (M)	6 0	12 08	Chesterfield	20 7 83	Sheffield U
Graves Wayne (M)	5 8	11 01	Scunthorpe	18 9 80	Trainee
Hayes Paul (F)	6 0	12 12	Dagenham	20 9 83	Norwich C
Jackson Mark (D)	6 0	12 02	Leeds	30 9 77	Leeds U
MacLean Steve (F)	5 10	11 01	Edinburgh	23 8 82	
Parton Andy (F)	5 10	12 00	Doncaster	29 9 83	Scholar
Ridley Lee (D)	5 9	11 11	Scunthorpe	5 12 81	Scholar
Sharp Kevin (D)	5 9	11 11	Ontario	19 9 74	Huddersfield T
Sparrow Matt (M)	5 11	10 10	London	3 10 81	Scholar
Stanton Nathan (D)	5 9	12 06	Nottingham	6 5 81	Trainee
Taylor Cleveland (M)	5 8	11 08	Leicester	9 9 83	Bolton W

League Appearances: Barwick, T. 27(3); Beagrie, P. 28(4); Butler, A. 34(1); Byrne, C. 39; Calvo-Garcia, A. 8(4); Evans, T. 36; Featherstone, L. 7(4); Graves, W. 12(9); Groves, P. 13; Gulliver, P. 2; Hayes, P. 12(23); Holloway, D. 5; Hunt, J. (1); Jackson, M. 15(2); Keegan, P. (2); Kell, R. 21(3); Kilford, I. 11(7); MacLean, S. 37(5); McCombe, J. 8(7); Parton, A. (3); Ridley, L. 15(3); Russell, S. 10; Sharp, K. 37(3); Smith, J. 1; Sparrow, M. 37(1); Stanton, N. 31(2); Taylor, C. 18(2); Torpey, S. 42(1); Williams, M. (1).

Goals – League (69): MacLean 23 (4 pens), Beagrie 11 (5 pens), Torpey 11, Groves 3, Sparrow 3, Taylor C 3, Butler 2, Calvo-Garcia 2, Hayes 2, Kell 2, Sharp 2 (1 pen), Barwick 1, Byrne 1, Holloway 1, Ridley 1, own goal 1.

Carling Cup (4): Hayes 2, Beagrie 1, MacLean 1.

FA Cup (7): Torpey 3, Hayes 2, McCombe 1, Parton 1.

LDV Vans Trophy (6): Hayes 1, Jackson 1, Kell 1, MacLean 1, Sparrow 1, Torpey 1.

Ground: Glanford Park, Scunthorpe, South Humberside DN15 8TD. Telephone (01724) 747670.

Record Attendance: Old Showground: 23,935 v Portsmouth, FA Cup 4th rd, 30 January 1954. Glanford Park: 8775 v Rotherham U, Division 4, 1 May 1989.

Capacity: 9182.

Manager: Brian Laws.

Secretary: A. D. Rowing.

Most League Goals: 88, Division 3 (N), 1957–58.

Highest League Scorer in Season: Barrie Thomas, 31, Division 2, 1961–62.

Most League Goals in Total Aggregate: Steve Cammack, 110, 1979–81, 1981–86.

Most Capped Player: None.

Most League Appearances: Jack Brownsword, 595, 1950–65.

Honours – Division 3 (N) Champions – 1957–58.

Colours: Claret shirts, blue shorts, white stockings.

SHEFFIELD UNITED

FL CHAMPIONSHIP

Allison Wayne (F)	6 1	15 07	Huddersfield	16 10 68	Tranmere R
Armstrong Chris (D)	5 9	11 00	Newcastle	5 8 82	Oldham Ath

Name	Ht	Wt	Birthplace	Date	Previous Club
Britton Andrew (G)	6 1	13 07	California	26 5 85	
Forte Jonathan (M)	6 0	12 02	Sheffield	25 7 86	Scholar
Francis Simon (D)	6 0	12 06	Nottingham	16 2 85	Bradford C
Gray Andy (M)	6 2	13 00	Harrogate	15 11 77	Bradford C
Jagielka Phil (M)	5 11	13 05	Manchester	17 8 82	Scholar
Kabba Steven (F)	5 10	11 12	Lambeth	7 3 81	Crystal Palace
Kenny Paddy (G)	6 0	15 00	Halifax	17 5 78	Bury
Kozluk Rob (D)	5 8	11 08	Sutton-in-Ashfield	5 7 77	Derby Co
Lester Jack (F)	5 11	11 00	Sheffield	8 10 75	Nottingham F
McCall Stuart (M)	5 8	10 02	Leeds	10 6 64	Bradford C
Montgomery Nick (M)	5 9	12 06	Leeds	28 10 81	Scholar
Morgan Chris (M)	6 1	12 09	Barnsley	9 11 77	Barnsley
Ndlovu Peter (F)	5 7	10 02	Bulawayo	25 2 73	Birmingham C
Page Robert (D)	5 11	13 12	Tylorstown	3 9 74	Watford
Parkinson Andy (F)	5 8	10 12	Liverpool	27 5 79	Tranmere R
Sestanovich Ashley (M)	6 3	13 00	London	18 9 81	Hampton & Richmond B
Shaw Paul (F)	5 11	13 03	Burnham	4 9 73	Gillingham
Tonge Michael (M)	6 0	13 02	Manchester	7 4 83	Scholar
Ward Ashley (F)	6 1	11 07	Manchester	24 11 70	Bradford C
Wright Alan (D)	5 4	9 09	Ashton-under-Lyme	28 9 71	Middlesbrough

League Appearances: Allison, W. 14(25); Armstrong, C. 4(8); Baxter, L. 1; Boussatta, D. 3(3); Brown, M. 14(1); Cryan, C. (1); Fettis, A. 2(1); Forte, J. 1(6); Francis, S. 4(1); Gerrard, P. 16; Gray, A. 14; Harley, J. 5; Jagielka, P. 43; Kabba, S. (1); Kenny, P. 27; Kozluk, R. 42; Lester, J. 25(7); McCall, S. 37; McLeod, I. 1(6); Montgomery, N. 32(4); Morgan, C. 32; Ndlovu, P. 28(8); Page, R. 30; Parkinson, A. 3(4); Peschisolido, P. 12(15); Rankine, M. 6(7); Robinson, C. 4(1); Sestanovich, A. (2); Shaw, P. 4(9); Sturridge, D. 2(2); Tonge, M. 46; Ward, A. 20(3); Whitlow, M. 13(4); Wright, A.

Goals – League (65): Lester 12 (6 pens), Gray 9 (1 pen), Ndlovu 9 (3 pens), Peschisolido 8, Tonge 4, Ward 4, Jagielka P 3, Montgomery 3, Brown 2 (2 pens), McCall 2, Allison 1, Armstrong 1, Kozluk 1, Morgan 1, Page 1, Shaw 1, Whitlow 1, Wright 1, own goal 1.

Carling Cup (2): Lester 2 (1 pen).

FA Cup (5): Allison 2, Lester 1 (pen), Morgan 1, Peschisolido 1.

Ground: Bramall Lane Ground, Sheffield S2 4SU. Telephone (0870) 787 1960.

Record Attendance: 68,287 v Leeds U, FA Cup 5th rd, 15 February 1936.

Capacity: 30,900.

Manager: Neil Warnock.

Secretary: Donna Fletcher.

Most League Goals: 102, Division 1, 1925–26.

Highest League Scorer in Season: Jimmy Dunne, 41, Division 1, 1930–31.

Most League Goals in Total Aggregate: Harry Johnson, 205, 1919–30.

Most Capped Player: Billy Gillespie, 25, Northern Ireland.

Most League Appearances: Joe Shaw, 629, 1948–66.

Honours – Football League: Division 1 Champions – 1897–98. Division 2 Champions – 1952–53. Division 4 Champions – 1981–82. **FA Cup:** Winners 1899, 1902, 1915, 1925.

Colours: Red and white striped shirts with white trim, red shorts and red stockings.

SHEFFIELD WEDNESDAY   FL CHAMPIONSHIP 1

Armstrong Craig (M)	5 11	12 09	South Shields	23 5 75	Huddersfield T
Brunt Chris (M)	6 1	12 13	Belfast	14 12 84	Middlesbrough
Carr Chris (D)	5 11	12 06	Newcastle	14 12 84	Trainee
Evans Richard (M)	5 10	12 09	Cardiff	19 6 83	Scholar
Hamshaw Matthew (M)	5 9	12 08	Rotherham	1 1 82	Trainee
Lee Graeme (D)	6 2	13 09	Middlesbrough	31 5 78	Hartlepool U
N'Dumbu Nsungu Guylain (M)	6 1	12 08	Kinshasa	26 12 82	
Olsen Kim (F)	6 4	13 07	Herning	11 2 79	
Proudlock Adam (F)	6 0	14 07	Wellington	9 5 81	Wolverhampton W
Shaw Jon (F)	6 0	12 12	Sheffield	10 11 83	Scholar
Smith Paul (M)	6 1	13 06	Easington	22 1 76	Hartlepool U
Tidman Ola (G)	6 2	12 08	Malmo	11 5 79	Stockport Co
Wood Richard (D)	6 3	12 01	Ossett	5 7 85	Scholar

League Appearances: Antoine-Curier, M. (1); Armstrong, C. 5(5); Barry-Murphy, B. 38(3); Beswetherick, J. 4(1); Bromby, L. 29; Brunt, C. 8(1); Burchill, M. 4(1); Carr, C. (2); Chambers, A. 8(3); Cooke, T. 19(4); Evans, R. 5(1); Geary, D. 41; Haslam, S. 16(9); Holt, G. 9(8); Kuqi, S. 7; Lee, G. 30; Lucas, D. 17; McLaren, P. 23(2); McMahon, L. 9(1); Mustoe, R. 22(3); N'Dumbu Nsungu, G. 20(4); Nixon, E. (1); Olsen, K. 6(4); Owusu, L. 12(8); Pressman, K. 20(1); Proudlock, A. 26(4); Quinn, A. 23(1); Reddy, M. 9(3); Robins, M. 14(1); Shaw, J. 7(7); Smith, D. 41; Smith, P. 12(7); Tidman, O. 9; Wilson, M. 3; Wood, R. 10(2).
Goals – League (48): N'Dumbu Nsungu 9 (3 pens), Kuqi 5, Owusu 5, Quinn 4, Lee 3, Proudlock 3, Robins 3, Brunt 2, Cooke 2, Holt 2, McLaren 2, Shaw J 2, Smith P 2, Bromby 1, Mustoe 1, Reddy 1, Smith D 1.
Carling Cup (2): Lee 1, Wood 1.
FA Cup (6): Proudlock 3 (1 pen), Holt 1, N'Dumbu-Nsungu 1, Owusu 1.
LDV Vans Trophy (9): Robins 4, Proudlock 3, Lee 1, Reddy 1.
Ground: Hillsborough, Sheffield, S6 1SW. Telephone (0114) 2212121
Record Attendance: 72,841 v Manchester C, FA Cup 5th rd, 17 February 1934.
Capacity: 39,814
Manager: Chris Turner.
Chief Executive: Karen Walker.
Most League Goals: 106, Division 2, 1958–59.
Highest League Scorer in Season: Derek Dooley, 46, Division 2, 1951–52.
Most League Goals in Total Aggregate: Andy Wilson, 199, 1900–20.
Most Capped Player: Nigel Worthington, 50 (66), Northern Ireland.
Most League Appearances: Andy Wilson, 501, 1900–20.
Honours – Football League: Division 1 Champions – 1902–03, 1903–04, 1928–29, 1929–30. Division 2 Champions – 1899–1900, 1925–26, 1951–52, 1955–56, 1958–59. **FA Cup winners** 1896, 1907, 1935. **Football League Cup winners** 1990–91.
Colours: Blue and white striped shirts, black shorts, blue stockings.

SHREWSBURY TOWN   FL CHAMPIONSHIP 2

Sam Aiston (M)	6 1	12 10	Newcastle	21 11 76	Sunderland
Jody Banim (F)			Manchester	1 4 78	Radcliffe Borough
Trevor Challis (D)	5 8	11 05	Paddington	23 10 75	Telford U

Colin Cramb (F)	5 11	12 04	Lanark	23 6 74	Bury
Duane Darby (F)	5 11	12 06	Birmingham	17 10 73	Rushden & D
Leon Drysdale (D)	5 10	11 11	Birmingham	3 2 81	Trainee
Ian Dunbavin (G)	6 2	13 00	Liverpool	27 5 80	Liverpool
Dave Edwards (M)	5 11	11 05	Shrewsbury	3 2 86	Trainee
Ian Fitzpatrick (M)	5 9	10 05	Manchester	22 9 80	Halifax T
Joe Hart (G)	6 3	13 03	Shrewsbury	19 4 87	Trainee
Scott Howie (G)	6 2	13 07	Glasgow	4 1 72	Bristol R
Ryan Lowe (M)	5 11	11 03	Liverpool	18 9 78	Burscough
Darren Moss (D)	5 10	11 00	Wrexham	24 5 81	Chester C
Martin O'Connor (M)	5 9	11 08	Walsall	10 12 67	Walsall
Dave Ridler (D)	6 1	12 02	Liverpool	12 3 76	Scarborough
Luke Rodgers (F)	5 7	11 00	Birmingham	1 1 82	Trainee
Jake Sedgemore (D)			Wolverhampton	10 10 78	Northwich Vic
Ross Stephens (M)	5 10	10 09	Landiloes	28 5 85	Trainee
Kevin Street (M)	5 10	10 08	Crewe	25 11 77	Bristol R
Darren Tinson (D)	6 0	12 12	Connah's Quay	15 11 69	Macclesfield T
Jamie Tolley (M)	6 0	11 03	Ludlow	12 5 83	Trainee

Ground: Gay Meadow, Abbey Foregate, Shrewsbury SY2 6AB. Telephone (01743) 360111.

Record Attendance: 18,917 v Walsall, Division 3, 26 April 1961. **Capacity:** 8000.

Manager: Jimmy Quinn.

Secretary: Mrs Judy Shone.

Most League Goals: 101, Division 4, 1958–59.

Highest League Scorer in Season: Arthur Rowley, 38, Division 4, 1958–59.

Most League Goals in Total Aggregate: Arthur Rowley, 152, 1958–65 (completing his League record of 434 goals).

Most Capped Player: Jimmy McLaughlin, 5 (12), Northern Ireland; Bernard McNally, 5, Northern Ireland.

Most League Appearances: Mickey Brown, 418, 1986–91; 1992–94; 1996–2001.

Honours – Football League: Division 3 Champions – 1978–79, 1993–94. **Welsh Cup winners** 1891, 1938, 1977, 1979, 1984, 1985.

Colours: Amber and blue shirts, blue shorts, blue stockings with amber trim.

SOUTHAMPTON   FA PREMIERSHIP

Anderson Stuart (M)			Banff	22 4 86	Scholar
Baird Chris (D)	5 10	11 11	Ballymoney	25 2 82	Scholar
Beattie James (F)	6 1	13 06	Lancaster	27 2 78	Blackburn R
Blayney Alan (G)	6 2	13 12	Belfast	9 10 81	Scholar
Crainey Stephen (D)	5 9	9 11	Glasgow	22 6 81	Celtic
Davies Arron (M)	5 9	10 00	Cardiff	22 6 84	Trainee
Delap Rory (M)	6 3	13 00	Sutton Coldfield	6 7 76	Derby Co
Delgado Agustin (F)	6 3	13 08	Ibarra	23 12 74	Necaxa
Dodd Jason (D)	5 10	12 11	Bath	2 11 70	Bath C
Fernandes Fabrice (M)	5 8	10 07	Aubervilliers	29 10 79	Rennes
Folly Yoann (M)	5 11	11 00	Togo	6 6 85	
Gillett Simon (M)	5 5	11 06	London	6 11 85	Trainee
Griffit Leandre (F)	5 11	11 01	Maubeuge	21 5 84	
Hall Fitz (D)	6 2	12 07	Leytonstone	20 12 80	Oldham Ath
Higginbotham Danny (D)	6 2	12 03	Manchester	29 12 78	Derby Co

Kenton Darren (D)	5 10	12 06	Wandsworth	13 9 78	Norwich C
Le Saux Graeme (D)	5 9	11 07	Jersey	17 10 68	Chelsea
Lundekvam Claus (D)	6 3	13 05	Austevoll	22 2 73	Brann
McCann Neil (M)	5 10	10 00	Greenock	11 8 74	Rangers
McDonald Chris (D)	6 1	13 00	Wycombe	28 12 85	Trainee
Niemi Antti (G)	6 1	13 00	Oulu	31 5 72	Hearts
Oakley Matthew (M)	5 10	12 06	Peterborough	17 8 77	Trainee
Ormerod Brett (F)	5 11	11 12	Blackburn	18 10 76	Blackpool
Pahars Marian (F)	5 8	10 08	Latvia	5 8 76	Skonto Riga
Phillips Kevin (F)	5 7	11 05	Hitchin	25 7 73	Sunderland
Poke Michael (G)	6 1	13 02	Spelthorne	21 11 85	Trainee
Prutton David (M)	5 10	12 03	Hull	12 9 81	Nottingham F
Smith Paul (G)	6 4	14 02	Epsom	17 12 79	Brentford
Surman Andrew (M)	5 10	11 05	Johannesburg	20 8 86	Trainee
Svensson Anders (M)	5 10	12 10	Gothenburg	17 7 76	Elfsborg
Svensson Michael (D)	6 2	13 07	Sweden	25 11 75	Troyes
Telfer Paul (M)	5 10	11 13	Edinburgh	21 10 71	Coventry C
Tessem Jo (M)	6 2	13 01	Orlandet	28 2 72	Molde
Williamson Mike (D)	6 4	13 03	Stoke	8 11 83	Trainee

League Appearances: Baird, C. 1(3); Beattie, J. 32(5); Blayney, A. 2; Crainey, S. 5; Cranie, M. 1; Delap, R. 26(1); Delgado, A. (4); Dodd, J. 27(1); Fernandes, F. 21(6); Folly, Y. 9; Griffit, L. 2(3); Hall, F. 7(4); Higginbotham, D. 24(3); Jones, P. 8; Kenton, D. 3(4); Le Saux, G. 19; Lundekvam, C. 31; Marsden, C. 9(4); McCann, N. 9(9); Niemi, A. 28; Oakley, M. 7; Ormerod, B. 14(8); Pahars, M. 6(8); Phillips, K. 28(6); Prutton, D. 22(5); Svensson, A. 17(13); Svensson, M. 26; Telfer, P. 33(4); Tessem, J. 1(2).
Goals – League (44): Beattie 14 (2 pens), Phillips 12, Ormerod 5, Griffit 2, Pahars 2, Svensson M 2, Delap 1, Fernandes 1, Lundekvam 1, Prutton 1, own goals 3.
Carling Cup (5): Beattie 3 (1 pen), Le Saux 1, Ormerod 1.
FA Cup (0).
UEFA Cup (1): Phillips 1.
Ground: The Friends Provident St Mary's Stadium, Britannia Road, Southampton SO14 5FP. Telephone (0870) 220 0000.
Record Attendance: 32,104 v Liverpool, FA Premier League, 18 January 2003.
Capacity: 32,689.
Manager: Paul Sturrock.
Secretary: Liz Coley.
Most League Goals: 112, Division 3 (S), 1957–58.
Highest League Scorer in Season: Derek Reeves, 39, Division 3, 1959–60.
Most League Goals in Total Aggregate: Mike Channon, 185, 1966–77, 1979–82.
Most Capped Player: Peter Shilton, 49 (125), England.
Most League Appearances: Terry Paine, 713, 1956–74.
Honours – Football League: Division 3 (S) Champions – 1921–22. Division 3 Champions – 1959–60. **FA Cup:** Winners 1975–76.
Colours: Red and white striped shirts, black shorts, red and white stockings.

SOUTHEND UNITED   FL CHAMPIONSHIP 2

Bentley Mark (M)	6 2	13 00	Hertford	7 1 78	
Bramble Tesfaye (F)	6 2	13 13	Ipswich	20 7 80	Cambridge C
Broughton Drewe (F)	6 2	13 06	Hitchin	25 10 78	Kidderminster H

Byrne Paul (M)	5 11	13 00	Dublin	30 6 72	Celtic
Dudfield Lawrie (F)	6 1	13 09	Southwark	7 5 80	Northampton T
Gower Mark (M)	5 8	12 02	Edmonton	5 10 78	Barnet
Husbands Michael (F)	5 8	10 10	Birmingham	13 11 83	Aston Villa
Jupp Duncan (D)	6 1	12 12	Guildford	25 1 75	Luton T
Kightly Michael (F)	5 10	10 00	Basildon	24 1 86	Scholar
Smith Jay (M)	5 7	10 11	London	24 9 81	Aston Villa

League Appearances: Bentley, M. 15(6); Bramble, T. 16(18); Broughton, D. 27(8); Clark, S. 2(4); Constantine, L. 40(3); Corbett, J. 13(4); Cort, L. 46; Dudfield, L. 13; Emberson, C. 6; Flahavan, D. 37; Fullarton, J. 7; Gower, M. 40; Hunt, L. 23(3); Husbands, M. 3(6); Jenkins, N. 7(9); Jupp, D. 39(1); Kightly, M. 2(9); Maher, K. 42; McSweeney, D. 16(5); Nicolau, N. 9; Nightingale, L. (4); Odunsi, L. 12; Pettefer, C. 11; Petterson, A. 1; Robinson, R. 2; Smith, J. 16(2); Stuart, J. 23(3); Tilson, S. (1); Warren, M. 27(5); Wilson, C. 11(3).

Goals – League (51): Constantine 21 (5 pens), Gower 6 (1 pen), Dudfield 5, Bramble 4, Bentley 2, Broughton 2, Warren 2, Corbett 1 (pen), Cort 1, Jenkins 1, Maher 1, McSweeney 1, Odunsi 1, Smith 1 (pen), own goals 2.

Carling Cup (2): Broughton 1, Maher 1.

FA Cup (8): Smith 3, Bramble 2, Gower 2, Corbett 1.

LDV Vans Trophy (15): Broughton 5, Constantine 4, Bramble 2, Clark 1, Corbett 1, Gower 1, Kightly 1.

Ground: Roots Hall Football Ground, Victoria Avenue, Southend-on-Sea SS2 6NQ. Telephone (0870) 174 2000.

Record Attendance: 31,090 v Liverpool FA Cup 3rd rd, 10 January 1979. **Capacity:** 12,268.

Manager: Steve Tilson.

Secretary: Miss Helen Giles.

Most League Goals: 92, Division 3 (S), 1950–51.

Highest League Scorer in Season: Jim Shankly, 31, 1928–29; Sammy McCrory, 1957–58, both in Division 3 (S).

Most League Goals in Total Aggregate: Roy Hollis, 122, 1953–60.

Most Capped Player: George Mackenzie, 9, Eire.

Most League Appearances: Sandy Anderson, 452, 1950–63.

Honours – Football League: Division 4 Champions – 1980–81.

Colours: All navy blue with white trim.

STOCKPORT COUNTY   FL CHAMPIONSHIP 1

Adams Danny (D)	5 8	13 09	Manchester	3 1 76	Macclesfield T
Bailey Matt (F)	6 4	11 06	Crewe	12 3 86	Nantwich T
Beckett Luke (F)	5 11	11 06	Sheffield	25 11 76	Chesterfield
Cartwright Lee (M)	5 8	11 00	Rawtenstall	19 9 72	Preston NE
Challinor Dave (D)	6 1	12 06	Chester	2 10 75	Tranmere R
Clare Rob (D)	6 1	11 07	Belper	28 2 83	Trainee
Daly Jon (F)	6 1	12 04	Dublin	8 1 83	Trainee
Goodwin Jim (D)	5 9	12 02	Waterford	20 11 81	
Griffin Danny (D)	5 10	10 12	Belfast	10 8 77	St Johnstone
Hardiker John (D)	6 0	11 04	Preston	17 2 82	Morecambe
Jackman Danny (D)	5 4	9 08	Worcester	3 1 83	Aston Villa
Jones Rob (D)	6 7	12 02	Stockton	30 11 79	
Lambert Ricky (M)	5 10	11 02	Liverpool	16 2 82	Macclesfield T

Lescott Aaron (M)	5 8	10 09	Birmingham	2 12 78	Sheffield W
McLachlan Fraser (M)	5 11	12 06	Knutsford	9 11 82	Scholar
Morrison Owen (M)	5 8	11 12	Derry	8 12 81	Sheffield U
Pemberton Martin (M)	5 11	12 06	Bradford	1 2 76	Mansfield T
Spencer James (G)	6 5	15 02	Stockport	11 4 85	Trainee
Welsh Andy (M)	5 8	9 08	Manchester	24 11 83	Scholar
Wilbraham Aaron (F)	6 3	12 04	Knutsford	21 10 79	Trainee
Williams Ashley (D)	6 0	11 02	Wolverhampton	23 8 84	Hednesford T
Williams Chris (F)	5 8	9 06	Manchester	2 2 85	Scholar

League Appearances: Adams, D. 12; Barlow, S. 15(15); Beckett, L. 6(2); Byrne, M. 1; Cartwright, L. 14(1); Challinor, D. 14(3); Clare, R. 36; Colgan, N. 14(1); Collins, W. (2); Daly, J. 19(6); Ellison, K. 10(4); Gibb, A. 23(3); Goodwin, J. 29(5); Griffin, D. 15; Hardiker, J. 38(1); Heath, M. 8; Jackman, D. 27; Jones, R. 14(2); Lambert, R. 39(1); Lescott, A. 12(2); Lynch, S. 9; McLachlan, F. 14(6); Morrison, O. 11(11); Myhill, B. 2; Pemberton, M. 5(1); Robertson, M. 9(3); Smith, S. 3(3); Spencer, J. 15; Walton, D. 7; Welsh, A. 24(10); Wilbraham, A. 32(9); Williams, Anthony 15; Williams, Ashley 10; Williams, C. 4(12).

Goals – League (62): Lambert 12 (5 pens), Barlow 8, Wilbraham 8, Beckett 4, Goodwin 4 (1 pen), Clare 3, Daly 3, Lynch 3, McLachlan 3, Williams C 3, Jackman 2, Jones R 2, Byrne 1, Ellison 1, Griffin 1, Morrison 1, Robertson 1, Welsh 1, own goal 1.

Carling Cup (1): Barlow 1.

FA Cup (1): Goodwin 1 (pen).

LDV Vans Trophy (7): Barlow 3, Goodwin 1 (pen), Lambert 1, Morrison 1, Williams C 1.

Ground: Edgeley Park, Hardcastle Road, Stockport, Cheshire SK3 9DD. Telephone (0161) 286 8888.

Record Attendance: 27,833 v Liverpool, FA Cup 5th rd, 11 February 1950.

Capacity: 10,817.

Manager: Sammy McIlroy.

Secretary: Gary Glendenning BA (HONS) FCCA.

Most League Goals: 115, Division 3 (N), 1933–34.

Highest League Scorer in Season: Alf Lythgoe, 46, Division 3 (N), 1933–34.

Most League Goals in Total Aggregate: Jack Connor, 132, 1951–56.

Most Capped Player: Jarkko Wiss, 9 (36), Finland.

Most League Appearances: Andy Thorpe, 489, 1978–86, 1988–92.

Honours – Football League: Division 3 (N) Champions – 1921–22, 1936–37. Division 4 Champions – 1966–67.

Colours: All blue.

STOKE CITY   FL CHAMPIONSHIP

Akinbiyi Ade (F)	6 1	12 08	Hackney	10 10 74	Crystal Palace
Asaba Carl (F)	6 2	14 02	London	28 1 73	Sheffield U
Cartwright Shaun (M)			Stoke-on-Trent	15 4 86	Scholar
Clarke Clive (D)	6 0	12 02	Dublin	14 1 80	Trainee
Commons Kris (D)	5 6	9 08	Nottingham	30 8 83	Scholar
De Goey Ed (G)	6 6	14 05	Gouda	20 12 66	Chelsea
Eustace John (M)	5 11	11 12	Solihull	3 11 79	Coventry C

Foster Ben (G)	6 2	12 06	Leamington Spa	3 4 83	Racing Club Warwick	
Greenacre Chris (F)	5 11	12 08	Halifax	23 12 77	Mansfield T	
Hall Marcus (D)	6 1	12 02	Coventry	24 3 76	Nottingham F	
Halls John (D)	6 0	11 00	Islington	14 2 82	Arsenal	
Henry Karl (M)	6 0	11 04	Wolverhampton	26 11 82	Trainee	
Hill Clint (D)	6 0	12 00	Liverpool	19 10 78	Oldham Ath	
Hutchison Ryan (M)					Scholar	
Neal Lewis (M)	5 10	10 11	Leicester	14 7 81		
Noel-Williams Gifton (F)	6 1	14 00	Islington	21 1 80	Watford	
Owen Gareth (D)	6 1	11 07	Stoke	21 9 82	Scholar	
Palmer Jermaine (F)	6 0	11 03	Nottingham	28 8 86	Scholar	
Russell Darel (M)	6 0	12 01	Mile End	22 10 80	Norwich C	
Thomas Wayne (D)	6 0	11 02	Gloucester	17 5 79	Torquay U	
Wilkinson Andy (D)	5 11	11 00	Stone	6 8 84	Scholar	
Williams Paul (D)	6 0	14 04	Burton	26 3 71	Southampton	

League Appearances: Akinbiyi, A. 23(7); Andrews, K. 16; Asaba, C. 26(11); Clarke, C. 41(1); Commons, K. 14(19); Cutler, N. 9(4); De Goey, E. 37; Eustace, J. 26; Goodfellow, M. (4); Greenacre, C. 8(5); Gunnarsson, B. 1(2); Hall, M. 34(1); Halls, J. 34; Henry, K. 14(6); Hill, C. 9(3); Hoekstra, P. 20(4); Iwelumo, C. 3(6); Johnson, R. 3(4); Marteinsson, P. 3; Neal, L. 6(13); Noel-Williams, G. 40(2); Owen, G. 1(2); Palmer, J. (3); Richardson, F. 6; Russell, D. 46; Svard, S. 9(4); Taggart, G. 21; Thomas, W. 39; Wilkinson, A. 1(2); Williams, P. 16(3); Wilson, B. (2).
Goals – League (58): Akinbiyi 10, Noel-Williams 10, Asaba 8 (2 pens), Eustace 5 (1 pen), Commons 4, Hoekstra 4 (2 pens), Russell 4, Clarke 3, Thomas 3, Greenacre 2, Taggart 2, Neal 1, Richardson 1, Svard 1.
Carling Cup (2): Goodfellow 1, Iwelumo 1.
FA Cup (1): Eustace 1.
Ground: Britannia Stadium, Stoke-on-Trent ST4 4EG. Telephone (01782) 592222.
Record Attendance: 51,380 v Arsenal, Division 1, 29 March 1937. **Capacity:** 28,232.
Manager: Tony Pulis.
Most League Goals: 92, Division 3 (N), 1926–27.
Highest League Scorer in Season: Freddie Steele, 33, Division 1, 1936–37.
Most League Goals in Total Aggregate: Freddie Steele, 142, 1934–49.
Most Capped Player: Gordon Banks, 36 (73), England.
Most League Appearances: Eric Skeels, 506, 1958–76.
Honours – Football League: Division 2 Champions – 1932–33, 1962–63, 1992–93. Division 3 (N) Champions – 1926–27. **Football League Cup:** Winners 1971–72.
Autoglass Trophy winners 1992. **Auto Windscreens Shield winners** 2000.
Colours: Red and white striped shirts, white shorts, white stockings.

SUNDERLAND   FL CHAMPIONSHIP

Alnwick Ben (G)	6 0	12 09	Sunderland	1 1 87	Scholar	
Arca Julio (D)	5 9	11 00	Quilmes	31 1 81	Argentinos Juniors	
Bell Ryan (D)	6 3	12 08	Ashington	30 3 86	Trainee	
Breen Gary (D)	6 2	11 12	London	12 12 73	West Ham U	
Brown Chris (F)	6 1	13 04	Doncaster	11 12 84	Trainee	
Butler Thomas (M)	5 7	10 06	Dublin	25 4 81	Trainee	
Clark Ben (D)	6 2	12 03	Shotley Bridge	24 1 83	Manchester U	
Dickman Jonjo (M)	5 8	10 05	Hexham	22 9 81		

Dodds Lewis (M)	5 8	10 07	Spennymoor	14 12 85	Trainee
Flynn Niall (M)	5 7	10 00	Dublin	22 1 86	Trainee
Healy Colin (M)	5 11	11 00	Cork	14 3 80	Celtic
Ingham Michael (G)	6 4	13 10	Preston	9 9 80	Malachians
Kingsberry Chris (M)	5 5	7 00	Lisburn	10 9 85	Trainee
Kyle Kevin (F)	6 3	13 00	Stranraer	7 6 81	
Leadbitter Grant (M)	5 9	10 03	Sunderland	7 1 86	Trainee
McCartney George (D)	5 11	10 10	Belfast	29 4 81	Trainee
McLean Euan (G)	6 3	13 07	Kilmarnock	9 1 86	Trainee
Medina Nicolas (M)	5 9	10 04	Buenos Aires	17 2 82	Argentinos Jun
Myhre Thomas (G)	6 4	13 12	Sarpsborg	16 10 73	Besiktas
Piper Matt (F)	6 0	13 00	Leicester	29 9 81	Leicester C
Poom Mart (G)	6 4	14 03	Tallinn	3 2 72	Derby Co
Ryan Richie (M)	5 10	10 07	Kilkenny	6 1 85	Scholar
Smith Daniel (D)	5 10	10 08	Sunderland	5 10 86	Scholar
Stewart Marcus (F)	5 10	11 08	Bristol	7 11 72	Ipswich T
Taylor Sean (D)	5 7	10 07	Amble	9 12 85	Trainee
Teggart Neil (F)	6 2	12 01	Downpatrick	16 9 84	Scholar
Thornton Sean (M)	5 11	12 03	Drogheda	18 5 83	Scholar
Williams Darren (D)	5 11	12 00	Middlebrough	28 4 77	York C
Wright Stephen (D)	6 0	12 08	Liverpool	8 2 80	Liverpool

League Appearances: Arca, J. 31; Babb, P. 22; Bjorklund, J. 19(6); Black, C. (1); Breen, G. 32; Butler, T. 7(5); Byfield, D. 8(9); Clark, B. 2(3); Cooper, C. (3); Cooper, K. (1); Downing, S. 7; Gray, M. (1); Healy, C. 16(4); James, C. 1; Kilbane, K. 5; Kyle, K. 36(8); McAteer, J. 18; McCartney, G. 40(1); Myhre, T. 3(1); Oster, J. 35(3); Piper, M. 4(5); Poom, M. 43; Proctor, M. 4(13); Quinn, A. 5(1); Robinson, J. 6(1); Smith, T. 22(13); Stewart, M. 28(12); Thirlwell, P. 21(8); Thornton, S. 14(8); Whitley, J. 33; Williams, D. 24(5); Wright, S. 20(2).

Goals – League (62): Stewart 14 (5 pens), Kyle 10, Byfield 5, Oster 5, Arca 4, Breen 4, Smith 4, Thornton 4, Downing 3 (1 pen), McAteer 2, Whitley 2, Poom 1, Proctor 1, Robinson 1, Wright 1, own goal 1.

Carling Cup (4): Kyle 3, own goal 1.

FA Cup (7): Smith 4, Arca 2, Kyle 1.

Play-Offs (4): Kyle 2, Stewart 2 (1 pen).

Ground: Stadium of Light, Sunderland, Tyne and Wear SR5 1SU. Telephone (0191) 551 5000.

Record Attendance: 75,118 v Derby Co, FA Cup 6th rd replay, 8 March 1933 (Roker Park). 48,353 v Liverpool, FA Premier League, 13 April 2002 (Stadium of Light). **Capacity:** 49,000.

Manager: Mick McCarthy.

Secretary: Jane Purdon.

Most League Goals: 109, Division 1, 1935–36.

Highest League Scorer in Season: Dave Halliday, 43, Division 1, 1928–29.

Most League Goals in Total Aggregate: Charlie Buchan, 209, 1911–25.

Most Capped Player: Charlie Hurley, 38 (40), Republic of Ireland.

Most League Appearances: Jim Montgomery, 537, 1962–77.

Honours – Football League: Division 1 Champions – 1891–92, 1892–93, 1894–95, 1901–02, 1912–13, 1935–36, 1995–96, 1998–99. Division 2 Champions – 1975–76. Division 3 Champions – 1987–88. **FA Cup:** Winners 1937, 1973.

Colours: Red and white striped shirts, black shorts, black stockings.

SWANSEA CITY   FL CHAMPIONSHIP 2

Britton Leon (M)	5 6	10 00	Merton	16 9 82	West Ham U
Connor Paul (F)	6 2	11 08	Bishop Auckland	12 1 79	Rochdale
Hylton Leon (D)	5 9	11 00	Birmingham	27 1 83	Aston Villa
Iriekpen Ezomo (D)	6 1	12 02	East London	14 5 82	West Ham U
Jones Stuart (D)	6 0	11 08	Aberystwyth	14 3 84	Scholar
Martinez Roberto (M)	5 9	12 02	Balaguer	13 7 73	Walsall
Maylett Brad (M)	5 10	10 04	Manchester	24 12 80	Burnley
Murphy Brian (G)	6 0	13 00	Waterford	7 5 83	Manchester C
Pritchard Mark (F)	5 10	12 04	Tredegar	23 11 85	
Robinson Andy (M)	5 8	11 04	Birkenhead	3 11 79	Cammell Laird
Tate Alan (D)	6 1	13 05	Easington	2 9 82	Manchester U
Thomas James (F)	6 0	13 05	Swansea	16 1 79	Blackburn R
Trundle Lee (F)	6 0	13 03	Liverpool	10 10 76	Wrexham

League Appearances: Britton, L. 42; Byrne, S. 9; Coates, J. 14(13); Connolly, K. 4(6); Connor, P. 12; Corbisierso, A. 1(4); Duffy, R. 16(2); Durkan, K. 11(4); Fieldwick, L. 4(1); Freestone, R. 35(2); Howard, M. 25; Hylton, L. 10(1); Iriekpen, E. 33(1); Jenkins, L. 8(3); Johnrose, L. 21(4); Jones, S. 16(8); Martinez, R. 24(3); Maxwell, L. 1(2); Maylett, B. 26(7); Murphy, B. 11; Nardiello, D. 3(1); Nugent, K. 31(8); O'Leary, K. 28(6); Pritchard, M. 1(3); Rees, M. 3; Rewbury, J. 1(1); Roberts, S. 8(4); Robinson, A. 34(3); Tate, A. 25(1); Thomas, J. 8(8); Trundle, L. 29(2); Wilson, M. 12.

Goals – League (58): Trundle 16 (3 pens), Nugent 8, Robinson 8 (1 pen), Connor 5, Maylett 5, Britton 3, Thomas 3, Wilson 2, Connolly 1, Duffy 1, Durkan 1, Iriekpen 1, Rees 1, Roberts 1, Tate 1, own goal 1.

Carling Cup (1): Connolly 1.

FA Cup (10): Trundle 5, Nugent 2, Robinson 2, Durkan 1.

LDV Vans Trophy (1): Nardiello 1.

Ground: Vetch Field, Swansea SA1 3SU. Telephone (01792) 633 400.

Record Attendance: 32,796 v Arsenal, FA Cup 4th rd, 17 February 1968. **Capacity:** 11,131.

Director of Football: Kenny Jackett.

Secretary: Jackie Rockey.

Most League Goals: 90, Division 2, 1956–57.

Highest League Scorer in Season: Cyril Pearce, 35, Division 2, 1931–32.

Most League Goals in Total Aggregate: Ivor Allchurch, 166, 1949–58, 1965–68.

Most Capped Player: Ivor Allchurch, 42 (68), Wales.

Most League Appearances: Wilfred Milne, 585, 1919–37.

Honours – Football League: Division 3 Champions – 1999–2000. Division 3 (S) Champions – 1924–25, 1948–49. **Autoglass Trophy:** Winners 1994. **Welsh Cup:** Winners 10 times.

Colours: All white.

SWINDON TOWN   FL CHAMPIONSHIP 1

Evans Rhys (G)	6 1	12 02	Swindon	27 1 82	Chelsea
Fallon Rory (F)	6 2	11 10	Gisborne	20 3 82	Barnsley
Gurney Andy (D)	5 10	11 06	Bristol	25 1 74	Reading
Hewlett Matt (M)	6 2	11 03	Bristol	25 2 76	Bristol C

Heywood Matthew (D)	6 2	14 00	Chatham	26 8 79	Burnley
Howard Brian (M)	5 8	11 05	Winchester	23 1 83	Southampton
Igoe Sammy (M)	5 6	10 00	Staines	30 9 75	Reading
Nicholas Andrew (D)	6 0	12 10	Liverpool	10 10 83	Liverpool
O'Hanlon Sean (D)	6 1	12 05	Southport	2 1 83	Everton
Parkin Sam (F)	6 2	13 00	Roehampton	14 3 81	Chelsea
Smith Grant (M)	6 1	12 07	Irvine	5 5 80	Sheffield U
Viveash Adrian (D)	6 2	12 13	Swindon	30 9 69	Reading

League Appearances: Burton, D. 4; Duke, D. 35(7); Evans, R. 41; Fallon, R. 6(13); Garrard, L. (1); Griemink, B. 5(1); Gurney, A. 42; Herring, I. 1; Hewlett, M. 43; Heywood, M. 39(1); Howard, B. 21(14); Ifil, J. 16; Igoe, S. 33(3); Lewis, J. 4; Miglioranzi, S. 34(1); Milner, J. 6; Mooney, T. 41(4); Nicholas, A. 28(3); O'Hanlon, S. 17(2); Parkin, S. 38(2); Reeves, A. 17(10); Robinson, S. 20(2); Ruster, S. (2); Smith, G. (7); Stevenson, J. 1(4); Viveash, A. 14(1).
Goals – League (76): Mooney 19, Parkin 19, Fallon 6, Gurney 6 (2 pens), Igoe 5, Howard 4, Miglioranzi 4, Hewlett 3, Milner 2, O'Hanlon 2, Burton 1, Duke 1, Heywood 1, Nicholas 1, Robinson S 1, own goal 1.
Carling Cup (5): Parkin 3, Gurney 1, Mooney 1.
FA Cup (1): Gurney 1 (pen).
LDV Vans Trophy (1): Robinson 1.
Play-Offs (2): Fallon 1, Parkin 1.
Ground: County Ground, Swindon, Wiltshire SN1 2ED. Telephone (0870) 443 1969.
Record Attendance: 32,000 v Arsenal, FA Cup 3rd rd, 15 January 1972. **Capacity:** 14,540.
Manager: Andy King.
Secretary: Linda Birrell.
Most League Goals: 100, Division 3 (S), 1926–27.
Highest League Scorer in Season: Harry Morris, 47, Division 3 (S), 1926–27.
Most League Goals in Total Aggregate: Harry Morris, 216, 1926–33.
Most Capped Player: Rod Thomas, 30 (50), Wales.
Most League Appearances: John Trollope, 770, 1960–80.
Honours – Football League: Division 2 Champions – 1995–96. Division 4 Champions – 1985–86. **Football League Cup:** Winners 1968–69. **Anglo-Italian Cup:** Winners 1970.
Colours: Red shirts, white shorts, red stockings, with white turnover.

TORQUAY UNITED   FL CHAMPIONSHIP 1

Bedeau Anthony (F)	5 10	11 00	Hammersmith	24 3 79	Trainee
Bond Kain (F)	5 9	10 10	Torquay	19 6 85	Scholar
Canoville Lee (M)	6 1	11 03	Ealing	14 3 81	Arsenal
Fowler Jason (M)	6 3	11 12	Bristol	20 8 74	Cardiff C
Graham David (F)	5 10	11 05	Edinburgh	6 10 78	Dunfermline Ath
Gritton Martin (F)	6 1	12 07	Glasgow	1 6 78	Plymouth Arg
Hockley Matthew (D)	5 10	11 07	Paignton	5 6 82	Trainee
McGlinchey Brian (D)	5 9	12 00	Derry	26 10 77	Plymouth Arg
Osei-Kuffour Jo (F)	5 7	10 06	Edmonton	17 11 81	Arsenal
Russell Alex (M)	5 9	11 07	Crosby	17 3 73	Cambridge U
Taylor Craig (D)	6 1	13 02	Plymouth	24 1 74	Plymouth Arg
Van Heusden Arjan (G)	6 3	14 07	Alphen	11 12 72	Mansfield T

League Appearances: Bedeau, A. 13(11); Benefield, J. 3(12); Bernard, N. (1); Bond, K. (1); Broad, J. 4(10); Canoville, L. 32(1); Dearden, K. 21(1); Fowler, J. 24(7); Graham, D. 41(4); Gritton, M. 17(14); Hankin, S. 1; Hazell, R. 12(7); Hill, K. 42(3); Hockley, M. 44(1); Killoughery, G. (3); McGlinchey, B. 34; McMahon, D. (1); Osei-Kuffour, J. 33(8); Rosenior, L. 9(1); Russell, A. 42(1); Taylor, C. 43; Van Heusden, A. 25; Williamson, M. 9(2); Wills, K. 7(16); Woods, S. 46; Woozley, D. 4(6).

Goals – League (68): Graham 22, Osei-Kuffour 10, Woods 6 (2 pens), Hill 5, Hockley 5, Gritton 4, Taylor 4, Wills 3, Fowler 2, Russell 2, Bedeau 1, Canoville 1, Hazell 1, own goals 2.

Carling Cup (1): Graham 1.
FA Cup (1): Benefield 1.
LDV Vans Trophy (2): Benefield 1, Wills 1.
Ground: Plainmoor Ground, Torquay, Devon TQ1 3PS. Telephone (01803) 328666.
Record Attendance: 21,908 v Huddersfield T, FA Cup 4th rd, 29 January 1955.
Capacity: 6269.
Manager: Leroy Rosenior.
Secretary: Heather Kindeleit-Badcock.
Most League Goals: 89, Division 3 (S), 1956–57.
Highest League Scorer in Season: Sammy Collins, 40, Division 3 (S), 1955–56.
Most League Goals in Total Aggregate: Sammy Collins, 204, 1948–58.
Most Capped Player: Rodney Jack, St Vincent.
Most League Appearances: Dennis Lewis, 443, 1947–59.
Honours – Nil
Colours: Yellow shirts, royal blue shorts, yellow stockings.

TOTTENHAM HOTSPUR   FA PREMIERSHIP

Barnard Lee (F)	5 10	10 10	Romford	18 7 84	Trainee
Brown Michael R (M)	5 9	12 04	Hartlepool	25 1 77	Sheffield U
Bunjevcevic Goran (D)	6 3	12 02	Karlovac	17 2 73	Red Star Belgrade
Burch Rob (G)	6 2	12 13	Yeovil	8 10 83	Trainee
Carr Stephen (D)	5 9	12 04	Dublin	29 8 76	Trainee
Davies Simon (M)	5 10	11 07	Haverfordwest	23 10 79	Peterborough U
Defoe Jermain (F)	5 7	10 04	Beckton	7 10 82	West Ham U
Doherty Gary (D)	6 2	13 01	Carndonagh	31 1 80	Luton T
Eyre Nicky (G)			Braintree	7 9 85	Trainee
Gardner Anthony (D)	6 3	14 00	Stafford	19 9 80	Port Vale
Hughes Mark (M)	5 10	12 04	Dungannon	16 9 83	Scholar
Jackson Johnnie (M)	6 1	12 00	Camden	15 8 82	Trainee
Kanoute Frederic (F)	6 3	13 08	Ste. Foy-Les-Lyon	2 9 77	West Ham U
Keane Robbie (F)	5 9	12 06	Dublin	8 7 80	Leeds U
Keller Kasey (G)	6 1	13 08	Washington	27 11 69	Rayo Vallecano
Kelly Stephen (D)	6 1	12 01	Dublin	6 9 83	
King Ledley (D)	6 2	14 05	Bow	12 10 80	Trainee
Mabizela Mbulelo (D)	5 10	12 06	Pietermaritzburg	16 9 80	Orlando P
Malcolm Michael (M)			Harrow	13 10 85	Trainee
Marney Dean (M)	5 9	11 04	Barking	31 1 84	Scholar
McKenna Kieran (M)			London	14 5 86	Academy
McKie Marcel (D)			Edmonton	22 9 84	Scholar
O'Donoghue Paul (D)	6 1	13 10	Lewisham	14 12 83	Scholar

Postiga Helder (F)	5 11	11 00	Povoa de Varzim	2	8 82	Porto
Price Owen (F)			London	20 10 85		
Rebrov Sergei (F)	5 8	11 00	Gorlovka	3	6 74	Dynamo Kiev
Redknapp Jamie (M)	6 0	13 03	Barton-on-Sea	25	6 73	Liverpool
Richards Dean (D)	6 2	13 01	Bradford	9	6 74	Southampton
Ricketts Rohan (M)	5 8	11 05	Clapham	22 12 82		Scholar
Robinson Paul (G)	6 4	15 07	Beverley	15 10 79		Leeds U
Slabber Jamie (F)	6 2	11 10	Enfield	31 12 84		Scholar
Taricco Mauricio (D)	5 8	11 07	Buenos Aires	10	3 73	Ipswich T
Yeates Mark (F)	5 9	10 07	Dublin	11	1 85	Trainee

League Appearances: Anderton, D. 16(4); Blondel, J. (1); Brown, M. 17; Bunjevcevic, G. 3(4); Carr, S. 32; Dalmat, S. 12(10); Davies, S. 17; Defoe, J. 14(1); Doherty, G. 16(1); Gardner, A. 33; Jackson, J. 9(2); Kanoute, F. 19(8); Keane, R. 31(3); Keller, K. 38; Kelly, S. 7(4); King, L. 28(1); Konchesky, P. 10(2); Mabizela, M. (6); Marney, D. 1(2); Postiga, H. 9(10); Poyet, G. 12(8); Redknapp, J. 14(3); Richards, D. 23; Ricketts, R. 12(12); Taricco, M. 31(1); Yeates, M. 1; Zamora, B. 6(10); Ziege, C. 7(1).

Goals – League (47): Keane 14 (3 pens), Defoe 7, Kanoute 7, Dalmat 3, Poyet 3, Davies 2, Anderton 1, Brown 1, Carr 1, Jackson 1, King 1, Mabizela 1, Postiga 1, Redknapp 1, Ricketts 1, Taricco 1, own goal 1.

Carling Cup (8): Anderton 2, Kanoute 2, Keane 1, Postiga 1, Ricketts 1, Zamora 1.

FA Cup (7): Kanoute 3, Doherty 1, Keane 1, King 1, Ziege 1.

Ground: 748 High Road, Tottenham, London N17 0AP. Telephone (020) 8365 5000.

Record Attendance: 75,038 v Sunderland, FA Cup 6th rd, 5 March 1938.

Capacity: 36,252.

Manager: Jacques Santini.

Secretary: John Alexander.

Most League Goals: 115, Division 1, 1960–61.

Highest League Scorer in Season: Jimmy Greaves, 37, Division 1, 1962–63.

Most League Goals in Total Aggregate: Jimmy Greaves, 220, 1961–70.

Most Capped Player: Pat Jennings, 74 (119), Northern Ireland.

Most League Appearances: Steve Perryman, 655, 1969–86.

Honours – Football League: Division 1 Champions – 1950–51, 1960–61. Division 2 Champions – 1919–20, 1949–50. **FA Cup:** Winners 1901 (as non-**League** club), 1921, 1961, 1962, 1967, 1981, 1982, 1991. **Football League Cup:** Winners 1970–71, 1972–73, 1998–99. **European Competitions:** European Cup-Winners' Cup winners: 1962–63. **UEFA Cup winners:** 1971–72, 1983–84.

Colours: White shirts, navy blue shorts, white stockings.

TRANMERE ROVERS   FL CHAMPIONSHIP 1

Achterberg John (G)	6 1	13 00	Utrecht	8	7 71	Eindhoven
Ashton Neil (M)	5 10	11 12	Liverpool	15	1 85	Scholar
Dagnall Chris (F)	5 8	12 09	Liverpool	15	4 86	Scholar
Harrison Danny (M)	5 11	12 04	Liverpool	4	11 82	Scholar
Howarth Russell (G)	6 2	14 05	York	27	3 82	York C
Hume Iain (F)	5 7	11 02	Brampton	31 10 83		
Jennings Steven (M)	5 7	11 07	Liverpool	28 10 84		Scholar
Jones Gary (M)	6 3	14 00	Chester	10	5 75	Nottingham F

102

Linwood Paul (D)	6 2	12 08	Birkenhead	24 10 83	Scholar
Loran Tyrone (D)	6 2	13 11	Amsterdam	29 6 81	
Navarro Alan (D)	5 10	11 07	Liverpool	31 5 81	Liverpool
Palethorpe Philip (G)			Liverpool	17 9 86	Scholar
Robinson Paul (F)	6 0	12 00	Newcastle	25 5 83	Scholar
Sharps Ian (D)	6 3	13 05	Warrington	23 10 80	Trainee
Taylor Ryan (D)	5 8	10 04	Liverpool	19 8 84	Scholar
Tremarco Carl (M)	5 11	12 03	Liverpool	11 10 85	Scholar

League Appearances: Achterberg, J. 45; Allen, G. 40(1); Ashton, N. (1); Beresford, D. 13(12); Connelly, S. 33(4); Dadi, E. 29(9); Dagnall, C. 5(5); Goodison, I. 12; Gray, K. 2; Hall, P. 9; Harrison, D. 32; Haworth, S. 21(1); Hay, A. 3(16); Howarth, R. 1; Hume, I. 32(8); Jennings, S. 1(3); Jones, G. 36(6); Linwood, P. 18(2); Loran, T. 26(2); Mellon, M. 39(4); Navarro, A. 9(10); Nicholson, S. 9(7); Onuora, I. 1(2); Roberts, G. 44; Sharps, I. 25(2); Taylor, R. 21(9).

Goals – League (59): Dadi 16 (1 pen), Hume 10, Jones 9, Haworth 6, Taylor 5 (4 pens), Hall 2, Harrison 2, Nicholson 2 (1 pen), Allen 1, Beresford 1, Dagnall 1, Roberts 1, Sharps 1, own goals 2.

Carling Cup (1): Dadi 1.

FA Cup (11): Hume 3, Dadi 2, Jones 2, Mellon 2 (1 pen), Haworth 1, Taylor 1 (pen).

LDV Vans Trophy (2): Hume 1, Nicholson 1.

Ground: Prenton Park, Prenton Road West, Birkenhead, Wirral CH42 9PY. Telephone (0151) 609 3333.

Record Attendance: 24,424 v Stoke C, FA Cup 4th rd, 5 February 1972.

Capacity: 16,500.

Manager: Brian Little.

Secretary: Mick Horton.

Most League Goals: 111, Division 3 (N), 1930–31.

Highest League Scorer in Season: Bunny Bell, 35, Division 3 (N), 1933–34.

Most League Goals in Total Aggregate: Ian Muir, 142, 1985–95.

Most Capped Player: John Aldridge, 30 (69), Republic of Ireland.

Most League Appearances: Harold Bell, 595, 1946–64 (incl. League record 401 consecutive appearances).

Honours – Football League Division 3 (N) Champions – 1937–38. **Welsh Cup:** Winners 1935. **Leyland Daf Cup:** Winners 1990.

Colours: All white.

WALSALL   FL CHAMPIONSHIP 1

Aranalde Zigor (D)	6 1	13 03	Ibarra	28 2 73	Logrones
Birch Gary (F)	6 0	12 03	Birmingham	8 10 81	Trainee
Corica Steve (M)	5 8	10 10	Cairns	24 3 73	Sanfrecce
Fryatt Matty (F)	5 10	11 00	Nuneaton	5 3 86	Scholar
Merson Paul (F)	6 0	12 10	Harlesden	20 3 68	Portsmouth
Osborn Simon (M)	5 9	11 04	New Addington	19 1 72	Gillingham
Roper Ian (D)	6 2	14 00	Nuneaton	20 6 77	Trainee
Taylor Kris (M)	5 9	11 05	Stafford	12 1 84	Manchester U
Wrack Darren (M)	5 9	12 03	Cleethorpes	5 5 76	Grimsby T
Wright Mark (M)	5 11	11 00	Wolverhampton	24 2 82	Scholar

League Appearances: Andrews, K. 10; Aranalde, Z. 29(7); Baird, C. 10; Bazeley, D. 35(4); Bennett, J. (1); Birch, G. 25(10); Bradbury, L. 7(1); Burley, C. 5; Burton, D. 2(1); Carbon, M. 7(1); Corica, S. 17(2); Dinning, T. 2(3); Emblen, N. 27(12); Fryatt, M. 4(7); Hay, D. 14(2); Lawrence, J. 8(9); Leitao, J. 29(10); Matias, P. 6(9); McSporran, J. 2(4); Merson, P. 31(3); O'Neil, G. 7; Oakes, S. 1(4); Osborn, S. 39(4); Petterson, A. 3; Ritchie, P. 33; Roper, I. 33; Samways, V. 29; Taylor, K. 5(6); Vincent, J. 12; Wales, G. 5(2); Walker, J. 43; Wrack, D. 23(4); Wright, M. 3(8).

Goals – League (45): Leitao 7, Wrack 6, Emblen 5, Birch 4, Merson 4, Osborn 3, Andrews 2, Corica 2 (1 pen), Samways 2, Wright 2, Bradbury 1 (pen), Fryatt 1, Lawrence 1, Matias 1, Ritchie 1, Taylor 1, Wales 1, own goal 1.

Carling Cup (3): Merson 2, Leitao 1.

FA Cup (1): Leitao 1.

Ground: Bescot Stadium, Bescot Cresent, Walsall WS1 4SA. Telephone (01922) 622791.

Record Attendance: 10,628 B International, England v Switzerland, 20 May 1991.

Capacity: 11,200.

Manager: Paul Merson.

Secretary/Commercial Manager: Roy Whalley.

Most League Goals: 102, Division 4, 1959–60.

Highest League Scorer in Season: Gilbert Alsop, 40, Division 3 (N), 1933–34 and 1934–35.

Most League Goals in Total Aggregate: Tony Richards, 184, 1954–63; Colin Taylor, 184, 1958–63, 1964–68, 1969–73.

Most Capped Player: Mick Kearns, 15 (18), Republic of Ireland.

Most League Appearances: Colin Harrison, 467, 1964–82.

Honours – Football League: Division 4 Champions – 1959–60.

Colours: Red shirts and shorts with black and white trim, red stockings.

WATFORD   FL CHAMPIONSHIP

Blizzard Dominic (M)	6 2	13 05	High Wycombe	2 9 83	Scholar
Brown Wayne (D)	6 1	12 10	Barking	20 8 77	Ipswich T
Cook Lee (M)	5 8	11 10	Hammersmith	3 8 82	Aylesbury U
Cox Neil (D)	5 11	13 08	Scunthorpe	8 10 71	Bolton W
Devlin Paul (M)	5 7	11 13	Birmingham	14 4 72	Birmingham C
Doyley Lloyd (D)	5 10	12 05	Whitechapel	1 12 82	Scholar
Dyer Bruce (F)	5 11	12 11	Ilford	13 4 75	Barnsley
Fisken Gary (M)	5 11	12 05	Watford	27 10 81	Scholar
Fitzgerald Scott (F)	5 11	12 00	Hillingdon	18 11 79	Northwood
Gayle Marcus (D)	6 3	14 03	Hammersmith	28 9 70	Rangers
Hand Jamie (M)	5 10	12 13	Uxbridge	7 2 84	Scholar
Helguson Heidar (F)	5 10	12 09	Akureyri	22 8 77	Lillestrom
Herd Ben (D)	5 9	10 12	Welwyn	21 6 85	Scholar
Ifil Jerel (D)	5 11	13 01	London	27 6 82	Academy
Lee Richard (G)	6 0	13 03	Oxford	5 10 82	Scholar
Mahon Gavin (M)	6 0	13 00	Birmingham	2 1 77	Brentford
Mayo Paul (D)	5 11	11 13	Lincoln	13 10 81	Lincoln C
McNamee Anthony (M)	5 6	9 11	Lambeth	13 7 84	Scholar
Norville Jason (F)	6 0	11 07	Trinidad & Tobago	9 9 83	Scholar
Smith Jack (D)	5 10	11 05	Hemel Hempstead	14 11 83	Scholar
Webber Danny (F)	5 8	11 00	Manchester	28 12 81	Manchester U
Young Ashley (M)	5 9	9 13	Stevenage	9 7 85	

League Appearances: Ardley, N. 35(3); Baird, C. 8; Blizzard, D. 1(1); Bouazza, H. 6(3); Brown, W. 12; Chamberlain, A. 20(1); Cook, L. 20(21); Cox, N. 35; Devlin, P. 39; Doyley, L. 7(2); Dyche, S. 22(3); Dyer, B. 18(14); Fisken, G. (1); Fitzgerald, S. 28(16); Gayle, M. 32; Hand, J. 16(6); Helguson, H. 20(2); Hyde, M. 28(5); Ifil, J. 9(1); Kelly, S. 13; Mahon, G. 32; Mayo, P. 12; McNamee, A. (2); Pidgeley, L. 26(1); Robinson, P. 10; Smith, J. 16(1); Vernazza, P. 17(12); Webber, D. 24(3); Young, A. (5).

Goals – League (54): Fitzgerald 10, Helguson 8 (1 pen) Cook 7, Webber 5, Cox 4 (4 pens), Devlin 3 (1 pen) Dyer 3, Young 3, Mahon 2, Smith 2, Ardley 1, Blizzard 1, Bouazza 1, Gayle 1, Hyde 1, own goals 2.

Carling Cup (1): Fitzgerald 1.

FA Cup (2): Helguson 1, Mahon 1.

Ground: Vicarage Road Stadium, Watford WD18 0ER. Telephone (0870) 111 1881.

Record Attendance: 34,099 v Manchester U, FA Cup 4th rd (replay), 3 February 1969. **Capacity:** 21,800.

Manager: Ray Lewington.

Secretary: Cathy Alexander.

Most League Goals: 92, Division 4, 1959–60.

Highest League Scorer in Season: Cliff Holton, 42, Division 4, 1959–60.

Most League Goals in Total Aggregate: Luther Blissett, 148, 1976–83, 1984–88, 1991–92.

Most Capped Player: John Barnes, 31 (79), England and Kenny Jackett, 31, Wales.

Most League Appearances: Luther Blissett, 415, 1976–83, 1984–88, 1991–92.

Honours – Football League: Division 3 Champions – 1968–69. Division 2 Champions – 1997–98. Division 4 Champions – 1977–78.

Colours: Yellow shirts, black shorts, black stockings.

WEST BROMWICH ALBION   FA PREMIERSHIP

Berthe Sekou (D)	6 3	13 02	Bamoko	7 10 77	Troyes
Brown Simon (M)	5 10	11 00	West Bromwich	18 9 83	Scholar
Chambers Adam (M)	5 10	11 12	Sandwell	20 11 80	Trainee
Chambers James (D)	5 10	11 10	Sandwell	20 11 80	Trainee
Clement Neil (D)	6 0	12 03	Reading	3 10 78	Chelsea
Dobie Scott (F)	6 1	12 05	Workington	10 10 78	Carlisle U
Dyer Lloyd (F)	5 10	11 04	Birmingham	13 9 82	
Gaardsoe Thomas (D)	6 2	12 08	Denmark	23 11 79	Ipswich T
Gregan Sean (M)	6 2	14 08	Guisborough	29 3 74	Preston NE
Haas Bernt (D)	6 1	12 08	Vienna	8 4 78	Sunderland
Horsfield Geoff (F)	5 10	11 02	Barnsley	1 11 73	Wigan Ath
Hoult Russell (G)	6 3	14 09	Ashby	22 11 72	Portsmouth
Hughes Lee (F)	5 10	12 00	Smethwick	22 5 76	Coventry C
Hulse Rob (F)	6 1	11 04	Crewe	25 10 79	Crewe Alex
Johnson Andy (M)	6 0	13 00	Bristol	2 5 74	Nottingham F
Koumas Jason (M)	5 10	11 02	Wrexham	25 9 79	Tranmere R
Marshall Lee (M)	6 0	11 10	Islington	21 1 79	Leicester C
Miotto Simon (G)	6 1	13 03	Tasmania	5 9 69	St Johnstone
Moore Darren (D)	6 2	15 07	Birmingham	22 4 74	Portsmouth
Murphy Joe (G)	6 2	13 06	Dublin	21 8 81	Tranmere R
O'Connor James (M)	5 8	11 06	Dublin	1 9 79	Stoke C
Robinson Paul (D)	5 9	11 12	Watford	14 12 78	Watford

Sakiri Artim (M)   5 11   12 00   Struga   23 9 73
Sigurdsson Larus (D)   6 0   11 00   Akureyri   4 6 73   Stoke C
Wallwork Ronnie (M)   5 10   12 09   Manchester   10 9 77   Manchester U

League Appearances: Berthe, S. 2(1); Chambers, A. ; Chambers, J. 14(3); Clement, N. 25(10); Dichio, D. 5(6); Dobie, S. 14(17); Dyer, L. 2(15); Facey, D. 2(7); Gaardsoe, T. 45; Gilchrist, P. 16(1); Gregan, S. 40(3); Haas, B. 36; Horsfield, G. 20; Hoult, R. 44; Hughes, L. 21(11); Hulse, R. 29(4); Johnson, A. 33(5); Kinsella, M. 15(3); Koumas, J. 37(5); Moore, D. 20(2); Murphy, J. 2(1); N'Dour, A. 2; O'Connor, J. 27(3); Robinson, P. 30(1); Sakiri, A. 6(19); Sigurdsson, L. 5; Skoubo, M. (2); Volmer, J. 10(5); Wallwork, R. 4(1).
Goals – League (64): Hughes 11 (2 pens), Hulse 10, Koumas 10, Horsfield 7, Dobie 5, Gaardsoe 4, Clement 2, Dyer 2, Johnson 2, Moore 2, Gregan 1, Haas 1, Kinsella 1, Sakiri 1, own goals 5.
Carling Cup (10): Hulse 3, Dobie 2, Haas 2, Clement 1, Hughes 1, own goal 1.
FA Cup (0).
Ground: The Hawthorns, West Bromwich B71 4LF. Telephone (0121) 525 8888.
Record Attendance: 64,815 v Arsenal, FA Cup 6th rd, 6 March 1937. **Capacity:** 28,000.
Manager: Gary Megson.
Secretary: Dr. John J. Evans BA, PHD. (Wales).
Most League Goals: 105, Division 2, 1929–30.
Highest League Scorer in Season: William 'Ginger' Richardson, 39, Division 1, 1935–36.
Most League Goals in Total Aggregate: Tony Brown, 218, 1963–79.
Most Capped Player: Stuart Williams, 33 (43), Wales.
Most League Appearances: Tony Brown, 574, 1963–80.
Honours – Football League: Division 1 Champions – 1919–20. Division 2 Champions – 1901–02, 1910–11. **FA Cup:** Winners 1888, 1892, 1931, 1954, 1968.
Football League Cup: Winners 1965–66.
Colours: Navy blue and white striped shirts, white shorts, navy blue stockings.

WEST HAM UNITED   FL CHAMPIONSHIP

Brevett Rufus (D)	5 8	11 13	Derby	24 9 69	Fulham
Bywater Steve (G)	6 2	12 00	Manchester	7 6 81	Trainee
Carrick Michael (M)	6 1	11 10	Wallsend	28 7 81	Trainee
Cohen Chris (D)	5 11	10 11	Norwich	5 3 87	Scholar
Cole Mitchell (M)			London	6 10 85	Trainee
Connolly David (F)	5 8	10 09	Willesden	6 6 77	Wimbledon
Dailly Christian (D)	6 0	12 10	Dundee	23 10 73	Blackburn R
Etherington Matthew (F)	5 9	10 12	Truro	14 8 81	Tottenham H
Ferdinand Anton (D)	6 0	11 00	Peckham	18 2 85	Trainee
Garcia Richard (F)	5 11	12 00	Perth	9 4 81	Trainee
Harewood Marlon (F)	6 1	13 07	Hampstead	25 8 79	Nottingham F
Horlock Kevin (M)	6 0	12 12	Erith	1 11 72	Manchester C
Hutchison Don (M)	6 1	11 08	Gateshead	9 5 71	Sunderland
Lomas Steve (M)	6 0	12 08	Hanover	14 3 72	Manchester C
McAnuff Jobi (M)	5 9	10 07	Edmonton	9 11 81	Wimbledon
Melville Andy (D)	6 1	12 13	Swansea	29 11 68	Fulham

Mullins Hayden (D)	6 0	11 12	Reading	27 3 79	Crystal Palace
Nowland Adam (M)	5 11	11 06	Preston	6 7 81	Wimbledon
Pearson Greg (F)			Birmingham	3 4 85	Trainee
Reo-Coker Nigel (M)	5 9	12 03	Southwark	14 5 84	Wimbledon
Repka Tomas (D)	6 0	12 04	Slavicin Zlin	2 1 74	Fiorentina
Sofiane Youssef (F)	5 8	11 00	Lyon	8 7 84	
Ward Elliott (D)			Harrow	19 1 85	Scholar
Zamora Bobby (F)	5 11	11 11	Barking	16 1 81	Tottenham H

League Appearances: Alexandersson, N. 5(3); Brevett, R. 2; Bywater, S. 17; Carole, S. (1); Carrick, M. 34(1); Cohen, C. 1(6); Connolly, D. 37(2); Dailly, C. 43; Deane, B. 9(17); Defoe, J. 19; Etherington, M. 34(1); Ferdinand, A. 9(11); Garcia, R. 2(5); Harewood, M. 28; Harley, J. 15; Horlock, K. 23(4); Hutchison, D. 10(14); James, D. 27; Kilgallon, M. 1(2); Lee, R. 12(4); Lomas, S. 5; McAnuff, J. 4(8); Mellor, N. 8(8); Melville, A. 11(3); Mullins, H. 27; Noble, D. (3); Nowland, A. 2(9); Pearce, I. 24; Quinn, W. 22; Reo-Coker, N. 13(2); Repka, T. 40; Sofiane, Y. (1); Srnicek, P. 2(1); Stockdale, R. 5(2); Zamora, B. 15(2).

Goals – League (67): Harewood 13 (3 pens), Defoe 11, Connolly 10 (2 pens), Deane 6, Etherington 5, Zamora 5, Hutchison 4, Dailly 2, Mellor 2, Reo-Coker 2, Carrick 1, Harley 1, Horlock 1, McAnuff 1, Pearce 1, own goals 2.

Carling Cup (6): Defoe 4 (1 pen), Connolly 2.

FA Cup (5): Connolly 2, Deane 1, Harewood 1, Mullins 1.

Play-Offs (2): Dailly 1, Etherington 1.

Ground: Boleyn Ground, Green Street, Upton Park, London E13 9AZ. Telephone (020) 8548 2748.

Record Attendance: 42,322 v Tottenham H, Division 1, 17 October 1970. **Capacity:** 35,056.

Manager: Alan Pardew.

Secretary: Peter Barnes.

Most League Goals: 101, Division 2, 1957–58.

Highest League Scorer in Season: Vic Watson, 42, Division 1, 1929–30.

Most League Goals in Total Aggregate: Vic Watson, 298, 1920–35.

Most Capped Player: Bobby Moore, 108, England.

Most League Appearances: Billy Bonds, 663, 1967–88.

Honours – Football League: Division 2 Champions – 1957–58, 1980–81. **FA Cup:** Winners 1964, 1975, 1980. **European Competitions: European Cup-Winners' Cup winners:** 1964–65. **Intertoto Cup winners:** 1999.

Colours: Sky blue shirts and shorts with claret trim, sky blue stockings.

WIGAN ATHLETIC   FL CHAMPIONSHIP

Baines Leighton (D)	5 8	11 10	Liverpool	11 12 84	
Breckin Ian (D)	6 2	13 05	Rotherham	24 2 75	Chesterfield
Bullard Jimmy (M)	5 10	11 07	Newham	23 10 78	Peterborough U
Dinning Tony (M)	6 0	13 00	Wallsend	12 4 75	Wolverhampton W
Eaden Nicky (D)	5 9	12 02	Sheffield	12 12 72	Birmingham C
Ellington Nathan (F)	5 10	13 01	Bradford	2 7 81	Bristol R
Filan John (G)	6 2	14 06	Sydney	8 2 70	Blackburn R
Flynn Mike (M)	5 10	12 10	Newport	17 10 80	Barry T
Jarrett Jason (M)	6 1	13 01	Bury	14 9 79	Bury
Mahon Alan (M)	5 8	11 10	Dublin	4 4 78	Blackburn R

McCulloch Lee (F)	6 1	13 00	Bellshill	14 5 78	Motherwell
McMillan Steve (D)	5 9	11 12	Edinburgh	19 1 76	Motherwell
Mitchell Paul (D)	5 9	11 12	Manchester	26 8 81	Scholar
Roberts Jason (F)	6 0	12 06	Park Royal	25 1 78	WBA
Roberts Neil (F)	5 10	12 08	Wrexham	7 4 78	Wrexham
Salisbury James (G)	6 1	13 00	Preston	10 3 84	Burnley
Teale Gary (F)	5 11	12 00	Glasgow	21 7 78	Ayr U
Vieira Magno (F)	5 9	11 00	Brazil	13 2 85	

League Appearances: Baines, L. 23(3); Breckin, I. 43(2); Bullard, J. 46; Burchill, M. 1(3); De Vos, J. 25(2); Dinning, T. 11(2); Eaden, N. 46; Ellington, N. 43(1); Farrelly, G. 3(4); Filan, J. 45; Flynn, M. 1(7); Horsfield, G. 16; Jackson, M. 23(1); Jarrett, J. 33(8); Kennedy, P. 10(2); Lawrence, J. (4); Liddell, A. 35(5); Mahon, A. 13(1); McCulloch, L. 31(10); McMillan, S. 13(2); Mitchell, P. 1(11); Roberts, J. 14; Roberts, N. 9(19); Rogers, A. 5; Teale, G. 15(13); Walsh, G. 1(2).
Goals – League (60): Ellington 18, Liddell 9 (3 pens), Roberts J 8, Horsfield 7, McCulloch 6, Bullard 2, De Vos 2, Roberts N 2, Teale 2, Jackson 1, Jarrett 1, Kennedy 1, Mahon 1.
Carling Cup (4): Bullard 1, Ellington 1, Jarrett 1, McCulloch 1.
FA Cup (1): own goal 1.
Ground: J. J. B. Stadium, Robin Park, Newtown, Wigan WN5 OU2. Telephone (01942) 774 000.
Record Attendance: 27,500 v Hereford U, FA Cup 2nd rd, 12 December 1953.
Capacity: 25,000
Manager: Paul Jewell.
Secretary: Stuart Hayton.
Most League Goals: 84, Division 3, 1996–97.
Highest League Scorer in Season: Graeme Jones, 31, Division 3, 1996–97.
Most League Goals in Total Aggregate: Andy Liddell, 70, 1998–2004.
Most Capped Player: Roy Carroll, 9 (14), Northern Ireland.
Most League Appearances: Kevin Langley, 317, 1981–86, 1990–94.
Honours – Football League: Division 2 Champions – 2002–03. Division 3 Champions – 1996–97. **Freight Rover Trophy:** Winners 1984–85. **Auto Windscreens Shield:** Winners 1998–99.
Colours: Blue shirts and shorts, white stockings.

WIMBLEDON (Now Milton Keynes Dons FC)
FL CHAMPIONSHIP 1

Chorley Ben (D)	6 3	13 02	Sidcup	30 9 82	Arsenal
Harding Ben (M)	5 10	11 02	Carshalton	6 9 84	Scholar
Herzig Nico (M)	5 10	11 00	Pobneck	10 12 83	Carl Zeiss Jena
Kamara Malvin (M)	5 11	13 07	London	17 11 83	Scholar
Lewington Dean (M)	5 11	11 02	London	18 5 84	Scholar
Mackie Jamie (F)	5 8	11 02	London	22 9 85	Leatherhead
Martin David (G)	6 1	13 07	Romford	22 1 86	Scholar
Small Wade (M)	5 7	11 07	Croydon	23 2 84	Scholar
Tapp Alex (M)	5 8	10 13	Redhill	7 6 82	Trainee

League Appearances: Agyemang, P. 23(3); Banks, S. 24; Barton, W. 5; Bevan, S. 10; Campbell-Ryce, J. 3(1); Chorley, B. 33(2); Darlington, J. 40(1); Gier, R. 24(1);

Gordon, M. 8(10); Gray, W. 20(13); Harding, B. 10(5); Hawkins, P. 16(2); Heald, P. 10; Herzig, N. 18(1); Holdsworth, D. 14(14); Holloway, D. 8(5); Jarrett, A. 3(6); Kamara, M. 15(12); Leigertwood, M. 27; Lewington, D. 28; Mackie, J. 8(5); Martin, D. 2; McAnuff, J. 25(2); McDonald, S. (2); McKoy, N. 1(2); Morgan, L. 2(1); Nowland, A. 24(1); Ntimban-Zeh, H. 9(1); Oyedele, S. 9; Puncheon, J. 6(2); Reo-Coker, N. 25; Small, W. 23(4); Smith, G. 10(1); Tapp, A. 12(2); Williams, M. 11; Worgan, L. (3).

Goals – League (41): Agyemang 7, McAnuff 5, Gray 4 (1 pen), Reo-Coker 4, Holdsworth 3 (1 pen), Nowland 3, Smith 3, Chorley 2, Kamara 2, Leigertwood 2, Darlington 1, Lewington 1, Small 1, Tapp 1, Williams 1, own goal 1.
Carling Cup (0).
FA Cup (2): Nowland 2.
Ground: The National Hockey Stadium, Silbury Boulevard, Central Milton Keynes, Buckinghamshire MK9 1FA. Telephone (01908) 607090.
Record Attendance: 30,115 v Manchester U, FA Premier **League**, 9 May 1993 (at Selhurst Park). **Capacity:** 8630.
Manager: Stuart Murdoch.
Secretary: Steve Rooke.
Most League Goals: 97, Division 3, 1983–84.
Highest League Scorer in Season: Alan Cork, 29, 1983–84.
Most League Goals in Total Aggregate: Alan Cork, 145, 1977–92.
Most Capped Player: Kenny Cunningham, 40 (57), Republic of Ireland.
Most League Appearances: Alan Cork, 430, 1977–92.
Honours – Football League: Division 4 Champions – 1982–83. **FA Cup:** Winners 1987–88.
Colours: All white with gold trim.

WOLVERHAMPTON WANDERERS
FL CHAMPIONSHIP

Andrews Keith (M)	6 0	13 05	Dublin	13 9 80	Trainee
Bonnar Thomas (M)			Letterkenny	20 10 85	Scholar
Camara Henri (F)	5 9	10 08	Dakar	10 5 77	Sedan
Cameron Colin (M)	5 8	11 00	Kirkcaldy	23 10 72	Hearts
Clarke Leon (F)	6 2	14 02	Birmingham	10 2 85	
Clingan Sammy (M)	5 11	11 06	Belfast	13 1 84	Scholar
Clyde Mark (D)	6 2	12 04	Limavady	27 12 82	Scholar
Cooper Kevin (M)	5 8	10 04	Derby	8 2 75	Wimbledon
Cort Carl (F)	6 4	12 07	Southwark	1 11 77	Newcastle U
Craddock Jody (D)	6 2	12 00	Bromsgrove	25 7 75	Sunderland
Flynn Patrick (M)			Dublin	13 1 85	Scholar
Gobern Lewis (M)			Birmingham	28 1 85	Scholar
Jones Paul (G)	6 3	15 02	Chirk	18 4 67	Southampton
Kennedy Mark (M)	5 11	11 09	Dublin	15 5 76	Manchester C
Lescott Jolean (D)	6 2	14 00	Birmingham	16 8 82	Trainee
Melligan John (M)	5 9	11 02	Dublin	11 2 82	Trainee
Miller Kenny (F)	5 10	11 04	Edinburgh	23 12 79	Rangers
Mulligan Gary (M)			Dublin	23 4 85	Scholar
Murray Matt (G)	6 4	13 10	Solihull	2 5 81	Trainee
Naylor Lee (D)	5 10	12 00	Bloxwich	19 3 80	Trainee
Newton Shaun (M)	5 8	11 00	Camberwell	20 8 75	Charlton Ath

O'Connor Kevin (M)			Dublin	19 10 85	Scholar
Oakes Michael (G)	6 2	14 00	Northwich	30 10 73	Aston Villa
Silas Jorge (M)	5 9	11 03	Lisbon	1 9 76	Uniao Leiria
Sturridge Dean (F)	5 8	12 02	Birmingham	27 7 73	Leicester C

League Appearances: Andrews, K. 1; Blake, N. 10(3); Butler, P. 37; Camara, H. 29(1); Cameron, C. 25(5); Clyde, M. 6(3); Cooper, K. (1); Cort, C. 13(3); Craddock, J. 31(1); Ganea, V. 6(10); Gudjonsson, J. 5(6); Ince, P. 32; Irwin, D. 30(2); Iversen, S. 11(5); Jones, P. 16; Kachloul, H. (4); Kennedy, M. 28(3); Luzhny, O. 4(2); Miller, K. 17(8); Murray, M. 1; Naylor, L. 37(1); Newton, S. 20(8); Oakes, M. 21; Oko-ronkwo, I. 7; Rae, A. 27(6); Silas, J. 2(7); Sturridge, D. 2(3).

Goals – League (38): Camara 7, Cort 5, Rae 5, Cameron 4 (1 pen), Iversen 4, Ganea 3, Ince 2, Kennedy 2, Miller 2, Blake 1, Butler 1, Craddock 1, own goal 1.

Carling Cup (5): Rae 2, Craddock 1, Gudjonsson 1, Miller 1.

FA Cup (4): Miller 2, Ganea 1, Rae 1.

Ground: Molineux Grounds, Wolverhampton WV1 4QR. Telephone (0870) 442 0123.

Record Attendance: 61,315 v Liverpool, FA Cup 5th rd, 11 February 1939.

Capacity: 28,666.

Manager: Dave Jones.

Secretary: Richard Skirrow.

Most League Goals: 115, Division 2, 1931–32.

Highest League Scorer in Season: Dennis Westcott, 38, Division 1, 1946–47.

Most League Goals in Total Aggregate: Steve Bull, 250, 1986–99.

Most Capped Player: Billy Wright, 105, England (70 consecutive).

Most League Appearances: Derek Parkin, 501, 1967–82.

Honours – Football League: Division 1 Champions – 1953–54, 1957–58, 1958–59. Division 2 Champions – 1931–32, 1976–77. Division 3 (N) Champions – 1923–24. Division 3 Champions – 1988–89. Division 4 Champions – 1987–88. **FA Cup:** Winners 1893, 1908, 1949, 1960. **Football League Cup:** Winners 1973–74, 1979–80. **Sherpa Van Trophy winners** 1988.

Colours: Gold shirts, black shorts, black stockings.

WREXHAM   FL CHAMPIONSHIP 1

Armstrong Chris (F)	6 0	13 03	Newcastle	19 6 71	Bolton W
Crowell Matt (M)	5 11	11 00	Bridgend	3 7 84	Southampton
Edwards Carlos (M)	5 11	11 01	Trinidad	24 10 78	
Ferguson Darren (M)	6 0	11 10	Glasgow	9 2 72	Wolverhampton W
Jones Mark (M)	5 11	10 12	Wrexham	15 8 83	Scholar
Llewellyn Chris (M)	6 0	11 06	Merthyr	29 8 79	Norwich C
Morgan Craig (D)	6 0	11 12	St Asaph	18 6 85	Scholar
Pejic Shaun (D)	6 0	11 07	Hereford	16 11 82	
Roberts Steve (D)	6 2	11 06	Wrexham	24 2 80	Trainee
Sam Hector (F)	5 9	11 05	Trinidad	25 2 78	San Juan Jabloteh

League Appearances: Armstrong, C. 19(7); Barrett, P. 19(8); Carey, B. 32(2); Crowell, M. 9(6); Dibble, A. 35; Edwards, C. 42; Edwards, P. 40(1); Ferguson, D. 39; Holmes, S. 3(10); Ingham, M. 11; Jones, L. 13(9); Jones, M. (13); Lawrence, D. 45; Llewellyn, C. 46; Mackin, L. 1; Morgan, C. 14(4); One, A. 2(1); Pejic, S. 20(1);

110

Roberts, S. 24(3); Sam, H. 24(13); Spender, S. 3(3); Thomas, S. 31(9); Whitfield, P. (2); Whitley, J. 34(2).

Goals – League (50): Sam 10, Llewellyn 8, Armstrong 5, Edwards C 5, Jones L 5 (2 pens), Lawrence 5, Barrett 2, Carey 2, Holmes 2, Thomas 2, Crowell 1, Ferguson 1, Jones M 1, own goal 1.

Carling Cup (0).

FA Cup (1): Armstrong 1.

LDV Vans Trophy (8): Jones L 3 (1 pen), Sam 2 (1 pen), Armstrong 1, Holmes 1, Jones M 1.

Ground: Racecourse Ground, Mold Road, Wrexham LL11 2AH. Telephone (01978) 262129.

Record Attendance: 34,445 v Manchester U, FA Cup 4th rd, 26 January 1957.

Capacity: 15,500.

Manager: Denis Smith.

Secretary: Bill Wingrove.

Most League Goals: 106, Division 3 (N), 1932–33.

Highest League Scorer in Season: Tom Bamford, 44, Division 3 (N), 1933–34.

Most League Goals in Total Aggregate: Tom Bamford, 175, 1928–34.

Most Capped Player: Joey Jones, 29 (72), Wales.

Most League Appearances: Arfon Griffiths, 592, 1959–61, 1962–79.

Honours – Football League: Division 3 Champions – 1977–78. **Welsh Cup:** Winners 22 times.

Colours: Red shirts, white shorts, red stockings.

WYCOMBE WANDERERS   FL CHAMPIONSHIP 2

Bloomfield Matt (M)	5 9	11 00	Ipswich	8	2 84	Ipswich T
Dixon Jonny (F)	5 9	11 01	Murcia	16	1 84	Scholar
Faulconbridge Craig (F)	6 1	13 00	Nuneaton	20	4 78	Wrexham
Harding Billy (F)	6 0	12 07	Carshalton	20	1 85	Scholar
Hole Stuart (D)	6 0	11 11	Oxford	17	7 85	Scholar
Johnson Roger (D)	6 3	11 00	Ashford	28	4 83	Trainee
Philo Mark (M)	5 11	11 05	Bracknell	5	10 84	Scholar
Reilly Andy (D)	5 10	12 08	Luton	26	10 85	Scholar
Ryan Keith (M)	5 10	12 06	Northampton	25	6 70	Berkhamsted T
Senda Danny (D)	5 10	10 02	Harrow	17	4 81	Southampton
Simpemba Ian (M)	6 2	12 08	Dublin	28	3 83	Scholar
Talia Frank (G)	6 1	13 06	Melbourne	20	7 72	Reading
Tyson Nathan (F)	5 10	10 02	Reading	4	5 82	Reading
Williams Steve (G)	6 6	13 10	Oxford	21	4 83	Scholar

League Appearances: Bell, A. 3(8); Bevan, S. 5; Bloomfield, M. 10(2); Branston, G. 9; Brown, S. 18(7); Bulman, D. 30(8); Cook, L. 1(4); Currie, D. 42; Dell, S. 3(1); Dixon, J. 2(6); Faulconbridge, C. 11(5); Harding, B. (2); Harris, R. 6(4); Henderson, W. 3; Hole, S. (1); Holligan, G. 8(5); Johnson, R. 28; Mapes, C. 10(5); Marshall, S. 8; McSporran, J. 29(4); Moore, L. 6; Nethercott, S. 22; Oliver, L. (2); Onuora, I. 6; Patterson, S. 3(1); Philo, M. 4(8); Reilly, A. 5; Roberts, S. 5(11); Rogers, M. 15; Ryan, K. 10(7); Senda, D. 37(3); Simpemba, I. 17(2); Simpson, M. 38; Talia, F. 17; Taylor, S. 6; Thomson, A. 11; Tyson, N. 21; Vinnicombe, C. 36; Williams, S. 19; Worgan, L. 2.

Goals – League (50): Tyson 9, Currie 7 (2 pens), McSporran 7, Moore 4, Bell 3, Mapes 3, Faulconbridge 2, Holligan 2, Johnson 2, Patterson 2, Simpemba 2, Simpson 2, Bloomfield 1, Brown 1 (pen), Nethercott 1, Ryan 1, Thomson 1.
Carling Cup (2): Harris 2.
FA Cup (7): McSporran 3, Currie 2, Holligan 1, Thomson 1.
LDV Vans Trophy (5): McSporran 2, Branston 1, Johnson 1, Thomson 1.
Ground: Adams Park, Hillbottom Road, Sands, High Wycombe HP12 4HJ. Telephone (01494) 472100.
Record Attendance: 9002 v West Ham U, FA Cup 3rd rd, 7 January 1995.
Capacity: 10,000 (7350 seats).
Manager: Tony Adams.
Secretary: Keith J. Allen.
Most League Goals: 67, Division 3, 1993–94.
Highest League Goalscorer in Season: Sean Devine, 23, 1999–2000.
Most League Goals in Total Aggregate: Dave Carroll, 41, 1993–2002.
Most Capped Player: Mark Rogers, 7, Canada.
Most League Appearances: Steve Brown, 371, 1994–2004.
Honours – GM Vauxhall Conference winners: 1993. **FA Trophy winners:** 1991, 1993.
Colours: Sky and navy blue quartered shirts, navy shorts, sky blue stockings.

YEOVIL TOWN   FL CHAMPIONSHIP 2

Name			Birthplace			Previous club
Collis Steve (G)	6 3	12 05	Barnet	18 3 81		Nottingham F
Elam Lee (M)	5 8	10 12	Bradford	24 9 76		
Gall Kevin (F)	5 9	10 08	Merthyr	4 2 82		Bristol R
Johnson Lee (M)	5 6	10 07	Newmarket	7 6 81		Brentford
Lindegaard Andy (F)	5 8	11 04	Taunton	10 9 80		
Lockwood Adam (D)	6 0	12 07	Wakefield	26 10 81		
Pluck Colin (D)	6 0	13 10	Edmonton	6 9 78		Morton
Reed Steve (D)	5 8	12 02	Barnstaple	18 6 85		
Skiverton Terry (D)	6 1	13 06	Mile End	26 6 75		Wycombe W
Terry Paul (M)	5 10	12 06	Barking	3 4 79		Dagenham & R
Way Darren (M)	5 6	10 00	Plymouth	21 11 79		
Weale Chris (G)	6 2	13 03	Yeovil	9 2 82		
Weatherstone Simon (F)	5 10	12 00	Reading	26 1 80		Boston U
Williams Gavin (M)	5 10	11 05	Merthyr	20 6 80		

League Appearances: Bishop, A. 4(1); Bull, R. 7; Collis, S. 11; Crittenden, N. 20(9); Edwards, J. 17(10); El Kholti, A. 19(4); Elam, L. 6(6); Gall, K. 39(4); Giles, C. (1); Gosling, J. 4(8); Jackson, K. 19(11); Johnson, L. 45; Lindegaard, A. 12(11); Lockwood, A. 43; Matthews, L. 2(2); O'Brien, R. 13; Pluck, C. 36; Reed, S. 3(2); Rodrigues, D. 3(1); Rodrigues, H. 23(11); Skiverton, T. 25(1); Stansfield, A. 7(25); Talbott, N. (1); Terry, P. 22(12); Way, D. 38(1); Weale, C. 35; Weatherstone, S. 11(4); Williams, G. 42.
Goals – League (70): Williams 9 (3 pens), Gall 8, Edwards 6, Stansfield 6, Jackson 5, Johnson 5 (1 pen), Way 5, Lockwood 4, Pluck 4, Rodrigues D 4, Bishop 2, Crittenden 2, Lindegaard 2, Skiverton 2, El Kholti 1, Elam 1, Gosling 1, Rodrigues H 1, Terry 1, Weatherstone 1.
Carling Cup (1): own goal 1.
FA Cup (9): Williams 3 (1 pen), Edwards 2, Pluck 2, Crittenden 1, Gall 1.
LDV Vans Trophy (4): Edwards 2, Gall 1, Williams 1 (pen).

Ground: Huish Park, Lufton Way, Yeovil, Somerset, BA22 8YF. Telephone (01935) 423662.
Record Attendance: 8612 v Arsenal, FA Cup 3rd rd, 2 January 1993 (16,318 v Sunderland at Huish). **Capacity:** 9564.
Manager: Gary Johnson.
Secretary: Jean Cotton.
Most League Goals: 70, Division 3, 2003–04.
Colours: Green and white hooped shirts, white shorts, white stockings.

YORK CITY   CONFERENCE NATIONAL

Brass Chris (M)	5 10	11 13	Easington	24	7 75	Burnley
Bullock Lee (M)	6 0	13 00	Stockton	22	5 81	Trainee
Dunning Darren (M)	5 7	11 12	Scarborough	8	1 81	Blackburn R
Merris Dave (D)	5 7	10 06	Rotherham	13 10 80		Harrogate T
Nogan Lee (F)	5 10	11 08	Cardiff	21	5 69	Darlington
Porter Chris (G)	6 2	12 10	Middlesbrough	10 11 79		Darlington

League Appearances: Arthur, A. 2(1); Ashcroft, K. 1(1); Bell, A. 3(7); Brackstone, S. 4(5); Brass, C. 39; Browne, G. 2(4); Bullock, L. 34(1); Coad, M. (3); Cooper, R. 26(11); Crowe, D. 2(3); Davies, S. 6(2); Dickman, J. 2; Dove, C. 1; Downes, S. 4(2); Dunning, D. 42; Edmondson, D. 26(1); Fox, C. 2(3); George, L. 14(8); Haw, R. (1); Hope, R. 36; Law, G. 2(2); Merris, D. 42(2); Newby, J. 6(1); Nogan, L. 38(1); Offiong, R. 2(2); Ovendale, M. 41; Parkin, J. 9(6); Porter, C. 5; Shaw, J. 5(3); Smith, C. 26(2); Stewart, B. 2(8); Walker, J. 7(2); Ward, M. 27(4); Wilford, A. 4(2); Wise, S. 18(1); Wood, L. 21(5); Yalcin, L. 5(10).
Goals – League (35): Nogan 8, Bullock 7, Dunning 3 (1 pen), George 3, Brackstone 2, Cooper 2, Hope 2, Parkin 2, Wilford 2, Bell 1, Brass 1, Edmondson 1, Wise 1.
Carling Cup (1): Morris 1.
FA Cup (1): Nogan 1.
LDV Vans Trophy (1): Dunning 1 (pen).
Ground: Bootham Crescent, York YO3 7AQ. Telephone (01904) 624447.
Record Attendance: 28,123 v Huddersfield T, FA Cup 6th rd, 5 March 1938.
Capacity: 9496.
Manager: Chris Brass.
Secretary: Keith Usher.
Most League Goals: 96, Division 4, 1983–84.
Highest League Scorer in Season: Bill Fenton, 31, Division 3 (N), 1951–52; Arthur Bottom, 31, Division 3 (N), 1954–55 and 1955–56.
Most League Goals in Total Aggregate: Norman Wilkinson, 125, 1954–66.
Most Capped Player: Peter Scott, 7 (10), Northern Ireland.
Most League Appearances: Barry Jackson, 481, 1958–70.
Honours – Football League: Division 4 Champions – 1983–84.
Colours: Red shirts, navy shorts, navy stockings.

LEAGUE POSITIONS: FA PREMIER from 1992–93 and DIVISION 1 1978–79 to 1991–92

	2002-03	2001-02	2000-01	1999-2000	1998-99	1997-98	1996-97	1995-96	1994-95	1993-94	1992-93	1991-92	1990-91
Arsenal	2	1	2	2	2	1	3	5	12	4	10	4	1
Aston Villa	16	8	8	6	6	7	5	4	18	10	2	7	17
Barnsley	–	–	–	–	–	19	–	–	–	–	–	–	–
Birmingham C	13	–	–	–	–	–	–	–	–	–	–	–	–
Blackburn R	6	10	–	–	19	6	13	7	1	2	4	–	–
Bolton W	17	16	–	–	–	18	–	20	–	–	–	–	–
Bradford C	–	–	20	17	–	–	–	–	–	–	–	–	–
Brighton & HA	–	–	–	–	–	–	–	–	–	–	–	–	–
Bristol C	–	–	–	–	–	–	–	–	–	–	–	–	–
Charlton Ath	12	14	9	–	18	–	–	–	–	–	–	–	–
Chelsea	4	6	6	5	3	4	6	11	11	14	11	14	11
Coventry C	–	–	19	14	15	11	17	16	16	11	15	19	16
Crystal Palace	–	–	–	–	–	–	–	19	–	20	10	3	
Derby Co	–	19	17	16	8	9	12	–	–	–	–	–	20
Everton	7	15	16	13	14	17	15	6	15	17	13	12	9
Fulham	14	13	–	–	–	–	–	–	–	–	–	–	–
Ipswich T	–	18	5	–	–	–	–	–	22	19	16	–	–
Leeds U	15	5	4	3	4	5	11	13	5	5	17	1	4
Leicester C	–	20	13	8	10	10	9	–	21	–	–	–	–
Liverpool	5	2	3	4	7	3	4	3	4	8	6	6	2
Luton T	–	–	–	–	–	–	–	–	–	–	–	20	18
Manchester C	9	–	18	–	–	–	–	18	17	16	9	5	5
Manchester U	1	3	1	1	1	2	1	1	2	1	1	2	6
Middlesbrough	11	12	14	12	9	–	19	12	–	–	21	–	–
Millwall	–	–	–	–	–	–	–	–	–	–	–	–	–
Newcastle U	3	4	11	11	13	13	2	2	6	3	–	–	–
Norwich C	–	–	–	–	–	–	–	–	20	12	3	18	15
Nottingham F	–	–	–	20	–	20	9	3	–	–	22	8	8
Notts Co	–	–	–	–	–	–	–	–	–	–	–	21	–
Oldham Ath	–	–	–	–	–	–	–	–	21	19	17	–	–
Oxford U	–	–	–	–	–	–	–	–	–	–	–	–	–
Portsmouth	–	–	–	–	–	–	–	–	–	–	–	–	–
QPR	–	–	–	–	–	–	–	19	8	9	5	11	12
Sheffield U	–	–	–	–	–	–	–	–	–	20	14	9	13
Sheffield W	–	–	19	12	16	7	15	13	7	7	3	–	–
Southampton	8	11	10	15	17	12	16	17	10	18	18	16	14
Stoke C	–	–	–	–	–	–	–	–	–	–	–	–	–
Sunderland	20	17	7	7	–	18	–	–	–	–	–	–	19
Swansea C	–	–	–	–	–	–	–	–	–	–	–	–	–
Swindon T	–	–	–	–	–	–	–	–	–	22	–	–	–
Tottenham H	10	9	12	10	11	14	10	8	7	15	8	15	10
Watford	–	–	–	20	–	–	–	–	–	–	–	–	–
WBA	19	–	–	–	–	–	–	–	–	–	–	–	–
West Ham U	18	7	15	9	5	8	14	10	14	13	–	22	–
Wimbledon	–	–	–	18	16	15	8	14	9	6	12	13	7
Wolv'hampton W	–	–	–	–	–	–	–	–	–	–	–	–	–

1989–90	1988–89	1987–88	1986–87	1985–86	1984–85	1983–84	1982–83	1981–82	1980–81	1979–80	1978–79	
4	1	6	4	7	7	6	10	5	3	4	7	Arsenal
2	17	–	22	16	10	10	6	11	1	7	8	Aston Villa
–	–	–	–	–	–	–	–	–	–	–	–	Barnsley
–	–	–	–	21	–	20	17	16	13	–	21	Birmingham C
–	–	–	–	–	–	–	–	–	–	–	–	Blackburn R
–	–	–	–	–	–	–	–	–	22	17	–	Bolton W
–	–	–	–	–	–	–	–	–	–	–	–	Bradford C
–	–	–	–	–	–	–	22	13	19	16	–	Brighton & HA
–	–	–	–	–	–	–	–	–	–	20	13	Bristol C
19	14	17	19	–	–	–	–	–	–	–	–	Charlton Ath
5	–	18	14	6	6	–	–	–	–	–	22	Chelsea
12	7	10	10	17	18	19	19	14	16	15	10	Coventry C
15	–	–	–	–	–	–	–	–	22	13	–	Crystal Palace
16	5	15	–	–	–	–	–	–	–	21	19	Derby Co
6	8	4	1	2	1	7	7	8	15	19	4	Everton
–	–	–	–	–	–	–	–	–	–	–	–	Fulham
–	–	–	–	20	17	12	9	2	2	3	6	Ipswich T
–	–	–	–	–	–	–	–	20	9	11	5	Leeds U
–	–	–	20	19	15	15	–	–	21	–	–	Leicester C
1	2	1	2	1	2	1	1	1	5	1	1	Liverpool
17	16	9	7	9	13	16	18	–	–	–	–	Luton T
14	–	–	21	15	–	–	20	10	12	17	15	Manchester C
13	11	2	11	4	4	4	3	3	8	2	9	Manchester U
–	18	–	–	–	–	–	–	22	14	9	12	Middlesbrough
20	10	–	–	–	–	–	–	–	–	–	–	Millwall
–	20	8	17	11	14	–	–	–	–	–	–	Newcastle U
10	4	14	5	–	20	14	14	–	20	12	16	Norwich C
9	3	3	8	8	9	3	5	12	7	5	2	Nottingham F
–	–	–	–	–	–	21	15	15	–	–	–	Notts Co
–	–	–	–	–	–	–	–	–	–	–	–	Oldham Ath
–	–	21	18	18	–	–	–	–	–	–	–	Oxford U
–	–	19	–	–	–	–	–	–	–	–	–	Portsmouth
11	9	5	16	13	19	5	–	–	–	–	20	QPR
–	–	–	–	–	–	–	–	–	–	–	–	Sheffield U
18	15	11	13	5	8	–	–	–	–	–	–	Sheffield W
7	13	12	12	14	5	2	12	7	6	8	14	Southampton
–	–	–	–	–	22	18	13	18	11	18	–	Stoke C
–	–	–	–	–	21	13	16	19	17	–	–	Sunderland
–	–	–	–	–	–	21	6	–	–	–	–	Swansea C
–	–	–	–	–	–	–	–	–	–	–	–	Swindon T
3	6	13	3	10	3	8	4	4	10	14	11	Tottenham H
–	–	20	9	12	11	11	2	–	–	–	–	Watford
–	–	–	–	22	12	17	11	17	4	10	3	WBA
–	19	16	15	3	16	9	8	9	–	–	–	West Ham U
8	12	7	6	–	–	–	–	–	–	–	–	Wimbledon
–	–	–	–	–	–	22	–	21	18	6	18	Wolv'hampton W

LEAGUE POSITIONS: DIVISION 1 from 1992–93 and DIVISION 2 1978–79 to 1991–92

	2002-03	2001-02	2000-01	1999-2000	1998-99	1997-98	1996-97	1995-96	1994-95	1993-94	1992-93	1991-92	1990-91
Aston Villa	–	–	–	–	–	–	–	–	–	–	–	–	–
Barnsley	–	23	16	4	13	–	2	10	6	18	13	16	8
Birmingham C	–	5	5	5	4	7	10	15	–	22	19	–	–
Blackburn R	–	–	2	11	–	–	–	–	–	–	–	6	19
Blackpool	–	–	–	–	–	–	–	–	–	–	–	–	–
Bolton W	–	–	3	6	6	–	1	–	3	14	–	–	–
Bournemouth	–	–	–	–	–	–	–	–	–	–	–	–	–
Bradford C	19	15	–	–	2	13	21	–	–	–	–	–	–
Brentford	–	–	–	–	–	–	–	–	–	–	22	–	–
Brighton & HA	23	–	–	–	–	–	–	–	–	–	–	23	6
Bristol C	–	–	–	24	–	–	–	–	23	13	15	17	9
Bristol R	–	–	–	–	–	–	–	–	–	24	13	13	–
Burnley	16	7	7	–	–	–	–	–	–	22	–	–	–
Bury	–	–	–	–	22	17	–	–	–	–	–	–	–
Cambridge U	–	–	–	–	–	–	–	–	–	–	23	5	–
Cardiff C	–	–	–	–	–	–	–	–	–	–	–	–	–
Carlisle U	–	–	–	–	–	–	–	–	–	–	–	–	–
Charlton Ath	–	–	–	1	–	4	15	6	15	11	12	7	16
Chelsea	–	–	–	–	–	–	–	–	–	–	–	–	–
Coventry C	20	11	–	–	–	–	–	–	–	–	–	–	–
Crewe Alex	–	22	14	19	18	11	–	–	–	–	–	–	–
Crystal Palace	14	10	21	15	14	–	6	3	–	1	–	–	–
Derby Co	18	–	–	–	–	–	–	2	9	6	8	3	–
Fulham	–	–	1	9	–	–	–	–	–	–	–	–	–
Gillingham	11	12	13	–	–	–	–	–	–	–	–	–	–
Grimsby T	24	19	18	20	11	–	22	17	10	16	9	19	–
Huddersfield T	–	–	22	8	10	16	20	8	–	–	–	–	–
Hull C	–	–	–	–	–	–	–	–	–	–	–	–	24
Ipswich T	7	–	–	3	3	5	4	7	–	–	–	1	14
Leeds U	–	–	–	–	–	–	–	–	–	–	–	–	–
Leicester C	2	–	–	–	–	–	–	5	–	4	6	4	22
Leyton Orient	–	–	–	–	–	–	–	–	–	–	–	–	–
Luton T	–	–	–	–	–	–	–	24	16	20	20	–	–
Manchester C	–	1	–	2	–	22	14	–	–	–	–	–	–
Mansfield T	–	–	–	–	–	–	–	–	–	–	–	–	–
Middlesbrough	–	–	–	–	2	–	–	–	1	9	–	2	7
Millwall	9	4	–	–	–	–	–	22	12	3	7	15	5
Newcastle U	–	–	–	–	–	–	–	–	–	–	1	20	11
Norwich C	8	6	15	12	9	15	13	16	–	–	–	–	–
Nottingham F	6	16	11	14	–	1	–	–	–	2	–	–	–
Notts Co	–	–	–	–	–	–	–	–	24	7	17	–	4
Oldham Ath	–	–	–	–	–	–	23	18	14	–	–	–	1
Oxford U	–	–	–	–	23	12	17	–	–	23	14	21	10
Peterborough U	–	–	–	–	–	–	–	–	–	24	10	–	–
Plymouth Arg	–	–	–	–	–	–	–	–	–	–	–	22	18
Port Vale	–	–	–	23	21	19	8	12	17	–	–	24	15
Portsmouth	1	17	20	18	19	20	7	21	18	17	3	9	17
Preston NE	12	8	4	–	–	–	–	–	–	–	–	–	–
QPR	–	–	23	10	20	21	9	–	–	–	–	–	–

1989-90	1988-89	1987-88	1986-87	1985-86	1984-85	1983-84	1982-83	1981-82	1980-81	1979-80	1978-79	
–	–	2	–	–	–	–	–	–	–	–	–	Aston Villa
19	7	14	11	12	11	14	10	6	–	–	–	Barnsley
–	23	19	19	–	2	–	–	–	–	3	–	Birmingham C
5	5	5	12	19	5	6	11	10	4	–	22	Blackburn R
–	–	–	–	–	–	–	–	–	–	–	–	Blackpool
–	–	–	–	–	–	–	22	19	18	–	–	Bolton W
22	12	17	–	–	–	–	–	–	–	–	–	Bournemouth
23	14	4	10	13	–	–	–	–	–	–	–	Bradford C
–	–	–	–	–	–	–	–	–	–	–	–	Brentford
18	19	–	22	11	6	9	–	–	–	–	2	Brighton & HA
–	–	–	–	–	–	–	–	–	21	–	–	Bristol C
–	–	–	–	–	–	–	–	–	22	19	16	Bristol R
–	–	–	–	–	–	–	21	–	–	21	13	Burnley
–	–	–	–	–	–	–	–	–	–	–	–	Bury
–	–	–	–	–	–	22	12	14	13	8	12	Cambridge U
–	–	–	–	–	21	15	–	20	19	15	9	Cardiff C
–	–	–	20	16	7	14	–	–	–	–	–	Carlisle U
–	–	–	–	2	17	13	17	13	–	22	19	Charlton Ath
–	1	–	–	–	–	1	18	12	12	4	–	Chelsea
–	–	–	–	–	–	–	–	–	–	–	–	Coventry C
–	–	–	–	–	–	–	–	–	–	–	–	Crewe Alex
–	3	6	6	5	15	18	15	15	–	–	1	Crystal Palace
–	–	–	1	–	20	13	16	6	–	–	–	Derby Co
–	–	–	–	22	9	11	4	–	20	10	–	Fulham
–	–	–	–	–	–	–	–	–	–	–	–	Gillingham
–	–	–	21	15	10	5	19	17	7	–	–	Grimsby T
–	–	23	17	16	13	12	–	–	–	–	–	Huddersfield T
14	21	15	14	6	–	–	–	–	–	–	–	Hull C
9	8	8	5	–	–	–	–	–	–	–	–	Ipswich T
1	10	7	4	14	7	10	8	–	–	–	–	Leeds U
13	15	13	–	–	–	–	3	8	–	1	17	Leicester C
–	–	–	–	–	–	–	–	22	17	14	11	Leyton Orient
–	–	–	–	–	–	–	–	1	5	6	18	Luton T
–	2	9	–	–	3	4	–	–	–	–	–	Manchester C
–	–	–	–	–	–	–	–	–	–	–	–	Mansfield T
21	–	3	–	21	19	17	16	–	–	–	–	Middlesbrough
–	–	1	16	9	–	–	–	–	–	–	21	Millwall
3	–	–	–	–	–	3	5	9	11	9	8	Newcastle U
–	–	–	–	1	–	–	–	3	–	–	–	Norwich C
–	–	–	–	–	–	–	–	–	–	–	–	Nottingham F
–	–	–	–	–	20	–	–	–	2	17	6	Notts Co
8	16	10	3	8	14	19	7	11	15	11	14	Oldham Ath
17	17	–	–	–	1	–	–	–	–	–	–	Oxford U
–	–	–	–	–	–	–	–	–	–	–	–	Peterborough U
16	18	16	7	–	–	–	–	–	–	–	–	Plymouth Arg
11	–	–	–	–	–	–	–	–	–	–	–	Port Vale
12	20	–	2	4	4	16	–	–	–	–	–	Portsmouth
–	–	–	–	–	–	–	–	–	20	10	7	Preston NE
–	–	–	–	–	–	–	1	5	8	5	–	QPR

LEAGUE POSITIONS: DIVISION 1 from 1992–93 and DIVISION 2 1978–79 to 1991–92 (cont.)

	2002-03	2001-02	2000-01	1999-2000	1998-99	1997-98	1996-97	1995-96	1994-95	1993-94	1992-93	1991-92	1990-91
Reading	4	–	–	–	–	24	18	19	2	–	–	–	–
Rotherham U	15	21	–	–	–	–	–	–	–	–	–	–	–
Sheffield U	3	13	10	16	8	6	5	9	8	–	–	–	–
Sheffield W	22	20	17	–	–	–	–	–	–	–	–	–	3
Shrewsbury T	–	–	–	–	–	–	–	–	–	–	–	–	–
Southampton	–	–	–	–	–	–	–	–	–	–	–	–	–
Southend U	–	–	–	–	–	–	24	14	13	15	18	12	–
Stockport Co	–	24	19	17	16	8	–	–	–	–	–	–	–
Stoke C	21	–	–	–	–	23	12	4	11	10	–	–	–
Sunderland	–	–	–	–	1	3	–	1	20	12	21	18	–
Swansea C	–	–	–	–	–	–	–	–	–	–	–	–	–
Swindon T	–	–	–	24	17	18	19	–	21	–	5	8	21
Tottenham H	–	–	–	–	–	–	–	–	–	–	–	–	–
Tranmere R	–	–	24	13	15	14	11	13	5	5	4	14	–
Walsall	17	18	–	22	–	–	–	–	–	–	–	–	–
Watford	13	14	9	–	5	–	23	7	19	16	10	20	–
WBA	–	2	6	21	12	10	16	11	19	21	–	–	23
West Ham U	–	–	–	–	–	–	–	–	–	–	2	–	2
Wimbledon	10	9	8	–	–	–	–	–	–	–	–	–	–
Wolv'hampton W	5	3	12	7	7	9	3	20	4	8	11	11	12
Wrexham	–	–	–	–	–	–	–	–	–	–	–	–	–

LEAGUE POSITIONS: DIVISION 2 from 1992–93 and DIVISION 3 1978–79 to 1991–92

	2002-03	2001-02	2000-01	1999-2000	1998-99	1997-98	1996-97	1995-96	1994-95	1993-94	1992-93	1991-92	1990-91
Aldershot	–	–	–	–	–	–	–	–	–	–	–	–	–
Barnet	–	–	–	–	–	–	–	–	–	–	24	–	–
Barnsley	19	–	–	–	–	–	–	–	–	–	–	–	–
Birmingham C	–	–	–	–	–	–	–	–	1	–	–	2	12
Blackburn R	–	–	–	–	–	–	–	–	–	–	–	–	–
Blackpool	12	16	–	22	14	12	7	3	12	20	18	–	–
Bolton W	–	–	–	–	–	–	–	–	–	–	2	13	4
Bournemouth	–	21	7	16	7	9	16	14	19	17	17	8	9
Bradford C	–	–	–	–	–	–	–	6	14	7	10	16	8
Brentford	16	3	14	17	–	21	4	15	2	16	–	1	6
Brighton & HA	–	1	–	–	–	–	–	23	16	14	9	–	–
Bristol C	3	7	9	9	–	2	5	13	–	–	–	–	–
Bristol R	–	–	21	7	13	5	17	10	4	8	–	–	–
Burnley	–	–	–	2	15	20	9	17	–	6	13	–	–
Bury	–	22	16	15	–	–	1	–	–	–	–	21	7
Cambridge U	–	24	19	19	–	–	–	–	20	10	–	–	1

1989–90	1988–89	1987–88	1986–87	1985–86	1984–85	1983–84	1982–83	1981–82	1980–81	1979–80	1978–79	
–	–	22	13	–	–	–	20	7	–	–	–	Reading
–	–	–	–	–	–	–	20	7	–	–	–	Rotherham U
2	–	21	9	7	18	–	–	–	–	–	20	Sheffield U
–	–	–	–	–	2	6	4	10	–	–	–	Sheffield W
–	22	18	18	17	8	8	9	18	14	13	–	Shrewsbury T
–	–	–	–	–	–	–	–	–	–	–	–	Southampton
–	–	–	–	–	–	–	–	–	–	–	–	Southend U
–	–	–	–	–	–	–	–	–	–	–	–	Stockport Co
24	13	11	8	10	–	–	–	–	–	–	3	Stoke C
6	11	–	20	18	–	–	–	–	–	2	4	Sunderland
–	–	–	–	–	21	–	–	3	12	–	–	Swansea C
4	6	12	–	–	–	–	–	–	–	–	–	Swindon T
–	–	–	–	–	–	–	–	–	–	–	–	Tottenham H
–	–	–	–	–	–	–	–	–	–	–	–	Tranmere R
–	24	–	–	–	–	–	–	–	–	–	–	Walsall
15	4	–	–	–	–	–	–	2	9	18	–	Watford
20	9	20	15	–	–	–	–	–	–	–	–	WBA
7	–	–	–	–	–	–	–	–	1	7	5	West Ham U
–	–	–	3	12	–	–	–	–	–	–	–	Wimbledon
10	–	–	–	22	–	2	–	–	–	–	–	Wolv'hampton W
–	–	–	–	–	–	–	–	21	16	16	15	Wrexham

1989–90	1988–89	1987–88	1986–87	1985–86	1984–85	1983–84	1982–83	1981–82	1980–81	1979–80	1978–79	
–	24	20	–	–	–	–	–	–	–	–	–	Aldershot
–	–	–	–	–	–	–	–	–	–	–	–	Barnet
–	–	–	–	–	–	–	–	2	11	–	–	Barnsley
7	–	–	–	–	–	–	–	–	–	–	–	Birmingham C
–	–	–	–	–	–	–	–	–	2	–	–	Blackburn R
23	19	10	9	12	–	–	–	–	23	18	12	Blackpool
6	10	–	21	18	17	10	–	–	–	–	–	Bolton W
–	–	–	1	15	10	17	14	–	–	–	–	Bournemouth
–	–	–	–	–	1	7	12	–	–	–	–	Bradford C
13	7	12	11	10	13	20	9	8	9	19	10	Brentford
–	–	2	–	–	–	–	–	–	–	–	–	Brighton & HA
2	11	5	6	9	5	–	–	23	–	–	–	Bristol C
1	5	8	19	16	6	5	7	15	–	–	–	Bristol R
–	–	–	–	21	12	–	1	8	–	–	–	Burnley
5	13	14	16	20	–	–	–	–	–	21	19	Bury
–	–	–	–	–	24	–	–	–	–	–	–	Cambridge U

LEAGUE POSITIONS: DIVISION 2 from 1992–93 and DIVISION 3 1978–79 to 1991–92 (cont.)

	2002-03	2001-02	2000-01	1999-2000	1998-99	1997-98	1996-97	1995-96	1994-95	1993-94	1992-93	1991-92	1990-91
Cardiff C	6	4	–	21	–	–	–	–	22	19	–	–	–
Carlisle U	–	–	–	–	23	–	21	–	–	–	–	–	–
Charlton Ath													
Cheltenham T	21	–	–	–	–	–	–	–	–	–	–	–	–
Chester C	–	–	–	–	–	–	–	–	23	–	24	18	19
Chesterfield	20	18	–	24	9	10	10	7	–	–	–	–	–
Colchester U	12	15	17	18	18	–	–	–	–	–	–	–	–
Crewe Alex	2	–	–	–	–	–	6	5	3	–	–	–	22
Crystal Palace													
Darlington	–	–	–	–	–	–	–	–	–	–	–	24	–
Derby Co													
Doncaster R													
Exeter C	–	–	–	–	–	–	–	–	–	22	19	20	16
Fulham	–	–	–	–	1	6	–	–	–	21	12	9	21
Gillingham	–	–	–	3	4	8	11	–	–	–	–	–	–
Grimsby T	–	–	–	–	–	3	–	–	–	–	–	3	–
Halifax T													
Hartlepool U	–	–	–	–	–	–	–	–	–	23	16	11	–
Hereford U													
Huddersfield T	22	6	–	–	–	–	–	–	5	11	15	3	11
Hull C	–	–	–	–	–	–	–	24	8	9	20	14	–
Leyton Orient	–	–	–	–	–	–	–	–	24	18	7	10	13
Lincoln C	–	–	–	–	23	–	–	–	–	–	–	–	–
Luton T	9	–	22	13	12	17	3	–	–	–	–	–	–
Macclesfield T	–	–	–	–	24	–	–	–	–	–	–	–	–
Manchester C	–	–	–	–	3	–	–	–	–	–	–	–	–
Mansfield T	23	–	–	–	–	–	–	–	–	–	22	–	24
Middlesbrough													
Millwall	–	–	1	5	10	18	14	–	–	–	–	–	–
Newport Co													
Northampton T	24	20	18	–	22	4	–	–	–	–	–	–	–
Notts Co	15	19	8	8	16	–	24	4	–	–	–	–	–
Oldham Ath	5	9	15	14	20	13	–	–	–	–	–	–	–
Oxford U	–	–	24	20	–	–	–	2	7	–	–	–	–
Peterborough U	11	17	12	–	–	–	21	19	15	–	–	6	–
Plymouth Arg	8	–	–	–	–	22	19	–	21	3	14	–	–
Portsmouth													
Port Vale	17	14	11	–	–	–	–	–	–	2	3	–	–
Preston NE	–	–	–	1	5	15	15	–	–	–	21	17	17
QPR	4	8	–	–	–	–	–	–	–	–	–	–	–
Reading	–	2	3	10	11	–	–	–	–	–	1	8	12	15
Rochdale													
Rotherham U	–	–	2	–	–	–	23	16	17	15	11	–	23
Scunthorpe U	–	–	–	23	–	–	–	–	–	–	–	–	–
Sheffield U													
Sheffield W													
Shrewsbury T	–	–	–	–	–	22	18	18	–	–	–	22	18
Southend U	–	–	–	–	–	24	–	–	–	–	–	–	2
Stockport Co	14	–	–	–	–	–	2	9	11	4	6	5	–
Stoke C	–	5	5	6	8	–	–	–	–	–	1	4	14

	1989-90	1988-89	1987-88	1986-87	1985-86	1984-85	1983-84	1982-83	1981-82	1980-81	1979-80	1978-79
Cardiff C	21	16	–	–	22	–	–	2	–	–	–	–
Carlisle U	–	–	22	–	–	–	–	2	19	6	6	–
Charlton Ath	–	–	–	–	–	–	–	–	–	3	–	–
Cheltenham T	–	–	–	–	–	–	–	–	–	–	–	–
Chester C	16	8	15	15	–	–	–	–	24	18	9	16
Chesterfield	–	22	18	17	17	–	–	24	11	5	4	20
Colchester U	–	–	–	–	–	–	–	–	–	22	5	7
Crewe Alex	12	–	–	–	–	–	–	–	–	–	–	–
Crystal Palace	–	–	–	–	–	–	–	–	–	–	–	–
Darlington	–	–	–	22	13	–	–	–	–	–	–	–
Derby Co	–	–	–	–	3	7	–	–	–	–	–	–
Doncaster R	–	–	24	13	11	14	–	23	19	–	–	–
Exeter C	–	–	–	–	–	24	19	18	11	8	9	–
Fulham	20	4	9	18	–	–	–	–	3	13	–	–
Gillingham	–	23	13	5	5	4	8	13	6	15	16	4
Grimsby T	–	22	–	–	–	–	–	–	–	–	1	–
Halifax T	–	–	–	–	–	–	–	–	–	–	–	–
Hartlepool U	–	–	–	–	–	–	–	–	–	–	–	–
Hereford U	–	–	–	–	–	–	–	–	–	–	–	–
Huddersfield T	8	14	–	–	–	–	–	3	17	4	–	–
Hull C	–	–	–	–	–	3	4	–	–	24	20	8
Leyton Orient	14	–	–	–	22	11	20	–	–	–	–	–
Lincoln C	–	–	–	21	19	14	6	4	–	–	–	24
Luton T	–	–	–	–	–	–	–	–	–	–	–	–
Macclesfield T	–	–	–	–	–	–	–	–	–	–	–	–
Manchester C	–	–	–	–	–	–	–	–	–	–	–	–
Mansfield T	15	15	19	10	–	–	–	–	–	–	23	18
Middlesbrough	–	–	–	2	–	–	–	–	–	–	–	–
Millwall	–	–	–	–	2	9	17	9	16	14	–	–
Newport Co	22	20	6	–	–	–	–	–	–	–	–	–
Northampton T	3	9	4	7	8	–	–	–	–	–	–	–
Notts Co	–	–	–	–	–	–	–	–	–	–	–	–
Oldham Ath	–	–	–	–	–	1	5	5	14	17	11	–
Oxford U	–	–	–	–	–	–	–	–	–	–	–	21
Peterborough U	–	–	–	2	15	19	8	10	7	15	15	–
Plymouth Arg	–	–	–	–	–	–	1	13	6	–	–	–
Portsmouth	–	3	11	12	–	–	23	–	–	–	–	–
Port Vale	19	6	16	–	23	16	16	14	–	–	–	–
Preston NE	–	–	–	–	–	–	–	–	–	–	–	–
QPR	10	18	–	1	9	–	21	12	10	7	–	–
Reading	–	–	–	–	–	–	–	–	–	–	–	–
Rochdale	9	–	21	14	14	12	18	–	–	1	13	17
Rotherham U	–	–	–	–	–	21	–	–	–	–	–	–
Scunthorpe U	–	2	–	–	–	3	11	–	21	12	–	–
Sheffield U	–	–	–	–	–	–	–	–	–	3	14	–
Sheffield W	11	–	–	–	–	–	–	–	–	–	–	1
Shrewsbury T	–	21	17	–	–	–	22	15	7	–	22	13
Southend U	–	–	–	–	–	–	–	–	–	–	–	–
Stockport Co	–	–	–	–	–	–	–	–	–	–	–	–
Stoke C	–	–	–	–	–	–	–	–	–	–	–	–

LEAGUE POSITIONS: DIVISION 2 from 1992–93 and DIVISION 3 1978–79 to 1991–92 (cont.)

	2002-03	2001-02	2000-01	1999-2000	1998-99	1997-98	1996-97	1995-96	1994-95	1993-94	1992-93	1991-92	1990-91
Sunderland	–	–	–	–	–	–	–	–	–	–	–	–	–
Swansea C	–	–	23	–	–	–	–	22	10	13	5	19	20
Swindon T	10	13	20	–	–	–	–	1	–	–	–	–	–
Torquay U	–	–	–	–	–	–	–	–	–	–	–	23	–
Tranmere R	7	12	–	–	–	–	–	–	–	–	–	–	5
Walsall	–	–	4	–	2	19	12	11	–	5	–	–	–
Watford	–	–	–	–	–	1	13	–	–	–	–	–	–
WBA	–	–	–	–	–	–	–	–	–	–	4	7	–
Wigan Ath	1	10	6	4	6	11	–	–	–	–	23	15	10
Wimbledon	–	–	–	–	–	–	–	–	–	–	–	–	–
Wolv'hampton W	–	–	–	–	–	–	–	–	–	–	–	–	–
Wrexham	–	23	10	11	17	7	8	8	13	12	–	–	–
Wycombe W	18	11	13	12	19	14	18	12	6	–	–	–	–
York C	–	–	–	–	21	16	20	20	9	5	–	–	–

LEAGUE POSITIONS: DIVISION 3 from 1992–93 and DIVISION 4 1978–79 to 1991–92

	2002-03	2001-02	2000-01	1999-2000	1998-99	1997-98	1996-97	1995-96	1994-95	1993-94	1992-93	1991-92	1990-91
Aldershot	–	–	–	–	–	–	–	–	–	–	–	*	23
Barnet	–	–	24	6	16	7	15	9	11	–	3	7	–
Barnsley	–	–	–	–	–	–	–	–	–	–	–	–	–
Blackpool	–	–	7	–	–	–	–	–	–	–	–	4	5
Bolton W	–	–	–	–	–	–	–	–	–	–	–	–	–
Boston U	15	–	–	–	–	–	–	–	–	–	–	–	–
Bournemouth	4	–	–	–	–	–	–	–	–	–	–	–	–
Bradford C	–	–	–	–	–	–	–	–	–	–	–	–	–
Brentford	–	–	–	–	–	–	–	–	–	–	–	–	–
Brighton & HA	–	–	1	11	17	23	23	–	–	–	–	–	–
Bristol C	–	–	–	–	–	–	–	–	–	–	–	–	–
Bristol R	20	23	–	–	–	–	–	–	–	–	–	–	–
Burnley	–	–	–	–	15	–	–	–	–	–	–	1	6
Bury	7	–	–	–	–	–	–	3	4	13	7	–	–
Cambridge U	12	–	–	–	2	16	10	16	–	–	–	–	–
Cardiff C	–	–	2	–	3	21	7	22	–	–	1	9	13
Carlisle U	22	17	22	23	23	–	3	–	1	7	18	22	20
Cheltenham T	–	4	9	8	–	–	–	–	–	–	–	–	–
Chester C	–	–	–	24	14	14	6	8	–	2	–	–	–
Chesterfield	–	–	3	–	–	–	–	–	3	8	12	13	18
Colchester U	–	–	–	–	–	4	8	7	10	17	10	–	–

*Record expunged

	1989–90	1988–89	1987–88	1986–87	1985–86	1984–85	1983–84	1982–83	1981–82	1980–81	1979–80	1978–79
Sunderland	–	–	1	–	–	–	–	–	–	–	–	–
Swansea C	17	12	–	–	24	20	–	–	–	–	–	3
Swindon T	–	–	–	3	–	–	–	–	22	17	10	5
Torquay U	–	–	–	–	–	–	–	–	–	–	–	–
Tranmere R	4	–	–	–	–	–	–	–	–	–	–	23
Walsall	24	–	3	8	6	11	6	10	20	20	–	22
Watford	–	–	–	–	–	–	–	–	–	–	–	2
WBA	–	–	–	–	–	–	–	–	–	–	–	–
Wigan Ath	18	17	7	4	4	16	15	18	–	–	–	–
Wimbledon	–	–	–	–	–	–	2	–	21	–	24	–
Wolv'hampton W	–	1	–	–	23	–	–	–	–	–	–	–
Wrexham	–	–	–	–	–	–	–	22	–	–	–	–
Wycombe W	–	–	–	–	–	–	–	–	–	–	–	–
York C	–	–	23	20	7	8	–	–	–	–	–	–

	1989–90	1988–89	1987–88	1986–87	1985–86	1984–85	1983–84	1982–83	1981–82	1980–81	1979–80	1978–79
Aldershot	22	–	–	6	16	13	5	18	16	6	10	5
Barnet	–	–	–	–	–	–	–	–	–	–	–	–
Barnsley	–	–	–	–	–	–	–	–	–	–	–	4
Blackpool	–	–	–	–	2	6	21	12	–	–	–	–
Bolton W	–	–	3	–	–	–	–	–	–	–	–	–
Boston U	–	–	–	–	–	–	–	–	–	–	–	–
Bournemouth	–	–	–	–	–	–	–	–	4	13	11	18
Bradford C	–	–	–	–	–	–	–	–	2	14	5	15
Brentford	–	–	–	–	–	–	–	–	–	–	–	–
Brighton & HA	–	–	–	–	–	–	–	–	–	–	–	–
Bristol C	–	–	–	–	–	4	14	–	–	–	–	–
Bristol R	–	–	–	–	–	–	–	–	–	–	–	–
Burnley	16	16	10	22	14	–	–	–	–	–	–	–
Bury	–	–	–	–	–	4	15	5	9	12	–	–
Cambridge U	6	8	15	11	22	–	–	–	–	–	–	–
Cardiff C	–	–	2	13	–	–	–	–	–	–	–	–
Carlisle U	8	12	23	–	–	–	–	–	–	–	–	–
Cheltenham T	–	–	–	–	–	–	–	–	–	–	–	–
Chester C	–	–	–	2	16	24	13	9	–	–	–	–
Chesterfield	7	–	–	–	1	13	–	–	–	–	–	–
Colchester U	24	22	9	5	6	7	8	6	6	–	–	–

LEAGUE POSITIONS: DIVISION 3 from 1992–93 and DIVISION 4 1978–79 to 1991–92 (cont.)

	2002-03	2001-02	2000-01	1999-2000	1998-99	1997-98	1996-97	1995-96	1994-95	1993-94	1992-93	1991-92	1990-91
Crewe Alex	–	–	–	–	–	–	–	–	–	3	6	6	–
Darlington	14	15	20	4	11	19	18	5	20	21	15	–	1
Doncaster R	–	–	–	–	–	24	19	13	9	15	16	21	11
Exeter C	23	16	19	21	12	15	22	14	22	–	–	–	–
Fulham	–	–	–	–	–	–	2	17	8	–	–	–	–
Gillingham	–	–	–	–	–	–	–	2	19	16	21	11	15
Grimsby T	–	–	–	–	–	–	–	–	–	–	–	–	–
Halifax T	–	24	23	18	10	–	–	–	–	–	22	20	22
Hartlepool U	2	7	4	7	22	17	20	20	18	–	–	–	3
Hereford U	–	–	–	–	–	–	24	6	16	20	17	17	17
Huddersfield T	–	–	–	–	–	–	–	–	–	–	–	–	–
Hull C	13	11	6	14	21	22	17	–	–	–	–	–	–
Kidderminster H	11	10	16	–	–	–	–	–	–	–	–	–	–
Leyton Orient	18	18	5	19	6	11	16	21	–	–	–	–	–
Lincoln C	6	22	18	15	–	3	9	18	12	18	8	10	14
Luton T	–	2	–	–	–	–	–	–	–	–	–	–	–
Macclesfield T	16	13	14	13	–	2	–	–	–	–	–	–	–
Maidstone U	–	–	–	–	–	–	–	–	–	–	–	18	19
Mansfield T	–	3	13	17	8	12	11	19	6	12	–	3	–
Newport Co	–	–	–	–	–	–	–	–	–	–	–	–	–
Northampton T	–	–	–	3	–	–	4	11	17	22	20	16	10
Notts Co	–	–	–	–	–	1	–	–	–	–	–	–	–
Oxford U	8	21	–	–	–	–	–	–	–	–	–	–	–
Peterborough U	–	–	–	5	9	10	–	–	–	–	–	–	4
Plymouth Arg	–	1	12	12	13	–	–	4	–	–	–	–	–
Portsmouth	–	–	–	–	–	–	–	–	–	–	–	–	–
Port Vale	–	–	–	–	–	–	–	–	–	–	–	–	–
Preston NE	–	–	–	–	–	–	–	1	5	5	–	–	–
Reading	–	–	–	–	–	–	–	–	–	–	–	–	–
Rochdale	19	5	8	10	19	18	14	15	15	9	11	8	12
Rotherham U	–	–	–	2	5	9	–	–	–	–	–	2	–
Rushden & D	1	6	–	–	–	–	–	–	–	–	–	–	–
Scarborough	–	–	–	–	24	6	12	23	21	14	13	12	9
Scunthorpe U	5	8	10	–	4	8	13	12	7	11	14	5	8
Sheffield U	–	–	–	–	–	–	–	–	–	–	–	–	–
Shrewsbury T	24	9	15	22	15	13	–	–	–	1	9	–	–
Southend U	17	12	11	16	18	–	–	–	–	–	–	–	–
Stockport Co	–	–	–	–	–	–	–	–	–	–	–	–	2
Swansea C	21	20	–	1	7	20	5	–	–	–	–	–	–
Swindon T	–	–	–	–	–	–	–	–	–	–	–	–	–
Torquay U	9	19	21	9	20	5	21	24	13	6	19	–	7
Tranmere R	–	–	–	–	–	–	–	–	–	–	–	–	–
Walsall	–	–	–	–	–	–	–	–	2	10	5	15	16
Watford	–	–	–	–	–	–	–	–	–	–	–	–	–
Wigan Ath	–	–	–	–	–	–	1	10	14	19	–	–	–
Wimbledon	–	–	–	–	–	–	–	–	–	–	–	–	–
Wolv'hampton W	–	–	–	–	–	–	–	–	–	–	–	–	–
Wrexham	3	–	–	–	–	–	–	–	–	–	2	14	24
Wycombe W	–	–	–	–	–	–	–	–	–	4	–	–	–
York C	10	14	17	20	–	–	–	–	–	–	4	19	21

1989-90	1988-89	1987-88	1986-87	1985-86	1984-85	1983-84	1982-83	1981-82	1980-81	1979-80	1978-79	
–	3	17	17	12	10	16	23	24	18	23	24	Crewe Alex
–	24	13	–	–	3	14	17	3	8	22	21	Darlington
20	23	–	–	–	2	–	–	3	12	22	–	Doncaster R
1	13	22	14	21	18	–	–	–	–	–	–	Exeter C
–	–	–	–	–	–	–	–	–	–	–	–	Fulham
14	–	–	–	–	–	–	–	–	–	–	–	Gillingham
2	9	–	–	–	–	–	–	–	–	–	2	Grimsby T
23	21	18	15	20	21	21	11	19	23	18	23	Halifax T
19	19	16	18	7	19	23	22	14	9	19	13	Hartlepool U
17	15	19	16	10	5	11	24	10	22	21	14	Hereford U
–	–	–	–	–	–	–	–	–	–	1	9	Huddersfield T
–	–	–	–	–	–	2	8	–	–	–	–	Hull C
–	–	–	–	–	–	–	–	–	–	–	–	Kidderminster H
–	6	8	7	5	–	–	–	–	–	–	–	Leyton Orient
10	10	–	24	–	–	–	–	–	2	7	–	Lincoln C
–	–	–	–	–	–	–	–	–	–	–	–	Luton T
–	–	–	–	–	–	–	–	–	–	–	–	Macclesfield T
5	–	–	–	–	–	–	–	–	–	–	–	Maidstone U
–	–	–	3	14	19	10	20	7	–	–	–	Mansfield T
–	–	24	–	–	–	–	–	–	–	3	8	Newport Co
–	–	–	1	8	23	18	15	22	10	13	19	Northampton T
–	–	–	–	–	–	–	–	–	–	–	–	Notts Co
–	–	–	–	–	–	–	–	–	–	–	–	Oxford U
9	17	7	10	17	11	7	9	5	5	8	–	Peterborough U
–	–	–	–	–	–	–	–	–	–	–	–	Plymouth Arg
–	–	–	–	–	–	–	–	–	–	4	7	Portsmouth
–	–	–	4	12	–	3	7	19	20	16	–	Port Vale
–	–	–	2	23	–	–	–	–	–	–	–	Preston NE
–	–	–	–	–	3	–	–	–	–	–	1	Reading
12	18	21	21	18	17	22	20	21	15	24	20	Rochdale
–	1	–	–	–	–	–	–	–	–	–	–	Rotherham U
–	–	–	–	–	–	–	–	–	–	–	–	Rushden & D
18	5	12	–	–	–	–	–	–	–	–	–	Scarborough
11	4	4	8	15	9	–	4	23	16	14	12	Scunthorpe U
–	–	–	–	–	–	–	1	–	–	–	–	Sheffield U
–	–	–	–	–	–	–	–	–	–	–	–	Shrewsbury T
3	–	–	3	9	20	–	–	–	1	–	–	Southend U
4	20	20	19	11	22	12	16	18	20	16	17	Stockport Co
–	–	6	12	–	–	–	–	–	–	–	–	Swansea C
–	–	–	–	1	8	17	8	–	–	–	–	Swindon T
15	14	5	23	24	24	9	12	15	17	9	11	Torquay U
–	2	14	20	19	6	10	19	11	21	15	–	Tranmere R
–	–	–	–	–	–	–	–	–	–	2	–	Walsall
–	–	–	–	–	–	–	–	–	–	–	–	Watford
–	–	–	–	–	–	3	11	6	6	–	–	Wigan Ath
–	–	–	–	–	–	–	1	–	4	–	3	Wimbledon
–	–	1	4	–	–	–	–	–	–	–	–	Wolv'hampton W
21	7	11	9	13	15	20	–	–	–	–	–	Wrexham
–	–	–	–	–	–	–	–	–	–	–	–	Wycombe W
13	11	–	–	–	–	1	7	17	24	17	10	York C

125

LEAGUE CHAMPIONSHIP HONOURS

FA PREMIER LEAGUE

Maximum points: 126

	First	Pts	Second	Pts	Third	Pts
1992–93	Manchester U	84	Aston Villa	74	Norwich C	72
1993–94	Manchester U	92	Blackburn R	84	Newcastle U	77
1994–95	Blackburn R	89	Manchester U	88	Nottingham F	77

Maximum points: 114

	First	Pts	Second	Pts	Third	Pts
1995–96	Manchester U	82	Newcastle U	78	Liverpool	71
1996–97	Manchester U	75	Newcastle U*	68	Arsenal*	68
1997–98	Arsenal	78	Manchester U	77	Liverpool	65
1998–99	Manchester U	79	Arsenal	78	Chelsea	75
1999–00	Manchester U	91	Arsenal	73	Leeds U	69
2000–01	Manchester U	80	Arsenal	70	Liverpool	69
2001–02	Arsenal	87	Liverpool	80	Manchester U	77
2002–03	Manchester U	83	Arsenal	78	Newcastle U	69
2003–04	Arsenal	90	Chelsea	79	Manchester U	75

DIVISION 1

Maximum points: 138

	First	Pts	Second	Pts	Third	Pts
1992–93	Newcastle U	96	West Ham U*	88	Portsmouth††	88
1993–94	Crystal Palace	90	Nottingham F	83	Millwall††	74
1994–95	Middlesbrough	82	Reading††	79	Bolton W	77
1995–96	Sunderland	83	Derby Co	79	Crystal Palace††	75
1996–97	Bolton W	98	Barnsley	80	Wolverhampton W††	76
1997–98	Nottingham F	94	Middlesbrough	91	Sunderland††	90
1998–99	Sunderland	105	Bradford C	87	Ipswich T††	86
1999–00	Charlton Ath	91	Manchester C	89	Ipswich T	87
2000–01	Fulham	101	Blackburn R	91	Bolton W	87
2001–02	Manchester C	99	WBA	89	Wolverhampton W††	86
2002–03	Portsmouth	98	Leicester C	92	Sheffield U††	80
2003–04	Norwich C	94	WBA	86	Sunderland††	79

DIVISION 2

Maximum points: 138

	First	Pts	Second	Pts	Third	Pts
1992–93	Stoke C	93	Bolton W	90	Port Vale††	89
1993–94	Reading	89	Port Vale	88	Plymouth Arg††	85
1994–95	Birmingham C	89	Brentford††	85	Crewe Alex††	83
1995–96	Swindon T	92	Oxford U	83	Blackpool††	82
1996–97	Bury	84	Stockport Co	82	Luton T††	78
1997–98	Watford	88	Bristol C	85	Grimsby T	72
1998–99	Fulham	101	Walsall	87	Manchester C	82
1999–00	Preston NE	95	Burnley	88	Gillingham	85
2000–01	Millwall	93	Rotherham U	91	Reading††	86
2001–02	Brighton & HA	90	Reading	84	Brentford*††	83
2002–03	Wigan Ath	100	Crewe Alex	86	Bristol C††	83
2003–04	Plymouth Arg	90	QPR	83	Bristol C††	82

DIVISION 3

Maximum points: 126

	First	Pts	Second	Pts	Third	Pts
1992–93	Cardiff C	83	Wrexham	80	Barnet	79
1993–94	Shrewsbury T	79	Chester C	74	Crewe Alex	73
1994–95	Carlisle U	91	Walsall	83	Chesterfield	81

Maximum points: 138

	First	Pts	Second	Pts	Third	Pts
1995–96	Preston NE	86	Gillingham	83	Bury	79
1996–97	Wigan Ath*	87	Fulham	87	Carlisle U	84
1997–98	Notts Co	99	Macclesfield T	82	Lincoln C	75

	First	Pts	Second	Pts	Third	Pts
1998–99	Brentford	85	Cambridge U	81	Cardiff C	80
1999–00	Swansea C	85	Rotherham U	84	Northampton T	82
2000–01	Brighton & HA	92	Cardiff C	82	Chesterfield¶	80
2001–02	Plymouth Arg	102	Luton T	97	Mansfield T	79
2002–03	Rushden & D	87	Hartlepool U	85	Wrexham	84
2003–04	Doncaster R	92	Hull C	88	Torquay U*	81

Won or placed on goal average (ratio)/goal difference.
†† *Not promoted after play-offs.* ¶ *9 pts deducted for irregularities.*

FOOTBALL LEAGUE
Maximum points: a 44; b 60

1888–89a	Preston NE	40	Aston Villa	29	Wolverhampton W	28
1889–90a	Preston NE	33	Everton	31	Blackburn R	27
1890–91a	Everton	29	Preston NE	27	Notts Co	26
1891–92b	Sunderland	42	Preston NE	37	Bolton W	36

DIVISION 1 to 1991–92
Maximum points: a 44; b 52; c 60; d 68; e 76; f 84; g 126; h 120; k 114.

1892–93c	Sunderland	48	Preston NE	37	Everton	36
1893–94c	Aston Villa	44	Sunderland	38	Derby Co	36
1894–95c	Sunderland	47	Everton	42	Aston Villa	39
1895–96c	Aston Villa	45	Derby Co	41	Everton	39
1896–97c	Aston Villa	47	Sheffield U*	36	Derby Co	36
1897–98c	Sheffield U	42	Sunderland	37	Wolverhampton W*	35
1898–99d	Aston Villa	45	Liverpool	43	Burnley	39
1899–1900d	Aston Villa	50	Sheffield U	48	Sunderland	41
1900–01d	Liverpool	45	Sunderland	43	Notts Co	40
1901–02d	Sunderland	44	Everton	41	Newcastle U	37
1902–03d	The Wednesday	42	Aston Villa*	41	Sunderland	41
1903–04d	The Wednesday	47	Manchester C	44	Everton	43
1904–05d	Newcastle U	48	Everton	47	Manchester C	46
1905–06e	Liverpool	51	Preston NE	47	The Wednesday	44
1906–07e	Newcastle U	51	Bristol C	48	Everton*	45
1907–08e	Manchester U	52	Aston Villa*	43	Manchester C	43
1908–09e	Newcastle U	53	Everton	46	Sunderland	44
1909–10e	Aston Villa	53	Liverpool	48	Blackburn R*	45
1910–11e	Manchester U	52	Aston Villa	51	Sunderland*	45
1911–12e	Blackburn R	49	Everton	46	Newcastle U	44
1912–13e	Sunderland	54	Aston Villa	50	Sheffield W	49
1913–14e	Blackburn R	51	Aston Villa	44	Middlesbrough*	43
1914–15e	Everton	46	Oldham Ath	45	Blackburn R*	43
1919–20f	WBA	60	Burnley	51	Chelsea	49
1920–21f	Burnley	59	Manchester C	54	Bolton W	52
1921–22f	Liverpool	57	Tottenham H	51	Burnley	49
1922–23f	Liverpool	60	Sunderland	54	Huddersfield T	53
1923–24f	Huddersfield T*	57	Cardiff C	57	Sunderland	53
1924–25f	Huddersfield T	58	WBA	56	Bolton W	55
1925–26f	Huddersfield T	57	Arsenal	52	Sunderland	48
1926–27f	Newcastle U	56	Huddersfield T	51	Sunderland	49
1927–28f	Everton	53	Huddersfield T	51	Leicester C	48
1928–29f	Sheffield W	52	Leicester C	51	Aston Villa	50
1929–30f	Sheffield W	60	Derby Co	50	Manchester C*	47
1930–31f	Arsenal	66	Aston Villa	59	Sheffield W	52
1931–32f	Everton	56	Arsenal	54	Sheffield W	50
1932–33f	Arsenal	58	Aston Villa	54	Sheffield W	51
1933–34f	Arsenal	59	Huddersfield T	56	Tottenham H	49
1934–35f	Arsenal	58	Sunderland	54	Sheffield W	49
1935–36f	Sunderland	56	Derby Co*	48	Huddersfield T	48

127

	First	Pts	Second	Pts	Third	Pts
1936–37f	Manchester C	57	Charlton Ath	54	Arsenal	52
1937–38f	Arsenal	52	Wolverhampton W	51	Preston NE	49
1938–39f	Everton	59	Wolverhampton W	55	Charlton Ath	50
1946–47f	Liverpool	57	Manchester U*	56	Wolverhampton W	56
1947–48f	Arsenal	59	Manchester U*	52	Burnley	52
1948–49f	Portsmouth	58	Manchester U*	53	Derby Co	53
1949–50f	Portsmouth*	53	Wolverhampton W	53	Sunderland	52
1950–51f	Tottenham H	60	Manchester U	56	Blackpool	50
1951–52f	Manchester U	57	Tottenham H*	53	Arsenal	53
1952–53f	Arsenal*	54	Preston NE	54	Wolverhampton W	51
1953–54f	Wolverhampton W	57	WBA	53	Huddersfield T	51
1954–55f	Chelsea	52	Wolverhampton W*	48	Portsmouth*	48
1955–56f	Manchester U	60	Blackpool*	49	Wolverhampton W	49
1956–57f	Manchester U	64	Tottenham H*	56	Preston NE	56
1957–58f	Wolverhampton W	64	Preston NE	59	Tottenham H	51
1958–59f	Wolverhampton W	61	Manchester U	55	Arsenal*	50
1959–60f	Burnley	55	Wolverhampton W	54	Tottenham H	53
1960–61f	Tottenham H	66	Sheffield W	58	Wolverhampton W	57
1961–62f	Ipswich T	56	Burnley	53	Tottenham H	52
1962–63f	Everton	61	Tottenham H	55	Burnley	54
1963–64f	Liverpool	57	Manchester U	53	Everton	52
1964–65f	Manchester U*	61	Leeds U	61	Chelsea	56
1965–66f	Liverpool	61	Leeds U*	55	Burnley	55
1966–67f	Manchester U	60	Nottingham F*	56	Tottenham H	56
1967–68f	Manchester C	58	Manchester U	56	Liverpool	55
1968–69f	Leeds U	67	Liverpool	61	Everton	57
1969–70f	Everton	66	Leeds U	57	Chelsea	55
1970–71f	Arsenal	65	Leeds U	64	Tottenham H*	52
1971–72f	Derby Co	58	Leeds U*	57	Liverpool*	57
1972–73f	Liverpool	60	Arsenal	57	Leeds U	53
1973–74f	Leeds U	62	Liverpool	57	Derby Co	48
1974–75f	Derby Co	53	Liverpool*	51	Ipswich T	51
1975–76f	Liverpool	60	QPR	59	Manchester U	56
1976–77f	Liverpool	57	Manchester C	56	Ipswich T	52
1977–78f	Nottingham F	64	Liverpool	57	Everton	55
1978–79f	Liverpool	68	Nottingham F	60	WBA	59
1979–80f	Liverpool	60	Manchester U	58	Ipswich T	53
1980–81f	Aston Villa	60	Ipswich T	56	Arsenal	53
1981–82g	Liverpool	87	Ipswich T	83	Manchester U	78
1982–83g	Liverpool	82	Watford	71	Manchester U	70
1983–84g	Liverpool	80	Southampton	77	Nottingham F*	74
1984–85g	Everton	90	Liverpool*	77	Tottenham H	77
1985–86g	Liverpool	88	Everton	86	West Ham U	84
1986–87g	Everton	86	Liverpool	77	Tottenham H	71
1987–88h	Liverpool	90	Manchester U	81	Nottingham F	73
1988–89k	Arsenal*	76	Liverpool	76	Nottingham F	64
1989–90k	Liverpool	79	Aston Villa	70	Tottenham H	63
1990–91k	Arsenal†	83	Liverpool	76	Crystal Palace	69
1991–92g	Leeds U	82	Manchester U	78	Sheffield W	75

No official competition during 1915–19 and 1939–46; Regional Leagues operating.
* Won or placed on goal average (ratio)/goal difference.
† 2 pts deducted

DIVISION 2 to 1991–92

Maximum points: a 44; b 56; c 60; d 68; e 76; f 84; g 126; h 132; k 138.

	First	Pts	Second	Pts	Third	Pts
1892–93a	Small Heath	36	Sheffield U	35	Darwen	30
1893–94b	Liverpool	50	Small Heath	42	Notts Co	39
1894–95c	Bury	48	Notts Co	39	Newton Heath*	38
1895–96c	Liverpool*	46	Manchester C	46	Grimsby T*	42

	First	Pts	Second	Pts	Third	Pts
1896–97c	Notts Co	42	Newton Heath	39	Grimsby T	38
1897–98c	Burnley	48	Newcastle U	45	Manchester C	39
1898–99d	Manchester C	52	Glossop NE	46	Leicester Fosse	45
1899–1900d	The Wednesday	54	Bolton W	52	Small Heath	46
1900–01d	Grimsby T	49	Small Heath	48	Burnley	44
1901–02d	WBA	55	Middlesbrough	51	Preston NE*	42
1902–03d	Manchester C	54	Small Heath	51	Woolwich A	48
1903–04d	Preston NE	50	Woolwich A	49	Manchester U	48
1904–05d	Liverpool	58	Bolton W	56	Manchester U	53
1905–06e	Bristol C	66	Manchester U	62	Chelsea	53
1906–07e	Nottingham F	60	Chelsea	57	Leicester Fosse	48
1907–08e	Bradford C	54	Leicester Fosse	52	Oldham Ath	50
1908–09e	Bolton W	52	Tottenham H*	51	WBA	51
1909–10e	Manchester C	54	Oldham Ath*	53	Hull C*	53
1910–11e	WBA	53	Bolton W	51	Chelsea	49
1911–12e	Derby Co*	54	Chelsea	54	Burnley	52
1912–13e	Preston NE	53	Burnley	50	Birmingham	46
1913–14e	Notts Co	53	Bradford PA*	49	Woolwich A	49
1914–15e	Derby Co	53	Preston NE	50	Barnsley	47
1919–20f	Tottenham H	70	Huddersfield T	64	Birmingham	56
1920–21f	Birmingham*	58	Cardiff C	58	Bristol C	51
1921–22f	Nottingham F	56	Stoke C*	52	Barnsley	52
1922–23f	Notts Co	53	West Ham U*	51	Leicester C	51
1923–24f	Leeds U	54	Bury*	51	Derby Co	51
1924–25f	Leicester C	59	Manchester U	57	Derby Co	55
1925–26f	Sheffield W	60	Derby Co	57	Chelsea	52
1926–27f	Middlesbrough	62	Portsmouth*	54	Manchester C	54
1927–28f	Manchester C	59	Leeds U	57	Chelsea	54
1928–29f	Middlesbrough	55	Grimsby T	53	Bradford PA*	48
1929–30f	Blackpool	58	Chelsea	55	Oldham Ath	53
1930–31f	Everton	61	WBA	54	Tottenham H	51
1931–32f	Wolverhampton W	56	Leeds U	54	Stoke C	52
1932–33f	Stoke C	56	Tottenham H	55	Fulham	50
1933–34f	Grimsby T	59	Preston NE	52	Bolton W*	51
1934–35f	Brentford	61	Bolton W*	56	West Ham U	56
1935–36f	Manchester U	56	Charlton Ath	55	Sheffield U*	52
1936–37f	Leicester C	56	Blackpool	55	Bury	52
1937–38f	Aston Villa	57	Manchester U*	53	Sheffield U	53
1938–39f	Blackburn R	55	Sheffield U	54	Sheffield W	53
1946–47f	Manchester C	62	Burnley	58	Birmingham C	55
1947–48f	Birmingham C	59	Newcastle U	56	Southampton	52
1948–49f	Fulham	57	WBA	56	Southampton	55
1949–50f	Tottenham H	61	Sheffield W*	52	Sheffield U*	52
1950–51f	Preston NE	57	Manchester C	52	Cardiff C	50
1951–52f	Sheffield W	53	Cardiff C*	51	Birmingham C	51
1952–53f	Sheffield U	60	Huddersfield T	58	Luton T	52
1953–54f	Leicester C*	56	Everton	56	Blackburn R	55
1954–55f	Birmingham C*	54	Luton T*	54	Rotherham U	54
1955–56f	Sheffield W	55	Leeds U	52	Liverpool*	48
1956–57f	Leicester C	61	Nottingham F	54	Liverpool	53
1957–58f	West Ham U	57	Blackburn R	56	Charlton Ath	55
1958–59f	Sheffield W	62	Fulham	60	Sheffield U*	53
1959–60f	Aston Villa	59	Cardiff C	58	Liverpool*	50
1960–61f	Ipswich T	59	Sheffield U	58	Liverpool	52
1961–62f	Liverpool	62	Leyton Orient	54	Sunderland	53
1962–63f	Stoke C	53	Chelsea*	52	Sunderland	52
1963–64f	Leeds U	63	Sunderland	61	Preston NE	56
1964–65f	Newcastle U	57	Northampton T	56	Bolton W	50
1965–66f	Manchester C	59	Southampton	54	Coventry C	53

	First	Pts	Second	Pts	Third	Pts
1966–67f	Coventry C	59	Wolverhampton W	58	Carlisle U	52
1967–68f	Ipswich T	59	QPR*	58	Blackpool	58
1968–69f	Derby Co	63	Crystal Palace	56	Charlton Ath	50
1969–70f	Huddersfield T	60	Blackpool	53	Leicester C	51
1970–71f	Leicester C	59	Sheffield U	56	Cardiff C*	53
1971–72f	Norwich C	57	Birmingham C	56	Millwall	55
1972–73f	Burnley	62	QPR	61	Aston Villa	50
1973–74f	Middlesbrough	65	Luton T	50	Carlisle U	49
1974–75f	Manchester U	61	Aston Villa	58	Norwich C	53
1975–76f	Sunderland	56	Bristol C*	53	WBA	53
1976–77f	Wolverhampton W	57	Chelsea	55	Nottingham F	52
1977–78f	Bolton W	58	Southampton	57	Tottenham H*	56
1978–79f	Crystal Palace	57	Brighton & HA*	56	Stoke C	56
1979–80f	Leicester C	55	Sunderland	54	Birmingham C*	53
1980–81f	West Ham U	66	Notts Co	53	Swansea C*	50
1981–82g	Luton T	88	Watford	80	Norwich C	71
1982–83g	QPR	85	Wolverhampton W	75	Leicester C	70
1983–84g	Chelsea*	88	Sheffield W	88	Newcastle U	80
1984–85g	Oxford U	84	Birmingham C	82	Manchester C	74
1985–86g	Norwich C	84	Charlton Ath	77	Wimbledon	76
1986–87g	Derby Co	84	Portsmouth	78	Oldham Ath††	75
1987–88h	Millwall	82	Aston Villa*	78	Middlesbrough	78
1988–89k	Chelsea	99	Manchester C	82	Crystal Palace	81
1989–90k	Leeds U*	85	Sheffield U	85	Newcastle U††	80
1990–91k	Oldham Ath	88	West Ham U	87	Sheffield W	82
1991–92k	Ipswich T	84	Middlesbrough	80	Derby Co	78

No official competition during 1915–19 and 1939–46; Regional Leagues operating.
* Won or placed on goal average (ratio)/goal difference.
†† Not promoted after play-offs.

DIVISION 3 to 1991–92

Maximum points: 92; 138 from 1981–82.

	First	Pts	Second	Pts	Third	Pts
1958–59	Plymouth Arg	62	Hull C	61	Brentford*	57
1959–60	Southampton	61	Norwich C	59	Shrewsbury T*	52
1960–61	Bury	68	Walsall	62	QPR	60
1961–62	Portsmouth	65	Grimsby T	62	Bournemouth*	59
1962–63	Northampton T	62	Swindon T	58	Port Vale	54
1963–64	Coventry C*	60	Crystal Palace	60	Watford	58
1964–65	Carlisle U	60	Bristol C*	59	Mansfield T	59
1965–66	Hull C	69	Millwall	65	QPR	57
1966–67	QPR	67	Middlesbrough	55	Watford	54
1967–68	Oxford U	57	Bury	56	Shrewsbury T	55
1968–69	Watford*	64	Swindon T	64	Luton T	61
1969–70	Orient	62	Luton T	60	Bristol R	56
1970–71	Preston NE	61	Fulham	60	Halifax T	56
1971–72	Aston Villa	70	Brighton & HA	65	Bournemouth*	62
1972–73	Bolton W	61	Notts Co	57	Blackburn R	55
1973–74	Oldham Ath	62	Bristol R*	61	York C	61
1974–75	Blackburn R	60	Plymouth Arg	59	Charlton Ath	55
1975–76	Hereford U	63	Cardiff C	57	Millwall	56
1976–77	Mansfield T	64	Brighton & HA	61	Crystal Palace*	59
1977–78	Wrexham	61	Cambridge U	58	Preston NE*	56
1978–79	Shrewsbury T	61	Watford*	60	Swansea C	60
1979–80	Grimsby T	62	Blackburn R	59	Sheffield W	58
1980–81	Rotherham U	61	Barnsley*	59	Charlton Ath	59
1981–82	Burnley*	80	Carlisle U	80	Fulham	78
1982–83	Portsmouth	91	Cardiff C	86	Huddersfield T	82
1983–84	Oxford U	95	Wimbledon	87	Sheffield U*	83
1984–85	Bradford C	94	Millwall	90	Hull C	87

	First	*Pts*	*Second*	*Pts*	*Third*	*Pts*
1985–86	Reading	94	Plymouth Arg	87	Derby Co	84
1986–87	Bournemouth	97	Middlesbrough	94	Swindon T	87
1987–88	Sunderland	93	Brighton & HA	84	Walsall	82
1988–89	Wolverhampton W	92	Sheffield U*	84	Port Vale	84
1989–90	Bristol R	93	Bristol C	91	Notts Co	87
1990–91	Cambridge U	86	Southend U	85	Grimsby T*	83
1991–92	Brentford	82	Birmingham C	81	Huddersfield T	78

* Won or placed on goal average (ratio)/goal difference.

DIVISION 4 (1958–1992)
Maximum points: 92; 138 from 1981–82.

	First	*Pts*	*Second*	*Pts*	*Third*	*Pts*
1958–59	Port Vale	64	Coventry C*	60	York C	60
1959–60	Walsall	65	Notts Co*	60	Torquay U	60
1960–61	Peterborough U	66	Crystal Palace	64	Northampton T*	60
1961–62†	Millwall	56	Colchester U	55	Wrexham	53
1962–63	Brentford	62	Oldham Ath*	59	Crewe Alex	59
1963–64	Gillingham*	60	Carlisle U	60	Workington	59
1964–65	Brighton & HA	63	Millwall*	62	York C	62
1965–66	Doncaster R*	59	Darlington	59	Torquay U	58
1966–67	Stockport Co	64	Southport*	59	Barrow	59
1967–68	Luton T	66	Barnsley	61	Hartlepools U	60
1968–69	Doncaster R	59	Halifax T	57	Rochdale*	56
1969–70	Chesterfield	64	Wrexham	61	Swansea C	60
1970–71	Notts Co	69	Bournemouth	60	Oldham Ath	59
1971–72	Grimsby T	63	Southend U	60	Brentford	59
1972–73	Southport	62	Hereford U	58	Cambridge U	57
1973–74	Peterborough U	65	Gillingham	62	Colchester U	60
1974–75	Mansfield T	68	Shrewsbury T	62	Rotherham U	59
1975–76	Lincoln C	74	Northampton T	68	Reading	60
1976–77	Cambridge U	65	Exeter C	62	Colchester U*	59
1977–78	Watford	71	Southend U	60	Swansea C*	56
1978–79	Reading	65	Grimsby T*	61	Wimbledon*	61
1979–80	Huddersfield T	66	Walsall	64	Newport Co	61
1980–81	Southend U	67	Lincoln C	65	Doncaster R	56
1981–82	Sheffield U	96	Bradford C*	91	Wigan Ath	91
1982–83	Wimbledon	98	Hull C	90	Port Vale	88
1983–84	York C	101	Doncaster R	85	Reading*	82
1984–85	Chesterfield	91	Blackpool	86	Darlington	85
1985–86	Swindon T	102	Chester C	84	Mansfield T	81
1986–87	Northampton T	99	Preston NE	90	Southend U	80
1987–88	Wolverhampton W	90	Cardiff C	85	Bolton W	78
1988–89	Rotherham U	82	Tranmere R	80	Crewe Alex	78
1989–90	Exeter C	89	Grimsby T	79	Southend U	75
1990–91	Darlington	83	Stockport Co*	82	Hartlepool U	82
1991–92§	Burnley	83	Rotherham U*	77	Mansfield T	77

* Won or placed on goal average (ratio)/goal difference.
†Maximum points: 88 owing to Accrington Stanley's resignation. *††Not promoted after play-offs.*
§Maximum points: 126 owing to Aldershot being expelled.

DIVISION 3—SOUTH (1920–1958)
1920–21 Season as Division 3.
Maximum points: a 84; b 92.

	First	*Pts*	*Second*	*Pts*	*Third*	*Pts*
1920–21a	Crystal Palace	59	Southampton	54	QPR	53
1921–22a	Southampton*	61	Plymouth Arg	61	Portsmouth	53
1922–23a	Bristol C	59	Plymouth Arg*	53	Swansea T	53
1923–24a	Portsmouth	59	Plymouth Arg	55	Millwall	54
1924–25a	Swansea T	57	Plymouth Arg	56	Bristol C	53
1925–26a	Reading	57	Plymouth Arg	56	Millwall	53

131

	First	Pts	Second	Pts	Third	Pts
1926–27a	Bristol C	62	Plymouth Arg	60	Millwall	56
1927–28a	Millwall	65	Northampton T	55	Plymouth Arg	53
1928–29a	Charlton Ath*	54	Crystal Palace	54	Northampton T*	52
1929–30a	Plymouth Arg	68	Brentford	61	QPR	51
1930–31a	Notts Co	59	Crystal Palace	51	Brentford	50
1931–32a	Fulham	57	Reading	55	Southend U	53
1932–33a	Brentford	62	Exeter C	58	Norwich C	57
1933–34a	Norwich C	61	Coventry C*	54	Reading*	54
1934–35a	Charlton Ath	61	Reading	53	Coventry C	51
1935–36a	Coventry C	57	Luton T	56	Reading	54
1936–37a	Luton T	58	Notts Co	56	Brighton & HA	53
1937–38a	Millwall	56	Bristol C	55	QPR*	53
1938–39a	Newport Co	55	Crystal Palace	52	Brighton & HA	49
1939–46	Competition cancelled owing to war.					
1946–47a	Cardiff C	66	QPR	57	Bristol C	51
1947–48a	QPR	61	Bournemouth	57	Walsall	51
1948–49a	Swansea T	62	Reading	55	Bournemouth	52
1949–50a	Notts Co	58	Northampton T*	51	Southend U	51
1950–51b	Nottingham F	70	Norwich C	64	Reading*	57
1951–52b	Plymouth Arg	66	Reading*	61	Norwich C	61
1952–53b	Bristol R	64	Millwall*	62	Northampton T	62
1953–54b	Ipswich T	64	Brighton & HA	61	Bristol C	56
1954–55b	Bristol C	70	Leyton Orient	61	Southampton	59
1955–56b	Leyton Orient	66	Brighton & HA	65	Ipswich T	64
1956–57b	Ipswich T*	59	Torquay U	59	Colchester U	58
1957–58b	Brighton & HA	60	Brentford*	58	Plymouth Arg	58

* Won or placed on goal average (ratio).

DIVISION 3—NORTH (1921–1958)
Maximum points: a 76; b 84; c 80; d 92.

	First	Pts	Second	Pts	Third	Pts
1921–22a	Stockport Co	56	Darlington*	50	Grimsby T	50
1922–23a	Nelson	51	Bradford PA	47	Walsall	46
1923–24b	Wolverhampton W	63	Rochdale	62	Chesterfield	54
1924–25b	Darlington	58	Nelson*	53	New Brighton	53
1925–26b	Grimsby T	61	Bradford PA	60	Rochdale	59
1926–27b	Stoke C	63	Rochdale	58	Bradford PA	55
1927–28b	Bradford PA	63	Lincoln C	55	Stockport Co	54
1928–29g	Bradford C	63	Stockport Co	62	Wrexham	52
1929–30b	Port Vale	67	Stockport Co	63	Darlington*	50
1930–31b	Chesterfield	58	Lincoln C	57	Wrexham*	54
1931–32c	Lincoln C*	57	Gateshead	57	Chester	50
1932–33b	Hull C	59	Wrexham	57	Stockport Co	54
1933–34b	Barnsley	62	Chesterfield	61	Stockport Co	59
1934–35b	Doncaster R	57	Halifax T	55	Chester	54
1935–36b	Chesterfield	60	Chester*	55	Tranmere R	55
1936–37b	Stockport Co	60	Lincoln C	57	Chester	53
1937–38b	Tranmere R	56	Doncaster R	54	Hull C	53
1938–39b	Barnsley	67	Doncaster R	56	Bradford C	52
1939–46	Competition cancelled owing to war.					
1946–47b	Doncaster R	72	Rotherham U	60	Chester	56
1947–48b	Lincoln C	60	Rotherham U	59	Wrexham	50
1948–49b	Hull C	65	Rotherham U	62	Doncaster R	50
1949–50b	Doncaster R	55	Gateshead	53	Rochdale*	51
1950–51d	Rotherham U	71	Mansfield T	64	Carlisle U	62
1951–52d	Lincoln C	69	Grimsby T	66	Stockport Co	59
1952–53d	Oldham Ath	59	Port Vale	58	Wrexham	56
1953–54d	Port Vale	69	Barnsley	58	Scunthorpe U	57
1954–55d	Barnsley	65	Accrington S	61	Scunthorpe U*	58

132

	First	Pts	Second	Pts	Third	Pts
1955–56*d*	Grimsby T	68	Derby Co	63	Accrington S	59
1956–57*d*	Derby Co	63	Hartlepools U	59	Accrington S*	58
1957–58*d*	Scunthorpe U	66	Accrington S	59	Bradford C	57

* Won or placed on goal average (ratio).

PROMOTED AFTER PLAY-OFFS
(Not accounted for in previous section)
1986–87 Aldershot to Division 3.
1987–88 Swansea C to Divison 3.
1988–89 Leyton Orient to Division 3.
1989–90 Cambridge U to Division 3; Notts Co to Division 2; Sunderland to Division 1.
1990–91 Notts Co to Division 1; Tranmere R to Division 2; Torquay U to Division 3.
1991–92 Blackburn R to Premier League; Peterborough U to Division 1.
1992–93 Swindon T to Premier League; WBA to Division 1; York C to Division 2.
1993–94 Leicester C to Premier League; Burnley to Division 1; Wycombe W to Division 2.
1994–95 Huddersfield T to Division 1.
1995–96 Leicester C to Premier League; Bradford C to Division 1; Plymouth Arg to Division 2.
1996–97 Crystal Palace to Premier League; Crewe Alex to Division 1; Northampton T to Division 2.
1997–98 Charlton Ath to Premier League; Colchester U to Division 2.
1998–99 Watford to Premier League; Scunthorpe to Division 2.
1999–00 Peterborough U to Division 2.
2000–01 Walsall to Division 1; Blackpool to Division 2.
2001–02 Birmingham C to Premier League; Stoke C to Division 1; Cheltenham T to Division 2.
2002–03 Wolverhampton W to Premier League; Cardiff C to Division 1; Bournemouth to Division 2.
2003–04 Crystal Palace to Premier League; Brighton & HA to Division 1; Huddersfield T to Division 2

RELEGATED CLUBS

FA PREMIER LEAGUE TO DIVISION 1

1992–93 Crystal Palace, Middlesbrough, Nottingham F.
1993–94 Sheffield U, Oldham Ath, Swindon T.
1994–95 Crystal Palace, Norwich C, Leicester C, Ipswich T.
1995–96 Manchester C, QPR, Bolton W.
1996–97 Sunderland, Middlesbrough, Nottingham F.
1997–98 Bolton W, Barnsley, Crystal Palace.
1998–99 Charlton Ath, Blackburn R, Nottingham F.
1999–90 Wimbledon, Sheffield W, Watford.
2000–01 Manchester C, Coventry C, Bradford C.
2001–02 Ipswich T, Derby Co, Leicester C.
2002–03 West Ham U, WBA, Sunderland.
2003–04 Leicester C, Leeds U, Wolverhampton W.

DIVISION 1 TO DIVISION 2

1898–99 Bolton W and Sheffield W
1899–1900 Burnley and Glossop
1900–01 Preston NE and WBA
1901–02 Small Heath and Manchester C
1902–03 Grimsby T and Bolton W
1903–04 Liverpool and WBA
1904–05 League extended. Bury and Notts Co, two bottom clubs in First Division, re-elected.
1905–06 Nottingham F and Wolverhampton W
1906–07 Derby Co and Stoke C
1907–08 Bolton W and Birmingham C
1908–09 Manchester C and Leicester Fosse
1909–10 Bolton W and Chelsea
1910–11 Bristol C and Nottingham F
1911–12 Preston NE and Bury
1912–13 Notts Co and Woolwich Arsenal

1913–14	Preston NE and Derby Co
1914–15	Tottenham H and Chelsea*
1919–20	Notts Co and Sheffield W
1920–21	Derby Co and Bradford PA
1921–22	Bradford C and Manchester U
1922–23	Stoke C and Oldham Ath
1923–24	Chelsea and Middlesbrough
1924–25	Preston NE and Nottingham F
1925–26	Manchester C and Notts Co
1926–27	Leeds U and WBA
1927–28	Tottenham H and Middlesbrough
1928–29	Bury and Cardiff C
1929–30	Burnley and Everton
1930–31	Leeds U and Manchester U
1931–32	Grimsby T and West Ham U
1932–33	Bolton W and Blackpool
1933–34	Newcastle U and Sheffield U
1934–35	Leicester C and Tottenham H
1935–36	Aston Villa and Blackburn R
1936–37	Manchester U and Sheffield W
1937–38	Manchester C and WBA
1938–39	Birmingham C and Leicester C
1946–47	Brentford and Leeds U
1947–48	Blackburn R and Grimsby T
1948–49	Preston NE and Sheffield U
1949–50	Manchester C and Birmingham C
1950–51	Sheffield W and Everton
1951–52	Huddersfield T and Fulham
1952–53	Stoke C and Derby Co
1953–54	Middlesbrough and Liverpool
1954–55	Leicester C and Sheffield W
1955–56	Huddersfield T and Sheffield U
1956–57	Charlton Ath and Cardiff C
1957–58	Sheffield W and Sunderland
1958–59	Portsmouth and Aston Villa
1959–60	Luton T and Leeds U
1960–61	Preston NE and Newcastle U
1961–62	Chelsea and Cardiff C
1962–63	Manchester C and Leyton Orient
1963–64	Bolton W and Ipswich T
1964–65	Wolverhampton W and Birmingham C
1965–66	Northampton T and Blackburn R
1966–67	Aston Villa and Blackpool
1967–68	Fulham and Sheffield U
1968–69	Leicester C and QPR
1969–70	Sunderland and Sheffield W
1970–71	Burnley and Blackpool
1971–72	Huddersfield T and Nottingham F
1972–73	Crystal Palace and WBA

1973–74	Southampton, Manchester U, Norwich C
1974–75	Luton T, Chelsea, Carlisle U
1975–76	Wolverhampton W, Burnley, Sheffield U
1976–77	Sunderland, Stoke C, Tottenham H
1977–78	West Ham U, Newcastle U, Leicester C
1978–79	QPR, Birmingham C, Chelsea
1979–80	Bristol C, Derby Co, Bolton W
1980–81	Norwich C, Leicester C, Crystal Palace
1981–82	Leeds U, Wolverhampton W, Middlesbrough
1982–83	Manchester C, Swansea C, Brighton & HA
1983–84	Birmingham C, Notts Co, Wolverhampton W
1984–85	Norwich C, Sunderland, Stoke C
1985–86	Ipswich T, Birmingham C, WBA
1986–87	Leicester C, Manchester C, Aston Villa
1987–88	Chelsea**, Portsmouth, Watford, Oxford U
1988–89	Middlesbrough, West Ham U, Newcastle U
1989–90	Sheffield W, Charlton Ath, Millwall
1990–91	Sunderland and Derby Co
1991–92	Luton T, Notts Co, West Ham U
1992–93	Brentford, Cambridge U, Bristol R
1993–94	Birmingham C, Oxford U, Peterborough U
1994–95	Swindon T, Burnley, Bristol C, Notts Co
1995–96	Millwall, Watford, Luton T
1996–97	Grimsby T, Oldham Ath, Southend U
1997–98	Manchester C, Stoke C, Reading
1998–99	Bury, Oxford U, Bristol C
1999–00	Walsall, Port Vale, Swindon T
2000–01	Huddersfield T, QPR, Tranmere R
2001–02	Crewe Alex, Barnsley, Stockport Co
2002–03	Sheffield W, Brighton & HA, Grimsby T
2003–04	Walsall, Bradford C, Wimbledon

**Relegated after play-offs.*
Subsequently re-elected to Division 1 when League was extended after the War.

DIVISION 2 TO DIVISION 3

1920–21	Stockport Co
1921–22	Bradford PA and Bristol C
1922–23	Rotherham Co and Wolverhampton W
1923–24	Nelson and Bristol C

1924–25	Crystal Palace and Coventry C
1925–26	Stoke C and Stockport Co
1926–27	Darlington and Bradford C
1927–28	Fulham and South Shields
1928–29	Port Vale and Clapton Orient

1929–30	Hull C and Notts Co
1930–31	Reading and Cardiff C
1931–32	Barnsley and Bristol C
1932–33	Chesterfield and Charlton Ath
1933–34	Millwall and Lincoln C
1934–35	Oldham Ath and Notts Co
1935–36	Port Vale and Hull C
1936–37	Doncaster R and Bradford C
1937–38	Barnsley and Stockport Co
1938–39	Norwich C and Tranmere R
1946–47	Swansea T and Newport Co
1947–48	Doncaster R and Millwall
1948–49	Nottingham F and Lincoln C
1949–50	Plymouth Arg and Bradford PA
1950–51	Grimsby T and Chesterfield
1951–52	Coventry C and QPR
1952–53	Southampton and Barnsley
1953–54	Brentford and Oldham Ath
1954–55	Ipswich T and Derby Co
1955–56	Plymouth Arg and Hull C
1956–57	Port Vale and Bury
1957–58	Doncaster R and Notts Co
1958–59	Barnsley and Grimsby T
1959–60	Bristol C and Hull C
1960–61	Lincoln C and Portsmouth
1961–62	Brighton & HA and Bristol R
1962–63	Walsall and Luton T
1963–64	Grimsby T and Scunthorpe U
1964–65	Swindon T and Swansea T
1965–66	Middlesbrough and Leyton Orient
1966–67	Northampton T and Bury
1967–68	Plymouth Arg and Rotherham U
1968–69	Fulham and Bury
1969–70	Preston NE and Aston Villa
1970–71	Blackburn R and Bolton W
1971–72	Charlton Ath and Watford
1972–73	Huddersfield T and Brighton & HA
1973–74	Crystal Palace, Preston NE, Swindon T
1974–75	Millwall, Cardiff C, Sheffield W
1975–76	Oxford U, York C, Portsmouth
1976–77	Carlisle U, Plymouth Arg, Hereford U
1977–78	Blackpool, Mansfield T, Hull C
1978–79	Sheffield U, Millwall, Blackburn R

1979–80	Fulham, Burnley, Charlton Ath
1980–81	Preston NE, Bristol C, Bristol R
1981–82	Cardiff C, Wrexham, Orient
1982–83	Rotherham U, Burnley, Bolton W
1983–84	Derby Co, Swansea C, Cambridge U
1984–85	Notts Co, Cardiff C, Wolverhampton W
1985–86	Carlisle U, Middlesbrough, Fulham
1986–87	Sunderland**, Grimsby T, Brighton & HA
1987–88	Huddersfield T, Reading, Sheffield U**
1988–89	Shrewsbury T, Birmingham C, Walsall
1989–90	Bournemouth, Bradford C, Stoke C
1990–91	WBA and Hull C
1991–92	Plymouth Arg, Brighton & HA, Port Vale
1992–93	Preston NE, Mansfield T, Wigan Ath, Chester C
1993–94	Fulham, Exeter C, Hartlepool U, Barnet
1994–95	Cambridge U, Plymouth Arg, Cardiff C, Chester C, Leyton Orient
1995–96	Carlisle U, Swansea C, Brighton & HA, Hull C
1996–97	Peterborough U, Shrewsbury T, Rotherham U, Notts Co
1997–98	Brentford, Plymouth Arg, Carlisle U, Southend U
1998–99	York C, Northampton T, Lincoln C, Macclesfield T
1999–00	Cardiff C, Blackpool, Scunthorpe U, Chesterfield
2000–01	Bristol R, Luton T, Swansea C, Oxford U
2001–02	Bournemouth, Bury, Wrexham, Cambridge U
2002–03	Cheltenham T, Huddersfield T, Mansfield T, Northampton T
2003–04	Grimsby T, Rushden & D, Notts Co, Wycombe W

DIVISION 3 TO DIVISION 4

1958–59	Rochdale, Notts Co, Doncaster R, Stockport Co
1959–60	Accrington S, Wrexham, Mansfield T, York C
1960–61	Chesterfield, Colchester U, Bradford C, Tranmere R
1961–62	Newport Co, Brentford, Lincoln C, Torquay U
1962–63	Bradford PA, Brighton & HA, Carlisle U, Halifax T
1963–64	Millwall, Crewe Alex, Wrexham, Notts Co

1964–65	Luton T, Port Vale, Colchester U, Barnsley
1965–66	Southend U, Exeter C, Brentford, York C
1966–67	Doncaster R, Workington, Darlington, Swansea T
1967–68	Scunthorpe U, Colchester U, Grimsby T, Peterborough U (demoted)
1968–69	Oldham Ath, Crewe Alex, Hartlepool, Northampton T

1969–70	Bournemouth, Southport, Barrow, Stockport Co
1970–71	Reading, Bury, Doncaster R, Gillingham
1971–72	Mansfield T, Barnsley, Torquay U, Bradford C
1972–73	Rotherham U, Brentford, Swansea C, Scunthorpe U
1973–74	Cambridge U, Shrewsbury T, Southport, Rochdale
1974–75	Bournemouth, Tranmere R, Watford, Huddersfield T
1975–76	Aldershot, Colchester U, Southend U, Halifax T
1976–77	Reading, Northampton T, Grimsby T, York C
1977–78	Port Vale, Bradford C, Hereford U, Portsmouth
1978–79	Peterborough U, Walsall, Tranmere R, Lincoln C
1979–80	Bury, Southend U, Mansfield T, Wimbledon
1980–81	Sheffield U, Colchester U, Blackpool, Hull C
1981–82	Wimbledon, Swindon T, Bristol C, Chester
1982–83	Reading, Wrexham, Doncaster R, Chesterfield
1983–84	Scunthorpe U, Southend U, Port Vale, Exeter C
1984–85	Burnley, Orient, Preston NE, Cambridge U
1985–86	Lincoln C, Cardiff C, Wolverhampton W, Swansea C
1986–87	Bolton W**, Carlisle U, Darlington, Newport Co
1987–88	Doncaster R, York C, Grimsby T, Rotherham U**
1988–89	Southend U, Chesterfield, Gillingham, Aldershot
1989–90	Cardiff C, Northampton T, Blackpool, Walsall
1990–91	Crewe Alex, Rotherham U, Mansfield T
1991–92	Bury, Shrewsbury T, Torquay U, Darlington

**Relegated after play-offs.

FOOTBALL LEAGUE PLAY-OFFS 2003–04

DIV 1 SEMI-FINALS FIRST LEG

| Crystal Palace | (0) 3 | Sunderland | (0) 2 |
| Ipswich T | (0) 1 | West Ham U | (0) 0 |

DIV 2 SEMI-FINALS FIRST LEG

| Hartlepool U | (0) 1 | Bristol C | (1) 1 |
| Swindon T | (0) 0 | Brighton & HA | (0) 1 |

DIV 3 SEMI-FINALS FIRST LEG

| Lincoln C | (0) 1 | Huddersfield T | (1) 2 |
| Northampton T | (0) 0 | Mansfield T | (1) 2 |

DIV 1 SEMI-FINALS SECOND LEG

| Sunderland | (2) 2 | Crystal Palace | (0) 1 |

aet; Crystal Palace won 5-4 on penalties

| West Ham U | (0) 2 | Ipswich T | (0) 0 |

DIV 2 SEMI-FINALS SECOND LEG

| Bristol C | (0) 2 | Hartlepool U | (0) 1 |
| Brighton & HA | (0) 1 | Swindon T | (0) 2 |

aet; Brighton & HA won 4-3 on penalties

DIV 3 SEMI-FINALS SECOND LEG

| Huddersfield T | (0) 2 | Lincoln C | (2) 2 |
| Mansfield T | (0) 1 | Northampton T | (2) 3 |

aet; Mansfield T won 5-4 on penalties

DIV 1 FINAL

| Crystal Palace | (0) 1 | West Ham U | (0) 0 |

DIV 2 FINAL

| Brighton & HA | (0) 1 | Bristol C | (0) 0 |

DIV 3 FINAL

| Huddersfield T | (0) 0 | Mansfield T | (0) 0 |

aet; Huddersfield T won 4-1 on penalties

LEAGUE TITLE WINS

FA PREMIER LEAGUE – Manchester U 8, Arsenal 3, Blackburn R 1.

LEAGUE DIVISION 1 – Liverpool 18, Arsenal 10, Everton 9, Sunderland 8, Aston Villa 7, Manchester U 7, Newcastle U 5, Sheffield W 4, Huddersfield T 3, Leeds U 3, Manchester C 3, Portsmouth 3, Wolverhampton W 3, Blackburn R 2, Burnley 2, Derby Co 2, Nottingham F 2, Preston NE 2, Tottenham H 2; Bolton W, Charlton Ath, Chelsea, Crystal Palace, Fulham, Ipswich T, Middlesbrough, Norwich C, Sheffield U, WBA 1 each.

LEAGUE DIVISION 2 – Leicester C 6, Manchester C 6, Birmingham C (one as Small Heath) 5, Sheffield W 5, Derby Co 4, Liverpool 4, Preston NE 4, Ipswich T 3, Leeds U 3, Middlesbrough 3, Notts Co 3, Stoke C 3, Aston Villa 2, Bolton W 2, Burnley 2, Bury 2, Chelsea 2, Fulham 2, Grimsby T 2, Manchester U 2, Millwall 2, Norwich C 2, Nottingham F 2, Tottenham H 2, WBA 2, West Ham U 2, Wolverhampton W 2; Blackburn R, Blackpool, Bradford C, Brentford, Brighton & HA, Bristol C, Coventry C, Crystal Palace, Everton, Huddersfield T, Luton T, Newcastle U, Plymouth Arg, QPR, Oldham Ath, Oxford U, Reading, Sheffield U, Sunderland, Swindon T, Watford, Wigan Ath 1 each.

LEAGUE DIVISION 3 – Brentford 2, Carlisle U 2, Oxford U 2, Plymouth Arg 2, Portsmouth 2, Preston NE 2, Shrewsbury T 2; Aston Villa, Blackburn R, Bolton W, Bournemouth, Bradford C, Brighton & HA, Bristol R, Burnley, Bury, Cambridge U, Cardiff C, Coventry C, Doncaster R, Grimsby T, Hereford U, Hull C, Leyton Orient, Mansfield T, Northampton T, Notts Co, Oldham Ath, QPR, Reading, Rotherham U, Rushden & D Southampton, Sunderland, Swansea C, Watford, Wigan Ath, Wolverhampton W, Wrexham 1 each.

LEAGUE DIVISION 4 – Chesterfield 2, Doncaster R 2, Peterborough U 2; Brentford, Brighton & HA, Burnley, Cambridge U, Darlington, Exeter C, Gillingham, Grimsby T, Huddersfield T, Lincoln C, Luton T, Mansfield T, Millwall, Northampton T, Notts Co, Port Vale, Reading, Rotherham U, Sheffield U, Southend U, Southport, Stockport Co, Swindon T, Walsall, Watford, Wimbledon, Wolverhampton W, York C 1 each.

To 1957–58

DIVISION 3 (South) – Bristol C 3, Charlton Ath 2, Ipswich T 2, Millwall 2, Notts Co 2, Plymouth Arg 2, Swansea T 2; Brentford, Brighton & HA, Bristol R, Cardiff C, Coventry C, Crystal Palace, Fulham, Leyton Orient, Luton T, Newport Co, Norwich C, Nottingham F, Portsmouth, QPR, Reading, Southampton 1 each.

DIVISION 3 (North) – Barnsley 3, Doncaster R 3, Lincoln C 3, Chesterfield 2, Grimsby T 2, Hull C 2, Port Vale 2, Stockport Co 2; Bradford C, Bradford PA, Darlington, Derby Co, Nelson, Oldham Ath, Rotherham U, Scunthorpe U, Stoke C, Tranmere R, Wolverhampton W 1 each.

LEAGUE STATUS FROM 1986–87

	RELEGATED FROM LEAGUE	PROMOTED TO LEAGUE
1986–87	Lincoln C	Scarborough
1987–88	Newport Co	Lincoln C
1988–89	Darlington	Maidstone U
1989–90	Colchester U	Darlington
1990–91	—	Barnet
1991–92	—	Colchester U
1992–93	Halifax T	Wycombe W
1993–94	—	—
1994–95	—	—
1995–96	—	—
1996–97	Hereford U	Macclesfield T
1997–98	Doncaster R	Halifax T
1998–99	Scarborough	Cheltenham T
1999–2000	Chester C	Kidderminster H
2000–01	Barnet	Rushden & D
2001–02	Halifax T	Boston U
2002–03	Shrewsbury T, Exeter C	Yeovil T, Doncaster R
2003–04	Carlisle U, York C	Chester C, Shrewsbury T

LEAGUE ATTENDANCES 2003–2004

FA BARCLAYCARD PREMIERSHIP ATTENDANCES

	Average Gate			Season 2003/04	
	2002/03	2003/04	+/–%	Highest	Lowest
Arsenal	38,040	38,079	+0.10	38,419	37,677
Aston Villa	35,081	36,622	+4.21	42,573	28,625
Birmingham City	28,813	29,078	+0.91	29,588	27,225
Blackburn Rovers	26,228	24,376	–7.60	30,074	19,939
Bolton Wanderers	24,965	26,718	+6.56	27,668	23,098
Charlton Athletic	26,235	26,278	+0.16	26,752	25,184
Chelsea	39,799	41,272	+3.57	41,932	40,491
Everton	38,468	38,837	+0.95	40,228	35,775
Fulham	16,685	16,240	–2.74	18,431	13,981
Leeds United	39,127	36,666	–6.71	40,153	30,544
Leicester City	29,219	30,983	+5.69	32,148	26,674
Liverpool	43,234	42,677	–1.31	44,374	34,663
Manchester City	34,451	46,830	+26.43	47,304	44,307
Manchester United	67,630	67,641	+0.02	67,758	67,346
Middlesbrough	31,005	30,395	–2.01	34,738	26,721
Newcastle United	51,920	51,966	+0.09	52,165	50,104
Portsmouth	18,934	20,054	+5.58	20,140	19,126
Southampton	30,680	31,717	+3.27	32,151	30,513
Tottenham Hotspur	35,899	34,872	–2.95	36,107	30,025
Wolverhampton Wanderers	25,745	28,864	+10.81	29,396	27,327

NATIONWIDE FOOTBALL LEAGUE: DIVISION ONE ATTENDANCES

	Average Gate			Season 2003/04	
	2002/03	2003/04	+/–%	Highest	Lowest
Bradford City	12,501	11,377	–9.9	17,143	9,011
Burnley	13,977	12,541	–11.5	18,852	9,473
Cardiff City	13,050	15,569	+16.2	19,202	13,021
Coventry City	14,813	14,816	+0.0	22,195	10,872
Crewe Alexandra	6,761	7,741	+12.7	10,014	5,867
Crystal Palace	16,867	17,344	+2.8	23,977	12,259
Derby County	25,470	22,200	–14.7	32,390	18,459
Gillingham	8,082	8,517	+5.1	11,418	6,923
Ipswich Town	25,455	24,520	–3.8	30,152	20,912
Millwall	8,512	10,497	+18.9	14,425	7,855
Norwich City	20,353	19,074	–6.7	23,942	16,082
Nottingham Forest	24,437	24,759	+1.3	29,172	20,168
Preston North End	13,853	14,150	+2.1	19,161	11,152
Reading	16,011	15,095	–6.1	21,718	10,543
Rotherham United	7,522	7,138	–5.4	11,455	5,450
Sheffield United	18,113	21,646	+16.3	27,008	17,396
Stoke City	14,588	14,425	–1.1	20,126	10,277
Sunderland	39,698	27,119	–46.4	36,278	22,167
Walsall	6,978	7,853	+11.1	11,049	6,395
Watford	13,405	14,856	+9.8	20,950	10,381
West Bromwich Albion	26,523	24,765	–7.1	27,195	22,048
West Ham United	34,404	31,167	–10.4	35,021	24,365
Wigan Athletic	7,288	9,505	+23.3	20,069	6,696
Wimbledon	2,786	4,751	+41.4	8,118	1,054

Premiership attendance averages and highest crowd figures for 2003–04 are official. Other attendances unofficial.

NATIONWIDE FOOTBALL LEAGUE: DIVISION TWO ATTENDANCES

	Average Gate			Season 2003/04	
	2002/03	2003/04	+/–%	Highest	Lowest
Barnsley	9,758	9,620	–1.4	20,438	7,547
Blackpool	6,991	6,326	–10.5	8,340	4,617
AFC Bournemouth	5,829	6,913	+15.7	8,909	5,837
Brentford	5,759	5,542	–3.9	9,485	3,818
Brighton & Hove Albion	6,651	6,248	–6.5	6,618	5,642
Bristol City	11,890	12,879	+7.7	19,101	9,365
Chesterfield	4,108	4,331	+5.1	7,695	3,123
Colchester United	3,387	3,536	+4.2	5,083	2,513
Grimsby Town	5,884	4,730	–24.4	6,856	3,143
Hartlepool United	4,943	5,419	+8.8	7,448	4,135
Luton Town	6,747	6,339	–6.4	8,499	5,002
Notts County	6,154	5,940	–3.6	9,601	4,145
Oldham Athletic	6,699	6,566	–2.0	13,007	4,990
Peterborough United	4,955	5,274	+6.0	10,194	3,855
Plymouth Argyle	8,981	12,654	+29.0	19,888	7,594
Port Vale	4,436	5,810	+23.6	7,958	4,523
Queens Park Rangers	13,206	14,785	+10.7	18,396	11,854
Rushden & Diamonds	4,330	4,457	+2.8	5,823	3,074
Sheffield Wednesday	20,327	22,336	+9.0	29,313	18,799
Stockport County	5,489	5,315	–3.3	8,617	3,683
Swindon Town	5,440	7,925	+31.4	14,540	5,313
Tranmere Rovers	7,877	7,606	–3.6	10,301	6,675
Wrexham	4,263	4,440	+4.0	8,497	3,035
Wycombe Wanderers	6,002	5,291	–13.4	7,634	4,401

NATIONWIDE FOOTBALL LEAGUE: DIVISION THREE ATTENDANCES

	Average Gate			Season 2003/04	
	2002/03	2003/04	+/–%	Highest	Lowest
Boston United	3,049	2,964	–2.9	5,708	2,147
Bristol Rovers	6,934	7,142	+2.9	9,812	5,333
Bury	3,226	2,892	–11.5	4,591	1,670
Cambridge United	4,173	3,919	–6.5	5,368	2,713
Carlisle United	4,776	5,617	+15.0	9,524	3,437
Cheltenham Town	4,655	4,116	–13.1	5,814	2,745
Darlington	3,312	5,023	+34.1	11,600	2,920
Doncaster Rovers	3,540	6,939	+49.0	9,720	4,716
Huddersfield Town	9,506	10,528	+9.7	18,633	8,275°
Hull City	12,843	16,847	+23.8	23,495	11,308
Kidderminster Harriers	2,895	2,980	+2.9	4,051	2,162
Leyton Orient	4,257	4,157	–2.4	6,119	3,475
Lincoln City	3,924	4,910	+20.1	8,154	3,441
Macclesfield Town	2,110	2,385	+11.5	3,801	1,513
Mansfield Town	4,887	5,207	+6.1	8,065	3,920
Northampton Town	5,211	5,306	+1.8	7,160	4,010
Oxford United	5,862	6,296	+6.9	9,477	4,962
Rochdale	2,740	3,277	+16.4	4,942	2,049
Scunthorpe United	3,692	3,840	+3.9	6,426	2,326
Southend United	3,951	4,535	+12.9	8,894	2,463
Swansea City	5,160	6,853	+24.7	9,800	4,400
Torquay United	3,132	3,460	+9.5	6,156	2,362
Yeovil Town	4,741	6,197	+23.5	8,760	4,867
York City	4,176	3,963	–5.4	7,923	2,676

TRANSFERS 2003–2004

May 2003	*From*	*To*
27 Loran, Tyrone	Manchester City	Tranmere Rovers
19 Reid, Paul M.	Rangers	Northampton Town

June 2003

11 Clark, Peter J.	Stockport County	Northampton Town
30 Finnan, Stephen J.	Fulham	Liverpool
17 Holland, Matthew R.	Ipswich Town	Charlton Athletic
23 Maylett, Bradley	Burnley	Swansea City

July 2003

10 Agogo, Manuel	Barnet	Bristol Rovers
12 Armstrong, Christopher	Oldham Athletic	Sheffield United
21 Bridge, Wayne M.	Southampton	Chelsea
19 Cochrane, Justin V.	Hayes	Crewe Alexandra
4 Coyne, Daniel	Grimsby Town	Leicester City
26 Duff, Damien A.	Blackburn Rovers	Chelsea
9 Dunn, David J.I.	Blackburn Rovers	Birmingham City
21 Francis, Damien J.	Wimbledon	Norwich City
15 Gower, Mark	Barnet	Southend United
8 Grazioli, Giuliano	Bristol Rovers	Barnet.
14 Hall, Fitz	Oldham Athletic	Southampton
25 Hignett, Craig J.	Blackburn Rovers	Leicester City
22 Hill, Clinton S.	Oldham Athletic	Stoke City
4 Howey, Stephen N.	Manchester City	Leicester City
11 Hulse, Robert W.	Crewe Alexandra	West Bromwich Albion
11 Hunt, David J.	Crystal Palace	Leyton Orient
22 Johnson, Glen M.C.	West Ham United	Chelsea
9 Kewell, Harry	Leeds United	Liverpool
21 Le Saux, Graeme P.	Chelsea	Southampton
31 Low, Joshua D.	Oldham Athletic	Northampton Town
31 McCann, Gavin P.	Sunderland	Aston Villa
30 Miller, Lee A.	Falkirk	Bristol City
9 Murray, Scott G.	Bristol City	Reading
10 Nelson, Michael J.	Bury	Hartlepool United
30 Reid, Steven J.	Millwall	Blackburn Rovers
24 Shipperley, Neil J.	Wimbledon	Crystal Palace
22 Sinclair, Trevor	West Ham United	Manchester City
17 Thatcher, Benjamin D.	Tottenham Hotspur	Leicester City
16 Webber, Daniel V.	Manchester United	Watford
22 Zamora, Robert L.	Brighton & Hove Albion	Tottenham Hotspur

Temporary transfers

15 Chadwick, Luke H. – Manchester U – Burnley;   28 Davies, Clint A. – Bradford C –
Halifax T;   7 Davis, James R.W. – Manchester U – Watford;   10 Gilbert, Peter –
Birmingham C – Plymouth Argyle;   24 Knight, Leon L. – Chelsea – Brighton & HA;   8
O'Neill, Joseph – Preston North End – Bury;   25 Patterson, Simon G. – Watford –
Wycombe W;   29 Stanley, Craig – Walsall – Raith R;   31 Stewart, Michael J. –
Manchester U – Nottingham Forest;   31 Warnock, Stephen – Liverpool – Coventry C

August 2003

26 Arphexad, Pegguy M.	Liverpool	Coventry City
11 Beaumont, James	Newcastle United	Nottingham Forest
8 Britton, Leon J.	West Ham United	Swansea City
29 Butler, Martin N.	Reading	Rotherham United
6 Cole, Joseph J.	West Ham United	Chelsea
8 Connolly, David J.	Wimbledon	West Ham United
20 Cooksey, Ernest G.	Crawley Town	Oldham Athletic
15 Craddock, Jody	Sunderland	Wolverhampton Wanderers
14 Crossley, Mark G.	Middlesbrough	Fulham
15 Curtis, John C.K.	Blackburn Rovers	Leicester City
8 Davis, Kelvin D.	Wimbledon	Ipswich Town
8 Etherington, Matthew	Tottenham Hotspur	West Ham United
11 Gardner, Ross	Newcastle United	Nottingham Forest
4 Goater, Shaun L.	Manchester City	Reading

8 Haas, Bernt	Sunderland	West Bromwich Albion
15 Horlock, Kevin	Manchester City	West Ham United
8 Hutchinson, Jonathan	Birmingham City	Darlington
8 Hylton, Leon D.	Aston Villa	Swansea City
15 Iversen, Steffen	Tottenham Hotspur	Wolverhampton Wanderers
15 Johnson, Michael O.	Birmingham City	Derby County
6 Kanoute, Frederic	West Ham United	Tottenham Hotspur
21 Knight, Leon L.	Chelsea	Brighton & Hove Albion
15 Langley, Richard B.M.	Queens Park Rangers	Cardiff City
15 Lee, Alan D.	Rotherham United	Cardiff City
29 McCann, Ryan P.	Celtic	Hartlepool United
7 McIndoe, Michael	Yeovil Town	Doncaster Rovers
22 McLeod, Kevin A.	Everton	Queens Park Rangers
14 Nash, Carlo J.	Manchester City	Middlesbrough
8 O'Connor, James K.	Stoke City	West Bromwich Albion
15 Phillips, Kevin M.	Sunderland	Southampton
29 Reyna, Claudio	Sunderland	Manchester City
8 Russell, Darel F.R.G.	Norwich City	Stoke City
14 Schemmel, Sebastien	West Ham United	Portsmouth
9 Sodje, Efetobore P.	Crewe Alexandra	Huddersfield Town
8 Sorensen, Thomas	Sunderland	Aston Villa
22 Stamp, Darryn	Northampton Town	Chester City
29 Sullivan, Neil	Tottenham Hotspur	Chelsea
27 Taylor, Gareth K.	Burnley	Nottingham Forest
29 Thome, Emerson A.	Sunderland	Bolton Wanderers
22 Thorpe, Anthony L.	Luton Town	Queens Park Rangers
26 Tonkin, Anthony	Stockport County	Crewe Alexandra
7 Veron, Juan S.	Manchester United	Chelsea
7 Wanless, Paul S.	Cambridge United	Oxford United
7 Wilkshire, Luke	Middlesbrough	Bristol City

Temporary transfers

16 Amankwaah, Kevin – Bristol C – Cheltenham T; 9 Andrews, Keith J. – Wolverhampton W – Stoke C; 8 Ashton, Jonathan J. – Leicester C – Oxford U; 27 Babbel, Markus – Liverpool – Blackburn R; 29 Bailey, John A.K. – Preston North End – Hamilton A; 22 Baldacchino, Ryan L. – Carlisle U – Gretna; 15 Beck, Daniel G. – Brighton & HA – Bognor Regis T; 8 Bishop, Andrew J. – Walsall – Kidderminster H; 8 Boucaud, Andre – Reading – Peterborough U; 14 Bradbury, Lee M. – Portsmouth – Derby Co; 21 Burchill, Mark J. – Portsmouth – Wigan Ath; 8 Caldwell, Gary – Newcastle U – Derby Co; 21 Callery, Alex J. – Worksop T – Ilkeston T; 8 Cameron, David A. – Chester C – Halifax T; 26 Chilvers, Liam C. – Arsenal – Colchester U; 14 Clarke, Lee – Peterborough U – Kettering T; 20 Cole, Carlton – Chelsea – Charlton Ath; 8 Colgan, Nick – Hibernian – Stockport Co; 29 Collin, Adam J. – Newcastle U – Oldham Ath; 28 Connell, Darren S. – Accrington Stanley – Burscough; 22 Corbett, Luke J. – Cheltenham T – Chelmsford C; 7 Danns, Neil A. – Blackburn R – Blackpool; 22 Donaldson, Clayton A. – Hull C – Scarborough; 7 Douglas, Jonathan – Blackburn R– Blackpool; 5 Fagan, Craig – Birmingham C – Colchester U; 29 Flitney, Ross D. – Fulham – Brighton & HA; 29 Forssell, Mikael K. – Chelsea – Birmingham C; 7 Fowler, Lee A. – Coventry C – Huddersfield T; 16 Furness, Adam – Stevenage Borough – Aveley; 8 Gamble, Joseph F. – Reading – Barnet; 29 Gerrard, Paul W. – Everton – Sheffield U; 7 Gill, Robert – Doncaster R– Chester C; 8 Gilroy, David M. – Bristol R– Forest Green R; 31 Gray, Michael – Sunderland – Celtic; 14 Hammond, Elvis Z. – Fulham – Norwich C; 29 Hawley, Karl L. – Walsall – Raith R; 22 Haworth, Robert J. – Hendon – Gravesend & Northfleet; 8 Henderson, Darius A. – Reading – Brighton & HA; 25 Hudson, Mark A. – Fulham – Oldham Ath; 27 Jenkins, Rory A. – Stevenage Borough – Oxford C; 6 Jones, Bradley – Middlesbrough – Rotherham U; 25 Jones, Darren L. – Bristol C – Cheltenham T; 16 Jones, Jimmi-Lee – Wolverhampton W – Forest Green R; 8 Jones, Lee – Stockport Co – Blackpool; 8 Jones, Mark A. – Hednesford T – Bromsgrove R; 1 Juan, Maldonado D. – Arsenal – Millwall; 23 Kilgallon, Matthew – Leeds U – West Ham U; 14 Kirkwood, Scott – Crawley T – Horsham; 29 Kuipers, Michael – Brighton & HA – Hull C; 8 Louis, Jefferson L. – Oxford U – Woking; 6 MacLean, Steven – Rangers – Scunthorpe U; 9 Manuella, Fiston – Aylesbury U – Aldershot T; 15 Marney, Daniel G. – Brighton & HA – Crawley T; 25 May, Ben S. – Millwall – Brentford; 29 McCormack, Alan – Preston North End – Leyton Orient; 15 McKenzie, Michael – Kettering T – Stamford; 18 McLeod, Kevin A. – Everton – Queens Park Rangers; 27 McPhail, Stephen J.P. – Leeds U – Nottingham Forest; 23 McSheffrey, Gary – Coventry C – Luton T; 7 Mellor, Neil A. – Liverpool –

141

West Ham U; 22 Mills, Daniel J. – Leeds U – Middlesbrough; 29 Murray, Adam D. – Derby Co – Kidderminster H; 8 Myhill, Glyn O. – Aston Villa – Macclesfield T; 8 Ndiwa, Lord-Kangana – Bolton W – Oldham Ath; 20 Onuora, Ifem – Sheffield U – Wycombe W; 30 Pell, Robert A. – Worksop T – Lancaster C; 20 Pennant, Jermaine – Arsenal – Leeds U; 2 Pitcher, Geoffrey – Brighton & HA – Stevenage Borough; 8 Pitt, Courtney L. – Portsmouth – Luton T; 11 Price, Jamie B. – Doncaster R– Halifax T; 2 Pullen, James – Ipswich T – Dagenham & Redbridge; 22 Richardson, Marcus G. – Hartlepool U – Lincoln C; 22 Ritchie, Paul M. – Manchester C – Walsall; 11 Robinson, Neil D. – Macclesfield T – Leigh RMI; 22 Russell, Samuel I. – Middlesbrough – Scunthorpe U; 8 Scott, Benjamin T. – Sheffield U – Hereford U; 18 Senior, Michael – Halifax T – Ossett T; 15 Shipperley, James A. – Hayes – Wealdstone; 7 Shuker, Christopher A. – Manchester C – Rochdale; 7 Singh, Harpal – Leeds U – Bury; 27 Smertin, Alexei – Chelsea – Portsmouth; 20 Stirling, Jude B. – Stevenage Borough – Hornchurch; 2 Strong, Greg – Hull C – Bury; 22 Svensson, Mattias – Charlton Ath – Derby Co; 8 Taylor, Maik S. – Fulham – Birmingham C; 8 Ten Heuvel, Laurens – Sheffield U – Grimsby T; 14 Thomas, Bradley M. – Peterborough U – Kettering T; 7 Vine, Rowan – Portsmouth – Colchester U; 8 Voltz, Moritz – Arsenal – Fulham; 8 Walters, Jonathan R. – Bolton W – Crewe Alex; 4 Williams, Thomas A. – Birmingham C – Queens Park Rangers; 11 Willock, Calum – Fulham – Bristol R; 30 Zenden, Boudewijn – Chelsea – Middlesbrough; 30 Zola Makongo, Calvin – Newcastle U – Oldham Ath

September 2003

15 Akinbiyi, Adeola P.	Crystal Palace	Stoke City
12 Ashton, Jonathan J.	Leicester City	Oxford United
17 Devlin, Paul J.	Birmingham City	Watford
25 France, Ryan	Alfreton Town	Hull City
25 Green, Francis J.	Peterborough United	Lincoln City
9 Horsfield, Geoffrey M.	Birmingham City	Wigan Athletic
2 Kilbane, Kevin D.	Sunderland	Everton
1 Martyn, Antony N.	Leeds United	Everton
23 Nolan, Matthew L.	Hitchin Town	Peterborough United
1 Pembridge, Mark	Everton	Fulham
6 Proudlock, Adam D.	Wolverhampton Wanderers	Sheffield Wednesday
5 Ritchie, Paul M.	Manchester City	Walsall
25 Smith, Thomas W.	Watford	Sunderland

Temporary transfers

2 Adams, Adrian – Forest Green R– Bath C; 11 Alexandersson, Niclas – Everton – West Ham U; 27 Allen, Daniel T. – Forest Green R– Evesham U; 17 Amankwaah, Kevin – Bristol C – Cheltenham T; 19 Ayres, Lee T. – Kidderminster H – Tamworth; 26 Baird, Christopher P. – Southampton – Walsall; 12 Bart-Williams, Christopher G. – Charlton Ath – Ipswich T; 15 Beck, Daniel G. – Brighton & HA – Bognor Regis T; 8 Beesley, Mark A. – Chester C – Southport; 20 Benjamin, Trevor J. – Leicester C – Gillingham; 1 Bent, Marcus N. – Ipswich T – Leicester C; 9 Bishop, Andrew – Walsall – Kidderminster H; 23 Blackman, Lloyd J. – Brentford – Scarborough; 7 Boucaud, Andre – Reading – Peterborough U; 12 Brannan, Gerard D. – Wigan Ath – Rochdale; 19 Branston, Guy P.B. – Rotherham U – Wycombe W; 6 Brayley, Albert P. – Canvey Island – Heybridge Swifts; 2 Brodie, Stephen E. – Chester C – Forest Green R; 19 Brown, Wayne L. – Watford – Gillingham; 4 Bull, Ronnie R. – Millwall – Yeovil T; 17 Burton, Deon J. – Portsmouth – Walsall; 25 Cade, Jamie W. – Middlesbrough – Chesterfield; 19 Cavill, Aaron – Northampton T – Bedford T; 17 Charles, Anthony D. – Aldershot T – Lewes; 26 Clark, Steven T. – Southend U – Macclesfield T; 28 Connell, Darren S. – Accrington Stanley – Burscough; 27 Cooper, Adam – Nuneaton Borough – Solihull Borough; 8 Crouch, Peter J. – Aston Villa – Norwich C; 26 Crowe, Dean A. – Luton T – York C; 5 Davies, Christopher M. – Lincoln C – Stamford; 16 Davies, Darren J. – Dover Ath – Molesey; 19 Dawes, Nicholas J. – Rotherham U – Grimsby T; 11 De Bolla, Mark – Charlton Ath – Chesterfield; 12 Devlin, Paul J. – Birmingham C – Watford; 24 Doherty, Sean A. – Fulham – Blackpool; 15 Doig, Christopher R. – Nottingham Forest – Northampton T; 12 Dolby, Christopher – Alfreton T – Wakefield & Emley; 5 Dyer, Lloyd R. – West Bromwich Albion – Kidderminster H; 1 Facey, Delroy M. – Bolton W – Burnley; 7 Fagan, Craig – Birmingham C – Colchester U; 1 Farrelly, Gareth – Bolton W – Burnley; 30 Flitney, Ross – Fulham – Brighton & HA; 23 Forde, David – West Ham U – Barnet; 12 Forrest, Martyn N. – Bury – Leigh RMI; 12 Gilroy, David M. – Bristol R– Clevedon T; 4 Gnohere, Arthur – Burnley – Queens Park Rangers; 5 Green, Dean – Farnborough T – Staines T; 16 Green, Francis J. – Peterborough U – Lincoln C; 9 Hall, Laurence W.L. – Stoke C – Tiverton T; 13 Hammond, Dean J. –

142

Brighton & HA – Aldershot T; 22 Hardie, Brian – Kettering T – Corby T; 16 Harley, Jon – Fulham – Sheffield U; 12 Harper, Kevin P. – Portsmouth – Norwich C; 19 Heath, Nicholas A. – Kidderminster H – Solihull Borough; 5 Henderson, Darius A. – Reading – Brighton & HA; 12 Henderson, Kevin M. – Hartlepool U – Carlisle U; 8 Henry, Solomon – Barnet – Berkhamsted T; 18 Hogg, Anthony T. – Gravesend & Northfleet – Folkestone Invicta; 19 Horrigan, Darren C. – Lincoln C – Cambridge C; 8 Horsfield, Geoffrey M. – Birmingham C – Wigan Ath; 12 Huckerby, Darren C. – Manchester C – Norwich C; 23 Hudson, Mark A. – Fulham – Oldham Ath; 4 Ifil, Jerel C. – Watford – Swindon T; 1 Jeffers, Francis – Arsenal – Everton; 26 Jones, Darren L. – Bristol C – Cheltenham T; 3 Kachloul, Hassan – Aston Villa – Wolverhampton W; 10 Kelly, James – Chester C – Scarborough; 24 Kelly, Stephen M. – Tottenham Hotspur – Watford; 4 Kielty, Gerrard T. – Leigh RMI – Stalybridge Celtic; 19 Kitamirike, Joel D. – Chelsea – Brentford; 1 Konchesky, Paul M. – Charlton Ath – Tottenham Hotspur; 26 Kuqi, Shefki – Sheffield Wednesday – Ipswich T; 5 Lewis, Matthew T. Kidderminster H – Hinckley U; 1 Little, Glen M. – Burnley – Bolton W; 5 Livesey, Daniel – Bolton W – Notts Co; 24 Logan, Richard J. – Boston U – Peterborough U; 11 Lucas, Adam – Leigh RMI – Burscough; 9 Mahon, Alan J. – Blackburn R– Ipswich T; 15 Marney, Daniel G. – Brighton & HA – Crawley T; 19 Martin, Ian – Leigh RMI – Rossendale U; 24 May, Ben S. – Millwall – Brentford; 1 McCarthy, David – Worksop T – Altrincham; 22 McCartney, David J. – Millwall – Egham T; 30 McCormack, Alan – Preston North End – Leyton Orient; 12 McGlinchey, Brian K. – Plymouth Argyle – Torquay U; 6 McGregor, Marc R. – Tamworth – Chippenham T; 12 McKenzie, Michael – Kettering T – Stamford; 19 McNamara, Niall A. – Lincoln C – Alfreton T; 17 McSheffrey, Gary – Coventry C – Luton T; 4 Milner, James P. – Leeds U – Swindon T; 12 Muller, Adam P. – Worksop T – Wakefield & Emley; 2 Mumford, Andrew O. – Swansea C – Newport Co; 19 Neill, Thomas E. – Farnborough T – Bishop's Stortford; 19 O'Brien, Robert L. – Doncaster R– Gainsborough Trinity; 13 Omoyinmi, Emmanuel – Oxford U – Margate; 26 O'Neil, Gary P. – Portsmouth – Walsall; 19 Onuora, Ifem –Sheffield U – Grimsby T; 5 Owen, Gareth J. – Stoke C – Tiverton T; 19 Penfold, Terry –Gravesend & Northfleet – Erith & Belvedere; 1 Perry, Christopher J. – Tottenham Hotspur – Charlton Ath; 16 Pidgeley, Leonard J. – Chelsea – Watford; 19 Pitt, Courtney L. – Portsmouth – Luton T; 6 Proudlock, Adam D. – Wolverhampton W – Sheffield Wednesday; 11 Quinn, Wayne R. – Newcastle U – West Ham U; 29 Rehman, Zeshan – Fulham – Brighton & HA; 23 Richardson, Marcus G. – Hartlepool U – Lincoln C; 8 Roache, Leigh P. – Barnet – Berkhamsted T; 1 Roberts, Jason A.D. – West Bromwich Albion – Portsmouth; 19 Robinson, Carl P. – Portsmouth – Rotherham U; 10 Robinson, Neil – Macclesfield T – Leigh RMI; 19 Ross, Neil J. – Macclesfield T – Northwich Victoria; 19 Russell, Matthew L. – Forest Green R– Farsley Celtic; 19 Russell, Samuel I. – Middlesbrough – Scunthorpe U; 12 Sale, Mark D. – Tamworth – Hucknall T; 7 Shuker, Christopher A. – Manchester C – Rochdale; 19 Simpemba, Ian F. – Wycombe W – Woking; 5 Smith, Gareth S. – Hull C – Stockport Co; 16 Stephens, Kevin – Leyton Orient – Billericay T; 22 Svensson, Mattias – Charlton Ath – Derby Co; 16 Tevendale, James R. – Hucknall T – Leek T; 4 Todd, Andrew J.J. – Blackburn R– Burnley; 26 Twigg, Gary – Derby Co – Burton Albion; 5 Walshe, Benjamin M. – Queens Park Rangers – Gravesend & Northfleet; 2 Westhead, Mark – Stevenage Borough – Hyde U; 29 Whelan, Glenn D. – Manchester C – Bury; 11 White, Andrew – Mansfield T – Boston U; 7 Whitman, Tristram – Doncaster R– Tamworth; 9 Wilkinson, Shaun F. – Brighton & HA – Havant & Waterlooville; 19 Williams, Benjamin W. – Manchester U – Altrincham; 15 Williamson, Michael J. – Southampton – Torquay U; 12 Wilson, Mark A. – Middlesbrough – Swansea C; 12 Wood, Neil A. – Manchester U – Peterborough U; 12 Wright, Thomas A. – Leicester C – Brentford

October 2003

31 Dean, Brian C.	Leicester City	West Ham United
16 Hatswell, Wayne	Chester City	Kidderminster Harriers
23 Ingimarsson, Ivar	Wolverhampton Wanderers	Reading
23 Mullins, Hayden I.	Crystal Palace	West Ham United
14 Quinn, Wayne R.	Newcastle United	West Ham United
14 Robinson, Paul P.	Watford	West Bromwich Albion

Temporary transfers

18 Abbott, Paul – Margate – Hitchin T; 24 Allaway, Shaun – Leeds
Arnison, Paul S. – Hartlepool U – Carlisle U; 27 Baird, Christoph
Walsall; 13 Barrowman, Andrew – Birmingham C – Crew
Christopher G. – Charlton Ath – Ipswich T; 3 Beck
Dagenham & Redbridge; 7 Bell, Lee – Crewe Alex
– Plymouth Argyle – Macclesfield T; 31 Black

21 Bouffong, Jonathon – Ford U – Berkhamsted T; 3 Brady, Matthew J. – Windsor & Eton – Mangotsfield U; 12 Brannan, Gerrard D. – Wigan Ath – Rochdale; 20 Branston, Guy – Rotherham U – Wycombe W; 4 Brayley, Albert P. – Canvey Island – Heybridge Swifts; 3 Brown, Christopher – Sunderland – Doncaster R; 5 Bull, Ronnie R. – Millwall – Yeovil T; 17 Burton, Deon J. – Portsmouth – Swindon T; 24 Burton, Steven P.G. – Hull C – Kidderminster H; 24 Buxton, Jake – Mansfield T – Alfreton T; 30 Buxton, Lewis E. – Portsmouth – AFC Bournemouth; 26 Cade, Jamie W. – Middlesbrough – Chesterfield; 23 Callery, Alex J. – Worksop T – Belper T; 18 Cameron, David A. – Chester C – Droylsden; 14 Camm, Mark L. – Lincoln C – King's Lynn; 24 Carbon, Matthew P. – Walsall – Lincoln C; 24 Clancy, Timothy – Millwall – Weymouth; 21 Clarke, Simon N. – Chelmsford C – Ford U; 17 Cooper, Shaun D. – Portsmouth – Leyton Orient; 24 Coulson, David W. – Lincoln C – Ilkeston T; 31 Cryan, Colin – Sheffield U – Scarborough; 13 De Bolla, Mark – Charlton Ath – Chesterfield; 17 Dichio, Daniele S.E. – West Bromwich Albion – Derby Co; 10 Dove, Craig – Middlesbrough – York C; 29 Downing, Stewart – Middlesbrough – Sunderland; 23 Drysdale, Leon A. – Shrewsbury T – Nuneaton Borough; 31 Elam, Lee P.G. – Halifax T – Yeovil T; 17 Evans, Louie – Gravesend & Northfleet – Bedford T; 31 Facey, Delroy M. – Bolton W – Burnley; 8 Fagan, Craig – Birmingham C – Colchester U; 31 Farrelly, Gareth – Bolton W – Burnley; 7 Folkes, Peter A. – Bradford C – Farsley Celtic; 11 Forde, David – West Ham U – Barnet; 17 Frost, Carl R. – Crewe Alex – Witton Albion; 18 Furness, Adam – Stevenage Borough – Hitchin T; 30 Gamble, Joseph – Reading – Barnet; 1 Gilbert, Peter – Birmingham C – Plymouth Argyle; 2 Gnohere, Arthur – Burnley – Queens Park Rangers; 10 Gore, Shane S. – Wimbledon – St Albans C; 13 Gray, Julian R. – Crystal Palace – Cardiff C; 10 Gulliver, Philip S. – Middlesbrough – Bury; 4 Halls, John – Arsenal – Stoke C; 17 Hammond, Dean J. – Brighton & HA – Leyton Orient; 10 Hanney, Joseph – Tamworth – Rothwell T; 23 Hardie, Brian – Kettering T – Corby T; 10 Harper, Kevin P. – Portsmouth – Norwich C; 14 Heathcote, Jonathan – Cambridge U – Grays Ath; 24 Heath, Matthew P. – Leicester C – Stockport Co; 13 Henderson, Kevin M. – Hartlepool U – Carlisle U; 26 Hogg, Anthony T. – Gravesend & Northfleet – Folkestone Invicta; 10 Hogg, Christopher – Ipswich T – Boston U; 17 Hooper, Ellis – Crawley T – Carshalton Ath; 24 Horrigan, Darren C. – Lincoln C – Ilkeston T; 28 Hunt, Lewis J. – Derby Co – Southend U; 31 Jackman, Daniel J. – Aston Villa – Stockport Co; 25 Jones, Darren L. – Bristol C – Cheltenham T; 31 Jones, Robert W. – Stockport Co – Macclesfield T; 21 Keegan, Paul A. – Leeds U – Scunthorpe U; 22 Kelly, Stephen M. – Tottenham Hotspur – Watford; 31 Kennedy, Peter H.J. – Wigan Ath – Derby Co; 10 Kirkwood, Scott – Crawley T – Fulham; 20 Kitamirike, Joel D. – Chelsea – Brentford; 6 Konchesky, Paul M. – Charlton Ath – Tottenham Hotspur; 17 Lee, David J.F. – Brighton & HA – Thurrock; 21 Lewis, Karl J. – Leicester C – Swindon T; 8 Lewis, Matthew T. – Kidderminster H – Hinckley U; 24 Leworthy, Craig – Havant & Waterlooville – Fleet T; 7 Livesey, Daniel – Bolton W – Notts Co; 9 Lovett, Jay – Farnborough T – Lewes; 1 Lucas, David A. – Preston North End – Sheffield Wednesday; 31 Martin, Ben – Swindon T – Lincoln C; 21 McCartney, David J. – Millwall – Egham T; 31 McCombe, Jamie – Scunthorpe U – Halifax T; 2 McCormack, Alan – Preston North End – Leyton Orient; 12 McGlinchey, Brian K. – Plymouth Argyle – Torquay U; 5 McGregor, Marc R. – Tamworth – Chippenham T; 7 McGregor, Marc R. – Tamworth – Weston-Super-Mare; 17 McKenzie, Michael – Kettering T – Stamford; 22 McSheffrey, Gary – Coventry C – Luton T; 3 Melligan, John J. – Wolverhampton W – Kidderminster H; 9 Mitchell, Craig R. – Mansfield T – Harrogate T; 2 Mkandawire, Tamika P. – West Bromwich Albion – Hereford U; 31 Moore, Paul – Telford U – Hucknall T; 10 Morgan, Alan W. – Blackburn R– Darlington; 22 Mullins, Hayden I. – Crystal Palace – West Ham U; 31 Murray, Karl A. – Shrewsbury T – Northwich Victoria; 24 Myhre, Thomas – Sunderland – Crystal Palace; 24 Nardiello, David A. – Manchester U – Swansea C; 20 O'Brien, Robert L. – Doncaster R– Gainsborough Trinity; 17 Omoyinmi, Emmanuel – Oxford U – Margate; 27 O'Neil, Gary – Portsmouth – Walsall; 17 Oshitola, Oloruntori O. – Grays Ath – Kettering T; 24 Pennant, Jermaine – Arsenal – Leeds U; 6 Perry, Christopher J. – Tottenham Hotspur – Charlton Ath; 15 Pidgeley, Leonard J. – Chelsea – Watford; 3 Pitcher, Geoffrey – Brighton & HA – Woking; 31 Pullen, James – Ipswich T – Peterborough U; 3 Quinn, Alan – Sheffield Wednesday – Sunderland; 3 Reddy, Michael – Sunderland – Sheffield Wednesday; 10 Rees, Matthew A. – Millwall – Aldershot T; 4 Reynolds, Craig J. – Arlesey T – St Albans C; 14 Roberts, Darren A. – Worksop T – Belper T; 19 Robinson, Carl P. – Portsmouth – Rotherham U; 24 Robinson, Ryan – Southend U – Wivenhoe T; 19 Russell, Matthew L. – Forest Green R– Farsley Celtic; 22 Russell, Samuel I. – Middlesbrough – Scunthorpe U; 31 Schumacher, Steven T. – Everton – Carlisle U; 31 Sestanovich, Ashley – Sheffield U – Scarborough; 18 Shields, Anthony G. – Peterborough U – Aldershot T; 21 Smith, Gareth S. – Hull C – Carlisle U; 24 Stark, Eastbourne Borough – Burgess Hill T; 23 Stockdale, Robert K. – Middlesbrough –

144

West Ham U; 20 Surey, Ben – Crystal Palace – Basingstoke T; 21 Svensson, Matthias – Charlton Ath – Derby Co; 12 Sykes, Alexander – Forest Green R– Bath C; 23 Tardif, Christopher L. – Portsmouth – Havant & Waterlooville; 24 Tate, Alan – Manchester U – Swansea C; 31 Traynor, Robert T. – Brentford – Chelmsford C; 17 Vincent, Jamie R. – Portsmouth – Walsall; 21 Walker, Richard M. – Blackpool – Northampton T; 7 Walshe, Benjamin M. – Queens Park Rangers – Gravesend & Northfleet; 13 Warne, Stephen J. – Chesterfield – Worksop T; 31 White, Andrew – Mansfield T – Kidderminster H; 6 Whitman, Tristram – Doncaster R– Tamworth; 12 Whittaker, Andrew – Southport – Kendal T; 16 Wilkinson, Shaun F. – Brighton & HA – Havant & Waterlooville; 30 Williams, Gareth A. – Crystal Palace – Cambridge U; 30 Williams, Ryan N. – Hull C – Bristol R; 16 Williamson, Michael J. – Southampton – Torquay U; 31 Willis, Adam P. – Kidderminster H – Burton Albion; 13 Willock, Calum D. – Fulham – Peterborough U; 31 Wright, Alan G. – Middlesbrough – Sheffield U; 13 Wright, Thomas – Leicester C – Brentford; 2 Zola Makongo, Calvin – Newcastle U – Oldham Ath

November 2003

27 Cade, Jamie W.	Middlesbrough	Colchester United
14 Fallon, Rory M.	Barnsley	Swindon Town
26 Harewood, Marlon A.	Nottingham Forest	West Ham United
20 Heathcote, Jonathan	Cambridge United	Hornchurch
27 King, Marlon F.	Gillingham	Nottingham Forest
28 Perry, Christopher J.	Tottenham Hotspur	Charlton Athletic
11 Rhodes, Alexander	Newmarket Town	Brentford
6 Rigoglioso, Adriano	Morecambe	Doncaster Rovers
19 Young, Philip N.	Vauxhall Motors	Northwich Victoria

Temporary transfers

24 Allaway, Shaun – Leeds U – Walsall; 28 Allen, Mark A. – Birmingham C – Bromsgrove R; 27 Arnison, Paul S. – Hartlepool U – Carlisle U; 14 Ashdown, Jamie L. – Reading – Rushden & Diamonds; 13 Bart-Williams, Christopher G. – Charlton Ath – Ipswich T; 3 Bell, Lee – Crewe Alex – Shrewsbury T; 14 Benjamin, Trevor J. – Leicester C – Rushden & Diamonds; 1 Beresford, David – Plymouth Argyle – Macclesfield T; 14 Bevan, Scott – Southampton – Woking; 20 Bishop, Andrew J. – Walsall – Rochdale; 14 Boyd, Adam M. – Hartlepool U – Boston U; 20 Bradbury, Lee M. – Portsmouth – Derby Co; 15 Brodie, Stephen E. – Chester C –Droylsden; 3 Brown, Christopher – Sunderland – Doncaster R; 24 Brown, Karl E. – Hednesford T – Northwich Victoria; 24 Brush, Richard J. – Coventry C – Tamworth; 25 Burton, Steven P.G. – Hull C – Kidderminster H; 1 Buttery, Luke – Cheltenham T – Chippenham T; 25 Byrne, Daniel T. – Manchester U – Hartlepool U; 21 Caines, Gavin L. – Walsall – Stafford Rangers; 10 Camm, Mark – Lincoln C – Kings Lyn; 8 Chard, Anthony J. – Burgess Hill T – Worthing; 26 Chadwick, Nicholas G. – Everton – Millwall; 7 Chilvers, Liam C. – Arsenal – Colchester U; 10 Clark, Dean W. – Woking – Lewes; 21 Clarke, Jamie C. – Grantham T – Corby T; 21 Clarke, Simon N. – Chelmsford C – Ford U; 14 Crofts, Andrew L. – Gillingham – Dover Ath; 10 Cropper, Dene J. – Lincoln C – Gainsborough Trinity; 21 Cryan, Colin – Sheffield U – Scarborough; 15 Cumberbatch, Mark – Barnet – Ashford C; 21 Curtis, Wayne J. – Morecambe – Barrow; 28 Danaher, Adam P. – Crawley T – Camberley T; 28 Delany, Dean – Port Vale – Macclesfield T; 20 Dinning, Tony – Wigan Ath – Walsall; 30 Browning, Stewart – Middlesbrough – Sunderland; 21 Drysdale, Leon A. – Shrewsbury T – Nuneaton Borough; 21 Edwards, Robert O. – Aston Villa – Crystal Palace; 14 Elliott, Steven W. – Derby Co – Blackpool; 7 Enckelman, Peter – Aston Villa – Blackburn R; 3 Fagan, Craig – Birmingham C – Colchester U; 28 Farrelly, Gareth – Bolton W – Bradford C; 21 Formann, Pascal – Nottingham Forest – Grantham T; 26 Forssell, Mikael K. – Chelsea – Birmingham C; 17 Frost, Carl R. – Crewe Alex – Witton Albion; 10 Garnett, Shaun M. – Halifax T – Morecambe; 10 Gill, Robert – Doncaster R– Dagenham & Redbridge; 20 Gulliver, Philip S. – Middlesbrough – Bury; 7 Haines, Danny – Tiverton T – Mangotsfield U; 21 Hallows, Marcus P. – Chorley – Altrincham; 2 Halls, John – Arsenal – Stoke C; 16 Hammond, Dean – Brighton & HA – Leyton Orient; 8 Hanney, Joseph – Tamworth – Rothwell T; 25 Harewood, Marlon A. – Nottingham Forest – West Ham U; 7 Heath, Nicholas A. – Kidderminster H – Cinderford T; 25 Heath, Matthew P. – Leicester C – Stockport Co; 28 Hudson, Mark A. – Fulham – Oldham Ath; 30 Hunt, Lewis J. – Derby Co – Southend U; 14 Ifil, Jerel C. – Watford – Swindon T; 14 Jackson, James T.W. – Dagenham & Redbridge – Dover Ath; 21 Jackson, Johnnie – Tottenham Hotspur – Coventry C; 14 James, Craig P. – Sunderland – Darlington; 28 Johnson, Jermaine – Bolton W – Oldham Ath; 1 Johnson, Paul M. – Staines T – Chertsey T; 4 Jones, Bradley – Middlesbrough – Blackpool; 26 Jones, Darren L. – Bristol C – Forest Green R; 13 Jones, Gary R. – Barnsley – Rochdale; 21 Kielty, Anthony – Hyde U – Kidsgrove Ath; 20 Kitamirike, Joel D. – Chelsea – Brentford; 10 Konchesky, Paul M. –

145

Charlton Ath – Tottenham Hotspur; 14 Larkin, Daniel – Folkestone Invicta – Chatham T; 20 Lawrence, James H. – Walsall – Wigan Ath; 14 Lindegaard, Andrew – Yeovil T – Weymouth; 3 Livesey, Daniel – Bolton W – Notts Co; 20 Lock, Anthony – Grays Ath – Ford U; 20 Lynn, Charles D. – Carlisle U – Workington; 26 Mahon, Alan – Blackburn R– Ipswich T; 18 Marshall, Andrew J. – Ipswich T – Wolverhampton W; 26 May, Ben S. – Millwall – Brentford; 25 McCombe, Jamie – Scunthorpe U – Halifax T; 17 McGlinchey, Brian K. – Plymouth Argyle – Torquay U; 4 McGregor, Marc R. – Tamworth – Weston-Super-Mare; 21 McGuire, Jamie A. – Tranmere R– Northwich Victoria; 24 McSheffrey, Gary – Coventry C – Luton T; 25 Meechan, Alexander T. – Dagenham & Redbridge – Forest Green R; 17 Melligan, John J. – Wolverhampton W – Doncaster R; 2 Mkandawire, Tamika – West Bromwich Albion – Hereford U; 21 Monk, Garry – Southampton – Barnsley; 14 Muller, Adam P. – Worksop T – Wakefield & Emley; 22 Myhill, Glyn O. – Aston Villa – Stockport Co; 21 Myhre, Thomas – Sunderland – Crystal Palace; 29 Neill, Thomas E. – Farnborough T – Chesham U; 28 O'Brien, Robert L. – Doncaster R– Gainsborough Trinity; 21 Oli, Dennis C. – Queens Park Rangers – Gravesend & Northfleet; 21 Onibuje, Folawiyo – Preston North End – Huddersfield T; 14 Pell, Robert A. – Worksop T – Wakefield & Emley; 20 Pennant, Jermaine – Arsenal – Leeds U; 10 Perry, Christopher J. – Tottenham Hotspur – Charlton Ath; 11 Pidgeley, Leonard J. – Chelsea – Watford; 21 Piper, Leonard H. – Dagenham & Redbridge – Margate; 21 Potter, Graham S. – Boston U – Shrewsbury T; 28 Protheroe, Lee – Canvey Island – Gravesend & Northfleet; 21 Quinn, Alan – Sheffield Wednesday – Sunderland; 9 Rees, Matthew R. – Millwall – Aldershot T; 14 Rehman, Zeshan – Fulham – Brighton & HA; 8 Richardson, Frazer – Leeds U – Stoke C; 14 Roberts, Darren A. – Worksop T – Belper T; 21 Roberts, Mark A. – Crewe Alex – Leek T; 20 Russell, Matthew L. – Forest Green R– Farsley Celtic; 21 Sadler, Matthew – Birmingham C – Northampton T; 21 Semple, Ryan D. – Peterborough U – Farnborough T; 28 Sestanovic, Ashley – Sheffield U – Scarborough; 14 Shaw, Jon S. – Sheffield Wednesday – York C; 13 Sheeran, Mark J. – Darlington – Whitby T; 10 Singh, Harpal – Leeds U – Bury; 8 Smissen, Michael – Dover Ath – Sittingbourne; 14 Smith, Gavin D. – Worksop T – Bradford Park Avenue; 28 Smith, Thomas – Northampton T – Gainsborough Trinity; 24 Stark, Paul – Eastbourne Borough – Burgess Hill T; 30 Stockdale, Robert K. – Middlesbrough – West Ham U; 17 Surey, Ben – Crystal Palace – Basingstoke T; 28 Tickle, David – Leigh RMI – Chorley; 14 Turnbull, Ross – Middlesbrough – Darlington; 17 Vincent, Jamie R. – Portsmouth – Walsall; 21 Walker, Richard M. – Blackpool – Northampton T; 9 Walshe, Benjamin M. – Queens Park Rangers – Gravesend & Northfleet; 12 Walters, Jonathan R. – Bolton W – Barnsley; 21 Watkins, Dale A. – Chelmsford C – Grantham T; 14 Westwood, Keiren – Manchester C – Oldham Ath; 2 Whelan, Glenn D. – Manchester C – Bury; 14 Whittaker, Andrew – Southport – Kendal T; 20 Wilkinson, Andrew G. – Stoke C – Telford U; 21 Williams, Anthony S. – Hartlepool U – Swansea C; 16 Willock, Calum – Fulham – Peterborough U; 13 Wright, Thomas – Leicester C – Brentford; 15 Yates, Adam P. – Crewe Alex – Halifax T; 14 Yeates, Mark S. – Tottenham Hotspur – Brighton & HA; 2 Zola Makongo, Calvin – Newcastle U – Oldham Ath

December 2003

12 Bart-Williams, Christopher G.	Charlton Athletic	Ipswich Town
24 Bloomfield, Matthew J.	Ipswich Town	Wycombe Wanderers
31 Brown, Michael R.	Sheffield United	Tottenham Hotspur
9 Elam, Lee P.G.	Halifax Town	Yeovil Town
5 Halls, John	Arsenal	Stoke City
18 Horsfield, Geoffrey M.	Wigan Athletic	West Bromwich Albion
27 Huckerby, Darren C.	Manchester City	Norwich City
31 Jackman, Daniel J.	Aston Villa	Stockport County
12 Jenkins, Lee D.	Swansea City	Kidderminster Harriers
30 Kitson, David B.	Cambridge United	Reading
2 Kuqi, Shefki	Sheffield Wednesday	Ipswich Town
4 Lewis, Matthew T.	Kidderminster Harriers	Hinckley United
4 Logan, Richard J.	Boston United	Peterborough United
15 McKenzie, Leon M.	Peterborough United	Norwich City
12 Myhill, Glyn O.	Aston Villa	Hull City
8 Robins, Mark G.	Rotherham United	Sheffield Wednesday
19 Svensson, Matthias	Charlton Athletic	Norwich City
30 Williams, Ryan N.	Hull City	Bristol Rovers
18 Willock, Calum D.	Fulham	Peterborough United

Temporary transfers

9 Allen, Mark A. – Birmingham C – Bromsgrove R; 27 Armstrong, Alun – Ipswich T –

Bradford C; 29 Arnison, Paul S. – Hartlepool U – Carlisle U; 31 Ashdown, Jamie – Reading – Rushden & Diamonds; 5 Baldwin, Patrick M. – Colchester U – St Albans C; 13 Baptiste, Alex – Mansfield T – Tamworth; 5 Beckford, Jermaine – Wealdstone – Uxbridge; 15 Benjamin, Trevor J. – Leicester C – Rushden & Diamonds; 21 Bishop, Andrew – Walsall – Rochdale; 2 Blackman, Lloyd J. – Brentford – Chelmsford C; 5 Bonfield, Darren – Hemel Hempstead T – Leighton T; 24 Bonsall, Scott M. – Harrogate T – Stalybridge Celtic; 6 Bowling, Ian – Worksop T – Stalybridge Celtic; 15 Boyd, Adam M. – Hartlepool U – Boston U; 29 Brayley, Albert P. – Canvey Island – Heybridge Swifts; 19 Brennan, Dean J.G. – Stevenage Borough – Hendon; 20 Brodie, Stephen E. – Chester C – Droylsden; 12 Brooks, Jamie P. – Oxford U – Maidenhead U; 3 Brown, Christopher – Sunderland – Doncaster R; 22 Brush, Richard J. – Coventry C – Tamworth; 11 Bryant, Simon C. – Bristol R– Tiverton T; 12 Budge, Kevin C. – Heybridge Swifts – Rothwell T; 24 Burchill, Mark J. – Portsmouth – Sheffield Wednesday; 31 Buxton, Lewis E. – Portsmouth – AFC Bournemouth; 22 Caines, Gavin L. – Walsall – Stafford Rangers; 11 Camm, Mark – Lincoln C – King's Lynn; 8 Causon, Stephen – Crawley T – Eastbourne Borough; 12 Cavill, Arran – Northampton T – Aylesbury U; 27 Chadwick, Nicholas G. – Everton – Millwall; 22 Corbett, Luke J. – Cheltenham T – Weston-Super-Mare; 19 Coulson, Mark D. – Peterborough U – Hitchin T; 16 Crofts, Andrew L. – Gillingham – Dover Ath; 14 Cumberbatch, Mark – Barnet – Ashford T; 30 Delany, Dean – Aston Villa – Macclesfield T; 19 Dell, Steven – Wycombe W – Eastbourne Borough; 29 Dixon, Jonathan J. – Wycombe W – Crawley T; 12 Duffy, Lee – Rochdale – Rossendale U; 1 Dyer, Kenneth – Dover Ath – Chatham T; 19 Easter, Jermaine M. – Hartlepool U – Spennymoor U; 15 Elliott, Steven W. – Derby Co – Blackpool; 5 Enckelman, Peter – Aston Villa – Blackburn R; 5 Fettis, Alan – Hull C – Sheffield U; 12 Fitzpatrick, Ian M. – Shrewsbury T – Leigh RMI; 24 Flitney, Ross D. – Fulham – Brighton & HA; 18 Fryatt, Matthew C. – Walsall – Carlisle U; 19 Furness, Adam – Stevenage Borough – Hertford T; 10 Goodwin, Mark C. – Eastbourne Borough – Burgess Hill T; 6 Green, Leon – Weymouth – Harrow Borough; 19 Green, Michael F. – Southampton – Chippenham T; 6 Haines, Danny – Tiverton· T – Mangotsfield U; 26 Hambley, Timothy J. – Welling U – Folkestone Invicta; 6 Hanney, Joseph – Tamworth – Rothwell T; 12 Harris, Richard L.S. – Wycombe W – Woking; 23 Harvey, Iain D. – Bath C – Yate T; 11 Hawkins, Darren M. – Bristol C – Bath C; 23 Heath, Matthew P. – Leicester C – Stockport Co; 7 Heath, Nicholas – Kidderminster H – Cinderford T; 9 Herring, Ian – Swindon T – Chippenham T; 12 Hogg, Christopher – Ipswich T – Boston U; 29 Holligan, Gavin V. – Wycombe W – Crawley T; 19 Holt, David A. – Stockport Co – Altrincham; 19 Huke, Shane – Peterborough U – Bedford T; 31 Hunt, Lewis J. – Derby Co – Scunthorpe U; 19 Hutton, Rory N. – Peterborough U – Hitchin T; 13 Hynes, Peter J. – Aston Villa – Doncaster R; 2 Jackman, Daniel J. – Aston Villa – Stockport Co; 16 Jackson, James T.W. – Dagenham & Redbridge – Dover Ath; 21 Jackson, Johnnie – Tottenham Hotspur – Coventry C; 14 James, Craig P. – Sunderland – Darlington; 29 Johnson, Jermaine – Bolton W – Oldham Ath; 13 Johnson, Simon A. – Leeds U – Blackpool; 3 Jones, Bradley – Middlesbrough – Blackpool; 30 Jones, Darren L. – Bristol C – Forest Green R; 3 Jones, Robert W. – Stockport Co – Macclesfield T; 16 Kelly, Stephen M. – Tottenham Hotspur – Watford; 16 Konchesky, Paul M. – Charlton Ath – Tottenham Hotspur; 15 Larkin, Daniel – Folkestone Invicta – Chatham T; 24 Larvin, Kevin – Leicester C – Hinckley T; 13 Lucas, David A. – Preston North End – Sheffield Wednesday; 12 Lynch, Simon – Preston North End – Stockport Co; 18 Lynn, Charles D. – Carlisle U – Workington; 17 Marshall, Andrew J. – Ipswich T – Wolverhampton W; 12 Martin, Simon – St Albans C – Cambridge C; 11 Matthews, Lee J. – Bristol C – Darlington; 23 McCafferty, Neil – Charlton Ath – Cambridge U; 15 McEveley, James – Blackburn R– Burnley; 19 McKenzie, Michael – Kettering U – Corby T; 19 McNamee, Anthony – Watford – Barnet; 19 McShane, Luke – Peterborough U – Stamford; 29 Melligan, John J. – Wolverhampton W – Doncaster R; 23 Monk, Garry – Southampton – Barnsley; 11 Moore, Luke I. – Aston Villa – Wycombe W; 5 Morison, Steve – Northampton T – Bishop's Stortford; 12 Morrow, Samuel – Ipswich T – Boston U; 23 Mumford, Andrew O. – Swansea C – Aldershot T; 30 Myhre, Thomas – Sunderland – Crystal Palace; 2 Niven, Derek – Bolton W – Chesterfield; 13 Northmore, Ryan – Woking – Bath C; 29 O'Brien, Robert L. – Doncaster R– Gainsborough Trinity; 21 Oli, Dennis C. – Queens Park Rangers – Gravesend & Northfleet; 22 Onibuje, Folawiyo – Preston North End – Huddersfield T; 23 Owusu, Lloyd M. – Sheffield Wednesday – Reading; 30 Pacquette, Richard – Queens Park Rangers – Dagenham & Redbridge; 12 Parton, Andrew – Scunthorpe U – Harrogate T; 24 Peat, Nathan N.M. – Hull C – Cambridge U; 20 Pennant, Jermaine – Arsenal – Leeds U; 12 Pitcher, Geoffrey – Brighton & HA – Barnet; 28 Pitt, Courtney L. – Portsmouth – Coventry C; 29 Protheroe, Lee – Canvey Island – Gravesend & Northfleet; 5 Reece, Dominic M.A. – Farnborough T – Halesowen

147

T; 7 Rees, Matthew R. – Millwall – Aldershot T; 19 Regan, Carl A. – Hull C – Chester C; 15 Rehman, Zeshan – Fulham – Brighton & HA; 8 Richardson, Marcus G. – Hartlepool U – Lincoln C; 31 Rickers, Paul S. – Northampton T – Leigh RMI; 9 Roache, Lee P. – Barnet – Bishop's Stortford; 19 Roberts, Darren A. – Worksop T – Belper T; 21 Roberts, Mark A. – Crewe Alex – Leek T; 8 Robins, Mark G. – Rotherham U – Sheffield Wednesday; 11 Robinson, Mark – Hartlepool U – Spennymoor U; 23 Robinson, Neil D. – Macclesfield T – Southport; 30 Rogers, Alan – Leicester C – Wigan Ath; 24 Rushbury, Andrew J. – Chesterfield – Alfreton T; 23 Sadler, Matthew – Birmingham C – Northampton T; 19 Semple, Ryan D. – Peterborough U – Farnborough T; 14 Shaw, Jon S. – Sheffield Wednesday – York C; 13 Shuker, Christopher A. – Manchester C – Hartlepool U; 8 Smissen, Michael – Dover Ath – Sittingbourne; 12 Smith, Gavin D. – Worksop T – Bradford Park Avenue; 19 Smith, Nicholas – Walsall – Tamworth; 6 Sollitt, Adam J. – Scarborough – Hucknall T; 31 Stephens, Kevin – Leyton Orient – Hornchurch; 30 Stockdale, Robert K. – Middlesbrough – West Ham U; 12 Strouts, James G. – Gravesend & Northfleet – Welling U; 14 Surey, Ben – Crystal Palace – Basingstoke T; 9 Taggart, Gerald P. – Leicester C – Stoke C; 19 Taylor, Jamie – Aldershot T – Carshalton Ath; 12 Taylor, Steven V. – Newcastle U – Wycombe W; 31 Tevendale, James R. – Hucknall T – Ilkeston T; 12 Thomas, Bradley M. – Peterborough U – Aldershot T; 2 Traynor, Robert – Brentford – Chelmsford C; 24 Tynan, Scott J. – Nottingham Forest – Telford U; 12 Uddin, Anwar – Bristol R– Hereford U; 24 Vaesen, Nico – Birmingham C – Gillingham; 31 Walters, Jonathan R. – Bolton W – Barnsley; 22 Watkins, Dale A. – Chelmsford C – Kings Lynn; 5 Weaver, Luke D.S. – Northampton T – Billericay T; 18 Webb, Daniel J. – Hull C – Cambridge U; 31 Westwood, Keiren – Manchester C – Oldham Ath; 23 Whelan, Glenn D. – Manchester C – Bury; 22 Whellans, Robert – Harrogate T – Radcliffe Borough; 31 White, Andrew – Mansfield T – Kidderminster H; 5 White, Robert – Nuneaton Borough – Corby T; 27 Whitworth, Neil A. – Southport – Radcliffe Borough; 11 Wilford, Aron L. – York C – Worksop T; 31 Wilkinson, Andrew G. – Stoke C – Telford U; 1 Willis, Adam P. – Kidderminster H – Burton Albion; 12 Wilson, Brian – Stoke C – Cheltenham T; 13 Woodards, Bradley – Ford U – Barking & East Ham U; 30 Wright, Thomas – Leicester C – Brentford; 15 Yeates, Mark – Tottenham Hotspur – Brighton & HA

January 2004

13 Agyemang, Patrick	Wimbledon	Gillingham
15 Bentley, Mark J.	Dagenham & Redbridge	Southend United
9 Berkovic, Eyal	Manchester City	Portsmouth
28 Cort, Carl E.R.	Newcastle United	Wolverhampton Wanderers
2 Dabizas, Nikos	Newcastle United	Leicester City
26 Duffy, Richard M.	Swansea City	Portsmouth
7 Enckelman, Peter	Aston Villa	Blackburn Rovers
9 Goodfellow, Marc D.	Stoke City	Bristol City
2 Henderson, Darius A.	Reading	Gillingham
30 Holt, Grant	Sheffield Wednesday	Rochdale
30 Howey, Stephen N.	Leicester City	Bolton Wanderers
9 Jackman, David J.	Aston Villa	Stockport County
14 James, David B.	West Ham United	Manchester City
29 Jones, Paul S.	Southampton	Wolverhampton Wanderers
29 Melville, Andrew R.	Fulham	West Ham United.
28 Nowland, Adam C.	Wimbledon	West Ham United
30 Parker, Scott M.	Charlton Athletic	Chelsea
2 Pearce, Ian A.	West Ham United	Fulham
27 Pouton, Alan	Grimsby Town	Gillingham
23 Reo-Coker, Nigel S.A.	Wimbledon	West Ham United
12 Richardson, Marcus G.	Hartlepool United	Lincoln City
13 Roberts, Jason A.D.	West Bromwich Albion	Wigan Athletic
31 Robertson, Hugh S.	Ross County	Hartlepool United
23 Saha, Louis	Fulham	Manchester United
12 Shaw, Paul	Gillingham	Sheffield United
27 Smith, Paul D.	Brentford	Southampton
29 Solano, Todco N.A.	Newcastle United	Aston Villa
30 Sutton, John W.M.	Raith Rovers	Millwall
16 Vincent, Jamie R.	Portsmouth	Derby County
16 Volz, Moritz	Arsenal	Fulham
23 Weatherstone, Simon	Boston United	Yeovil Town
12 Wright, Alan G.	Middlesbrough	Sheffield United

Temporary transfers

16 Abidallah, Nabil – Ipswich T – Northampton T; 1 Allaway, Shaun – Leeds U – Walsall;
1 Allen, Daniel T. – Forest Green R– Clevedon T; 23 Bankole, Ademola – Crewe Alex –
Barnet; 2 Bannister, Patrick T. – Bradford C – Hednesford T; 15 Beardsley, Christopher
K. – Mansfield T – Worksop T; 5 Beckford, Jermaine – Wealdstone – Uxbridge; 16
Benjamin, Trevor J. – Leicester C – Brighton & HA; 16 Beswetherick, Jonathan B. –
Sheffield Wednesday – Macclesfield T; 30 Betts, Thomas G. – Crewe Alex – Vauxhall
Motors; 16 Bevan, Scott – Southampton – Wycombe W; 23 Boertien, Paul – Derby Co –
Notts Co; 29 Bonsall, Scott M. – Harrogate T – Rossendale U; 23 Bowker, Terrence –
Stalybridge Celtic – Radcliffe Borough; 30 Boyd, Adam M. – Hartlepool U – Boston U;
16 Bradley, John – Hornchurch – Boreham Wood; 23 Brayley, Albert P. – Canvey Island
– Hornchurch; 19 Brush, Richard J. – Coventry C – Tamworth; 7 Bull, Ronnie R. –
Millwall – Brentford; 30 Byrne, Shaun R. – West Ham U – Swansea C; 16 Caig,
Anthony – Newcastle U – Barnsley; 22 Caines, Gavin L. – Walsall – Stafford Rangers;
16 Campbell, Jamie – Woking – Havant & Waterlooville; 9 Challinor, David P. –
Stockport Co – Bury; 8 Coates, Steven – Ilkeston T – Shepshed Dynamo; 30 Cobb, Paul
M. – East Thurrock U – Tilbury; 1 Connolly, Gary M. – Bashley – Havant &
Waterlooville; 23 Cook, Lewis L. – Wycombe W – Weymouth; 6 Cooke, Stephen L. –
Aston Villa – AFC Bournemouth; 6 Cooper, Kevin L. – Wolverhampton W –
Sunderland; 20 Corbett, Luke J. – Cheltenham T – Weston-Super-Mare; 19 Coulsen,
Mark D. – Peterborough U – Hitchin T; 15 Cumberbatch, Mark – Barnet – Ashford T; 2
Daly, Jonathan M. – Stockport Co – Bury; 17 Daws, Nicholas J. – Rotherham U –
Grimsby T; 20 Dell, Steven – Wycombe W – Eastbourne Borough; 13 Dichio, Daniele
S.E. – West Bromwich Albion – Millwall; 23 Dinning, Tony – Wigan Ath – Blackpool;
16 Downey, Gareth – Scarborough – Spennymoor U; 16 Duffy, Lee – Rochdale –
Rossendale U; 16 Edwards, Nathan M. – Chippenham T – Swindon Supermarine; 9
Edwards, Robert O. – Aston Villa – Derby Co; 24 Essandoh, Roy K. – Bishop's Stortford
– Gravesend & Northfleet; 30 Facey, Delroy M. – Bolton W – West Bromwich Albion; 2
Fettis, Alan – Hull C – Sheffield U; 9 Foran, Richard – Carlisle U – Oxford U; 9 Forbes,
Dean – Bromley – Tonbridge Angels; 17 Forbes, Scott – Canvey Island – Bishop's
Stortford; 23 Frost, Carl R. – Crewe Alex – Leek T; 19 Fryatt, Matthew C. – Walsall –
Carlisle U; 23 Furness, Adam – Stevenage Borough – Braintree T; 16 Glover, Simon D.
– Dover Ath – Ashford T; 17 Goodwin, Mark C. – Eastbourne Borough – Hastings U;
30 Gradley, Patrick – Gravesend & Northfleet – Boreham Wood; 7 Green, Leon –
Weymouth – Harrow Borough; 16 Gulliver, Philip S. – Middlesbrough – Scunthorpe U;
6 Haines, Danny – Tiverton T – Mangotsfield U; 16 Hall, Laurence W.L. – Stoke C –
Gresley R; 26 Hambley, Timothy J. – Welling U – Folkestone Invicta; 16 Harley, Jon –
Fulham – West Ham U; 13 Harris, Richard – Wycombe W – Woking; 26 Harvey, Iain
D. – Bath C – Yate T; 11 Hawkins, Darren M. – Bristol C – Bath C; 13 Henry, Karl L.D.
– Stoke C – Cheltenham T; 18 Holt, David – Stockport Co – Altrincham; 16 Hudson,
Mark A. – Fulham – Crystal Palace; 19 Hutton, Rory N. – Peterborough U – Hitchin T;
23 Hynes, Peter J. – Aston Villa – Cheltenham T; 23 Jackson, Kirk S.S. – Yeovil T –
Dagenham & Redbridge; 15 Jephcott, Avun C. – Coventry C – Notts Co; 25 Jones,
Darren L. – Bristol C – Forest Green R; 14 Jones, Gary R. – Barnsley – Rochdale; 9
Jones, Paul S. – Southampton – Liverpool; 1 Jones, Robert W. – Stockport Co –
Macclesfield T; 23 Jorgensen, Claus B. – Coventry C – AFC Bournemouth; 13 Lever,
Mark – Ilkeston T – Ossett T; 19 Lucas, David A. – Preston North End – Sheffield
Wednesday; 13 Lynch, Simon – Preston/North End – Stockport Co; 15 Lynn, Charles D.
– Carlisle U – Workington; 16 Marney, Dean E. – Tottenham Hotspur – Queens Park
Rangers; 23 Marshall, Andrew J. – Ipswich T – Millwall; 23 Marshall, Lee K. – West
Bromwich Albion – Hull C; 31 Martin, Andrew – Hornchurch – East Thurrock U; 13
Matthews, Lee J. – Bristol C – Bristol R; 3 Maynard, Tony D. – Hornchurch – Braintree
T; 27 McCafferty, Neil – Charlton Ath – Cambridge U; 19 McEvilly, Lee R. – Rochdale
– Accrington Stanley; 9 McGuire, Liam J. – Southport – Prescot Cables; 7 McMaster,
Jamie – Leeds U – Chesterfield; 3 McShane, Luke – Peterborough U – Stamford; 16
Melville, Andrew R. – Fulham – West Ham U; 23 Mings, Adrian – Chippenham T –
Gloucester C; 14 Mitchell, Craig R. – Mansfield T – Northwich Victoria; 21 Monk,
Garry – Southampton – Barnsley; 19 Myhre, Thomas – Sunderland – Crystal Palace; 27
Nardiello, Daniel A. – Manchester U – Barnsley; 8 Neill, Thomas E. – Farnborough T –
Chesham U; 2 Nethercott, Stuart – Millwall – Wycombe W; 23 Niven, Derek – Bolton
W – Chesterfield; 23 Nolan, Matthew L. – Peterborough U – Cambridge C; 23
O'Hanlon, Sean P. – Everton – Swindon T; 17 Omoyinmi, Emmanuel – Oxford U –
Margate; 29 Orr, Bradley J. – Newcastle U – Burnley; 26 Osman, Leon – Everton –
Derby Co; 16 Owen, Gareth J. – Stoke C – Oldham Ath; 20 Owusu, Lloyd – Sheffield
Wednesday – Reading; 6 Pacquette, Richard F. – Queens Park Rangers – Dagenham &
Redbridge; 16 Palmer, Christopher L. – Derby Co – Hereford U; 15 Parkinson, Andrew

149

J. – Sheffield U – Notts Co; 23 Pattison, Matthew – Farnborough T – Kingstonian; 25 Pears, Richard J. – Tiverton T – Mangotsfield U; 26 Peat, Nathan N.M. – Hull C – Cambridge U; 9 Pemberton, Martin C. – Stockport Co – Rochdale; 30 Penfold, Terry – Gravesend & Northfleet – Chelmsford C; 20 Pennant, Jermaine – Arsenal – Leeds U; 16 Pethick, Robert J. – Brighton & HA – Weymouth; 15 Pipe, David R. – Coventry C – Notts Co; 31 Poate, Brett – Havant & Waterlooville – Bognor Regis T; 18 Pouton, Alan – Grimsby T – Gillingham; 26 Protheroe, Lee – Canvey Island – Gravesend & Northfleet; 4 Pulman, Ian J. – Margate – Eastbourne Borough; 9 Quinn, Barry S. – Coventry C – Rushden & Diamonds; 29 Rachubka, Paul S. – Charlton Ath – Burnley; 30 Raw, Thomas D. – Scarborough – Chorley; 23 Reece, Dominic M.A. – Farnborough T – Sutton Coldfield T; 23 Rees, Matthew R. – Millwall – Dagenham & Redbridge; 23 Roache, Lee P. – Barnet – Windsor & Eton; 30 Roberts, Mark A. – Crewe Alex – Vauxhall Motors; 30 Robinson, Carl P. – Portsmouth – Sheffield U; 14 Rogers, Mark A. – Wycombe W – Stevenage Borough; 26 Rushbury, Andrew J. – Chesterfield – Alfreton T; 15 Sam, Lloyd E. – Charlton Ath – Leyton Orient; 2 Scott, Richard P. – Peterborough U – Stevenage Borough; 9 Semple, Ryan D. – Peterborough U – Farnborough T; 16 Shaaban, Rami – Arsenal – West Ham U; 12 Shuker, Christopher A. – Manchester C – Hartlepool U; 23 Skora, Eric – Preston North End – Kilmarnock; 16 Smith, Jeff – Bolton W – Scunthorpe U; 24 Stark, Paul – Eastbourne Borough – Burgess Hill T; 2 St Ledger-Hall, Sean P. – Peterborough U – Stevenage Borough; 16 Stowe, Christopher J. – Hampton & Richmond Borough – Billericay T; 12 Strouts, James G. – Gravesend & Northfleet – Welling U; 2 Sturridge, Dean C. – Wolverhampton W – Sheffield U; 1 Svard, Sebastian – Arsenal – Stoke C; 6 Taggart, Gerald P. – Leicester C – Stoke C; 16 Taylor, Cleveland – Bolton W – Scunthorpe U; 30 Tierney, Paul T. – Manchester U – Colchester U; 30 Traynor, Robert T. – Brentford – Crawley T; 27 Tucker, Anthony – Walton & Hersham – Hayes; 25 Tynan, Scott J. – Nottingham Forest – Telford U; 2 Tyson, Nathan – Reading – Wycombe W; 14 Uddin, Anwar – Bristol R– Hereford U; 16 Vieira, Magno S. – Wigan Ath – Northampton T; 30 Wales, Gary – Heart of Midlothian – Walsall; 8 Walker, Justin – Cambridge U – York C; 22 Wallwork, Ronald – West Bromwich Albion – Bradford C; 21 Watkins, Dale A. – Chelmsford C – Kings Lynn; 6 Weaver, Luke D.S. – Northampton T – Billericay T; 19 Webb, Daniel J. – Hull C – Cambridge U; 7 White, Robert – Nuneaton Borough – Corby T; 23 Williams, Anthony S. – Hartlepool U – Stockport Co; 2 Williams, Thomas A. – Birmingham C – Peterborough U; 16 Willis, Scott L. – Lincoln C – Northwich Victoria; 10 Wilson, Brian – Stoke C – Cheltenham T; 22 Wilson, Mark A. – Middlesbrough – Sheffield Wednesday; 30 Wood, Neil A. – Manchester U – Burnley

February 2004

2 Arnison, Paul S.	Hartlepool United	Carlisle United
12 Boulding, Michael	Grimsby Town	Barnsley
6 Byfield, Darren	Rotherham United	Sunderland
2 Defoe, Jermain C.	West Ham United	Tottenham Hotspur
27 Dichio, Daniele S.E.	West Bromwich Albion	Millwall
2 Facey, Delroy M.	Bolton Wanderers	West Bromwich Albion
19 Gnohere, Arthur	Burnley	Queens Park Rangers
27 Gray, Andrew D.	Bradford City	Sheffield United
13 Haddrell, Matt	Macclesfield Town	Leek Town
14 Keates, Dean S.	Hull City	Kidderminster Harriers
2 Leigertwood, Mikele B.	Wimbledon	Crystal Palace
6 Mahon, Alan	Blackburn Rovers	Wigan Athletic
4 McAnuff, Joel J.F.M.	Wimbledon	West Ham United
2 Morris, Lee	Derby County	Leicester City
2 Nelson, Stuart	Hucknall Town	Brentford
20 Parkin, Jonathan	York City	Macclesfield Town
10 Proctor, Michael A.	Sunderland	Rotherham United
17 Scoffham, Steven	Gedling Town	Notts County
2 Stead, Jonathan	Huddersfield Town	Blackburn Rovers
6 Tate, Alan	Manchester United	Swansea City
2 Taylor, Martin	Blackburn Rovers	Birmingham City
2 Thomas, Jerome W.	Arsenal	Charlton Athletic
5 Walters, Jonathan R.	Bolton Wanderers	Hull City
26 Webb, Daniel J.	Hull City	Cambridge United

Temporary transfers

7 Abbott, Paul – Margate – Braintree T; 16 Abbott, Pawel T.H. – Preston North End – Huddersfield T; 13 Adams, Adrian – Forest Green R– Bashley; 6 Allen, Daniel T. – Forest Green R– Bashley; 24 Armstrong, Alun – Ipswich T – Bradford C; 24

Armstrong, Craig S. – Sheffield Wednesday – Grimsby T;   6 Awuah, Jones – Gillingham – Dover Ath;   6 Baptiste, Alex – Mansfield T – Burton Albion;   19 Baptiste, Liam D. – Waltham Forest – Barking & East Ham U;   27 Barmby, Nicholas J. – Leeds U – Nottingham Forest;   6 Bishop, Andrew J. – Walsall – Yeovil T;   20 Bowker, Terrence – Stalybridge Celtic – Radcliffe Borough;   7 Bradshaw, Craig R.J. – Portsmouth – Dorchester T;   25 Branston, Guy P.B. – Rotherham U – Peterborough U;   2 Bridges, Michael – Leeds U – Newcastle U;   13 Brodie, Stephen E. – Chester C – Leigh RMI;   27 Brooker, Paul – Leicester C – Reading;   6 Brooks, Jamie P. – Oxford U – Tamworth;   17 Brown, Wayne L. – Watford – Colchester U;   9 Bull, Ronnie R. – Millwall – Brentford;   27 Buttery, Luke – Cheltenham T – Swindon Supermarine;   2 Caldwell, Stephen – Newcastle U – Leeds U;   6 Campbell-Ryce, Jamal J. – Charlton Ath – Wimbledon;   8 Challinor, David P. – Stockport Co – Bury;   19 Chambers, Adam C. – West Bromwich Albion – Sheffield Wednesday;   7 Chopra, Rocky M. – Newcastle U – Nottingham Forest;   25 Clancy, Timothy – Millwall – Weymouth;   13 Clarke, Peter M. – Everton – Coventry C;   7 Coates, Steven – Ilkeston T – Shepshed Dynamo;   1 Connolly, Gary M. – Bashley – Havant & Waterlooville;   24 Cook, James S. – Stevenage Borough – Bath C;   27 Cumberbatch, Mark – Barnet – Wealdstone;   2 Daly, Jonathan M. – Stockport Co – Bury;   13 Davies, Arron R. – Southampton – Barnsley;   23 Daws, Nicholas J. – Rotherham U – Grimsby T;   10 Dichio, Daniele S.E. – West Bromwich Albion – Millwall;   25 Dickman, Jonjo – Sunderland – York C;   27 Dinning, Tony – Wigan Ath – Blackpool;   6 Donaldson, Clayton A. – Hull C – Halifax T;   12 Downey, Gareth – Scarborough – Spennymoor U;   5 Dudfield, Lawrie G. – Northampton T – Southend U;   6 Easter, Jermaine M. – Hartlepool U – Cambridge U;   6 Evans, Louie – Gravesend & Northfleet – King's Lynn;   10 Fettis, Alan – Hull C – Sheffield U;   18 Forbes, Scott – Canvey Island – Bishop's Stortford;   10 Foster, James I. – Chester C – Kidderminster H;   12 Frendo, John – Hendon – Ware;   23 Frost, Carl R. – Crewe Alex – Leek T;   2 Fry, Adam G. – Peterborough U – Rothwell T;   13 Giles, Christopher – Yeovil T – Woking;   21 Glover, Simon D. – Dover Ath – Ashford T;   19 Goodwin, Mark C. – Eastbourne Borough – Hastings U;   13 Grainger, Martin R. – Birmingham C – Coventry C;   27 Green, Michael F. – Southampton – Chippenham T;   27 Groves, Paul – Grimsby T – Scunthorpe U;   27 Hambley, Timothy J. – Welling U – Folkestone Invicta;   17 Harley, Jon – Fulham – West Ham U;   11 Hawkins, Darren M. – Bristol C – Bath C;   27 Hemmings, Anthony G. – Alfreton T – Halesowen T;   10 Henry, Karl – Stoke C – Cheltenham T;   20 Hignett, Craig J. – Leicester C – Crewe Alex;   27 Hirschfeld, Lars – Tottenham Hotspur – Gillingham;   16 Holligan, Gavin V. – Wycombe W – Hornchurch;   27 Holloway, Darren – Wimbledon – Scunthorpe U;   6 Howells, Lee – Cheltenham T – Merthyr Tydfil;   14 Hudson, Mark A. – Fulham – Crystal Palace;   13 Impey, Andrew R. – Leicester C – Nottingham Forest;   2 Johnson, Jermaine – Bolton W – Oldham Ath;   24 Jorgensen, Claus B. – Coventry C – AFC Bournemouth;   10 Keates, Dean S. – Hull C – Kidderminster H;   27 Langmead, Kelvin S. – Preston North End – Carlisle U;   20 Lee, Kris – Thurrock – Heybridge Swifts;   19 Lever, Mark – Ilkeston T – Ossett T;   25 Lewis, Karl J. – Leicester C – Hull C;   2 Lindley, James E. – Tamworth – Hucknall T;   6 Livesey, Daniel – Bolton W – Rochdale;   3 Lua-Lua, Lomano T. – Newcastle U – Portsmouth;   28 Lucas, Richard – Gainsborough Trinity – Stocksbridge Park Steels;   20 Marney, Daniel G. – Brighton & HA – Crawley T;   27 Marshall, Andrew J. – Ipswich T – Millwall;   23 Marshall, Lee – West Bromwich Albion – Hull C;   28 Martin, Andrew – Hornchurch – East Thurrock U;   17 Matthews, Lee J. – Bristol C – Bristol R;   20 McClements, Eddie – Gravesend & Northfleet – Dartford;   20 McEvilly, Lee – Rochdale – Accrington Stanley;   6 McGuire, Liam J. – Southport – Prescot Cables;   9 McMaster, Jamie – Leeds U – Chesterfield;   20 Mkandawire, Tamika P. – West Bromwich Albion – Hereford U;   20 Moore, Neil – Nuneaton Borough – Stafford Rangers;   29 Nardiello, Daniel A. – Manchester U – Barnsley;   6 Ndiwa, Kangana L. – Bolton W – Rochdale;   3 Nethercott, Stuart – Millwall – Wycombe W;   11 Nicholls, Ashley – Darlington – Cambridge U;   27 Noble, David J. – West Ham U – Boston U;   22 Nolan, Matthew N. – Peterborough U – Cambridge C;   23 O'Hanlon, Sean P. – Everton – Swindon T;   17 Oli, Dennis C. – Queens Park Rangers – Farnborough T;   27 Omoyinmi, Emmanuel – Oxford U – Gravesend & Northfleet;   10 Oshitola, Oloruntori – Grays Ath – Great Wakering R;   23 Osman, Leon – Everton – Derby Co;   2 Otsemobor, John – Liverpool – Bolton W;   17 Owen, Gareth J. – Stoke C – Oldham Ath;   20 Owusu, Lloyd M. – Sheffield Wednesday – Reading;   6 Pacquette, Richard F. – Queens Park Rangers – Mansfield T;   6 Parsons, Phil – Woking – Walton & Hersham;   27 Pearson, Gregory – West Ham U – Barnet;   29 Penfold, Terry – Gravesend & Northfleet – Chelmsford C;   20 Pennant, Jermaine – Arsenal – Leeds U;   10 Pettefer, Carl J. – Portsmouth – Southend U;   17 Pipe, David R. – Coventry C – Notts Co;   7 Pitcher, Geoffrey – Brighton & HA – Havant & Waterlooville;   13 Placid, Darren – Heybridge Swifts – Waltham Forest;   13 Pressman, Kevin P. – Sheffield Wednesday – West Bromwich Albion;   6 Proctor, Michael A. – Sunderland – Rotherham U;   27 Proffitt, Darryl S. –

151

Manchester C – Coventry C; 27 Pullen, James D.C. – Peterborough U – Heybridge Swifts;
9 Pulman, Ian J. – Margate – Eastbourne Borough; 20 Randall, Martin J. – Hendon –
Ashford T (Middlesex); 12 Rankin, Isiah – Barnsley – Grimsby T; 26 Reece, Dominic
M.A. – Farnborough T – Sutton Coldfield T; 24 Roache, Lee P. – Barnet – Windsor &
Eton; 27 Roberts, Mark A. – Crewe Alex – Vauxhall Motors; 24 Roberts, Stuart I. –
Wycombe W – Swansea C; 28 Robinson, Mark – Hartlepool U – Scarborough; 19
Robinson, Neil D. – Macclesfield T – Southport; 13 Rocastle, Craig A. – Chelsea –
Barnsley; 13 Rogers, Alan – Leicester C – Nottingham Forest; 16 Rogers, Mark A. –
Wycombe W – Stevenage Borough; 22 Rushbury, Andrew J. – Chesterfield – Alfreton T;
14 Sam, Lloyd – Charlton Ath – Leyton Orient; 20 Saxby, Gavin A. – Alfreton T –
Ilkeston T; 10 Shuker, Christopher A. – Manchester C – Hartlepool U; 14 Smith, Gavin
D. – Worksop T – Ilkeston T; 4 Smith, Jeff – Bolton W – Rochdale; 20 Srnicek, Pavel –
Portsmouth – West Ham U; 20 Stockdale, Robert K. – Middlesbrough – Rotherham U;
12 Strouts, James G. – Gravesend & Northfleet – Welling U; 6 Tansley, Anthony –
Alfreton T – Belper T; 16 Taylor, Cleveland – Bolton W – Scunthorpe U; 6 Teggart,
Neil – Sunderland – Darlington; 6 Thorpe, Lee A. – Leyton Orient – Grimsby T; 29
Traynor, Robert – Brentford – Crawley T; 6 Turner, Iain R. – Everton – Chester C; 3
Tyson, Scott J. – Nottingham Forest – Telford U; 2 Tyson, Nathan – Reading – Wycombe
W; 13 Vaesen, Nico – Birmingham C – Bradford C; 16 Vieira, Magno S. – Wigan Ath –
Northampton T; 26 Wallwork, Ronald – West Bromwich Albion – Bradford C; 6
Walton, David L. – Derby Co – Stockport Co; 19 White, Andrew – Mansfield T – Burton
Albion; 14 White, Robert – Nuneaton Borough – Corby T; 13 Wilford, Aron L. – York
C – Harrogate T; 22 Williams, Anthony S. – Hartlepool U – Stockport Co; 20 Williams,
Daniel I.L. – Kidderminster H – Chester C; 20 Williams, Gareth A. – Crystal Palace –
AFC Bournemouth; 4 Williams, Lee – Grays Ath – Hornchurch; 1 Williams, Thomas A.
– Birmingham C – Peterborough U; 26 Willis, Scott L. – Lincoln C – Hereford U; 2
Zayed, Eamon – Bray W – Crewe Alex;

March 2004

15 Abbott, Pawel T.H.	Preston North End	Huddersfield Town
12 Adams, Daniel B.	Macclesfield Town	Stockport County
25 Anderson, John	Hull City	Bristol Rovers
12 Banks, Steven	Wimbledon	Gillingham
25 Burton, Steven P.G.	Hull City	Kidderminster Harriers
5 Close, Brian A.	Middlesbrough	Darlington
12 Connor, Paul	Rochdale	Swansea City
26 Cropper, Dene J.	Lincoln City	Boston United
25 De Bolla, Mark	Charlton Athletic	Chesterfield
1 Dudfield, Lawrie G.	Northampton Town	Southend United
26 Evans, Paul S.	Bradford City	Nottingham Forest
25 Fagan, Craig	Birmingham City	Colchester United
17 Francis, Simon C.	Bradford City	Sheffield United
25 Heald, Gregory J.	Leyton Orient	Rochdale
25 Henriksen, Bo	Kidderminster Harriers	Bristol Rovers
18 Iwelumo, Chris	Stoke City	Brighton & Hove Albion
12 Johnson, Jermaine	Bolton Wanderers	Oldham Athletic
2 Keates, Dean S.	Hull City	Kidderminster Harriers
8 Mayo, Paul	Lincoln City	Watford
25 McSporran, Jermaine	Wycombe Wanderers	Walsall
19 Melton, Stephen	Hull City	Boston United
26 Murray, Scott G.	Reading	Bristol City
11 Niven, Derek	Bolton Wanderers	Chesterfield
24 Noble, David J.	West Ham United	Boston United
25 O'Hanlon, Sean P.	Everton	Swindon Town
25 Owusu, Lloyd M.	Sheffield Wednesday	Reading
9 Patten, Ben	Ford United	Ipswich Town
5 Payne, Stephen J.	Chesterfield	Macclesfield Town
25 Peschisolido, Paul P.	Sheffield United	Derby County
25 Rankin, Isaiah	Barnsley	Grimsby Town
12 Sabin, Eric	Queens Park Rangers	Northampton Town
17 Shuker, Christopher A.	Manchester City	Barnsley
4 Smith, Jeff	Bolton Wanderers	Preston North End
9 Sobers, Jerrome	Ford United	Ipswich Town
22 Srnicek, Pavel	Portsmouth	West Ham United
12 Strong, Greg	Hull City	Boston United
16 Taylor, Cleveland K.W.	Bolton Wanderers	Scunthorpe United
31 Taylor, Maik S.	Fulham	Birmingham City

19 Thomas, Danny J.	AFC Bournemouth	Boston United
12 Tyson, Nathan	Reading	Wycombe Wanderers
24 Wales, Gary	Heart of Midlothian	Walsall
19 Walker, Richard M.	Blackpool	Oxford United
4 Wilkinson, Wesley	Nantwich Town	Oldham Athletic
25 Williams, Daniel I.L.	Kidderminster Harriers	Bristol Rovers
31 Wilson, Brian	Stoke City	Cheltenham Town

Temporary transfers

5 Adams, Daniel B. – Macclesfield T – Stockport Co; 25 Adebola, Bamberdele O. – Coventry C – Burnley; 17 Allen, Daniel T. – Forest Green R– Taunton T; 13 Andrews, Keith J. – Wolverhampton W – Walsall; 25 Armstrong, Craig – Sheffield Wednesday – Grimsby T; 11 Arphexad, Pegguy M. – Coventry C – Notts Co; 11 Ashcroft, Lee – Southport – Chorley; 8 Baguley, Jamie C. – Stockport Co – Altrincham; 8 Bailey, Mathew J. – Stockport Co – Altrincham; 16 Baird, Christopher P. – Southampton – Watford; 19 Baptiste, Liam D. – Waltham Forest – Barking & East Ham U; 24 Barnard, Lee J. – Tottenham Hotspur – Stevenage Borough; 26 Bates, Tom – Coventry C – Bedworth U; 25 Birch, Gary S. – Walsall – Barnsley; 31 Bixby, Robert – Hayes – Berkhamsted T; 25 Blackman, Lloyd J. – Brentford – Cambridge C; 25 Branston, Guy– Rotherham U – Peterborough U; 30 Britton, Andrew – Sheffield U – Bradford Park Avenue; 31 Brooker, Paul – Leicester C – Reading; 25 Brown, Jermaine A.A. – Boston U – King's Lynn; 25 Brown, Simon A. – West Bromwich Albion – Kidderminster H; 19 Brown, Wayne L. – Watford – Colchester U; 9 Bull, Ronnie R. – Millwall – Brentford; 11 Bullock, Lee – York C – Cardiff C; 12 Camp, Lee M.J. – Derby Co – Queens Park Rangers; 25 Cartwright, Shaun – Stoke C – Leek T; 19 Chadwick, Nicholas G. – Everton – Millwall; 9 Challinor, David P. – Stockport Co – Bury; 20 Chambers, Adam – West Bromwich Albion – Sheffield Wednesday; 25 Clarke, Leon M. – Wolverhampton W – Kidderminster H; 13 Coates, Steven – Ilkeston T – Shepshed Dynamo; 15 Cobb, Paul M. – East Thurrock U – Tilbury; 5 Coleano, Rudi A. – Farsley Celtic – Guiseley; 4 Connolly, Gary M. – Bashley – Havant & Waterlooville; 31 Cook, James S. – Stevenage Borough – Bath C; 27 Cook, Lewis L. – Wycombe W – Cambridge C; 12 Cooper, Colin T. – Middlesbrough – Sunderland; 19 Cooper, Kevin – Wolverhampton W – Norwich C; 25 Cooper, Shaun D. – Portsmouth – Leyton Orient; 12 Danns, Neil A. – Blackburn R– Hartlepool U; 5 De Bolla, Mark – Charlton Ath – Chesterfield; 24 Donnelly, Ciaran – Blackburn R– Blackpool; 16 Donovan, James – Millwall – Farnborough T; 5 Downer, Simon – Leyton Orient – Aldershot T; 13 Dudfield, Lawrie G. – Northampton T – Southend U; 9 Duffield, Peter – Boston U – Carlisle U; 4 Dunbavin, Ian S. – Shrewsbury T – Morecambe; 9 Easter, Jermaine – Hartlepool U – Cambridge U; 25 Elam, Lee P.G. – Yeovil T – Chester C; 16 Elliott, Matthew S. – Leicester C – Ipswich T; 12 Ellison, Kevin – Stockport Co – Lincoln C; 25 Evans, Paul S. – Bradford C – Nottingham Forest; 11 Fettis, Alan – Hull C – Grimsby T; 25 Fieldwick, Lee P. – Brentford – Swansea C; 16 Fitzgerald, Scott B. – Colchester U – Brentford; 22 Fitzpatrick, Ian A. – Shrewsbury T – Forest Green R; 15 Flood, William R. – Manchester C – Rochdale; 5 Foster, Benjamin – Stoke C – Stafford Rangers; 11 Foster, James I. – Chester C – Kidderminster H; 19 Fotiadis, Andrew – Peterborough U – Heybridge Swifts; 16 Francis, Simon – Bradford C – Sheffield U; 31 Furness, Adam – Stevenage Borough – Ware; 22 Gemmill, Scott – Everton – Preston North End; 25 Gerrard, Paul W. – Everton – Nottingham Forest; 12 Gilchrist, Philip A. – West Bromwich Albion – Rotherham U; 12 Gill, Robert – Doncaster R– Burton Albion; 23 Gordon, Dean D. – Coventry C – Reading; 19 Gosling, Jamie J. – Yeovil T – Aldershot T; 22 Gourlay, William – Kettering T – Corby T; 31 Gradley, Patrick – Gravesend & Northfleet – Boreham Wood; 19 Graham, Daniel A.W. – Middlesbrough – Darlington; 19 Grainger, Martin R. – Birmingham C – Coventry C; 19 Gunnarsson, Brynjar B. – Nottingham Forest – Stoke C; 11 Hackworth, Anthony – Notts Co – Scarborough; 19 Hardie, Brian – Kettering T – Corby T; 25 Harkins, Gary – Blackburn R– Huddersfield C; 30 Harris, Richard L.S. – Wycombe W – Maidenhead U; 5 Haworth, Robert J. – Gravesend & Northfleet – Maidenhead U; 30 Hemmings, Anthony G. – Alfreton T – Grantham T; 12 Henderson, Wayne – Aston Villa – Tamworth; 22 Hignett, Craig J. – Leicester C – Crewe Alex; 23 Hill, Stephen B. – Rochdale – Morecambe; 25 Howe, Edward J.F. – Portsmouth – Swindon T; 31 Hughes, Stephen T. – Brentford – Basingstoke T; 25 Hunt, Warren D. – Portsmouth – Leyton Orient; 25 Hurst, Kevan – Sheffield U – Boston U; 15 Impey, Andrew R. – Leicester C – Nottingham Forest; 16 Ingham, Michael G. – Sunderland – Wrexham; 16 Iwelumo, Chris – Stoke C – Brighton & HA; 19 James, Craig P. – Sunderland – Port Vale; 19 John, Jerome L. – Billericay T – Great Wakering R; 25 Jorgensen, Claus B. – Coventry C – AFC Bournemouth; 17 Kerr, Brian – Newcastle U – Coventry C; 19 King, Jordan – Hereford U – Hednesford T; 6 Knight, Glen J. – Dagenham & Redbridge – Bromley; 29 Langmead, Kelvin S. – Preston North End –

153

Carlisle U; 22 Lawrence, Lee A. – Manchester U – Shrewsbury T; 25 Lescott, Aaron A. – Stockport Co – Bristol R; 8 Livesey, Daniel – Bolton W – Rochdale; 29 Lucas, Richard – Gainsborough Trinity – Stocksbridge Park Steels; 25 Matias, Pedro M.M. – Walsall – Blackpool; 20 Matthews, Lee J. – Bristol C – Yeovil T; 8 May, Rory J. – Lincoln C – Halifax T; 31 McCarthy, David – Worksop T – Stalybridge Celtic; 25 McClements, Eddie – Gravesend & Northfleet – Fisher Ath; 12 McLeod, Izale M. – Derby Co – Sheffield U; 24 McMahon, Daryl – West Ham U – Torquay U; 29 McSweeney, David – Southend U – Welling U; 12 Murphy, David P. – Middlesbrough – Barnsley; 5 Nethercott, Stuart – Millwall – Wycombe W; 25 Newby, Jon P.R. – Huddersfield T – York C; 12 Nicholson, Kevin J. – Notts Co – Scarborough; 25 Nicolau, Nicky G. – Arsenal – Southend U; 5 Noble, Stuart W. – Fulham – Woking; 19 Northmore, Ryan – Woking – Yeovil T; 12 Offiong, Richard – Newcastle U – York C; 17 Olszar, Sebastian – Portsmouth – Coventry C; 29 Omoyinmi, Emmanuel – Oxford U – Gravesend & Northfleet; 24 Osman, Leon – Everton – Derby Co; 24 Owen, Gareth J. – Stoke C – Oldham Ath; 19 Parker, Daniel – Worcester C – Evesham U; 19 Parkinson, Andrew J. – Sheffield U – Notts Co; 29 Pearson, Gregory – West Ham U – Barnet; 20 Pennant, Jermaine – Arsenal – Leeds U; 12 Pettefer, Carl J. – Portsmouth – Southend U; 22 Pipe, David R. – Coventry C – Notts Co; 19 Pitcher, Geoffrey – Brighton & HA – Farnborough T; 25 Platt, Matthew – Crewe Alex – Runcorn FC Halton; 25 Price, Michael D. – Scarborough – Leigh RMI; 27 Pullen, James – Peterborough U – Heybridge Swifts; 3 Quinn, Barry S. – Coventry C – Oxford U; 2 Rachubka, Paul S. – Charlton Ath – Huddersfield T; 5 Ralph, Andrew O. – Northwich Victoria – Stalybridge Celtic; 4 Raw, Thomas D. – Scarborough – Spennymoor U; 25 Rees, Matthew R. – Millwall – Swansea C; 4 Rioch, Gregor J. – Shrewsbury T – Northwich Victoria; 5 Roberts, Darren A. – Worksop T – Farsley Celtic; 22 Roberts, Mark A. – Crewe Alex – Vauxhall Motors; 25 Robinson, Carl P. – Portsmouth – Sunderland; 25 Rocastle, Craig A. – Chelsea – Lincoln C; 19 Rogers, Alan – Leicester C – Nottingham Forest; 25 Rogers, Kristian R. – Sheffield U – Macclesfield T; 19 Rosenior, Liam J. – Fulham – Torquay U; 13 Ruffer, Carl J. – Chester C – Droylsden; 3 Sabin, Eric – Queens Park Rangers – Boston U; 5 Salisbury, James A. – Wigan Ath – Leigh RMI; 4 Schumacher, Steven T. – Everton – Oldham Ath; 6 Simpson, Sekani – Bristol C – Forest Green R; 22 Smith, Gary S. – Middlesbrough – Wimbledon; 11 Smith, Mark – Chesterfield – Frickley Ath; 31 Standen, Dean – Welling U – Erith & Belvedere; 22 Stockdale, Robert K. – Middlesbrough – Rotherham U; 25 Surey, Ben D. – Crystal Palace – Gravesend & Northfleet; 24 Symes, Michael – Everton – Crewe Alex; 25 Talbot, Daniel B. – Rushden & Diamonds – Stevenage Borough; 8 Tansley, Anthony – Alfreton T – Belper T; 5 Teesdale, Richard – Hereford U – Moor Green; 7 Teggart, Neil – Sunderland – Darlington; 5 Thomas, Daniel K. – Brentford – Staines T; 8 Turner, Iain R. – Everton – Chester C; 16 Twigg, Gary – Derby Co – Bristol R; 5 Tyson, Nathan – Reading – Wycombe W; 17 Uddin, Anwar – Bristol R– Telford U; 18 Vaesen, Nico – Birmingham C – Crystal Palace; 12 Venus, Mark – Cambridge U – Dagenham & Redbridge; 2 Viveash, Adrian L. – Swindon T – Kidderminster H; 17 Walker, Richard M. – Blackpool – Oxford U; 9 Walton, David L. – Derby Co – Stockport Co; 29 Warne, Stephen J. – Chesterfield – Matlock T; 19 Whitman, Tristram – Scarborough – Leigh RMI; 19 Williams, Benjamin P. – Manchester U – Crewe Alex; 22 Williams, Gareth A. – Crystal Palace – Colchester U; 12 Williams, Gareth – Southampton – Tiverton T; 24 Williamson, Michael J. – Southampton – Doncaster R; 4 Williams, Thomas A. – Birmingham C – Peterborough U; 28 Willis, Scott L. – Lincoln C – Hereford U; 25 Wilson, Brian – Stoke C – Cheltenham T; 1 Wood, Neil A. – Manchester U – Burnley;

April 2004

7 Bull, Ronnie R.	Millwall	Brentford
24 Gilbert, Peter	Birmingham City	Plymouth Argyle
6 James, Craig P.	Sunderland	Port Vale

Temporary transfers

10 Allen, Daniel T. – Forest Green R– Taunton T; 8 Baguley, Jamie C. – Stockport Co – Altrincham; 8 Bailey, Matthew – Stockport Co – Altrincham; 19 Baird, Christopher P. – Southampton – Watford; 25 Brown, Simon – West Bromwich Albion – Kidderminster H; 13 Camp, Lee M.J. – Derby Co – Queens Park Rangers; 16 Danns, Neil A. – Blackburn R– Hartlepool U; 25 Donnelly, Ciaran – Blackburn R– Blackpool; 5 Downer, Simon – Leyton Orient – Aldershot T; 8 Easter, Jermaine – Hartlepool U – Cambridge U; 16 Elliott, Matthew S. – Leicester C – Ipswich T; 13 Ellison, Kevin – Stockport Co – Lincoln C; 13 Gilchrist, Philip A. – West Bromwich Albion – Rotherham U; 18 Gosling, Jamie J. – Yeovil T – Aldershot T; 20 Graham, Daniel A.W. – Middlesbrough – Darlington; 14 Hackworth, Anthony – Notts Co – Scarborough; 22 Harkins, Gary – Blackburn R– Huddersfield T; 23 Henderson, Wayne – Aston Villa –

154

Wycombe W;   20 Hignett, Craig J. – Leicester C – Crewe Alex;   13 Hudson, Mark A. –
Fulham – Crystal Palace;   18 King, Jordan – Hereford U – Hednesford T;   23 Lawrence,
Lee A. – Manchester U – Shrewsbury T;   8 Livesey, Daniel – Bolton W – Rochdale;   22
MacKenzie, Christopher – Telford U – Hereford U;   16 Matthews, Lee J. – Bristol C –
Yeovil T;   7 Murphy, David P. – Middlesbrough – Barnsley;   14 Nicholson, Kevin J. –
Notts Co – Scarborough;   14 Northmore, Ryan – Woking – Yeovil T;   25 Pearson,
Gregory – West Ham U – Barnet;   20 Pennant, Jermaine – Arsenal – Leeds U;   4 Quinn,
Barry S. – Coventry C – Oxford U;   4 Rachubka, Paul S. – Charlton Ath – Huddersfield
T;   1 Reece, Dominic M.A. – Farnborough T – Sutton Coldfield T;   1 Rioch, Gregor J. –
Shrewsbury T – Northwich Victoria;   5 Roberts, Darren A. – Worksop T – Farsley Celtic;
15 Rosenior, Liam – Fulham – Torquay U;   22 Smith, Gary S. – Middlesbrough –
Wimbledon;   16 Symes, Michael – Everton – Crewe Alex;   4 Teesdale, Richard –
Hereford U – Moor Green;   3 Thomas, Daniel K. – Brentford – Staines T;   15 Turnbull,
Ross – Middlesbrough – Barnsley;   16 Twigg, Gary – Derby Co – Bristol R;   29 Ward,
Gavin J. – Coventry C – Barnsley;   13 Williams, Benjamin W. – Manchester U – Crewe
Alex;   12 Worgan, Lee J. – Wimbledon – Wycombe W

May 2004

25 Lucas, David A.	Preston North End	Sheffield Wednesday
27 Pugh, Daniel	Manchester United	Leeds United
16 Robinson, Paul W.	Leeds United	Tottenham Hotspur
24 Scimeca, Riccardo	Leicester City	West Bromwich Albion
26 Smith, Alan	Leeds United	Manchester United

Temporary transfers

2 Bradshaw, Craig R.J. – Portsmouth – Dorchester T;   13 Danns, Neil A. – Blackburn R–
Hartlepool U;   4 Downer, Simon – Leyton Orient – Aldershot T;   11 Ellison, Kevin –
Stockport Co – Lincoln C;   6 Henderson, Wayne – Aston Villa – Wycombe W;   2 King,
Jordan – Hereford U – Hednesford T;   10 Rachubka, Paul S. – Charlton Ath –
Huddersfield T;   7 Robinson, Carl P. – Portsmouth – Sunderland;   6 Turnbull, Ross –
Middlesbrough – Barnsley

FOREIGN TRANSFERS 2003–2004

May 2003

15 Dugarry, Christophe	Bordeaux	Birmingham City
30 Neumayr, Markus M.	Eintracht Frankfurt	Manchester United

July 2003

9 Ambrosio, Marco	Chievo	Chelsea
15 Amoruso, Lorenzo	Rangers	Blackburn Rovers
29 Bosvelt, Paul	Feyenoord	Manchester City
22 Campo, Ivan R.	Real Madrid	Bolton Wanderers
29 Djemba Djemba, Eric D.	Nantes	Manchester United
21 Emerton, Brett	Feyenoord	Blackburn Rovers
31 Folly, Yoann	St Etienne	Southampton
16 Giannakopoulos, Stelios	Olympiakos	Bolton Wanderers
23 Griffit, Leandre	Amiens	Southampton
28 Doriva, Guidoni D.	Celta Vigo	Middlesbrough
22 Howard, Timothy M.	New York/New Jersey MetroStars	Manchester United
15 Laville, Florent	Lyon	Bolton Wanderers
18 Le Tallec, Anthony	Le Havre	Liverpool
1 Makabu-Ma-Kalamby, Yves	PSV Eindhoven	Chelsea
16 Nalis, Lilian B.P.	Chievo	Leicester City
30 Okoronkwo, Isaac	Shakhtjor Donetsk	Wolverhampton Wanderers
18 Postiga, Helder M.M.	Porto	Tottenham Hotspur
18 Senderos, Philippe	Servette	Arsenal
21 Silas, Jorge M.F.	Uniao Leiria	Wolverhampton Wanderers
18 Sinama-Pongolle, Florent	Le Havre	Liverpool
30 Stefanovic, Dejan	Vitesse	Portsmouth
9 Tarnat, Michael	Bayern Munich	Manchester City
11 Wapenaar, Harald	Utrecht	Portsmouth
22 Yelldell, David R.	Stuttgart Kickers	Blackburn Rovers
10 Yobo, Joseph	Marseille	Everton
17 Zivkovic, Boris	Leverkusen	Portsmouth

August 2003

1 Bonnissel, Jerome	Rangers	Fulham
6 Camara, Henri	Sedan	Wolverhampton Wanderers
1 Camara, Zoumana	Lens	Leeds United
6 Clichy, Gael	Cannes	Arsenal
29 Crespo, Herman	Internazionale	Chelsea
12 Domi, Didier	Paris St Germain	Leeds United
14 Faye, Andy M.	Auxerre	Portsmouth
1 Figueroa, Luciano G.	Rosario Central	Birmingham City
1 Geremi N.F.S.	Real Madrid	Chelsea
7 Gresko, Vratislav	Parma	Blackburn Rovers
29 Gudjonsson, Johannes K.	Betis	Wolverhampton Wanderers
15 Jardel, Mario D.A.R.	Sporting Lisbon	Bolton Wanderers
29 Karbassiyon, Danny	Roanoke Star	Arsenal
13 Kleberson, Pereira J.	Atletico Paranaense	Manchester United
5 Lehmann, Jens	Borussia Dortmund	Arsenal
14 Leite, Sergio	Boavista	Charlton Athletic
26 Mabizela, Mbulelo O.	Orlando Pirates	Tottenham Hotspur
30 McManaman, Steve	Real Madrid	Manchester City
29 Medjani, Carl	St Etienne	Liverpool
26 Mendieta-Zabala, Gaizka	Lazio	Middlesbrough
19 Mutu, Adrian	Parma	Chelsea
31 Olembe, Salomon R.O.	Marseille	Leeds United
1 Pericard, Vincent D.P.	Juventus	Portsmouth
14 Ronaldo, Cristiano Dos Santos A.	Sporting Lisbon	Manchester United
14 Sakho, Lamine	Marseille	Leeds United
14 Schemmel, Sebastien	West Ham United	Portsmouth
7 Sibierski, Antoine	Lens	Manchester City
26 Smertin, Alexei	Bordeaux	Chelsea

September 2003

1 Baggio, Dino	Lazio	Blackburn Rovers
12 Ba, Ibrahim	AC Milan	Bolton Wanderers
3 Chapuis, Cyril S.T.	Marseille	Leeds United
1 Dalmat, Stephane	Internazionale	Tottenham Hotspur
1 Makelele, Claude	Real Madrid	Chelsea
1 Papadopoulos, Michal	Banik Ostrava	Arsenal
1 Roque Junior, Jose V.	AC Milan	Leeds United
1 Srnicek, Pavel	Brescia	Portsmouth

October 2003

24 Fabregas, Cese	Barcelona	Arsenal

January 2004

31 Andresen, Martin	Stabaek	Blackburn Rovers
16 Arason, Arni G.	Rosenborg	Manchester City
14 Bocanegra, Carlos	Chicago Fire	Fulham
31 John, Collins	Twente	Fulham
31 Freund, Steffen	Kaiserslautern	Leicester City
1 Ganea, Viorel I.	Bursaspor	Wolverhampton Wanderers
27 McBride, Brian R.	Columbus Crewe	Fulham
7 Moreno, Javi V.	Atletico Madrid	Bolton Wanderers
30 Mornar, Ivica	Anderlecht	Portsmouth
30 Olszar, Sebastian	Admira Modling	Portsmouth
5 Pasanen, Petri M.	Ajax	Portsmouth
30 Reyes, Jose Antonio	Sevilla	Arsenal
1 Ricketts, Donovan	Village United	Bolton Wanderers
31 Van Buyten, Daniel	Marseille	Manchester City

Summer transfers to be found in Stop Press on page 6.

FA CUP REVIEW 2003–2004

For what is traditionally known as the competition proper the FA Cup went into the serious business of itself just off the M25 at Thurrock on a Friday evening in November and ended in May several hours drive away at the Millennium Stadium in Cardiff.

In between the minnows and giant-killers were largely swept away having had their moments, but for a change there was a final appearance for one team outside the Premier League. Millwall had held strong hopes of forcing themselves into a play-off berth in the First Division. But the attack on two fronts cost them dearly in the League once they had secured a tie to be savoured against a Manchester United chasing the only hope of silverware in the season.

The outcome was as predicted a fairly easy 3-0 win for United with Ronaldo's sparkling performance illuminating an otherwise low key affair, which in no way diminished the Lions' achievement in getting there in the first place.

But back to the beginning and Thurrock who used to be Purfleet, holding Luton to a draw. The following day there were the usual ups and downs for the aspiring teams. Gainsborough crashed 7-1 at Brentford and Bishop Stortford leaked six at Mansfield. Yet Scarborough were winners over re-instated League side Doncaster and Stevenage accounted for Stockport. Ford of the Ryman League held Port Vale in the Potteries.

Sunday had more surprises with Canvey drawing locally at Southend, Hornchurch disposing of Darlington 2-0 and Accrington beating Huddersfield 1-0. This more than compensated for Shildon's 7-2 reverse at Notts County.

Neither of the three drawing upstarts survived replays, but all that Port Vale received from their win was to lose at home in the second round to Scarborough. But Telford did as well in their 3-0 win over Brentford and Accrington earned a replay from the visit to Bournemouth before winning it on a penalty shoot-out.

Telford's reward was a trip to Crewe and they returned with 1-0 win. Accrington held Colchester at home and Scarborough did likewise at Southend. With the big guns entering there were casualties of Premiership proportions with Charlton losing 3-2 at Gillingham while Bolton were held at Tranmere, Chelsea at Watford and Wolves at Kidderminster. Millwall began modestly with a 2-1 win over Walsall. The following day in the same third round, Manchester United won 2-1 at Aston Villa.

In extra time Tranmere tripped up Bolton and Scarborough edged out Southend for another place in the fourth round. Their lucky dip was pulling out moneybags Chelsea at home. Moreover they were by no means disgraced by the slender 1-0 defeat. Telford's tie with Millwall was knocked out by a waterlogged pitch.

The Sunday offering saw Wolves ousted by West Ham 3-1 at Molineux, while Manchester United had a comfortable 3-0 victory at Northampton. Indeed because of the vagaries of the various pairings, the fifth round had only half of its number representing the Premier League, and included Colchester and Tranmere from Division Two, Swansea from the Third. Worse still for the top echelon, three of the ties would account for another trio.

When playtime arrived there was even the possibility of Fulham losing a replay at West Ham and Sunderland overturning Birmingham at the second attempt as well. United won the Mancunian derby 4-2, Arsenal kept up their record over Chelsea, but Portsmouth and Liverpool had to replay. Swansea went out at Tranmere, as did Colchester at Sheffield United. Millwall having won through the twice-postponed affair with Telford, defeated Burnley 1-0.

Sunderland did in fact survive over Birmingham in extra time, but Fulham won convincingly at West Ham and because of Liverpool's European commitments, their Pompey replay had to be squeezed into a weekend but they lost it 1-0.

Incredibly the sixth round draw locked the four remaining Premier sides together. Manchester United beat Fulham 2-1 and Arsenal accounted for Portsmouth 5-1 at Fratton Park. Sunderland beat Sheffield United 1-0 but Tranmere held Millwall at the New Den only to lose at home 2-1.

Against most expectations the draw again saw Arsenal and Manchester United paired, leaving Sunderland and Millwall to fight the Football League corner. Arguably neither favourites came through, one goal enough for United at Villa Park and similarly for Millwall at Old Trafford.

In statistical terms Manchester United collected their 11th FA Cup success to push them two ahead in the rankings over Arsenal. Millwall with three earlier semi-finals to their credit added to their own CV.

THE FA CUP 2003–2004

FIRST ROUND

Thurrock	(0) 1	Luton T	(1) 1
Barnet	(2) 2	Stalybride C	(1) 2
Blackpool	(2) 4	Boreham Wood	(0) 0
Bournemouth	(1) 1	Bristol R	(0) 0
Brentford	(1) 7	Gainsborough T	(0) 1
Bury	(0) 1	Rochdale	(1) 2
Cheltenham T	(1) 3	Hull C	(0) 1
Chester C	(0) 0	Gravesend & N	(1) 1
Colchester U	(1) 1	Oxford U	(0) 0
Farnborough T	(0) 0	Weston-Super-Mare	(1) 1
Grantham T	(1) 1	Leyton Orient	(1) 2
Grays Ath	(0) 1	Aldershot T	(0) 2
Grimsby T	(0) 1	QPR	(0) 0
Hartlepool U	(2) 4	Whitby T	(0) 0
Kidderminster H	(1) 2	Northwich Vic	(0) 1
Lancaster C	(1) 1	Cambridge U	(1) 2
Lincoln C	(2) 3	Brighton & HA	(0) 1
Macclesfield T	(1) 3	Boston U	(0) 0
Mansfield T	(4) 6	Bishop's Stortford	(0) 0
Northampton T	(1) 3	Plymouth Arg	(1) 2
Oldham Ath	(2) 3	Carlisle U	(0) 0
Peterborough U	(0) 2	Hereford U	(0) 0
Port Vale	(0) 2	Ford U	(1) 2
Scarborough	(0) 1	Doncaster R	(0) 0
Scunthorpe U	(1) 2	Shrewsbury T	(0) 1
Stevenage B	(2) 2	Stockport Co	(0) 1
Swansea C	(1) 3	Rushden & D	(0) 0
Telford U	(0) 3	Crawley T	(2) 2
Torquay U	(0) 1	Burton Alb	(1) 2
Tranmere R	(1) 3	Chesterfield	(0) 2
Woking	(3) 3	Histon	(1) 1
Wycombe W	(1) 4	Swindon T	(0) 1
Yeovil T	(1) 4	Wrexham	(0) 1
Accrington S	(0) 1	Huddersfield T	(0) 0
Bradford PA	(2) 2	Bristol C	(2) 5
Hornchurch	(1) 2	Darlington	(0) 0
Notts Co	(3) 7	Shildon	(0) 2
Sheffield W	(1) 4	Salisbury C	(0) 0
Southend U	(1) 1	Canvey Island	(1) 1
York C	(1) 1	Barnsley	(1) 2

FIRST ROUND REPLAYS

Luton T	(1) 3	Thurrock	(0) 1
Stalybridge C	(0) 0	Barnet	(1) 2
Canvey Island	(2) 2	Southend U	(1) 3
Ford U	(0) 1	Port Vale	(1) 2
(aet.)			

SECOND ROUND

Wycombe W	(0) 1	Mansfield T	(0) 1
Bournemouth	(0) 1	Accrington S	(1) 1
Bristol C	(0) 0	Barnsley	(0) 0
Cheltenham T	(2) 3	Leyton Orient	(0) 1
Colchester U	(0) 1	Aldershot T	(0) 0
Gravesend & N	(1) 1	Notts Co	(0) 2

Hornchurch	(0) 0	Tranmere R	(1) 1
Macclesfield T	(1) 1	Cambridge U	(1) 1
Northampton T	(1) 4	Weston-Super-Mare	(0) 1
Oldham Ath	(0) 2	Blackpool	(3) 5
Peterborough U	(1) 3	Grimsby T	(1) 2
Rochdale	(0) 0	Luton T	(1) 2
Scunthorpe U	(1) 2	Sheffield W	(0) 2
Southend U	(1) 3	Lincoln C	(0) 0
Swansea C	(1) 2	Stevenage B	(0) 1
Telford U	(1) 3	Brentford	(0) 0
Woking	(0) 0	Kidderminster H	(1) 3
Yeovil T	(3) 5	Barnet	(1) 1
Burton Alb	(0) 0	Hartlepool U	(0) 1
Port Vale	(0) 0	Scarborough	(0) 1

SECOND ROUND REPLAYS

Accrington S	(0) 0	Bournemouth	(0) 0
(aet; Accrington S won 5-3 on penalties.)			
Barnsley	(2) 2	Bristol C	(0) 1
Cambridge U	(0) 2	Macclesfield T	(1) 2
(aet; Macclesfield T won 4-2 on penalties.)			
Mansfield T	(1) 3	Wycombe W	(0) 2
Sheffield W	(0) 0	Scunthorpe U	(0) 0
(aet; Scunthorpe U won 3-1 on penalties.)			

THIRD ROUND

Accrington S	(0) 0	Colchester U	(0) 0
Barnsley	(0) 0	Scunthorpe U	(0) 0
Birmingham C	(2) 4	Blackburn R	(0) 0
Bradford C	(0) 1	Luton T	(1) 2
Cardiff C	(0) 0	Sheffield U	(0) 1
Coventry C	(0) 2	Peterborough U	(0) 1
Crewe Alex	(0) 0	Telford U	(1) 1
Everton	(2) 3	Norwich C	(1) 1
Gillingham	(3) 3	Charlton Ath	(1) 2
Ipswich T	(0) 3	Derby Co	(0) 0
Kidderminster H	(0) 1	Wolverhampton W	(0) 1
Manchester C	(1) 2	Leicester C	(1) 2
Mansfield T	(0) 0	Burnley	(1) 2
Middlesbrough	(1) 2	Notts Co	(0) 0
Millwall	(2) 2	Walsall	(1) 1
Northampton T	(0) 1	Rotherham U	(0) 1
Nottingham F	(0) 1	WBA	(0) 0
Portsmouth	(1) 2	Blackpool	(1) 1
Preston NE	(3) 3	Reading	(3) 3
Southampton	(0) 0	Newcastle U	(2) 3
Southend U	(1) 1	Scarborough	(0) 1
Sunderland	(0) 1	Hartlepool U	(0) 0
Swansea C	(1) 2	Macclesfield T	(0) 1
Tottenham H	(2) 3	Crystal Palace	(0) 0
Tranmere R	(0) 1	Bolton W	(0) 1
Watford	(2) 2	Chelsea	(2) 2
Wigan Ath	(0) 1	West Ham U	(0) 2
Wimbledon	(0) 1	Stoke C	(1) 1
Aston Villa	(1) 1	Manchester U	(0) 2
Fulham	(1) 2	Cheltenham T	(1) 1
Leeds U	(1) 1	Arsenal	(2) 4
Yeovil T	(0) 0	Liverpool	(0) 2

THIRD ROUND REPLAYS

Bolton W	(0) 1	Tranmere R	(0) 2
(aet.)			
Colchester U	(1) 2	Accrington S	(0) 1
Reading	(0) 1	Preston NE	(1) 2
Rotherham U	(1) 1	Northampton T	(1) 2
Scunthorpe U	(1) 2	Barnsley	(0) 0
Stoke C	(0) 0	Wimbledon	(1) 1
Wolverhampton W	(1) 2	Kidderminster H	(0) 0
Chelsea	(2) 4	Watford	(0) 0
Leicester C	(0) 1	Manchester C	(1) 3
Scarborough	(0) 1	Southend U	(0) 0

FOURTH ROUND

Arsenal	(2) 4	Middlesbrough	(1) 1
Birmingham C	(1) 1	Wimbledon	(0) 0
Burnley	(2) 3	Gillingham	(0) 1
Coventry C	(1) 1	Colchester U	(1) 1
Ipswich T	(0) 1	Sunderland	(1) 2
Liverpool	(1) 2	Newcastle U	(1) 1
Luton T	(0) 0	Tranmere R	(0) 1
Portsmouth	(1) 2	Scunthorpe U	(0) 1
Scarborough	(0) 0	Chelsea	(1) 1
Swansea C	(0) 2	Preston NE	(0) 1
Everton	(0) 1	Fulham	(0) 1
Manchester C	(1) 1	Tottenham H	(0) 1
Northampton T	(0) 0	Manchester U	(1) 3
Nottingham F	(0) 0	Sheffield U	(1) 3
Wolverhampton W	(1) 1	West Ham U	(3) 3
Telford U	(0) 0	Millwall	(1) 2

FOURTH ROUND REPLAYS

Colchester U	(2) 3	Coventry C	(1) 1
Fulham	(0) 2	Everton	(0) 1
(aet.)			
Tottenham H	(3) 3	Manchester C	(0) 4

FIFTH ROUND

Fulham	(0) 0	West Ham U	(0) 0
Manchester U	(1) 4	Manchester City	(0) 2
Millwall	(0) 1	Burnley	(0) 0
Sunderland	(1) 1	Birmingham C	(1) 1
Tranmere R	(1) 2	Swansea C	(1) 1
Arsenal	(0) 2	Chelsea	(1) 1
Liverpool	(1) 1	Portsmouth	(0) 1
Sheffield U	(0) 1	Colchester U	(0) 0

FIFTH ROUND REPLAYS

Portsmouth	(0) 1	Liverpool	(0) 0
West Ham U	(0) 0	Fulham	(0) 3
Birmingham C	(0) 0	Sunderland	(0) 2
(aet.)			

SIXTH ROUND

Manchester U	(1) 2	Fulham	(1) 1
Portsmouth	(0) 1	Arsenal	(3) 5
Millwall	(0) 0	Tranmere R	(0) 0
Sunderland	(1) 1	Sheffield U	(0) 0

160

SIXTH ROUND REPLAY

Tranmere R	(1) 1	Millwall	(2) 2

SEMI-FINAL

Arsenal	(0) 0	Manchester U	(1) 1
Sunderland	(0) 0	Millwall	(1) 1

THE FA CUP FINAL

Saturday, 22 May 2004

(at Millennium Stadium, Cardiff, attendance 72,350)

Manchester U (1) 3 *(Ronaldo 42, Van Nistelrooy 64 (pen), 80)*   **Millwall (0) 0**

Manchester U: Howard (Carroll); Neville G, O'Shea, Brown, Keane, Silvestre, Ronaldo (Solskjaer), Fletcher (Butt), Van Nistelrooy, Scholes, Giggs.

Millwall: Marshall; Elliott, Ryan (Cogan), Cahill, Lawrence, Ward, Ifill, Wise (Weston), Harris (McCammon), Livermore, Sweeney.

Referee: J. Winter (Stockton).

PAST FA CUP FINALS

Details of one goalscorer is not available in 1878.

Year	Team	Score	Opponent	Score
1872	The Wanderers *Betts*	1	Royal Engineers	0
1873	The Wanderers *Kinnaird, Wollaston*	2	Oxford University	0
1874	Oxford University *Mackarness, Patton*	2	Royal Engineers	0
1875	Royal Engineers *Renny-Tailyour*	1	Old Etonians *Bonsor*	1*
Replay	Royal Engineers *Renny-Tailyour, Stafford*	2	Old Etonians	0
1876	The Wanderers *Edwards*	1	Old Etonians *Bonsor*	1*
Replay	The Wanderers *Wollaston, Hughes 2*	3	Old Etonians	0
1877	The Wanderers *Lindsay, Kenrick*	2	Oxford University *Kinnaird (og)*	1*
1878	The Wanderers *Kenrick 2, Kinnaird*	3	Royal Engineers *Unknown*	1
1879	Old Etonians *Clerke*	1	Clapham Rovers	0
1880	Clapham Rovers *Lloyd-Jones*	1	Oxford University	0
1881	Old Carthusians *Wyngard, Parry, Todd*	3	Old Etonians	0
1882	Old Etonians *Anderson*	1	Blackburn Rovers	0
1883	Blackburn Olympic *Costley, Matthews*	2	Old Etonians *Goodhart*	1*
1884	Blackburn Rovers *Sowerbutts, Forrest*	2	Queen's Park, Glasgow *Christie*	1
1885	Blackburn Rovers *Forrest, Brown*	2	Queen's Park, Glasgow	0
1886	Blackburn Rovers	0	West Bromwich Albion	0
Replay	Blackburn Rovers *Brown, Sowerbutts*	2	West Bromwich Albion	0
1887	Aston Villa *Hunter, Hodgetts*	2	West Bromwich Albion	0
1888	West Bromwich Albion *Woodhall, Bayliss*	2	Preston NE *Dewhurst*	1
1889	Preston NE *Dewhurst, J. Ross, Thompson*	3	Wolverhampton W	0
1890	Blackburn Rovers *Walton, John Southworth, Lofthouse, Townley 3*	6	Sheffield W *Bennett*	1
1891	Blackburn Rovers *Dewar, John Southworth, Townley*	3	Notts Co *Oswald*	1

1892	West Bromwich Albion 3	Aston Villa 0
	Geddes, Nicholls, Reynolds	
1893	Wolverhampton W 1	Everton 0
	Allen	
1894	Notts Co...........................4	Bolton W 1
	Watson, Logan 3	*Cassidy*
1895	Aston Villa 1	West Bromwich Albion 0
	J. Devey	
1896	Sheffield W 2	Wolverhampton W 1
	Spiksley 2	*Black*
1897	Aston Villa 3	Everton 2
	Campbell, Wheldon,	*Boyle, Bell*
	Crabtree	
1898	Nottingham F 3	Derby Co 1
	Cape 2, McPherson	*Bloomer*
1899	Sheffield U.........................4	Derby Co 1
	Bennett, Beers, Almond,	*Boag*
	Priest	
1900	Bury..................................4	Southampton.....................................0
	McLuckie 2, Wood, Plant	
1901	Tottenham H.......................2	Sheffield U.......................................2
	Brown 2	*Bennett, Priest*
Replay	Tottenham H.......................3	Sheffield U.......................................1
	Cameron, Smith, Brown	*Priest*
1902	Sheffield U.........................1	Southampton.....................................1
	Common	*Wood*
Replay	Sheffield U.........................2	Southampton.....................................1
	Hedley, Barnes	*Brown*
1903	Bury..................................6	Derby Co 0
	Ross, Sagar, Leeming 2,	
	Wood, Plant	
1904	Manchester C 1	Bolton W 0
	Meredith	
1905	Aston Villa 2	Newcastle U 0
	Hampton 2	
1906	Everton 1	Newcastle U 0
	Young	
1907	Sheffield W 2	Everton 1
	Stewart, Simpson	*Sharp*
1908	Wolverhampton W 3	Newcastle U 1
	Hunt, Hedley, Harrison	*Howey*
1909	Manchester U.......................1	Bristol C...0
	A. Turnbull	
1910	Newcastle U 1	Barnsley...1
	Rutherford	*Tufnell*
Replay	Newcastle U 2	Barnsley...0
	Shepherd 2 (1 pen)	
1911	Bradford C..........................0	Newcastle U 0
Replay	Bradford C..........................1	Newcastle U 0
	Speirs	
1912	Barnsley 0	West Bromwich Albion 0
Replay	Barnsley 1	West Bromwich Albion 0*
	Tufnell	

1913	Aston Villa 1		Sunderland 0	
	Barber			
1914	Burnley 1		Liverpool 0	
	Freeman			
1915	Sheffield U 3		Chelsea 0	
	Simmons, Masterman, Kitchen			
1920	Aston Villa 1		Huddersfield T 0*	
	Kirton			
1921	Tottenham H 1		Wolverhampton W 0	
	Dimmock			
1922	Huddersfield T 1		Preston NE 0	
	Smith (pen)			
1923	Bolton W 2		West Ham U 0	
	Jack, J.R. Smith			
1924	Newcastle U 2		Aston Villa 0	
	Harris, Seymour			
1925	Sheffield U 1		Cardiff C 0	
	Tunstall			
1926	Bolton W 1		Manchester C 0	
	Jack			
1927	Cardiff C 1		Arsenal 0	
	Ferguson			
1928	Blackburn Rovers 3		Huddersfield T 1	
	Roscamp 2, McLean		*A. Jackson*	
1929	Bolton W 2		Portsmouth 0	
	Butler, Blackmore			
1930	Arsenal 2		Huddersfield T 0	
	James, Lambert			
1931	West Bromwich Albion 2		Birmingham 1	
	W.G. Richardson 2		*Bradford*	
1932	Newcastle U 2		Arsenal 1	
	Allen 2		*John*	
1933	Everton 3		Manchester C 0	
	Stein, Dean, Dunn			
1934	Manchester C 2		Portsmouth 1	
	Tilson 2		*Rutherford*	
1935	Sheffield W 4		West Bromwich Albion 2	
	Rimmer 2, Palethorpe,		*Boyes, Sandford*	
	Hooper			
1936	Arsenal 1		Sheffield U 0	
	Drake			
1937	Sunderland 3		Preston NE 1	
	Gurney, Carter, Burbanks		*F. O'Donnell*	
1938	Preston NE 1		Huddersfield T 0*	
	Mutch (pen)			
1939	Portsmouth 4		Wolverhampton W 1	
	Parker 2, Barlow,		*Dorsett*	
	Anderson			
1946	Derby Co 4		Charlton Ath 1*	
	H. Turner (og), Doherty,		*H. Turner*	
	Stamps 2			

1947	Charlton Ath ....1 *Duffy*		Burnley 0*	
1948	Manchester U ....4 *Rowley 2, Pearson, Anderson*		Blackpool ....2 *Shimwell (pen), Mortensen*	
1949	Wolverhampton W ....3 *Pye 2, Smyth,*		Leicester C ....1 *Griffiths*	
1950	Arsenal.....................................2 *Lewis 2*		Liverpool 0	
1951	Newcastle U ....2 *Milburn 2*		Blackpool 0	
1952	Newcastle U ....1 *G. Robledo*		Arsenal 0	
1953	Blackpool..................................4 *Mortensen 3, Perry*		Bolton W ....3 *Lofthouse, Moir, Bell*	
1954	West Bromwich Albion ....3 *Allen 2 (1 pen), Griffin*		Preston NE ....2 *Morrison, Wayman*	
1955	Newcastle U ....3 *Milburn, Mitchell, Hannah*		Manchester C................................1 *Johnstone*	
1956	Manchester C ....3 *Hayes, Dyson, Johnstone*		Birmingham C................................1 *Kinsey*	
1957	Aston Villa ....2 *McParland 2*		Manchester U ....1 *T. Taylor*	
1958	Bolton W ....2 *Lofthouse 2*		Manchester U 0	
1959	Nottingham F ....2 *Dwight, Wilson*		Luton T..1 *Pacey*	
1960	Wolverhampton W ....3 *McGrath (og), Deeley 2*		Blackburn Rovers...........................0	
1961	Tottenham H.............................2 *Smith, Dyson*		Leicester C 0	
1962	Tottenham H.............................3 *Greaves, Smith, Blanchflower (pen)*		Burnley ....1 *Robson*	
1963	Manchester U ....3 *Herd 2, Law*		Leicester C ....1 *Keyworth*	
1964	West Ham U ....3 *Sissons, Hurst, Boyce*		Preston NE ....2 *Holden, Dawson*	
1965	Liverpool ....2 *Hunt, St John*		Leeds U ....1* *Bremner*	
1966	Everton ....3 *Trebilcock 2, Temple*		Sheffield W ....2 *McCalliog, Ford*	
1967	Tottenham H..............................2 *Robertson, Saul*		Chelsea ....1 *Tambling*	
1968	West Bromwich Albion .....1 *Astle*		Everton 0*	
1969	Manchester C ....1 *Young*		Leicester C 0	
1970	Chelsea.....................................2 *Houseman, Hutchinson*		Leeds U ....2* *Charlton, Jones*	

Replay	Chelsea.................................2	Leeds U 1*
	Osgood, Webb	*Jones*
1971	Arsenal.................................2	Liverpool 1*
	Kelly, George	*Heighway*
1972	Leeds U 1	Arsenal 0
	Clarke	
1973	Sunderland 1	Leeds U 0
	Porterfield	
1974	Liverpool 3	Newcastle 0
	Keegan 2, Heighway	
1975	West Ham U...........................2	Fulham 0
	A. Taylor 2	
1976	Southampton.........................1	Manchester U 0
	Stokes	
1977	Manchester U........................2	Liverpool 1
	Pearson, J. Greenhoff	*Case*
1978	Ipswich T 1	Arsenal 0
	Osborne	
1979	Arsenal.................................3	Manchester U 2
	Talbot, Stapleton,	*McQueen, McIlroy*
	Sunderland	
1980	West Ham U...........................1	Arsenal 0
	Brooking	
1981	Tottenham H..........................1	Manchester C.........................1*
	Hutchison (og)	*Hutchison*
Replay	Tottenham H..........................3	Manchester C.........................2
	Villa 2, Crooks	*MacKenzie, Reeves (pen)*
1982	Tottenham H..........................1	QPR 1*
	Hoddle	*Fenwick*
Replay	Tottenham H..........................1	QPR 0
	Hoddle (pen)	
1983	Manchester U........................2	Brighton & HA.......................2*
	Stapleton, Wilkins	*Smith, Stevens*
Replay	Manchester U........................4	Brighton & HA.......................0
	Robson 2, Whiteside, Muhren (pen)	
1984	Everton 2	Watford.................................0
	Sharp, Gray	
1985	Manchester U........................1	Everton 0*
	Whiteside	
1986	Liverpool 3	Everton 1
	Rush 2, Johnston	*Lineker*
1987	Coventry C 3	Tottenham H..........................2*
	Bennett, Houchen,	*C. Allen, Kilcline (og)*
	Mabbutt (og)	
1988	Wimbledon 1	Liverpool 0
	Sanchez	
1989	Liverpool 3	Everton 2*
	Aldridge, Rush 2	*McCall 2*
1990	Manchester U........................3	Crystal Palace 3*
	Robson, Hughes 2	*O'Reilly, Wright 2*
Replay	Manchester U........................1	Crystal Palace 0
	Martin	

1991	Tottenham H.....................2	Nottingham F.......................................1*
	Stewart, Walker (og)	*Pearce*
1992	Liverpool 2	Sunderland 0
	Thomas, Rush	
1993	Arsenal................................1	Sheffield W...1*
	Wright	*Hirst*
Replay	Arsenal................................2	Sheffield W...1*
	Wright, Linighan	*Waddle*
1994	Manchester U......................4	Chelsea 0
	Cantona 2 (2 pens),	
	Hughes, McClair	
1995	Everton 1	Manchester U 0
	Rideout	
1996	Manchester U......................1	Liverpool 0
	Cantona	
1997	Chelsea................................2	Middlesbrough......................................0
	Di Matteo, Newton	
1998	Arsenal................................2	Newcastle U 0
	Overmars, Anelka	
1999	Manchester U......................2	Newcastle U 0
	Sheringham, Scholes	
2000	Chelsea................................1	Aston Villa 0
	Di Matteo	
2001	Liverpool 2	Arsenal 1
	Owen 2	*Ljungberg*
2002	Arsenal................................2	Chelsea 0
	Parlour, Ljungberg	
2003	Arsenal................................1	Southampton..0
	Pires	
2004	Manchester U......................3	Millwall 0
	Ronaldo, Van Nistelrooy 2 (1 pen)	

*After extra time

SUMMARY OF FA CUP WINNERS SINCE 1872

Manchester United	11
Arsenal	9
Tottenham Hotspur	8
Aston Villa	7
Blackburn Rovers	6
Liverpool	6
Newcastle United	6
Everton	5
The Wanderers	5
West Bromwich Albion	5
Bolton Wanderers	4
Manchester City	4
Sheffield United	4
Wolverhampton Wanderers	4
Chelsea	3
Sheffield Wednesday	3
West Ham United	3
Bury	2
Nottingham Forest	2
Old Etonians	2
Preston North End	2
Sunderland	2
Barnsley	1
Blackburn Olympic	1
Blackpool	1
Bradford City	1
Burnley	1
Cardiff City	1
Charlton Athletic	1
Clapham Rovers	1
Coventry City	1
Derby County	1
Huddersfield Town	1
Ipswich Town	1
Leeds United	1
Notts County	1
Old Carthusians	1
Oxford University	1
Portsmouth	1
Royal Engineers	1
Southampton	1
Wimbledon	1

APPEARANCES IN FA CUP FINAL

Arsenal	16
Manchester United	16
Newcastle United	13
Everton	12
Liverpool	12
Aston Villa	10
West Bromwich Albion	10
Tottenham Hotspur	9
Blackburn Rovers	8
Manchester City	8
Wolverhampton Wanderers	8
Bolton Wanderers	7
Chelsea	7
Preston North End	7
Old Etonians	6
Sheffield United	6
Sheffield Wednesday	6
Huddersfield Town	5
The Wanderers	5
Derby County	4
Leeds United	4
Leicester City	4
Oxford University	4
Royal Engineers	4
Southampton	4
Sunderland	4
West Ham United	4
Blackpool	3
Burnley	3
Nottingham Forest	3
Portsmouth	3
Barnsley	2
Birmingham City	2
Bury	2
Cardiff City	2
Charlton Athletic	2
Clapham Rovers	2
Notts County	2
Queen's Park (Glasgow)	2
Blackburn Olympic	1
Bradford City	1
Brighton & Hove Albion	1
Bristol City	1
Coventry City	1
Crystal Palace	1
Fulham	1
Ipswich Town	1
Luton Town	1
Middlesbrough	1
Millwall	1
Old Carthusians	1
Queen's Park Rangers	1
Watford	1
Wimbledon	1

CARLING CUP REVIEW 2003–2004

For its first association with the Football League Cup, the Carling appendage ensured a new name on the overall trophy in that neither Bolton Wanderers nor Middlesbrough had succeeded in respectively one and two previous final attempts.

In consecutive years 1997 and 1998 Boro had been thwarted first by Leicester, then Chelsea but not without a fight as both matches needed extra time. In 1995 Bolton had lost to Liverpool.

Thus it was on Leap Year Day Middlesbrough took a two minute lead over Bolton, increased it with a penalty five minutes later and were pulled back in the 21st minute where the scoring ended to make it third time lucky for the north-east club and their first major honour having won the old Amateur Cup for a second time in 1898.

After a quiet first round there was a long pause of well over a month before the second round and the introduction of at least those from the elite without European commitments. Then the shocks started. Birmingham lost 1-0 at Blackpool, Fulham went down similarly at Wigan and Charlton required an 8-7 penalty shoot-out win to dislodge Luton after sharing four goals with them. Bolton beat Walsall 3-1, but Boro needed extra time to eliminate Brighton.

The third round drew in the European contingent, but they had their problems from the word go. Arsenal with a reserve-looking line-up had to go to a 9-8 penalty shoot-out themselves after being held by Rotherham and Manchester United similarly tailored, only defeated Leeds who had been frightened by Swindon previously, in the extra period. Not so fortunate were Newcastle beaten 2-1 at St James Park by West Bromwich Albion.

Bolton with a 2-0 win over Gillingham and Boro 2-1 at Wigan made it to the fourth round among a healthy looking thirteen Premier survivors. Ironically the upset came at West Bromwich where another cosmetic Manchester United offering lost 2-0. The two other Football League teams enjoyed less fortune; Crystal Palace were beaten 3-0 at Aston Villa, while Reading lost 1-0 at home to Chelsea.

Conversely, Arsenal gave the opportunity to several of their promising younger players and more senior members infrequently used on first team duty in the Premier League, and had a splendid 5-1 win over Wolves. Southampton won the south coast derby 2-0 against Portsmouth and Tottenham accounted for Manchester City 3-1 at White Hart Lane.

Oddly enough both Bolton and Middlesbrough left it late in their encounters. Bolton needed an injury penalty to clinch a surprise 3-2 win at Liverpool, while Boro were forced into a penalty shoot-out after being held to a goalless draw by Everton and came through 5-4 on spot kicks.

As far as the quarter-finals were concerned, where United had failed at West Bromwich, Arsenal succeeded keeping faith with the policy which had seen them safely through up to this point. They won 2-0 at The Hawthorns.

Villa caused something of a shock when they beat Chelsea 2-1 at Villa Park, but again both Bolton and Boro were pushed hard by their opposition before reaching the semi-final stage.

Southampton fought through the 90 minutes and only conceded a goal with five minutes remaining of the extra period. The following day Middlesbrough equalised late at Tottenham and were again required to resort to penalties before moving on. History repeated itself on the final scoreline 5-4 on penalty kicks.

Thus most of the competition had been wrapped up before the Christmas period and the semi-finals were opened in the third week in January. Middlesbrough had to go to Highbury for the first leg against Arsenal, who adhered to their previous stance of team selection only for Boro to take a slender 1-0 lead into the return.

The following day Bolton won a goalscoring spree against Villa 5-2 to apparently set up a sure thing for a final appearance. But despite having a player sent off just before the interval, Villa gave Bolton a couple of shocks before winning the game 2-0 but losing the tie on a 5-4 aggregate.

Moreover Bolton had to wait a week before knowing their opponents, because although the Riverside Stadium pitch had been passed fit for play, the surrounding area was treacherous and the game had to be postponed. Arsenal's task was made more difficult at Middlesbrough in that they also were reduced by dismissal to ten players before the interval and eventually lost this second leg 2-1.

CARLING CUP 2003–2004

FIRST ROUND

Barnsley	(0) 1	Blackpool	(2) 2
Bradford C	(0) 0	Darlington	(0) 0
(aet; Darlington won 5-3 on penalties.)			
Bristol R	(0) 0	Brighton & HA	(0) 1
Cambridge U	(1) 1	Gillingham	(0) 2
Cardiff C	(2) 4	Leyton Orient	(0) 1
Cheltenham T	(1) 1	QPR	(1) 2
Chesterfield	(0) 0	Burnley	(0) 0
(aet; Burnley won 3-2 on penalties.)			
Colchester U	(2) 2	Plymouth Arg	(1) 1
Crewe Alex	(0) 2	Wrexham	(0) 0
Doncaster R	(0) 3	Grimsby T	(1) 2
Huddersfield T	(0) 2	Derby Co	(1) 1
Lincoln C	(0) 0	Stockport Co	(0) 1
Luton T	(1) 4	Yeovil T	(0) 1
Macclesfield T	(1) 1	Sheffield U	(1) 2
Millwall	(0) 0	Oxford U	(0) 1
Northampton T	(1) 1	Norwich C	(0) 0
Port Vale	(0) 0	Nottingham F	(0) 0
(aet; Nottingham F won 3-2 on penalties.)			
Preston NE	(0) 0	Notts Co	(0) 0
(aet; Notts Co won 7-6 on penalties.)			
Rotherham U	(2) 2	York C	(1) 1
Scunthorpe U	(0) 2	Oldham Ath	(0) 1
Southend U	(2) 2	Swindon T	(1) 3
Torquay U	(0) 1	Crystal Palace	(1) 1
(aet; Crystal Palace won 3-1 on penalties.)			
Tranmere R	(0) 1	Bury	(0) 0
WBA	(1) 4	Brentford	(0) 0
Walsall	(1) 2	Carlisle U	(1) 1
Watford	(0) 1	Bournemouth	(0) 0
(aet.)			
Wigan Ath	(1) 2	Hull C	(0) 0
Wycombe W	(1) 2	Wimbledon	(0) 0
Boston U	(0) 1	Reading	(1) 3
Bristol C	(1) 4	Swansea C	(1) 1
(aet.)			
Coventry C	(0) 2	Peterborough U	(0) 0
Ipswich T	(0) 1	Kidderminster H	(0) 0
(aet.)			
Mansfield T	(0) 1	Sunderland	(1) 2
Sheffield W	(0) 2	Hartlepool U	(0) 2
(aet; Hartlepool U won 5-4 on penalties.)			
West Ham U	(2) 3	Rushden & D	(1) 1
Stoke C	(1) 2	Rochdale	(0) 1

SECOND ROUND

Blackpool	(1) 1	Birmingham C	(0) 0
Bristol C	(0) 1	Watford	(0) 0
(aet.)			
Cardiff C	(2) 2	West Ham U	(1) 3
Charlton Ath	(1) 4	Luton T	(2) 4
(aet; Charlton Ath won 8-7 on penalties.)			
Crystal Palace	(2) 2	Doncaster R	(0) 1
Hartlepool U	(1) 1	WBA	(0) 2

Leicester C	(0) 1	Crewe Alex	(0) 0
Notts Co	(2) 2	Ipswich T	(1) 1
Portsmouth	(3) 5	Northampton T	(0) 2
Rotherham U	(1) 1	Colchester U	(1) 1
Scunthorpe U	(1) 2	Burnley	(2) 3
Sheffield U	(0) 0	QPR	(2) 2
Stoke C	(0) 0	Gillingham	(1) 2
Sunderland	(1) 2	Huddersfield T	(2) 4
Tranmere R	(0) 0	Nottingham F	(0) 0

(aet; Nottingham F won 4-1 on penalties.)

Wigan Ath	(0) 1	Fulham	(0) 0
Wolverhampton W	(1) 2	Darlington	(0) 0
Wycombe W	(0) 0	Aston Villa	(2) 5
Bolton W	(1) 3	Walsall	(0) 1
Coventry C	(0) 0	Tottenham H	(2) 3
Everton	(2) 3	Stockport Co	(0) 0
Leeds U	(0) 2	Swindon T	(1) 2

(aet; Leeds U won 4-3 on penalties.)

Middlesbrough	(0) 1	Brighton & HA	(0) 0

(aet.)

Oxford U	(0) 1	Reading	(0) 3

THIRD ROUND

Arsenal	(1) 1	Rotherham U	(0) 1

(aet; Arsenal won 9-8 on penalties.)

Blackpool	(0) 1	Crystal Palace	(1) 3
Bolton W	(1) 2	Gillingham	(0) 0
Bristol C	(0) 0	Southampton	(1) 3
Leeds U	(0) 2	Manchester U	(0) 3

(aet.)

QPR	(0) 0	Manchester C	(1) 3
Reading	(0) 1	Huddersfield T	(0) 0
Wolverhampton W	(0) 2	Burnley	(0) 0
Aston Villa	(0) 1	Leicester C	(0) 0
Blackburn R	(1) 3	Liverpool	(1) 4
Chelsea	(2) 4	Notts Co	(1) 2
Everton	(1) 1	Charlton Ath	(0) 0
Newcastle U	(0) 1	WBA	(1) 2

(aet.)

Nottingham F	(1) 2	Portsmouth	(0) 4

(aet.)

Tottenham H	(0) 1	West Ham U	(0) 0

(aet.)

Wigan Ath	(0) 1	Middlesbrough	(1) 2

FOURTH ROUND

Arsenal	(1) 5	Wolverhampton W	(0) 1
Southampton	(1) 2	Portsmouth	(0) 0
Aston Villa	(1) 3	Crystal Palace	(0) 0
Liverpool	(0) 2	Bolton W	(1) 3
Middlesbrough	(0) 0	Everton	(0) 0

(aet; Middlesbrough won 5-4 on penalties.)

Reading	(0) 0	Chelsea	(0) 1
Tottenham H	(2) 3	Manchester C	(0) 1
WBA	(1) 2	Manchester U	(0) 0

FIFTH ROUND

Bolton W	(0) 1	Southampton	(0) 0

(aet.)

WBA	(0) 0	Arsenal	(1) 2
Aston Villa	(1) 2	Chelsea	(0) 1
Tottenham H	(1) 1	Middlesbrough	(0) 1

(aet; Middlesbrough won 5-4 on penalties.)

SEMI-FINAL FIRST LEG

| Arsenal | (0) 0 | Middlesbrough | (0) 1 |
| Bolton W | (3) 5 | Aston Villa | (1) 2 |

SEMI-FINAL SECOND LEG

| Aston Villa | (1) 2 | Bolton W | (0) 0 |
| Middlesbrough | (0) 2 | Arsenal | (0) 1 |

CARLING CUP FINAL

Sunday, 29 February 2004

(at Millennium Stadium, Cardiff, attendance 72,634)

Middlesbrough (2) 2 *(Job 2, Zenden 7 (pen))*   **Bolton W (1) 1** *(Davies 21)*

Middlesbrough: Schwarzer; Mills, Queudrue, Southgate, Ehiogu, Doriva, Mendieta, Boateng, Job (Ricketts), Juninho, Zenden.

Bolton W: Jaaskelainen; Hunt (Giannakopoulos), Charlton, Campo, N'Gotty, Emerson, Nolan (Javi Moreno), Frandsen (Pedersen), Davies, Djorkaeff, Okocha.

Referee: M. Riley (W. Yorkshire).

PAST LEAGUE CUP FINALS

Played as two legs up to 1966

1961	Rotherham U ....2 *Webster, Kirkman*	Aston Villa 0
	Aston Villa ....3 *O'Neill, Burrows, McParland*	Rotherham U 0*
1962	Rochdale ....0 *Lythgoe 2, Punton*	Norwich C 3
	Norwich C ....1 *Hill*	Rochdale 0
1963	Birmingham C ....3 *Leek 2, Bloomfield*	Aston Villa ....1 *Thomson*
	Aston Villa 0	Birmingham C 0
1964	Stoke C ....1 *Bebbington*	Leicester C ....1 *Gibson*
	Leicester C ....3 *Stringfellow, Gibson, Riley*	Stoke C ....2 *Viollet, Kinnell*
1965	Chelsea ....3 *Tambling, Venables (pen),* *McCreadie*	Leicester C ....2 *Appleton, Goodfellow*
	Leicester C 0	Chelsea 0
1966	West Ham U ....2 *Moore, Byrne*	WBA ....1 *Astle*
	WBA ....4 *Kaye, Brown, Clark, Williams*	West Ham U ....1 *Peters*
1967	QPR ....3 *Morgan R, Marsh, Lazarus*	WBA ....2 *Clark C 2*
1968	Leeds U ....1 *Cooper*	Arsenal 0
1969	Swindon T ....3 *Smart, Rogers 2*	Arsenal ....1* *Gould*
1970	Manchester C ....2 *Doyle, Pardoe*	WBA ....1* *Astle*
1971	Tottenham H ....2 *Chivers 2*	Aston Villa 0
1972	Chelsea ....1 *Osgood*	Stoke C ....2 *Conroy, Eastham*
1973	Tottenham H ....1 *Coates*	Norwich C 0
1974	Wolverhampton W ....2 *Hibbitt, Richards*	Manchester C ....1 *Bell*
1975	Aston Villa ....1 *Graydon*	Norwich C 0
1976	Manchester C ....2 *Barnes, Tueart*	Newcastle U ....1 *Gowling*
1977	Aston Villa 0	Everton 0
Replay	Aston Villa ....1 *Kenyon (og)*	Everton ....1* *Latchford*
Replay	Aston Villa ....3 *Little 2, Nicholl*	Everton ....2* *Latchford, Lyons*
1978	Nottingham F 0	Liverpool 0*
Replay	Nottingham F ....1 *Robertson (pen)*	Liverpool 0
1979	Nottingham F ....3 *Birtles 2, Woodcock*	Southampton ....2 *Peach, Holmes*
1980	Wolverhampton W ....1 *Gray*	Nottingham F 0

1981	Liverpool ...1 *Kennedy A*	West Ham U ...1* *Stewart (pen)*
Replay	Liverpool ...2 *Dalglish, Hansen*	West Ham U ...1 *Goddard*
1982	Liverpool ...3 *Whelan 2, Rush*	Tottenham H ...1* *Archibald*
1983	Liverpool ...2 *Kennedy A, Whelan*	Manchester U ...1* *Whiteside*
1984	Liverpool ...0	Everton ...0*
Replay	Liverpool ...1 *Souness*	Everton ...0
1985	Norwich C ...1 *Chisholm (og)*	Sunderland ...0
1986	Oxford U ...3 *Hebberd, Houghton, Charles*	QPR ...0
1987	Arsenal ...2 *Nicholas 2*	Liverpool ...1 *Rush*
1988	Luton T ...3 *Stein B 2, Wilson*	Arsenal ...2 *Hayes, Smith*
1989	Nottingham F ...3 *Clough 2, Webb*	Luton T ...1 *Harford*
1990	Nottingham F ...1 *Jemson*	Oldham Ath ...0
1991	Sheffield W ...1 *Sheridan*	Manchester U ...0
1992	Manchester U ...1 *McClair*	Nottingham F ...0
1993	Arsenal ...2 *Merson, Morrow*	Sheffield W ...1 *Harkes*
1994	Aston Villa ...3 *Atkinson, Saunders 2 (1 pen)*	Manchester U ...1 *Hughes*
1995	Liverpool ...2 *McManaman 2*	Bolton W ...1 *Thompson*
1996	Aston Villa ...3 *Milosevic, Taylor, Yorke*	Leeds U ...0
1997	Leicester C ...1 *Heskey*	Middlesbrough ...1* *Ravanelli*
Replay	Leicester C ...1 *Claridge*	Middlesbrough ...0*
1998	Chelsea ...2 *Sinclair, Di Matteo*	Middlesbrough ...0*
1999	Tottenham H ...1 *Nielsen*	Leicester C ...0
2000	Leicester C ...2 *Elliott 2*	Tranmere R ...1 *Kelly*
2001	Liverpool ...1 *Fowler*	Birmingham C ...1 *Purse (pen)*

Liverpool won 5-4 on penalties.

2002	Blackburn ...2 *Jansen, Cole*	Tottenham H ...1 *Ziege*
2003	Liverpool ...2 *Gerrard, Owen*	Manchester U ...0
2004	Middlesbrough ...2 *Job, Zenden (pen)*	Bolton W ...1 *Davies*

*After extra time

LDV VANS TROPHY 2003–2004

NORTHERN SECTION FIRST ROUND

Blackpool	(3) 3	Tranmere R	(0) 2
Carlisle U	(1) 2	Rochdale	(0) 0
Chester C	(0) 0	Doncaster R	(0) 1
Chesterfield	(2) 2	Macclesfield T	(1) 1
Darlington	(0) 1	Hull C	(2) 3
Halifax T	(1) 2	York C	(0) 1
Lincoln C	(1) 3	Telford U	(0) 1
Mansfield T	(0) 1	Stockport Co	(1) 2
Oldham Ath	(2) 3	Hartlepool U	(1) 3

(aet; Oldham Ath won 5-3 on penalties.)

Scarborough	(0) 2	Port Vale	(1) 1
Scunthorpe U	(0) 2	Shrewsbury T	(1) 1
Wrexham	(1) 4	Morecambe	(0) 1
Notts Co	(0) 0	Barnsley	(0) 0

(aet; Barnsley won 4-2 on penalties.)

Sheffield W	(0) 1	Grimsby T	(1) 1

(aet; Sheffield W won 5-4 on penalties.)

SOUTHERN SECTION FIRST ROUND

Brighton & HA	(1) 2	Forest Green R	(0) 0
Barnet	(2) 3	Brentford	(0) 3

(aet; Brentford won 3-1 on penalties.)

Cheltenham T	(1) 1	Colchester U	(1) 3
Peterborough U	(2) 3	Torquay U	(2) 2

(aet; Peterborough U won on slow death.)

Plymouth Arg	(2) 4	Bristol C	(0) 0
QPR	(1) 2	Kidderminster H	(0) 0
Southend U	(1) 2	Bristol R	(1) 1

(aet.)

Stevenage B	(0) 0	Luton T	(0) 1
Wycombe W	(1) 1	Cambridge U	(0) 0
Yeovil T	(0) 2	Bournemouth	(0) 0
Boston U	(1) 2	Swindon T	(1) 1
Dagenham & R	(0) 4	Leyton Orient	(0) 1
Oxford U	(0) 0	Rushden & D	(1) 1
Hereford U	(0) 2	Exeter C	(0) 0

NORTHERN SECTION SECOND ROUND

Bury	(1) 2	Oldham Ath	(0) 1
Blackpool	(0) 1	Doncaster R	(0) 0
Carlisle U	(2) 2	Huddersfield T	(0) 0
Hull C	(0) 1	Scunthorpe U	(1) 3
Lincoln C	(1) 4	Chesterfield	(1) 3

(aet; Lincoln C won on slow death.)

Scarborough	(0) 0	Halifax T	(0) 1
Stockport Co	(2) 5	Wrexham	(2) 4

(aet; Stockport Co won on slow death.)

Sheffield W	(0) 1	Barnsley	(0) 0

SOUTHERN SECTION SECOND ROUND

Brighton & HA	(1) 3	Boston U	(0) 1

(aet; Brighton & HA won on slow death.)

Hereford U	(0) 1	Northampton T	(0) 1

(aet; Northampton T won 4-3 on penalties.)

Peterborough U	(1) 3	Brentford	(1) 2

Plymouth Arg	(2) 2	Wycombe W	(2) 2

(aet; Wycombe W won 4-2 on penalties.)

QPR	(1) 2	Dagenham & R	(0) 1
Rushden & D	(1) 1	Luton T	(2) 2
Swansea C	(0) 1	Southend U	(0) 2
Yeovil T	(1) 2	Colchester U	(1) 2

(aet; Colchester U won 4-2 on penalties.)

NORTHERN SECTION QUARTER-FINALS

Bury	(0) 0	Scunthorpe U	(0) 1

(aet; Scunthorpe U won on slow death.)

Carlisle U	(0) 0	Sheffield W	(1) 3
Stockport Co	(0) 0	Blackpool	(0) 1

(aet.)

Halifax T	(1) 1	Lincoln C	(0) 0

SOUTHERN SECTION QUARTER-FINALS

QPR	(2) 2	Brighton & HA	(0) 1
Northampton T	(0) 2	Peterborough U	(0) 1

(aet; Northampton T won on slow death.)

Southend U	(2) 3	Luton T	(0) 0
Wycombe W	(1) 2	Colchester U	(2) 3

(aet.)

NORTHERN SECTION SEMI-FINALS

Blackpool	(2) 3	Halifax T	(2) 2
Sheffield W	(2) 4	Scunthorpe U	(0) 0

SOUTHERN SECTION SEMI-FINALS

Northampton T	(1) 2	Colchester U	(0) 3

(aet; Colchester U won on slow death.)

Southend U	(1) 4	QPR	(0) 0

NORTHERN FINAL FIRST LEG

Blackpool	(0) 1	Sheffield W	(0) 0

NORTHERN FINAL SECOND LEG

Sheffield W	(0) 0	Blackpool	(2) 2

SOUTHERN FINAL FIRST LEG

Colchester U	(1) 2	Southend U	(2) 3

SOUTHERN FINAL SECOND LEG

Southend U	(1) 1	Colchester U	(1) 1

LDV VANS TROPHY FINAL

Sunday, 21 March 2004

(at Millennium Stadium, Cardiff, attendance 34,031)

Blackpool (1) 2 *(Murphy 2, Coid 55)*   **Southend U (0) 0**

Blackpool: Jones L; Grayson, Jaszczun, Dinning, Flynn, Elliott, Wellens (McMahon), Bullock (Richardson), Murphy, Sheron (Blinkhorn), Coid.

Southend U: Flahavan; Jupp, Wilson (Bramble), Maher, Cort, Warren, Pettefer, Hunt, Broughton, Constantine, Gower (Jenkins).

Referee: R. Pearson (Peterlee).

FA CHARITY SHIELD WINNERS 1908–2003

1908	Manchester U v QPR	
	4-0 after 1-1 draw	
1909	Newcastle U v Northampton T	2-0
1910	Brighton v Aston Villa	1-0
1911	Manchester U v Swindon T	8-4
1912	Blackburn R v QPR	2-1
1913	Professionals v Amateurs	7-2
1920	Tottenham H v Burnley	2-0
1921	Huddersfield T v Liverpool	1-0
1922	Not played	
1923	Professionals v Amateurs	2-0
1924	Professionals v Amateurs	3-1
1925	Amateurs v Professionals	6-1
1926	Amateurs v Professionals	6-3
1927	Cardiff C v Corinthians	2-1
1928	Everton v Blackburn R	2-1
1929	Professionals v Amateurs	3-0
1930	Arsenal v Sheffield W	2-1
1931	Arsenal v WBA	1-0
1932	Everton v Newcastle U	5-3
1933	Arsenal v Everton	3-0
1934	Arsenal v Manchester C	4-0
1935	Sheffield W v Arsenal	1-0
1936	Sunderland v Arsenal	2-1
1937	Manchester C v Sunderland	2-0
1938	Arsenal v Preston NE	2-1
1948	Arsenal v Manchester U	4-3
1949	Portsmouth v Wolverhampton W	1-1*
1950	World Cup Team v	4-2
	Canadian Touring Team	
1951	Tottenham H v Newcastle U	2-1
1952	Manchester U v Newcastle U	4-2
1953	Arsenal v Blackpool	3-1
1954	Wolverhampton W v WBA	4-4*
1955	Chelsea v Newcastle U	3-0
1956	Manchester U v Manchester C	1-0
1957	Manchester U v Aston Villa	4-0
1958	Bolton W v Wolverhampton W	4-1
1959	Wolverhampton W v	3-1
	Nottingham F	
1960	Burnley v Wolverhampton W	2-2*
1961	Tottenham H v FA XI	3-2

1962	Tottenham H v Ipswich T	5-1
1963	Everton v Manchester U	4-0
1964	Liverpool v West Ham U	2-2*
1965	Manchester U v Liverpool	2-2*
1966	Liverpool v Everton	1-0
1967	Manchester U v Tottenham H	3-3*
1968	Manchester C v WBA	6-1
1969	Leeds U v Manchester C	2-1
1970	Everton v Chelsea	2-1
1971	Leicester C v Liverpool	1-0
1972	Manchester C v Aston Villa	1-0
1973	Burnley v Manchester C	1-0
1974	Liverpool† v Leeds U	1-1
1975	Derby Co v West Ham U	2-0
1976	Liverpool v Southampton	1-0
1977	Liverpool v Manchester U	0-0*
1978	Nottingham F v Ipswich T	5-0
1979	Liverpool v Arsenal	3-1
1980	Liverpool v West Ham U	1-0
1981	Aston Villa v Tottenham H	2-2*
1982	Liverpool v Tottenham H	1-0
1983	Manchester U v Liverpool	2-0
1984	Everton v Liverpool	1-0
1985	Everton v Manchester U	2-0
1986	Everton v Liverpool	1-1*
1987	Everton v Coventry C	1-0
1988	Liverpool v Wimbledon	2-1
1989	Liverpool v Arsenal	1-0
1990	Liverpool v Manchester U	1-1*
1991	Arsenal v Tottenham H	0-0*
1992	Leeds U v Liverpool	4-3
1993	Manchester U† v Arsenal	1-1
1994	Manchester U v Blackburn R	2-0
1995	Everton v Blackburn R	1-0
1996	Manchester U v Newcastle U	4-0
1997	Manchester U† v Chelsea	1-1
1998	Arsenal v Manchester U	3-0
1999	Arsenal v Manchester U	2-1
2000	Chelsea v Manchester U	2-0
2001	Liverpool v Manchester U	2-1
2002	Arsenal v Liverpool	1-0
2003	Manchester U† v Arsenal	1-1

*Each club retained shield for six months. †Won on penalties.

THE FA COMMUNITY SHIELD 2003

Sunday, 10 August 2003

(at Millennium Stadium, Cardiff, attendance 59,293)

Manchester U (1) 1   Arsenal (1) 1

Manchester U: Howard; Neville P (Forlan), Fortune (O'Shea), Ferdinand, Keane, Silvestre, Solskjaer, Butt (Djemba Djemba), Van Nistelrooy, Giggs, Scholes.
Scorer: Silvestre 15.
Arsenal: Lehmann; Lauren, Cole, Vieira, Campbell, Toure, Parlour (Wiltord), Silva (Edu), Henry (Pires), Bergkamp (Jeffers■), Ljungberg (Van Bronckhorst).
Scorer: Henry 20.
(Manchester U won 4-3 on penalties.)
Referee: S. Bennett (Kent).   ■ *Denotes player sent off.*

177

SCOTTISH LEAGUE REVIEW 2003–2004

Having started the season modestly enough with a goalless draw at Dunfermline Athletic, Celtic made up for this partial disappointment by reducing the Scottish Premier League to a one horse race in the shortest possible time.

Incredibly they did not drop another point until held 1-1 at Parkhead by Motherwell on 14 March, having created a record 25 successive wins in the top echelon. By this time and another 1-0 victory over Rangers, Celtic were 16 points ahead at the top with third placed Hearts 12 points below Rangers. So much for competition.

By the time of the split after 33 matches the title was already assured for Celtic of course and the only interest remained in the placings to get into Europe and whether Partick Thistle at the bottom of the table would get a reprieve because the only two real candidates for promotion Clyde and Inverness Caledonian, would both have to find a groundshare option to be allowed up. In the event, Caley made it but were initially turned down by the SPL clubs, before being admitted though Partick appealed the decision.

Actually the first domestic honour of the season went to Caley who beat Airdrie United 2-0 in the Bell's League Cup final. The CIS Insurance Cup also finished with the same scoreline, Livingston beating Hibernian. The Hi-Bees had pulled off the not unremarkable feat of beating Rangers 4-3 on penalties after a 1-1 draw in the semi-final, having knocked out Celtic 2-1 in the fourth round! Yet they had not made the cut in the League.

Celtic did achieve the double beating Dunfermline, the team they had started the season drawing against in the League, 3-1 in the final with Henrik Larsson scoring twice. He finished his illustrious Celtic career with 242 competitive goals to his credit.

However, if domestic performances had been paramount for Celtic, their European adventure was not as satisfying as it had been the previous term when they had reached the final of the UEFA Cup. This time round they were unable to breach the group stage of the Champions League in the new format which cut out the second such round, it being replaced by earlier knock-out rounds. Similar fate befell Rangers.

Naturally it is not the end of European competition to be bounced out of the Champions League; consolation can come in the UEFA Cup for those narrowly missing out in the former tournament. Thus Celtic it was who appeared in the third round of the latter competition. Drawn at home to Teplice they took a respectable 3-0 lead from the first leg and only lost 1-0 away.

Barcelona provided severe opposition in the fourth round and in a stormy encounter Celtic edged home 1-0 but the Spaniards finished with nine players, Celtic ten. Displaying one of their finest defensive exhibitions of the season in Spain, the Bhoys pulled off a sensational goalless draw to go through.

Alas the quarter-finals were something of an anti-climax, in that another Spanish team Villarreal proved more of a stumbling block. A 1-1 draw at Parkhead was clearly not good enough and Celtic lost 2-0 in the second leg.

In the UEFA Cup Hearts appeared to have achieved the difficult task of winning the away leg of the second round 1-0 in Bordeaux, but were beaten 2-0 at Tynecastle. Dundee had gone out to Perugia in the first round.

On the financial front there were problems of varying proportions for Dundee, Livingston, Dunfermline and Motherwell. Administration was either knocking on the door or had been admitted previously.

As far as the Scottish League was concerned, Caley having battled with Clyde and overtaken them in the penultimate match by winning there 2-1, must have been relieved that a groundsharing hope with Aberdeen had been sanctioned.

Ayr United and Brechin City were relegated to the Second Division, their places being taken by Airdrie and Hamilton Academical both of whom had a season to remember since they were trailing in the wake of Morton and Berwick Rangers for much of the season. Airdrie having rallied convincingly to head affairs, Hamilton were rather slower to react but on 10 April signalled their intentions with a 6-1 win over Morton, eventually overtaking their rivals on points in the last match.

East Fife and Stenhousemuir found themselves relegated to the Third Division with free-scoring Stranraer catching Stirling Albion for that championship, but both being promoted.

SCOTTISH LEAGUE TABLES 2003–2004

Premier League

		Home					Away					Total						
	P	W	D	L	F	A	W	D	L	F	A	W	D	L	F	A	Gd	Pts
1 Celtic	38	15	2	2	62	15	16	3	0	43	10	31	5	2	105	25	80	98
2 Rangers	38	16	0	3	48	11	9	6	4	28	22	25	6	7	76	33	43	81
3 Hearts	38	12	5	2	32	17	7	6	6	24	23	19	11	8	56	40	16	68
4 Dunfermline	38	9	7	3	28	19	5	4	10	17	33	14	11	13	45	52	−7	53
5 Dundee U	38	8	6	5	28	27	5	4	10	19	33	13	10	15	47	60	−13	49
6 Motherwell	38	7	7	5	25	22	5	3	11	17	27	12	10	16	42	49	−7	46
7 Dundee	38	8	3	8	21	20	4	7	8	27	37	12	10	16	48	57	−9	46
8 Hibernian	38	6	5	8	25	28	5	6	8	16	32	11	11	16	41	60	−19	44
9 Livingston	38	6	9	4	24	18	4	4	11	24	39	10	13	15	48	57	−9	43
10 Kilmarnock	38	8	3	8	29	31	4	3	12	22	43	12	6	20	51	74	−23	42
11 Aberdeen	38	5	3	11	22	29	4	4	11	17	34	9	7	22	39	63	−24	34
12 Partick T	38	5	4	10	24	32	1	4	14	15	35	6	8	24	39	67	−28	26

First Division

		Home					Away					Total						
	P	W	D	L	F	A	W	D	L	F	A	W	D	L	F	A	Gd	Pts
1 Inverness CT	36	13	4	1	37	12	8	3	7	30	21	21	7	8	67	33	34	70
2 Clyde	36	11	4	3	34	17	9	5	4	30	23	20	9	7	64	40	24	69
3 St Johnstone	36	8	5	5	34	27	7	7	4	25	18	15	12	9	59	45	14	57
4 Falkirk	36	8	4	6	20	16	7	6	5	23	21	15	10	11	43	37	6	55
5 Queen of the S	36	9	6	3	24	16	6	3	9	22	32	15	9	12	46	48	−2	54
6 Ross Co	36	8	6	4	24	17	4	7	7	25	24	12	13	11	49	41	8	49
7 St Mirren	36	6	9	3	27	23	3	5	10	12	23	9	14	13	39	46	−7	41
8 Raith R	36	5	5	8	18	28	3	5	10	19	29	8	10	18	37	57	−20	34
9 Ayr U	36	4	7	7	21	29	2	6	10	16	29	6	13	17	37	58	−21	31
10 Brechin C	36	5	3	10	21	33	1	6	11	16	40	6	9	21	37	73	−36	27

Second Division

		Home					Away					Total						
	P	W	D	L	F	A	W	D	L	F	A	W	D	L	F	A	Gd	Pts
1 Airdrie U	36	10	6	2	36	19	10	4	4	28	17	20	10	6	64	36	28	70
2 Hamilton A	36	9	3	6	32	21	9	5	4	38	26	18	8	10	70	47	23	62
3 Dumbarton	36	12	3	3	31	13	6	3	9	25	28	18	6	12	56	41	15	60
4 Morton	36	8	8	2	37	30	8	3	7	29	28	16	11	9	66	58	8	59
5 Berwick R	36	8	2	8	31	31	6	4	8	30	36	14	6	16	61	67	−6	48
6 Forfar Ath	36	7	4	7	25	30	5	7	6	24	27	12	11	13	49	57	−8	47
7 Alloa	36	6	6	6	33	26	6	2	10	22	29	12	8	16	55	55	0	44
8 Arbroath	36	5	6	7	17	27	6	4	8	24	30	11	10	15	41	57	−16	43
9 East Fife	36	7	2	9	24	24	4	6	8	14	21	11	8	17	38	45	−7	41
10 Stenhousemuir	36	4	1	13	12	29	3	3	12	16	36	7	4	25	28	65	−37	25

Third Division

		Home					Away					Total						
	P	W	D	L	F	A	W	D	L	F	A	W	D	L	F	A	Gd	Pts
1 Stranraer	36	13	2	3	51	14	11	5	2	36	16	24	7	5	87	30	57	79
2 Stirling Alb	36	10	5	3	37	12	13	2	4	41	15	23	8	5	78	27	51	77
3 Gretna	36	9	5	4	29	18	11	3	4	30	21	20	8	8	59	39	20	68
4 Peterhead	36	10	5	3	38	13	8	2	8	29	24	18	7	11	67	37	30	61
5 Cowdenbeath	36	7	5	6	25	27	8	7	3	21	12	15	10	11	46	39	7	55
6 Montrose	36	7	4	7	31	34	5	8	5	21	29	12	12	12	52	63	−11	48
7 Queen's Park	36	5	5	8	20	24	5	6	7	21	29	10	11	15	41	53	−12	41
8 Albion R	36	6	2	10	16	35	6	2	10	30	40	12	4	20	66	75	−9	40
9 Elgin C	36	4	5	9	23	34	2	2	14	25	59	6	7	23	48	93	−45	25
10 East Stirlingshire	36	2	2	14	22	51	0	0	18	8	67	2	2	32	30	118	−88	8

BANK OF SCOTLAND SCOTTISH LEAGUE—PREMIER LEAGUE

RESULTS 2003–2004

	Aberdeen	Celtic	Dundee	Dundee U	Dunfermline Ath	Hearts	Hibernian	Kilmarnock	Livingston	Motherwell	Partick Th	Rangers
Aberdeen	—	1-3	2-2 1-2	0-1	1-2	0-1	3-1 0-1	3-1	0-3	0-3	2-1	2-3
Celtic	4-0	—	3-2	3-0	2-0	5-0	6-0	5-1	1-2	0-2	0-0	1-1
Dundee	1-2	0-1	—	5-0 2-1	5-0 1-2	2-2	1-1	1-2 2-0	5-1	3-0	3-1	3-0 1-0
Dundee U	2-0 3-2	1-2	1-1	—	0-2 0-1	2-1 0-2	2-2	1-1	2-1 2-0	0-1	1-0	0-2
Dunfermline Ath	2-2	1-5	2-2	3-2 0-1	—	2-1	1-2	2-3	2-1	0-2	0-0	1-3 3-3
Hearts	2-0 1-0	0-0	2-0	2-0	1-0 3-2	—	0-0	2-1	2-0	1-0	2-1	2-0
Hibernian	0-1 1-1	0-1	1-1	2-0	1-0 2-1	1-0	—	3-1 3-0	3-1 0-2	1-0 3-0	1-0	2-0 2-3
Kilmarnock	1-3 4-0	1-2	3-1	1-1	1-2	0-2	0-2 2-0	—	0-2 3-1	0-0 3-2	3-2 1-2	0-4
Livingston	1-0	0-4	1-1	0-0	1-1	1-1	1-0 4-1	1-2	—	0-2	2-1	1-1
Motherwell	0-3 2-0	0-5	5-3	2-3	4-1	1-1	0-1	2-4 2-2	1-1	—	2-1	0-1
Partick T	3-0	1-4	3-1	3-1 0-1	4-0	1-0	5-2	4-0	1-1 5-2	4-0	—	1-1
Rangers	3-0	0-1 1-2	4-0	2-1	4-1	2-1 0-1	3-0	2-0	1-0	1-0 4-0	2-0	—

BELL'S SCOTTISH LEAGUE—DIVISION ONE RESULTS 2003–2004

	Ayr U	Brechin C	Clyde	Falkirk	Inverness CT	Queen of the South	Raith R	Ross Co	St Johnstone	St Mirren
Ayr U	—	3-2	2-2	1-1	0-3	1-4	1-0	1-3	1-1	0-2
Brechin C	3-1	—	1-1	2-3	1-1	1-1	1-0	1-2	1-1	2-0
Clyde	0-3	2-1	—	2-2	0-2	0-1	0-3	4-2	0-1	1-1
Falkirk	3-0	0-0	2-5	—	2-4	2-1	1-0	1-0	0-2	2-0
Inverness CT	2-1	3-0	0-2	1-2	—	3-1	4-1	2-2	2-3	2-2
Queen of the South	0-1	5-0	1-1	4-2	1-2	—	3-2	1-0	0-3	0-0
Raith R	0-0	5-0	0-0	1-2	2-1	0-2	—	0-2	0-1	1-0
Ross Co	1-0	1-0	3-1	0-0	2-1	0-0	2-1	—	1-0	1-2
St Johnstone	2-1	1-0	4-1	2-0	3-2	4-1	3-0	1-1	—	1-0
St Mirren	4-1	2-2	0-1	0-1	2-1	4-1	0-2	2-0	1-1	—

BELL'S SCOTTISH LEAGUE—DIVISION TWO RESULTS 2003–2004

	Airdrie U	Alloa Ath	Arbroath	Berwick R	Dumbarton	East Fife	Forfar Ath	Hamilton	Morton A	Stenhousemuir
Airdrie U	—	1-0	2-1	1-1	2-0	1-1	3-3	3-0	1-6	2-0
Alloa Ath	1-4	—	0-1	6-0	1-1	2-1	2-2	1-1	2-0	4-0
Arbroath	0-1	2-2	—	2-3	1-2	2-0	1-1	1-3	0-1	2-2
Berwick R	1-1	3-1	4-0	—	3-0	1-1	0-0	2-2	3-3	1-0
Dumbarton	0-4	3-2	1-2	1-0	—	0-0	0-1	0-2	0-4	2-1
East Fife	0-1	3-0	1-3	4-1	1-0	—	3-1	2-4	2-0	2-1
Forfar Ath	3-1	1-0	1-0	3-1	1-3	1-0	—	0-3	1-0	3-0
Hamilton A	1-1	0-1	1-2	2-2	3-1	1-0	2-3	—	0-0	0-1
Morton	3-1	2-2	2-2	1-3	2-2	2-1	2-1	4-3	—	5-2
Stenhousemuir	0-3	0-1	0-3	3-1	1-2	0-1	0-2	0-4	0-2	—

BELL'S SCOTTISH LEAGUE—DIVISION THREE RESULTS 2003–2004

	Albion R	Cowdenbeath	East Stirling	Elgin C	Gretna	Montrose	Peterhead	Queen's Park	Stirling A	Stranraer
Albion R	—	1-2 / 2-4	5-0 / 5-1	1-2 / 1-2	1-3 / 1-2	0-1 / 3-0	2-0 / 3-3	3-1 / 3-1	0-3 / 3-5	1-1 / 1-4
Cowdenbeath	1-4 / 1-1	—	2-1 / 2-0	3-2 / 2-0	0-1 / 1-2	3-3 / 0-0	2-0 / 0-3	0-1 / 0-1	2-0 / 0-5	0-1 / 1-2
East Stirling	3-4 / 1-8	1-1 / 0-1	—	3-1 / 2-1	0-1 / 2-4	3-0 / 1-1	1-3 / 0-3	5-1 / 1-2	2-4 / 0-3	1-2 / 1-3
Elgin C	1-5 / 1-2	0-4 / 0-0	3-1 / 3-0	—	3-3 / 1-1	1-4 / 1-1	2-3 / 1-0	2-4 / 2-2	0-2 / 0-1	0-0 / 1-1
Gretna	3-1 / 3-0	1-0 / 0-1	2-1 / 5-1	2-2 / 2-1	—	1-2 / 2-1	3-2 / 1-1	1-3 / 1-1	0-1 / 1-0	0-0 / 2-4
Montrose	1-0 / 3-1	1-3 / 1-1	5-1 / 1-0	3-3 / 4-3	2-0 / 1-4	—	0-1 / 2-1	1-1 / 0-0	1-3 / 1-4	1-4 / 1-2
Peterhead	2-1 / 5-0	0-1 / 0-0	6-0 / 0-0	5-1 / 3-1	2-0 / 2-1	0-0 / 1-2	—	1-1 / 4-1	2-2 / 0-0	2-0 / 0-4
Queen's Park	1-1 / 0-1	0-0 / 1-2	1-0 / 5-1	5-2 / 4-0	0-1 / 4-1	1-1 / 1-1	1-0 / 1-0	—	0-2 / 1-4	0-2 / 1-0
Stirling A	2-1 / 3-0	0-0 / 1-1	5-1 / 6-0	3-0 / 6-1	0-1 / 1-3	1-1 / 1-0	3-1 / 1-0	1-0 / 0-0	—	2-2 / —
Stranraer	5-0 / 4-0	2-0 / 1-0	4-0 / 7-1	4-3 / 6-0	1-2 / 3-2	2-0 / 6-0	0-2 / 1-1	1-0 / 3-1	0-1 / 1-1	—

ABERDEEN   PREMIER LEAGUE

Ground: Pittodrie Stadium, Aberdeen AB24 5QH (01224) 650400
Ground capacity: 21,487. **Colours:** All red with white trim.
Manager: Jim Calderwood.
League Appearances: Anderson R 25; Bird M (2); Booth S 20(1); Buckley R 6(2);
Clark C 18(5); Considine A 1; Deloumeaux E 8(3); Diamond A 17(2); Donald D
(1); Esson R 2; Foster R 12(6); Hart M 10(1); Heikkinen M 38; Higgins C 4; Hinds
L 23(7); Lombardi M (1); Mackie D 4(12); McCulloch M 1(2); McGuire P 16(1);
McNaughton K 15(2); McQuilken J 7; Morrison S 26(1); Muirhead S 24(8);
O'Leary R 2; Preece D 36; Prunty B 6(12); Rutkiewicz K 16; Sheerin P 27(6);
Souter K 1(2); Stewart J 3(5); Tarditi S (1); Tiernan F 3(3); Tosh S 24(2); Zdrilic D
23(8).
Goals – League (39): Booth 8 (1 pen), Hinds 6, Anderson 5, Zdrilic 4, Tosh 3,
Deloumeaux 2, Diamond 2, McGuire 2, Prunty 2, Clark 1, Foster 1, Morrison 1,
Sheerin 1, own goal 1
Scottish Cup (6): Zdrilic 2, Booth 1, Clark 1, Heikkinen 1, Muirhead 1
CIS Cup (10): Tosh 3, Hinds 2, Zdrilic 2, Booth 1, Muirhead 1, Sheerin 1
Honours – Division 1: Champions – 1954-55, **Premier Division:** Champions – 1979-
80, 1983-84, 1984-85. **Scottish Cup winners** 1947, 1970, 1982, 1983, 1984, 1986, 1990.
League Cup winners 1956, 1977, 1986, 1990, 1996. **European Cup-Winners' Cup
winners** 1983.

AIRDRIE UNITED   DIV. 1

Ground: Shyberry Excelsior Stadium, Airdrie ML6 8QZ (01236) 622000
Ground capacity: 10,000 (all seated). **Colours:** White shirts with red diamond,
white shorts.
Manager: Sandy Stewart.
League Appearances: Black K 4; Christie K 10(3); Coyle O 23; Docherty S 27;
Dunn D 25(3); Glancy M 14(12); Gow A 26(6); Lovering P 18; McGeown M 36;
McGowan N 32; McKenna S 1; McKeown S 10(18); McLaren W 18(3); McManus
A 28(1); Roberts M 19(11); Ronald P 7(6); Singbo F 3(3); Stewart A 13(1);
Vareille J 21(12); Wilson M 25(8); Wilson S 16(3); Wilson W 21(2).
Goals – League (64): Coyle 12, Gow 12 (2 pens), McLaren 10, Vareille 9, Docherty
4, Dunn 4, McKeown 4, Glancy 3, Lovering 2, Christie 1, Roberts 1, Ronald 1, Wil-
son S 1
Scottish Cup (5): Coyle 2, McKeown 1, Roberts 1, Stewart 1
CIS Cup (3): Glancy 1, Roberts 1, Ronald 1
Challenge Cup (8): Dunn 2, McKeown 2, Gow 1, Roberts 1, Vareille 1, Wilson S 1
Honours – Second Division: Champions – 2003–04; **Division II:** Champions – 1902-
03, 1954-55, 1973-74. **Scottish Cup winners** 1924. **B&Q Cup winners** 1995. **Bell's
League Challenge winners** 2000-01, 2001-02.

ALBION ROVERS   DIV. 3

Ground: Cliftonhill Stadium, Main Street, Coatbridge ML5 3RB (01236) 606334
Ground capacity: 2496. **Colours:** Scarlet and yellow shirts, scarlet shorts.
Manager: Kevin McAllister.
League Appearances: Bennett N 26(1); Bradford J 14(6); Carr M 1; Connolly C
5(3); Cormack P 17(4); Crabbe S 13; Denham G 1; Diack I 5(8); Fahey C 9; Farrell
D 16(1); Kerr C 6(2); Kerr S (1); Low A 4(6); McAllister K 12(2); McBride K 5(7);
McCaig J 21(2); McCaul G 18; McKenzie M 3(11); McManus P 33(1); Mercer J 33;
Molloy M 2(3); Paterson A 29(2); Patrick R 12(1); Potter K 3(2); Selkirk A (2); Sil-

vestro C 3; Skinner S (2); Smith J 27(2); Stirling J 31(2); Sweeney S 21; Valentine J (1); Yardley M 26(1).
Goals – League (66): McManus 18, Yardley 11, Mercer 10, Stirling 7 (2 pens), Bradford 4, McBride 2, McKenzie 2, Smith 2, Crabbe 1, Diack 1, Farrell 1, McAllister 1, McCaul 1 Patrick 1, Sweeney 1, own goals 3
Scottish Cup (2): Mercer 1, own goal 1
CIS Cup (2): McAllister 1, McManus 1
Challenge Cup (3): Diack 2, McManus 1
Honours – Division II: Champions – 1933-34. **Second Division:** Champions 1988-89.

ALLOA ATHLETIC   DIV. 2

Ground: Recreation Park, Alloa FK10 1RY (01259) 722695
Ground capacity: 3100. **Colours:** Gold shirts with black trim, black shorts with gold stripe.
Manager: Tom Hendrie.
League Appearances: Bolochowescyj M 20; Callaghan S 35; Clark D 6(1); Crabbe S 1(9); Daly M 8(9); Evans G 1(5); Evans J 4(2); Ferguson A 33(1); Hamilton R 35; Janczyk N 10(2); Kelbie K (8); Little I 33(1); McGlynn G 32; McGowan J 34; McLaughlin P 8(4); Nicolson I 35; Seaton A 20; Stevenson J 2(11); Valentine C 33; Walker R 35; Walker S 11; Watson M (4).
Goals – League (55): Hamilton 13, Little 11, Callaghan 6 (2 pens), McGowan 5, Walker R 5, Ferguson 3, Nicolson 3, Daly 2, Janczyk 2, Stevenson 2, Bolochowescyj 1, Clark 1, own goal 1
Scottish Cup (6): Ferguson 2, Hamilton 1, McGowan 1, Walker R 1, Walker S 1
CIS Cup (0)
Challenge Cup (1): Callaghan (pen)
Honours – Division II: Champions – 1921-22. **Third Division:** Champions – 1997-98. **Bell's League Challenge winners** 1999-2000.

ARBROATH   DIV. 2

Ground: Gayfield Park, Arbroath DD11 1QB (01241) 872157
Ground capacity: 4020. **Colours:** Maroon shirts with white trim, white shorts.
Manager: Steve Kirk.
League Appearances: Browne P 17(4); Cargill A 25; Collier J (1); Cusick J 24; Denham C 3; Diack I 21(1); Dow A 18; Durno J 3(8); Farquharson P (12); Graham E 2(3); Graham J 14(1); Henslee C 20(11); Herkes J 7(8); Kerrigan S 3(3); King D 33; Kirk S (1); McAulay J 8(10); McCulloch M 21; McGlashan J 34; McLean D 12(4); McMullen K 32(2); Miller G 15(1); Mitchell A 2; Newall C (3); Peat M 33; Rennie S 32; Shaw G (1); Swankie G 16(14); Watson C (1); Woodcock T 1(1).
Goals – League (41): McGlashan 10, Cargill 7, Diack 7 (1 pen), McLean 6, Cusick 5 (3 pens), Dow 2, Durno 1, Graham J 1, Henslee 1, McMullen 1
Scottish Cup (3): McGlashan 3
CIS Cup (4): McGlashan 2, Cusick 1, Graham J 1
Challenge Cup (3): McGlashan 2, Graham J 1
Honours – Nil.

AYR UNITED   DIV. 2

Ground: Somerset Park, Ayr KA8 9NB (01292) 263435
Ground capacity: 10,243 (1549 seated). **Colours:** White shirts with black trim, black shorts.
Director of Football: Campbell Money.

League Appearances: Black A 17(2); Brown G 12(3); Burgess R 4(4); Campbell M 25; Chaplain S 29(5); Conway C (8); Craig D 33; Crawford S 1; Doyle J 6(1); Dunlop M 18(5); Ferguson A 16(15); Ferguson S 9; Hardy L 24; Hillcoat J 1(1); Kean S 36; Kerr C 5(4); Kinniburgh W 7; Latta J 1(2); Lyle W 26(5); McColl M 2(12); McGrady S 11(9); Miller S 1(5); Mullen B (5); Ramsay D 29; Roy L 35; Smyth M 30(4); Tait J 11; Whalen S 7(2).
Goals – League (37): Kean 9, Ferguson A 7, Chaplain 4, Hardy 4 (1 pen), Brown 2, Campbell 2, Dunlop 2, Black 1, Craig 1, Doyle 1, Ramsay 1, Smyth 1, Whalen 1, own goal 1
Scottish Cup (1): Craig 1
CIS Cup (1): Smyth 1
Challenge Cup (1): Kean 1
Honours – Division II: Champions – 1911-12, 1912-13, 1927-28, 1936-37, 1958-59, 1965-66. **Second Division:** Champions – 1987-88, 1996-97.

BERWICK RANGERS   DIV. 2

Ground: Shielfield Park, Berwick-on-Tweed TD15 2EF (01289) 307424
Ground capacity: 4131. **Colours:** Black with broad gold stripe, black shorts with white trim.
Manager: Paul Smith.
League Appearances: Bain C (1); Bennett J 30(4); Birrell J (1); Blackley D (5); Bracks K (1); Connell G 25(2); Connelly S 9; Forrest G 18; Godfrey R 11(1); Gordon K 3(10); Hampshire P 32(3); Hilland F 9(4); Hutchison G 36; Inglis N 25; Kerrigan S (6); Macdonald S (1); McAllister J 1(2); McCormick M (4); McCutcheon G 33(1); McNicoll G 32; Murie D 35; Neill M 16(4); Neill A 20(2); Noon D 1; Robertson M (3); Smith D 7(12); Waldie C 11(2).
Goals – League (61): Hutchison 22, McCutcheon 14, Forrest 8, Cowan 4, Hampshire 4, Connelly 3, Bennett 2 (2 pens), Hilland 2, McNicoll 1, Neill M 1
Scottish Cup (4): Hutchison 3, own goal 1
CIS Cup (0)
Challenge Cup (1): McNicoll 1
Honours – Second Division: Champions – 1978-79.

BRECHIN CITY   DIV. 2

Ground: Glebe Park, Brechin DD9 6BJ (01356) 622856
Ground capacity: 3980. **Colours:** Red with white trim.
Manager: Dick Campbell.
League Appearances: Beith G 2(2); Black R 5(5); Boylan C 1(12); Budinauckas K 8(1); Clark D 3(3); Davidson I 3(1); Deas P 32; Dowie A 15; Duffy D 8; Fotheringham K 8(4); Gibson G 11(16); Hampshire S 27; Hay D 16(2); Jablonski N 15(1); Jackson C 1; Johnson G 25; King C 27(5); McCulloch M 3(3); McCulloch S 22(8); McLeish K 11(9); Millar M 19(1); Miller G 7(10); Mitchell A 27(2); Shields D (2); Smith J 26(2); Soutar D 12; Stein J 2(4); Templeman C 22(11); Walker S 1; White D 27(1); Winter C 10.
Goals – League (37): Templeman 5 (1 pen), Gibson 4, Hampshire 4, Duffy 3, King 3, Fotheringham 2 (2 pens), McCulloch S 2, McLeigh 2, Millar M 2 (2 pens), Mitchell 2, Smith 2, White 2, Winter 2, Beith 1, Jablonski 1
Scottish Cup (1): King 1
CIS Cup (5): Fotheringham 1, Gibson 1, Hampshire 1, Templeman 1, White 1
Challenge Cup (7): Fotheringham 2, Templeman 2, Johnston 1, King 1, White 1
Honours – Second Division: Champions – 1982-83, 1989-90. **Third Division:** Champions – 2001-02. **C Division:** Champions – 1953-54.

CELTIC   PREMIER LEAGUE

Ground: Celtic Park, Glasgow G40 3RE (0141) 556 2611
Ground capacity: 60,355 (all seated). **Colours:** Green and white hooped shirts, white shorts.
Manager: Martin O'Neill.
League Appearances: Agathe D 26(1); Balde D 30(1); Beattie C 2(8); Crainey S 1(1); Douglas R 15(1); Gray M 2(5); Hartson J 14(1); Hedman M 12; Kennedy J 9(3); Lambert P 9(4); Larsson H 36(1); Lennon N 35; Maloney S 9(10); Marshall D 11; McGeady A 3(1); McManus S 5; McNamara J 26(1); Miller L 13(12); Mjällby J 10(3); Pearson S 16(1); Petrov S 33(2); Smith J 2(7); Sutton C 25; Sylla M 5(9); Thompson A 26; Valgaeren J 4(3); Varga S 35; Wallace R 4(4).
Goals – League (105): Larsson 30, Sutton 19 (6 pens), Thompson 11 (3 pens), Hartson 9, Petrov 6, Varga 6, Agathe 5, Maloney 5, Pearson 3, Balde 2, Miller 2, Beattie 1, Kennedy 1, Lambert 1, McGeady 1, McNamara 1, Wallace 1, own goal 1
Scottish Cup (12): Larsson 5, Petrov 3, Sutton 2, Hartson 1, Lambert 1
CIS Cup (3): Beattie 1, Smith 1, Varga 1
Honours – Division I: Champions – 1892-93, 1893-94, 1895-96, 1897-98, 1904-05, 1905-06, 1906-07, 1907-08, 1908-09, 1909-10, 1913-14, 1914-15, 1915-16, 1916-17, 1918-19, 1921-22, 1925-26, 1935-36, 1937-38, 1953-54, 1965-66, 1966-67, 1967-68, 1968-69, 1969-70, 1970-71, 1971-72, 1972-73, 1973-74. **Premier Division:** Champions – 1976-77, 1978-79, 1980-81, 1981-82, 1985-86, 1987-88, 1997-98. **Premier League:** 2000-01, 2001-02, 2003–04. **Scottish Cup winners** 1892, 1899, 1900, 1904, 1907, 1908, 1911, 1912, 1914, 1923, 1925, 1927, 1931, 1933, 1937, 1951, 1954, 1965, 1967, 1969, 1971, 1972, 1974, 1975, 1977, 1980, 1985, 1988, 1989, 1995, 2001, 2004. **League Cup winners** 1957, 1958, 1966, 1967, 1968, 1969, 1970, 1975, 1983, 1998, 2000, 2001, 2004. **European Cup winners** 1967.

CLYDE   DIV. 1

Ground: Broadwood Stadium, Cumbernauld G68 9NE (01236) 451511
Ground capacity: 8200. **Colours:** White shirts with red and black trim, black shorts.
Manager: Billy Reid.
League Appearances: Doyle P 1(6); Fotheringham K 9(4); Fraser J 16(2); Gibson J 26(1); Gilhaney M 6(27); Hagen D 22(9); Halliwell B 20; Harty J 29(5); Keogh P 10(15); Kernaghan A 22; Marshall C 24(2); McCann H 6; McCluskey S 17; McConalogue S 17(7); McGroarty C 12; McLaughlin M 29(2); Mensing S 30(1); Millen A 14(3); Morrison A 16(1); Potter J 11(1); Ross J 35; Smith A 24(9).
Goals – League (64): Harty 15 (3 pens), Keogh 12, Smith 10, McConalogue 7, McLaughlin 5, Gibson 4, Fotheringham 2, Gilhaney 2, Marshall 2, Ross 2, Hagen 1, McCluskey 1, own goal 1
Scottish Cup (3): Smith 2, Ross 1
CIS Cup (4): Gilhaney 2, Keogh 1, Millen 1
Challenge Cup (2): Fraser 1, McConalogue 1
Honours – Division II: Champions – 1904-05, 1951-52, 1956-57, 1961-62, 1972-73. **Second Division:** Champions – 1977-78, 1981-82, 1992-93, 1999-2000. **Scottish Cup winners** 1939, 1955, 1958.

COWDENBEATH   DIV. 3

Ground: Central Park, Cowdenbeath KY4 9EY (01383) 610166
Ground capacity: 5268. **Colours:** Royal blue with white cuffs and collar, white shorts.
Manager: Keith Wright.

League Appearances: Bathgate S (1); Boyle S 2; Bristow S (1); Brown G 12(2); Buchanan L 8(17); Campbell A 18(3); Carlin A 33; Fallon J 3(4); Fleming A 3(1); Fusco G 22(5); Gilfillan B 32(1); Gordon K 7(8); Kelly J 4(6); Matheson R 3(6); Mauchlen I 14(10); McCallum R 1(12); McGuinness S 11(5); McInally D 29(5); McKeown J 32(1); Moffat A 2(2); Morris I 5; Mowat D 33(3); Orhue P (1); Ritchie I 29(1); Shand C 30(1); Shields D 30(1); Skinner S 8(1); Slaven J 1(2); Stewart S 3(1); Winter C 21.
Goals – League (46): Shields 12, Buchanan 8, Gilfillan 6, Brown 5, Ritchie 4, Morris 2, Skinner 2, Winter 2, Fusco 1, McInally 1, Mauchlen 1, Stewart 1, own goal 1
Scottish Cup (10): Gordon 2, Mauchlen 2, Buchanan 1, Fusco 1, Gilfillan 1, Shields 1, Winter 1, own goal 1
CIS Cup (3): McInally 2, Morris 1
Challenge Cup (1): Brown 1
Honours – Division II: Champions – 1913-14, 1914-15, 1938-39.

DUMBARTON   DIV. 2

Ground: Strathclyde Homes Stadium, Dumbarton G82 1JJ.
Ground capacity: 2050. **Colours:** Yellow shirts with black facing, shorts yellow with black stripe.
Manager: Brian Fairley.
League Appearances: Bonar S 35; Boyle C 17(11); Bradley M 18(6); Brittain C 32; Collins N 29(1); Dillon J 31(5); Dobbins I 12(5); Donald B 24(2); Duffy N 8(1); English I 8(1); Flannery P 9(2); Grindlay S 34; Herd G 11(9); Laidler S (6); Mallan S 3(2); McEwan C 19(4); McKinstry J 35; Obidile E 8(2); Okoli J 2; Renicks S 7(11); Robertson K 2; Rodgers A 7(4); Ronald P 13(1); Russell I 26(7); Skjelbred B 2(6); Smith D 4(1); Wight J (1).
Goals – League (56): Russell 10, Dillon 8, Herd 8, Bonar 5, Boyle 4, McEwan 4, Rodgers 4, Flannery 3, Ronald 3, Bradley 2, Collins 2, Brittain 1, English 1, Skjelbred 1
Scottish Cup (0)
CIS Cup (3): Bonar 1, Flannery 1, Obidile 1
Challenge Cup (0)
Honours – Division I: Champions – 1890-91 (Shared), 1891-92. **Division II:** Champions – 1910-11, 1971-72. **Second Division:** Champions – 1991-92. **Scottish Cup winners** 1883.

DUNDEE   PREMIER LEAGUE

Ground: Dens Park, Dundee DD3 7JY (01382) 889966
Ground capacity: 11,760 (all seated). **Colours:** Navy shirts with white and red shoulder and sleeve flashes, white shorts with navy and red piping, navy stockings with two white hoops.
Manager: Jim Duffy.
League Appearances: Barrett N 10(2); Brady G 35(2); Burley C 1(1); Caballero F 9(4); Cameron D 6(5); Carranza L 2(3); Clark N (2); Cowan T 4(1); Fotheringham M 19(5); Hegarty C 1(3); Hernandez J 27(2); Hutchinson T 8(4); Jablonski N 3(9); Kneissl S 5(6); Linn R 3(9); Lovell S 15(6); Macdonald C 6; Mackay D 34(1); Mair L 36; McCafferty J (1); McLean D 3(1); McNally S 1(1); Milne S 15(5); Nemsadze G 9; Novo I 34(1); Rae G 11(2); Ravanelli F 5; Robb S 9(6); Sancho B 20(1); Sara J 3(7); Smith B 27(2); Soutar D 1; Speroni J 37; Wilkie L 21; Youngson A (1).
Goals – League (48): Novo 20 (2 pens), Milne 8, Lovell 5, Fotheringham 4, Rae 2, Smith 2, Cowan 1, Hernandez 1, Hutchinson 1, Kneissl 1, McLean 1, Mair 1, Willkie 1
Scottish Cup (2): Novo 1, Robb 1
CIS Cup (6): Ravanelli 3, Linn 1, Novo 1, Wilkie 1

Honours – Division I: Champions – 1961-62. **First Division: Champions** – 1978-79, 1991-92, 1997-98. **Division II: Champions** – 1946-47. **Scottish Cup winners** 1910. **League Cup winners** 1952, 1953, 1974. **B&Q (Centenary) Cup winners** 1991.

DUNDEE UNITED   PREMIER LEAGUE

Ground: Tannadice Park, Dundee DD3 7JW (01382) 833166
Ground capacity: 14,223. **Colours:** Tangerine shirts, tangerine shorts.
Manager: Ian McCall.
League Appearances: Archibald A 38; Bollan G 1(1); Bullock A 5; Conway A (1); Coyle O (3); Dodds W 23(10); Duff S 10(8); Easton C 10(12); Gallacher P 33; Griffin D 9(4); Holmes G (3); Innes C 29; Kerr M 30(3); McCracken D 32; McInnes D 34(1); McIntyre J 27(3); McLaren A 26(1); Miller C 22(4); Paterson J 10(6); Paterson S 2(1); Robson B 25(3); Samuel C 11(15); Scotland J 10(11); Wilson M 31(1).
Goals – League (47): Dodds 10 (1 pen), McIntyre 10 (1 pen), Miller 5, Scotland 4, McLaren 3, Robson 3, Samuel 3, Wilson 3 (1 pen), Archibald 2, Innes 1, Kerr 1, McCracken 1, McInnes 1
Scottish Cup (1): McInnes 1
CIS Cup (3): McIntyre 2, McLaren 1
Honours – Premier Division: Champions – 1982-83. **Division II: Champions** – 1924-25, 1928-29. **Scottish Cup winners** 1994. **League Cup winners** 1980, 1981.

DUNFERMLINE ATHLETIC   PREMIER LEAGUE

Ground: East End Park, Dunfermline KY12 7RB (01383) 724295
Ground capacity: 12,500. **Colours:** Black and white striped shirts, white shorts.
Manager: David Hay.
League Appearances: Brewster C 23(3); Bullen L 19(8); Byrne R 10(3); Clark P 1(1); Crawford S 33(1); Dair J (1); Dempsey G 15(17); Greenhill G (1); Grondin D 9(5); Hunt N 5(8); Kilgannon S 4(7); Labonte A 8(13); Mason G 32; McDermott A 5(1); McGarty M (1); McGroarty C 2; McGuire K (1); Mehmet W 5(13); Nicholson B 36; Ruitenbeek M 1; Shields G 15(2); Skerla A 35; Stillie D 37; Thomson SM 15(1); Tod A 22(8); Wilson C 1; Wilson S 28; Young Darren 32; Young Derek 25(3).
Goals – League (45): Crawford 13, Brewster 5, Dempsey 5, Nicholson 5 (1 pen), Derek Young 4, Bullen 2, Hunt 2, Tod 2, Mehmet 1, Shields 1, Thomson SM 1, Wilson S 1, Darren Young 1, own goals 2
Scottish Cup (14): Brewster 4, Nicholson 4, Crawford 2, Bullen 1, Byrne 1, Skerla 1, Darren Young 1
CIS Cup (4): Crawford 2, Brewster 1, Darren Young 1
Honours – First Division: Champions – 1988-89, 1995-96. **Division II: Champions** – 1925-26. **Second Division: Champions** – 1985-86. **Scottish Cup winners** 1961, 1968.

EAST FIFE   DIV. 3

Ground: Bayview Park, Methil, Fife KY8 3RW (01333) 426323
Ground capacity: 2000 (all seated). **Colours:** Gold and black shirts, white shorts.
Manager: James Moffat.
League Appearances: Bain K 10(1); Blair B 15(7); Byle L 2; Deuchar K 31(5); Donaldson E 31(1); Fairbairn B 10(20); Gilbert G 11(11); Graham M 2; Hall M 27; Herkes J 8(7); Kelly P 24(1); Love G 1(2); Lumsden C 21(2); Lynes C 3(3); Mathie G 16; McDonald G 31(3); McDonald I 9; McMillan C 36; Miller C 6; Mitchell J 14(10); Mortimer P 9(7); Nicholas S 10(1); O'Connor G 34; Russell G 9(1); Stein J 12(1); Stewart W 14(7).

Goals – League (38): Deuchar 11, McDonald G 9, Donaldson 3, Fairbairn 3, McMillan 3, Hall 2, Nicholas 2, Lynes 1, Mitchell 1, Mortimer 1, Stein 1, own goal 1
Scottish Cup (6): Deuchar 1, Hall 1, McDonald G 1, Nicholas 1, own goals 2
CIS Cup (0)
Challenge Cup (0)
Honours – Division II: Champions – 1947-48. **Scottish Cup winners** 1938. **League Cup winners** 1948, 1950, 1954.

EAST STIRLINGSHIRE DIV. 3

Ground: Firs Park, Falkirk FK2 7AY (01324) 623583
Ground capacity: 1880. **Colours:** Black shirts with white hoops, black shorts with white and red stripes.
Head Coach: Dennis Newall.
League Appearances: Baldwin C 23(1); Boyle G 1(7); Carnaghan G 1; Connolly J 19; Ford K 9(1); Gilpin R 4; Hare R 11(4); Irvine S 1(2); Kane P (3); Kelly S 20(11); Leishman J 14(6); Livingstone S 29(3); Lynch C 2(3); Mackay J 12(3); Maughan R 26; McAuley S 24(5); McCann K 5; McCulloch G 1(2); McGhee G 35(1); McLaren G 30(2); Millar D 8(2); Mulholland B 13(3); Newell C 15; Oates S 16; Ogilvie F (1); Ormiston D 7; Penman C 1; Polwart D 14(4); Reid C 9(2); Reid M (1); Rodden P 7(12); Todd C 13(1); Ure D 26(2).
Goals – League (30): Ure 9, Kelly 7 (2 pens), McAuley 3, Millar 2, Baldwin 1, Leishman 1, Livingstone 1, Ormiston 1, Polwart 1, Reid C 1, Rodden 1, own goals 2
Scottish Cup (0)
CIS Cup (1): Rodden
Challenge Cup (2): Baldwin 1, Kelly 1
Honours – Division II: Champions – 1931-32. **C Division:** Champions – 1947-48.

ELGIN CITY DIV. 3

Ground: Borough Briggs, Elgin IV30 1AP (01343) 551114
Ground capacity: 5000 (478 seated). **Colours:** Black and white vertical stripes, black shorts.
Manager: David Robertson.
League Appearances: Addicoat W 4; Allison J 32; Anderson R (1); Bone A 30(3); Bremner F 4(2); Campbell C 28; Charlesworth M (1); Coulter R 16(1); Dempsie A 21; Dickson H 18(1); Dickson M 1(1); Donald M (4); Gallagher J 3(2); Goram A 5; Hamilton P 3; Hind D 28(3); Martin W 30(4); McCormick S 14(2); McKenzie J 14; McLean C 2; McLean N 19(7); McMillan A 19(2); McMullan R 18(10); Murphy J 6(1); Ogboke C 9(10); Pirie M 28; Ralph J 1; Read C (1); Reid P 2(4); Steele K 9(13); Teasdale M 1; Thomson R (1); Tully C 17; Vigurs I 1(2); White J 13(3); Wood G (1).
Goals – League (48): Bone 15, Martin 8, Ogboke 6, Tully 5, Hind 2, McCormick 2, Steele 2, White 2, Allison 1, Bremner 1, Coulter 1, McKenzie 1, McMillan 1, McMullan 1
Scottish Cup (1): Campbell 1
CIS Cup (0)
Challenge Cup (0)

FALKIRK DIV. 1

Ground: Brockville Park, Falkirk FK1 5AX (01324) 624121
Ground capacity: 9706. **Colours:** Navy blue shirts with white seams, navy shorts.
Head Coach: John Hughes.

League Appearances: Barr D (1); Christie K 2; Colquhoun D 7(8); Creaney P (1); Ferguson A 17; Henry J 5(2); Hill D 19(1); Hughes J 27; James K 13; Latapy R 32; Lawrie A 34(1); Lee J 27(2); MacSween I 5(5); Mackenzie S 26(1); Manson S (1); May E 2(2); McAnespie K 12(14); McCluskey S 1; McLaren A 1(1); McMenamin C 13(4); McPherson C 35; McStay R 2(4); Nicholls D 13(9); O'Neil J 30; Rahim B 19(7); Ramsay M (2); Rodgers A 2(4); Scally N 12(8); Sharp J 30; Twaddle M (3); Xausa D 10(5).
Goals – League (43): Lee 8, Latapy 7, Henry 4, McMenamin 4, O'Neil 4 (1 pen). McAnespie 3, Colquhoun 2, Hughes 2, Lawrie 2, Scally 2, James 1, McPherson 1, Nicholls 1, Sharp 1, own goal 1
Scottish Cup (2): Lee 1, Xausa 1
CIS Cup (5): Nicholls 2, Latapy 1, McMenamin 1, Rodgers 1
Challenge Cup (0)
Honours – Division II: Champions – 1935-36, 1969-70, 1974-75. **First Division:** Champions – 1990-91, 1993-94, 2002-03. **Second Division:** Champions – 1979-80. **Scottish Cup winners** 1913, 1957. **League Challenge Cup winners** 1998.

FORFAR ATHLETIC   DIV. 2

Ground: Station Park, Forfar, Angus (01307) 463576
Ground capacity: 4640. **Colours:** Navy shirts with sky blue side panels, sky blue shorts with navy side panels.
Manager: Raymond Stewart.
League Appearances: Bremner C (1); Brown M 32; Byers K 20(5); Davidson H 33(1); Ferrie N 4(2); Ferry M 11(7); Florence S 8(6); Forbes B (1); Henderson D 25(1); Horn R 28; King M 11(5); Lowing D 16(5); Lunan P 29(2); MacNicol S 12; Maher M 11(17); McClune D 28(1); Ogunmade D 2(3); Rattray A 23; Sellars B 28(1); Shields P 25(8); Stewart D 11; Taylor S 3(10); Tosh P 31(1); Vella S 4; Williams D 1(6).
Goals – League (49): Tosh 18, Shields 9, Davidson 4, Ferry M 4, Henderson 4, Rattray 2, Sellars 2, Taylor 2, Lunan 1, McClune 1, Maher 1, own goal 1
Scottish Cup (4): Tosh 3 (1 pen), Rattray 1
CIS Cup (4): Henderson 2, Tosh 2
Challenge Cup (8): Shields 4, Maher 2, Davidson 1, Tosh 1
Honours – Second Division: Champions – 1983-84. **Third Division:** Champions – 1994-95.

GRETNA   DIV. 3

Ground: Raydale Park, Gretna DG16 5AP (01461) 337602
Ground capacity: 2200. **Colours:** Black shirt with white troops, black shorts with white trim.
Manager: Rowan Alexander.
League Appearances: Allan J 2(4); Baldacchino R 33; Birch M 23; Cameron M 24(2); Cohen G 14(12); Cosgrove S (4); Eccles M 5(5); Galloway M 34(1); Gordon W 4(15); Grainger D 1; Holdsworth D 27; Hore J 1; Irons D 32(1); Knox K 2(1); Lennon D 34(1); Maddison L 29; Mathieson D 35; May K 1(2); McGuffie R 19(7); O'Neill P 2; Prokas R 27(3); Robb R 1; Skelton G 30(1); Skinner S 1; Spence C 1; Stevens I 23(5); Summersgill C 1; Townsley D 15; Wake B 6(5).
Goals – League (59): Cameron 17 (2 pens), Stevens 10, Townsley 9, Wake 5, Baldacchino 4, Birch 3, Galloway 3, Skelton 2, Gordon 1, Irons 1, McGuffie 1, Maddison 1, own goals 2
Scottish Cup (9): Sevens 3, Skelton 2, Baldacchino 1, Cohen 1, Gordon 1, Holdsworth 1
CIS Cup (1): McGuffie 1
Challenge Cup (0)

HAMILTON ACADEMICAL   DIV. 1

Ground: New Douglas Park, Cadzow Avenue, Hamilton ML3 0FT (01698) 368650
Ground capacity: 5396. **Colours:** Red and white hooped shirts, white shorts.
Manager: Allan Maitland.
League Appearances: Aitken C 32(1); Anderson D (1); Arbuckle A 23(6); Bailey J
4(3); Blackadder R 10(5); Carrigan B 30(1); Convery S 12(4); Corcoran M 22(13);
Donnelly C 1(8); Ferguson D 3(1); Fitter J 5; Forbes B 4(4); Gemmell J (8);
Gribben D 4(19); Hodge S 31(1); Jellema R (1); Lumsden T 33(1); Maxwell D 2;
McEwan D 36; McPhee B 31; Paterson N (3); Quitongo J 14(4); Sherry J 22(4);
Thomson S 36; Waddell A (5); Waddell R 8(1); Walker R 21(2); Whiteford A
12(5).
Goals – League (70): McPhee 19 (3 pens), Carrigan 14 (3 pens), Aitken 8,
Quitongo 5, Convery 4, Corcoran 3, Thomson 3, Walker R 3, Bailey 2 (1 pen),
Gribben 2, Lumsden 2, Whiteford 2, Gemmell 1, Hodge 1, Waddell A 1
Scottish Cup (4): McPhee 2, Corcoran 1, Quitongo 1
CIS Cup (5): McPhee 2, Aitken 1, Carrigan 1, Corcoran 1
Challenge Cup (2): Aitken 1, McPhee 1
Honours – First Division: Champions – 1985-86, 1987-88. **Divison II:** Champions –
1903-04. **Division III:** Champions – 2000-01. **B&Q Cup winners** 1992, 1993.

HEART OF MIDLOTHIAN   PREMIER LEAGUE

Ground: Tynecastle Park, Gorgie Road, Edinburgh EH11 2NL (0131) 200 7200
Ground capacity: 18,000. **Colours:** Maroon shirts, white shorts.
Manager: Craig Levein.
League Appearances: Berra C 3(3); Boyack S 3(5); De Vries M 26(5); Gordon C
29; Hamill J 12(6); Hartley P 29(1); Janczyk N 4(7); Kirk A 14(10); Kisnorbo P
28(3); Macfarlane N 24(6); Maybury A 32(1); McCann H 6; McKenna K 22(10);
McMullan P 1(1); Moilanen T 9; Neilson R 25(4); Pressley S 31; Severin S 24(2);
Simmons S 1(6); Sloan R 9(4); Stamp P 23(2); Tierney G 1; Valois J 5(6); Wales G
(1); Webster A 31(1); Weir G 7(11); Wyness D 19(9).
Goals – League (56): De Vries 12, Kirk 8, Wyness 7, McKenna 6, Pressley 5 (2
pens), Hartley 3, Hamill 2, Maybury 2, Stamp 2, Webster 2, Severin 1, Simmons 1,
Weir 1, own goals 4
Scottish Cup (2): Hamill 1, own goal 1
CIS Cup (2): De Vries 1, Kirk 1
Honours – Division I: Champions – 1894-95, 1896-97, 1957-58, 1959-60. **First Divi-
sion:** Champions – 1979-80. **Scottish Cup winners** 1891, 1896, 1901, 1906, 1956,
1998. **League Cup winners** 1955, 1959, 1960, 1963.

HIBERNIAN   PREMIER LEAGUE

Ground: Easter Road Stadium, Edinburgh EH7 5QG (0131) 661 2159
Ground capacity: 17,500. **Colours:** Green shirts with white sleeves and collar, white
shorts with green stripe.
Manager: Tony Mowbray.
League Appearances: Andersson D 38; Baillie J 2; Brebner G 22; Brown S 34(2);
Caldwell G 16(1); Dobbie S 7(20); Doumbe M 33; Edge R 20; Fletcher S 1(4);
Glass S 9(3); Kane J (1); McCluskey J (1); McDonald K (1); McManus T 18(14);
Murdock C 32; Murray I 14; Nicol K 11(4); O'Connor G 27(6); Orman A 13(5);
Reid A 16(4); Riordan D 27(7); Shields J 1; Smith G 19; Thomson K 23; Whittaker
S 15(13); Wiss J 13; Zambernardi Y 7(1).
Goals – League (41): Riordan 15, McManus 4 (1 pen), O'Connor 4, Brown S 3,
Murdock 3, Dobbie 2, Doumbe 2, Brebner 1, Caldwell 1, Murray 1, Nicol 1, Reid
1, Thomson 1, Whittaker 1, own goal 1

192

Scottish Cup (0)
CIS Cup (14): Dobbie 4, Riordan 3, O'Connor 2, Brebner 1, Brown S 1, Murray 1,
Thomson 1, own goal 1
Honours – Division I: Champions – 1902-03, 1947-48, 1950-51, 1951-52. **First Division:** Champions – 1980-81, 1998-99. **Division II:** Champions – 1893-94, 1894-95,
1932-33. **Scottish Cup winners** 1887, 1902. **League Cup winners** 1973, 1992.

INVERNESS CALEDONIAN THISTLE
PREMIER LEAGUE

Ground: Caledonian Stadium, East Longman, Inverness IV1 1FF (01463) 715816
Ground capacity: 6500. **Colours:** Royal blue shirts with red stripes, royal blue shorts.
Manager: John Robertson.
League Appearances: Bingham D 31(2); Brown M 36; Christie C 2(1); Duncan R
33; Golabek S 34; Hart R 15(5); Hislop S 18(8); Keogh L 21(8); Low A (1);
MacMillan C (10); Mackie D 5(1); Macrae D (2); Mann R 33; McBain R 32;
McCaffrey S 34; McKinnon L (1); Munro G 8(7); Procter D 4(7); Ritchie P 23(11);
Thomson D 7(14); Tokely R 34; Wilson B 26(3).
Goals – League (67): Ritchie 14, Bingham 13, Wilson 11 (4 pens), Hislop 9, McCaffrey 4, Keogh 3, McBain 3, Tokely 3, Duncan 1, Golabek 1, Hart 1, Mann 1, Munro
1, Thomson 1, own goal 1
Scottish Cup (10): Ritchie 5, Bingham 2, McBain 1, Thomson 1, Wilson 1
CIS Cup (1): Ritchie 1
Challenge Cup (14): Hislop 5, Ritchie 3, Bingham 2, Hart 2, Wilson 2
Honours – First Division: Champions – 2003–04. **Third Division:** Champions –
1996-97. **Bell's League Challenge winners** 2004.

KILMARNOCK
PREMIER LEAGUE

Ground: Rugby Park, Kilmarnock KA1 2DP (01563) 525184
Ground capacity: 18,128. **Colours:** Blue and white striped shirts, blue shorts.
Manager: Jim Jefferies.
League Appearances: Boyd K 31(5); Canero P 12(1); Canning M 4(1); Dargo C
3(9); Di Giacomo P 4(3); Dillon S 2; Dindeleux F 33; Dodds R 9(2); Dubourdeau F
19; Fowler J 25(7); Fulton S 21; Greer G 23(2); Hardie M 8(8); Hay G 30; Hessey S
7; Innes C 1; Invincibile D 19(3); Lilley D 14; Locke G 18(2); Mahood A 2(3);
McDonald G 15(8); McLaughlin B 14(2); McSwegan G 13(18); Meldrum C 16(1);
Murray S 22(7); Naismith S (1); Nish C 15(15); Samson C 1; Shields G 19; Skora E
16(1); Smith G 2(1).
Goals – League (51): Boyd 15, Nish 9, McSwegan 6, Invincibile 5, Dargo 3,
McDonald 3, Canero 2, Skora 2, Canning 1, Dindeleux 1, Hardie 1, Hessey 1, Lilley 1, Shields 1
Scottish Cup (3): McDonald 1, McSwegan 1, Nish 1
CIS Cup (0)
Honours – Division I: Champions – 1964-65. **Division II:** Champions – 1897-98,
1898-99. **Scottish Cup winners** 1920, 1929, 1997.

LIVINGSTON
PREMIER LEAGUE

Ground: Almondvale Stadium, Livingston EH54 7DN (01506) 417 000
Ground capacity: 10,024. **Colours:** Gold shirts, black shorts, white stockings.
Team Manager: Allan Preston.
League Appearances: Andrews M 38; Brittain R 4(8); Camacho J (6); Capin S 2;
Dorado E 29; Fernandez D 25(2); Ipoua G (1); Kerr B 11(2); Lilley D 29(7); Lovell
S 24(1); Main A 3; Makel L 36; McAllister J 34; McGovern J 11(16); McKenzie R

35; McLaughlin S 8(9); McMenamin C 6(9); McNamee D 30; McPake J (1); O'Brien B 28(5); Pasquinelli F 16(5); Quino F 6(6); Rubio O 36(1); Snowdon W (2); Toure-Maman C 1; Whitmore T 2(1); Wilson B 4; Xausa D (1).
Goals – League (48): Lilley 12 (2 pens), Makel 8, McMenamin 7, O'Brien 5, Fernandez 3, McNamee 3, Pasquinelli 3, Camacho 1, Lovell 1, McAllister 1, McGovern 1, McLaughlin 1, Rubio 1, Quino 1
Scottish Cup (8): Lilley 3, Fernandez 2, McMenamin 1, O'Brien 1, own goal 1
CIS Cup (10): Lilley 3, Makel 3, McAllister 1, Pasquinelli 1, Quino 1, own goal 1
Honours – First Division: Champions – 2000-01. **Second Division:** Champions – 1986-87, 1998-99. **Third Division:** Champions – 1995-96. **League Cup winners** 2004.

MONTROSE   DIV. 3

Ground: Links Park, Montrose DD10 8QD (01674) 673200
Ground capacity: 3292. **Colours:** Royal blue shirts and shorts.
Manager: Henry Hall.
League Appearances: Black R 10(1); Brash K 3; Budd A 2; Butter J 30; Conway F 6; Coulston D 2(4); Donachie B 31(1); Farnan C 6(7); Ferguson S 36; Gibson K 19(4); Hall E 1(9); Hankinson M 6(1); Henderson R 4(16); Kerrigan S 32; McQuillan J 33; Michie S 30(1); Sharp G 13(16); Simpson M 10(1); Smart C 24(2); Smith E 28; Smith G 9(4); Spink D 5(5); Stephen N 1(2); Thomson G 2; Watt J 1(9); Webster K 26(6); Wood M 26(3).
Goals – League (52): Muchie 14, Kerrigan 8, Smart 8, Gibson 5, Black 4, Smith E 4, Webster 2, Wood 2, Farnan 1, Henderson 1, McQuillan 1, Sharp 1, Simpson 1
Scottish Cup (5): Michie 2, Wood 2, Ferguson 1
CIS Cup (2): Kerrigan 1, Smart 1
Challenge Cup (0)
Honours – Second Division: Champions – 1984-85.

MORTON   DIV. 2

Ground: Cappielow Park, Greenock (01475) 723571
Ground capacity: 11,612. **Colours:** Royal blue and white hooped shirts, white shorts with royal blue panel down side.
Manager: John McCormack.
League Appearances: Adam J 2(3); Bannerman S 17(8); Bottiglieri E 32(2); Cannie P 11(10); Collins D 28; Coyle C 36; Gaughan P 1(2); Greacen S 32; Hawke W 1(11); Henderson R 20(1); MacGregor D 25(1); Maisano J 29; Maisano M 28(3); McAlister J 1(8); McGlinchy P (7); McLeod C 5(1); Millar C 35(1); Uotinen J 5(15); Walker P 31(2); Weatherson P 31; Williams A 26(9).
Goals – League (66): Williams 15 (1 pen), Weatherson 14, Greacen 7, Maisano J 7, Walker 6, Bannerman 3, Cannie 3, Maisano M 3, Millar 3, Bottiglieri 2, Collins 1, Henderson 1, Uotinen 1
Scottish Cup (4): Williams 2, Millar 1, Weatherson 1
CIS Cup (3): Bannerman 1, Bottiglieri 1, Weatherson 1
Challenge Cup (5): Weatherson 3 (1 pen), Hawke 1, Maisano J 1
Honours – First Division: Champions – 1977-78, 1983-84, 1986-87. **Division II:** Champions – 1949-50, 1963-64, 1966-67. **Second Division:** Champions – 1994-95. **Third Division:** Champions 2002-03. **Scottish Cup winners** 1922.

MOTHERWELL   PREMIER LEAGUE

Ground: Fir Park, Motherwell ML1 2QN (01698) 333333
Ground capacity: 13,742. **Colours:** Amber shirts with claret hoop and trim, amber shorts, amber stockings with claret trim.
First Team Coach: Terry Butcher.

League Appearances: Adams D 31; Bollan G 1(2); Burns A 29(4); Clarkson D 32(6); Corr B 5; Corrigan M 38; Cowan D (1); Craig S 16(8); Craigan S 36; Dair J 19(10); Fagan S 9(4); Fitzpatrick M 1(1); Hammell S 37; Kinniburgh W (1); Lasley K 33; Leitch DS 20; MacDonald K 1(3); Marshall G 33; McDonald S 10(5); McFadden J 2(1); O'Donnell P 7(2); Partridge D 15; Pearson S 17(1); Quinn P 24(2); Wright K 2(12).
Goals – League (42): Clarkson 11, Adams 7 (1 pen), Pearson 4, Craig 3, Lasley 3, McFadden 3 (1 pen), Burns 2, Dair 2, McDonald S 2, Corrigan 1, Fagan 1, Hammell 1, Quinn 1, Wright 1
Scottish Cup (6): Burns 2, Clarkson 2, Adams 1, McDonald S 1
CIS Cup (3): Craig 1, Lasley 1, Pearson 1
Honours – Division I: Champions – 1931-32. **First Division:** Champions – 1981-82, 1984-85. **Division II:** Champions – 1953-54, 1968-69. **Scottish Cup winners** 1952, 1991. **League Cup winners** 1951.

PARTICK THISTLE   DIV. 1

Ground: Firhill Park, Glasgow G20 7AL (0141) 579 1971
Ground capacity: 13,141. **Colours:** Red and yellow striped shirts, red shorts.
Joint Managers: Gerry Britton and Derek Whyte.
League Appearances: Anis J 20(4); Arthur K 22; Bonnes S 11(9); Britton G 15(12); Cadete J 1(4); Chiarini D 5(1); English T (2); Fleming D 20(4); Forrest E 3(2); Gemmell J (5); Gibson A 4(7); Gibson W 16; Grady J 32(1); Howie W 5(5); Langfield J 10; Lilley D 15; Madaschi A 23(1); McBride J 19(2); Mikkelsen J 5; Milne K 25; Mitchell J 30(2); Murray G 36; Panther E (8); Pinkowski S 1; Ross A 11(8); Ross I 15(3); Rowson D 35; Strachan A 2(3); Taylor S 6(7); Thomson A 13(8); Waddell R 3(4); Whyte D 15.
Goals – League (39): Grady 15 (1 pen), Thomson 5 (1 pen), Britton 4, Mitchell 4, Madaschi 2, Rowson 2, Bonnes 1, McBride 1, Milne 1, Ross A 1, Taylor 1, Waddell A 1, own goal 1
Scottish Cup (8): Britton 2, Grady 2, Bonnes 1, McBride 1, Mitchell 1, Rowson 1
CIS Cup (2): Milne 1, Mitchell 1
Honours – First Division: Champions – 1975-76, 2001-02. **Division II:** Champions – 1896-97, 1899-1900, 1970-71. **Second Division:** Champions 2000-01. **Scottish Cup winners** 1921. **League Cup winners** 1972.

PETERHEAD   DIV. 3

Ground: Balmoor Stadium, Peterhead AB42 1EU (01779) 478256
Ground capacity: 3250 (1000 seated). **Colours:** Royal blue with white shirts, royal blue shorts.
Manager: Iain Stewart.
League Appearances: Bain K 11(2); Bavidge M 33(1); Beith G 9(3); Brash K 6(4); Buchan M 15; Buchanan R 3; Duncan R 20(8); Gibson K 6; Good I 22(1); Grant R 3(4); Johnston M 28(5); Mackay S 11(8); Mathers P 33; McGuinness K 20(3); McSkimming S 20(2); Milne D 1(4); Perry M 33; Raeside R 30(1); Robertson S 16; Roddie A 25(2); Shand R 1; Smith D 11(12); Stewart D 1(9); Stewart G 4(3); Stewart I 17(4); Tindal K 17(4).
Goals – League (67): Johnston 18 (2 pens), Bavidge 16, Raeside 6, Stewart I 6, Buchan 3, Robertson 3, Roddie 3, Beith 2, Mackay 2, Tindal 2, Duncan 1, Gibson 1, Good 1, Perry 1, Smith 1, Stewart G 1
Scottish Cup (2): Bavidge 2
CIS Cup (4): Stewart I 3, Mackay 1
Challenge Cup (4): Grant 1, Raeside 1, Stewart D 1, Stewart I 1

QUEEN OF THE SOUTH   DIV. 1

Ground: Palmerston Park, Dumfries DG2 9BA (01387) 254853
Ground capacity: 8352. **Colours:** Royal blue shirts with white sleeves, white shorts with blue piping.
Manager: Ian Scott.
League Appearances: Aitken A 24(7); Allan D 15(3); Bagan D 29(2); Bowey S 33; Burke A 27(7); Burns P 23(6); Dodds J 12(1); Gibson W 14(2); Jaconelli E 11(6); Lyle D 8(7); McAlpine J 19(3); McColligan B 18(5); McMullan P 3(9); O'Connor S 19(8); Paton E 35; Payne S 4(6); Reid B 33; Robertson K 2; Samson C 12; Scott C 10; Talbot P 3(1); Thomson J 26(1); Wood G 16(5).
Goals – League (46): Burke 13, O'Connor 12, Bowey 7, Wood 4, Jaconelli 3, Bagan 2, Paton 2, Lyle 1, McColligan 1, Reid 1
Scottish Cup (3): O'Connor 3
CIS Cup (6): Burke 3, Bagan 1, Burns 1, Wood 1
Challenge Cup (1): Lyle 1
Honours – Division II: Champions – 1950-51. **Second Division:** Champions – 2001-02. **Challenge Cup winners** 2003

QUEEN'S PARK   DIV. 3

Ground: Hampden Park, Glasgow G42 9BA (0141) 632 1275
Ground capacity: 52,000. **Colours:** Black and white hooped shirts, white shorts.
Coach: Kenneth Brannigan.
League Appearances: Agostini D 20(3); Bonnar M 7(6); Canning S 25(3); Carcary D 16(6); Carroll F 17(7); Clark R 27(2); Conlin R 1(1); Crawford D 1(1); Dunning A 12(2); Fallon S 20(1); Ferry D 24(2); Gallagher P 4(6); Graham A 20(1); Harvey P 19(6); Kettlewell S 15(12); McAuley S 13(4); McCallum D 18(1); McCue B (1); Menelaws D 3(3); Moffat S 8(3); Quinn A (2); Reilly S 27; Scrimgour D 35; Sinclair R 20(1); Stewart D 13(2); Thompson J 5(4); Trouten A (1); Weatherston D (5); Whelan J 26(7).
Goals – League (41): Reilly 7 (3 pens), McAuley 6, Carcary 5, Whelan 5, Canning 4, Carroll 3, Graham 3, Gallagher 2, McCallum 2, Dunning 1, Harvey 1, Stewart 1, own goal 1
Scottish Cup (1): McAuley 1
CIS Cup (3): Clark 1, Graham 1, Reilly 1
Challenge Cup (2): Clark 1, Graham 1
Honours – Division II: Champions – 1922-23. **B Division:** Champions – 1955-56. **Second Division:** Champions – 1980-81. **Third Division:** Champions – 1999-2000. **Scottish Cup winners** 1874, 1875, 1876, 1880, 1881, 1882, 1884, 1886, 1890, 1893.

RAITH ROVERS   DIV. 1

Ground: Stark's Park, Pratt Street, Kirkcaldy KY1 1SA (01592) 263514
Ground capacity: 10,104 (all seated). **Colours:** Navy blue shirts with white sleeves, white shorts with navy blue and red edges.
Manager: Claude Anelka.
League Appearances: Berthelot D 14; Blackadder R 8(9); Bornes J 13; Boyle J 3(12); Brady D 24(5); Brittain R 9(4); Brown I 13(3); Calderon A 26(3); Capin S 11(1); Carranza L 2(1); Dennis S 23; Dow A 9; Evans D 2(6); Ferrero S 12; Glynn D 1; Gonzalez R 17(1); Hawley K 4(7); Henry J 2(1); Irons S (1); Jack M 6; Langfield J 5; Leiper C (1); Malcolm C 1(4); Martin J 1(4); Maxwell D 2(5); Millar P 1(1); Neito J 11(1); O'Reilly C 2(2); Patino C 20; Peers M 2(3); Pereira Gomez R 10; Prest M 8(3); Raffell B (1); Rivas F 33; Robb S 8(3); Smart J 9(3); Stanic G 28(1); Stanley C 18(2); Sutton J 20(1); Talio V 9(1); Young L 9(5).
Goals – League (37): Sutton 13, Pereira Gomez 6, Calderon 3, Ferrero 3, Hawley

196

2, Rivas 2, Blackadder 1, Brittain 1, Brown 1, Dennis 1, O'Reilly 1, Patino 1, Stanley 1, own goal 1
Scottish Cup (1): Talio 1
CIS Cup (0)
Challenge Cup (10): Prest 3, Sutton 3, Calderon 1, Henry 1, Peers 1, Stanley 1
Honours – First Division: Champions – 1992-93, 1994-95. **Second Division:** Champions – 1907-08, 1909-10 (Shared), 1937-38, 1948-49. **League Cup winners** 1995.

RANGERS   PREMIER LEAGUE

Ground: Ibrox Stadium, Glasgow G51 2XD (0870) 600 1972
Ground capacity: 50,444. **Colours:** Royal blue shirts with red chevrons and white collar, white shorts with royal blue and red trim.
Manager: Alex McLeish.
League Appearances: Adams C 1(1); Arteta M 23; Arveladze S 17(2); Ball M 30(2); Berg H 20; Burke C 11(9); Capucho N 18(4); Davidson R (1); Duffy D (1); Emerson 13(1); Ferguson B 3; Fetai B (1); Hughes S 17(5); Hutton A 11; Khizanishvili Z 25(1); Klos S 34; Lovenkrands P 22(3); Malcolm R 8(6); McCormack R 1(1); McGregor A 4; McKenzie G (2); Mols M 29(6); Moore C (1); Namouchi H 4(3); Nerlinger C 11(3); Ostenstad E 2(9); Rae G 9(1); Rickse.. r 29(1); Ross M 10(10); Thompson S 9(7); Vanoli P 14(9); Walker A (2); de Boer F 15; de Boer R 12(4).
Goals – League (76): Arveladze 12 (1 pen). Mols 9, Arteta 8 (2 pens), Lovenkrands 8, Thompson 8 (2 pens). Capucho 5, Burke 3, Hughes 3, Namouchi 3, de Boer F 2, de Boer R 2, Moore 2 (1 pen), Rae 2, Ball 1, Hutton 1, McCormack 1 (1 pen), Nerlinger 1, Ricksen 1, Ross 1, Vanoli 1, own goals 2
Scottish Cup (4): Arveladze 2, de Boer R 1, Lovenkrands 1
CIS Cup (10): Nerlinger 3, Mols 2, Ostenstad 2, Burke 1, Capucho 1, Lovenkrands 1
Honours – Division I: Champions – 1890-91 (Shared), 1898-99, 1899-1900, 1900-01, 1901-02, 1910-11, 1911-12, 1912-13, 1917-18, 1919-20, 1920-21, 1922-23, 1923-24, 1924-25, 1926-27, 1927-28, 1928-29, 1929-30, 1930-31, 1932-33, 1933-34, 1934-35, 1936-37, 1938-39, 1946-47, 1948-49, 1949-50, 1952-53, 1955-56, 1956-57, 1958-59, 1960-61, 1962-63, 1963-64, 1974-75. **Premier Division:** Champions – 1975-76, 1977-78, 1986-87, 1988-89, 1989-90, 1990-91, 1991-92, 1992-93, 1993-94, 1994-95, 1995-96, 1996-97. **Premier League:** Champions – 1998-99, 1999-2000, 2002-03. **Scottish Cup winners** 1894, 1897, 1898, 1903, 1928, 1930, 1932, 1934, 1935, 1936, 1948, 1949, 1950, 1953, 1960, 1962, 1963, 1964, 1966, 1973, 1976, 1978, 1979, 1981, 1992, 1993, 1996, 1999, 2000, 2002, 2003. **League Cup winners** 1947, 1949, 1961, 1962, 1964, 1965, 1971, 1976, 1978, 1979, 1982, 1984, 1985, 1987, 1988, 1989, 1991, 1993, 1994, 1997, 1999, 2002, 2003. **European Cup-Winners' Cup winners** 1972.

ROSS COUNTY   DIV. 1

Ground: Victoria Park, Dingwall IV15 9QW (01349) 860860
Ground capacity: 6700. **Colours:** Navy blue with white and red pin stripe on collar and sleeves, white shorts with navy and red side stripe, navy stockings.
Manager: Alex Smith.
League Appearances: Bayne G 16(9); Canning M 14(1); Cowie D 8(15); Fridge L (1); Gethins C 6(13); Hamilton J 12(10); Hannah D 32; Higgins S 15(11); Lauchlan J 17; MacDonald N 1; Mackay S 20(1); Malcolm S 23(1); McCulloch M 33(3); McCunnie J 35; McGarry S 19(9); O'Donnell S 15(11); Ogunmade D (4); Rankin J 35; Robertson H 18(2); Smith G 20; Stewart C 16; Tait J 8(1); Webb S 12(2); Winters D 21(11).
Goals – League (49): Winters 10 (2 pens), Bayne 6, Hamilton 5 (1 pen), Higgins 5, McGarry 5, Rankin 5, O'Donnell 3, Gethins 2, Robertson 2, Hannah 1 (1 pen), Mackay 1, Tait 1, Webb 1, own goals 2

Scottish Cup (0)
CIS Cup (2): Cowie 1, Mackay 1
Challenge Cup (7): Winters 3, Hamilton 2, Rankin 1, own goal 1
Honours – Third Division: Champions – 1998-99.

ST JOHNSTONE   DIV. 1

Ground: McDiarmid Park, Crieff Road, Perth PH1 2SJ (01738) 459090
Ground capacity: 10,673. **Colours:** Royal blue shirts with white trim, white shorts.
Manager: John Connolly.
League Appearances: Baxter M 11(5); Bernard P 24(1); Cuthbert K 29; Dods D 24(2); Donnelly S 35(1); Ferry M 1; Forsyth R 18(4); Fotheringham M 3(4); Fraser S 2; Hay C 10(12); Lovering P 4(1); MacDonald P 11(4); Malone E 5(4); Maxwell I 33; McLaughlin B 23(7); McQuilken J 15; Nelson C 7; Paatelainen M 28(5); Parker K 13(18); Reilly M 25(2); Robertson J 27; Robertson M 8(1); Stevenson R 8(4); Taylor S 8(1); Vata R 15; Weir J 9.
Goals – League (59): Paatelainen 11, Hay 9, Donnelly 8 (2 pens), MacDonald 8, Parker 8, McLaughlin 3, Bernard 2, Baxter 1, Dods 1, Fotheringham 1, McQuilken 1, Malone 1, Maxwell 1, Robertson J 1, Robertson M 1, Taylor 1, own goal 1
Scottish Cup (0)
CIS Cup (8): Dods 2, Donnelly 2, Paatelainen 2, MacDonald 1, McLaughlin 1
Challenge Cup (5): Parker 2, Donnelly 1, Forsyth 1, Paatelainen 1
Honours – First Division: Champions – 1982-83, 1989-90, 1996-97. **Division II:** Champions – 1923-24, 1959-60, 1962-63.

ST MIRREN   DIV. 1

Ground: St Mirren Park, Paisley PA3 2EJ (0141) 889 2558, 840 1337
Ground capacity: 10,866 (all seated). **Colours:** Black and white striped shirts, white shorts with black trim.
Manager: Gus MacPherson.
League Appearances: Annand E 6(3); Broadfoot K 28(3); Crilly M 18(7); Dempsie M 20(3); Dunn R 11(16); Ellis L 21(2); Gemmill S (3); Gillies R 33(3); Hinchcliffe C 28; Lappin S 23(1); Lavety B 4(9); MacPherson A 9; McCay R 1; McGinty B 23(5); McGowne K 29(1); McGroarty C 12(1); McKenna D 1(8); McKnight P (4); Millen A 19; Molloy C 1(1); Muir A (3); Murray H 27(3); O'Neil J 23(6); Russell A 17(9); Twaddle K 1(2); Van Zanten D 32(3); Walker S 1; Woods S 8.
Goals – League (39): Gillies 8 (1 pen), McGinty 6 (2 pens), Lappin 4, O'Neil 4, Russell 4, Broadfoot 3, Dunn 2, Murray 2, Van Zanten 2, Crilly 1, McGowne 1, Millen 1, own goal 1
Scottish Cup (2): Lavety 1, McKenna 1
CIS Cup (0)
Challenge Cup (7): O'Neil 3, Crilly 1, Gillies 1 (1 pen), McGinty 1, Russell 1
Honours – First Division: Champions – 1976-77, 1999-2000. **Division II:** Champions – 1967-68. **Scottish Cup winners** 1926, 1959, 1987.

STENHOUSEMUIR   DIV. 3

Ground: Ochilview Park, Stenhousemuir FK5 5QL (01324) 562992
Ground capacity: 2374. **Colours:** Maroon shirts, white shorts.
Joint Managers: Des McKeown and Tony Smith.
League Appearances: Bonar P 7(5); Booth M 23(6); Brown A 27(5); Cairney C 2(2); Carr D 18(7); Cosgrove S 11(5); Craig J 3(2); Crawford B 1(3); Donnelly K 3(1); Easton S 1(4); Flannery P 6(4); Gaughan K 15; Hamilton S 24(3); Hardie A 2; Harty M 19(13); Johnstone D 1(2); Kerrigan S 5; Knox J 3(3); Knox K 17; Lauchlan M 21(7); Mallan S 5(1); McCloy B 4(2); McCulloch G 13(3); McCulloch W 34; McDowell M 2; McGowan M 9(1); McKenna G 17(5); McKenzie J 16; McQuilter

R 8; Miller C 6(1); Morrison D 5(2); Murphy P 18; Murphy S 10(3); Savage J 3; Scott C (1); Sinclair T (1); Smith A 21(3); Tully C 6(1); Waldie C 11(1).
Goals – League (28): Brown 5, Murphy S 4, McKenzie 3, Booth 2 (1 pen), Carr 2, Harty 2, Savage 2, Crawford 1, Donnelly 1, Knox J 1, Lauchlan 1, McQuilter 1, Mallan 1, own goals 2
Scottish Cup (1): Brown 1
CIS Cup (1): Harty 1
Challenge Cup (0)
Honours – League Challenge Cup: Winners – 1996.

STIRLING ALBION   DIV. 2

Ground: Forthbank Stadium, Springkerse Industrial Estate, Stirling FK7 7UJ (01786) 450399
Ground capacity: 3808. **Colours:** Red and white halved shirts, shorts red with white piping.
Player Coach: Allan Moore.
League Appearances: Anderson D 25(3); Beveridge R 1(3); Davidson R 21(11); Devine S 19(7); Elliot B 3(16); Ferguson C 4(15); Gibson A 15(1); Hay P 24(7); Hogarth M 35; Kelly G 7(12); Lyle D 19; McKinnon C 26(2); McLean S 30(1); McNally M 22; Morrison S 1; Nugent P 22(1); O'Brien D 32(3); Rowe G 36; Scotland C 13; Smith A 30(2); Wilson D 11(8).
Goals – League (78): McLean 21 (1 pen), McKinnon 11, Lyle 10, O'Brien 10, Davidson 9, Devine 3, Ferguson 3, Rowe 3, Elliot 1, Gibson 1, Hay 1, Kelly 1, Wilson 1, own goals 3
Scottish Cup (4): Kelly 2, O'Brien 1, Rowe 1
CIS Cup (0)
Challenge Cup (3): Elliot 2, McLean 1
Honours – Division II: Champions – 1952-53, 1957-58, 1960-61, 1964-65. **Second Division:** Champions – 1976-77, 1990-91, 1995-96.

STRANRAER   DIV. 2

Ground: Stair Park, Stranraer DG9 8BS (01776) 703271
Ground capacity: 5600. **Colours:** Blue shirts with white side panels, blue shorts with white side panels.
Manager: Neil Watt.
League Appearances: Aitken S 31(2); Collins L 11(1); Crawford B 2(9); Cruickshank C 1(5); Essler A 1; Finlayson K 32(1); Gaughan K (1); Graham D 30(2); Grant A 2(9); Guy G 1(1); Henderson M 35; Jenkins A 35(1); Kerr P 2(6); Marshall S 1(6); McAllister T 3(7); McCondichie A 36; McPhee G 1(2); Moore M 30(1); Sharp L 35; Swift S 36; Turnbull D 1(13); Wingate D 36; Wright F 34.
Goals – League (87): Moore 24, Graham 19, Finlayson 10, Swift 7, Jenkins 6, Henderson 5, Crawford 3, Sharp 3, Grant 2, Wright 2, Aitken 1, Collins 1, Kerr 1, Turnbull 1, Wingate 1, own goal 1
Scottish Cup (2): Jenkins 1, Moore 1
CIS Cup (0)
Challenge Cup (2): Moore 2
Honours – Second Division: Champions – 1993-94, 1997-98. **Third Division:** Champions – 2003–04. **League Challenge Cup winners** 1997.

SCOTTISH LEAGUE HONOURS

*On goal average (ratio)/difference. †Held jointly after indecisive play-off.
‡Won on deciding match. ††Held jointly. ¶Two points deducted for fielding ineligible
player. Competition suspended 1940–45 during war; Regional Leagues operating.
‡‡Two points deducted for registration irregularities.

PREMIER LEAGUE

Maximum points: 108

	First	Pts	Second	Pts	Third	Pts
1998–99	Rangers	77	Celtic	71	St Johnstone	57
1999–00	Rangers	90	Celtic	69	Hearts	54

Maximum points: 114

	First	Pts	Second	Pts	Third	Pts
2000–01	Celtic	97	Rangers	82	Hibernian	66
2001–02	Celtic	103	Rangers	85	Livingston	58
2002–03	Rangers*	97	Celtic	97	Hearts	63
2003–04	Celtic	98	Rangers	81	Hearts	68

PREMIER DIVISION

Maximum points: 72

	First	Pts	Second	Pts	Third	Pts
1975–76	Rangers	54	Celtic	48	Hibernian	43
1976–77	Celtic	55	Rangers	46	Aberdeen	43
1977–78	Rangers	55	Aberdeen	53	Dundee U	40
1978–79	Celtic	48	Rangers	45	Dundee U	44
1979–80	Aberdeen	48	Celtic	47	St Mirren	42
1980–81	Celtic	56	Aberdeen	49	Rangers*	44
1981–82	Celtic	55	Aberdeen	53	Rangers	43
1982–83	Dundee U	56	Celtic*	55	Aberdeen	55
1983–84	Aberdeen	57	Celtic	50	Dundee U	47
1984–85	Aberdeen	59	Celtic	52	Dundee U	47
1985–86	Celtic*	50	Hearts	50	Dundee U	47

Maximum points: 88

	First	Pts	Second	Pts	Third	Pts
1986–87	Rangers	69	Celtic	63	Dundee U	60
1987–88	Celtic	72	Hearts	62	Rangers	60

Maximum points: 72

	First	Pts	Second	Pts	Third	Pts
1988–89	Rangers	56	Aberdeen	50	Celtic	46
1989–90	Rangers	51	Aberdeen*	44	Hearts	44
1990–91	Rangers	55	Aberdeen	53	Celtic*	41

Maximum points: 88

	First	Pts	Second	Pts	Third	Pts
1991–92	Rangers	72	Hearts	63	Celtic	62
1992–93	Rangers	73	Aberdeen	64	Celtic	60
1993–94	Rangers	58	Aberdeen	55	Motherwell	54

Maximum points: 108

	First	Pts	Second	Pts	Third	Pts
1994–95	Rangers	69	Motherwell	54	Hibernian	53
1995–96	Rangers	87	Celtic	83	Aberdeen*	55
1996–97	Rangers	80	Celtic	75	Dundee U	60
1997–98	Celtic	74	Rangers	72	Hearts	67

DIVISION 1

Maximum points: 52

	First	Pts	Second	Pts	Third	Pts
1975–76	Partick T	41	Kilmarnock	35	Montrose	30

Maximum points: 78

	First	Pts	Second	Pts	Third	Pts
1976–77	St Mirren	62	Clydebank	58	Dundee	51
1977–78	Morton*	58	Hearts	58	Dundee	57
1978–79	Dundee	55	Kilmarnock*	54	Clydebank	54
1979–80	Hearts	53	Airdrieonians	51	Ayr U*	44
1980–81	Hibernian	57	Dundee	52	St Johnstone	51
1981–82	Motherwell	61	Kilmarnock	51	Hearts	50

1982–83	St Johnstone	55	Hearts	54	Clydebank	50
1983–84	Morton	54	Dumbarton	51	Partick T	46
1984–85	Motherwell	50	Clydebank	48	Falkirk	45
1985–86	Hamilton A	56	Falkirk	45	Kilmarnock	44

Maximum points: 88

| 1986–87 | Morton | 57 | Dunfermline Ath | 56 | Dumbarton | 53 |
| 1987–88 | Hamilton A | 56 | Meadowbank T | 52 | Clydebank | 49 |

Maximum points: 78

1988–89	Dunfermline Ath	54	Falkirk	52	Clydebank	48
1989–90	St Johnstone	58	Airdrieonians	54	Clydebank	44
1990–91	Falkirk	54	Airdrieonians	53	Dundee	52

Maximum points: 88

1991–92	Dundee	58	Partick T*	57	Hamilton A	57
1992–93	Raith R	65	Kilmarnock	54	Dunfermline Ath	52
1993–94	Falkirk	66	Dunfermline Ath	65	Airdrieonians	54

Maximum points: 108

1994–95	Raith R	69	Dunfermline Ath*	68	Dundee	68
1995–96	Dunfermline Ath	71	Dundee U*	67	Morton	67
1996–97	St Johnstone	80	Airdrieonians	60	Dundee*	58
1997–98	Dundee	70	Falkirk	65	Raith R*	60
1998–99	Hibernian	89	Falkirk	66	Ayr U	62
1999–00	St Mirren	76	Dunfermline Ath	71	Falkirk	68
2000–01	Livingston	76	Ayr U	69	Falkirk	56
2001–02	Partick T	66	Airdrieonians	56	Ayr U	52
2002–03	Falkirk	81	Clyde	72	St Johnstone	67
2003–04	Inverness CT	70	Clyde	69	St Johnstone	57

DIVISION 2

Maximum points: 52

| 1975–76 | Clydebank* | 40 | Raith R | 40 | Alloa | 35 |

Maximum points: 78

1976–77	Stirling A	55	Alloa	51	Dunfermline Ath	50
1977–78	Clyde*	53	Raith R	53	Dunfermline Ath	48
1978–79	Berwick R	54	Dunfermline Ath	52	Falkirk	50
1979–80	Falkirk	50	East Stirling	49	Forfar Ath	46
1980–81	Queen's Park	50	Queen of the S	46	Cowdenbeath	45
1981–82	Clyde	59	Alloa*	50	Arbroath	50
1982–83	Brechin C	55	Meadowbank T	54	Arbroath	49
1983–84	Forfar Ath	63	East Fife	47	Berwick R	43
1984–85	Montrose	53	Alloa	50	Dunfermline Ath	49
1985–86	Dunfermline Ath	57	Queen of the S	55	Meadowbank T	49
1986–87	Meadowbank T	55	Raith R*	52	Stirling A*	52
1987–88	Ayr U	61	St Johnstone	59	Queen's Park	51
1988–89	Albion R	50	Alloa	45	Brechin C.	43
1989–90	Brechin C	49	Kilmarnock	48	Stirling A	47
1990–91	Stirling A	54	Montrose	46	Cowdenbeath	45
1991–92	Dumbarton	52	Cowdenbeath	51	Alloa	50
1992–93	Clyde	54	Brechin C*	53	Stranraer	53
1993–94	Stranraer	56	Berwick R	48	Stenhousemuir*	47

Maximum points: 108

1994–95	Morton	64	Dumbarton	60	Stirling A	58
1995–96	Stirling A	81	East Fife	67	Berwick R	60
1996–97	Ayr U	77	Hamilton A	74	Livingston	64
1997–98	Stranraer	61	Clydebank	60	Livingston	59
1998–99	Livingston	77	Inverness CT	72	Clyde	53
1999–00	Clyde	65	Alloa	64	Ross County	62
2000–01	Partick T	75	Arbroath	58	Berwick R*	54

2001–02	Queen of the S	67	Alloa	59	Forfar Ath	53
2002–03	Raith R	59	Brechin C	55	Airdrie U	54
2003–04	Airdrie U	70	Hamilton A	62	Dumbarton	60

DIVISION 3

Maximum points: 108

1994–95	Forfar Ath	80	Montrose	67	Ross Co	60
1995–96	Livingston	72	Brechin C	63	Caledonian T	57
1996–97	Inverness CT	76	Forfar Ath*	59	Ross Co	67
1997–98	Alloa	76	Arbroath	68	Ross Co*	67
1998–99	Ross Co	77	Stenhousemuir	64	Brechin C	59
1999–00	Queen's Park	69	Berwick R	64	Forfar Ath	61
2000–01	Hamilton A*	76	Cowdenbeath	76	Brechin C	72
2001–02	Brechin C	73	Dumbarton	61	Albion R	59
2002–03	Morton	72	East Fife	71	Albion R	70
2003–04	Stranraer	79	Stirling A	77	Gretna	68

DIVISION 1 to 1974–75

Maximum points: a 36; b 44; c 40; d 52; e 60; f 68; g 76; h 84.

	First	Pts	Second	Pts	Third	Pts
1890–91a	Dumbarton††	29	Rangers††	29	Celtic	21
1891–92b	Dumbarton	37	Celtic	35	Hearts	34
1892–93a	Celtic	29	Rangers	28	St Mirren	20
1893–94a	Celtic	29	Hearts	26	St Bernard's	23
1894–95a	Hearts	31	Celtic	26	Rangers	22
1895–96a	Celtic	30	Rangers	26	Hibernian	24
1896–97a	Hearts	28	Hibernian	26	Rangers	25
1897–98a	Celtic	33	Rangers	29	Hibernian	22
1898–99a	Rangers	36	Hearts	26	Celtic	24
1899–1900a	Rangers	32	Celtic	25	Hibernian	24
1900–01c	Rangers	35	Celtic	29	Hibernian	25
1901–02a	Rangers	28	Celtic	26	Hearts	22
1902–03b	Hibernian	37	Dundee	31	Rangers	29
1903–04d	Third Lanark	43	Hearts	39	Celtic*	38
1904–05d	Celtic‡	41	Rangers	41	Third Lanark	35
1905–06e	Celtic	49	Hearts	43	Airdrieonians	38
1906–07f	Celtic	55	Dundee	48	Rangers	45
1907–08f	Celtic	55	Falkirk	51	Rangers	50
1908–09f	Celtic	51	Dundee	50	Clyde	48
1909–10f	Celtic	54	Falkirk	52	Rangers	46
1910–11f	Rangers	52	Aberdeen	48	Falkirk	44
1911–12f	Rangers	51	Celtic	45	Clyde	42
1912–13f	Rangers	53	Celtic	49	Hearts*	41
1913–14g	Celtic	65	Rangers	59	Hearts*	54
1914–15g	Celtic	65	Hearts	61	Rangers	50
1915–16g	Celtic	67	Rangers	56	Morton	51
1916–17g	Celtic	64	Morton	54	Rangers	53
1917–18f	Rangers	56	Celtic	55	Kilmarnock*	43
1918–19f	Celtic	58	Rangers	57	Morton	47
1919–20h	Rangers	71	Celtic	68	Motherwell	57
1920–21h	Rangers	76	Celtic	66	Hearts	50
1921–22h	Celtic	67	Rangers	66	Raith R	51
1922–23g	Rangers	55	Airdrieonians	50	Celtic	46
1923–24g	Rangers	59	Airdrieonians	50	Celtic	46
1924–25g	Rangers	60	Airdrieonians	57	Hibernian	52
1925–26g	Celtic	58	Airdrieonians*	50	Hearts	50
1926–27g	Rangers	56	Motherwell	51	Celtic	49
1927–28g	Rangers	60	Celtic*	55	Motherwell	55
1928–29g	Rangers	67	Celtic	51	Motherwell	50

1929–30g	Rangers	60	Motherwell	55	Aberdeen	53
1930–31g	Rangers	60	Celtic	58	Motherwell	56
1931–32g	Motherwell	66	Rangers	61	Celtic	48
1932–33g	Rangers	62	Motherwell	59	Hearts	50
1933–34g	Rangers	66	Motherwell	62	Celtic	47
1934–35g	Rangers	55	Celtic	52	Hearts	50
1935–36g	Celtic	66	Rangers*	61	Aberdeen	61
1936–37g	Rangers	61	Aberdeen	54	Celtic	52
1937–38g	Celtic	61	Hearts	58	Rangers	49
1938–39g	Rangers	59	Celtic	48	Aberdeen	46
1946–47e	Rangers	46	Hibernian	44	Aberdeen	39
1947–48e	Hibernian	48	Rangers	46	Partick T	36
1948–49e	Rangers	46	Dundee	45	Hibernian	39
1949–50e	Rangers	50	Hibernian	49	Hearts	43
1950–51e	Hibernian	48	Rangers	38	Dundee	38
1951–52e	Hibernian	45	Rangers	41	East Fife	37
1952–53e	Rangers*	43	Hibernian	43	East Fife	39
1953–54e	Celtic	43	Hearts	38	Partick T	35
1954–55e	Aberdeen	49	Celtic	46	Rangers	41
1955–56f	Rangers	52	Aberdeen	46	Hearts*	45
1956–57f	Rangers	55	Hearts	53	Kilmarnock	42
1957–58f	Hearts	62	Rangers	49	Celtic	46
1958–59f	Rangers	50	Hearts	48	Motherwell	44
1959–60f	Hearts	54	Kilmarnock	50	Rangers*	42
1960–61f	Rangers	51	Kilmarnock	50	Third Lanark	42
1961–62f	Dundee	54	Rangers	51	Celtic	46
1962–63f	Rangers	57	Kilmarnock	48	Partick T	46
1963–64f	Rangers	55	Kilmarnock	49	Celtic*	47
1964–65f	Kilmarnock*	50	Hearts	50	Dunfermline Ath	49
1965–66f	Celtic	57	Rangers	55	Kilmarnock	45
1966–67f	Celtic	58	Rangers	55	Clyde	46
1967–68f	Celtic	63	Rangers	61	Hibernian	45
1968–69f	Celtic	54	Rangers	49	DunfermlineAth	45
1969–70f	Celtic	57	Rangers	45	Hibernian	44
1970–71f	Celtic	56	Aberdeen	54	St Johnstone	44
1971–72f	Celtic	60	Aberdeen	50	Rangers	44
1972–73f	Celtic	57	Rangers	56	Hibernian	45
1973–74f	Celtic	53	Hibernian	49	Rangers	48
1974–75f	Rangers	56	Hibernian	49	Celtic	45

DIVISION 2 to 1974–75

Maximum points: a 76; b 72; c 68; d 52; e 60; f 36; g 44.

1893–94f	Hibernian	29	Cowlairs	27	Clyde	24
1894–95f	Hibernian	30	Motherwell	22	Port Glasgow	20
1895–96f	Abercorn	27	Leith Ath	23	Renton	21
1896–97f	Partick T	31	Leith Ath	27	Kilmarnock*	21
1897–98f	Kilmarnock	29	Port Glasgow	25	Morton	22
1898–99f	Kilmarnock	32	Leith Ath	27	Port Glasgow	25
1899–1900f	Partick T	29	Morton	28	Port Glasgow	20
1900–01f	St Bernard's	25	Airdrieonians	23	Abercorn	21
1901–02g	Port Glasgow	32	Partick T	31	Motherwell	26
1902–03g	Airdrieonians	35	Motherwell	28	Ayr U*	27
1903–04g	Hamilton A	37	Clyde	29	Ayr U	28
1904–05g	Clyde	32	Falkirk	28	Hamilton A	27
1905–06g	Leith Ath	34	Clyde	31	Albion R	27
1906–07g	St Bernard's	32	Vale of Leven*	27	Arthurlie	27
1907–08g	Raith R	30	Dumbarton‡‡	27	Ayr U	27
1908–09g	Abercorn	31	Raith R*	28	Vale of Leven	28
1909–10g	Leith Ath‡	33	Raith R	33	St Bernard's	27

203

1910–11*g*	Dumbarton	31	Ayr U	27	Albion R	25
1911–12*g*	Ayr U	35	Abercorn	30	Dumbarton	27
1912–13*d*	Ayr U	34	Dunfermline Ath	33	East Stirling	32
1913–14*g*	Cowdenbeath	31	Albion R	27	Dunfermline Ath*	26
1914–15*d*	Cowdenbeath*	37	St Bernard's*	37	Leith Ath	37
1921–22*a*	Alloa	60	Cowdenbeath	47	Armadale	45
1922–23*a*	Queen's Park	57	Clydebank ¶	50	St Johnstone ¶	45
1923–24*a*	St Johnstone	56	Cowdenbeath	55	Bathgate	44
1924–25*a*	Dundee U	50	Clydebank	48	Clyde	47
1925–26*a*	Dunfermline Ath	59	Clyde	53	Ayr U	52
1926–27*a*	Bo'ness	56	Raith R	49	Clydebank	45
1927–28*a*	Ayr U	54	Third Lanark	45	King's Park	44
1928–29*b*	Dundee U	51	Morton	50	Arbroath	47
1929–30*a*	Leith Ath*	57	East Fife	57	Albion R	54
1930–31*a*	Third Lanark	61	Dundee U	50	Dunfermline Ath	47
1931–32*a*	East Stirling*	55	St Johnstone	55	Raith R*	46
1932–33*c*	Hibernian	54	Queen of the S	49	Dunfermline Ath	47
1933–34*c*	Albion R	45	Dunfermline Ath*	44	Arbroath	44
1934–35*c*	Third Lanark	52	Arbroath	50	St Bernard's	47
1935–36*c*	Falkirk	59	St Mirren	52	Morton	48
1936–37*c*	Ayr U	54	Morton	51	St Bernard's	48
1937–38*c*	Raith R	59	Albion R	48	Airdrieonians	47
1938–39*c*	Cowdenbeath	60	Alloa*	48	East Fife	48
1946–47*d*	Dundee	45	Airdrieonians	42	East Fife	31
1947–48*e*	East Fife	53	Albion R	42	Hamilton A	40
1948–49*e*	Raith R*	42	Stirling A	42	Airdrieonians*	41
1949–50*e*	Morton	47	Airdrieonians	44	Dunfermline Ath*	36
1950–51*e*	Queen of the S*	45	Stirling A	45	Ayr U*	36
1951–52*e*	Clyde	44	Falkirk	43	Ayr U	39
1952–53*e*	Stirling A	44	Hamilton A	43	Queen's Park	37
1953–54*e*	Motherwell	45	Kilmarnock	42	Third Lanark*	36
1954–55*e*	Airdrieonians	46	Dunfermline Ath	42	Hamilton A	39
1955–56*b*	Queen's Park	54	Ayr U	51	St Johnstone	49
1956–57*b*	Clyde	64	Third Lanark	51	Cowdenbeath	45
1957–58*b*	Stirling A	55	Dunfermline Ath	53	Arbroath	47
1958–59*b*	Ayr U	60	Arbroath	51	Stenhousemuir	46
1959–60*b*	St Johnstone	53	Dundee U	50	Queen of the S	49
1960–61*b*	Stirling A	55	Falkirk	54	Stenhousemuir	50
1961–62*b*	Clyde	54	Queen of the S	53	Morton	44
1962–63*b*	St Johnstone	55	East Stirling	49	Morton	48
1963–64*b*	Morton	67	Clyde	53	Arbroath	46
1964–65*b*	Stirling A	59	Hamilton A	50	Queen of the S	45
1965–66*b*	Ayr U	53	Airdrieonians	50	Queen of the S	47
1966–67*a*	Morton	69	Raith R	58	Arbroath	57
1967–68*b*	St Mirren	62	Arbroath	53	East Fife	49
1968–69*b*	Motherwell	64	Ayr U	53	East Fife*	48
1969–70*b*	Falkirk	56	Cowdenbeath	55	Queen of the S	50
1970–71*b*	Partick T	56	East Fife	51	Arbroath	46
1971–72*b*	Dumbarton*	52	Arbroath	52	Stirling A	50
1972–73*b*	Clyde	56	Dumfermline Ath	52	Raith R*	47
1973–74*b*	Airdrieonians	60	Kilmarnock	58	Hamilton A	55
1974–75*a*	Falkirk	54	Queen of the S*	53	Montrose	53

Elected to Division 1: 1894 Clyde; 1895 Hibernian; 1896 Abercorn; 1897 Partick T; 1899 Kilmarnock; 1900 Morton and Partick T; 1902 Port Glasgow and Partick T; 1903 Airdrieonians and Motherwell; 1905 Falkirk and Aberdeen; 1906 Clyde and Hamilton A; 1910 Raith R; 1913 Ayr U and Dumbarton.

RELEGATED CLUBS

From Premier League

1998–99 Dunfermline Ath
1999–00 *No relegated team*
2000–01 St Mirren
2001–02 St Johnstone
2002–03 *No relegated team*
2003–04 Partick T

From Premier Division

1974–75 *No relegation due to League reorganisation*
1975–76 Dundee, St Johnstone
1976–77 Hearts, Kilmarnock
1977–78 Ayr U, Clydebank
1978–79 Hearts, Motherwell
1979–80 Dundee, Hibernian
1980–81 Kilmarnock, Hearts
1981–82 Partick T, Airdrieonians
1982–83 Morton, Kilmarnock
1983–84 St Johnstone, Motherwell
1984–85 Dumbarton, Morton
1985–86 *No relegation due to League reorganisation*
1986–87 Clydebank, Hamilton A
1987–88 Falkirk, Dunfermline Ath, Morton
1988–89 Hamilton A
1989–90 Dundee
1990–91 None
1991–92 St Mirren, Dunfermline Ath
1992–93 Falkirk, Airdrieonians
1993–94 *See footnote*
1994–95 Dundee U
1995–96 Partick T, Falkirk
1996–97 Raith R
1997–98 Hibernian

From Division 1

1974–75 *No relegation due to League reorganisation*
1975–76 Dunfermline Ath, Clyde
1976–77 Raith R, Falkirk
1977–78 Alloa Ath, East Fife
1978–79 Montrose, Queen of the S
1979–80 Arbroath, Clyde
1980–81 Stirling A, Berwick R
1981–82 East Stirling, Queen of the S
1982–83 Dunfermline Ath, Queen's Park
1983–84 Raith R, Alloa
1984–85 Meadowbank T, St Johnstone
1985–86 Ayr U, Alloa

1986–87 Brechin C, Montrose
1987–88 East Fife, Dumbarton

1988–89 Kilmarnock, Queen of the S
1989–90 Albion R, Alloa
1990–91 Clyde, Brechin C
1991–92 Montrose, Forfar Ath —
1992–93 Meadowbank T, Cowdenbeath
1993–94 *See footnote*
1994–95 Ayr U, Stranraer
1995–96 Hamilton A, Dumbarton
1996–97 Clydebank, East Fife
1997–98 Partick T, Stirling A
1998–99 Hamilton A, Stranraer
1999–00 Clydebank
2000–01 Morton, Alloa
2001–02 Raith R
2002–03 Alloa, Arbroath
2003–04 Ayr U, Brechin C

From Division 2

1994–95 Meadowbank T, Brechin C
1995–96 Forfar Ath, Montrose
1996–97 Dumbarton, Berwick R
1997–98 Stenhousemuir, Brechin C
1998–99 East Fife, Forfar Ath
1999–00 Hamilton A**
2000–01 Queen's Park, Stirling A
2001–02 Morton
2002–03 Stranraer, Cowdenbeath
2003–04 East Fife, Stenhousemuir

From Division 1 1973–74

1921–22 *Queen's Park, Dumbarton, Clydebank
1922–23 Albion R, Alloa Ath
1923–24 Clyde, Clydebank
1924–25 Third Lanark, Ayr U
1925–26 Raith R, Clydebank
1926–27 Morton, Dundee U
1927–28 Dunfermline Ath, Bo'ness
1928–29 Third Lanark, Raith R
1929–30 St Johnstone, Dundee U
1930–31 Hibernian, East Fife
1931–32 Dundee U, Leith Ath
1932–33 Morton, East Stirling
1933–34 Third Lanark, Cowdenbeath
1934–35 St Mirren, Falkirk
1935–36 Airdrieonians, Ayr U
1936–37 Dunfermline Ath, Albion R
1937–38 Dundee, Morton
1938–39 Queen's Park, Raith R
1946–47 Kilmarnock, Hamilton A
1947–48 Airdrieonians, Queen's Park
1948–49 Morton, Albion R
1949–50 Queen of the S, Stirling A

1950–51 Clyde, Falkirk
1951–52 Morton, Stirling A
1952–53 Motherwell, Third Lanark
1953–54 Airdrieonians, Hamilton A
1954–55 *No clubs relegated*
1955–56 Stirling A, Clyde
1956–57 Dunfermline Ath, Ayr U
1957–58 East Fife, Queen's Park
1958–59 Queen of the S, Falkirk
1959–60 Arbroath, Stirling A
1960–61 Ayr U, Clyde
1961–62 St Johnstone, Stirling A
1962–63 Clyde, Raith R
1963–64 Queen of the S, East Stirling
1964–65 Airdrieonians, Third Lanark
1965–66 Morton, Hamilton A
1966–67 St Mirren, Ayr U
1967–68 Motherwell, Stirling A
1968–69 Falkirk, Arbroath
1969–70 Raith R, Partick T
1970–71 St Mirren, Cowdenbeath
1971–72 Clyde, Dunfermline Ath
1972–73 Kilmarnock, Airdrieonians
1973–74 East Fife, Falkirk

*Season 1921–22 – only 1 club promoted, 3 clubs relegated.
**15 pts deducted for failing to field a team.*

Scottish League championship wins: Rangers 50, Celtic 38, Aberdeen 4, Hearts 4, Hibernian 4, Dumbarton 2, Dundee 1, Dundee U 1, Kilmarnock 1, Motherwell 1, Third Lanark 1.

The Scottish Football League was reconstructed into three divisions at the end of the 1974–75 season, so the usual relegation statistics do not apply. Further reorganization took place at the end of the 1985–86 season. From 1986–87, the Premier and First Division had 12 teams each. The Second Division remained at 14. From 1988–89, the Premier Division reverted to 10 teams, and the First Division to 14 teams but in 1991–92 the Premier and First Division reverted to 12. At the end of the 1997–98 season, the top nine clubs in Premier Division broke away from the Scottish League to form a new competition, the Scottish Premier League, with the club promoted from Division One. At the end of the 1999–2000 season two teams were added to the Scottish League. There was no relegation from the Premier League but two promoted from the First Division and three from each of the Second and Third Divisions. One team was relegated from the First Division and one from the Second Division, leaving 12 teams in each division. In season 2002–03, Falkirk were not promoted to the Premier League due to the failure of their ground to meet League standards. Inverness CT were promoted after a previous refusal in 2003–04 because of ground sharing.

PAST SCOTTISH LEAGUE CUP FINALS

Season	Winner		Runner-up	
1946–47	Rangers	4	Aberdeen	0
1947–48	East Fife	0 4	Falkirk	0* 1
1948–49	Rangers	2	Raith Rovers	0
1949–50	East Fife	3	Dunfermline	0
1950–51	Motherwell	3	Hibernian	0
1951–52	Dundee	3	Rangers	2
1952–53	Dundee	2	Kilmarnock	0
1953–54	East Fife	3	Partick Thistle	2
1954–55	Hearts	4	Motherwell	2
1955–56	Aberdeen	2	St Mirren	1
1956–57	Celtic	0 3	Partick Thistle	0 0
1957–58	Celtic	7	Rangers	1
1958–59	Hearts	5	Partick Thistle	1
1959–60	Hearts	2	Third Lanark	1
1960–61	Rangers	2	Kilmarnock	0
1961–62	Rangers	1 3	Hearts	1 1
1962–63	Hearts	1	Kilmarnock	0
1963–64	Rangers	5	Morton	0
1964–65	Rangers	2	Celtic	1
1965–66	Celtic	2	Rangers	1
1966–67	Celtic	1	Rangers	0
1967–68	Celtic	5	Dundee	3
1968–69	Celtic	6	Hibernian	2
1969–70	Celtic	1	St Johnstone	0
1970–71	Rangers	1	Celtic	0
1971–72	Partick Thistle	4	Celtic	1
1972–73	Hibernian	2	Celtic	1
1973–74	Dundee	1	Celtic	0
1974–75	Celtic	6	Hibernian	3
1975–76	Rangers	1	Celtic	0
1976–77	Aberdeen	2	Celtic	1
1977–78	Rangers	2	Celtic	1*
1978–79	Rangers	2	Aberdeen	1
1979–80	Aberdeen	0 0	Dundee U	0* 3
1980–81	Dundee	0	Dundee U	3
1981–82	Rangers	2	Dundee U	1
1982–83	Celtic	2	Rangers	1
1983–84	Rangers	3	Celtic	2
1984–85	Rangers	1	Dundee U	0
1985–86	Aberdeen	3	Hibernian	0
1986–87	Rangers	2	Celtic	1
1987–88	Rangers†	3	Aberdeen	3*
1988–89	Aberdeen	2	Rangers	3*
1989–90	Aberdeen	2	Rangers	1
1990–91	Rangers	2	Celtic	1
1991–92	Hibernian	2	Dunfermline Ath	0
1992–93	Rangers	2	Aberdeen	1*
1993–94	Rangers	2	Hibernian	1
1994–95	Raith R†	2	Celtic	2*
1995–96	Aberdeen	2	Dundee	0
1996–97	Rangers	4	Hearts	3
1997–98	Celtic	3	Dundee U	0
1998–99	Rangers	2	St Johnstone	1
1999–2000	Celtic	2	Aberdeen	0
2000–01	Celtic	3	Kilmarnock	0
2001–02	Rangers	4	Ayr U	0
2002–03	Rangers	2	Celtic	1
2003–04	Livingston	2	Hibernian	0

†Won on penalties *After extra time

CIS SCOTTISH LEAGUE CUP 2003–2004

FIRST ROUND

Arbroath	(0) 1	Raith R	(0) 0
Ayr U	(0) 1	Dumbarton	(1) 2
Cowdenbeath	(0) 3	Alloa Ath	(0) 0
East Fife	(0) 0	Airdrie U	(1) 2
East Stirling	(0) 1	Ross Co	(0) 2
Elgin C	(0) 0	Brechin C	(1) 4
Forfar Ath	(0) 1	Berwick R	(0) 0
Gretna	(1) 1	Peterhead	(0) 2
Hamilton A	(2) 3	Albion R	(0) 2
Inverness CT	(1) 1	Queen's Park	(1) 2
Montrose	(0) 2	Stirling Albion	(0) 0
St Mirren	(0) 0	St Johnstone	(0) 2
(aet)			
Stenhousemuir	(1) 1	Queen of the S	(1) 2
Morton	(1) 2	Stranraer	(0) 0

SECOND ROUND

Aberdeen	(2) 3	Dumbarton	(0) 1
Arbroath	(0) 3	Falkirk	(1) 4
(aet)			
Brechin C	(1) 1	Kilmarnock	(0) 0
Clyde	(0) 2	Airdrie U	(0) 1
Dundee U	(2) 3	Morton	(0) 1
Forfar Ath	(1) 3	Motherwell	(1) 3
(aet; Forfar Ath won 4-2 on penalties.)			
Hibernian	(4) 9	Montrose	(0) 0
Queen's Park	(0) 1	Livingston	(2) 3
Ross Co	(0) 0	Queen of the S	(2) 3
St Johnstone	(0) 3	Hamilton A	(0) 2
(aet)			
Dunfermline Ath	(0) 2	Cowdenbeath	(0) 0
Peterhead	(1) 2	Partick T	(1) 2
(aet; Partick T won 4-3 on penalties.)			

THIRD ROUND

Aberdeen	(4) 5	Brechin C	(0) 0
Hibernian	(2) 2	Queen of the S	(0) 1
Rangers	(2) 6	Forfar Ath	(0) 0
St Johnstone	(1) 3	Dunfermline Ath	(0) 2
Clyde	(1) 2	Dundee	(1) 5
Dundee U	(0) 0	Livingston	(1) 1
Hearts	(0) 2	Falkirk	(0) 1
Partick T	(0) 0	Celtic	(1) 2

QUARTER FINALS

Aberdeen	(1) 2	Livingston	(1) 3
(aet)			
Dundee	(0) 1	Hearts	(0) 0
(aet)			
Rangers	(1) 3	St Johnstone	(0) 0
Hibernian	(0) 2	Celtic	(0) 1

SEMI-FINALS

Dundee	(0) 0	Livingston	(0) 1
Hibernian	(0) 1	Rangers	(1) 1
(aet; Hibernian won 4-3 on penalties)			

FINAL

Livingston	(0) 2	Hibernian	(0) 0

BELL'S LEAGUE CHALLENGE 2003–2004

FIRST ROUND

Airdrie U	(0) 2	Montrose	(0) 0
Albion R	(0) 1	East Fife	(0) 0
Alloa Ath	(0) 1	Clyde	(1) 2
Ayr U	(0) 1	Stirling Albion	(1) 2
(aet)			
Brechin C	(0) 1	Falkirk	(0) 0
Cowdenbeath	(1) 1	Ross Co	(1) 2
East Stirling	(0) 2	Raith R	(1) 5
Forfar Ath	(0) 4	Elgin C	(0) 0
Gretna	(0) 0	Inverness CT	(1) 5
Hamilton A	(1) 2	St Johnstone	(0) 3
(aet)			
Morton	(3) 4	Arbroath	(1) 3
St Mirren	(0) 3	Queen's Park	(2) 2
(aet)			
Stenhousemuir	(0) 0	Peterhead	(0) 3
Stranraer	(1) 2	Queen of the S	(0) 1

SECOND ROUND

Brechin C	(2) 3	Stirling Albion	(0) 1
Clyde	(0) 0	St Johnstone	(0) 1
Forfar Ath	(1) 4	Albion R	(1) 2
(aet)			
Morton	(0) 1	Airdrie U	(0) 2
Peterhead	(0) 1	Inverness CT	(1) 2
Raith R	(0) 2	Stranraer	(0) 0
Ross Co	(1) 5	Dumbarton	(0) 0
St Mirren	(1) 2	Berwick R	(0) 1

QUARTER FINALS

Forfar Ath	(0) 0	Airdrie U	(0) 2
Inverness CT	(0) 1	Ross Co	(0) 0
Raith R	(2) 3	St Mirren	(1) 2
St Johnstone	(0) 1	Brechin C	(2) 2

SEMI-FINALS

Raith R	(0) 0	Inverness CT	(3) 4
Brechin C	(1) 1	Airdrie U	(1) 2
(aet)			

FINAL

Inverness CT	(0) 2	Airdrie U	(0) 0

TENNENT'S SCOTTISH CUP 2003–2004

FIRST ROUND

Clachnacuddin	(0) 0	Stranraer	(2) 2
Cowdenbeath	(4) 5	Edinburgh C	(0) 0
Elgin C	(1) 1	Peterhead	(2) 2
Forfar Ath	(0) 1	East Fife	(0) 1
Gretna	(1) 4	Dumbarton	(0) 0
Montrose	(0) 1	Albion R	(1) 1
Spartans	(3) 6	Buckie T	(1) 1
Stirling Albion	(0) 3	Queen's Park	(1) 1

FIRST ROUND REPLAYS

Albion R	(1) 1	Montrose	(0) 3
East Fife	(1) 3	Forfar Ath	(0) 3

(aet; East Fife won 4-1 on penalties)

SECOND ROUND

Alloa Ath	(3) 3	Spartans	(2) 3
Berwick R	(3) 4	Huntly	(1) 2
East Stirling	(0) 0	Cowdenbeath	(1) 5
Gretna	(1) 5	Stenhousemuir	(0) 1
Inverurie Locos	(0) 1	Airdrie U	(3) 5
Peterhead	(0) 0	East Fife	(1) 2
Stirling Albion	(1) 1	Arbroath	(1) 2
Montrose	(0) 1	Threave R	(0) 0
Morton	(2) 4	Vale of Leithen	(0) 0
Stranraer	(0) 0	Hamilton A	(0) 1

SECOND ROUND REPLAY

Spartans	(1) 5	Alloa Ath	(2) 3

(aet)

THIRD ROUND

Aberdeen	(0) 0	Dundee	(0) 0
Arbroath	(1) 1	Spartans	(2) 4
Ayr U	(1) 1	Falkirk	(1) 2
Celtic	(0) 2	Ross Co	(0) 0
Clyde	(0) 3	Gretna	(0) 0
Dunfermline Ath	(2) 3	Dundee U	(1) 1
East Fife	(0) 0	Queen of the S	(0) 1
Hamilton A	(1) 2	Cowdenbeath	(0) 0
Hearts	(1) 2	Berwick R	(0) 0
Hibernian	(0) 0	Rangers	(1) 2
Inverness CT	(3) 5	Brechin C	(0) 1
Livingston	(1) 1	Montrose	(0) 0
Morton	(0) 0	Partick T	(1) 3
Raith R	(0) 1	Kilmarnock	(3) 3
St Johnstone	(0) 0	Motherwell	(2) 3
St Mirren	(0) 2	Airdrie U	(0) 0

THIRD ROUND REPLAY

Dundee	(1) 2	Aberdeen	(1) 3

FOURTH ROUND

Clyde	(1) 1	Dunfermline Ath	(2) 2

(Match abandoned after 57 minutes – heavy snow.)

Falkirk	(0) 0	Aberdeen	(0) 2
Hearts	(0) 0	Celtic	(2) 3
Motherwell	(3) 3	Queen of the S	(0) 2
Partick T	(1) 5	Hamilton A	(0) 1
St Mirren	(0) 0	Inverness CT	(0) 1
Kilmarnock	(0) 0	Rangers	(0) 2
Spartans	(0) 0	Livingston	(0) 4
Clyde	(0) 0	Dunfermline Ath	(3) 3

QUARTER-FINALS

Aberdeen	(0) 1	Livingston	(0) 1
Motherwell	(0) 0	Inverness CT	(1) 1
Partick T	(0) 0	Dunfermline Ath	(2) 3
Celtic	(0) 1	Rangers	(0) 0

QUARTER FINAL REPLAY

Livingston	(1) 1	Aberdeen	(0) 0

SEMI-FINALS

Inverness CT	(1) 1	Dunfermline Ath	(0) 1
Livingston	(0) 1	Celtic	(1) 3

SEMI-FINAL REPLAY

Inverness CT	(1) 2	Dunfermline Ath	(1) 3

FINAL

Dunfermline Ath	(1) 1	Celtic	(0) 3

PAST LEAGUE CHALLENGE FINALS

1991	Dundee	3	Ayr U	2
1992	Hamilton A	1	Ayr U	0
1993	Hamilton A	3	Morton	2
1994	St Mirren	9	Falkirk	3
1995	Airdrieonians	3	Dundee	2
1996	Stenhousemuir	0	Dundee U	0
	(Stenhousemuir won 5-4 on penalties)			
1997	Stranraer	1	St Johnstone	0
1998	Falkirk	1	Qeeen of the South	0
1999	no competition			
2000	Alloa	4	Inverness CT	4
	(Alloa won 5-4 on penalties)			
2001	Airdrieonians	2	Livingston	2
	(Airdrieonians won 3-2 on penalties)			
2002	Airdrieonians	2	Alloa	1
2003	Queen of the S	2	Brechin C	0
2004	Inverness CT	2	Airdrie U	0

PAST SCOTTISH CUP FINALS

Year	Team	Score	Team	Score
1874	Queen's Park	2	Clydesdale	0
1875	Queen's Park	3	Renton	0
1876	Queen's Park	1 2	Third Lanark	1 0
1877	Vale of Leven	0 1 3	Rangers	0 1 2
1878	Vale of Leven	1	Third Lanark	0
1879	Vale of Leven	1	Rangers	1

Vale of Leven awarded cup, Rangers did not appear for replay

Year	Team	Score	Team	Score
1880	Queen's Park	3	Thornliebank	0
1881	Queen's Park	2 3	Dumbarton	1 1

Replayed because of protest

Year	Team	Score	Team	Score
1882	Queen's Park	2 4	Dumbarton	2 1
1883	Dumbarton	2 2	Vale of Leven	2 1

Queen's Park awarded cup when Vale of Leven did not appear for the final

Year	Team	Score	Team	Score
1885	Renton	0 3	Vale of Leven	0 1
1886	Queen's Park	3	Renton	1
1887	Hibernian	2	Dumbarton	1
1888	Renton	6	Cambuslang	1
1889	Third Lanark	3 2	Celtic	0 1

Replayed because of protest

Year	Team	Score	Team	Score
1890	Queen's Park	1 2	Vale of Leven	1 1
1891	Hearts	1	Dumbarton	0
1892	Celtic	1 5	Queen's Park	0 1

Replayed because of protest

Year	Team	Score	Team	Score
1893	Queen's Park	2	Celtic	1
1894	Rangers	3	Celtic	1
1895	St Bernards	3	Renton	1
1896	Hearts	3	Hibernian	1
1897	Rangers	5	Dumbarton	1
1898	Rangers	2	Kilmarnock	0
1899	Celtic	2	Rangers	0
1900	Celtic	4	Queen's Park	3
1901	Hearts	4	Celtic	3
1902	Hibernian	1	Celtic	0
1903	Rangers	1 0 2	Hearts	1 0 0
1904	Celtic	3	Rangers	2
1905	Third Lanark	0 3	Rangers	0 1
1906	Hearts	1	Third Lanark	0
1907	Celtic	3	Hearts	0
1908	Celtic	5	St Mirren	1
1909	*After two drawn games between Celtic and Rangers, 2.2, 1.1, there was a riot and the cup was withheld*			
1910	Dundee	2 0 2	Clyde	2 0 1
1911	Celtic	0 2	Hamilton Acad	0 0
1912	Celtic	2	Clyde	0
1913	Falkirk	2	Raith R	0
1914	Celtic	0 4	Hibernian	0 1
1920	Kilmarnock	3	Albion R	2
1921	Partick Th	1	Rangers	0
1922	Morton	1	Rangers	0
1923	Celtic	1	Hibernian	0
1924	Airdrieonians	2	Hibernian	0
1925	Celtic	2	Dundee	1
1926	St Mirren	2	Celtic	0
1927	Celtic	3	East Fife	1
1928	Rangers	4	Celtic	0
1929	Kilmarnock	2	Rangers	0
1930	Rangers	0 2	Partick Th	0 1
1931	Celtic	2 4	Motherwell	2 2
1932	Rangers	1 3	Kilmarnock	1 0
1933	Celtic	1	Motherwell	0

Year	Winner		Opponent	
1934	Rangers	5	St Mirren	0
1935	Rangers	2	Hamilton Acad	1
1936	Rangers	1	Third Lanark	0
1937	Celtic	2	Aberdeen	1
1938	East Fife	1 4	Kilmarnock	1 2
1939	Clyde	4	Motherwell	0
1947	Aberdeen	2	Hibernian	1
1948	Rangers	1 1	Morton	1 0
1949	Rangers	4	Clyde	1
1950	Rangers	3	East Fife	0
1951	Celtic	1	Motherwell	0
1952	Motherwell	4	Dundee	0
1953	Rangers	1 1	Aberdeen	1 0
1954	Celtic	2	Aberdeen	1
1955	Clyde	1 1	Celtic	1 0
1956	Hearts	3	Celtic	1
1957	Falkirk	1 2	Kilmarnock	1 1
1958	Clyde	1	Hibernian	0
1959	St Mirren	3	Aberdeen	1
1960	Rangers	2	Kilmarnock	0
1961	Dunfermline Ath	0 2	Celtic	0 0
1962	Rangers	2	St Mirren	0
1963	Rangers	1 3	Celtic	1 0
1964	Rangers	3	Dundee	1
1965	Celtic	3	Dunfermline Ath	2
1966	Rangers	0 1	Celtic	0 0
1967	Celtic	2	Aberdeen	0
1968	Dunfermline Ath	3	Hearts	1
1969	Celtic	4	Rangers	0
1970	Aberdeen	3	Celtic	1
1971	Celtic	1 2	Rangers	1 1
1972	Celtic	6	Hibernian	1
1973	Rangers	3	Celtic	2
1974	Celtic	3	Dundee U	0
1975	Celtic	3	Airdrieonians	1
1976	Rangers	3	Hearts	1
1977	Celtic	1	Rangers	0
1978	Rangers	2	Aberdeen	1
1979	Rangers	0 0 3	Hibernian	0 0 2
1980	Celtic	1	Rangers	0
1981	Rangers	0 4	Dundee U	0 1
1982	Aberdeen	4	Rangers	1 (aet)
1983	Aberdeen	1	Rangers	0 (aet)
1984	Aberdeen	2	Celtic	1 (aet)
1985	Celtic	2	Dundee U	1
1986	Aberdeen	3	Hearts	0
1987	St Mirren	1	Dundee U	0 (aet)
1988	Celtic	2	Dundee U	1
1989	Celtic	1	Rangers	0
1990	Aberdeen†	0	Celtic	0
1991	Motherwell	4	Dundee U	3 (aet)
1992	Rangers	2	Airdrieonians	1
1993	Rangers	2	Aberdeen	1
1994	Dundee U	1	Rangers	0
1995	Celtic	1	Airdrieonians	0
1996	Rangers	5	Hearts	1
1997	Kilmarnock	1	Falkirk	0
1998	Hearts	2	Rangers	1
1999	Rangers	1	Celtic	0
2000	Rangers	4	Aberdeen	0
2001	Celtic	3	Hibernian	0
2002	Rangers	3	Celtic	2
2003	Rangers	1	Dundee	0
2004	Celtic	3	Dunfermline Ath	1

†won on penalties

213

WELSH LEAGUE 2003–2004

JT HUGHES/MITSUBISHI WELSH PREMIER LEAGUE

				Home			Away					Total						
		P	W	D	L	F	A	W	D	L	F	A	W	D	L	F	A	Gd	Pts
1	Rhyl	32	13	3	0	45	10	10	5	1	31	16	23	8	1	76	26	50	77
2	TNS	32	13	1	2	40	14	11	3	2	37	14	24	4	4	77	28	49	76
3	Haverfordwest C	32	10	5	1	22	10	7	6	3	18	13	17	11	4	40	23	17	62
4	Aberystwyth T	32	10	3	3	30	16	8	2	6	29	23	18	5	9	59	39	20	59
5	Caersws	32	8	5	3	30	18	7	5	4	33	23	15	10	7	63	41	22	55
6	Bangor City	32	7	5	4	37	25	9	2	5	35	22	16	6	10	72	47	25	54
7	Cwmbran Town	32	7	3	6	22	20	8	0	8	26	24	15	3	14	48	44	4	48
8	Connah's Quay N	32	6	3	7	29	28	5	6	5	29	27	11	9	12	58	55	3	42
9	Caernarfon Town	32	6	5	5	38	31	5	4	7	27	34	11	9	12	65	65	0	42
10	Newtown	32	7	4	5	22	22	5	1	10	21	28	12	5	15	43	50	-7	41
11	Port Talbot T	32	6	3	7	25	26	5	3	8	16	25	11	6	15	41	51	-10	39
12	Porthmadog	32	7	3	6	26	23	4	0	12	15	31	11	3	18	41	54	-13	36
13	Newi Cefn Druids	32	6	2	8	25	31	5	0	11	19	28	11	2	19	44	59	-15	35
14	Afan Lido	32	4	5	7	15	19	4	3	9	16	35	8	8	16	31	54	-23	32
15	Welshpool Town	32	4	4	8	21	32	2	3	11	14	39	6	7	19	35	71	-36	25
16	Carmarthen Town	32	3	3	10	13	32	0	8	8	15	37	3	11	18	28	69	-41	20
17	Barry Town*	32	3	1	12	17	37	0	6	10	13	40	3	7	22	30	77	-47	16

NORTHERN IRELAND LEAGUE 2003–2004

DAILY MIRROR IRISH LEAGUE PREMIER DIVISION

				Home			Away					Total						
		P	W	D	L	F	A	W	D	L	F	A	W	D	L	F	A	Gd	Pts
1	Linfield	30	12	3	0	35	7	10	4	1	32	9	22	7	1	67	16	51	73
2	Portadown	30	11	3	1	35	7	11	1	3	36	15	22	4	4	71	22	49	70
3	Lisburn	30	10	3	2	26	13	6	4	5	19	17	16	7	7	45	30	15	55
4	Coleraine	30	10	2	3	30	17	4	7	4	18	19	14	9	7	48	36	12	51
5	Glentoran	30	9	1	5	26	11	6	4	5	22	16	15	5	10	48	27	21	50
6	Ballymena	30	7	4	4	22	17	6	4	5	19	18	13	8	9	41	35	6	47
7	Limavady	30	7	2	6	20	23	5	3	7	21	20	12	5	13	41	43	-2	41
8	Ards	30	5	7	3	21	20	4	4	7	15	26	9	11	10	36	46	-10	38
9	Crusaders	30	4	4	7	16	19	6	2	7	17	19	10	6	11	33	38	-5	36
10	Dungannon Swifts	30	6	4	5	24	26	4	2	9	12	22	10	6	14	36	48	-12	36
11	Institute	30	5	4	6	16	24	4	3	8	21	29	9	7	14	37	53	-16	34
12	Newry	30	6	6	3	20	13	2	3	10	15	40	8	9	13	35	53	-18	33
13	Omagh	30	5	2	8	21	32	4	2	9	16	26	9	4	17	37	58	-21	31
14	Larne	30	4	2	9	20	31	3	6	6	22	20	7	8	15	42	51	-9	29
15	Cliftonville	30	4	3	8	13	20	2	5	8	14	25	6	8	16	27	45	-18	26
16	Glenavon*	30	1	4	10	11	32	3	0	12	13	35	4	4	22	24	67	-43	16

*Relegated.

PROMOTION/RELEGATION PLAY-OFF
First Leg
Armagh City 0, Cliftonville 3 *(at Holm Park, Armagh)*

Second Leg
Cliftonville 1, Armagh City 1 *(at Solitude, Belfast)*

Leading goalscorers: 34 Ferguson (Linfield); 27 Hamilton (Portadown); 23 Arkins (Portadown); 21 Fitzgerald (Ards); 20 Smith A (Glentoran); 19 Parkhouse (Institute); 18 Kennedy (Ards), Hamill (Coleraine); 14 Morgan (Linfield), Halliday (Glentoran).

REPUBLIC OF IRELAND LEAGUE

	P	W	D	L	F	A	GD	Pts
Shelbourne	36	19	12	5	52	28	24	69
Bohemians	36	18	10	8	58	37	21	64
Cork City	36	13	14	9	43	33	10	53
Longford Town	36	12	12	12	46	44	2	48
St Patrick's Athletic	36	10	16	10	48	48	0	46
Waterford United	36	11	12	13	44	58	−14	45
Shamrock Rovers	36	10	14	12	45	46	−1	44
Drogheda United	36	9	10	17	38	50	−12	37
Derry City	36	7	15	14	33	51	−18	36
UCD	36	7	13	16	27	39	−12	34

HIGHLAND LEAGUE

	P	W	D	L	F	A	GD	Pts
Clachnacuddin	28	21	3	4	61	25	+36	66
Buckie Thistle	28	18	7	3	56	32	+24	61
Fraserburgh	28	18	5	5	81	36	+45	59
Deveronvale	28	18	1	9	77	41	+36	55
Keith	28	17	2	9	70	36	+34	53
Huntly	28	16	5	7	73	47	+26	53
Inverurie Loco Works	28	13	10	5	76	51	+25	49
Forres Mechanics	28	13	4	11	63	49	+14	43
Nairn County	28	9	5	14	40	60	−20	32
Cove Rangers	28	7	6	15	46	61	−15	27
Wick Academy	28	6	5	17	42	65	−23	23
Brora Rangers	28	5	6	17	34	71	−37	21
Lossiemouth	28	4	8	16	41	74	−33	20
Rothes	28	2	9	17	19	62	−43	15
Fort William	28	3	4	21	20	89	−69	13

EUROPEAN REVIEW 2003–2004

Favourites have a habit of falling and failing in horse races, but football is no protector of the fancied. Take the Champions League which produced Porto and Monaco as its finalists having the previous week listed Valencia and Marseille as the UEFA Cup's remaining pair.

The Gothenburg final of the Champions League was a remarkable achievement for Porto coach Jose Mourinho already being touted as a likely successor to Claudio Ranieri for the Chelsea job. Having masterminded the Portuguese club's success in the 2002–03 UEFA Cup final, a hard-earned 3-2 win over Celtic in extra time, he achieved the rare feat of taking the Champions League prize in the following season.

Porto had a pretty comfortable win over Monaco who themselves had a curious campaign highlighted by one outstanding victory 8-3 over Deportivo La Coruna and an even better performance against Real Madrid. In contrast, Porto's campaign had been one of scraping draws and narrow wins with their coach having to work strenuously to achieve his ultimate goal.

So much for the finale, the drama for the more favoured candidates had arrived earlier. In the semi-final, Porto had been held at home by La Coruna in a goalless draw. The Spaniards had a player sent off late in the match as well. But in the second leg Porto had gone ahead in the 60th minute from the penalty spot before La Coruna were again reduced to ten players. Porto saw out the remaining time.

In the other semi-final, Monaco finished the first leg with ten players from the 53rd minute, but still managed to defeat Chelsea 3-1. Manager Ranieri held up his hand for the outcome because after a useful 1-1 first half he made some ill-judged substitutions which cost him the game. The return leg at Stamford Bridge ended 2-2 after Chelsea had led 2-0.

However, it had been in the quarter-final stage that the three more favoured teams had fallen unexpectedly. Arsenal, considered by many experts to be England's one real prospect of lifting the Champions League, finally found their hoodoo over Chelsea removed. After a 1-1 draw at Chelsea, the Blues snatched a 2-1 win at Highbury.

Neither Real Madrid nor AC Milan fared any better. Real had seemingly floated into the semi-final after taking a 4-2 lead over Monaco only to be shocked when their opponents gave them a goal start in the first half then proceeded to score three times themselves and go through on the away goals rule.

Oddly enough Porto had had arguably their most effective two matches with Lyon at this stage, taking a 2-0 lead at home and finishing 2-2 in France. But if Monaco had staged a dramatic revival, it was nothing to the achievement of La Coruna against Milan.

Having initially given the Spaniards a goal start, Milan cruised to a 4-1 lead at the end and must have been brimming over with confidence for the return. Alas they were trailing 3-0 at the interval and losing 4-0 on the night, crashed out 5-4 on aggregate.

The UEFA Cup did not manage to provide such excitement, but was hard-fought nonetheless. In the final Marseille lost goalkeeper Fabien Barthez, sent off just on the interval. They found the handicap of ten men for an entire half too much having gone a goal down from the penalty spot as a result of the incident and conceded a second goal after the resumption.

There had been English hopes in the UEFA Cup, too, as Newcastle United had forced their way to the semi-finals having lost out in the earlier stages of the Champions League on penalties to Partizan Belgrade having done the difficult part of the job by winning in Serbia.

But Marseille were United's opponents in the semi-final of the UEFA Cup and following a goalless draw at St James Park, the French won the second leg 2-0. The other semi was an all-Spanish affair with one penalty for Valencia settling the game over two legs.

Valencia had also won the Spanish League title, the Champions League demise causing Real Madrid to drop behind Barcelona and La Coruna into the strangely unaccustomed berth of fourth place in La Liga in what was David Beckham's first season abroad.

Despite their European reverse, Milan held the Italian Serie A title, while in Germany it was Werder Bremen who took the Bundesliga. For the French it was Lyon who provided a personal hat-trick of championships.

UEFA CHAMPIONS LEAGUE 2003–2004

FIRST QUALIFYING ROUND FIRST LEG

BATE Borisov	(1) 1	Bohemians		(0) 0
Dynamo Tbilisi	(2) 3	SK Tirana		(0) 0
Glentoran	(0) 0	HJK Helsinki		(0) 0
Grevenmacher	(0) 0	Leotar		(0) 0
HB Torshavn	(0) 0	Kaunas		(0) 1
Omonia	(0) 0	Irtysh		(0) 0
Pyunik	(0) 1	KR Reykjavik		(0) 0
Serif	(0) 1	Flora Tallinn		(0) 0
Sliema Wanderers	(0) 2	Skonto Riga		(0) 0
Vardar	(1) 3	Barry Town		(0) 0

FIRST QUALIFYING ROUND SECOND LEG

Barry Town	(1) 2	Vardar		(0) 1
Bohemians	(2) 3	BATE Borisov		(0) 0
Flora Tallinn	(0) 1	Serif		(0) 1
HJK Helsinki	(0) 1	Glentoran		(0) 0
Irtysh	(1) 1	Omonia		(0) 2
KR Reykjavik	(0) 1	Pyunik		(0) 1
Kaunas	(3) 4	HB Torshavn		(1) 1
Leotar	(0) 0	Grevenmacher		(0) 0
SK Tirana	(1) 3	Dynamo Tbilisi		(0) 0
(aet; SK Tirana won 4-2 on penalties.)				
Skonto Riga	(1) 3	Sliema Wanderers		(0) 1

SECOND QUALIFYING ROUND FIRST LEG

Bohemians	(0) 0	Rosenborg		(1) 1
CSKA Moscow	(0) 1	Vardar		(0) 1
FC Copenhagen	(3) 4	Sliema Wanderers		(0) 1
Kaunas	(0) 0	Celtic		(2) 4
Leotar	(1) 1	Slavia Prague		(1) 2
MTK Budapest	(2) 3	HJK Helsinki		(0) 1
Maribor	(1) 1	Dynamo Zagreb		(1) 1
Partizan Belgrade	(0) 1	Djurgaarden		(0) 1
Pyunik	(0) 0	CSKA Sofia		(1) 2
Rapid Bucharest	(0) 0	Anderlecht		(0) 0
SK Tirana	(1) 1	Graz		(3) 5
Serif	(0) 0	Shakhtjor Donetsk		(0) 0
Wisla	(3) 5	Omonia		(0) 0
Zilina	(0) 1	Maccabi Tel Aviv		(0) 0

SECOND QUALIFYING ROUND SECOND LEG

Anderlecht	(0) 3	Rapid Bucharest		(2) 2
CSKA Sofia	(0) 1	Pyunik		(0) 0
Celtic	(1) 1	Kaunas		(0) 0
Djurgaarden	(1) 2	Partizan Belgrade		(0) 2
Dynamo Zagreb	(0) 2	Maribor		(1) 1
Graz	(1) 2	SK Tirana		(0) 1
HJK Helsinki	(0) 1	MTK Budapest		(0) 0
Maccabi Tel Aviv	(1) 1	Zilina		(1) 1
Omonia	(1) 2	Wisla		(1) 2
Rosenborg	(1) 4	Bohemians		(0) 0
Shakhtjor Donetsk	(0) 2	Serif		(0) 0
Slavia Prague	(1) 2	Leotar		(0) 0
Sliema Wanderers	(0) 0	FC Copenhagen		(3) 6
Vardar	(0) 1	CSKA Moscow		(1) 1

THIRD QUALIFYING ROUND FIRST LEG

Celta Vigo	(1) 3	Slavia Prague		(0) 0

Dynamo Kiev	(2) 3	Dynamo Zagreb	(1) 1
Graz	(0) 1	Ajax	(0) 1
Anderlecht	(2) 3	Wisla	(0) 1
FC Brugge	(2) 2	Borussia Dortmund	(0) 1
FK Austria	(0) 0	Marseille	(1) 1
Galatasaray	(3) 3	CSKA Sofia	(0) 0
Grasshoppers	(0) 1	AEK Athens	(0) 0
Lazio	(1) 3	Benfica	(0) 1
MTK Budapest	(0) 0	Celtic	(2) 4
Partizan Belgrade	(0) 0	Newcastle United	(1) 1
Rangers	(1) 1	FC Copenhagen	(0) 1
Rosenborg	(0) 0	La Coruna	(0) 0
Shakhtjor Donetsk	(0) 1	Lokomotiv Moscow	(0) 0
Vardar	(0) 2	Sparta Prague	(2) 3
Zilina	(0) 0	Chelsea	(1) 2

THIRD QUALIFYING ROUND SECOND LEG

Chelsea	(1) 3	Zilina	(0) 0
La Coruna	(1) 1	Rosenborg	(0) 0
Sparta Prague	(1) 2	Vardar	(0) 2
Wisla	(0) 0	Anderlecht	(0) 1
AEK Athens	(3) 3	Grasshoppers	(0) 1
Ajax	(1) 2	Graz	(1) 1
Benfica	(0) 0	Lazio	(1) 1
Borussia Dortmund	(1) 2	FC Brugge	(1) 1

(aet; FC Brugge won 4-2 on penalties.)

CSKA Sofia	(0) 0	Galatasaray	(1) 3
Celtic	(1) 1	MTK Budapest	(0) 0
Dynamo Zagreb	(0) 0	Dynamo Kiev	(0) 2
FC Copenhagen	(0) 1	Rangers	(0) 2
Lokomotiv Moscow	(2) 3	Shakhtjor Donetsk	(0) 1
Marseille	(0) 0	FK Austria	(0) 0
Newcastle United	(0) 0	Partizan Belgrade	(0) 1

(aet; Partizan Belgrade won 4-3 on penalties.)

| Slavia Prague | (2) 2 | Celta Vigo | (0) 0 |

GROUP A

Bayern Munich	(0) 2	Celtic	(0) 1
Lyon	(1) 1	Anderlecht	(0) 0
Anderlecht	(0) 1	Bayern Munich	(0) 1
Celtic	(0) 2	Lyon	(0) 0
Anderlecht	(0) 1	Celtic	(0) 0
Lyon	(0) 1	Bayern Munich	(1) 1
Bayern Munich	(1) 1	Lyon	(1) 2
Celtic	(3) 3	Anderlecht	(0) 1
Anderlecht	(0) 1	Lyon	(0) 0
Celtic	(0) 0	Bayern Munich	(0) 0
Bayern Munich	(1) 1	Anderlecht	(0) 0
Lyon	(1) 3	Celtic	(1) 2

Group A Final Table	P	W	D	L	F	A	Pts
Lyon	6	3	1	2	7	7	10
Bayern Munich	6	2	3	1	6	5	9
Celtic	6	2	1	3	8	7	7
Anderlecht	6	2	1	3	4	6	7

GROUP B

Arsenal	(0) 0	Internazionale	(3) 3
Dynamo Kiev	(0) 2	Lokomotiv Moscow	(0) 0
Internazionale	(1) 2	Dynamo Kiev	(1) 1
Lokomotiv Moscow	(0) 0	Arsenal	(0) 0
Dynamo Kiev	(1) 2	Arsenal	(0) 1

Lokomotiv Moscow	(1) 3	Internazionale	(0) 0
Arsenal	(0) 1	Dynamo Kiev	(0) 0
Internazionale	(1) 1	Lokomotiv Moscow	(0) 1
Internazionale	(1) 1	Arsenal	(1) 5
Lokomotiv Moscow	(2) 3	Dynamo Kiev	(1) 2
Arsenal	(1) 2	Lokomotiv Moscow	(0) 0
Dynamo Kiev	(0) 1	Internazionale	(0) 1

Group B Final Table	P	W	D	L	F	A	Pts
Arsenal	6	3	1	2	9	6	10
Lokomotiv Moscow	6	2	2	2	7	7	8
Internazionale	6	2	2	2	8	11	8
Dynamo Kiev	6	2	1	3	8	8	7

GROUP C

AEK Athens	(0) 1	La Coruna	(1) 1
PSV Eindhoven	(0) 1	Monaco	(1) 2
La Coruna	(1) 2	PSV Eindhoven	(0) 0
Monaco	(2) 4	AEK Athens	(0) 0
AEK Athens	(0) 0	PSV Eindhoven	(1) 1
La Coruna	(0) 1	Monaco	(0) 0
Monaco	(5) 8	La Coruna	(2) 3
PSV Eindhoven	(0) 2	AEK Athens	(0) 0
La Coruna	(1) 3	AEK Athens	(0) 0
Monaco	(1) 1	PSV Eindhoven	(0) 1
AEK Athens	(0) 0	Monaco	(0) 0
PSV Eindhoven	(1) 3	La Coruna	(0) 2

Group C Final Table	P	W	D	L	F	A	Pts
Monaco	6	3	2	1	15	6	11
La Coruna	6	3	1	2	12	12	10
PSV Eindhoven	6	3	1	2	8	7	10
AEK Athens	6	0	2	4	1	11	2

GROUP D

Juventus	(1) 2	Galatasaray	(1) 1
Real Sociedad	(0) 1	Olympiakos	(0) 0
Galatasaray	(0) 1	Real Sociedad	(1) 2
Olympiakos	(1) 1	Juventus	(1) 2
Galatasaray	(1) 1	Olympiakis	(0) 0
Juventus	(3) 4	Real Sociedad	(0) 2
Olympiakos	(2) 3	Galatasaray	(0) 0
Real Sociedad	(0) 0	Juventus	(0) 0
Olympiakos	(0) 2	Real Sociedad	(1) 2
Galatasaray	(0) 2	Juventus	(0) 0
(In Dortmund.)			
Juventus	(4) 7	Olympiakos	(0) 0
Real Sociedad	(0) 1	Galatasaray	(1) 1

Group D Final Table	P	W	D	L	F	A	Pts
Juventus	6	4	1	1	15	6	13
Real Sociedad	6	2	3	1	8	8	9
Galatasaray	6	2	1	3	6	8	7
Olympiakos	6	1	1	4	6	13	4

GROUP E

Manchester United	(4) 5	Panathinaikos	(0) 0
Rangers	(0) 2	Stuttgart	(1) 1
Panathinaikos	(0) 1	Rangers	(1) 1
Stuttgart	(0) 2	Manchester United	(0) 1
Rangers	(0) 0	Manchester United	(1) 1
Stuttgart	(2) 2	Panathinaikos	(0) 0
Manchester United	(2) 3	Rangers	(0) 0

Panathinaikos	(0) 1	Stuttgart	(0) 3
Panathinaikos	(0) 0	Manchester United	(0) 1
Stuttgart	(1) 1	Rangers	(0) 0
Manchester United	(1) 2	Stuttgart	(0) 0
Rangers	(1) 1	Panathinaikos	(1) 3

Group E Final Table	P	W	D	L	F	A	Pts
Manchester United	6	5	0	1	13	2	15
Stuttgart	6	4	0	2	9	6	12
Panathinaikos	6	1	1	4	5	13	4
Rangers	6	1	1	4	4	10	4

GROUP F

Partizan Belgrade	(0) 1	Porto	(1) 1
Real Madrid	(2) 4	Marseille	(1) 2
Marseille	(0) 3	Partizan Belgrade	(0) 0
Porto	(1) 1	Real Madrid	(2) 3
Marseille	(1) 2	Porto	(2) 3
Real Madrid	(1) 1	Partizan Belgrade	(0) 0
Partizan Belgrade	(0) 0	Real Madrid	(0) 0
Porto	(1) 1	Marseille	(0) 0
Marseille	(0) 1	Real Madrid	(1) 2
Porto	(1) 2	Partizan Belgrade	(0) 1
Partizan Belgrade	(0) 1	Marseille	(0) 1
Real Madrid	(1) 1	Porto	(1) 1

Group F Final Table	P	W	D	L	F	A	Pts
Real Madrid	6	4	2	0	11	5	14
Porto	6	3	2	1	9	8	11
Marseille	6	1	1	4	9	11	4
Partizan Belgrade	6	0	3	3	3	8	3

GROUP G

Besiktas	(0) 0	Lazio	(1) 2
Sparta Prague	(0) 0	Chelsea	(0) 1
Chelsea	(0) 0	Besiktas	(2) 2
Lazio	(0) 2	Sparta Prague	(2) 2
Chelsea	(0) 2	Lazio	(1) 1
Sparta Prague	(0) 2	Besiktas	(0) 1
Besiktas	(0) 1	Sparta Prague	(0) 0
Lazio	(0) 0	Chelsea	(1) 4
Chelsea	(0) 0	Sparta Prague	(0) 0
Lazio	(0) 1	Besiktas	(1) 1
Besiktas	(0) 0	Chelsea	(0) 2
(In Gelsenkirchen.)			
Sparta Prague	(0) 1	Lazio	(0) 0

Group G Final Table	P	W	D	L	F	A	Pts
Chelsea	6	4	1	1	9	3	13
Sparta Prague	6	2	2	2	5	5	8
Besiktas	6	2	1	3	5	7	7
Lazio	6	1	2	3	6	10	5

GROUP H

AC Milan	(0) 1	Ajax	(0) 0
FC Brugge	(0) 1	Celta Vigo	(0) 1
Ajax	(1) 2	FC Brugge	(0) 0
Celta Vigo	(0) 0	AC Milan	(0) 0
AC Milan	(0) 0	FC Brugge	(1) 1
Ajax	(0) 1	Celta Vigo	(0) 0
Celta Vigo	(2) 3	Ajax	(0) 2
FC Brugge	(0) 0	AC Milan	(0) 1
Ajax	(0) 0	AC Milan	(0) 1

Celta Vigo	(0) 1	FC Brugge	(0) 1
AC Milan	(1) 1	Celta Vigo	(1) 2
FC Brugge	(1) 2	Ajax	(1) 1

Group H Final Table	P	W	D	L	F	A	Pts
AC Milan	6	3	1	2	4	3	10
Celta Vigo	6	2	3	1	7	6	9
FC Brugge	6	2	2	2	5	6	8
Ajax	6	2	0	4	6	7	6

KNOCK-OUT ROUND FIRST LEG

Bayern Munich	(0) 1	Real Madrid	(0) 1
Celta Vigo	(1) 2	Arsenal	(1) 3
Lokomotiv Moscow	(1) 2	Monaco	(0) 1
Sparta Prague	(0) 0	AC Milan	(0) 0
La Coruna	(1) 1	Juventus	(0) 0
Porto	(1) 2	Manchester United	(0) 1
Real Sociedad	(0) 0	Lyon	(1) 1
Stuttgart	(0) 0	Chelsea	(1) 1

KNOCK-OUT ROUND SECOND LEG

Chelsea	(0) 0	Stuttgart	(0) 0
Juventus	(0) 0	La Coruna	(1) 1
Lyon	(0) 1	Real Sociedad	(0) 0
Manchester United	(1) 1	Porto	(0) 1
AC Milan	(1) 4	Sparta Prague	(0) 1
Arsenal	(2) 2	Celta Vigo	(0) 0
Monaco	(0) 1	Lokomotiv Moscow	(0) 0
Real Madrid	(1) 1	Bayern Munich	(0) 0

QUARTER-FINALS FIRST LEG

AC Milan	(1) 4	La Coruna	(1) 1
Porto	(1) 2	Lyon	(0) 0
Chelsea	(0) 1	Arsenal	(0) 1
Real Madrid	(0) 4	Monaco	(1) 2

QUARTER-FINALS SECOND LEG

Arsenal	(1) 1	Chelsea	(0) 2
Monaco	(1) 3	Real Madrid	(1) 1
La Coruna	(3) 4	AC Milan	(0) 0
Lyon	(1) 2	Porto	(1) 2

SEMI-FINAL FIRST LEG

| Monaco | (1) 3 | Chelsea | (1) 1 |
| Porto | (0) 0 | La Coruna | (0) 0 |

SEMI-FINAL SECOND LEG

| La Coruna | (0) 0 | Porto | (0) 1 |
| Chelsea | (2) 2 | Monaco | (1) 2 |

UEFA CHAMPIONS LEAGUE FINAL 2004

Porto (1) 3 *(Carlos Alberto 39, Deco 71, Alenichev 75)*   **Monaco (0) 0**

Wednesday, 26 May 2004

(at Arena AufSchalke, Gelsenkirchen, Germany, 52,000)

Porto: Vitor Baia; Paulo Ferreira, Nuno Valente, Costinha, Jorge Costa, Ricardo Carvalho, Pedro Mendes, Deco (Pedro Emanuel 85), Carlos Alberto (Alenichev 60), Derlei (McCarthy 78), Maniche.

Monaco: Roma; Ibarra, Evra, Zikos, Givet (Squillaci 73), Rodriguez, Cisse (Nonda 64), Bernardi, Giuly (Prso 23), Morientes, Rothen.

Referee: K.M. Nielsen (Denmark)

UEFA CHAMPIONS LEAGUE 2004–2005

NEW SYSTEM
The 2004–05 season will see the start of UEFA's club licensing system. In order for a club to be admitted to any of the UEFA club competitions, minimum standards in areas including sporting matters, infrastructure, personnel and administration, legal matters and financial matters must be fulfilled.

UEFA CHAMPIONS LEAGUE PARTICIPATING CLUBS
FC Porto; Valencia CF; FC Barcelona; RC Deportivo La Coruña; Real Madrid CF; AC Milan ; AS Roma; Juventus FC; FC Internazionale; Arsenal FC; Chelsea FC ; Manchester United FC; Liverpool FC; SV Werder Bremen; FC Bayern München; Bayer 04 Leverkusen; Olympique Lyonnais; Paris Saint-Germain FC; AS Monaco FC; Panathinaikos FC; Olympiacos CFP ; FC PAOK; SL Benfica; AFC Ajax; PSV Eindhoven; Celtic FC; Rangers FC; Fenerbahçe SK; Trabzonspor; RSC Anderlecht; Club Brugge KV; FC Baník Ostrava; AC Sparta Praha; FC Basel 1893; BSC Young Boys; FC Dynamo Kyiv; FC Shakhtar Donetsk ; Maccabi Haifa FC; Maccabi Tel-Aviv FC; Grazer AK; Wisła Kraków; PFC CSKA Moskva; FK Crvena Zvezda; Rosenborg BK; PFC Lokomotiv Plovdiv; HNK Hajduk Split; Djurgårdens IF ; FC København; MŠK Žilina; FC Dinamo Bucuresti; Ferencvárosi TC; APOEL FC; NK Gorica; HJK Helsinki ; FC Skonto; FC Sheriff; FC WIT Georgia; NK Široki Brijeg; FBK Kaunas; KR Reykjavík ; FK Pobeda; FC Gomel; Shelbourne FC; Sliema Wanderers; FC Pyunik; Rhyl FC; KF Tirana; FC Flora; Linfield FC; AS Jeunesse Esch; HB Tórshavn ; FK Neftchi

INTERTOTO CUP 2003

1st leg home team v 1st leg away team, first leg score, second leg score, aggregate score

FIRST ROUND
Partizani* v M. Netanya 2-0, 1-3, 3-3
Brno* v Kotayk 1-0, 2-3, 3-3
Györ* v Achnas 1-1, 2-2, 3-3
Bangor v Gloria 0-1, 2-5, 2-6
Dubnica v Olympiakos 3-0, 4-1, 7-1
Dacia v Gí 4-1, 1-0, 5-1
Sloboda v KA 1-1, 1-1, 2-2
aet: Sloboda won 3-2 on penalties.
Shakhtyor v Omagh 1-0, 7-1, 8-1
OFK v Trans 6-1, 5-3, 11-4
Dinaburg v Wil 1-0, 0-2, 1-2
Odra v Shamrock Rovers 1-2, 0-1, 1-3
Spartak v Pobeda 1-5, 1-2, 2-7
Allianssi v Hibernians 1-0, 1-1, 2-1
Pasching* v WIT 1-0, 1-2, 2-2
Koper v Zagreb 1-0, 2-2, 3-2
Zalgiris v Örgryte 1-1, 0-3, 1-4
Encamp v Lierse 0-3, 1-4, 1-7
Videoton v Marek 2-2, 2-3, 4-5
Polonia v Tobol 0-3, 1-2, 1-5
Tampere* v Ceahlaul 1-0, 1-2, 2-2
Sutjeska v US Luxembourg 3-0, 1-1, 4-1

SECOND ROUND
Örgryte v Nice* 3-2, 1-2, 4-4
Thun v Brno 2-3, 1-1, 3-4
Brescia v Gloria 2-1, 1-1, 3-2
Marek v Wolfsburg 1-1, 0-2, 1-3
Shakhtyor v Cibalia 1-1, 2-4, 3-5
Willem II v Wil 2-1, 1-3, 3-4
Pobeda v Pasching 1-1, 1-2, 2-3
Sloboda v Lierse 1-0, 1-5, 2-5
Dacia v Partizani 2-0, 3-0, 5-0
Koper* v Dubnica 1-0, 2-3, 3-3

Sint-Truiden v Tobol 0-2, 0-1, 0-3
Synot v OFK 1-0, 3-3, 4-3
Racing* v Györ 1-0, 1-2, 2-2
Liberec v Shamrock Rovers
  2-0, 2-0, 4-0
Akratitos v Allianssi 0-1, 0-0, 0-1
Tampere v Sutjeska 0-0, 1-0, 1-0

THIRD ROUND
Tobol v Pasching 0-1, 0-3, 0-4
Perugia v Allianssi 2-0, 2-0, 4-0
Egaleo v Koper 2-3, 2-2, 4-5
Nantes v Wil 2-1, 3-2, 5-3
Nice v Werder Bremen 0-0, 0-1, 0-1
Villarreal v Brescia 2-0, 1-1, 3-1
Guingamp v Brno 2-1, 2-4, 4-5
Dacia v Schalke 0-1, 1-2, 1-3
Racing v Liberec 0-1, 1-2, 1-3
Synot v Wolfsburg 0-1, 0-2, 0-3
Tampere v Cibalia 0-2, 1-0, 1-2
Heerenveen v Lierse 4-1, 1-0, 5-1

SEMI-FINAL
Nantes v Perugia 0-1, 0-0, 0-1
Pasching v Werder Bremen 4-0, 1-1, 5-1
Brno v Villarreal 1-1, 0-2, 1-3
Schalke v Liberec 2-1, 0-0, 2-1
Heerenveen v Koper 2-0, 0-1, 2-1
Cibalia v Wolfsburg 1-4, 0-4, 1-8

FINALS
Pasching v Schalke 0-2, 0-0, 0-2
Heerenveen v Villarreal 1-2, 0-0, 1-2
Perugia v Wolfsburg 1-0, 2-0, 3-0

* Won on away goals rule.

UEFA CUP 2003–2004

QUALIFYING ROUND, FIRST LEG

AIK Stockholm	(0) 1	Fylkir	(0) 0
Atyrau	(0) 1	Levski	(4) 4
Birkirkara	(0) 0	Ferencvaros	(1) 5
Brondby	(2) 3	Dynamo Minsk	(0) 0
Cement	(0) 0	Katowice	(0) 0
Dinamo Bucharest	(2) 5	Metalurgs	(1) 2
Dinamo Tirana	(0) 0	Lokeren	(3) 4
Ekranas	(1) 1	Debrecen	(0) 1
Esbjerg	(3) 5	Santa Coloma	(0) 0
Etzella	(1) 1	Kamen	(1) 2
Groclin	(1) 2	Atlantas	(0) 0
Haka	(2) 2	Hajduk Split	(1) 1
Hapoel Tel Aviv (*in Rotterdam*)	(1) 1	Banants	(0) 1
Karnten	(1) 2	Grindavik	(0) 1
Lens	(0) 3	Torpedo Kutaisi	(0) 0
Levadia	(0) 1	Varteks	(1) 3
Liteks	(0) 0	Zimbru Chisinau	(0) 0
Molde	(2) 2	KI	(0) 0
MyPa	(2) 3	Young Boys	(1) 2
Neman	(0) 1	Steaua	(0) 1
Nordsjaelland	(2) 4	Shirak	(0) 0
NSI	(0) 1	Lyn	(2) 3
Odense	(1) 1	VMK	(0) 1
Petrzalka	(1) 1	Dudelange	(0) 0
Matador Puchov	(1) 3	Sioni	(0) 0
Publikum	(4) 7	Belasica	(0) 2
Red Star Belgrade	(3) 5	Otaci	(0) 0
Sarajevo	(0) 1	Sartid	(1) 1
Torpedo Moscow	(2) 5	Domagnano	(0) 0
Vaduz	(0) 0	Dnepr	(0) 1
Valletta	(0) 0	Neuchatel Xamax	(2) 2
Ventspils	(0) 1	Plock	(1) 1
Viktoria Zizkov	(0) 3	Zhenis	(0) 0
Zeljeznicar	(0) 1	Anorthosis	(0) 0
Apoel	(1) 2	Derry City	(1) 1
Coleraine	(2) 2	Uniao Leiria	(1) 1
Cwmbran Town	(0) 0	Maccabi Haifa	(2) 3
Malmo	(2) 4	Portadown	(0) 0
Manchester City	(1) 5	TNS	(0) 0
Olimpija	(0) 1	Shelbourne	(0) 0
Vllaznia	(0) 0	Dundee	(1) 2

QUALIFYING ROUND, SECOND LEG

Anorthosis	(1) 1	Zeljeznicar	(2) 3
Atlantas	(0) 1	Groclin	(2) 4
Banants	(0) 1	Hapoel Tel Aviv	(1) 2
Belasica	(0) 0	Publikum	(2) 5
Debrecen	(1) 2	Ekranas	(0) 1
Dnepr	(0) 1	Vaduz	(0) 0
Domagnano	(0) 0	Torpedo Moscow	(1) 4
Dudelange	(0) 0	Petrzalka	(0) 1
Dynamo Minsk	(0) 0	Brondby	(1) 2
Ferencvaros	(0) 1	Birkirkara	(0) 0
Fylkir	(0) 0	AIK Stockholm	(0) 0
Grindavik	(0) 1	Karnten	(0) 1
Hajduk Split	(1) 1	Haka	(0) 0

223

Kamen	(1) 7	Etzella	(0) 0
Katowice	(0) 1	Cement	(1) 1
KI	(0) 0	Molde	(2) 4
Levski	(1) 2	Atyrau	(0) 0
Lokeren	(1) 3	Dinamo Tirana	(1) 1
Lyn	(3) 6	NSI	(0) 0
Metalurgs	(1) 1	Dinamo Bucharest	(1) 1
Neuchatel Xamax	(1) 2	Valletta	(0) 0
Otaci	(1) 2	Red Star Belgrade	(2) 3
Plock	(2) 2	Ventspils	(0) 2
Santa Coloma	(1) 1	Esbjerg	(3) 4
Sartid	(1) 3	Sarajevo	(0) 0
Shirak	(0) 0	Nordsjaelland	(1) 2
Sioni	(0) 0	Matador Puchov	(3) 3
Steaua	(0) 0	Neman	(0) 0
Torpedo Kutaisi	(0) 0	Lens	(2) 2
Varteks	(1) 3	Levadia	(0) 2
VMK	(0) 0	Odense	(0) 3
Young Boys	(1) 2	MyPa	(0) 2
Zhenis	(0) 1	Viktoria Zizkov	(2) 3
Zimbru Chisinau	(0) 2	Liteks	(0) 0
Derry City	(0) 0	Apoel	(1) 3
Dundee	(2) 4	Vllaznia	(0) 0
Maccabi Haifa (*in Izmir*)	(2) 3	Cwmbran Town	(0) 0
Portadown	(0) 0	Malmo	(0) 2
Shelbourne	(1) 2	Olimpija	(2) 3
TNS	(0) 0	Manchester City	(1) 2
Uniao Leiria	(0) 5	Coleraine	(0) 0

FIRST ROUND FIRST LEG

AIK Stockholm	(0) 0	Valencia	(0) 1
Apoel	(0) 1	Mallorca	(1) 2
Auxerre	(1) 1	Neuchatel Xamax	(0) 0
Bordeaux	(2) 2	Petrzalka	(1) 1
Brondby	(0) 1	Viktoria Zizkov	(0) 0
Cement	(0) 0	Lens	(0) 1
CSKA Sofia	(1) 1	Torpedo Moscow	(0) 1
Dinamo Bucharest	(0) 2	Shakhtjor Donetsk	(0) 0
Dynamo Zagreb	(1) 3	MTK Budapest	(1) 1
Feyenoord	(0) 2	Karnten	(0) 1
Ferencvaros	(0) 1	FC Copenhagen	(1) 1
FK Austria	(1) 1	Borussia Dortmund	(1) 2
Gaziantep	(0) 1	Hapoel Tel Aviv	(0) 0
Grasshoppers	(1) 1	Hajduk Split	(0) 1
Hamburg	(0) 2	Dnepr	(1) 1
Hapoel Ramat Gan (*in Streda*)	(0) 0	Levski	(0) 1
Hertha Berlin	(0) 0	Groclin	(0) 1
Kaiserslautern	(0) 1	Teplice	(1) 2
Kamen	(0) 0	Schalke	(0) 0
La Louviere	(1) 1	Benfica	(0) 1
Maccabi Haifa (*in Izmir*)	(1) 2	Publikum	(0) 1
Malatya	(0) 0	Basle	(1) 2
Metalurgs	(1) 1	Parma	(0) 1
MyPa	(0) 0	Sochaux	(1) 1
Odense	(1) 2	Red Star Belgrade	(1) 2
Panionios	(2) 2	Nordsjaelland	(0) 0
PAOK Salonika	(0) 0	Lyn	(1) 1
Matador Puchov	(0) 1	Barcelona	(0) 1
Roma	(2) 4	Vardar	(0) 0

Salzburg	(0) 0	Udinese	(1) 1
Sartid	(0) 1	Slavia Prague	(2) 2
Spartak Moscow	(2) 2	Esbjerg	(0) 0
Sporting Lisbon	(1) 2	Malmo	(0) 0
Uniao Leiria	(0) 1	Molde	(0) 0
Utrecht	(1) 2	Zilina	(0) 0
Varteks	(1) 1	Debrecen	(1) 3
Ventspils	(0) 1	Rosenborg	(3) 4
Villarreal	(0) 0	Trabzonspor	(0) 0
Valerenga	(0) 0	Graz	(0) 0
Wisla	(1) 2	NEC Nijmegen	(0) 1
Zimbru Chisinau	(0) 1	Aris Salonika	(1) 1
Dundee	(0) 1	Perugia	(0) 2
Genclerbirligi	(2) 3	Blackburn Rovers	(0) 1
Hearts	(1) 2	Zeljeznicar	(0) 0
Manchester City	(1) 3	Lokeren	(2) 2
Newcastle United	(2) 5	NAC Breda	(0) 0
Southampton	(0) 1	Steaua	(1) 1
Olimpija	(0) 1	Liverpool	(0) 1

FIRST ROUND, SECOND LEG

Aris Salonika	(1) 2	Zimbru Chisinau	(1) 1
Barcelona	(3) 8	Matador Puchov	(0) 0
Basle	(0) 1	Malatya	(0) 2
Benfica	(0) 1	La Louviere	(0) 0
Borussia Dortmund	(1) 1	FK Austria	(0) 0
Debrecen	(2) 3	Varteks	(1) 2
Dnepr	(1) 3	Hamburg	(0) 0
Esbjerg	(0) 1	Spartak Moscow	(1) 1
FC Copenhagen	(0) 1	Ferencvaros	(0) 1
(aet; FC Copenhagen won 4-3 on penalties.)			
Graz	(1) 1	Valerenga	(0) 1
Groclin	(0) 1	Hertha Berlin	(0) 0
Hajduk Split	(0) 0	Grasshoppers	(0) 0
Hapoel Tel Aviv (*in Rotterdam*)	(0) 0	Gaziantep	(0) 0
Karnten	(0) 0	Feyenoord	(1) 1
Lens	(2) 5	Cement	(0) 0
Levski	(1) 4	Hapoel Ramat Gan	(0) 0
Lyn	(0) 0	PAOK Salonika	(0) 3
MTK	(0) 0	Dynamo Zagreb	(0) 0
Mallorca	(1) 4	Apoel Nicosia	(1) 2
Malmo	(0) 0	Sporting Lisbon	(0) 1
Molde	(1) 3	Uniao Leiria	(1) 1
Neuchatel Xamax	(0) 0	Auxerre	(0) 1
NEC Nijmegen	(1) 1	Wisla	(1) 2
Nordsjaelland	(0) 0	Panionios	(0) 1
Parma	(1) 3	Metalurg	(0) 0
Petrzalka	(0) 1	Bordeaux	(0) 1
Publikum	(1) 2	Maccabi Haifa	(0) 2
Red Star Belgrade	(3) 4	Odense	(2) 3
Rosenborg	(3) 6	Ventspils	(0) 0
Schalke	(0) 1	Kamen	(0) 0
Shakhtjor Donetsk	(2) 2	Dinamo Bucharest	(1) 3
Slavia Prague	(2) 2	Sartid	(0) 1
Sochaux	(0) 2	MyPa	(0) 0
Teplice	(0) 1	Kaiserslautern	(0) 0
Torpedo Moscow	(1) 1	CSKA Sofia	(0) 1
(aet; Torpedo Moscow won 3-2 on penalties.)			
Trabzonspor	(0) 2	Villarreal	(0) 3
Udinese	(1) 1	Salzburg	(0) 2

Valencia	(0) 1	AIK Stockholm	(0) 0
Vardar	(1) 1	Roma	(0) 1
Viktoria Zizkov	(0) 0	Brondby	(0) 1
Zilina	(0) 0	Utrecht	(1) 4
Blackburn Rovers	(0) 1	Genclerbirligi	(0) 1
Liverpool	(2) 3	Olimpija	(0) 0
Lokeren	(0) 0	Manchester City	(0) 1
NAC Breda	(0) 0	Newcastle United	(0) 1
Perugia	(0) 1	Dundee	(0) 0
Steaua	(0) 1	Southampton	(0) 0
Zeljeznicar	(0) 0	Hearts	(0) 0

SECOND ROUND, FIRST LEG

Benfica	(1) 3	Molde	(0) 1
Borussia Dortmund	(0) 2	Sochaux	(2) 2
Dynamo Zagreb	(0) 0	Dnepr	(1) 2
FC Copenhagen	(1) 1	Mallorca	(1) 2
Feyenoord	(0) 0	Teplice	(1) 2
Gaziantep	(1) 3	Lens	(0) 0
Genclerbirligi	(0) 1	Sporting Lisbon	(0) 1
PAOK Salonika	(1) 1	Debrecen	(1) 1
Panionios	(0) 0	Barcelona	(1) 3
Perugia	(0) 2	Aris Salonika	(0) 0
Roma	(0) 1	Hajduk Split	(0) 0
Rosenborg	(0) 0	Red Star Belgrade	(0) 0
Salzburg	(0) 0	Parma	(0) 4
Schalke	(0) 2	Brondby	(1) 1
Slavia Prague	(1) 2	Levski	(0) 2
Spartak Moscow	(1) 4	Dinamo Bucharest	(0) 0
Utrecht	(0) 0	Auxerre	(0) 0
Valencia	(0) 0	Maccabi Haifa	(0) 0
Valerenga	(0) 0	Wisla	(0) 0
Villarreal	(0) 2	Torpedo Moscow	(0) 0
Basle	(2) 2	Newcastle United	(2) 3
Bordeaux	(0) 0	Hearts	(0) 1
Manchester City	(1) 1	Groclin	(0) 1
Steaua	(0) 1	Liverpool	(1) 1

SECOND ROUND, SECOND LEG

Aris Salonika	(0) 1	Perugia	(1) 1
Auxerre	(2) 4	Utrecht	(0) 0
Barcelona	(2) 2	Panionios	(0) 0
Brondby	(1) 2	Schalke	(0) 1
(aet; Brondby won 3-1 on penalties.)			
Debrecen	(0) 0	PAOK Salonika	(0) 0
Dynamo Bucharest	(1) 3	Spartak Moscow	(0) 1
Dnepr	(0) 1	Dynamo Zagreb	(0) 1
Hajduk Split	(1) 1	Roma	(0) 1
Lens	(0) 1	Gaziantep	(1) 3
Levski	(0) 0	Slavia Prague	(0) 0
Maccabi Haifa (*in Rotterdam*)	(0) 0	Valencia	(2) 4
Mallorca	(0) 0	FC Copenhagen	(0) 1
Molde	(0) 0	Benfica	(2) 2
Parma	(3) 5	Salzburg	(0) 0
Red Star Belgrade	(0) 0	Rosenborg	(0) 1
Sochaux	(1) 4	Borussia Dortmund	(0) 0
Sporting Lisbon	(0) 0	Genclerbirligi	(2) 3
Teplice	(1) 1	Feyenoord	(1) 1
Torpedo Moscow	(0) 1	Villarreal	(0) 0
Wisla	(0) 0	Valerenga	(0) 0
(aet; Valerenga won 4-3 on penalties.)			

Groclin	(0) 0	Manchester City	(0) 0
Hearts	(0) 0	Bordeaux	(1) 2
Liverpool	(0) 1	Steaua	(0) 0
Newcastle United	(1) 1	Basle	(0) 0

THIRD ROUND, FIRST LEG

Auxerre	(0) 0	Panathinaikos	(0) 0
Benfica	(0) 1	Rosenborg	(0) 0
Brondby	(0) 0	Barcelona	(0) 1
FC Brugge	(1) 1	Debrecen	(0) 0
Galatasaray	(1) 2	Villarreal	(2) 2
Gaziantep	(1) 1	Roma	(0) 0
Groclin	(0) 0	Bordeaux	(0) 1
Marseille	(0) 1	Dnepr	(0) 0
Parma	(0) 0	Genclerbirligi	(0) 1
Perugia	(0) 0	PSV Eindhoven	(0) 0
Sochaux	(0) 2	Internazionale	(1) 2
Spartak Moscow	(0) 0	Mallorca	(0) 3
Valencia	(2) 3	Besiktas	(2) 2
Celtic	(2) 3	Teplice	(0) 0
Liverpool	(0) 2	Levski	(0) 0
Valerenga	(0) 1	Newcastle United	(1) 1

THIRD ROUND, SECOND LEG

Barcelona	(2) 2	Brondby	(0) 1
Besiktas	(0) 0	Valencia	(1) 2
Bordeaux	(2) 4	Groclin	(0) 1
Debrecen	(0) 0	FC Brugge	(0) 0
Dnepr	(0) 0	Marseille	(0) 0
Genclerbirligi	(1) 3	Parma	(0) 0
Internazionale	(0) 0	Sochaux	(0) 0
Mallorca	(0) 0	Spartak Moscow	(1) 1
Panathinaikos	(0) 0	Auxerre	(0) 1
PSV Eindhoven	(2) 3	Perugia	(0) 1
Roma	(2) 2	Gaziantep	(0) 0
Rosenborg	(2) 2	Benfica	(1) 1
Villarreal	(0) 3	Galatasaray	(0) 0
Levski	(2) 2	Liverpool	(3) 4
Newcastle United	(1) 3	Valerenga	(1) 1
Teplice	(1) 1	Celtic	(0) 0

FOURTH ROUND, FIRST LEG

Auxerre	(1) 1	PSV Eindhoven	(0) 1
Benfica	(0) 0	Internazionale	(0) 0
Bordeaux	(0) 3	FC Brugge	(0) 1
Genclerbirligi	(1) 1	Valencia	(0) 0
Villarreal	(2) 2	Roma	(0) 0
Celtic	(0) 1	Barcelona	(0) 0
Liverpool	(0) 1	Marseille	(0) 1
Newcastle United	(0) 4	Mallorca	(0) 1

FOURTH ROUND, SECOND LEG

FC Brugge	(0) 0	Bordeaux	(0) 1
Internazionale	(1) 4	Benfica	(1) 3
PSV Eindhoven	(2) 3	Auxerre	(0) 0
Roma	(1) 2	Villarreal	(0) 1
Valencia	(0) 2	Genclerbirligi	(0) 0
(aet; Valencia won on sudden death.)			
Barcelona	(0) 0	Celtic	(0) 0
Mallorca	(0) 0	Newcastle United	(0) 3
Marseille	(1) 2	Liverpool	(1) 1

QUARTER-FINALS, FIRST LEG

Bordeaux	(1) 1	Valencia	(0) 2
Marseille	(0) 1	Internazionale	(0) 0
Celtic	(0) 1	Villarreal	(1) 1
PSV Eindhoven	(1) 1	Newcastle United	(1) 1

QUARTER-FINALS, SECOND LEG

Internazionale	(0) 0	Marseille	(0) 1
Valencia	(0) 2	Bordeaux	(0) 1
Newcastle United	(1) 2	PSV Eindhoven	(0) 1
Villarreal	(1) 2	Celtic	(0) 0

SEMI-FINALS, FIRST LEG

Villarreal	(0) 0	Valencia	(0) 0
Newcastle United	(0) 0	Marseille	(0) 0

SEMI-FINALS, SECOND LEG

Valencia	(1) 1	Villarreal	(0) 0
Marseille	(1) 2	Newcastle United	(0) 0

UEFA CUP FINAL 2004

Wednesday, 19 May 2004

(in Gothenburg, 40,000)

Valencia (1) 2 *(Vicente 45 (pen), Mista 47)*   **Marseille (0) 0**

Valencia: Canizares; Curro Torres, Carboni, Baraja, Ayala, Marchena (Pellegrino 86), Rufete (Aimar 64), Albelda, Angulo (Sissoko 83), Mista, Vicente.

Marseille: Barthez[a]; Ferreira, Dos Santos, Beye, Hemdani, Meite, Flamini (Batiles 71), Meriem (Gavanon 45), Marlet, Drogba, N'Diaye (Celestini 84).

Referee: P. Collina (Italy).

UEFA CUP 2004–2005
From the 2004–05 season, the UEFA Cup will adopt a new format that will include a group stage alongside the traditional two-legged format, with the final continuing as a single match.

ALTERED FORMAT
Two qualifying rounds and the first round proper will open the competition, at which point 40 clubs will advance to the group stage. This part of the competition comprises eight groups of five teams with two matches at home and two matches away for each team in each group. The winners, runners-up and third-placed team advance to the knock-out phase, at which point they are joined by the eight clubs which finish in third place in each of the groups in the UEFA Champions League group phase. From this point, the 32 clubs embark on a knock-out competition, playing two matches against each other on a home and away basis. The club scoring the greater aggregate of goals qualifying for the next round. In the event of both teams scoring the same number of goals, the team which scores more goals away qualifies. The final is decided by a single match.

ENGLISH PARTICIPATING CLUBS
England: Newcastle U, Middlesbrough, Millwall.

PAST EUROPEAN CUP FINALS

1956	Real Madrid	4	Stade de Rheims	3
1957	Real Madrid	2	Fiorentina	0
1958	Real Madrid	3	AC Milan	2*
1959	Real Madrid	2	Stade de Rheims	0
1960	Real Madrid	7	Eintracht Frankfurt	3
1961	Benfica	3	Barcelona	2
1962	Benfica	5	Real Madrid	3
1963	AC Milan	2	Benfica	1
1964	Internazionale	3	Real Madrid	1
1965	Internazionale	1	SL Benfica	0
1966	Real Madrid	2	Partizan Belgrade	1
1967	Celtic	2	Internazionale	1
1968	Manchester U	4	Benfica	1*
1969	AC Milan	4	Ajax	1
1970	Feyenoord	2	Celtic	1*
1971	Ajax	2	Panathinaikos	0
1972	Ajax	2	Internazionale	0
1973	Ajax	1	Juventus	0
1974	Bayern Munich	1 4	Atletico Madrid	1 0
1975	Bayern Munich	2	Leeds U	0
1976	Bayern Munich	1	St Etienne	0
1977	Liverpool	3	Borussia Moenchengladbach	1
1978	Liverpool	1	FC Brugge	0
1979	Nottingham F	1	Malmö	0
1980	Nottingham F	1	Hamburg	0
1981	Liverpool	1	Real Madrid	0
1982	Aston Villa	1	Bayern Munich	0
1983	Hamburg	1	Juventus	0
1984	Liverpool†	1	Roma	1
1985	Juventus	1	Liverpool	0
1986	Steaua Bucharest†	0	Barcelona	0
1987	Porto	2	Bayern Munich	1
1988	PSV Eindhoven†	0	Benfica	0
1989	AC Milan	4	Steaua Bucharest	0
1990	AC Milan	1	Benfica	0
1991	Red Star Belgrade†	0	Marseille	0
1992	Barcelona	1	Sampdoria	0

PAST UEFA CHAMPIONS LEAGUE FINALS

1993	Marseille	1	AC Milan	0
(Marseille subsequently stripped of title)			
1994	AC Milan	4	Barcelona	0
1995	Ajax	1	AC Milan	0
1996	Juventus†	1	Ajax	1
1997	Borussia Dortmund	3	Juventus	1
1998	Real Madrid	1	Juventus	0
1999	Manchester U	2	Bayern Munich	1
2000	Real Madrid	3	Valencia	0
2001	Bayern Munich†	1	Valencia	1
2002	Real Madrid	2	Leverkusen	1
2003	AC Milan†	0	Juventus	0
2004	Porto	3	Monaco	0

† aet; won on penalties.
* aet.

229

PAST EUROPEAN CUP-WINNERS FINALS

Year	Winner		Runner-up	
1961	Fiorentina	4	Rangers	1‡
1962	Atletico Madrid	1 3	Fiorentina	1 0
1963	Tottenham H.	5	Atletico Madrid	1
1964	Sporting Lisbon	3 1	MTK Budapest	3* 0
1965	West Ham U.	2	Munich 1860	0
1966	Borussia Dortmund	2	Liverpool	1*
1967	Bayern Munich	1	Rangers	0*
1968	AC Milan	2	Hamburg	0
1969	Slovan Bratislava	3	Barcelona	2
1970	Manchester C	2	Gornik Zabrze	1
1971	Chelsea	1 2	Real Madrid	1* 1*
1972	Rangers	3	Dynamo Moscow	2
1973	AC Milan	1	Leeds U	0
1974	Magdeburg	2	AC Milan	0
1975	Dynamo Kiev	3	Ferencvaros	0
1976	Anderlecht	4	West Ham U	2
1977	Hamburg	2	Anderlecht	0
1978	Anderlecht	4	Austria Vienna	0
1979	Barcelona	4	Fortuna Dusseldorf	3*
1980	Valencia†	0	Arsenal	0
1981	Dynamo Tbilisi	2	Carl Zeiss Jena	1
1982	Barcelona	2	Standard Liege	1
1983	Aberdeen	2	Real Madrid	1*
1984	Juventus	2	Porto	1
1985	Everton	3	Rapid Vienna	1
1986	Dynamo Kiev	3	Atletico Madrid	0
1987	Ajax	1	Lokomotiv Leipzig	0
1988	Mechelen	1	Ajax	0
1989	Barcelona	2	Sampdoria	0
1990	Sampdoria	2	Anderlecht	0
1991	Manchester U	2	Barcelona	1
1992	Werder Bremen	2	Monaco	0
1993	Parma	3	Antwerp	1
1994	Arsenal	1	Parma	0
1995	Real Zaragoza	2	Arsenal	1*
1996	Paris St Germain	1	Rapid Vienna	0
1997	Barcelona	1	Paris St Germain	0
1998	Chelsea	1	Stuttgart	0
1999	Lazio	2	Mallorca	1

PAST FAIRS CUP FINALS

Year	Winner		Runner-up	
1958	Barcelona	8	London	2‡
1960	Barcelona	4	Birmingham C	1‡
1961	Roma	4	Birmingham C	2‡
1962	Valencia	7	Barcelona	3‡
1963	Valencia	4	Dynamo Zagreb	1‡
1964	Real Zaragoza	2	Valencia	1
1965	Ferencvaros	1	Juventus	0
1966	Barcelona	4	Real Zaragoza	3‡
1967	Dynamo Zagreb	2	Leeds U	0‡
1968	Leeds U	1	Ferencvaros	0‡
1969	Newcastle U	6	Ujpest Dozsa	2‡
1970	Arsenal	4	Anderlecht	3‡
1971	Leeds U**	3	Juventus	3‡

*After extra time   **Won on away goals   †Won on penalties   ‡Aggregate score

PAST UEFA CUP FINALS

Year	Winner			Runner-up		
1972	Tottenham H	2	1	Wolverhampton W	1	1
1973	Liverpool	3	0	Borussia Moenchengladbach	0	2
1974	Feyenoord	2	2	Tottenham H	2	0
1975	Borussia Moenchengladbach	0	5	Twente Enschede	0	1
1976	Liverpool	3	1	FC Brugge	2	1
1977	Juventus**	1	1	Athletic Bilbao	0	2
1978	PSV Eindhoven	0	3	SEC Bastia	0	0
1979	Borussia Moenchengladbach	1	1	Red Star Belgrade	1	0
1980	Borussia Moenchengladbach	3	0	Eintracht Frankfurt**	2	1
1981	Ipswich T	3	2	AZ 67 Alkmaar	0	4
1982	IFK Gothenburg	1	3	SV Hamburg	0	0
1983	Anderlecht	1	1	Benfica	0	1
1984	Tottenham H†	1	1	RSC Anderlecht	1	1
1985	Real Madrid	3	0	Videoton	0	1
1986	Real Madrid	5	0	Cologne	1	2
1987	IFK Gothenburg	1	1	Dundee U	0	1
1988	Bayer Leverkusen†	0	3	Espanol	0	3
1989	Napoli	2	3	Stuttgart	1	3
1990	Juventus	3	0	Fiorentina	1	0
1991	Internazionale	2	0	AS Roma	0	1
1992	Ajax**	0	2	Torino	0	2
1993	Juventus	3	3	Borussia Dortraund	1	0
1994	Internazionale	1	1	Salzburg	0	0
1995	Parma	1	1	Juventus	0	1
1996	Bayern Munich	2	3	Bordeaux	0	1
1997	Schalke*†	1	0	Internazionale	0	1
1998	Internazionale		3	Lazio		0
1999	Parma		3	Marseille		0
2000	Galatasaray†		0	Arsenal		0
2001	Liverpool§		5	Alaves		4
2002	Feyenoord		3	Borussia Dortmund		2
2003	Porto*		3	Celtic		2
2004	Valencia		2	Marseille		0

*After extra time   **Won on away goals   †Won on penalties
§Won on sudden death.

EURO 2004 REVIEW

The Greeks clearly have a word or two for it, roughly translated means something along the lines of surprise packets. Starting the final stages of Euro 2004 with scarcely the best record in the competition throughout its history, or any other major tournament for that matter, they were ranked 20th in terms of achievement in the European Championships. Such statistics count for nothing of course, especially when you go on to win it.

Opening with victory over the host nation Portugal was just the start. Then came the elimination of the favourites France and already Greece entered the record books as the first country to beat the hosts and then the holders in the same final tournament. The icing on this particular Greek dish came with the mouth-watering reprise for them of beating Portugal again in the final itself.

In between though there had been the narrow squeak of losing to Russia, arguably the only match they might have been expected to win at all! This was after being held to a draw by Spain before taking the French on and beating them in the quarter-finals. The Czech Republic had been the sole 100 per cent team in the competition, but the Greeks kept up a tremendous work rate and snatched the crucial silver goal in the dying moments.

Perhaps it was no surprise in a competition where the fancied fell by the wayside. The old order casualties numbered the perennial under-achievers Spain, Italy, Germany and Holland, not to mention England. At one stage after losing their opening fixture against France in overtime, England began to score goals freely and seemed a threat when other more favoured entries were being knocked out.

It came to a halt against Portugal who had reorganised after the initial defeat by Greece. But the match went to extra time and penalties before the Portuguese came through. The Dutch were always chasing the game with Portugal and only really mounted a threat when gifted an own goal to reduce the deficit to 2-1. Wily coach Felipe Scolari who had led Brazil to their 2002 World Cup triumph was on the threshold of another major trophy. But it was not to be.

Greece's German born coach Otto Rehhagel had had a modest playing career in the 1960s with Hertha Berlin and Kaiserslautern before taking a clutch of German clubs under his wing to varying degrees of success. He took over the national spot in Greece in 2001. His final opponent Luiz Felipe Scolari had only been in charge of Portugal from January 2003 and with no qualification required as the host nation he had the difficult task of selecting and watching his players perform without the aid of competitive football.

This may have accounted for the disappointing display in the opening match with Greece. But he made swift changes to the team and pulled them together with the help of the support of the Portuguese people who like Greece had never seen their team win a major tournament.

Other than Greece, the team who probably surpassed their wildest expectations were Latvia who arrived at the finals via the play-offs where they defeated Turkey, the team which had won plaudits back in the 2002 World Cup.

Lativa led the Czechs, could have beaten the Germans and only in the last match with Holland did they concede three goals and finish well beaten. The Dutch again showed a lack of discipline at times and tactically were criticised at home and abroad. Spain lived up to their reputation of never managing to reach the level of performance many of their leading players achieve at club level.

However for the French, Germans and Italians this was seen by many to be a turning point in their fortunes – for the worst. The French had come into the competition with expectations after the woeful displays in the 2002 World Cup and after a run of success in non-competitive matches afterwards. Germany gave arguably their poorest showing in a major final, while the Italians looked lacklustre in the extreme.

The Swedes and Danes had their moments without convincing anyone they could win a tournament of surprises, nor the Swiss, Croats and Russians failed to impress overall, while Bulgaria as expected made their traditional early exit. Failure from the penalty spot again proved the excuse for England's ticket home.

In the final Greece man-marked to perfection, defended resolutely and ran all night. Portugal needed better performances from their three stars Figo, Deco and Ronaldo than they received. The final ball was invariably weak and ill-directed. Rui Costa might have improved matters had he been introduced earlier. As it was Charisteas' header from a poorly defended corner was enough.

EURO 2004 QUALIFYING RESULTS

■ *Denotes player sent off.*
NB: Places for teams level on points determined by results between them.

GROUP 1

Nicosia, 7 September 2002, 11,898

Cyprus (1) 1 *(Okkas 14)*   **France (1) 2** *(Cisse 39, Wiltord 52)*
Cyprus: Panayiotou N; Theodotou, Daskalakis (Michael 68), Ioakim, Konnafis, Spyrou, Kaiafas, Satsias, Nicolaou N (Agathocleous 74), Rauffmann (Yiasoumi 62), Okkas.
France: Coupet; Thuram, Christanval, Desailly, Silvestre, Wiltord (Kapo 79), Makelele, Zidane, Vieira, Marlet (Govou 70), Cisse.
Referee: Fandel (Germany).

Ljubljana, 7 September 2002, 15,000

Slovenia (1) 3 *(Debono 37 (og), Siljak 59, Cimerotic 90)*   **Malta (0) 0**
Slovenia: Simeunovic; Vugdalic, Bulajic, Knavs, Karic, Sukalo (Gajser 74), Acimovic (Radosavljevic 86), Zahovic, Pavlin, Siljak, Cimerotic.
Malta: Muscat; Said, Dimech, Carabott, Debono, Chetcuti, Agius, Giglio■, Mallia (Bogdanovic 71), Nwoko, Michael Mifsud (Mifsud A 88).
Referee: Borovilos (Greece).

Stade de France, 12 October 2002, 77,619

France (2) 5 *(Vieira 10, Marlet 35, 64, Wiltord 79, Govou 86)*   **Slovenia (0) 0**
France: Barthez; Thuram (Sagnol 84), Silvestre, Vieira, Gallas, Desailly, Wiltord (Cheyrou 87), Makelele, Marlet (Govou 80), Zidane, Henry.
Slovenia: Simeunovic; Gajser■, Karic (Filekovic 88), Sukalo, Vugdalic, Cipot, Zahovic, Radosavljevic (Zlogar 68), Siljak, Pavlin, Cimerotic (Ceh N 46).
Referee: Nielsen (Denmark).

Valletta, 12 October 2002, 4000

Malta (0) 0   **Israel (0) 2** *(Balili 57, Revivo 77)*
Malta: Muscat; Said, Dimech, Chetcuti, Carabott, Debono, Agius (Mallia 84), Turner, Brincat (Mifsud A 76), Nwoko (Bogdanovic 64), Michael Mifsud.
Israel: Auat; Zano, Domb, Banin, Badir, Benado, Keissi, Balili (Benayoun 71), Revivo, Tal (Antebi 82), Berkovic.
Referee: Shebek (Ukraine).

Valletta, 16 October 2002, 12,000

Malta (0) 0   **France (2) 4** *(Henry 25, 35, Wiltord 59, Carriere 84)*
Malta: Muscat; Carabott, Chetcuti, Debono (Miguel Mifsud 87), Said, Dimech, Agius, Michael Mifsud, Giglio, Nwoko (Bogdanovic 46), Brincat (Mallia 69).
France: Barthez; Thuram, Silvestre, Vieira (Dacourt 70), Gallas (Mexes 84), Desailly, Wiltord, Makelele, Marlet, Zidane, Henry (Carriere 78).
Referee: Tudor (Romania).

Nicosia, 20 November 2002, 5000

Cyprus (0) 2 *(Rauffmann 50, Okkas 74)*   **Malta (0) 1** *(Michael Mifsud 90)*
Cyprus: Panayiotou N; Konnafis, Ioakim, Spyrou, Okkarides, Theodotou, Satsias (Michael), Kaiafas, Okkas, Rauffmann (Yiasoumi 71), Constantinou M (Nicolaou N 66).
Malta: Muscat; Said, Mamo (Miguel Mifsud 74), Giglio (Theuma 80), Chetcuti, Carabott, Agius, Dimech, Michael Mifsud, Bogdanovic, Mifsud A (Mallia 61).
Referee: Guenov (Bulgaria).

Limassol, 29 March 2003, 5000

Cyprus (0) 1 *(Rauffmann 61)*   **Israel (1) 1** *(Afek 2)*
Cyprus: Panayiotou N; Okkarides, Ioakim (Nicolaou N 46) (Daskalakis 77), Konnafis, Spyrou, Theodotou, Engomitis (Rauffmann 60), Kaiafas, Tomic, Constantinou M, Okkas.
Israel: Auat; Benado, Ben-Haim, Keissi, Harazi A (Abuksis 85), Banin, Badir, Afek (Benayoun 73), Zandberg (Nimny 66), Tal, Revivo.
Referee: McCurry (Scotland).

Lens, 29 March 2003, 40,775

France (2) 6 *(Wiltord 36, Henry 38, 54, Zidane 57 (pen), 81, Trezeguet 70)*   Malta (0) 0
France: Barthez; Thuram (Sagnol 65), Lizarazu, Pedretti, Gallas, Silvestre, Wiltord (Govou 75), Makelele, Trezeguet, Zidane, Henry (Rothen 80).
Malta: Muscat; Carabott, Ciantar, Said, Vella, Mamo (Chetcuti 71), Bogdanovic (Turner 62), Dimech, Mallia, Michael Mifsud, Nwoko.
Referee: Bozinovski (Macedonia).

Palermo, 2 April 2003, 5000

Israel (1) 1 *(Afek 2)*   France (2) 2 *(Trezeguet 23, Zidane 45)*
Israel: Auat; Benado, Ben-Haim, Keissi, Harazi A, Abuksis, Banin (Benayoun 74), Tal (Badir 56), Afek, Turgeman (Zandberg 46), Revivo.
France: Barthez; Thuram, Lizarazu, Vieira, Gallas, Silvestre, Wiltord (Govou 66), Makelele, Trezeguet (Cisse 74), Zidane, Henry.
Referee: Barber (England).

Ljubljana, 2 April 2003, 5000

Slovenia (4) 4 *(Siljak 5, 14, Zahovic 39 (pen), Ceh A 43)*   Cyprus (1) 1 *(Constantinou M 10)*
Slovenia: Simeunovic; Cipot, Karic, Vugdalic, Bulajic, Zahovic, Ceh A, Pavlin, Sukalo, Koren (Zlogar 85), Siljak (Rakovic 90).
Cyprus: Panayiotou N; Konnafis (Ioakim 46), Daskalakis, Spyrou (Constantinou G 75), Theodotou, Kaiafas, Okkarides, Rauffmann (Charalambides 46), Tomic, Okkas, Constantinou M.
Referee: Gomes (Portugal).

Palermo, 30 April 2003, 1000

Israel (0) 2 *(Badir 88, Holtzman 90)*   Cyprus (0) 0
Israel: Elimelech; Zano, Afek, Benado, Ben-Haim, Banin (Badir 85), Keissi, Abuksis, Revivo, Turgeman (Benayoun 52), Zandberg (Holtzman 67).
Cyprus: Panayiotou N; Konnafis, Germanou, Nicolaou N, Tomic (Kaiafas 62), Engomitis (Chrisostomos 80), Theodotou, Nicolaou C (Yiasoumi 89), Okkarides, Okkas, Constantinou M.
Referee: Benes (Czech Republic).

Valletta, 30 April 2003, 2500

Malta (0) 1 *(Michael Mifsud 90)*   Slovenia (2) 3 *(Zahovic 15, Siljak 36, 57)*
Malta: Muscat; Ciantar, Vella, Carabott, Said, Turner, Dimech, Giglio (Camenzuli 69), Mallia, Michael Mifsud, Nwoko (Bogdanovic 63).
Slovenia: Simeunovic; Cipot, Vugdalic, Karic, Oslaj (Snofl 61), Sukalo, Ceh N, Zahovic, Pavlin, Siljak (Rakovic 90), Gajser (Koren 78).
Referee: Hanacsek (Hungary).

Antalya, 7 June 2003, 2500

Israel (0) 0   Slovenia (0) 0
Israel: Elimelech; Benado, Banin, Keissi, Afek (Zandberg 71), Nimny, Tal (Bachar 76), Abuksis (Holtzman 86), Revivo, Zano, Benayoun.
Slovenia: Simeunovic; Cipot, Vugdalic, Knavs, Gajser (Koren 71), Sukalo, Pavlin, Karic, Zahovic, Acimovic (Snofl 86), Siljak.
Referee: Busacca (Switzerland).

Ta'Qali, 7 June 2003, 3000

Malta (0) 1 *(Dimech 72)*   Cyprus (1) 2 *(Constantinou M 23 (pen), 52)*
Malta: Darmanin[a]; Camenzuli, Said (Bogdanovic 86), Carabott, Vella, Giglio, Dimech, Mallia (Agius 66), Turner, Michael Mifsud, Nwoko (Muscat 23).
Cyprus: Panayiotou N; Konnafis, Charalambides (Garpozis 90), Daskalakis (Foukaris 65), Christodoulou, Satsias, Okkarides, Michael, Ilia, Okkas (Yiasoumi 78), Constantinou M.
Referee: Brugger (Austria).

Saint-Denis, 6 September 2003, 55,000

France (3) 5 *(Trezeguet 7, 82, Wiltord 20, 41, Henry 59)*   **Cyprus (0) 0**
France: Barthez; Thuram (Sagnol 65), Lizarazu, Makelele, Desailly, Silvestre, Wiltord, Vieira (Dacourt 71), Trezeguet, Henry (Marlet 78), Pires.
Cyprus: Panayiotou N; Okkarides, Georghiou N, Theodotou, Konnafis (Ioakim 46), Engomitis (Michael C 58), Nicolaou N, Kaiafas, Satsias, Okkas, Constantinou M (Yiasoumi 67).
Referee: Irvine (Northern Ireland).

Ljubljana, 6 September 2003, 8000

Slovenia (2) 3 *(Siljak 35, Knavs 37, Ceh N 78)*   **Israel (0) 1** *(Revivo 69)*
Slovenia: Simeunovic; Cipot, Karic, Snofl, Knavs, Sukalo, Ceh N (Rudonja 89), Zahovic, Kapic (Seslar 84), Acimovic, Siljak (Cimerotic 64).
Israel: Elimelech; Harazi, Ben-Haim[*], Benado, Keissi (Balili 46), Abuksis (Badir 77), Tal, Berkovic, Benayoun, Revivo, Nimny[*].
Referee: Fandel (Germany).

Antalya, 10 September 2003, 300

Israel (1) 2 *(Revivo 16, Abuksis 78)*   **Malta (0) 2** *(Michael Mifsud 51 (pen), Carabott 52)*
Israel: Elimelech; Harazi, Benado, Gershon, Zandberg (Benayoun 62), Revivo, Abuksis, Berkovic (Afek 43), Tal, Balili, Badir.
Malta: Muscat; Barbara, Chetcuti, Carabott, Said, Camenzuli, Turner, Giglio (Theuma 79), Michael Mifsud, Bogdanovic (Galea 69), Nwoko (Mifsud A 88).
Referee: Blareau (Bulgaria).

Ljubljana, 10 September 2003, 8000

Slovenia (0) 0   France (1) 2 *(Trezeguet 10, Dacourt 71)*
Slovenia: Simeunovic; Vugdalic (Snofl 83), Knavs, Cipot, Karic, Acimovic, Sukalo (Kapic 55), Pavlin, Ceh N, Zahovic (Cimerotic 65), Siljak.
France: Barthez; Thuram, Lizarazu, Makelele[*], Desailly, Silvestre, Wiltord (Sagnol 76), Vieira, Trezeguet (Dacourt 69), Henry, Zidane (Pires 79).
Referee: Messina (Italy).

Limassol, 11 October 2003, 2346

Cyprus (0) 2 *(Georgiou S 74, Yiasoumi 84)*   **Slovenia (2) 2** *(Siljak 12, 42)*
Cyprus: Panayiotou N; Georgiou S, Georgiou N (Lambrou 80), Antoniou, Nicolaou N, Ilia, Constantinou M (Charalambous 46), Yiasoumi, Okkarides, Iakovou, Engomitis (Eleftheriou 42).
Slovenia: Simeunovic; Cipot (Bulajic 26), Vugdalic, Knavs, Sukalo, Ceh N, Siljak, Pavlin, Rudonja (Koren 85), Kapic, Acimovic.
Referee: Ovrebo (Norway).

Saint-Denis, 11 October 2003, 57,009

France (3) 3 *(Henry 9, Trezeguet 25, Boumsong 43)*   **Israel (0) 0**
France: Barthez; Reveillere, Thuram, Boumsong, Lizarazu, Dacourt, Pedretti, Pires (Giuly 85), Zidane, Henry (Cisse 77), Trezeguet (Marlet 85).
Israel: Davidovich; Harazi, Benado, Gershon, Keissi, Zeituni (Balili 89), Tal, Badir (Udi 76), Benayoun, Zandberg (Abuksis 46), Revivo.
Referee: Bolognino (Italy).

Group 1 Final Table	P	W	D	L	F	A	Pts
France	8	8	0	0	29	2	24
Slovenia	8	4	2	2	15	12	14
Israel	8	2	3	3	9	11	9
Cyprus	8	2	2	4	9	18	8
Malta	8	0	1	7	5	24	1

GROUP 2

Sarajevo, 7 September 2002, 4500

Bosnia (0) 0   Romania (3) 3 *(Chivu 8, Munteanu D 10, Ganea 28)*
Bosnia: Piplica; Beslija (Brkic 41), Music, Hibic, Rizvic, Hota, Ikanovic (Huric 37), Bajramovic (Akrapovic 46), Salihamidzic, Muratovic, Mulina.

235

Romania: Stelea (Vintila 33); Contra, Radoi, Popescu, Chivu, Codrea (Ghioane 84), Munteanu D, Munteanu V, Mutu, Ganea, Niculae (Cernat 66).
Referee: Cardoso (Portugal).

Oslo, 7 September 2002, 25,114

Norway (0) 2 *(Riise 55, Carew 90)*   **Denmark (1) 2** *(Tomasson 23, 72)*
Norway: Grodas; Basma, Berg, Johnsen R, Bergdolmo, Leonhardsen (Strand 77), Andersen T (Carew 77), Bakke (Larsen S 88), Riise, Iversen, Solskjaer.
Denmark: Sorensen; Helveg, Laursen, Lustu, Jensen N, Rommedahl (Michaelsen 59), Poulsen, Gravesen, Gronkjaer (Jensen C 70), Tomasson (Nielsen P 90), Sand.
Referee: Dallas (Scotland).

Copenhagen, 12 October 2002, 40,259

Denmark (0) 2 *(Tomasson 51 (pen), Sand 71)*   **Luxembourg (0) 0**
Denmark: Jensen S; Bogelund, Jensen N, Gravesen, Henriksen, Poulsen, Rommedahl (Gronkjaer 67), Jensen C (Lovenkrands 67), Tomasson, Sand, Jorgensen (Roll 75).
Luxembourg: Besic; Ferron, Deville F, Reiter, Hoffmann, Strasser, Remy, Holtz (Di Domenico 72), Leweck, Braun G (Huss 79), Cardoni.
Referee: Bede (Hungary).

Bucharest, 12 October 2002, 21,000

Romania (0) 0   Norway (0) 1 *(Iversen 84)*
Romania: Vintila; Contra, Rat, Radoi, Popescu, Chivu, Codrea, Munteanu D (Pancu 85), Ganea (Niculae 64), Moldovan (Ilie 64), Mutu.
Norway: Myhre; Bergdolmo, Basma, Bakke, Lundekvam, Berg, Iversen, Andersen T, Carew (Leonhardsen 80), Solskjaer (Rushfeldt 89), Riise.
Referee: Ivanov (Russia).

Luxembourg, 16 October 2002, 2056

Luxembourg (0) 0   Romania (4) 7 *(Moldovan 2, 5, Radoi 24, Contra 45, 47, 86, Ghioane 80)*
Luxembourg: Besic; Ferron, Deville F, Leweck, Hoffmann, Strasser, Holtz (Rohmann 76), Reiter, Remy, Braun G (Huss 71), Cardoni (Schneider 60).
Romania: Vintila; Contra, Rat, Munteanu D, Radoi, Popescu, Codrea (Ghioane 36), Moldovan (Cernat 69), Ilie, Ganea (Pancu 46), Miu.
Referee: Lajuks (Latvia).

Oslo, 16 October 2002, 24,169

Norway (2) 2 *(Lundekvam 7, Riise 27)*   **Bosnia (0) 0**
Norway: Olsen; Basma, Bergdolmo, Andersen T (Larsen S 90), Berg, Lundekvam, Leonhardsen (Carew 65), Bakke, Solskjaer (Rushfeldt 89), Iversen, Riise.
Bosnia: Tolja; Bosnjak (Mujcin 65), Papac, Bajramovic, Hibic, Konjic, Salihamidzic (Miskovic 85), Grujic, Baljic, Sabic (Huric 57), Music.
Referee: Benes (Czech Republic).

Zenica, 29 March 2003, 12,000

Bosnia (0) 2 *(Bolic 54, Barbarez 77)*   **Luxembourg (0) 0**
Bosnia: Hasagic; Biscevic (Berberovic 68), Konjic, Alihodzic, Bajramovic, Bolic (Turkovic 82), Beslija (Hrgovic 80), Baljic, Grujic, Music, Barbarez.
Luxembourg: Besic; Peters, Hoffmann, Strasser, Federspiel, Schauls, Remy, Molitor, Christophe (Huss 86), Braun G (Schneider 88), Leweck (Di Domenico 79).
Referee: Hyytia (Finland).

Bucharest, 29 March 2003, 50,000

Romania (1) 2 *(Mutu 5, Munteanu D 47)*   **Denmark (1) 5** *(Rommedahl 9, 90, Gravesen 53, Tomasson 71, Contra 73 (og))*
Romania: Lobont; Radoi, Popescu, Filipescu, Chivu, Contra, Codrea (Reghecampf 60), Munteanu D, Pancu (Bratu 68), Ganea, Mutu.
Denmark: Sorensen; Rytter (Michaelsen 34), Henriksen, Laursen, Jensen N, Rommedahl, Poulsen (Weighorst 68), Gravesen, Lovenkrands (Jorgensen 56), Tomasson, Sand.
Referee: Gonzalez (Spain).

236

Copenhagen, 2 April 2003, 30,845

Denmark (0) 0   Bosnia (2) 2 *(Barbarez 23, Baljic 29)*
Denmark: Sorensen; Michaelsen, Henriksen, Albrechtsen, Jensen N (Frandsen 81), Rommedahl, Jensen C (Wieghorst 60), Gravesen, Jorgensen, Tomasson (Berg S 85), Sand.
Bosnia: Hasagic; Berberovic, Music, Konjic, Bajramovic, Hibic, Beslija (Mulina 84), Hrgovic (Grujic 67), Biscevic, Baljic (Blatnjak 77), Barbarez.
Referee: Stredak (Slovakia).

Luxembourg, 2 April 2003, 3000

Luxembourg (0) 0   Norway (0) 2 *(Rushfeldt 60, Solskjaer 74)*
Luxembourg: Besic; Peters, Federspiel, Hoffmann, Strasser, Remy, Schauls, Molitor, Braun G (Schneider 75), Leweck (Lassine 89), Christophe (Huss 83).
Norway: Olsen; Bergdolmo, Johnsen, Berg, Basma, Rudi (Tessem 46), Andersen T, Bakke (Larsen S 86), Riise, Flo T (Rushfeldt 46), Solskjaer.
Referee: Dobrinov (Bulgaria).

Copenhagen, 7 June 2003, 41,824

Denmark (1) 1 *(Gronkjaer 6)*   **Norway (0) 0**
Denmark: Sorensen; Helveg, Laursen, Henriksen, Jensen N, Wieghorst, Gravesen, Gronkjaer (Rommedahl 70), Jensen C (Larsen 62), Jorgensen (Nielsen P 83), Sand.
Norway: Olsen; Basma, Johnsen R, Lundekvam, Bakke, Iversen, Andersen T (Bergdolmo 46), Leonhardsen (Flo T 62), Riise, Carew, Solskjaer (Flo H 89).
Referee: Poll (England).

Craiova, 7 June 2003, 37,000

Romania (0) 2 *(Mutu 46, Ganea 88)*   **Bosnia (0) 0**
Romania: Lobont; Contra, Iencsi, Chivu, Rat, Radoi, Codrea (Bundea 66), Pancu, Ganea, Mutu (Miu 86), Ilie (Soava 73).
Bosnia: Hasagic; Berberovic (Blatnjak 73), Music, Konjic, Bajramovic, Hibic, Bolic, Beslija (Bartolovic 47), Grujic, Barbarez, Hrgovic.
Referee: Bossen (Holland).

Luxembourg, 11 June 2003, 6869

Luxembourg (0) 0   Denmark (1) 2 *(Jensen C 22, Gravesen 50)*
Luxembourg: Besic; Federspiel, Schauls, Strasser, Remy, Reiter, Molitor, Leweck, Braun G (Christophe 70), Posing, Braun M.
Denmark: Sorensen; Bogelund (Larsen 52), Laursen, Henriksen, Jensen N, Wieghorst, Gravesen, Gronkjaer (Rommedahl 63), Jensen C, Jorgensen, Sand (Skoubo 74).
Referee: Baskakov (Russia).

Oslo, 11 June 2003, 24,890

Norway (0) 1 *(Solskjaer 78 (pen))*   **Romania (0) 1** *(Ganea 64)*
Norway: Olsen; Bergdolmo, Berg (Lundekvam 86), Johnsen R, Basma, Solskjaer, Bakke, Andersen T, Johnsen F (Flo T 70), Riise, Carew (Iversen 81).
Romania: Lobont; Contra, Iencsi, Chivu, Rat, Radoi, Soava, Pancu (Bratu 86), Ganea, Mutu, Ilie (Stoica 46).
Referee: Michel (Slovakia).

Zenica, 6 September 2003, 18,000

Bosnia (0) 1 *(Bajramovic 86)*   **Norway (0) 0**
Bosnia: Hasagic; Spahic, Konjic, Hibic, Papac, Salihamidzic (Beslija 66), Bajramovic, Grujic, Barbarez (Biscevic 87), Music (Hrgovic 70), Bolic.
Norway: Johnsen E; Basma, Berg H, Johnsen R, Bergdolmo, Solskjaer (Iversen 85), Andresen, Hangeland, Strand R (Solli 87), Riise, Carew (Flo T 77).
Referee: Bre (France).

Ploiesti, 6 September 2003, 4500

Romania (3) 4 *(Mutu 39, Pancu 42, Ganea 44, Bratu 77)*   **Luxembourg (0) 0**
Romania: Lobont; Stoican, Rat, Iencsi, Chivu (Soava 46), Radoi, Dumitru, Munteanu D, Ganea, Mutu (Bratu 46), Pancu (Stoica A 76).
Luxembourg: Besic; Peters, Federspiel, Hoffmann, Strasser, Remy, Schauls, Reiter, Leweck, Cardoni (Mannon 84), Braun G (Huss 84).
Referee: Yefet (Israel).

237

Copenhagen, 10 September 2003, 42,049

Denmark (1) 2 *(Tomasson 35 (pen), Laursen 90)*   **Romania (0) 2** *(Mutu 61, Pancu 72)*
Denmark: Sorensen; Wieghorst (Poulsen 64), Henriksen, Laursen, Jensen N, Helveg, Gravesen, Gronkjaer (Rommedahl 80), Tomasson (Jensen C 55), Martin Jorgensen, Sand.
Romania: Lobont; Stoican, Iencsi, Chivu, Rat, Dumitru (Cernat 70), Radoi, Pancu, Munteanu D, Ganea (Bratu 77), Mutu (Soava 90).
Referee: Meier (Switzerland).

Luxembourg, 10 September 2003, 3500

Luxembourg (0) 0   Bosnia (1) 1 *(Barbarez 36)*
Luxembourg: Besic; Peters, Federspiel (Engeldinger 55), Hoffmann, Strasser, Remy, Schauls, Reiter, Leweck, Braun G (Mannon 22), Huss.
Bosnia: Hasagic; Spahic, Turkovic, Konjic, Bajramovic, Hibic, Bolic (Beslija 62), Huric (Biscevic 62), Barbarez, Salihamidzic, Hrgovic (Papac 78).
Referee: Kapitanis (Cyprus).

Sarajevo, 11 October 2003, 35,500

Bosnia (1) 1 *(Bolic 39)*   **Denmark (1) 1** *(Martin Jorgensen 12)*
Bosnia: Hasagic; Spahic (Baljic 46), Music, Konjic (Hrgovic 79), Hibic, Bajramovic, Grujic (Biscevic 85), Barbarez, Salihamidzic, Beslija, Bolic.
Denmark: Sorensen; Wieghorst, Henriksen, Laursen, Helveg, Jensen N (Nielsen P 90), Gravesen■, Gronkjaer (Larsen 85), Poulsen, Tomasson, Martin Jorgensen (Rommedahl 55).
Referee: Barber (England).

Oslo, 11 October 2003, 22,255

Norway (1) 1 *(Flo T 18)*   **Luxembourg (0) 0**
Norway: Johnsen E; Basma, Lundekvam, Berg H, Riise, Strand R, Andresen, Winsnes (Andersen 80), Flo H (Johnsen F 69), Flo T (Rushfeldt 85), Brattbakk.
Luxembourg: Besic; Peters, Hoffmann, Schauls, Federspiel, Mannon (Di Domenico 71), Remy, Strasser, Leweck, Braun G, Huss.
Referee: Szabo (Hungary).

Group 2 Final Table	P	W	D	L	F	A	Pts
Denmark	8	4	3	1	15	9	15
Norway	8	4	2	2	9	5	14
Romania	8	4	2	2	21	9	14
Bosnia	8	4	1	3	7	8	13
Luxembourg	8	0	0	8	0	21	0

GROUP 3

Vienna, 7 September 2002, 18,300

Austria (2) 2 *(Herzog 4 (pen), 30 (pen))*   **Moldova (0) 0**
Austria: Manninger; Dospel, Baur, Martin Hiden, Panis, Schopp (Wimmer 58), Aufhauser, Herzog, Flogel, Vastic (Wagner 81), Wallner (Krankl 68).
Moldova: Hmaruc; Covalenco, Rebeja, Olexic, Sosnovschi, Priganiuc (Boret 68), Boicenco (Cebotari 46), Berco (Catinsus 46), Rogaciov, Ivanov, Clescenco.
Referee: Dougal (Scotland).

Eindhoven, 7 September 2002, 34,000

Holland (2) 3 *(Davids 35, Kluivert 37, Hasselbaink 73)*   **Belarus (0) 0**
Holland: Van der Sar; Ricksen, Stam, Frank de Boer, Zenden, Van der Meyde, Van Bommel, Cocu, Davids (Van der Vaart 70) (Reiziger 83), Kluivert, Van Nistelrooy (Hasselbaink 70).
Belarus: Shantalosov (Khomutovski 88); Kulchi, Lukhvich, Ostrovski, Shtanyuk, Gurenko, Khatskevich (Kovba 82), Hleb, Omelyunchuk (Shuneiko 76), Romashchenko■, Kutuzov.
Referee: Barber (England).

238

Minsk, 12 October 2002, 23,000

Belarus (0) 0   Austria (0) 2 *(Schopp 57, Akagunduz 89)*
Belarus: Tumilovich; Hleb, Gurenko, Lukhvich■, Ostrovski, Shtanyuk, Kulchi, Yaskovich (Omelyanchuk 51), Shuneiko (Vasilyuk 64), Khatskevich, Kutuzov (Ryndyuk 83).
Austria: Manninger; Schopp, Cerny, Martin Hiden, Baur, Dospel, Kovacevic (Aufhauser 90), Flogel, Kahraman (Herzog 82), Wallner (Akagunduz 75), Wagner.
Referee: Poulat (France).

Chisinau, 12 October 2002, 3000

Moldova (0) 0   Czech Republic (0) 2 *(Jankulovski 70 (pen), Rosicky 80)*
Moldova: Hmaruc; Catinsus, Cebotari, Sosnovschi■, Olexic, Covalenco, Rebeja, Pusca, Covalciuc (Budanov 70), Clescenco (Patula 46), Boret (Ivanov 65).
Czech Republic: Cech; Grygera, Jankulovski, Galasek (Jarosik 55), Bolf, Ujfalusi, Poborsky, Rosicky (Lokvenc 84), Vachousek (Dostalek 88), Koller, Stajner.
Referee: Irvine (Northern Ireland).

Vienna, 16 October 2002, 46,300

Austria (0) 0   Holland (3) 3 *(Seedorf 16, Cocu 20, Makaay 30)*
Austria: Manninger; Schopp, Weissenberger (Akagunduz 76), Martin Hiden■, Baur, Dospel, Flogel, Herzog (Aufhauser 46), Wallner (Scharner 80), Wagner, Cerny.
Holland: Van der Sar; Ricksen, Zenden (Bouma 69), Van Bommel (Ronald de Boer 77), Frank de Boer, Stam, Seedorf, Cocu, Makaay (Hasselbaink 80), Kluivert, Davids.
Referee: Collina (Italy).

Teplice, 16 October 2002, 12,850

Czech Republic (2) 2 *(Poborsky 7, Baros 23)*   **Belarus (0) 0**
Czech Republic: Cech; Jiranek (Grygera 86), Bolf, Ujfalusi, Poborsky, Galasek, Rosicky (Jarosik 90), Koller (Vachousek 56), Baros, Jankulovski, Nedved.
Belarus: Tumilovich; Yaskovich (Lavrik 26), Khrapkovski, Shuneiko (Omelyunchuk 46), Shantyuk, Romashchenko, Gurenko, Kulchi, Hleb (Ryndyuk 69), Khatskevich, Kutuzov.
Referee: Fleischer (Germany).

Minsk, 29 March 2003, 8000

Belarus (1) 2 *(Kutuzov 43, Gurenko 58)*   **Moldova (1) 1** *(Cebotari 14)*
Belarus: Tumilovich; Omelyunchuk, Kulchi, Ostrovski, Lavrik, Gurenko, Hleb (Romashchenko 80), Belkevich, Shuneiko, Khatskevich, Kutuzov (Kovba 87).
Moldova: Hmaruc; Olexic, Catinsus, Priganiuc, Covalenco, Testimitanu, Rebeja, Rogaciov (Popovich 25) (Berco 62) Covalciuc, Cebotari (Golban 79) Clescenco.
Referee: Verbist (Belgium).

Rotterdam, 29 March 2003, 45,000

Holland (1) 1 *(Van Nistelrooy 45)*   **Czech Republic (0) 1** *(Koller 68)*
Holland: Waterreus; Ricksen, Stam, Frank de Boer, Van Bronckhorst (Van der Vaart 39), Seedorf, Van Bommel, Davids, Zenden, Kluivert, Van Nistelrooy (Makaay 81).
Czech Republic: Cech; Grygera, Bolf, Ujfalusi, Jankulovski, Poborsky, Galasek, Rosicky, Nedved, Smicer (Jiranek 79), Koller (Lokvenc 88).
Referee: Nielsen (Denmark).

Prague, 2 April 2003, 17,150

Czech Republic (2) 4 *(Nedved 19, Koller 32, 62, Jankulovski 57 (pen))*   **Austria (0) 0**
Czech Republic: Cech; Grygera, Bolf, Ujfalusi, Jankulovski, Poborsky, Galasek, Smicer (Rosicky 63), Nedved (Vachousek 74), Baros, Koller (Lokvenc 79).
Austria: Mandl; Schamer, Stranzl, Hieblinger, Pogatetz, Schopp, Aufhauser, Flogel (Wagner 46), Weissenberger, Herzog (Kovacevic■ 53), Haas (Dospel 64).
Referee: Lopez (Spain).

Tiraspol, 2 April 2003, 13,000

Moldova (1) 1 *(Boret 16)*   **Holland (1) 2** *(Van Nistelrooy 37, Van Bommel 84)*
Moldova: Hmaruc; Covalenco, Olexic, Testimitanu, Catinsus, Priganiuc, Covalciuc (Berco 79), Ivanov, Boret, Cebotari (Pogreban 88), Clescenco (Golban 63).
Holland: Waterreus; Reiziger, Stam (Ricksen 63), Frank de Boer, Van Bommel, Davids, Seedorf (Ronald de Boer 65), Van der Vaart (Van Hooijdonk 74), Van Nistelrooy, Kluivert, Zenden.
Referee: Sars (France).

Minsk, 7 June 2003, 8000

Belarus (0) 0   Holland (0) 2 *(Overmars 62, Kluivert 68)*
Belarus: Tumilovich; Ostrovski, Lukhvich, Shtanyuk (Omelyunchuk 90), Shuneiko (Kovba 75), Belkevich, Romashchenko (Hleb 52), Gurenko, Kulchi, Kutuzov, Lavrik.
Holland: Van der Sar; Reiziger (Bosvelt 46), Frank de Boer, Stam, Van Bronckhorst (Overmars 60), Seedorf, Van Bommel, Cocu, Zenden, Kluivert, Van Nistelrooy (Van der Vaart 75).
Referee: Ovrevo (Norway).

Tiraspol, 7 June 2003, 10,000

Moldova (0) 1 *(Frunza 60)*   **Austria (0) 0**
Moldova: Hmaruc; Testimitanu, Priganiuc, Catinsus, Olexic, Ivanov, Frunza (Valuta 84), Covalciuc, Cebotari (Patula 77), Boret (Andriuta 67), Rogaciov.
Austria: Mandl; Schamer (Eder 79), Dospel (Cerny 56), Stranzl, Ehmann, Aufhauser, Schopp, Flogel, Wagner (Wallner 69), Haas, Kirchler.
Referee: Da Silva (Portugal).

Innsbruck, 11 June 2003, 8100

Austria (1) 5 *(Aufhauser 33, Haas 47, Kirchler 52, Wallner 62, Cerny 69)*   **Belarus (0) 0**
Austria: Mandl (Payer 85); Schamer, Dospel, Stranzl (Hieblinger 46), Ehmann, Aufhauser, Cerny, Flogel, Wagner, Haas (Wallner 60), Kirchler.
Belarus: Tumilovich; Kulchi, Ostrovski, Lukhvich, Shtanyuk (Khraphovsky 66), Gurenko, Omelyunchuk, Lavrik, Belkevich (Kovba 55), Romashchenko, Kutuzov (Vasilyuk 46).
Referee: Frojdfeldt (Sweden).

Olomouc, 11 June 2003, 12,097

Czech Republic (1) 5 *(Smicer 41, Koller 72 (pen), Stajner 81, Lokvenc 88, 90)*
Moldova (0) 0
Czech Republic: Cech; Grygera, Bolf, Ujfalusi, Jankulovski, Poborsky (Stajner 65), Galasek, Smicer (Baros 59), Rosicky, Nedved, Koller (Lokvenc 79).
Moldova: Hmaruc; Testimitanu, Priganiuc*, Catinsus, Olexic, Covalenca, Ivanov, Covalciuc (Pogreban 83), Cebotari (Frunza 76), Boret, Rogaciov (Patula 76).
Referee: Jakobsson (Iceland).

Minsk, 6 September 2003, 11,000

Belarus (1) 1 *(Bulyga 14)*   **Czech Republic (1) 3** *(Nedved 37, Baros 54, Smicer 85)*
Belarus: Tumilovich; Kulchi, Ostrovski, Lukhvich, Shtanyuk, Rovneiko (Khraphovsky 90), Kutuzov (Hleb 56), Romashchenko, Geraschenko, Gurenko (Volodenkov 82), Bulyga.
Czech Republic: Cech; Grygera, Ujfalusi, Bolf, Jankulovski, Poborsky, Tyce (Smicer 35), Rosicky (Vachousek 83), Nedved, Koller, Baros (Hubschman 66).
Referee: McCurry (Scotland).

Rotterdam, 6 September 2003, 47,000

Holland (1) 3 *(Van der Vaart 30, Kluivert 60, Cocu 64)*   **Austria (1) 1** *(Pogatetz 34)*
Holland: Van der Sar; Reiziger, Frank de Boer, Stam, Van der Meyde (Robben 72), Cocu, Van Bommel, Davids (Van Hooijdonk 46), Zenden (Overmars 46), Kluivert, Van der Vaart.
Austria: Mandl; Dospel, Ehmann, Martin Hiden, Pogatetz, Schopp, Aufhauser, Flogel, Ivanschitz (Dollinger 84), Glieder (Kirchler 66), Kollmann (Haas 66).
Referee: Poulat (France).

Prague, 10 September 2003, 18,356

Czech Republic (2) 3 *(Koller 15 (pen), Poborsky 38, Baros 90)*   **Holland (0) 1** *(Van der Vaart 62)*
Czech Republic: Cech; Grygera (Hubschman 25), Ujfalusi, Galasek, Bolf, Smicer (Vachousek 81), Poborsky, Jiranek, Rosicky (Baros 60), Nedved, Koller.
Holland: Van der Sar; Reiziger, Stam, Frank de Boer (Ooijer 46), Cocu, Van Bommel, Overmars (Bosvelt 20), Davids*, Van Nistelrooy (Van Hooijdonk 71), Kluivert, Van der Vaart.
Referee: Batista (Portugal).

Tiraspol, 10 September 2003, 7000

Moldova (1) 2 *(Dadu 23, Covalciuc 88)* **Belarus (0) 1** *(Vasilyuk 89 (pen))*
Moldova: Hmaruc; Covalenco (Savinov 74), Olexic, Barisev, Catinsus, Valuta (Boret 69), Covalciuc, Ivanov, Rogaciov, Cebotari, Dadu (Clescenco 68).
Belarus: Tumilovich; Kulchi, Ostrovski, Lukhvich, Shtanyuk (Omelyunchuk 40), Gurenko, Rovneiko, Geraschenko, Bulyga, Romashchenko (Vasilyuk 66), Kutuzov (Volodenkov 52).
Referee: Delevic (Serbia).

Vienna, 11 October 2003, 32,350

Austria (0) 2 *(Haas 51, Ivanschitz 77)* **Czech Republic (1) 3** *(Jankulovski 27, Vachousek 79, Koller 90)*
Austria: Mandl; Standfest, Stranzl, Martin Hiden, Pogatetz, Aufhauser, Schopp■, Flogel (Dospel 68), Glieder (Wagner 68), Ivanschitz, Haas (Linz 76).
Czech Republic: Cech; Petrous, Galasek, Boli, Jankulovski (Vorisek 83), Heinz (Koller 68), Stajner, Nedved, Lokvenc, Vachousek, Jiranek (Tyce 41).
Referee: Kasnaferis (Greece).

Eindhoven, 11 October 2003, 30,995

Holland (1) 5 *(Kluivert 43, Sneider 51, Van Hooijdonk 74 (pen), Van der Vaart 80, Robben 89)* **Moldova (0) 0**
Holland: Van der Sar; Reiziger (Makaay 33), Stam, Ooijer, Van Bronckhorst, Van der Meyde, Cocu, Sneider, Overmars (Robben 65), Kluivert (Van Hooijdonk 71), Van der Vaart.
Moldova: Hmaruc; Covalenco (Testimitanu 63), Savinov, Valuta, Catinsus, Covalciuc, Priganiuc, Ivanov (Miterev 82), Cebotari, Barisev, Dadu (Golban 74).
Referee: Siric (Croatia).

Group 3 Final Table	P	W	D	L	F	A	Pts
Czech Republic	8	7	1	0	23	5	22
Holland	8	6	1	1	20	6	19
Austria	8	3	0	5	12	14	9
Moldova	8	2	0	6	5	19	6
Belarus	8	1	0	7	4	20	3

GROUP 4

Riga, 7 September 2002, 9000

Latvia (0) 0 Sweden (0) 0
Latvia: Kolinko; Stepanovs IN, Astafjevs, Zemlinsky, Laizans, Blagonadezhdin, Isakov, Bleidelis, Rubins, Pahars (Stolcers 80), Verpakovsky.
Sweden: Hedman; Mellberg, Jakobsson, Michael Svensson, Antonelius, Linderoth, Alexandersson, Farnerud (Jonson 56), Magnus Svensson (Johansson 76), Ibrahimovic (Kallstrom 65), Allback.
Referee: De Bleeckere (Belgium).

Serravalle, 7 September 2002, 2000

San Marino (0) 0 Poland (0) 2 *(Kaczorowski 75, Kukielka 88)*
San Marino: Gasperoni F; Gennari, Vannucci (Selva R 83), Matteoni, Albani, Bacciocchi, Mauro Marani, Michele Marani, Moretti L (Zonzini 70), Selva A, Ugolini (De Luigi 78).
Poland: Kowalewski; Glowacki, Klos, Bak J, Kaczorowski, Kukielka, Kaluzny (Marcin Zewlakow 60), Kosowski, Wichniarek (Dawidowski 46), Zurawski, Olisadebe (Lewandowski M 80).
Referee: McKeon (Republic of Ireland).

Warsaw, 12 October 2002, 12,000

Poland (0) 0 Latvia (1) 1 *(Laizans 30)*
Poland: Dudek; Hajto, Michal Zewlakow (Surma 46), Kukielka, Zielinski, Ratajczak, Dawidowski, Lewandowski M, Wichniarek (Marcin Zewlakow 46), Zurawski, Kosowski (Mieciel 63).
Latvia: Kolinko; Blagonadezhdin, Laizans, Rubins, Stepanovs IN, Zemlinsky, Isakov, Astafjevs, Verpakovsky (Stolcers 89), Pahars (Prohorenkovs 58), Bleidelis.
Referee: Busacca (Switzerland).

Stockholm, 12 October 2002, 35,084

Sweden (0) 1 *(Ibrahimovic 76)*   **Hungary (1) 1** *(Kenesei 5)*
Sweden: Isaksson; Mellberg, Antonelius (Jonson 67), Linderoth, Jakobsson, Michael Svensson, Alexandersson (Kallstrom 59), Ljungberg, Andersson A, Ibrahimovic (Allback 76), Anders Svensson.
Hungary: Kiraly; Feher C, Low, Urban, Dragoner, Gyepes, Lipcsei, Lisztes, Tokoli (Feher M 59), Kenesei (Gera 70), Dardai.
Referee: Stark (Germany).

Budapest, 16 October 2002, 8000

Hungary (0) 3 *(Gera 49, 60, 85)*   **San Marino (0) 0**
Hungary: Kiraly; Feher C, Low, Urban, Dragoner, Gyepes, Lipcsei, Lisztes (Miriuta 84), Tokoli, Kenesei (Gera 46), Dardai (Feher M 78).
San Marino: Gasperoni F; Gennari, Gobbi, Bacciocchi, Valentini C (Zonzini 81), Albani, Moretti L (Selva R 55), Michele Marani, Muccioli (Montagna 73), Selva A, Vannucci.
Referee: Orrason (Iceland).

Serravalle, 20 November 2002, 600

San Marino (0) 0   Latvia (0) 1 *(Valentini C 89 (og))*
San Marino: Gasperoni F; Valentini C, Matteoni, Gobbi, Gennari (Albani 86), Bacciocchi, Muccioli, Michele Marani (Zonzini 53), Selva A, Vannucci, Montagna (De Luigi 59).
Latvia: Kolinko; Stepanovs IN, Kolesnichenko (Prohorenkovs 57), Blagonadezhdin, Astafjevs, Zemlinsky, Isakov, Bleidelis (Stolcers 46), Rubins, Pahars, Verpakovsky (Mikholap 63).
Referee: Khudiev (Azerbaijan).

Chorzow, 29 March 2003, 48,000

Poland (0) 0   Hungary (0) 0
Poland: Dudek; Bak J, Hajto, Stolarczyk, Szymkowiak, Kaluzny, Swierczewski, Kosowski, Zajac (Dawidowski 71), Kuzba, Olisadebe.
Hungary: Kiraly; Feher C, Urban, Dragoner, Juhar, Lipcsei, Dardai, Lisztes, Low, Tokoli (Boor 85), Kenesei (Sebok 69).
Referee: De Santis (Italy).

Budapest, 2 April 2003, 30,000

Hungary (0) 1 *(Lisztes 65)*   **Sweden (1) 2** *(Allback 34, 66)*
Hungary: Kiraly; Feher C, Juhar, Urban (Bodnar 61), Dragoner, Lipcsei (Boor 80), Dardai, Lisztes, Low, Tokoli (Sebok 68), Kenesei.
Sweden: Isaksson; Lucic, Michael Svensson, Edman, Mellberg, Andersson A, Anders Svensson (Kallstrom 61), Mjallby, Ljungberg, Larsson, Allback (Jonson 90).
Referee: Bastista (Portugal).

Ostrowiec, 2 April 2003, 8500

Poland (2) 5 *(Szymkowiak 4, Kosowski 27, Kuzba 55, 90, Karwan 82)*   **San Marino (0) 0**
Poland: Dudek; Bak J (Wasilewski 63), Zielinski, Sznaucner, Zajac (Karwan 46), Szymkowiak, Burkhardt, Kosowski, Zurawski, Kuzba, Olisadebe (Krzynowek 39).
San Marino: Gasperoni F; Albani, Bacciocchi, Matteoni, Michele Marani, Zonzini (Gasperoni B 67), Moretti L, Muccioli, Selva A (Ugolini 89), Vannucci, Montagna (De Luigi 74).
Referee: Loizou (Cyprus).

Riga, 30 April 2003, 7500

Latvia (2) 3 *(Prohorenkovs 9, Bleidelis 20, 74)*   **San Marino (0) 0**
Latvia: Kolinko; Zirnis, Stepanovs IN, Zemlinsky, Laizans, Isakov, Prohorenkovs, Rubins, Bleidelis (Dobretsov 83), Verpakovsky (Rimkus 60), Mikholap (Stolcers 78).
San Marino: Gasperoni F; Valentini F, Gennari, Albani, Bacciocchi, Matteoni (Moretti 77), Muccioli (Gasperoni B 90), Michele Marani, Selva A, Vannucci, Montagna (De Luigi 64).
Referee: Byrne (Republic of Ireland).

242

Budapest, 7 June 2003, 3000

Hungary (0) 3 *(Szabics 51, 58, Gera 87)*   **Latvia (1) 1** *(Verpakovsky 38)*
Hungary: Vegh; Urban, Dragoner (Gera 40), Juhar■, Feher C, Lisztes (Boor 77), Dardai, Lipcsei, Low, Kenesei (Lendvai 64), Szabics.
Latvia: Kolinko; Blagonadezhdin, Stepanovs IN, Zemlinsky, Isakov, Rubins, Astafjevs (Semyonov 85), Laizans, Bleidelis (Stolcers 79), Verpakovsky, Lobanov (Mikholap 71).
Referee: Merk (Germany).

Serravalle, 7 June 2003, 2184

San Marino (0) 0   Sweden (1) 6 *(Jonson 16, 59, 70, Allback 52, 85, Ljungberg 53)*
San Marino: Gasperoni F; Valentini C (Zonzini 66), Albani, Matteoni, Gennari, Moretti L (Selva R 86), Bacciocchi, Selva A, Gasperoni B, Montagna, Vannucci (De Luigi 77).
Sweden: Isaksson; Lucic, Mellberg, Jakobsson, Edman, Mjallby (Nilsson 73), Andersson A, Kallstrom (Anders Svensson 57), Ljungberg (Johansson 73), Allback, Jonson.
Referee: Delevic (Serbia).

Serravalle, 11 June 2003, 1000

San Marino (0) 0   Hungary (2) 5 *(Boor 5, Lisztes 20, 82, Kenesei 62, Szabics 77)*
San Marino: Gasperoni F; Valentini C, Albani, Matteoni, Mauro Marani, Bacciocchi, Gasperoni B, Zonzini, De Luigi (Montagna 74), Selva R, Vannucci (Gennari 65).
Hungary: Vegh; Bodog, Dragoner, Szekeres (Fuzi 56), Boor, Lipcsei (Lendvai 74), Dardai (Zavadszky 80), Lisztes, Low, Kenesei, Szabics.
Referee: Clark (Scotland).

Stockholm, 11 June 2003, 35,220

Sweden (2) 3 *(Anders Svensson 16, 71, Allback 43)*   **Poland (0) 0**
Sweden: Isaksson; Lucic (Michael Svensson 87), Mellberg, Jakobsson, Edman, Ljungberg, Mjallby, Nilsson, Anders Svensson, Allback, Jonson (Magnus Svensson 72).
Poland: Dudek; Baszczynski (Klos 46), Bak J, Hajto, Stolarczyk, Szymkowiak (Burkhardt 76), Dawidowski, Zdebel, Kosowski (Zajac 64), Krzynowek, Wichniarek.
Referee: Veissiere (France).

Riga, 6 September 2003, 9000

Latvia (0) 0   Poland (2) 2 *(Szymkowiak 36, Klos 38)*
Latvia: Kolinko; Isakov, Zemlinsky, Stepanovs IN, Blagonadezhdin, Bleidelis, Lobanov, Laizans■, Rubins (Semyonov 77), Prohorenkovs (Rimkus 80), Verpakovsky (Stolcers 82).
Poland: Dudek; Klos, Bak J, Hajto, Ratajczyk, Lewandowski M (Kosowski 68), Sobolewski, Szymkowiak (Zdebel 89), Krzynowek, Zurawski, Kryszalowicz (Saganowski 46).
Referee: Vassaras (Greece).

Gothenburg, 6 September 2003, 31,098

Sweden (1) 5 *(Jonson M 33, Jakobsson 49, Ibrahimovic 56, 83 (pen), Kallstrom 68 (pen)*   **San Marino (0) 0**
Sweden: Isaksson; Lucic, Mellberg, Michael Svensson, Edman, Jakobsson (Linderoth 65), Nilsson M, Anders Svensson (Johansson A 65), Kallstrom, Ibrahimovic, Jonson M (Skoog 73).
San Marino: Gasperoni F; Albani, Matteoni, Bacciocchi, Valentini C, Vannucci, Moretti L, Michele Marani, Gennari (Nanni 26), Gasperoni A (Zonzini 9) (Selva A 85), Montagna.
Referee: Messner (Austria).

Riga, 10 September 2003, 7500

Latvia (2) 3 *(Verpakovsky 38, 51, Bleidelis 42)*   **Hungary (0) 1** *(Lisztes 53)*
Latvia: Kolinko; Stepanovs IN, Astafjevs, Zemlinsky, Lobanov, Blagonadezhdin, Zirnis, Bleidelis, Verpakovsky (Kolesnichenko 89), Rubins, Rimkus (Semyonov 75).
Hungary: Kiraly; Feher C, Dragoner, Lovv (Boor 46), Juhar, Lipcsei, Szabics, Dardai, Feher M (Kenesei 46), Lisztes, Gera (Kovacs 86).
Referee: Larsen (Denmark).

243

Chorzow, 10 September 2003, 20,000

Poland (0) 0   Sweden (2) 2 *(Nilsson M 2, Mellberg 36)*
Poland: Dudek; Klos, Sobolewski, Michal Zewlakow, Szymkowiak, Bak J, Hajto■, Krzynowek, Lewandowski M (Kosowski 68), Saganowski (Rasiak 64), Zurawski (Kryszalowicz 73).
Sweden: Isaksson; Lucic, Mellberg, Michael Svensson, Edman, Jakobsson, Nilsson M, Anders Svensson, Ljungberg, Allback (Ibrahimovic 87), Jonson M (Anders Andersson 84).
Referee: Riley (England).

Budapest, 11 October 2003, 15,500

Hungary (0) 1 *(Szabics 49)*   **Poland (1) 2** *(Niedzielan 10, 62)*
Hungary: Kiraly; Bodog, Dragoner, Juhar, Boor, Lipcsei (Gera 46), Dardai, Fuzi, Lisztes, Feher M (Kenesei 65), Szabics.
Poland: Dudek; Klos, Bak J, Rzasa, Michal Zewlakow, Sobolewski, Szymkowiak (Lewandowski M 85), Mila (Kosowski 53), Krzynowek, Rasiak, Niedzielan (Saganowski 87).
Referee: Gonzalez (Spain).

Stockholm, 11 October 2003, 32,095

Sweden (0) 0   Latvia (1) 1 *(Verpakovsky 23)*
Sweden: Isaksson; Lucic (Dorsin 46), Mellberg, Michael Svensson, Andersson C (Johansson A 81), Jakobsson, Nilsson M, Anders Svensson, Kallstrom (Ibrahimovic 64), Allback, Jonson M.
Latvia: Kolinko; Stepanovs IN, Astafjevs, Zemlinsky, Lobanov, Blagonadezhdin, Zirnis■, Bleidelis, Verpakovsky (Stolcers 87), Rubins (Pucinsks 81), Rimkus (Isakov 75).
Referee: De Santis (Italy).

Group 4 Final Table	P	W	D	L	F	A	Pts
Sweden	8	5	2	1	19	3	17
Latvia	8	5	1	2	10	6	16
Poland	8	4	1	3	11	7	13
Hungary	8	3	2	3	15	9	11
San Marino	8	0	0	8	0	30	0

GROUP 5

Toftir, 7 September 2002, 4000

Faeroes (2) 2 *(Petersen J 7, 13)*   **Scotland (0) 2** *(Lambert 62, Ferguson B 83)*
Faeroes: Knudsen; Johannesen O, Hansen JK, Thorsteinsson, Jacobsen JR, Elltor (Lakjuni 89), Benjaminsen, Johnsson, Jacobsen C (Jacobsen R 76), Borg, Petersen J (Flotum 80).
Scotland: Douglas; Ross (Alexander 75), Crainey, Ferguson B, Weir, Dailly, Lambert, Dobie (Thompson 83), Dickov (Crawford 46), Kyle, Johnston.
Referee: Granat (Poland).

Kaunas, 7 September 2002, 8500

Lithuania (0) 0   Germany (1) 2 *(Ballack 25, Stankevicius 58 (og))*
Lithuania: Stauce; Skarbalius, Stankevicius, Gleveckas, Dedura, Semberas, Zutautas, Razanauskas (Morinas 71), Mikalajunas, Poskus, Jankauskas (Fomenka 77).
Germany: Kahn; Linke, Ramelow, Metzelder, Frings, Schneider (Jeremies 85), Hamann, Ballack, Bohme, Jancker (Neuville 68), Klose.
Referee: Poll (England).

Reykjavik, 12 October 2002, 6611

Iceland (0) 0   Scotland (1) 2 *(Dailly 7, Naysmith 63)*
Iceland: Arason; Thorsteinsson, Vidarsson (Baldvinsson 66), Ingimarsson, Sigurdsson L, Hreidarsson, Gudnason (Gudjonsson B 77), Kristinsson R, Gudjohnsen E, Sigurdsson H (Helguson 46), Gunnarsson.
Scotland: Douglas; Ross, Naysmith (Anderson R 90), Dailly, Pressley, Wilkie, Lambert, Ferguson B, Crawford, Thompson S (Severin 89), McNamara (Davidson 34).
Referee: Sars (France).

Kaunas, 12 October 2002, 4000

Lithuania (2) 2 *(Razanauskas 23 (pen), Poskus 37)*   **Faeroes (0) 0**
Lithuania: Stauce; Zutautas (Barasa 75), Cesnauskis D (Slavickas 77) (Stankevicius 84), Skarbalius, Poskus, Gleveckas, Razanauskas, Skerla, Fomenka, Dziaukstas, Mikalajunas.
Faeroes: Mikkelsen; Johannesen O, Jacobsen C (Flotum 60), Johnsson J (Jacobsen R 68), Petersen J, Thorsteinsson (Joensen J 73), Jacobsen JR, Hansen O, Benjaminsen, Hansen JK, Borg.
Referee: Delevic (Yugoslavia).

Hanover, 16 October 2002, 36,000

Germany (1) 2 *(Ballack 2 (pen), Klose 59)*   **Faeroes (1) 1** *(Friedrich 45 (og))*
Germany: Kahn; Schneider (Kehl 87), Frings, Friedrich, Ramelow (Freier 46), Worns, Jeremies, Hamann, Jancker (Neuville 69), Klose, Ballack.
Faeroes: Mikkelsen; Thorsteinsson, Hansen JK, Benjaminsen, Johannesen O, Jacobsen JR, Borg (Elltor 71), Johnsson, Petersen J (Petersen H 87), Flotum (Jacobsen C 78), Hansen O.
Referee: Koren (Israel).

Reykjavik, 16 October 2002, 5000

Iceland (0) 3 *(Helguson 50, Gudjohnsen E 60, 73)*   **Lithuania (0) 0**
Iceland: Arason; Thorsteinsson (Gudjonsson B 37), Vidarsson, Ingimarsson, Gunnarsson, Hreidarsson, Gudnason, Stigsson (Einarsson 65), Helguson, Gudjohnsen E, Gudjonsson J (Sigurdsson H 75).
Lithuania: Stauce; Dziaukstas, Gleveckas, Skerla, Stankevicius, Cesnauskis D▪, Razanauskas, Mikalajunas, Barasa, Fomenka, Poskus.
Referee: Gilewski (Poland).

Nuremberg, 29 March 2003, 40,754

Germany (1) 1 *(Ramelow 8)*   **Lithuania (0) 1** *(Razanauskas 73)*
Germany: Kahn; Friedrich, Worns, Rau (Freier 83), Frings, Ramelow, Hamann, Bohme (Rehmer 46), Schneider, Klose, Bobic (Kuranyi 72).
Lithuania: Stauce; Semberas, Zvirgdauskas, Dedura, Barasa, Morinas, Petrenko (Dziaukstas 87), Pukelevicius (Maciulevicius 46), Mikalajunas, Razanauskas, Jankauskas (Fomenka 90).
Referee: Torres (Spain).

Glasgow, 29 March 2003, 37,938

Scotland (1) 2 *(Miller 12, Wilkie 70)*   **Iceland (0) 1** *(Gudjohnsen E 48)*
Scotland: Douglas; Wilkie, Alexander, Ferguson, Pressley, Dailly, Lambert, Hutchison (Devlin 66), Crawford, Miller (McNamara 82), Naysmith.
Iceland: Arason; Thorsteinsson, Sigurdsson L, Bergsson, Gunnarsson (Gudjonsson T 74), Kristinsson R, Gudjonsson J, Ingimarsson, Vidarsson (Sigurdsson I 83), Gudjohnsen E (Gudmundsson T 89), Gretarsson.
Referee: Temmink (Holland).

Kaunas, 2 April 2003, 8000

Lithuania (0) 1 *(Razanauskas 74 (pen))*   **Scotland (0) 0**
Lithuania: Stauce; Semberas, Zvirgdauskas, Dedura, Barasa, Morinas, Petrenko (Maciulevicius 71), Razanauskas, Gleveckas, Mikalajunas (Buitkus 89), Jankauskas (Fomenka 63).
Scotland: Gallacher; Alexander, Naysmith, Wilkie, Pressley, Dailly, McNamara (Gray 81), Lambert, Crawford (Devlin 57), Miller, Hutchison (Cameron 78).
Referee: Stuchlik (Austria).

Reykjavik, 7 June 2003, 6038

Iceland (0) 2 *(Sigurdsson H 49, Gudmundsson T 89)*   **Faeroes (0) 1** *(Jacobsen JR 62)*
Iceland: Arason; Sigurdsson I (Gudmundsson T 75), Bergsson, Hreidarsson, Vidarsson, Kristinsson R, Sigurdsson L, Gudjonsson J, Sigurdsson H (Gretarsson 75), Gudjohnsen E, Gudjonsson T.
Faeroes: Mikkelsen; Jacobsen C, Joensen J, Jacobsen JR, Olsen, Borg, Jacobsen R, Petersen H (Johnsson 61), Benjaminsen, Petersen J, Flotum (Elltor 64).
Referee: Liba (Czech Republic).

245

Glasgow, 7 June 2003, 48,047

Scotland (0) 1 *(Miller 69)*   **Germany (1) 1** *(Bobic 23)*
Scotland: Douglas; Ross (McNamara 75), Naysmith, Dailly, Pressley, Webster, Devlin (Rae 60), Cameron, Crawford, Miller (Thompson 90), Lambert.
Germany: Kahn; Frings, Rau (Freier 57), Friedrich, Ramelow, Worns, Jeremies, Ballack, Bobic, Klose (Neuville 74), Schneider (Kehl 86).
Referee: Messina (Italy).

Torshavn, 11 June 2003, 6130

Faeroes (0) 0   Germany (0) 2 *(Klose 89, Bobic 90)*
Faeroes: Mikkelsen; Johannesen O, Joensen J, Thorsteinsson, Jacobsen JR, Jacobsen R, Benjaminsen, Johnsson, Borg (Elltor 61), Petersen J, Jacobsen C (Petersen JI 77).
Germany: Kahn (Rost 46); Friedrich, Freier, Rau (Hartmann 72), Ramelow, Worns, Jeremies (Klose 65), Kehl, Bobic, Neuville, Schneider.
Referee: Wegereef (Holland).

Kaunas, 11 June 2003, 8000

Lithuania (0) 0   Iceland (0) 3 *(Gudjonsson T 60, Gudjohnsen E 72, Hreidarsson 90)*
Lithuania: Stauce; Semberas■, Dedura, Barasa (Maciulevicius 72), Petrenko, Zvirgzdauskas, Zutautas (Karcemarskas 70), Morinas, Razanauskas, Jankauskas (Danilevicius 79), Skarbalius.
Iceland: Arason; Sigurdsson L, Bergsson, Hreidarsson, Vidarsson, Gunnarsson, Kristinsson R, Gudjonsson J (Gretarsson 89), Sigurdsson H (Gudmundsson T 82), Gudjohnsen E, Gudjonsson T.
Referee: Corpodea (Romania).

Torshavn, 20 August 2003, 3416

Faeroes (0) 1 *(Jacobsen R 65)*   **Iceland (1) 2** *(Gudjohnsen E 5, Marteinsson 70)*
Faeroes: Mikkelsen; Thorsteinsson (Joensen J 78), Jacobsen JR, Johannesen, Olsen, Jacobsen C, Johnsson J, Petersen JI, Jacobsen R, Petersen J (Petersen H 78), Flotum (Elltor 56).
Iceland: Arason; Marteinsson, Bjarnason, Hreidarsson, Gudjonsson T, Gudjonsson J, Gunnarsson B (Gretarsson 71), Kristinsson R (Helguson 77), Vidarsson, Gudjohnsen E, Sigurdsson H (Sigurdsson I 84).
Referee: Gonzalez (Spain).

Reykjavik, 6 September 2003, 7035

Iceland (0) 0   Germany (0) 0
Iceland: Arason; Sigurdsson L, Bjarnason, Hreidarsson, Gudjonsson T, Gudjonsson J, Marteinsson (Gretarsson 75), Kristinsson R, Sigurdsson I (Vidarsson 83), Gudjohnsen E, Helguson (Sigurdsson H 78).
Germany: Kahn; Friedrich, Worns, Baumann, Schneider (Deisler 76), Ramelow, Ballack, Kehl, Rahn (Hartmann 60), Klose, Neuville (Kuranyi 46).
Referee: Barber (England).

Glasgow, 6 September 2003, 40,909

Scotland (2) 3 *(McCann 7, Dickov 45, McFadden 74)*   **Faeroes (0) 1** *(Johnsson J 35)*
Scotland: Douglas; McNamara, Naysmith, Ferguson B, Webster, Wilkie, Devlin (McFadden 59), Cameron, Dickov (Rae 68), Crawford (Thompson S 75), McCann.
Faeroes: Mikkelsen; Petersen JI, Thorsteinsson, Jacobsen JR, Johannesen, Petersen H (Akselsen 66), Benjaminsen, Johnsson J (Danielsen 85), Borg (Holst 85), Jacobsen R, Petersen J.
Referee: Ceferen (Slovenia).

Toftir, 10 September 2003, 2175

Faeroes (1) 1 *(Olsen 43)*   **Lithuania (1) 3** *(Morinas 23, 57, Vencevicius 88)*
Faeroes: Knudsen; Hansen HF, Olsen, Thorsteinsson (Jacobsen R 50), Jacobsen JR, Petersen JI, Benjaminsen, Johnsson J (Danielsen 85), Borg (Akselsen 70), Petersen J, Jacobsen C.
Lithuania: Kurskis; Dziaukstas, Dedura, Barasa, Cesnauskis E, Zvirgzdauskas, Morinas (Kucys 78), Cesnauskis D, Jankauskas, Poderis (Tamosauskas 46), Vencevicius (Guscinas 90).
Referee: Trivkovic (Croatia).

Dortmund, 10 September 2003, 67,000

Germany (1) 2 *(Bobic 25, Ballack 50 (pen))*   **Scotland (0) 1** *(McCann 60)*
Germany: Kahn; Friedrich, Baumann, Worns, Schneider (Kehl 81), Rehmer, Ramelow, Rau, Ballack, Bobic (Klose 76), Kuranyi.
Scotland: Douglas; McNamara, Naysmith, Ferguson B, Pressley, Dailly, McFadden (Rae 53), Lambert (Ross■ 46), Thompson S, Cameron, McCann.
Referee: Frisk (Sweden).

Hamburg, 11 October 2003, 50,780

Germany (1) 3 *(Ballack 9, Bobic 59, Kuranyi 79)*   **Iceland (0) 0**
Germany: Kahn; Friedrich, Ramelow, Worns, Hinkel, Baumann, Rahn, Schneider, Ballack, Bobic (Klose 70), Kuranyi (Neuville 85).
Iceland: Arason; Bjarnason, Vidarsson, Hreidarsson, Sigurdsson I (Dadason 65), Gretarsson (Gunnarsson V 80), Kristinsson R, Ingimarsson, Gudjonsson T, Gudjohnsen E, Sigurdsson H (Gunnarsson B 80).
Referee: Ivanov (Russia).

Glasgow, 11 October 2003, 50,343

Scotland (0) 1 *(Fletcher 70)*   **Lithuania (0) 0**
Scotland: Douglas; McNamara, Naysmith, Cameron (Fletcher 65), Pressley, Dailly, Rae, Ferguson, Crawford, Miller (Hutchison 65), McFadden (Alexander 90).
Lithuania: Stauce; Dziaukstas, Zvirgzdauskas (Cesnauskis D 46), Dedura, Regelskis (Beniusis 85), Barasa, Razanauskas, Vencevicius (Maciulevicius 79), Baravicius, Jankauskas, Poskus.
Referee: Colombo (France).

Group 5 Final Table	P	W	D	L	F	A	Pts
Germany	8	5	3	0	13	4	18
Scotland	8	4	2	2	12	8	14
Iceland	8	4	1	3	11	9	13
Lithuania	8	3	1	4	7	11	10
Faeroes	8	0	1	7	7	16	1

GROUP 6

Erevan, 7 September 2002, 9000

Armenia (0) 2 *(Art Petrossian 73, Sarkissian 90)*   **Ukraine (2) 2** *(Serebrennikov 2, Zubov 33)*
Armenia: Berezovski; Artur Mkrtchian (Sarkissian 60), Hovsepian, Vardanian, Minasian (Voskanian 46), Khachatrian R, Art Petrossian, Bilibio, Dokhoyan, Art Karamian, Arm Karamian (Movsisian 71).
Ukraine: Reva; Luzhny, Tymoshchuk, Yezersky■, Nesmachni, Kormiltsev, Serebrennikov, Gusin (Maksimioek 65) (Popov 90), Moroz, Zubov (Spivak 69), Vorobei.
Referee: Vuorela (Finland).

Athens, 7 September 2002, 17,000

Greece (0) 0   Spain (1) 2 *(Raul 8, Valeron 76)*
Greece: Nikopolidis; Patsatzoglou, Dabizas, Dellas, Fyssas (Vryzas 72), Konstantinidis (Karagounis 40), Zagorakis (Basinas 46), Tsartas, Giannakopoulos, Charisteas, Nikolaidis.
Spain: Casillas; Michel Salgado, Marchena, Garcia Calvo, Raul Bravo, Joaquin (Mendieta 59), Xavi (Baraja 59), Valeron (Cesar 87), Helguera, Vicente, Raul.
Referee: Merk (Germany).

Albacete, 12 October 2002, 16,000

Spain (1) 3 *(Baraja 19, 88, Guti 59)*   **Northern Ireland (0) 0**
Spain: Casillas; Michel Salgado, Raul Bravo, Xavi, Puyol, Helguera, Joaquin (Mendieta 79), Baraja, Raul (Morientes 63), Guti (Capi 59), Vicente.
Northern Ireland: Taylor; Hughes A, McCartney, Murdock, Taggart (McCann 70), Lomas, Johnson D, Mulryne, Gillespie, McVeigh (Healy 65), Horlock (Hughes M 65).
Referee: Dobrinov (Bulgaria).

Kiev, 12 October 2002, 55,000

Ukraine (0) 2 *(Vorobei 51, Voronin 90)*   **Greece (0) 0**
Ukraine: Reva; Tymoshchuk, Luzhny, Starostiak, Moroz (Radchenko 25), Gusin, Kormiltsev (Rebrov 71), Zubov, Kalinitchenko, Vorobei, Serebrennikov (Voronin 24).
Greece: Nikopolidis; Seitaridis, Lakis (Giannakopoulos 66), Dabizas, Dellas, Venetidis, Zagorakis (Basinas 69), Karagounis, Tsartas, Nikolaidis (Vryzas 66), Charisteas.
Referee: Temmink (Holland).

Athens, 16 October 2002, 5500

Greece (1) 2 *(Nikolaidis 2, 59)*   **Armenia (0) 0**
Greece: Nikopolidis; Seitaridis, Georgiadis (Giannakopoulos 46), Dellas, Dabizas, Venetidis (Vryzas 60), Basinas, Kafes, Charisteas, Nikolaidis, Tsartas (Zagorakis 46).
Armenia: Berezovski; Sarkissian (Melikian 82), Vardanian, Khachatrian R (Minasian 46), Bilibio, Hovsepian, Art Petrossian, Art Karamian, Arm Karamian (Mkhitarian 66), Voskanian, Dokhoyan.
Referee: Ceferin (Slovenia).

Belfast, 16 October 2002, 9288

Northern Ireland (0) 0   Ukraine (0) 0
Northern Ireland: Taylor; Lomas, Horlock, Mulryne (McCann 80), Hughes A, McCartney, Gillespie, Johnson D (Murdock 84), McVeigh (Kirk 65), Healy, Hughes M.
Ukraine: Reva; Starostiak, Luzhny, Tymoshchuk, Kormiltsev (Lysytski 89), Gusin, Zubov, Kalynychenko (Rebrov 54), Voronin, Radchenko, Vorobei (Melashchenko 76).
Referee: Bolognino (Italy).

Erevan, 29 March 2003, 9000

Armenia (0) 1 *(Art Petrossian 87)*   **Northern Ireland (0) 0**
Armenia: Berezovski; Melikian, Dokhoyan, Hovsepian, Vardanian, Bilibio, Art Petrossian (Mkhitarian 89), Voskanian, Sarkissian (Artur Mkrtchian 89), Art Karamian (Agvan Mkrtchian 89), Arm Karamian.
Northern Ireland: Taylor; Hughes A, McCann, Lomas, Williams, Craigan, Gillespie, Johnson D, Healy, Quinn (Elliott 70), McVeigh.
Referee: Beck (Liechtenstein).

Kiev, 29 March 2003, 82,000

Ukraine (1) 2 *(Voronin 11, Gorchkov 90)*   **Spain (0) 2** *(Raul 83, Etxeberria 87)*
Ukraine: Shovkovskyi; Nesmachni, Dmitrulin, Fedorov, Tymoshchuk, Kormiltsev (Kalynychenko 62), Gusin, Gorchkov, Voronin, Vorobei, Shevchenko (Serebrennikov 67).
Spain: Casillas; Michel Salgado, Aranzabal, Albelda (Xavi 65), Marchena, Cesar, Etxeberria, Baraja, Guti (Valeron 65), Raul, Vicente (Diego Tristan 77).
Referee: Riley (England).

Belfast, 2 April 2003, 7196

Northern Ireland (0) 0   Greece (1) 2 *(Charisteas 2, 55)*
Northern Ireland: Taylor; Hughes A, McCartney, Lomas, Williams, Craigan, Gillespie■, Johnson D, Healy (Kirk 68), Quinn■, McCann (McVeigh 68).
Greece: Nikopolidis; Giannakopoulos, Venetidis (Fyssas 70), Dabizas, Kyrgiakos, Konstantinidis, Zagorakis, Tsartas (Kafes 75), Charisteas, Nikolaidis (Vryzas 41), Karagounis.
Referee: Gilewski (Poland).

Amilivia, 2 April 2003, 13,500

Spain (0) 3 *(Diego Tristan 63, Helguera 69, Joaquin 90)*   **Armenia (0) 0**
Spain: Casillas; Michel Salgado, Bravo, Albelda, Helguera, Marchena, Etxeberria (Joaquin 46), Xavi (Vicente 54), Valeron (Baraja 63), Raul, Diego Tristan.
Armenia: Berezovski; Dokhoyan, Vardanian, Melikian, Hovsepian, Art Petrossian (Mkhitarian 81) (Minasian 84), Khachatrian R, Voskanian, Sarkissian, Art Karamian (Bilibio 89), Arm Karamian.
Referee: Yefet (Israel).

248

Zaragoza, 7 June 2003, 32,000

Spain (0) 0   Greece (1) 1 *(Giannakopoulos 42)*
Spain: Casillas; Michel Salgado, Raul Bravo, Marchena (Sergio 76), Puyol, Helguera, Etxeberria (Joaquin 57), Valeron, Raul, Morientes, Vicente (De Pedro 57).
Greece: Nikopolidis; Seitaridis, Dellas, Dabizas, Kapsis, Venetidis■, Zagorakis, Tsartas (Karagounis 36), Giannakopoulos, Vryzas, Charisteas (Lakis 34).
Referee: Sars (France).

Lvov, 7 June 2003, 30,000

Ukraine (1) 4 *(Gorchkov 28, Shevchenko 65 (pen), 70, Fedorov 90)*   **Armenia (1) 3**
(Sarkissian 13 (pen), 50, Art Petrossian 72 (pen))
Ukraine: Shutkov; Luzhny, Fedorov, Nesmachni, Zakarlyuka (Radchenko 63), Popov (Kalynychenko 65), Gorchkov, Voronin, Rebrov (Venhlynsky 80), Shevchenko, Vorobei.
Armenia: Berezovski; Partsikian, Dokhoyan, Vardanian, Hovsepian, Art Petrossian (Bilibio 75), Khachatrian B, Voskanian, Sarkissian, Art Karamian (Arutiunian 83), Arm Karamian.
Referee: Albrecht (Germany).

Athens, 11 June 2003, 15,000

Greece (0) 1 *(Charisteas 86)*   **Ukraine (0) 0**
Greece: Nikopolidis; Seitaridis, Dabizas, Dellas, Fyssas, Kapsis, Zagorakis (Tsartas 72), Lakis (Houtos 65), Karagounis, Vryzas (Charisteas 46), Giannakopoulos.
Ukraine: Shovkovskyi; Nesmachni, Fedorov, Golovko, Tymoshchuk, Gusin, Shevchuk, Zakarlyuka, Voronin, Shevchenko, Rebrov (Vorobei 61).
Referee: De Bleeckere (Belgium).

Belfast, 11 June 2003, 11,365

Northern Ireland (0) 0   Spain (0) 0
Northern Ireland: Taylor; Baird, Kennedy, Griffin, Hughes A, McCartney, Healy, Johnson, Smith (Williams 90), Jones (McVeigh 73), Doherty (Toner 80).
Spain: Casillas; Puyol, Juanfran, Sergio (Joaquin 66), Marchena, Helguera, Etxeberria (De Pedro 78), Baraja, Valeron, Raul, Vicente (Morientes 66).
Referee: Larsen (Denmark).

Erevan, 6 September 2003, 6500

Armenia (0) 0   Greece (1) 1 *(Vryzas 34)*
Armenia: Berezovski; Melikian, Bilibio, Zeciu, Vardanian, Khachatrian R, Art Petrossian, Voskanian, Sarkissian, Art Karamian, Arm Karamian (Movsesian 65).
Greece: Nikopolidis; Seitaridis, Fyssas, Antzas, Dellas, Basinas, Kapsis, Vryzas, Karagounis (Zagorakis 89), Giannakopoulos (Nikolaidis 87), Charisteas.
Referee: Temmink (Holland).

Donetsk, 6 September 2003, 24,000

Ukraine (0) 0   Northern Ireland (0) 0
Ukraine: Shovkovskyi; Luzhny, Fedorov, Tymoshchuk, Nesmachni, Horshkov, Gusin (Gusev 16), Zubov, Rebrov (Melaschenko 72), Voronin, Vorobei.
Northern Ireland: Taylor; Baird, Kennedy, Griffin, Hughes A, McCartney, Gillespie, Doherty (Mulryne 67), Johnson D, Healy (Smith 62), Hughes M (Jones 81).
Referee: Stark (Germany).

Belfast, 10 September 2003, 8616

Northern Ireland (0) 0   Armenia (1) 1 *(Arm Karamian 29)*
Northern Ireland: Taylor; Baird, McCann, Griffin, Hughes A, McCartney, Gillespie (Jones 29), Doherty (Mulryne 29), Johnson D, Healy (McVeigh 78), Smith.
Armenia: Berezovski; Melikian, Bilibio, Hovsepian, Zeciu, Khachatrian R, Art Petrossian (Arm Karamian 12), Voskanian, Sarkissian, Art Karamian (Partsikian 87), Movsesian (Hakobian A 75).
Referee: Stredak (Slovakia).

Elche, 10 September 2003, 38,000

Spain (0) 2 *(Raul 59, 71)*   **Ukraine (0) 1** *(Shevchenko 84)*
Spain: Casillas; Michel Salgado, Juanito, Marchena, Puyol, Etxeberria, Alonso, Baraja (Xavi 85), Vicente (Valeron 64), Raul, Fernando Torres (Reyes 64).
Ukraine: Shovkovskyi; Luzhny, Fedorov, Tymoshchuk, Nesmachni, Dmitrulin (Zubov 65), Popov (Serebrennikov 18), Horshkov, Voronin (Gusev 52), Shevchenko, Vorobei.
Referee: Hauge (Norway).

Erevan, 11 October 2003, 15,000

Armenia (0) 0   Spain (1) 4 *(Valeron 7, Raul 76, Reyes 87, 90)*
Armenia: Berezovski; Melikian, Dokhoyan K, Hovsepian, Vardanian, Khachatrian R, Secu (Bilibio 88), Voskanian (Movsesian 78), Sarkissian, Art Karamian, Arm Karamian (Petrossian G 87).
Spain: Casillas; Michel Salgado, Helguera, Marchena, Puyol, Baraja (Xabi Alonso 66), Albelda, Etxeberria, Valeron, Vicente (Reyes 62), Raul (Luque 78).
Referee: Meier (Switzerland).

Athens, 11 October 2003, 15,500

Greece (0) 1 *(Tsartas 69 (pen))*   **Northern Ireland (0) 0**
Greece: Nikopolidis; Dabizas (Venetidis 46), Dellas, Antzas, Seitaridis, Basinas (Zagorakis 90), Tsartas, Vryzas, Fyssas, Charisteas (Nikolaidis 46), Giannakopoulos.
Northern Ireland: Taylor; Baird, Kennedy, Griffin (Jones 88), Hughes A, McCartney▪, Gillespie (Smith 63), Whitley Jeff, Healy, Elliott (Murdock 70), Hughes M.
Referee: Batista (Portugal).

Group 6 Final Table	P	W	D	L	F	A	Pts
Greece	8	6	0	2	8	4	18
Spain	8	5	2	1	16	4	17
Ukraine	8	2	4	2	11	10	10
Armenia	8	2	1	5	7	16	7
Northern Ireland	8	0	3	5	0	8	3

GROUP 7

Vaduz, 7 September 2002, 1200

Liechtenstein (0) 1 *(Michael Stocklasa 90)*   **Macedonia (1) 1** *(Hristov 7)*
Liechtenstein: Jehle; Ritter, Gigon (Burgmeier 83), Hasler D, Michael Stocklasa, Martin Stocklasa, Telser (D'Elia 83), Frick M, Gerster, Beck T, Beck M (Buchel 46).
Macedonia: Milosevski; Braga (Grncarov 85), Sedloski, Nikolovski, Petrov, Mitreski I, Sumolikoski, Sakiri, Pandev (Stoikov 70), Hristov (Popov 58), Mitreski A.
Referee: Goduljan (Ukraine).

Istanbul, 7 September 2002, 20,000

Turkey (2) 3 *(Serhat 14, Arif 45, 65)*   **Slovakia (0) 0**
Turkey: Rustu; Fatih, Bulent K, Alpay, Hakan Unsal, Okan (Nihat 63), Tugay, Emre B (Cihan 78), Basturk, Serhat (Umit D 87), Arif.
Slovakia: Bucek; Karhan, Spilar, Dzurik, Labant (Michalik 61), Kisel, Cisovski, Kozlej (Reiter 55), Gresko (Hlinka 72), Janocko, Vittek.
Referee: Nieto (Spain).

Skopje, 12 October 2002, 12,000

Macedonia (1) 1 *(Grozdanovski 2)*   **Turkey (1) 2** *(Okan 29, Nihat 54)*
Macedonia: Milosevski; Mitreski I, Vasovski, Sedloski, Stojanovski, Mitreski A, Trajanov (Nacevski 68), Sumolikoski (Petrov 46), Sakiri, Hristov (Popov 46), Grozdanovski.
Turkey: Rustu; Fatih, Bulent K, Alpay, Tugay (Serhat 46), Emre B, Basturk, Arif (Hasan Sas 46), Nihat, Ergun.
Referee: Fisker (Denmark).

Bratislava, 12 October 2002, 30,000

Slovakia (1) 1 *(Nemeth S 24)*   **England (0) 2** *(Beckham 65, Owen 82)*
Slovakia: Konig; Pinte (Kozlej 88), Leitner, Zeman, Dzurik, Hlinka, Karhan, Janocko (Mintal 88), Nemeth S, Petras, Vittek (Reiter 80).
England: Seaman; Neville G, Ashley Cole, Southgate, Woodgate, Butt, Beckham, Gerrard (Dyer 77), Heskey (Smith 90), Owen (Hargreaves 46), Scholes.
Referee: Messina (Italy).

Southampton, 16 October 2002, 32,095

England (2) 2 *(Beckham 14, Gerrard 36)*   **Macedonia (2) 2** *(Sakiri 11, Trajanov 25)*
England: Seaman; Neville G, Ashley Cole, Gerrard (Butt 56), Campbell, Woodgate, Beckham, Scholes, Smith*, Owen, Bridge (Vassell 58).
Macedonia: Milosevski; Popov, Petrov, Sumolikoski, Sedloski, Vasovski, Grozdanovski, Mitreski A, Sakiri, Trajanov (Stojanovski 90), Toleski (Pandev 62).
Referee: Ibanez (Spain).

Istanbul, 16 October 2002, 15,000

Turkey (3) 5 *(Okan 7, Umit D 14, Ilhan 23, Serhat 81, 90)*   **Liechtenstein (0) 0**
Turkey: Rustu; Umit D, Ergun, Bulent K (Fatih 46), Alpay, Tugay, Okan (Hakan Unsal 60), Emre B, Ilhan (Serhat 79), Arif, Nihat.
Liechtenstein: Jehle; Telser, Michael Stocklasa, Nigg (Burgmeier 72), Hasler D, D'Elia, Martin Stocklasa (Beck M 79), Buchel (Ospelt 85), Beck T, Frick M, Gerster.
Referee: Baskakov (Russia).

Vaduz, 29 March 2003, 3548

Liechtenstein (0) 0   **England (1) 2** *(Owen 28, Beckham 53)*
Liechtenstein: Jehle; Telser, Hasler D, Michael Stocklasa, D'Elia, Beck T, Martin Stocklasa, Buchel (Beck M 86), Zech (Burgmeier 62), Frick (Nigg 82), Gerster.
England: James; Neville G, Bridge, Gerrard (Butt 66), Ferdinand, Southgate, Beckham (Murphy 70), Scholes, Heskey (Rooney 80), Owen, Dyer.
Referee: Kasnaferis (Greece).

Skopje, 29 March 2003, 8000

Macedonia (0) 0   **Slovakia (1) 2** *(Petras 28, Reiter 90)*
Macedonia: Milosevski; Braga, Lazarevski (Stoikov 81), Sedloski, Mitreski I, Sumolikovski (Naumoski 52), Jancevski, Krstev M, Sakiri, Krstev S (Grozdanovski 61), Pandev.
Slovakia: Konig; Petras, Klimpl, Hlinka, Leitner, Karhan (Hanek 90), Demo (Labant 81), Michalik, Janocko, Nemeth S (Reiter 75), Vittek.
Referee: Duhamel (France).

Sunderland, 2 April 2003, 47,667

England (0) 2 *(Vassell 76, Beckham 90 (pen))*   **Turkey (0) 0**
England: James; Neville G, Bridge, Butt, Campbell, Ferdinand, Beckham, Scholes, Rooney (Dyer 89), Owen (Vassell 58), Gerrard.
Turkey: Rustu; Fatih (Hakan Sukur 79), Ergun, Alpay, Bulent K, Tugay, Okan (Umit D 59), Emre B, Basturk (Hasan Sas 70), Nihat, Ilhan.
Referee: Meier (Switzerland).

Trnava, 2 April 2003

Slovakia (1) 4 *(Reiter 18, Nemeth S 51, 64, Janocko 90)*   **Liechtenstein (0) 0**
Slovakia: Konig; Petras, Klimpl, Hlinka, Leitner, Karhan (Hanek 90), Demo (Labant 68), Michalik (Mintal 81), Janocko, Kozlej (Nemeth S 46), Reiter.
Liechtenstein: Jehle; Telser, Hasler D, Michael Stocklasa, D'Elia, Beck T, Martin Stocklasa, Buchel (Gigon 71), Burgmeier, Frick M (Nigg 60), Gerster (Ospelt 85).
Match played behind closed doors.
Referee: Ceferen (Slovenia).

Skopje, 7 June 2003, 6000

Macedonia (1) 3 *(Sedloski 39 (pen), Krstev M 52, Stoikov 82)*   **Liechtenstein (1) 1**
(Beck T 20)
Macedonia: Milosevski; Sumolikoski, Sedloski, Vasovski, Lazarevski, Trajanov (Jancevski 60), Mitreski A, Sakiri (Bajevski 55), Stoikov, Naumoski (Dimitrovski 46), Krstev M.
Liechtenstein: Jehle; Ospelt, Hasler D, Gigon, Maierhofer (Wolfinger 89), D'Elia, Gerster, Frick M, Telser, Beck M (Vogt 89), Beck T (Rohrer 79).
Referee: Jara (Czech Republic).

Bratislava, 7 June 2003, 15,000

Slovakia (0) 0   Turkey (1) 1 *(Nihat 12)*
Slovakia: Konig; Zeman, Hlinka (Vittek 46), Klimpl, Labant, Karhan (Mintal 71), Janocko, Petras, Demo, Michalik (Kisel 77), Nemeth S.
Turkey: Rustu; Fatih, Alpay, Bulent K, Ergun, Okan (Tayfun 58), Basturk (Volkan 80), Tugay, Emre B (Ibrahim 90), Nihat, Hakan Sukur.
Referee: Hauge (Norway).

Middlesbrough, 11 June 2003, 35,000

England (0) 2 *(Owen 62 (pen), 73)*   **Slovakia (1) 1** *(Janocko 31)*
England: James; Mills (Hargreaves 43), Ashley Cole, Neville P, Southgate, Upson, Gerrard, Scholes, Rooney (Vassell 58), Owen, Lampard.
Slovakia: Konig; Hanek, Labant (Debnar 38), Zabavnik, Zeman, Petras, Demo (Mintal 55), Janocko, Nemeth S (Reiter 75), Vittek, Michalik.
Referee: Stark (Germany).

Istanbul, 11 June 2003, 22,000

Turkey (1) 3 *(Nihat 27, Gokdeniz 48, Hakan Sukur 59)*   **Macedonia (2) 2** *(Grozdanovski 23, Sakiri 29)*
Turkey: Rustu; Fatih, Alpay (Yildirin 72), Bulent K, Ergun, Emre B (Gokdeniz 43), Tayfun (Okan 46), Tugay, Ibrahim, Hakan Sukur (Volkan 78), Nihat.
Macedonia: Milosevski; Sumolikoski, Sedloski, Vasovski, Lazarevski, Bozinovski (Poleski 76), Mitreski A, Sakiri, Stoikov, Grozdanovski (Nuhiji 56), Jancevski.
Referee: Rosetti (Italy).

Vaduz, 6 September 2003, 3548

Liechtenstein (0) 0   Turkey (2) 3 *(Tumer 14, Okan 41, Hakan Sukur 50)*
Liechtenstein: Jehle; Telser, Michael Stocklasa (Maierhofer 80), Hasler D, Ritter, Martin Stocklasa, Beck T (Beck R 59), Gerster, D'Elia, Frick M, Burgmeier (Buchel 59).
Turkey: Rustu; Umit D, Bulent K (Deniz 64), Alpay, Ibrahim, Tumer (Hasan Sas 64), Tugay, Okan (Gokdeniz 75), Ergun, Hakan Sukur, Tuncay.
Referee: Van Egmond (Holland).

Skopje, 6 September 2003, 20,500

Macedonia (1) 1 *(Hristov 28)*   **England (0) 2** *(Rooney 53, Beckham 63 (pen))*
Macedonia: Milosevski; Stojanovski, Mitreski I, Stavrevski, Grozdanovski (Braga 56), Trajanov, Pandev (Gjuzelov 48), Sumolikoski, Sakiri, Naumoski, Hristov (Dimitrovski 88).
England: James; Neville G, Ashley Cole, Lampard (Heskey 46), Terry, Campbell, Beckham, Butt, Rooney (Neville P 74), Owen (Dyer 86), Hargreaves.
Referee: De Bleeckere (Belgium).

Old Trafford, 10 September 2003, 64,931

England (0) 2 *(Owen 46, Rooney 52)*   **Liechtenstein (0) 0**
England: James; Neville G, Bridge, Gerrard (Hargreaves 58), Terry, Upson, Beckham (Neville P 58), Rooney (Cole J 69), Beattie, Owen, Lampard.
Liechtenstein: Jehle; Telser, Michael Stocklasa (Maierhofer 46), Hasler D, Ritter, Martin Stocklasa, Burgmeier, Gerster, Beck R (Beck T 57), D'Elia (Buchel 73), Frick M.
Referee: Fisker (Denmark).

Zilina, 10 September 2003, 2286

Slovakia (1) 1 *(Nemeth S 25)*   **Macedonia (0) 1** *(Dimitrovski 62)*
Slovakia: Konig; Petras, Labant V, Klimpl, Zabavnik, Labant B, Durica (Kisel 71), Oravec, Janocko (Sninsky 89), Mintal (Urban 71), Nemeth S.
Macedonia: Milosevski; Stojanovski, Mitreski I, Stavrevski, Sedloski, Jancevski, Pandev (Kapinkovski 73), Trajanov, Grozdanovski (Georgievski 90), Sakiri, Naumoski (Dimitrovski 33).
Referee: Sundell (Sweden).

Vaduz, 11 October 2003, 1500

Liechtenstein (0) 0   Slovakia (0) 2 *(Vittek 40, 56)*
Liechtenstein: Heeb; Telser, Maierhofer, Hasler D, Michael Stocklasa, Ritter, Beck T (Beck R 46), Beck M (Rohrer 46), D'Elia (Buchel 76), Frick M, Burgmeier.

252

Slovakia: Konig; Klimpl, Leitner, Labant B, Varga, Zabavnik, Kisel (Urban 46), Michalik (Babnic 84), Janocko, Nemeth S (Oravec 76), Vittek.
Referee: Hyylia (Finland).

Istanbul, 11 October 2003, 42,000

Turkey (0) 0   England (0) 0
Turkey: Rustu; Fatih, Alpay, Bulent K, Ibrahim, Okan (Ilhan 67), Tugay, Emre B (Ergun 79), Sergen (Tuncay 61), Nihat, Hakan Sukur.
England: James; Neville G, Ashley Cole, Gerrard, Campbell, Terry, Beckham, Butt, Rooney (Dyer 73), Heskey (Vassell 68), Scholes (Lampard 90).
Referee: Collina (Italy).

Group 7 Final Table	P	W	D	L	F	A	Pts
England	8	6	2	0	14	5	20
Turkey	8	6	1	1	17	5	19
Slovakia	8	3	1	4	11	9	10
Macedonia	8	1	3	4	11	14	6
Liechtenstein	8	0	1	7	2	22	1

GROUP 8

Brussels, 7 September 2002, 20,000

Belgium (0) 0   Bulgaria (1) 2 *(Jankovic 17, Stilian Petrov 63)*
Belgium: De Vlieger; Vreven, Van Buyten, Simons, Van der Heyden (Peeters B 64), Englebert (Mpenza M 53), Vanderhaeghe, Baseggio, Goor, Mpenza E (Thijs 70), Sonck.
Bulgaria: Zdravkov; Kishishev, Kirilov, Petov I, Petrov M, Peev (Petkov G 83), Stilian Petrov, Balakov, Petov M (Zagorcic 90), Pazin, Jankovic (Chilikov 77).
Referee: Hauge (Norway).

Osijek, 7 September 2002, 12,000

Croatia (0) 0   Estonia (0) 0
Croatia: Pletikosa; Zivkovic, Babic, Simic D, Tokic, Vugrinec, Tapalovic, Saric (Tomas 79), Maric T (Petric 60), Olic, Maric S (Rapajic 46).
Estonia: Poom; Allas, Stepanovs, Piroja, Saviauk, Rooba M, Reim, Kristal, Lindpere (Rooba U 59), Zelinski, Oper.
Referee: Marin (Spain).

Andorra, 12 October 2002, 700

Andorra (0) 0   Belgium (0) 1 *(Sonck 61)*
Andorra: Koldo; Ayala, Txema (Escura 66), Jonas, Lima A, Fernandez (Silva 6), Emiliano, Jimenez (Lucendo 75), Juli Sanchez, Ruiz, Sonejee.
Belgium: De Vlieger; De Cock, Dheedene, Buffel, Valgaeren, Simons, Vanderhaeghe, Baseggio (Thijs 81), Sonck (Soeters 90), Van Houdt, Goor.
Referee: Nalbandian (Armenia).

Sofia, 12 October 2002, 43,000

Bulgaria (2) 2 *(Stilian Petrov 22, Berbatov 37)*   **Croatia (0) 0**
Bulgaria: Zdravkov; Kishishev, Petov I, Stilian Petrov, Pazin, Kirilov, Peev (Ivanov G 90), Jankovic, Berbatov (Chilikov 39), Petrov M (Petrov G 66), Balakov.
Croatia: Pletikosa; Simic D (Olic 18), Zivkovic, Tomas, Kovac R, Tudor, Vugrinec, Leko, Rapajic (Maric M 46), Boksic (Maric S 69), Stanic.
Referee: Frisk (Sweden).

Sofia, 16 October 2002, 38,000

Bulgaria (1) 2 *(Chilikov 37, Balakov 59)*   **Andorra (0) 1** *(Lima A 81)*
Bulgaria: Zdravkov; Kishishev, Jankovic (Gonzo 77), Peev, Pazin, Kirilov, Stilian Petrov, Balakov (Svetoslav Petrov 62), Petrov M (Manchev 75), Chilikov, Petkov I.
Andorra: Koldo; Ayala, Jonas, Lima A■, Fernandez, Escura, Emiliano (Silva 64), Lima I, Jimenez (Marc 80), Sonejee, Ruiz.
Referee: Richards (Wales).

Tallinn, 16 October 2002, 4000

Estonia (0) 0   Belgium (1) 1 *(Sonck 2)*
Estonia: Poom; Allas, Rooba U, Anniste (Haavistu 46), Stepanovs, Piiroja, Reim, Kristal (Lindpere 83), Oper, Zelinski, Terehhov (Viikmae 60).
Belgium: De Vlieger; De Cock, Dheedene, Vanderhaeghe, Valgaeren, Simons, Buffel (Van Hout 89), Baseggio, Sonck, Van Houdt, Goor.
Referee: Riley (England).

Zagreb, 29 March 2003, 22,000

Croatia (1) 4 *(Srna 9, Prso 53, Maric T 68, Leko 76)*   **Belgium (0) 0**
Croatia: Pletikosa; Simic D, Simunic, Kovac R, Zivkovic, Rapajic, Tudor (Kovac N 77), Srna, Rosso (Leko 46), Prso (Stanic 70), Maric T.
Belgium: Vandendriessche; De Cock (Deflandre 57), Valgaeren (Van Damme 67), Van Buyten, Van der Heyden, Buffel, Simons, Englebert (Baseggio 55), Goor, Sonck, Mpenza E.
Referee: Fandel (Germany).

Varazdin, 2 April 2003, 10,000

Croatia (2) 2 *(Rapajic 11 (pen), 44)*   **Andorra (0) 0**
Croatia: Pletikosa; Simic D, Simunic (Kovac N 46), Kovac R, Zivkovic, Rapajic (Babic 65), Tudor, Srna, Leko, Prso, Maric T (Stanic 46).
Andorra: Koldo; Ayala, Txema, Jonas, Fernandez, Sonejee, Emiliano (Motwani 89), Marc, Pol Perez (Lucendo 79), Jimenez (Escura 55), Juli Sanchez.
Referee: Salomir (Romania).

Tallinn, 2 April 2003, 3200

Estonia (0) 0   Bulgaria (0) 0
Estonia: Poom; Allas, Lemsalu, Jaager, Rooba U, Leetma, Kristal, Oper, Haavistu (Reinumae 63), Terehov, Zelinski (Viikmae 63).
Bulgaria: Zdravkov; Kishishev, Pazin, Petkov I, Kirilov, Stilian Petrov, Peev, Balakov, Petrov M (Petkov M 70), Berbatov, Jankovic (Todorov 46).
Referee: Plautz (Austria).

La Vella, 30 April 2003, 500

Andorra (0) 0   Estonia (1) 2 *(Zelinski 26, 74)*
Andorra: Koldo; Ayala (Silva 90), Txema, Escura, Fernandez, Emiliano, Marc (Alvarez 80), Sonejee, Juli Sanchez,Ruiz, Jimenez (Lucendo 71).
Estonia: Poom; Allas, Stepanovs, Lemsalu, Rooba U, Reim, Haavistu (Reinumae 69), Kristal, Terehhov (Lindpere 55), Viikmae (Rooba M 89), Zelinski.
Referee: Aydin (Turkey).

Sofia, 7 June 2003, 42,000

Bulgaria (0) 2 *(Berbatov 53, Todorov 71 (pen))*   **Belgium (1) 2** *(Stilian Petrov 31 (og), Clement 57)*
Bulgaria: Zdravkov; Stankov, Kirilov, Stoyanov, Petkov I, Borimirov, Stilian Petrov, Hristov (Manchev 72), Petrov M, Dimitrov (Alexandrov 81), Berbatov (Todorov 54).
Belgium: De Vlieger; Deflandre, Simons, Van Buyten, Dheedene, Mpenza M, Baseggio, Clement, Goor, Buffel, Sonck (Mpenza E 73).
Referee: Collina (Italy).

Tallinn, 7 June 2003, 2700

Estonia (2) 2 *(Allas 22, Viikmae 31)*   **Andorra (0) 0**
Estonia: Poom; Allas, Stepanovs, Piroja, Rooba U (Saviauk 49), Leetma, Kristal, Zahovalko, Haavistu (Rooba M 70), Viikmae, Lindpere (Reinumae 88).
Andorra: Koldo; Escura, Txema, Juli, Lima A, Lima I, Emiliano (Silva 83), Jimenez (Marc 53), Sonejee, Ruiz, Juli Sanchez.
Referee: Juhos (Hungary).

Ghent, 11 June 2003, 12,000

Belgium (2) 3 *(Goor 20, 65, Sonck 44)*   **Andorra (0) 0**
Belgium: De Vlieger; De Cock, Simons, Van Buyten, Dheedene (Van der Heyden 79), Clement, Baseggio, Goor (Soetars 83), Mpenza M, Sonck, Buffel (Martens 73).
Andorra: Koldo; Ayala, Txema, Jonas, Sonejee (Lucendo 81), Lima A, Lima I, Emiliano (Alvarez 70), Juli Sanchez (Escura 58), Fernandez, Marc.
Referee: Shmolik (Belarus).

254

Tallinn, 11 June 2003, 6000

Estonia (0) 0   Croatia (0) 1 *(Kovac N 77)*
Estonia: Poom; Allas (Zahovalko 82), Stepanovs, Piiroja, Rooba U, Leetma, Kristal, Oper, Rooba M (Reinumae 71), Lindpere (Lemsalu 83), Zelinski.
Croatia: Pletikosa; Simunic, Tomas, Zivkovic, Simic D (Maric T 61), Babic (Leko 73), Rapajic (Rosso 79), Kovac N, Srna, Olic, Prso.
Referee: Hamer (Luxembourg).

La Vella, 6 September 2003, 800

Andorra (0) 0   Croatia (2) 3 *(Kovac N 4, Simunic 16, Rosso 71)*
Andorra: Koldo; Ramirez, Txema, Jonas (Garcia 68), Lima A, Fernandez, Ayala, Juli Sanchez, Sonejee, Emiliano (Silva 49), Ruiz.
Croatia: Pletikosa; Simic D, Simunic, Tomas, Kovac R, Leko (Tudor 46), Rapajic, Rosso, Mornar, Kovac N (Vranjes 32), Olic (Prso 57).
Referee: Liba (Czech Republic).

Sofia, 6 September 2003, 25,128

Bulgaria (1) 2 *(Petrov M 16, Berbatov 67)*   **Estonia (0) 0**
Bulgaria: Ivankov; Borimirov, Kirilov, Stoyanov (Zhelev 88), Petkov I, Stilian Petrov, Hristov, Dimitrov (Peev 71), Jankovic (Krastev 63), Petrov M, Berbatov.
Estonia: Poom; Allas, Stepanovs, Jaager, Rooba U, Leetma, Rooba M (Reinumae 60), Kristal, Viikmae, Oper*, Lindpere (Klavan 74).
Referee: Wack (Germany).

La Vella, 10 September 2003, 1000

Andorra (0) 0   Bulgaria (2) 3 *(Berbatov 10, 23, Hristov 58)*
Andorra: Koldo; Ramirez, Txema, Jonas (Juli Sanchez 60), Lima A, Ayala (Escura 80), Sonejee, Jimenez, Fernandez, Marc, Ruiz (Lucendo 90).
Bulgaria: Ivankov; Borimirov, Kirilov, Pazin, Petkov I, Stilian Petrov, Peev (Manchev 63), Hristov, Jankovic (Dimitrov 59), Petrov M, Berbatov.
Referee: Mikulski (Poland).

Brussels, 10 September 2003, 35,000

Belgium (2) 2 *(Sonck 34, 42)*   **Croatia (1) 1** *(Simic D 35)*
Belgium: De Vlieger; Deflandre, Simons, Van Buyten, Van Damme, Baseggio, Goor, Clement, Walasiak, Buffel (Martens 88), Sonck (Soetars 90).
Croatia: Pletikosa; Simic D, Simunic*, Tomas, Kovac R, Zivkovic, Rapajic (Maric 78), Rosso (Srna 65), Mornar, Kovac N, Olic (Prso 46).
Referee: Poll (England).

Liege, 11 October 2003, 26,000

Belgium (1) 2 *(Reinumae 45 (og), Buffel 61)*   **Estonia (0) 0**
Belgium: De Vlieger; Deflandre, Van Buyten, Simons, Van Damme (Deschacht 56), Mpenza M, Baseggio, Clement, Goor, Sonck (Mpenza E 80), Buffel (Roussel 87).
Estonia: Poom; Jaager, Lemsalu, Piroja, Rooba U, Reinumae, Haavistu (Zahhoraiko 78), Reim, Rooba M, Klavan (Terehhov 64), Viikmae.
Referee: Busacca (Switzerland).

Zagreb, 11 October 2003, 37,000

Croatia (0) 1 *(Olic 48)*   **Bulgaria (0) 0**
Croatia: Pleitkosa; Simic D, Vranjes, Kovac R, Tudor, Zivkovic, Rapajic (Babic 54), Srna (Olic 46), Prso, Leko, Mornar (Rosso 76).
Bulgaria: Zdravkov; Krastev, Kirilov, Petkov I, Pazin, Borimirov, Dimitrov (Manchev 62), Peev (Jankov 72), Hristov, Stilian Petrov, Berbatov.
Referee: Veissiere (France).

Group 8 Final Table	P	W	D	L	F	A	Pts
Bulgaria	8	5	2	1	13	4	17
Croatia	8	5	1	2	12	4	16
Belgium	8	5	1	2	11	9	16
Estonia	8	2	2	4	4	6	8
Andorra	8	0	0	8	1	18	0

GROUP 9

Baku, 7 September 2002, 37,000

Azerbaijan (0) 0   Italy (1) 2 *(Akhmedov 32 (og), Del Piero 63)*
Azerbaijan: Kramarenko; Kuliyev K, Kerimov A, Akhmedov, Kuliyev E, Imamaliev, Kurbanov M (Musayev 68), Aliyev, Kurbanov K (Ismailov 90), Sadykhov, Agayev (Nabiev 88).
Italy: Buffon; Panucci, Nesta, Cannavaro, Coco, Gattuso, Di Biagio (Ambrosini 57), Del Piero, Tommasi, Inzaghi (Pirlo 78), Vieri (Montella 57).
Referee: Vassaras (Greece).

Helsinki, 7 September 2002, 35,833

Finland (0) 0   Wales (1) 2 *(Hartson 30, Davies 72)*
Finland: Niemi; Nylund (Johansson 69), Saarinen (Kopteff 78), Hyypia, Tihinen, Nurmela (Kottila 86), Riihilahti, Tainio, Kolkka, Litmanen, Kuqi.
Wales: Jones; Delaney, Gabbidon, Savage, Melville, Pembridge, Speed, Johnson (Bellamy 76), Hartson, Davies, Giggs.
Referee: Plautz (Austria).

Helsinki, 12 October 2002, 11,853

Finland (1) 3 *(Akhmedov 14 (og), Tihinen 59, Hyypia 71)*   **Azerbaijan (0) 0**
Finland: Niemi; Pasanen, Saarinen, Riihilahti, Tihinen, Hyypia (Kuivasto 79), Nurmela, Tainio (Wiss 74), Sumiala (Kuqi 85), Litmanen, Kolkka.
Azerbaijan: Gasanzade; Kerimov A, Akhmedov, Agayev, Kuliyev K, Kuliyev E, Mamedov R (Mamedov F 90), Kurbanov M (Sadykhov 65), Kurbanov G, Aliyev, Imamaliev (Vasilyev 83).
Referee: Hamer (Luxembourg).

Naples, 12 October 2002, 42,661

Italy (1) 1 *(Del Piero 39)*   **Yugoslavia (1) 1** *(Mijatovic 28)*
Italy: Buffon; Panucci, Zauri (Oddo 32), Pirlo (Ambrosini 34), Nesta, Cannavaro, Tommasi, Doni (Montella 46), Inzaghi, Del Piero, Gattuso.
Yugoslavia: Jevric; Lazetic, Dragutinovic, Vidic, Mihajlovic, Krstajic, Trobok, Mirkovic (Duljaj 8), Kovacevic D (Milosevic 69), Mijatovic (Kezman 66), Stankovic D.
Referee: Gonzalez (Spain).

Cardiff, 16 October 2002, 70,000

Wales (1) 2 *(Davies 12, Bellamy 71)*   **Italy (1) 1** *(Del Piero 32)*
Wales: Jones P; Delaney, Speed, Pembridge, Melville, Gabbidon, Davies, Savage, Hartson, Bellamy (Blake 90), Giggs.
Italy: Buffon; Panucci, Zauri, Pirlo, Nesta, Cannavaro, Tommasi, Di Biagio (Gattuso 65) (Marazzina 85), Del Piero, Montella (Maccarone 70), Ambrosini.
Referee: Veissiere (France).

Belgrade, 16 October 2002, 35,000

Yugoslavia (0) 2 *(Kovacevic D 56, Mihajlovic 84 (pen))*   **Finland (0) 0**
Yugoslavia: Jevric; Njegus (Krstajic 46), Dragutinovic, Stankovic D, Vidic, Mihajlovic, Lazetic, Duljaj, Kovacevic D (Milosevic 71), Kezman (Brnovic N 62), Mijatovic.
Finland: Niemi; Saarinen, Kuivasto, Pasanen (Reini² 63), Hyypia, Riihilahti, Nurmela, Tainio (Kuqi 82), Litmanen, Kolkka, Sumiala (Johansson 57).
Referee: Van Hulten (Holland).

Baku, 20 November 2002, 8000

Azerbaijan (0) 0   Wales (1) 2 *(Speed 9, Hartson 68)*
Azerbaijan: Gasanzade; Kerimov A (Mamedov F 46), Niftaliev, Sadykhov, Yadullayev, Akhmedov (Asadov 76), Kurbanov M (Ismailov 64), Imamaliev, Kurbanov A, Vasilyev, Aliyev.
Wales: Jones P; Delaney (Weston 71), Barnard, Robinson C (Trollope 90), Melville, Page, Davies, Speed, Earnshaw (Roberts N 89), Hartson, Giggs.
Referee: Huyghe (Belgium).

Podgorica, 13 February 2003, 8000

Yugoslavia (1) 2 *(Mijatovic 33 (pen), Lazetic 52)*   **Azerbaijan (0) 2** *(Kurbanov G 58, 77)*
Yugoslavia: Jevric; Djordjevic, Dudic, Bunjevcevic, Vukic, Lazetic (Markovic 74), Boskovic, Stankovic D, Mijatovic (Ljuboja 70), Kezman (Duljaj 59), Milosevic.
Azerbaijan: Gasanzade; Kuliyev K, Sadykhov, Kuliyev E, Akhmedov, Kurbanov M (Mamedov F 90), Mamedov R, Imamaliev, Aliyev (Mamedov K 87), Kurbanov G, Ismailov (Musayev 55).
Referee: Granat (Poland).

Palermo, 29 March 2003, 34,074

Italy (2) 2 *(Vieri 6, 22)*   **Finland (0) 0**
Italy: Buffon; Panucci, Zambrotta, Zanetti C, Cannavaro, Nesta, Perrotta, Camoranesi, Totti (Miccoli 86), Delvecchio (Birindelli 69), Vieri (Corradi 82).
Finland: Niemi; Pasanen, Tihinen, Hyypia, Saarinen, Riihilahti (Johansson 36), Ilola, Nurmela (Kopteff 75), Tainio, Kolkka (Kuqi 89), Forssell.
Referee: Ivanov (Russia).

Cardiff, 29 March 2003, 72,500

Wales (3) 4 *(Bellamy 1, Speed 40, Hartson 44, Giggs 52)*   **Azerbaijan (0) 0**
Wales: Jones; Davies, Speed (Trollope 46), Pembridge, Melville, Page, Oster, Savage (Robinson C 19), Hartson, Bellamy (Edwards 71), Giggs.
Azerbaijan: Gasanzade; Akhmedov, Kuliyev K, Aliyev (Tagizade 76), Kuliyev E (Yadullayev 46), Hajiyev (Mamedov F 46), Kurbanov M, Mamedov R, Kurbanov G, Imamaliev, Musayev.
Referee: Leuba (Switzerland).

Helsinki, 7 June 2003, 17,343

Finland (2) 3 *(Hyypia 20, Kolkka 45, Forssell 57)*   **Serbia-Montenegro (0) 0**
Finland: Jaaskelainen; Pasanen, Hyypia, Tihinen, Saarinen, Valakari, Nurmela (Riihilahti 88), Vayrynen, Litmanen, Forssell (Kuqi 81), Kolkka (Kopteff 67).
Serbia-Montenegro: Jevric; Mirkovic (Kovacevic M 81), Vidic, Mihajlovic■, Dmitrovic, Duljaj, Markovic, Krstajic, Mijatovic (Vukic 46), Kovacevic D, Milosevic (Jestrovic 46).
Referee: Colombo (France).

Baku, 11 June 2003, 3500

Azerbaijan (0) 2 *(Kurbanov G 88 (pen), Aliyev 90)*   **Serbia-Montenegro (1) 1** *(Boskovic 27)*
Azerbaijan: Kramarenko; Agayev (Tagizade 84), Akhmedov, Kuliyev E, Kerimov, Kuliyev K, Kurbanov M, Sadykhov, Aliyev, Kurbanov G (Yadullayev 90), Musayev (Ismailov 59).
Serbia-Montenegro: Jevric (Zilic 46); Mirkovic, Njegus, Djordjevic N, Malbasa, Duljaj (Milosevic 88), Vukic, Krstajic, Boskovic, Kovacevic D, Mijatovic (Kovacevic N 68).
Referee: Fisker (Denmark).

Helsinki, 11 June 2003, 36,850

Finland (0) 0   Italy (1) 2 *(Totti 32, Del Piero 73)*
Finland: Jaaskelainen; Pasanen, Hyypia, Tihinen, Saarinen, Valakari (Riihilahti 82), Nurmela (Kopteff 69), Vayrynen, Litmanen, Forssell, Kolkka (Johansson 79).
Italy: Buffon; Panucci, Zambrotta, Perrotta, Nesta, Cannavaro (Legrottaglie 90), Zanetti C, Fiore (Oddo 83), Totti, Del Piero, Corradi (Delvecchio 85).
Referee: Siric (Croatia).

Belgrade, 20 August 2003, 25,000

Serbia-Montenegro (0) 1 *(Mladenovic 73)*   **Wales (0) 0**
Serbia-Montenegro: Jevric; Gavrancic, Krstajic, Stefanovic, Cirkovic, Mladenovic, Dragutinovic, Stankovic D (Djordjevic P 81), Vukic (Ilic 68), Kovacevic D, Kezman (Milosevic 71).
Wales: Jones P; Delaney, Speed, Pembridge, Page, Gabbidon, Davies, Savage, Blake (Earnshaw), Bellamy, Giggs.
Referee: Frisk (Sweden).

Baku, 6 September 2003, 450

Azerbaijan (0) 1 *(Ismailov 89)*   **Finland (0) 2** *(Tainio 52, Nurmela 76)*
Azerbaijan: Kramarenko; Agayev (Musayev 11), Akhmedov**■**, Kuliyev E, Kuliyev K, Kurbanov M, Yadullayev, Sadykhov, Ismailov, Aliyev, Vasilyev.
Finland: Niemi; Saarinen, Hyypia, Pasanen, Vayrynen (Riihilahti 69), Nurmela, Tainio (Valakari 86), Kolkka, Reini, Forssell, Johansson (Kopteff 46).
Referee: Hrinak (Slovakia).

Milan, 6 September 2003, 68,000

Italy (0) 4 *(Inzaghi 59, 63, 70, Del Piero 76 (pen))*   **Wales (0) 0**
Italy: Buffon; Panucci (Oddo 58), Nesta, Cannavaro, Zambrotta, Camoranesi, Perrotta (Fiore 86), Zanetti C, Del Piero, Inzaghi (Gattuso 74), Vieri.
Wales: Jones P; Delaney, Speed, Pembridge (Johnson 79), Page, Savage, Koumas (Earnshaw 71), Davies, Hartson (Blake 82), Bellamy, Giggs.
Referee: Merk (Germany).

Belgrade, 10 September 2003, 35,000

Serbia-Montenegro (0) 1 *(Ilic 82)*   **Italy (1) 1** *(Inzaghi 22)*
Serbia-Montenegro: Jevric; Gavrancic, Krstajic, Stefanovic, Cirkovic, Mladenovic, Dragutinovic (Boskovic 70), Ilic, Djordjevic P, Kezman (Ljuboja 60), Milosevic.
Italy: Buffon; Panucci, Nesta, Cannavaro, Zambrotta, Tacchinardi, Perrotta, Camoranesi (Gattuso 51), Del Piero, Inzaghi (Fiore 64), Vieri (Corradi 79).
Referee: Hamer (Luxembourg).

Cardiff, 10 September 2003, 72,500

Wales (1) 1 *(Davies 3)*   **Finland (0) 1** *(Forssell 79)*
Wales: Jones P; Weston (Johnson 72), Speed, Pembridge, Page, Melville, Davies, Koumas**■**, Hartson (Blake 81), Earnshaw, Giggs.
Finland: Niemi; Pasanen (Kopteff 81), Hyypia, Tihinen, Saarinen (Reini 46), Nurmela, Riihilahti, Tainio, Vayrynen (Kuqi 57), Kolkka, Forssell.
Referee: Ibanez (Spain).

Reggio Calabria, 11 October 2003, 30,000

Italy (2) 4 *(Vieri 16, Inzaghi 24, 88, Di Vaio 65)*   **Azerbaijan (0) 0**
Italy: Buffon; Oddo, Nesta (Ferrari 77), Cannavaro, Zambrotta, Camoranesi (Gattuso 87), Zanetti, Perrotta, Totti, Inzaghi, Vieri (Di Vaio 55).
Azerbaijan: Kramarenko (Gasanzade 56); Agayev, Kerimov, Imamaliev, Kuliyev E, Kuliyev K, Kurbanov M (Mamedov R 84), Tagizade (Vasilyev 74), Yadullayev, Sadykhov, Aliyev.
Referee: Dougal (Scotland).

Cardiff, 11 October 2003, 72,514

Wales (1) 2 *(Hartson 24 (pen), Earnshaw 90)*   **Serbia-Montenegro (1) 3** *(Vukic 4, Milosevic 82, Ljuboja 87)*
Wales: Jones P; Weston (Edwards 73), Barnard, Speed, Gabbidon, Delaney, Robinson C (Oster 88), Bellamy, Earnshaw, Hartson (Blake 86), Giggs.
Serbia-Montenegro: Jevric; Gavrancic, Bunjevcevic, Djordjevic N, Cirkovic (Brnovic 74), Vukic, Mladenovic, Boskovic, Sarac, Kezman (Milosevic 60), Kovacevic D (Ljuboja 75).
Referee: Stuchlik (Austria).

Group 9 Final Table	P	W	D	L	F	A	Pts
Italy	8	5	2	1	17	4	17
Wales	8	4	1	3	13	10	13
Serbia-Montenegro	8	3	3	2	11	11	12
Finland	8	3	1	4	9	10	9
Azerbaijan	8	1	1	6	5	20	4

Serbia-Montenegro: changed name from Yugoslavia in February 2003.

GROUP 10

Moscow, 7 September 2002, 23,000

Russia (2) 4 *(Kariaka 20, Bestchastnykh 24, Kerzhakov 71, Babb 88 (og))*   **Republic of Ireland (0) 2** *(Doherty 69, Morrison 76)*
Russia: Ovchinnikov; Loskov, Yanovsky, Ignachevitch, Onopko, Nizhegorodov, Kariaka, Aldonin, Bestchastnykh (Kerzhakov 46), Semak (Khokhlov 75), Gusev (Solomatin 28).

258

Republic of Ireland: Given; Finnan, Harte, Cunningham, Breen, Kinsella, McAteer (Doherty 65), Holland, Robbie Keane, Duff (Morrison 18), Kilbane (Babb 85).
Referee: Colombo (France).

Basle, 7 September 2002, 20,500

Switzerland (1) 4 *(Frei 37, Yakin H 63, Muller P 74, Chapuisat 82)*   **Georgia (0) 1** *(Arveladze A 62)*
Switzerland: Stiel; Haas, Henchoz, Yakin M, Magnin (Berner 83), Cabanas, Vogel (Celestini 68), Muller P, Frei, Chapuisat, Yakin H (Wicky 74).
Georgia: Gvaramadze; Kobiashvili, Shekiladze, Kaladze, Sajaia (Rekhviashvili 46) (Kavelashvili 84), Nemsadze, Tskitishvili, Jamarauli, Demetradze, Arveladze A, Kinkladze (Burduli 46).
Referee: Krinak (Slovakia).

Tirana, 12 October 2002, 15,000

Albania (0) 1 *(Murati 79)*   **Switzerland (1) 1** *(Yakin M 38)*
Albania: Strakosha; Fakaj, Duro (Sina 88), Murati, Cipi, Xhumba, Hasi, Lala, Vata F, Tare (Myrtaj 71), Haxhi (Bushi 60).
Switzerland: Stiel; Haas, Magnin, Cabanas (Cantaluppi 81), Yakin M, Muller P, Vogel, Yakin H (Celestini 63), Frei (Thurre 84), Chapuisat, Wicky.
Referee: Erdemir (Turkey).

Dublin, 16 October 2002, 40,000

Republic of Ireland (0) 1 *(Magnin 78 (og))*   **Switzerland (1) 2** *(Yakin H 45, Celestini 87)*
Republic of Ireland: Given; Kelly G, Harte (Doherty 86), Holland, Breen, Cunningham, Healy, Kinsella, Robbie Keane, Duff (Butler 82), Kilbane (Morrison 61).
Switzerland: Stiel; Haas, Magnin, Vogel, Yakin M, Muller, Cabanas, Yakin H (Celestini 84), Frei (Thurre 70), Chapuisat, Wicky (Cantaluppi 84).
Referee: Pedersen (Norway).

Moscow, 16 October 2002, 15,000

Russia (2) 4 *(Kerzhakov 3, Semak 42, 55, Onopko 52)*   **Albania (1) 1** *(Duro 13)*
Russia: Ovchinnikov; Nizhegorodov, Ignachevitch, Smertin, Semak, Yanovsky, Onopko, Gusev (Yevseyev 81), Solomatin, Loskov (Aldonin 46), Kerzhakov (Popov 64).
Albania: Strakosha; Cipi, Xhumba, Fakaj, Murati, Hasi, Lala, Duro, Vata F (Sina 60), Tare (Myrtaj 69), Haxhi (Bushi 56).
Referee: Sundell (Sweden).

Tirana, 29 March 2003, 16,000

Albania (1) 3 *(Rraklli 20, Lala 80, Tare 83)*   **Russia (0) 1** *(Kariaka 77)*
Albania: Strakosha; Beqiri, Cipi, Aliaj, Duro, Lala, Hasi, Murati (Bellai 68), Skela (Dede 84), Rraklli (Myrtaj 71), Tare.
Russia: Ovchinnikov; Nizhegorodov, Ignachevitch, Berezutski, Gusev (Bestchastnykh 56), Aldonin, Smertin (Yanovsky 73), Tochilin (Kariaka 46), Loskov, Semak, Kerzhakov.
Referee: Alaerts (Belgium).

Tbilisi, 29 March 2003, 15,000

Georgia (0) 1 *(Kobiashvili 61)*   **Republic of Ireland (1) 2** *(Duff 18, Doherty 84)*
Georgia: Lomaia; Khizanishvili, Shashiashvili, Amisulashvili, Nemsadze, Tskitishvili, Jamarauli, Kinkladze (Didava 70), Kobiashvili, Ketsbaia (Demetradze 46), Iashvili.
Republic of Ireland: Given; Carr, O'Shea, Kinsella, Breen, Cunningham, Carsley, Holland, Doherty, Kilbane, Duff.
Referee: Vassaras (Greece).

Tirana, 2 April 2003, 17,000

Albania (0) 0   Republic of Ireland (0) 0
Albania: Strakosha; Duro, Murati (Bellai 67), Beqiri, Cipi, Aliaj, Lala, Hasi, Skela (Bushi 86), Rraklli (Myrtaj 69), Tare.
Republic of Ireland: Given; Carr, O'Shea, Holland, Green, Cunningham, Carsley, Kinsella, Keane (Doherty 67), Duff, Kilbane.
Referee: Farina (Italy).

Tbilisi, 2 April 2003, 10,000

Georgia (0) 0   Switzerland (0) 0
Georgia: Lomaia; Khizanishvili, Kemoklidze, Khizaneishvili, Kvirkvelia, Tskitishvili, Nemsadze (Didava 46), Rekhviashvili, Kobiashvili, Demetradze (Ashvetia 72), Iashvili (Arveladze S 46).
Switzerland: Zuberbuhler; Haas, Berner, Vogel, Yakin M, Meyer, Cabanas (Cantaluppi 68), Yakin H (Thurre 90), Frei (Celestini 59), Chapuisat, Wicky.
Referee: Trivkovic (Croatia).

Tbilisi, 30 April 2003, 11,000

Georgia (1) 1 *(Asatiani 11)*   **Russia (0) 0**
Georgia: Lomaia; Khizanishvili, Khizaneishvili, Kaladze, Tskitishvili, Nemsadze, Kvirkvelia, Burduli (Shashiashvili 80), Ashvetia (Alexidze 84), Asatiani (Didava 75), Demetradze.
Russia: Mandrykin; Nizhegorodov, Ignachevitch (Evsikov 14), Onopko, Aldonin (Sychev 79), Alenichev, Smertin, Titov, Kariaka, Semak, Izmailov (Kerzhakov 46).
Referee: Wack (Germany).

Dublin, 7 June 2003, 33,000

Republic of Ireland (1) 2 *(Keane 6, Aliaj 90)*   **Albania (1) 1** *(Skela 9)*
Republic of Ireland: Given; Carr, O'Shea, Kinsella (Carsley 55), Cunningham, Breen, Kilbane (Reid 76), Holland, Robbie Keane, Connolly (Doherty 65), Duff.
Albania: Strakosha (Beqaj 77); Beqiri, Cipi, Aliaj, Duro, Lala, Hasi, Skela, Murati (Bellai 57), Rraklli (Myrtaj 86), Tare.
Referee: Mikulski (Poland).

Basle, 7 June 2003, 30,500

Switzerland (2) 2 *(Frei 14, 16)*   **Russia (1) 2** *(Ignachevitch 24, 68 (pen))*
Switzerland: Stiel; Haas, Yakin M, Muller P (Henchoz 82), Magnin (Berner 61), Cabanas, Celestini, Wicky (Vogel 71), Yakin H, Frei, Chapuisat.
Russia: Ovchinnikov; Berezutski, Ignachevitch, Kovtun, Gusev, Smertin, Yanovski, Aldonin, Karyaka (Bystrov 52), Popov (Sychev 46), Semak (Evsikov 82).
Referee: Ibanez (Spain).

Dublin, 11 June 2003, 36,000

Republic of Ireland (1) 2 *(Doherty 43, Robbie Keane 59)*   **Georgia (0) 0**
Republic of Ireland: Given; Carr, O'Shea, Carsley, Cunningham, Breen, Healy (Kinsella 86), Holland, Robbie Keane, Doherty (Lee 88), Kilbane.
Georgia: Lomaia; Khizanishvili, Khizaneishvili, Kaladze, Rekhviashvili, Burduli, Didava (Aleksidze 76), Asatiani, Amisulashvili, Demetradze (Daraselia 62), Arveladze S.
Referee: Gonzalez (Spain).

Geneva, 11 June 2003, 26,000

Switzerland (2) 3 *(Haas 10, Frei 32, Cabanas 72)*   **Albania (1) 2** *(Lala 23, Skela 86 (pen))*
Switzerland: Stiel; Haas, Henchoz (Zwyssig 75), Yakin M, Berner, Cabanas, Vogel, Wicky (Spycher 64), Yakin H, Frei (Celestini 83), Chapuisat.
Albania: Strakosha; Beqiri, Cipi (Cana 46), Aliaj, Duro (Dragusha 74), Hasi, Lala, Skela, Bellai, Bushai (Rraklli 62), Tare.
Referee: Bennett (England).

Tbilisi, 6 September 2003, 18,000

Georgia (3) 3 *(Arveladze S 9, 44, Ashvetia 18)*   **Albania (0) 0**
Georgia: Lomaia; Khizanishvili, Kemoklidze, Burduli (Rekhviashvili 70), Kvirkvelia, Kobiashvili, Nemsadze, Iashvili, Ashvetia, Jamarauli (Asatiani 58), Arveladze S (Demetradze 60).
Albania: Strakosha; Cipi, Dede (Jupi 10), Cana, Hasi, Murati, Bushai (Tare 61), Aliaj, Skela, Bellai (Duro 46), Dragusha.
Referee: Voliquartz (Denmark).

Dublin, 6 September 2003, 36,000

Republic of Ireland (1) 1 *(Duff 35)*   **Russia (1) 1** *(Ignachevitch 42)*
Republic of Ireland: Given; Carr, O'Shea, Carsley, Cunningham, Breen, Carsley (Reid 46), Kilbane, Holland, Morrison (Doherty 73), Healy, Duff.
Russia: Ovchinnikov; Evseev, Ignachevitch, Onopko, Sennikov, Gusev, Smertin, Mostovoi, Yesipov (Kerzhakov 33), Alenichev (Aldonin 39), Bulykin.
Referee: Michel (Slovakia).

Tirana, 10 September 2003, 10,500

Albania (0) 3 *(Hasi 52, Tare 54, Bushi 80)*   **Georgia (0) 1** *(Arveladze S 63)*
Albania: Strakosha; Beqiri, Cipi, Cana (Myrtaj 85), Hasi, Murati (Haxhi 18), Shkembi, Rraklli (Bushi 58), Aliaj, Tare, Duro.
Georgia: Lomaia; Khizanishvili, Kemoklidze (Rekhviashvili 40), Didava (Kinkladze 54), Kvirkvelia, Kobiashvili, Nemsadze, Ashvetia, Iashvili (Demetradze 54), Jamarauli, Arveladze S.
Referee: Salomir (Romania).

Moscow, 10 September 2003, 29,000

Russia (2) 4 *(Bulykin 20, 33, 59, Mostovoi 72)*   **Switzerland (1) 1** *(Karyaka 12 (og))*
Russia: Ovchinnikov; Radimov, Solomatin (Sennikov 46), Karyaka, Ignachevitch, Onopko, Gusev (Izmailov 58), Smertin, Kerzhakov (Sychev 77), Mostovoi, Bulykin.
Switzerland: Zuberbuhler; Meyer, Berner (Wicky 71), Henchoz, Yakin M, Vogel, Cabanas■, Muller P (Huggel 64), Frei (Rama 79), Celestini, Chapuisat.
Referee: Collina (Italy).

Moscow, 11 October 2003, 30,000

Russia (2) 3 *(Bulykin 29, Titov 45, Sychev 73)*   **Georgia (1) 1** *(Iashvili 5)*
Russia: Ovchinnikov; Evseev, Sennikov, Titov, Karayaka (Izmailov 46), Ignachevitch, Onopko, Gusev (Aldonin 63), Bulykin, Mostovoi, Kerzhakov (Sychev 56).
Georgia: Lomaia; Khizanishvili, Kemoklidze, Kobiashvili, Kvirkvelia, Tskitishvili (Asatiani 54), Nemsadze, Ashvetia (Daraselia 58), Iashvili, Jamarauli (Burduli 46), Demetradze.
Referee: Plautz (Austria).

Basle, 11 October 2003, 31,006

Switzerland (1) 2 *(Yakin H 6, Frei 60)*   **Republic of Ireland (0) 0**
Switzerland: Stiel; Haas, Yakin M, Muller P, Spycher, Huggel, Vogel, Yakin H (Celestini 55), Wicky, Frei (Henchoz 90), Chapuisat (Streller 68).
Republic of Ireland: Given; Carr, Harte, Holland (Kinsella 74), Breen, O'Shea, Duff, Healy, Robbie Keane, Connolly (Morrison 56), Kilbane (Finnan 74).
Referee: Frisk (Sweden).

Group 10 Final Table	P	W	D	L	F	A	Pts
Switzerland	8	4	3	1	15	11	15
Russia	8	4	2	2	19	12	14
Republic of Ireland	8	3	2	3	10	11	11
Albania	8	2	2	4	11	15	8
Georgia	8	2	1	5	8	14	7

PLAY-OFFS FIRST LEG

Zagreb, 15 November 2003, 35,000

Croatia (1) 1 *(Prso 5)*   **Slovenia (1) 1** *(Siljak 22)*
Croatia: Pleitkosa; Simic D, Neretjak, Tomas, Tudor, Zivkovic (Srna 59), Mornar, Leko (Rosso 46), Kovac N, Prso, Olic (Rapajic 46).
Slovenia: Dabanovic; Cipot, Karic, Vugdalic, Knavs, Sukalo, Ceh N (Bulajic 86), Zahovic, Pavlin, Acimovic (Kapic 76), Siljak (Cesar 89).
Referee: Merk (Germany).

Riga, 15 November 2003, 8000

Latvia (1) 1 *(Verpakovsky 29)*   **Turkey (0) 0**
Latvia: Kolinko; Isakov, Lobanov, Stepanovs IN, Astafjevs, Korabiovs, Laizans, Bleidelis, Rubins (Pucinsks 83), Rimkus (Stolcers 86), Verpakovsky (Kolesnichenko 89).
Turkey: Rustu; Fatih, Bulent K, Ibrahim, Emre A■, Tugay, Ergun, Emre B (Tumer 88), Okan (Gokdeniz 84), Nihat (Deniz 77), Ilhan.
Referee: Veissiere (France).

Moscow, 15 November 2003, 29,000

Russia (0) 0   Wales (0) 0
Russia: Ovchinnikov; Evseev, Ignachevitch, Onopko, Sennikov, Smertin (Gusev 59), Mostovoi, Alenichev, Loskov, Sychev (Izmailov 46), Bulykin.
Wales: Jones P; Delaney, Barnard, Speed, Gabbidon, Melville, Johnson, Savage, Hartson (Blake 83), Koumas, Giggs.
Referee: Batista (Portugal).

Glasgow, 15 November 2003, 50,670

Scotland (1) 1 *(McFadden 22)*   **Holland (0) 0**
Scotland: Douglas; McNamara, Naysmith, Dailly, Pressley, Wilkie, Fletcher, Ferguson, Dickov (Miller 66), McFadden (Hutchison 90), McCann (Pearson 71).
Holland: Van der Sar; Ooijer, Stam, Frank de Boer, Van Bronckhorst (Seedorf 46), Van der Meyde, Cocu, Davids (Van der Vaart 60), Overmars, Kluivert (Makaay 77), Van Nistelrooy.
Referee: Hauge (Norway).

Valencia, 15 November 2003, 53,000

Spain (1) 2 *(Raul 20, Berg H 85 (og))*   **Norway (1) 1** *(Iversen 14)*
Spain: Casillas; Michel Salgado, Helguera, Marchena, Puyol, Etxeberria (Joaquin 77), Albelda, Baraja, Reyes (Vicente 77), Raul, Fernando Torres (Valeron 68).
Norway: Johnsen E; Basma, Berg H, Lundekvam, Riise, Strand R (Brattbakk 25), Iversen (Johnsen F 77), Andresen (Berg R 87), Andersen, Solli, Flo T.
Referee: Poll (England).

PLAY-OFFS SECOND LEG

Amsterdam, 19 November 2003, 51,000

Holland (3) 6 *(Sneider 14, Ooijer 32, Van Nistelrooy 37, 51, 67, Frank de Boer 65)*
Scotland (0) 0
Holland: Van der Sar; Reiziger, Ooijer (Frank de Boer 46), Cocu, Bouma (Seedorf 68), Van der Meyde, Sneider, Davids, Overmars, Van der Vaart, Van Nistelrooy (Kluivert 77).
Scotland: Douglas; McNamara, Naysmith (Ross 46), Ferguson, Pressley, Wilkie, Fletcher, Rae, Dickov (Crawford 46), McFadden, McCann (Miller 62).
Referee: Michel (Slovakia).

Oslo, 19 November 2003, 25,106

Norway (0) 0   Spain (1) 3 *(Raul 34, Vicente 49, Etxeberria 55)*
Norway: Johnsen E (Olsen 61); Basma, Lundekvam, Johnsen R, Stensaas, Iversen, Andresen (Johnsen F 73), Andersen (Flo H 46), Solli, Riise, Flo T.
Spain: Casillas; Michel Salgado, Helguera, Cesar, Puyol, Xabi Alonso, Albelda (Baraja 84), Etxeberria (Joaquin 77), Valeron (Guti 73), Vicente, Raul.
Referee: Collina (Italy).

Ljubljana, 19 November 2003, 9000

Slovenia (0) 0   Croatia (0) 1 *(Prso 61)*
Slovenia: Dabanovic; Cipot (Bulajic 90), Karic, Vugdalic, Knavs, Sukalo (Rakovic 69), Ceh N, Zahovic, Pavlin, Rudonja (Kapic 46), Acimovic.
Croatia: Pletikosa; Srna, Simunic (Babic 53), Kovac R, Tudor■, Zivkovic, Rapajic (Tomas 69), Rosso, Prso (Leko 76), Kovac N, Sokota.
Referee: Meier (Switzerland).

Istanbul, 19 November 2003, 25,000

Turkey (1) 2 *(Ilhan 21, Hakan Sukur 64)*   **Latvia (0) 2** *(Laizans 66, Verpakovsky 77)*
Turkey: Omer; Umit D (Hasan Sas 78), Bulent K, Ibrahim, Deniz, Emre B, Tumer (Gokdeniz 60), Tugay (Tuncay 80), Nihat, Hakan Sukur, Ilhan.
Latvia: Kolinko; Stepanovs IN, Astafjevs, Zemlinsky, Laizans, Zirnis, Isakov, Bleidelis, Verpakovsky, Rubins, Rimkus (Stolcers 79).
Referee: Frisk (Sweden).

Cardiff, 19 November 2003, 73,062

Wales (0) 0   Russia (1) 1 *(Evseev 23)*
Wales: Jones P; Delaney, Barnard, Speed, Gabbidon, Melville, Koumas (Blake 74), Johnson (Earnshaw 58), Hartson, Savage, Giggs.
Russia: Malafeev; Evseev, Ignachevitch, Onopko, Sennikov, Smertin, Gusev, Titov (Radimov 59), Alenichev, Izmailov, Bulykin.
Referee: Gonzalez (Spain).

EURO 2004 FINAL COMPETITION

GROUP A

Estadio Dragao, Oporto, 12 June 2004, 52,000

Portugal (0) 1 *(Ronaldo 90)*   **Greece (1) 2** *(Karagounis 7, Basinas 51 (pen))*

Portugal: Ricardo; Paulo Ferreira, Rui Jorge, Rui Costa, Jorge Andrade, Fernando Couto, Figo, Costinha (Nuno Gomes 66), Simao Sabrosa (Ronaldo 46), Pauleta, Maniche.
Greece: Nikopolidis; Seitaridis, Fyssas, Karagounis (Katsouranis 46), Dellas, Kapsis, Zagorakis, Basinas, Charisteas (Lakis 74), Vryzas, Giannakopoulos (Nikolaidis 68).
Referee: Collina (Italy).

Faro-Loule, 12 June 2004, 30,000

Spain (0) 1 *(Valeron 60)*   **Russia (0) 0**

Spain: Casillas; Puyol, Raul Bravo, Baraja (Xabi Alonso 58), Helguera, Marchena, Albelda, Etxeberria, Raul (Torres 77), Morientes (Valeron 58), Vicente.
Russia: Ovchinnikov; Evseyev, Sennikov, Gusev (Radinov 46), Sharonov⌐, Smertin, Aldonin (Sychev 67), Mostovoi, Bulykin, Izmailov (Kirlia 73), Alenichev.
Referee: Meier (Switzerland).

Estadio Do Bessa Sec. XXI, 16 June 2004, 25,444

Greece (0) 1 *(Charisteas 66)*   **Spain (1) 1** *(Morientes 28)*

Greece: Nikopolidis; Seitaridis, Fyssas (Venetidis 85), Karagounis (Tsartas 52), Dellas, Kapsis, Giannakopoulos (Nikolaidis 49), Zagorakis, Charisteas, Vryzas, Katsouranis.
Spain: Casillas; Puyol, Raul Bravo, Baraja, Helguera, Marchena, Etxeberria (Joaquin 46), Albelda, Raul (Torres 80), Morientes (Valeron 65), Vicente.
Referee: Michel (Slovakia).

Estadio Da Luz, Lisbon, 16 June 2004, 58,000

Russia (0) 0   Portugal (1) 2 *(Maniche 7, Rui Costa 89)*

Russia: Ovchinnikov⌐; Evseyev, Sennikov, Aldonin, Smertin, Bugayev, Alenichev, Loskov, Izmailov (Bystrov 72), Kerzkhov, Kariaka (Bulykin 80).
Portugal: Ricardo; Miguel, Nuno Valente, Costinha, Jorge Andrade, Ricardo Carvalho, Simao Sabrosa (Rui Costa 63), Maniche, Deco, Pauleta, Figo (Ronaldo 78).
Referee: Hauge (Norway).

Faro-Loule, 20 June 2004, 25,000

Russia (2) 2 *(Kirichenko 2, Bulykin 17)*   **Greece (1) 1** *(Vryzas 43)*

Russia: Malafeyev; Anyukov, Evseyev, Gusev, Sharanov (Sennikov 56), Bugayev, Alenichev, Radimov, Bulykin (Sychev 46), Kariaka, Kirichenko.
Greece: Nikopolidis; Seitaridis, Venetidis (Fyssas 89), Katsouranis, Dellas, Kapsis, Basinas (Tsartas 42), Zagorakis, Papadopoulos (Nikolaidis 69), Charisteas, Vryzas.
Referee: Veissiere (France).

Estadio Jose Alvalade XXI, 20 June 2004, 47,491

Spain (0) 0   Portugal (0) 1 *(Nuno Gomes 57)*

Spain: Casillas; Puyol, Raul Bravo, Xabi Alonso, Helguera, Juanito (Morientes 80), Joaquin (Luque 72), Albelda (Baraja 66), Raul, Torres, Vicente.
Portugal: Ricardo; Miguel, Nuno Valente, Costinha, Jorge Andrade, Ricardo Carvalho, Figo (Petit 78), Maniche, Pauleta (Nuno Gomes 46), Deco, Ronaldo (Fernando Couto 84).
Referee: Frisk (Sweden).

GROUP A FINAL TABLE

	P	W	L	D	F	A	GD	Pts
Portugal	3	2	1	0	4	2	2	6
Greece	3	1	1	1	4	4	0	4
Spain	3	1	1	1	2	2	0	4
Russia	3	1	2	0	2	4	−2	3

GROUP B

Estadio Da Luz, Lisbon, 13 June 2004, 64,000

France (0) 2 *(Zidane 89, 90 (pen))*   **England (1) 1** *(Lampard 38)*
France: Barthez; Gallas, Lizarazu, Makelele, Thuram, Silvestre (Sagnol 79), Vieira, Zidane, Trezeguet, Henry, Pires (Wiltord 76).
England: James; Neville G, Cole A, Gerrard, Campbell, King, Beckham, Lampard, Rooney (Heskey 76), Owen (Vassell 69), Scholes (Hargreaves 76).
Referee: Merk (Germany).

Leiria, 13 June 2004, 25,000

Switzerland (0) 0   Croatia (0) 0
Switzerland: Stiel; Haas, Spycher, Vogel, Yakin M, Muller P, Huggel, Wicky (Henchoz 83), Chapuisat (Celestini 55), Frei, Yakin H (Gygax 85).
Croatia: Butina; Simic D (Srna 61), Zivkovic, Bjelica (Rosso 73), Kovac R, Simunic, Mornar, Kovac N, Sokota, Prso, Olic (Rapaic 46).
Referee: Batista (Portugal).

Leiria, 17 June 2004, 30,000

Croatia (0) 2 *(Rapaic 48, Prso 52)*   **France (1) 2** *(Tudor 22 (og), Trezeguet 64)*
Croatia: Butina; Simic D, Simunic, Rosso, Kovac R, Tudor, Bjelica (Leko 68), Kovac N, Sokota (Olic 73), Prso, Rapaic (Mornar 87).
France: Barthez; Gallas (Sagnol 81), Silvestre, Vieira, Thuram, Desailly, Wiltord (Pires 70), Dacourt (Pedretti 78), Trezeguet, Henry, Zidane.
Referee: Nielsen (Denmark).

Coimbra, 17 June 2004, 30,616

England (1) 3 *(Rooney 23, 75, Gerrard 82)*   **Switzerland (0) 0**
England: James; Neville G, Cole A, Gerrard, Campbell, Terry, Beckham, Lampard, Rooney (Dyer 83), Owen (Vassell 72), Scholes (Hargreaves 70).
Switzerland: Stiel; Haas, Spycher, Celestini (Cabanas 53), Yakin M, Muller P, Huggel, Wicky, Chapuisat (Gygaz 46), Frei, Yakin H (Vonlanthen 83).
Referee: Ivanov (Russia).

Estadio Da Luz, Lisbon, 21 June 2004, 63,000

Croatia (1) 2 *(Kovac N 5, Tudor 73)*   **England (2) 4** *(Scholes 40, Rooney 45, 68, Lampard 79)*
Croatia: Butina; Simic D (Srna 67), Simunic, Rosso, Kovac R (Mornar 46), Tudor, Kovac N, Zivkovic, Prso, Rapaic (Olic 55), Sokota.
England: James; Neville G, Cole A, Lampard (Neville P 84), Campbell, Terry, Beckham, Gerrard, Rooney (Vassell 71), Owen, Scholes (King 70).
Referee: Collina (Italy).

Coimbra, 21 June 2004, 30,000

Switzerland (1) 1 *(Vonlanthen 26)*   **France (1) 3** *(Zidane 20, Henry 76, 84)*
Switzerland: Stiel; Henchoz (Magnin 85), Spycher, Vogel, Yakin M, Muller P, Cabanas, Gygax (Rama 85), Wicky, Yakin H (Huggel 60), Vonlanthen.
France: Barthez; Sagnol (Gallas 46), Lizarazu, Makelele, Thuram, Silvestre, Vieira, Zidane, Trezeguet (Saha 75), Henry, Pires.
Referee: Michel (Slovakia).

GROUP B FINAL TABLE

	P	W	L	D	F	A	GD	Pts
France	3	2	0	1	7	4	3	7
England	3	2	1	0	8	4	4	6
Croatia	3	0	1	2	4	6	-2	2
Switzerland	3	0	2	1	1	6	-5	1

GROUP C

Guimaraes, 14 June 2004, 29,595

Denmark (0) 0   Italy (0) 0
Denmark: Sorensen; Helveg, Jensen N, Jensen D, Laursen, Henriksen, Poulsen (Priske 76), Jorgensen (Perez 72), Rommedahl, Sand (Jensen C 69), Tomasson.

Italy: Buffon; Panucci, Zambrotta, Perrotta, Nesta, Cannavaro, Zanetti C (Gattuso 57), Camoranesi (Fiore 68), Del Piero (Cassano 64), Vieri, Totti.
Referee: Gonzalez (Spain).

Estadio Jose Alvalade XXI, Lisbon, 14 June 2004, 52,000

Sweden (1) 5 *(Ljungberg 32, Larsson 57, 58, Ibrahimovic 78 (pen), Allback 90)*
Bulgaria (0) 0

Sweden: Isaksson; Lucic (Wilhelmsson 41), Edman, Linderoth, Mellberg, Jakobsson, Nilsson, Svensson A (Kallstrom 77), Ibrahimovic (Allback 81), Larsson, Ljungberg.
Bulgaria: Zdravkov; Ivanov, Petkov I, Hristov, Pazin, Kirilov, Peev, Petrov S, Berbatov (Manchev 76), Jankovic (Dimitrov 62), Petrov M (Lazarov 84).
Referee: Riley (England).

Braga, 18 June 2004, 24,131

Bulgaria (0) 0   Denmark (1) 2 *(Tomasson 44, Gronkjaer 90)*
Bulgaria: Zdravkov; Ivanov (Lazarov 51), Petkov I (Zagorcic 40), Hristov, Kirilov, Stoianov, Peev, Petrov S, Berbatov, Yankovich (Petkov M 81), Petrov M.
Denmark: Sorensen; Helveg, Jensen N, Gravesen, Laursen, Henriksen, Tomasson, Jensen D, Rommedahl (Gronkjaer 23), Sand, Jorgensen (Jensen C 72).
Referee: Batista (Portugal).

Estadio Dragao, Oporto, 18 June 2004, 44,926

Italy (0) 1 *(Cassano 37)*   **Sweden (0) 1** *(Ibrahimovic 85)*
Italy: Buffon; Panucci, Zambrotta, Pirlo, Nesta, Cannavaro, Gattuso (Favalli 76), Perrotta, Del Piero (Camoranesi 82), Vieri, Cassano (Fiore 70).
Sweden: Isaksson; Nilsson, Edman (Allback 76), Linderoth, Mellberg, Jakobsson, Wilhelmsson (Jonson 65), Svensson A (Kallstrom 55), Ibrahimovic, Larsson, Ljungberg.
Referee: Meier (Switzerland).

Estadio Do Bessa Sec. XXI, 22 June 2004, 29,000

Denmark (1) 2 *(Tomasson 28, 66)*   **Sweden (0) 2** *(Larsson 47 (pen), Jonson 89)*
Denmark: Sorensen; Helveg, Jensen N (Bogelund 46), Gravesen, Laursen, Henriksen, Tomasson, Jensen D (Poulsen 66), Sand, Jorgensen (Rommedahl 57), Gronkjaer.
Sweden: Isaksson; Nilsson, Edman, Jonson, Mellberg, Jakobsson, Andersson A (Allback 82), Kallstrom (Wilhelmsson 72), Ibrahimovic, Larsson, Ljungberg.
Referee: Merk (Germany).

Guimaraes, 22 June 2004, 16,002

Italy (0) 2 *(Perrotta 48, Cassano 90)*   **Bulgaria (1) 1** *(Petrov M 45)*
Italy: Buffon; Panucci, Zambrotta, Pirlo, Nesta, Materazzi (Di Vaio 83), Fiore, Perrotta (Oddo 68), Del Piero, Corradi (Vieri 54), Cassano.
Bulgaria: Zdravkov; Borimirov, Stoianov, Yankovich (Bozhinov 46), Zagorcic, Pazin (Kotev 64), Petov M, Lazarov, Berbatov, Petrov M, Hristov (Dimitrov 79).
Referee: Ivanov (Russia).

GROUP C FINAL TABLE

	P	W	L	D	F	A	GD	Pts
Sweden	3	1	0	2	8	3	5	5
Denmark	3	1	0	2	4	2	2	5
Italy	3	1	0	2	3	2	1	5
Bulgaria	3	0	3	0	1	9	–8	0

GROUP D

Aveiro, 15 June 2004, 25,000

Czech Republic (0) 2 *(Baros 73, Heinz 85)*   **Latvia (1) 1** *(Verpakovsky 45)*
Czech Republic: Cech; Grygera (Heinz 56), Jankulovski, Galasek (Smicer 64), Bolf, Ujfalusi, Poborsky, Rosicky, Baros (Jiranek 87), Koller, Nedved.
Latvia: Kolinko; Isakov, Blagonadezdin, Lobanov (Rimkus 90), Zemlinsky, Stepanovs IN, Astafjevs, Bleidelis, Verpakovsky (Pahars 82), Prohorenkovs (Laizans 71), Rubins.
Referee: Veissiere (France).

Estadio Dragao, Oporto, 15 June 2004, 46,000

Germany (1) 1 *(Frings 30)*   **Holland (0) 1** *(Van Nistelrooy 81)*
Germany: Kahn; Friedrich, Lahm, Hamann, Worns, Nowotny, Baumann, Schneider (Schweinsteiger 68), Kuranyi (Bobic 85), Frings (Ernst 79), Ballack.
Holland: Van der Sar; Heitinga (Van Hooijdonk 74), Van Bronckhorst, Cocu, Stam, Bouma, Davids (Sneijder 46), Van der Vaart, Van Nistelrooy, Van der Meyde, Zenden (Overmars 46).
Referee: Frisk (Sweden).

Aveiro, 19 June 2004, 29,935

Holland (2) 2 *(Bouma 4, Van Nistelrooy 19)*   **Czech Republic (1) 3** *(Koller 23, Baros 71, Smicer 88)*
Holland: Van der Sar; Heitinga¹, Van Bronckhorst, Cocu, Stam, Bouma, Seedorf (Van der Vaart 85), Davids, Van Nistelrooy, Van der Meyde (Reiziger 79), Robben (Bosvelt 60).
Czech Republic: Cech; Grygera (Smicer 25), Galasek (Heinz 62), Poborsky, Ujfalusi, Jiranek, Rosicky, Jankulovski, Koller (Rozehnal 75), Baros, Nedved.
Referee: Gonzalez (Spain).

Estadio Do Bessa Sec. XXI, 19 June 2004, 30,000

Latvia (0) 0   Germany (0) 0
Latvia: Kolinko; Izakov, Blagonadezdin, Lobanov (Laizans 70), Stepanovs IN, Zemlinsky, Bleidelis, Astafjevs, Verpakovsky (Zirnis 90), Prohorenkovs (Pahars 67), Rubins.
Germany: Kahn; Friedrich, Lahm, Hamann, Worns, Baumann, Schneider (Schweinsteiger 46), Ballack, Kuranyi (Brdaric 78), Bobic (Klose 67), Frings.
Referee: Riley (England).

Estadio Jose Alvalade XXI, 23 June 2004, 46,849

Germany (1) 1 *(Ballack 21)*   **Czech Republic (1) 2** *(Heinz 30, Baros 77)*
Germany: Kahn; Frings (Podolski 46), Schweinsteiger (Jeremies 86), Friedrich, Nowotny, Worns, Lahm, Hamann (Klose 79), Kuranyi, Ballack, Schneider.
Czech Republic: Blazek; Jiranek, Mares, Plasil, Bolf, Rozehnal, Tyce, Galasek (Hubschman 46), Heinz, Lokvenc (Baros 59), Vachousek.
Referee: Hauge (Norway).

Braga, 23 June 2004, 30,000

Holland (2) 3 *(Van Nistelrooy 27 (pen), 35, Makaay 84)*   **Latvia (0) 0**
Holland: Van der Sar; Reiziger, Van Bronckhorst, Van der Meyde (Overmars 63), De Boer Frank, Stam, Seedorf, Cocu, Van Nistelrooy (Makaay 71), Davids (Sneijder 72), Robben.
Latvia: Kolinko; Isakov, Blagonadezdin, Lobanov, Zemlinsky, Stepanovs IN, Bleidelis (Stolcers 83), Rubins, Verpakovsky (Pahars 62), Prohorenkovs (Laizans 74), Astafjevs.
Referee: Nielsen (Denmark).

GROUP D FINAL TABLE

	P	W	L	D	F	A	GD	Pts
Czech Republic	3	3	0	0	7	4	3	9
Netherlands	3	1	1	1	6	4	2	4
Germany	3	0	1	2	2	3	-1	2
Latvia	3	0	2	1	1	5	-4	1

QUARTER-FINALS

Estadio Da Luz, Lisbon, 24 June 2004, 65,000

Portugal (0) 2 *(Postiga 83, Rui Costa 110)*   **England (1) 2** *(Owen 3, Lampard 115)*
Portugal: Ricardo; Miguel (Rui Costa 77), Nuno Valente, Maniche, Ricardo Carvalho, Jorge Andrade, Costinha (Simao Sabrosa 62), Deco, Figo (Postiga 74), Nuno Gomes, Ronaldo.
England: James; Neville G, Cole A, Gerrard (Hargreaves 81), Terry, Campbell, Beckham, Lampard, Rooney (Vassell 27), Owen, Scholes (Neville P 56).
aet; Portugal won 6-5 on penalties: Beckham missed, Deco scored, Owen scored, Simao Sabrosa scored, Lampard scored, Rui Costa missed,Terry scored, Ronaldo scored, Hargreaves scored, Maniche scored, Cole scored, Postiga scored, Vassell saved, Ricardo scored.
Referee: Meier (Switzerland).

Estadio Jose Alvalade XXI, 25 June 2004, 45,390

France (0) 0   Greece (0) 1 *(Charisteas 65)*
France: Barthez; Gallas, Lizarazu, Makelele, Thuram, Silvestre, Dacourt (Wiltord 70), Zidane, Trezeguet (Saha 70), Henry, Pires (Rothen 70).
Greece: Nikopolidis; Seitaridis, Fyssas, Basinas (Tsartas 85), Kapsis, Dellas, Zagorakis, Karagounis, Charisteas, Nikolaidis (Lakis 60), Katsouranis.
Referee: Frisk (Sweden).

Faro-Loule, 26 June 2004, 30,000

Sweden (0) 0   Holland (0) 0
Sweden: Isaksson; Ostlund, Nilsson, Linderoth, Mellberg, Jakobsson, Jonson (Wilhelmsson 65), Svensson A (Kallstrom 81), Ibrahimovic, Larsson, Ljungberg.
Holland: Van der Sar; Reiziger, Van Bronckhorst, Cocu, De Boer (Bouma 36), Stam, Seedorf, Van der Meyde (Makaay 87), Van Nistelrooy, Davids (Heitinga 62), Robben.
aet; Holland won 5-4 on penalties: Kalstrom scored, Van Nistelrooy scored, Larsson scored, Heitinga scored, Ibrahimovic missed, Reiziger scored, Ljungberg scored, Cocu hit post, Wilhelmsson scored, Makaay scored, Mellberg saved, Robben scored.
Referee: Michel (Slovakia).

Estadio Dragao, Oporto, 27 June 2004, 41,092

Czech Republic (0) 3 *(Koller 49, Baros 63, 65)*   **Denmark (0) 0**
Czech Republic: Cech; Jiranek (Grygera 39), Jankulovski, Galasek, Ujfalusi, Bolf, Poborsky, Rosicky, Koller, Baros (Heinz 71), Nedved.
Denmark: Sorensen; Helveg, Bogelund, Gravesen, Laursen, Henriksen, Poulsen, Jensen C (Madsen 71), Tomasson, Jorgensen (Lovenkrands 85), Gronkjaer (Rommedahl 77).
Referee: Ivanov (Russia).

SEMI-FINALS

Estadio Jose Alvalade XXI, 30 June 2004, 46,679

Portugal (1) 2 *(Ronaldo 26, Maniche 58)*   **Holland (0) 1** *(Jorge Andrade 63 (og))*
Portugal: Ricardo; Miguel, Nuno Valente, Maniche (Fernando Couto 87), Ricardo Carvalho, Jorge Andrade, Costinha, Figo, Pauleta (Nuno Gomes 74), Deco, Ronaldo (Petit 67).
Holland: Van der Sar; Reiziger, Van Bronckhorst, Cocu, Bouma (Van der Vaart 55), Stam, Seedorf, Davids, Van Nistelrooy, Robben (Van Hooijdonk 81), Overmars (Makaay 46).
Referee: Frisk (Sweden).

Estadio Dragao, Oporto, 1 July 2004, 45,000

Greece (0) 1 *(Dellas 105)*   **Czech Republic (0) 0**
Greece: Nikopolidis; Seitaridis, Fyssas, Basinas (Giannakopoulos 72), Kapsis, Dellas, Zakorakis, Karagounis, Charisteas, Vryzas (Tsartas 90), Katsouranis.
Czech Republic: Cech; Grygera, Jankulovski, Galasek, Ujfalusi, Bolf, Poborsky, Rosicky, Koller, Baros, Nedved (Smicer 40).
aet; Greece won on slow death.
Referee: Collina (Italy).

FINAL

Estadio Da Luz, Lisbon, 4 July 2004, 62,865

Greece (0) 1 *(Charisteas 57)*   **Portugal (0) 0**
Greece: Nikopolidis; Seitaridis, Fyssas, Basinas, Kapsis, Dellas, Katsouranis, Zagorakis, Charisteas, Vryzas (Papadopoulos 81), Giannakopoulos (Venetidis 76).
Portugal: Ricardo; Miguel (Paulo Ferreira 43), Nuno Valente, Costinha (Rui Costa 58), Jorge Andrade, Ricardo Carvalho, Figo, Maniche, Pauleta (Nuno Gomes 74), Deco, Ronaldo.
Referee: Merk (Germany).

PAST EUROPEAN CHAMPIONSHIP FINALS

Year	Winners		Runners-up		Venue	Attendance
1960	USSR	2	Yugoslavia	1	Paris	17,966
1964	Spain	2	USSR	1	Madrid	120,000
1968	Italy	2	Yugoslavia	0	Rome	60,000
	(After 1-1 draw)					75,000
1972	West Germany	3	USSR	0	Brussels	43,437
1976	Czechoslovakia	2	West Germany	2	Belgrade	45,000
	(Czechoslovakia won on penalties)					
1980	West Germany	2	Belgium	1	Rome	47,864
1984	France	2	Spain	0	Paris	48,000
1988	Holland	2	USSR	0	Munich	72,308
1992	Denmark	2	Germany	0	Gothenburg	37,800
1996	Germany	2	Czech Republic	1	Wembley	73,611
	(Germany won on sudden death)					
2000	France	2	Italy	1	Rotterdam	50,000
	(France won on sudden death)					
2004	Greece	1	Portugal	0	Lisbon	62,865

PAST WORLD CUP FINALS

Year	Winners		Runners-up		Venue	Att.	Referee
1930	Uruguay	4	Argentina	2	Montevideo	90,000	Langenus (B)
1934	Italy	2	Czechoslovakia	1	Rome	50,000	Eklind (Se)
	(after extra time)						
1938	Italy	4	Hungary	2	Paris	45,000	Capdeville (F)
1950	Uruguay	2	Brazil	1	Rio de Janeiro	199,854	Reader (E)
1954	West Germany	3	Hungary	2	Berne	60,000	Ling (E)
1958	Brazil	5	Sweden	2	Stockholm	49,737	Guigue (F)
1962	Brazil	3	Czechoslovakia	1	Santiago	68,679	Latychev (USSR)
1966	England	4	West Germany	2	Wembley	93,802	Dienst (Sw)
	(after extra time)						
1970	Brazil	4	Italy	1	Mexico City	107,412	Glockner (EG)
1974	West Germany	2	Holland	1	Munich	77,833	Taylor (E)
1978	Argentina	3	Holland	1	Buenos Aires	77,000	Gonella (I)
	(after extra time)						
1982	Italy	3	West Germany	1	Madrid	90,080	Coelho (Br)
1986	Argentina	3	West Germany	2	Mexico City	114,580	Filho (Br)
1990	West Germany	1	Argentina	0	Rome	73,603	Mendez (Mex)
1994	Brazil	0	Italy	0	Los Angeles	94,194	Puhl (H)
	(Brazil won 3-2 on penalties aet)						
1998	France	3	Brazil	0	St-Denis	75,000	Belqola (Mor)
2002	Brazil	2	Germany	0	Yokohama	69,029	Collina (I)

WORLD CUP 2006 RESULTS AND FIXTURES

SOUTH AMERICA

Top four qualify for finals; fifth placed team enters play-off against Oceania winners for a place in finals.

QUALIFYING RESULTS

Argentina	(2) 2	Chile	(0) 2
Ecuador	(1) 2	Venezuela	(0) 0
Peru	(2) 4	Paraguay	(1) 1
Colombia	(1) 1	Brazil	(1) 2
Uruguay	(2) 5	Bolivia	(0) 0
Chile	(1) 2	Peru	(0) 1
Venezuela	(0) 0	Argentina	(3) 3
Bolivia	(2) 4	Colombia	(0) 0
Brazil	(1) 1	Ecuador	(0) 0
Paraguay	(1) 4	Uruguay	(1) 1
Argentina	(0) 3	Bolivia	(0) 0
Colombia	(0) 0	Venezuela	(1) 1
Paraguay	(1) 2	Ecuador	(0) 1
Uruguay	(1) 2	Chile	(1) 1
Chile	(0) 0	Paraguay	(1) 1
Peru	(0) 1	Brazil	(1) 1
Venezuela	(0) 2	Bolivia	(0) 1
Colombia	(0) 1	Argentina	(1) 1
Ecuador	(0) 0	Peru	(0) 0
Brazil	(2) 3	Uruguay	(0) 3
Argentina	(0) 1	Ecuador	(0) 0
Bolivia	(0) 0	Chile	(1) 2
Paraguay	(0) 0	Brazil	(0) 0
Peru	(0) 0	Colombia	(2) 2
Uruguay	(0) 0	Venezuela	(1) 3
Bolivia	(1) 2	Paraguay	(1) 1
Uruguay	(0) 1	Peru	(2) 3
Venezuela	(0) 0	Chile	(0) 1
Brazil	(1) 3	Argentina	(0) 1
Ecuador	(1) 2	Colombia	(0) 1
Ecuador	(3) 3	Bolivia	(0) 2
Argentina	(0) 0	Paraguay	(0) 0
Chile	(0) 1	Brazil	(1) 1
Colombia	(3) 5	Uruguay	(0) 0
Peru	(0) 0	Venezuela	(0) 0

REMAINING FIXTURES

04/05.09.04 – Brazil v Bolivia; Chile v Colombia; Paraguay v Venezuela; Peru v Argentina; Uruguay v Ecuador

09/10.10.04 – Argentina v Uruguay; Bolivia v Peru; Colombia v Paraguay; Ecuador v Chile; Venezuela v Brazil

12/13.10.04 – Bolivia v Uruguay; Brazil v Colombia; Chile v Argentina; Paraguay v Peru; Venezuela v Ecuador

16/17.11.04 – Argentina v Venezuela; Colombia v Bolivia; Ecuador v Brazil; Peru v Chile; Uruguay v Paraguay

26/27.03.05 – Bolivia v Argentina; Brazil v Peru; Chile v Uruguay; Ecuador v Paraguay; Venezuela v Colombia

29/30.03.05 – Argentina v Colombia; Bolivia v Venezuela; Paraguay v Chile; Peru v Ecuador; Uruguay v Brazil

04/05.06.05 – Brazil v Paraguay; Chile v Bolivia; Colombia v Peru; Ecuador v Argentina; Venezuela v Uruguay

07/08.06.05 – Argentina v Brazil; Chile v Venezuela; Colombia v Ecuador; Paraguay v Bolivia; Peru v Uruguay

03/04.09.05 – Bolivia v Ecuador; Brazil v Chile; Paraguay v Argentina; Uruguay v Colombia; Venezuela v Peru

08/09.10.05 – Argentina v Peru; Bolivia v Brazil; Colombia v Chile; Ecuador v Uruguay; Venezuela v Paraguay

11/12.10.05 – Brazil v Venezuela; Chile v Ecuador; Paraguay v Colombia; Peru v Bolivia; Uruguay v Argentina

EUROPE

Group winners and two best runners-up qualify for finals. Remaining six runners-up paired in two leg play-off matches, the winners of which also qualify for finals. Group runners-up ranked according to results against teams finishing in order in their respective groups.

FIXTURES

GROUP 1

18.08.04 – Macedonia v Armenia; Romania v Finland

04.09.04 – Finland v Andorra; Romania v Macedonia

08.09.04 – Andorra v Romania; Armenia v Finland; Holland v Czech Republic

09.10.04 – Czech Republic v Romania; Finland v Armenia; Macedonia v Holland

13.10.04 – Andorra v Macedonia; Armenia v Czech Republic; Holland v Finland

17.11.04 – Andorra v Holland; Armenia v Romania; Macedonia v Czech Republic

09.02.05 – Macedonia v Andorra

26.03.05 – Armenia v Andorra; Czech Republic v Finland; Romania v Holland

30.03.05 – Armenia v Czech Republic; Holland v Armenia; Macedonia v Romania

04.06.05 – Armenia v Macedonia; Czech Republic v Andorra; Holland v Romania

08.06.05 – Czech Republic v Macedonia; Finland v Holland; Romania v Armenia

17.08.05 – Macedonia v Finland; Romania v Andorra

03.09.05 – Andorra v Finland; Armenia v Holland; Romania v Czech Republic

07.09.05 – Czech Republic v Armenia; Finland v Macedonia; Holland v Andorra

08.10.05 – Czech Republic v Holland; Finland v Romania

12.10.05 – Andorra v Armenia; Finland v Czech Republic; Holland v Macedonia

GROUP 2

04.09.04 – Albania v Greece; Denmark v Ukraine; Turkey v Georgia

08.09.04 – Georgia v Albania; Greece v Turkey; Kazakhstan v Ukraine

09.10.04 – Albania v Denmark; Turkey v Kazakhstan; Ukraine v Greece

13.10.04 – Denmark v Turkey; Kazakhstan v Albania; Ukraine v Georgia

17.11.04 – Georgia v Denmark; Greece v Kazakhstan; Turkey v Ukraine

09.02.05 – Albania v Ukraine; Greece v Denmark; Kazakhstan v Georgia

26.03.05 – Denmark v Kazakhstan; Georgia v Greece; Turkey v Albania

30.03.05 – Georgia v Turkey; Greece v Albania; Ukraine v Denmark

04.06.05 – Albania v Georgia; Turkey v Greece; Ukraine v Kazakhstan

08.06.05 – Denmark v Albania; Greece v Ukraine; Kazakhstan v Turkey

03.09.05 – Albania v Kazakhstan; Georgia v Ukraine; Turkey v Denmark

07.09.05 – Denmark v Georgia; Kazakhstan v Greece; Ukraine v Turkey

08.10.05 – Denmark v Greece; Georgia v Kazakhstan; Ukraine v Albania

12.10.05 – Albania v Turkey; Greece v Georgia; Kazakhstan v Denmark

GROUP 3

18.08.04 – Liechtenstein v Estonia; Slovakia v Luxembourg

04.09.04 – Estonia v Luxembourg; Latvia v Portugal; Russia v Slovakia

08.09.04 – Luxembourg v Latvia; Portugal v Estonia; Slovakia v Liechtenstein

09.10.04 – Liechtenstein v Portugal; Luxembourg v Russia; Slovakia v Latvia

13.10.04 – Latvia v Estonia; Luxembourg v Liechtenstein; Portugal v Russia

17.11.04 – Liechtenstein v Latvia; Luxembourg v Portugal; Russia v Estonia

26.03.05 – Estonia v Slovakia; Liechtenstein v Russia

30.03.05 – Estonia v Russia; Latvia v Luxembourg; Slovakia v Portugal

04.06.05 – Estonia v Liechtenstein; Portugal v Slovakia; Russia v Latvia

08.06.05 – Estonia v Portugal; Latvia v Liechtenstein; Luxembourg v Slovakia

17.08.05 – Latvia v Russia; Liechtenstein v Slovakia

03.09.05 – Estonia v Latvia; Portugal v Luxembourg; Russia v Liechtenstein

07.09.05 – Latvia v Slovakia; Liechtenstein v Luxembourg; Russia v Portugal

08.10.05 – Portugal v Liechtenstein; Russia v Luxembourg; Slovakia v Estonia

12.10.05 – Luxembourg v Estonia; Portugal v Latvia; Slovakia v Russia

GROUP 4
04.09.04 – France v Israel; Republic of Ireland v Cyprus; Switzerland v Faeroes
08.09.04 – Faeroes v France; Israel v Cyprus; Switzerland v Republic of Ireland
09.10.04 – Cyprus v Faeroes; France v Republic of Ireland; Israel v Switzerland
13.10.04 – Cyprus v France; Republic of Ireland v Faeroes
17.11.04 – Cyprus v Israel
26.03.05 – Israel v Republic of Ireland; France v Switzerland
30.03.05 – Israel v France; Switzerland v Cyprus
04.06.05 – Faeroes v Switzerland; Republic of Ireland v Israel
08.06.05 – Faeroes v Republic of Ireland
17.08.05 – Faeroes v Cyprus
03.09.05 – France v Faeroes; Switzerland v Israel
07.09.05 – Cyprus v Switzerland; Faeroes v Israel; Republic of Ireland v France
08.10.05 – Cyprus v Republic of Ireland; Switzerland v France
08.10.05 – Israel v Faeroes
12.10.05 – France v Cyprus; Republic of Ireland v Switzerland

GROUP 5
04.09.04 – Italy v Norway; Slovenia v Moldova
08.09.04 – Moldova v Italy; Norway v Belarus; Scotland v Slovenia
09.10.04 – Belarus v Moldova; Scotland v Norway; Slovenia v Italy
13.10.04 – Italy v Belarus; Moldova v Scotland; Norway v Slovenia
28.03.05 – Italy v Scotland
30.03.05 – Moldova v Norway; Slovenia v Belarus
04.06.05 – Belarus v Slovenia; Norway v Italy; Scotland v Moldova
08.06.05 – Belarus v Scotland
03.09.05 – Moldova v Belarus; Scotland v Italy; Slovenia v Norway
07.09.05 – Belarus v Italy; Moldova v Slovenia; Norway v Scotland
08.10.05 – Italy v Slovenia; Norway v Moldova; Scotland v Belarus
12.10.05 – Belarus v Norway; Italy v Moldova; Slovenia v Scotland

GROUP 6
04.09.04 – Austria v England; Azerbaijan v Wales; Northern Ireland v Poland
08.09.04 – Austria v Azerbaijan; Poland v England; Wales v Northern Ireland
09.10.04 – Austria v Poland; Azerbaijan v Northern Ireland; England v Wales
13.10.04 – Azerbaijan v England; Northern Ireland v Austria; Wales v Poland

26.03.05 – England v Northern Ireland; Poland v Azerbaijan; Wales v Austria
30.03.05 – Austria v Wales; England v Azerbaijan; Poland v Northern Ireland
04.06.05 – Azerbaijan v Poland
03.09.05 – Northern Ireland v Azerbaijan; Poland v Austria; Wales v England
07.09.05 – Azerbaijan v Austria; Northern Ireland v England; Poland v Wales
08.10.05 – England v Austria; Northern Ireland v Wales
12.10.05 – Austria v Northern Ireland; England v Poland; Wales v Azerbaijan

GROUP 7
04.09.04 – Belgium v Lithuania; San Marino v Serbia & M
08.09.04 – Bosnia v Spain; Lithuania v San Marino
09.10.04 – Bosnia v Serbia & M; Spain v Belgium
13.10.04 – Lithuania v Spain; Serbia & M v San Marino
17.11.04 – Belgium v Serbia & M; San Marino v Lithuania
09.02.05 – Spain v San Marino
26.03.05 – Belgium v Bosnia
30.03.05 – Bosnia v Lithuania; San Marino v Belgium; Serbia & M v Spain
04.06.05 – San Marino v Bosnia; Serbia & M v Belgium; Spain v Lithuania
08.06.05 – Spain v Bosnia
03.09.05 – Bosnia v Belgium; Serbia & M v Lithuania
07.09.05 – Belgium v San Marino; Lithuania v Bosnia; Spain v Serbia & M
08.10.05 – Belgium v Spain; Bosnia v San Marino; Lithuania v Serbia & M
12.10.05 – Lithuania v Belgium; San Marino v Spain; Serbia & M v Bosnia

GROUP 8
04.09.04 – Croatia v Hungary; Iceland v Bulgaria; Malta v Sweden
08.09.04 – Hungary v Iceland; Sweden v Croatia
09.10.04 – Croatia v Bulgaria; Malta v Iceland; Sweden v Hungary
13.10.04 – Bulgaria v Malta; Iceland v Sweden
17.11.04 – Malta v Hungary
26.03.05 – Bulgaria v Sweden; Croatia v Iceland
30.03.05 – Croatia v Malta; Hungary v Bulgaria
04.06.05 – Bulgaria v Croatia; Iceland v Hungary; Sweden v Malta
08.06.05 – Iceland v Malta
03.09.05 – Hungary v Malta; Iceland v Croatia; Sweden v Bulgaria
07.09.05 – Bulgaria v Iceland; Hungary v Sweden; Malta v Croatia
08.10.05 – Bulgaria v Hungary; Croatia v Sweden
12.10.05 – Hungary v Croatia; Malta v Bulgaria; Sweden v Iceland

WORLD CLUB CHAMPIONSHIP

Played annually up to 1974 and intermittently since then between the winners of the European Cup and the winners of the South American Champions Cup — known as the Copa Libertadores. In 1980 the winners were decided by one match arranged in Tokyo in February 1981 and the venue has been the same since. AC Milan replaced Marseille who had been stripped of their European Cup title in 1993.

1960   Real Madrid beat Penarol 0-0, 5-1
1961   Penarol beat Benfica 0-1, 5-0, 2-1
1962   Santos beat Benfica 3-2, 5-2
1963   Santos beat AC Milan 2-4, 4-2, 1-0
1964   Inter-Milan beat Independiente 0-1, 2-0, 1-0
1965   Inter-Milan beat Independiente 3-0, 0-0
1966   Penarol beat Real Madrid 2-0, 2-0
1967   Racing Club beat Celtic 0-1, 2-1, 1-0
1968   Estudiantes beat Manchester United 1-0, 1-1
1969   AC Milan beat Estudiantes 3-0, 1-2
1970   Feyenoord beat Estudiantes 2-2, 1-0
1971   Nacional beat Panathinaikos* 1-1, 2-1
1972   Ajax beat Independiente 1-1, 3-0
1973   Independiente beat Juventus* 1-0
1974   Atlético Madrid* beat Independiente 0-1, 2-0
1975   Independiente and Bayern Munich could not agree dates; no matches.
1976   Bayern Munich beat Cruzeiro 2-0, 0-0
1977   Boca Juniors beat Borussia Moenchengladbach* 2-2, 3-0
1978   Not contested
1979   Olimpia beat Malmö* 1-0, 2-1
1980   Nacional beat Nottingham Forest 1-0
1981   Flamengo beat Liverpool 3-0
1982   Penarol beat Aston Villa 2-0
1983   Gremio Porto Alegre beat SV Hamburg 2-1
1984   Independiente beat Liverpool 1-0
1985   Juventus beat Argentinos Juniors 4-2 on penalties after a 2-2 draw
1986   River Plate beat Steaua Bucharest 1-0
1987   FC Porto beat Penarol 2-1 after extra time
1988   Nacional (Uru) beat PSV Eindhoven 7-6 on penalties after 1-1 draw
1989   AC Milan beat Atletico Nacional (Col) 1-0 after extra time
1990   AC Milan beat Olimpia 3-0
1991   Red Star Belgrade beat Colo Colo 3-0
1992   Sao Paulo beat Barcelona 2-1
1993   Sao Paulo beat AC Milan 3-2
1994   Velez Sarsfield beat AC Milan 2-0
1995   Ajax beat Gremio Porto Alegre 4-3 on penalties after 0-0 draw
1996   Juventus beat River Plate 1-0
1997   Borussia Dortmund beat Cruzeiro 2-0
1998   Real Madrid beat Vasco da Gama 2-1
1999   Manchester U beat Palmeiras 1-0
2000   Boca Juniors beat Real Madrid 2-1
2001   Bayern Munich beat Boca Juniors 1-0 after extra time
2002   Real Madrid beat Olimpia 2-0

*European Cup runners-up; winners declined to take part.

2003

14 December 2003, in Yokohama

Boca Juniors (1) 1 *(Donnet 29)* **AC Milan (1) 1** *(Tomasson 24)*   68,000

aet; Boca Juniors won 3-1 on penalties: Schiavi, Donnet and Cascini scored for Boca Juniors; Rui Costa for AC Milan. Battaglia missed for Boca Juniors, Pirlo, Seedorf and Costacurta missed for AC Milan.

Boca Juniors: Abbondanzieri; Perea, Schiavi, Burdisso, Rodriguez, Donnet, Battaglia, Cascini, Cagna, Iarley, Schelotto (Tevez 73).

AC Milan: Dida; Cafu, Pancaro, Pirlo, Costacurta, Maldini, Gattuso (Ambrosini 102), Kaka (Rui Costa 78), Shevchenko, Tomasson (Inzaghi 60), Seedorf.

Referee: M. Ivanov (Russia).

EUROPEAN SUPER CUP

Played annually between the winners of the European Champions' Cup and the European Cup-Winners' Cup (UEFA Cup from 2000). AC Milan replaced Marseille in 1993–94.

Previous Matches

1972	Ajax beat Rangers 3-1, 3-2
1973	Ajax beat AC Milan 0-1, 6-0
1974	Not contested
1975	Dynamo Kiev beat Bayern Munich 1-0, 2-0
1976	Anderlecht beat Bayern Munich 4-1, 1-2
1977	Liverpool beat Hamburg 1-1, 6-0
1978	Anderlecht beat Liverpool 3-1, 1-2
1979	Nottingham F beat Barcelona 1-0, 1-1
1980	Valencia beat Nottingham F 1-0, 1-2
1981	Not contested
1982	Aston Villa beat Barcelona 0-1, 3-0
1983	Aberdeen beat Hamburg 0-0, 2-0
1984	Juventus beat Liverpool 2-0
1985	Juventus v Everton not contested due to UEFA ban on English clubs
1986	Steaua Bucharest beat Dynamo Kiev 1-0
1987	FC Porto beat Ajax 1-0, 1-0
1988	KV Mechelen beat PSV Eindhoven 3-0, 0-1
1989	AC Milan beat Barcelona 1-1, 1-0
1990	AC Milan beat Sampdoria 1-1, 2-0
1991	Manchester U beat Red Star Belgrade 1-0
1992	Barcelona beat Werder Bremen 1-1, 2-1
1993	Parma beat AC Milan 0-1, 2-0
1994	AC Milan beat Arsenal 0-0, 2-0
1995	Ajax beat Zaragoza 1-1, 4-0
1996	Juventus beat Paris St Germain 6-1, 3-1
1997	Barcelona beat Borussia Dortmund 2-0, 1-1
1998	Chelsea beat Real Madrid 1-0
1999	Lazio beat Manchester U 1-0
2000	Galatasaray beat Real Madrid 2-1
	(aet; Galatasaray won on sudden death.)
2001	Liverpool beat Bayern Munich 3-2
2002	Real Madrid beat Feyenoord 3-1

2003–04

29 August 2003, Monaco

AC Milan (1) 1 *(Shevchenko 10)*   **Porto (0) 0**   18,500

AC Milan: Dida; Simic, Nesta, Maldini, Pancaro, Gattuso, Pirlo, Rui Costa (Cafu 86), Seedorf (Ambrosini 70), Shevchenko (Rivaldo 76), Inzaghi.

Porto: Vitor Baia; Paulo Ferreira, Jorge Costa, Ricardo Carvalho, Ricardo Costa, Alenichev (Ricardo Fernandes 76), Deco, Costinha (Bosingwa 67), Maniche, McCarthy (Jankauskas 60), Derlei.

Referee: P.Barber (England).

OTHER BRITISH AND IRISH INTERNATIONAL MATCHES 2003–2004

FRIENDLIES

Ipswich, 20 August 2003, 28,700

England (1) 3 *(Beckham 10 (pen), Owen 51, Lampard 80)*   **Croatia (0) 1** *(Mornar 78)*

England: James (Robinson 46); Neville P (Mills 82), Cole A (Bridge 60), Butt (Lampard 27), Terry, Ferdinand (Upson 60), Beckham (Sinclair 60), Gerrard (Murphy 82), Heskey (Beattie 77), Owen (Dyer 60), Scholes (Cole J 60).
Croatia: Pletikosa (Butina 70); Simic (Babic 46), Zivkovic (Seric 73), Tomas, Kovac R, Simunic, Leko (Rosso 60), Maric (Mornar 46), Olic, Kovac N (Agic 73), Rapaic (Srna 46).
Referee: Bo Larsen (Denmark).

Old Trafford, 16 November 2003, 64,159

England (2) 2 *(Rooney 5, Cole J 9)*   **Denmark (2) 3** *(Jorgensen 8, 30 (pen), Tomasson 82)*

England: James (Robinson 46); Neville G (Johnson 16), Cole A (Bridge 46), Butt (Neville P 46), Terry, Upson, Beckham (Jenas 66), Lampard, Heskey (Beattie 46), Rooney (Parker 66), Cole J (Murphy 76).
Denmark: Sorensen; Helveg (Priske 46), Jensen N, Gravesen, Nielsen (Gaardsoe 71), Henriksen, Wieghorst (Jensen D 29), Jorgensen (Madsen 84), Rommedahl (Perez 19), Sand (Tomasson 46), Gronkjaer (Lovenkrands 61).
Referee: Hrinak (Slovakia).

Faro-Loule, 18 February 2004, 27,000

Portugal (0) 1 *(Pauleta 70)*   **England (0) 1** *(King 47)*

Portugal: Ricardo; Paulo Ferreira, Rui Jorge (Valente 46), Petit (Viana 83), Jorge Andrade (Ricardo Carvalho 75), Fernando Couto (Beto 83), Costinha (Deco 46), Figo (Boa Morte 66), Simao Sabrosa (Ronaldo 46), Pauleta (Almeida 78), Rui Costa
England: James; Neville P (Mills 46), Cole A (Bridge 18) (Carragher 86), Butt (Jenas 86), Southgate, King, Beckham (Hargreaves 86), Scholes (Dyer 46), Lampard (Cole J 46), Rooney (Heskey 71), Owen (Smith 71).
Referee: Kassai (Hungary).

Gothenburg, 31 March 2004, 40,464

Sweden (0) 1 *(Ibrahimovic 54)*   **England (0) 0**

Sweden: Isaksson (Kihlstedt 46); Lucic, Edman, Andersson A (Kallstrom 46), Mellberg, Mjallby (Linderoth 46), Nilsson, Svensson A (Jonson 46), Ibrahimovic (Ostlund 90), Elmander (Hansson 46), Wilhelmsson.
England: James; Neville P, Carragher, Butt (Parker 78), Terry (Gardner 46), Woodgate (Southgate 46), Hargreaves (Jenas 60), Gerrard (Cole J 60), Rooney (Smith 60), Vassell (Defoe 12), Thompson (Heskey 60).
Referee: Ovrebo (Norway).

City of Manchester, 1 June 2004, 38,581

England (1) 1 *(Owen 22)*   **Japan (0) 1** *(Ono 53)*

England: James; Neville G (Neville P 86), Cole A, Gerrard (Hargreaves 82), Terry (King 88), Campbell, Beckham (Cole J 82), Lampard (Butt 82), Rooney (Heskey 77), Owen (Vassell 77), Scholes (Dyer 77).
Japan: Narazaki; Kaji, Santos, Tauboi, Miyamoto, Nakazawa, Inamoto (Fukunishi 90), Nakamura, Tamada (Suzuki 60), Kubo (Yanagisawa 60), Ono.
Referee: Rosetti (Italy).

City of Manchester, 5 June 2004, 43,500

England (3) 6 *(Lampard 25, Rooney 27, 38, Vassell 57, 77, Bridge 68)*

Iceland (1) 1 *(Helguson 42)*

England: Robinson (Walker 61); Neville G (Neville P 46), Cole A (Bridge 46), Gerrard (Hargreaves 46), Carragher (Defoe 83), Campbell (King 46), Beckham (Dyer 46), Lampard (Butt 46), Rooney (Vassell 46), Owen (Heskey 46), Scholes (Cole J 46).
Iceland: Arason; Gudjonsson T (Gudmundsson J 77), Sigurdsson I (Jonsson 77), Ingimarsson, Marteinsson (Saevarsson K 46), Hreidarsson, Gudjonsson J (Helgason 86), Gretarsson, Helguson (Gudmundsson T 84), Sigurdsson H (Gudjonsson B 68), Gudjohnsen.
Referee: Wegereef (Holland).

Oslo, 20 August 2003, 12,858

Norway (0) 0   Scotland (0) 0

Norway: Johnsen E; Basma (Aas 70), Bergdolmo (Iversen S 68), Hangeland (Andersen T 46), Berg (Johnsen R 46), Lundekvam, Andresen, Johnsen F (Solli 46), Solskjaer, Carew (Flo H 81), Riise.

Scotland: Douglas; Ross (Fletcher 60), Dailly, Ferguson B, Webster, Pressley, Cameron (Rae 84), Lambert, Crawford (Devlin 80), Hutchison, Naysmith.

Referee: Vuorela (Finland).

Hampden Park, 31 March 2004, 20,433

Scotland (0) 1 *(McFadden 57)*   **Romania (1) 2** *(Chivu 37, Pancu 51)*

Scotland: Gallacher; Alexander, McCann, Kennedy (Crainey 18), Pressley, Dailly, Caldwell G, Rae, Miller (McFadden 51), Thompson S (Crawford 63), Cameron.

Romania: Stelea (Lobont 46); Stoican, Rat, Petre O, Iensci, Chivu, Petre F (Mitea 46), Pancu (Danciulescu 89), Cernat (Soava 63), Ganea (Cristea 81), Mutu.

Referee: Hyyria (Finland).

Copenhagen, 28 April 2004, 22,885

Denmark (0) 1 *(Sand 60)*   **Scotland (0) 0**

Denmark: Sorensen; Helveg, Jensen N (Perez 46), Jensen C (Sennels 46), Laursen, Henriksen (Kroldrup 66), Jensen D, Wieghorst (Retov 80), Jorgensen (Rommedahl 66), Tomasson (Sand 46), Gronkjaer (Rasmussen 88).

Scotland: Gallacher; Caldwell G, Crainey, Holt (Canero 16), Pressley, Mackay, Cameron (McCann 46), Fletcher, Kyle, McFadden, Dailly.

Referee: Ingvarsson (Sweden).

Tallinn, 27 May 2004, 4000

Estonia (0) 0   Scotland (0) 1 *(McFadden 76)*

Estonia: Kaalma; Allas, Stepanov, Jaager, Klavan, Rahn, Terehov (Reinumae 85), Reim, Viikmae, Oper, Lindpere (Kink 75).

Scotland: Gallacher; McNamee, Hughes, Caldwell G, Mackay, Pressley (Webster 46), Fletcher, Holt, Miller (Crawford 79), McFadden (Kerr 89), Quashie.

Referee: Poulsen (Denmark).

Easter Road, 30 May 2004, 16,187

Scotland (4) 4 *(Fletcher 6, Holt 14, Caldwell G 23, Quashie 34)*

Trinidad & Tobago (0) 1 *(John 55)*

Scotland: Gordon; McNamara, McAllister, Caldwell G (Caldwell S 80), Pressley, Mackay (McNamee 85), Quashie (Hughes 72), Fletcher, Crawford (Miller 67), McFadden (Webster 85), Holt.

Trinidad & Tobago: Ince; Edwards (Theobald 90), Mason, Sancho, Cox, Andrews, Eve (Jermot 82), Dwarika (Nixon 74), John, Glen (Boucard 28), Jones (Rojas 46).

Referee: Vink (Holland).

Cardiff, 18 February 2004, 47,124

Wales (2) 4 *(Earnshaw 1, 35, 58, Taylor 78)*   **Scotland (0) 0**

Wales: Crossley (Ward 46); Edwards, Gabbidon, Speed (Robinson C 72), Melville (Symons 67), Page, Oster, Savage (Fletcher 72), Earnshaw, Giggs (Taylor 46), Davies (Parry 33).

Scotland: Douglas; McNamara, Naysmith (Murty 46), Caldwell S, Ritchie, Dailly, Fletcher (Webster 86), Cameron (Gallagher 68), Pearson (McFadden 46), Miller, Dickov.

Referee: Ross (Northern Ireland).

Budapest, 31 March 2004, 15,000

Hungary (1) 1 *(Kenesei 17 (pen))*   **Wales (1) 2** *(Koumas 20, Earnshaw 81)*

Hungary: Babos; Bodnar, Low (Bodor 89), Peto, Stark, Komiosi (Dveri 89), Molnar, Lisztes (Toth 52), Kenesei (Szabics 46), Torghelle (Sebok J 69), Gera.

Wales: Jones P (Coyne 46); Gabbidon, Thatcher (Edwards 54), Robinson C (Fletcher 89), Melville, Page, Koumas, Savage, Earnshaw, Taylor, Vaughan (Roberts G 64).
Referee: Meyer (Germany).

Oslo, 27 May 2004, 14,137
Norway (0) 0   Wales (0) 0
Norway: Myhre; Basma, Riise, Helstad (Flo T 61), Johnsen R (Andersen 88), Berg (Lundekvam 17), Andresen, Hoset, Solskjaer (Solli 61), Saeternes (Lange 46), Pedersen (Bergdolmo 46).
Wales: Coyne; Delaney, Thatcher, Robinson C (Edwards 75), Collins, Gabbidon, Oster (Barnard 90), Fletcher, Earnshaw (Roberts N 71), Bellamy (Llewellyn 80), Parry (Roberts G 71).
Referee: Hansson (Sweden).

Wrexham, 30 May 2004, 10,805
Wales (1) 1 *(Parry 21)*   **Canada (0) 0**
Wales: Coyne (Margetson 46); Delaney, Thatcher, Robinson C (Edwards 79), Collins, Gabbidon, Oster, Fletcher, Bellamy, Giggs (Llewellyn 89), Parry (Earnshaw 67).
Canada: Onstad; Imhof, Jazic, De Guzman, Watson, De Vos, Hulme (Occean 79), Hutchinson (Peschisolido 46), Radzinski (McKenna 72), De Rosario (Klukowski 83), Brennan (Bircham 46).
Referee: McKeon (Republic of Ireland).

Windsor Park, 18 February 2004, 11,288
Northern Ireland (0) 1 *(Healy 56)*
Norway (3) 4 *(Pedersen 17, 35, Iversen 43, Gillespie 57 (og))*
Northern Ireland: Taylor; Baird, Kennedy (Jones 77), Hughes A, McCartney, Griffin (Williams 46), Gillespie (McVeigh 73), Johnson, Healy, Smith, Hughes M.
Norway: Myhre (Holtan 70); Andresen, El Fakiri, Hangeland, Helstad (Hoiland 89), Hoseth, Iversen, Johnsen F, Riise (Hanstveit 70), Rushfeldt (Flo H 46), Pedersen (Odegaard 80).
Referee: Thomson (Scotland).

Tallinn, 31 March 2004, 2000
Estonia (0) 0   Northern Ireland (1) 1 *(Healy 45)*
Estonia: Kaalma; Jaager, Stepanov, Piiroja (Rahn 81), Klavan, Reim, Smirnov (Reinumae 85), Kristal, Zelinski (Teever 64), Rooba M (Lindpere 73), Kink (Terehhov 71).
Northern Ireland: Taylor; Baird, Capaldi, Craigan, Williams, Sonner (Duff M 78), Mulryne (McCann 68), Jeff Whitley, Healy, Smith, Jones.
Referee: Petteri (Finland).

Windsor Park, 28 April 2004, 9690
Northern Ireland (1) 1 *(Quinn 17)*   **Serbia-Montenegro (1) 1** *(Paunovic 7)*
Northern Ireland: Taylor (Carroll 46); Baird, Capaldi, Craigan, Williams, Doherty (Hughes M 78), Gillespie (Jones 46), Jeff Whitley (Sonner 78), Healy (Hamilton 46), Quinn (Smith 78), Mulryne (McVeigh 46).
Serbia-Montenegro: Kovacevic; Cirkovic (Markoski 83), Dudic, Gavrancic, Dragutinovic (Milivoje Vitakic 46), Nadj, Trobok (Vladimir Ivic 46), Vukic, Kezman, Petokvic, Paunovic (Kolakovic 69).
Referee: Richards (Wales).

Waterford, 30 May 2004, 1500
Barbados (1) 1 *(Skinner 40)*   **Northern Ireland (0) 1** *(Healy 71)*
Barbados: Chase; Braithwaite, Burrowes, James, Parris, Forde (Goodridge 46), Grosvenor, Hall, Lovell (Hawkesworth), Lucas (Burgess), Skinner (Riley 65).
Northern Ireland: Taylor; Baird (Jones 67), Capaldi (Elliott 67), Craigan, Williams⁸, Johnson, Gillespie (Murdock 46), Sonner (McVeigh 67), Healy (Hamilton 80), Quinn, Mulryne (Smith 46).
Referee: Brizan (Trinidad & Tobago).

Basseterre, 2 June 2004, 1800

St Kitts & Nevis (0) 0   Northern Ireland (0) 2 *(Healy 81, Jones 86)*

St Kitts & Nevis: Byron (Benjamin 85); Lewis, Eddy (Lawrence 87), Leader, Saddler K (Sargeant 75), Isaac, Huggins (Saddler A 75), Burton (Riley 54), Gomez, Lake (Francis 59), Gumbs.

Northern Ireland: Taylor; Baird, Capaldi, Craigan, Murdock, Jeff Whitley (Johnson 65), McVeigh (Mulryne 65), Sonner (Jones 52), Hamilton (Healy 65), Smith, Elliott (Gillespie 65).

Referee: Matthews (St Kitts & Nevis).

Bacolet, 6 June 2004, 5100

Trinidad & Tobago (0) 0   Northern Ireland (2) 3 *(Healy 4, 65, Elliott 41)*

Trinidad & Tobago: Ince; Sancho (Thomas 46), Cox, Andrews, Rougier (Roberts 76), Eve, Jemmott (Theobald 83), Boucard (Fitzwilliams 68), Edwards, Mason (Yorke 46), John.

Northern Ireland: Taylor (Mannus 82); Baird, Capaldi, Craigan (Murdock 46), Williams, Jeff Whitley, Johnson (Gillespie 72), Mulryne (Sonner 72), Healy (McVeigh 66), Quinn (Smith 61), Elliott (Jones 46).

Referee: Callender (Barbados).

Dublin, 19 August 2003, 37,200

Republic of Ireland (0) 2 *(O'Shea 74, Morrison 81)* **Australia (0) 1** *(Viduka 49)*

Republic of Ireland: Colgan; Carr (Harte 57), O'Shea, Holland (Healy 19), Breen (O'Brien 46), Cunningham (Dunne 84), Finnan (Kilbane 66), Kinsella, Doherty (Morrison 57), Robbie Keane (Connolly 46), Duff (Quinn 80).

Australia: Schwarzer; Neill, Lazaridis, Okon (Grelia 66), Foxe, Popovic, Emerton, Bresciano, Viduka (Aloisi 78), Chipperfield, Tiatto (Vidmar 69).

Referee: Vidlak (Czech Republic).

Dublin, 9 September 2003, 27,000

Republic of Ireland (1) 2 *(Connolly 35, Dunne 90)*   **Turkey (0) 2** *(Hakan Sukur 51, Okan Y 86)*

Republic of Ireland: Colgan (Murphy 72); Finnan, Harte (Carr 90), Healy (McPhail 86), Breen (Morrison 86), O'Brien (Dunne 72), Kinsella, Connolly, Doherty, Kilbane, Duff (Reid S 46).

Turkey: Rustu (Omer 61) (Zafer 86); Fatih, Ergun, Tugay (Ahmet 72), Bulent K (Umit D 86), Tayfun (Deniz 46), Alpay (Okan B 46), Emre (Gokdeniz 61), Hakan Sukur (Tumer 86), Tuncay (Okan Y 72), Hasan Sas (Ibrahim 46).

Referee: Wegereef (Holland).

Dublin, 18 November 2003, 23,253

Republic of Ireland (0) 3 *(Duff 23, Robbie Keane 60, 84)*   **Canada (0) 0**

Republic of Ireland: Given (Colgan 82); Carr (Harte 46), O'Shea (Thompson 87), Kavanagh (Holland 11), Dunne, Cunningham, Reid S (Delap 61), Reid A (McPhail 73), Doherty (Morrison 46), Robbie Keane, Duff (Kilbane 87).

Canada: Hirschfeld; Stalteri, Jazic, Bircham (Nash 79), De Vos (Rogers 82), McKenna, Bent, Imhof, Radzinski, Peschisolido (Bernier 75), Hastings (Fenwick 87).

Referee: Whitby (Wales).

Dublin, 18 February 2004, 44,000

Republic of Ireland (0) 0   Brazil (0) 0

Republic of Ireland: Given; Carr, O'Shea, Holland, O'Brien, Cunningham, Kilbane, Kavanagh, Robbie Keane, Morrison, Reid A (McAteer 64).

Brazil: Dida; Cafu, Roberto Carlos, Silva (Edmilson 14), Roque Junior, Lucio, Kleberson (Julio Baptista 46), Kaka, Ronaldo, Ronaldinho, Ze Roberto.

Referee: Frisk (Sweden).

Dublin, 31 March 2004, 42,000
Republic of Ireland (0) 2 *(Harte 52, Robbie Keane 90)*
Czech Republic (0) 1 *(Baros 81)*
Republic of Ireland: Given (Kenny 82); Maybury, Harte, Holland, Doherty (Miller 70), Cunningham, Reid A (Delap 66), Kilbane, Robbie Keane, Morrison (Lee 76), Duff (Kinsella 76).
Czech Republic: Cech (Vaniak 46); Giranek (Plasil 69), Jankulovski, Galasek, Bolf (Rozehnal 58), Ujfalusi, Sionko (Stajner 46), Tyce, Baros (Vorisek 84), Koller (Lokvenc 46), Nedved (Heinz 46).
Referee: Fisker (Denmark).

Bydgoszcz, 28 April 2004, 18,000
Poland (0) 0   Republic of Ireland (0) 0
Poland: Dudek (Boruc 58); Zewlakow (Kaczorowski 83), Rzasa, Szymkowiak (Radomski 85), Klos (Bosacki 80), Glowacki (Hajto 46), Lewandowski, Zurawski, Olisadebe (Niedzielan 46), Krzynowek (Kosowski 46), Mila (Smolarek 65).
Republic of Ireland: Given (Colgan 70); O'Shea, Harte (Maybury 63), Miller, Doherty (O'Brien 80), Cunningham, Reid S, Kinsella, Reid A (Douglas 80), Morrison (Byrne 89), Lee (Barrett 63).
Referee: Shebek (Ukraine).

Dublin, 27 May 2004, 42,356
Republic of Ireland (0) 1 *(Holland 85)*   **Romania (0) 0**
Republic of Ireland: Given; Finnan, Maybury, Roy Keane, O'Brien, Cunningham, Miller, Holland, Robbie Keane, Morrison, Reid A (Rowlands 78).
Romania: Lobont (Stelea 46); Dumitru, Dancia (Petre M 78), Plesan (Alluta 61), Icensi (Barcuan 90), Ghianes, Radoi (Constianin 84), Soava (Petre O 90), Danciulescu (Neaga 61), Ganea (Niculae 88), Dica (Alexa 78).
Referee: Jara (Czech Republic).

Charlton, 29 May 2004, 7438
Republic of Ireland (0) 0   Nigeria (1) 3 *(Ogbeche 36, 69, Martins 49)*
Republic of Ireland: Colgan; Finnan, Maybury (Clarke 46), Holland (Douglas 67), Doherty, Cunningham, Miller (Rowlands 46), Kinsella, Robbie Keane (Barrett 84), Lee, McPhail.
Nigeria: Rotimi; Abbey (Adamu 90), Lawal, Olofinjana (Obiefule 86), Olajengbesi, Enakhire, Utaka, Obodo, Martins (Showunmi 84), Ogbeche (Baita 72), Ekwueme.
Referee: D'Urso (England).

Charlton, 2 June 2004, 6155
Republic of Ireland (1) 1 *(Barrett 26)*   **Jamaica (0) 0**
Republic of Ireland: Kenny; Maybury, O'Shea (Clarke 46), Quinn (Holland 83), Doherty, O'Brien, Barrett, Kinsella, Morrison, Lee (McGeady 83), Reid A (Rowlands 77).
Jamaica: Ricketts; Neil, Reid, Chin-Sue (Langley 66), Stewart, Goodison, Davis, Hyde, Lisbie (Johnson 83), King (Dobson 85), Burton (Bernard 83).
Referee: Styles (England).

Amsterdam, 5 June 2004, 43,000
Holland (0) 0   Republic of Ireland (1) 1 *(Robbie Keane 45)*
Holland: Van der Sar; Reiziger (Heitinga 46), Van Bronckhorst, Cocu, Stam, Bouma (Van Hooijdonk 84), Sneijder (Seedorf 46) (Bosvelt 63), Van der Vaart, Davids (Robben 63), Van Nistelrooy (Makaay 66), Kluivert (Van der Meyde 46).
Republic of Ireland: Given; Finnan, Maybury (Doyle 88), Holland, Cunningham, O'Brien, Barrett, Quinn, Robbie Keane, Morrison (Lee 83), Reid A.
Referee: Dean (England).

ENGLAND UNDER-21 TEAMS 2003–2004

■*Denotes player sent off.*

West Ham, 19 August 2003, 11,008

England (0) 0
Croatia (1) 3 *(Ljubojevic 12, 52, Pranjic 90)*
England: Murray; Johnson, Konchesky, Prutton, Parnaby, Clarke (Jagielka 73), Pennant■, Jenas, Jeffers (Cole C 70), Defoe, Barry (Sidwell 46).

Skopje, 5 September 2003, 2700

Macedonia (0) 1 *(Stojkov 60)*
England (1) 1 *(Jagielka 35)*
England: Kirkland; Johnson, Konchesky, Barton, Clarke, Jagielka, Pennant (Wright-Phillips 62), Sidwell, Jeffers, Ameobi, Defoe (Tonge 71).

Everton, 9 September 2003, 23,744

England (1) 1 *(Barton 37)*
Portugal (1) 2 *(Quaresma 4, Postiga 78)*
England: Grant; Jagielka, Konchesky, Barton, Dawson, Clarke, Johnson, Prutton (Defoe 78), Jeffers, Ameobi, Barry.

Istanbul, 10 October 2003, 4000

Turkey (1) 1 *(Sonkaya 2)*
England (0) 0
England: Grant; Johnson■, Taylor M, Prutton (Bent D 80), Davies, Jagielka, Wright-Phillips, Sidwell (Reo-Coker 61), Jenas, Ameobi, Defoe.

Hull, 17 February 2004, 25,280

England (1) 3 *(Ashton 23, Bentley 72, Bent D 87)*
Holland (0) 2 *(Tuyp 47, Huntelaar 74)*
England: Carson; Hunt (Hoyte 46), Ridgewell, Reo-Coker (Chaplow 84), Johnson, Taylor S, Bentley, Welsh, Ashton (Stead 69), Cole C (Bent D 84), Downing (Whittingham 69).

Kristiansund, 30 March 2004, 7330

Sweden (0) 2 *(Nilsson P 58, Andersson J 70)*
England (1) 2 *(Ashton 14, Chopra 90)*
England: Carson (Grant 69); Hoyte, Ridgewell, Reo-Coker (Jones 79), Dawson, Taylor S (Kilgallon 63), Bentley (Chopra 79), Tonge (Ambrose 63), Ashton (Stead 63), Cole C (Bent D 69), Downing (Milner 79).

POST-WAR INTERNATIONAL APPEARANCES

As at July 2004 *(Season of first cap given)*

ENGLAND

A'Court, A. (5) 1957/8 Liverpool
Adams, T. A. (66) 1986/7 Arsenal
Allen, C. (5) 1983/4 QPR, Tottenham H
Allen, R. (5) 1951/2 WBA
Allen, T. (3) 1959/60 Stoke C
Anderson, S. (2) 1961/2 Sunderland
Anderson, V. (30) 1978/9 Nottingham F, Arsenal, Manchester U
Anderton, D. R. (30) 1993/4 Tottenham H
Angus, J. (1) 1960/1 Burnley
Armfield, J. (43) 1958/9 Blackpool
Armstrong, D. (3) 1979/80 Middlesbrough, Southampton
Armstrong, K. (1) 1954/5 Chelsea
Astall, G. (2) 1955/6 Birmingham C
Astle, J. (5) 1968/9 WBA
Aston, J. (17) 1948/9 Manchester U
Atyeo, J. (6) 1955/6 Bristol C

Bailey, G. R. (2) 1984/5 Manchester U
Bailey, M. (2) 1963/4 Charlton
Baily, E. (9) 1949/50 Tottenham H
Baker, J. (8) 1959/60 Hibernian, Arsenal
Ball, A. (72) 1964/5 Blackpool, Everton, Arsenal
Ball, M. J. (1) 2000/01 Everton
Banks, G. (73) 1962/3 Leicester C, Stoke C
Banks, T. (6) 1957/8 Bolton W
Bardsley, D. (2) 1992/3 QPR
Barham, M. (2) 1982/3 Norwich C
Barlow, R. (1) 1954/5 WBA
Barmby, N. J. (23) 1994/5 Tottenham H, Middlesbrough, Everton, Liverpool
Barnes, J. (79) 1982/3 Watford, Liverpool
Barnes, P. (22) 1977/8 Manchester C, WBA, Leeds U
Barrass, M. (3) 1951/2 Bolton W
Barrett, E. D. (3) 1990/1 Oldham Ath, Aston Villa
Barry, G. (8) 1999/00 Aston Villa
Barton, W. D. (3) 1994/5 Wimbledon, Blackburn R
Batty, D. (42) 1990/1 Leeds U, Blackburn R, Newcastle U, Leeds U
Baynham, R. (3) 1955/6 Luton T
Beardsley, P. A. (59) 1985/6 Newcastle U, Liverpool, Newcastle U
Beasant, D. J. (2) 1989/90 Chelsea
Beattie, J. S. (5) 2002/03 Southampton

Beattie, T. K. (9) 1974/5 Ipswich T
Beckham, D. R. J. (72) 1996/7 Manchester U, Real Madrid
Bell, C. (48) 1967/8 Manchester C
Bentley, R. (12) 1948/9 Chelsea
Berry, J. (4) 1952/3 Manchester U
Birtles, G. (3) 1979/80 Nottingham F, Manchester U
Blissett, L. (14) 1982/3 Watford, AC Milan
Blockley, J. (1) 1972/3 Arsenal
Blunstone, F. (5) 1954/5 Chelsea
Bonetti, P. (7) 1965/6 Chelsea
Bould, S. A. (2) 1993/4 Arsenal
Bowles, S. (5) 1973/4 QPR
Bowyer, L. D. (1) 2002/03 Leeds U
Boyer, P. (1) 1975/6 Norwich C
Brabrook, P. (3) 1957/8 Chelsea
Bracewell, P. W. (3) 1984/5 Everton
Bradford, G. (1) 1955/6 Bristol R
Bradley, W. (3) 1958/9 Manchester U
Bridge, W. M. (17) 2001/02 Southampton, Chelsea
Bridges, B. (4) 1964/5 Chelsea
Broadbent, P. (7) 1957/8 Wolverhampton W
Broadis, I. (14) 1951/2 Manchester C, Newcastle U
Brooking, T. (47) 1973/4 West Ham U
Brooks, J. (3) 1956/7 Tottenham H
Brown, A. (1) 1970/1 WBA
Brown, K. (1) 1959/60 West Ham U
Brown, W. M. (7) 1998/9 Manchester U
Bull, S. G. (13) 1988/9 Wolverhampton W
Butcher, T. (77) 1979/80 Ipswich T, Rangers
Butt, N. (35) 1996/7 Manchester U
Byrne, G. (2) 1962/3 Liverpool
Byrne, J. (11) 1961/2 Crystal P, West Ham U
Byrne, R. (33) 1953/4 Manchester U

Callaghan, I. (4) 1965/6 Liverpool
Campbell, S. (62) 1995/6 Tottenham H, Arsenal
Carragher, J. L. (12) 1998/9 Liverpool
Carrick, M. (2) 2000/01 West Ham U
Carter, H. (7) 1946/7 Derby Co
Chamberlain, M. (8) 1982/3 Stoke C
Channon, M. (46) 1972/3 Southampton, Manchester C
Charles, G. A. (2) 1990/1 Nottingham F

280

Charlton, J. (35) 1964/5 Leeds U
Charlton, R. (106) 1957/8 Manchester U
Charnley, R. (1) 1961/2 Blackpool
Cherry, T. (27) 1975/6 Leeds U
Chilton, A. (2) 1950/1 Manchester U
Chivers, M. (24) 1970/1 Tottenham H
Clamp, E. (4) 1957/8 Wolverhampton W
Clapton, D. (1) 1958/9 Arsenal
Clarke, A. (19) 1969/70 Leeds U
Clarke, H. (1) 1953/4 Tottenham H
Clayton, R. (35) 1955/6 Blackburn R
Clemence, R (61) 1972/3 Liverpool, Tottenham H
Clement, D. (5) 1975/6 QPR
Clough, B. (2) 1959/60 Middlesbrough
Clough, N. H. (14) 1988/9 Nottingham F
Coates, R. (4) 1969/70 Burnley, Tottenham H
Cockburn, H. (13) 1946/7 Manchester U
Cohen, G. (37) 1963/4 Fulham
Cole, Andy (15) 1994/5 Manchester U
Cole, Ashley (30) 2000/01 Arsenal
Cole, J. J. (17) 2000/01 West Ham U, Chelsea
Collymore, S. V. (3) 1994/5 Nottingham F
Compton, L. (2) 1950/1 Arsenal
Connelly, J. (20) 1959/60 Burnley, Manchester U
Cooper, C. T. (2) 1994/5 Nottingham F
Cooper, T. (20) 1968/9 Leeds U
Coppell, S. (42) 1977/8 Manchester U
Corrigan, J. (9) 1975/6 Manchester C
Cottee, A. R. (7) 1986/7 West Ham U, Everton
Cowans, G. (10) 1982/3 Aston Villa, Bari, Aston Villa
Crawford, R. (2) 1961/2 Ipswich T
Crowe, C. (1) 1962/3 Wolverhampton W
Cunningham, L. (6) 1978/9 WBA, Real Madrid
Curle, K. (3) 1991/2 Manchester C
Currie, A. (17) 1971/2 Sheffield U, Leeds U

Daley, A. M. (7) 1991/2 Aston Villa
Davenport, P. (1) 1984/5 Nottingham F
Deane, B. C. (3) 1990/1 Sheffield U
Deeley, N. (2) 1958/9 Wolverhampton W
Defoe, J. C. (2) 2003/04 Tottenham H
Devonshire, A. (8) 1979/80 West Ham U
Dickinson, J. (48) 1948/9 Portsmouth
Ditchburn, E. (6) 1948/9 Tottenham H

Dixon, K. M. (8) 1984/5 Chelsea
Dixon, L. M. (22) 1989/90 Arsenal
Dobson, M. (5) 1973/4 Burnley, Everton
Dorigo, A. R. (15) 1989/90 Chelsea, Leeds U
Douglas, B. (36) 1957/8 Blackburn R
Doyle, M. (5) 1975/6 Manchester C
Dublin, D. (4) 1997/8 Coventry C, Aston Villa
Dunn, D. J. I. (1) 2002/03 Blackburn R
Duxbury, M. (10) 1983/4 Manchester U
Dyer, K. C. (23) 1999/00 Newcastle U

Eastham, G. (19) 1962/3 Arsenal
Eckersley, W. (17) 1949/50 Blackburn R
Edwards, D. (18) 1954/5 Manchester U
Ehiogu, U. (4) 1995/6 Aston Villa, Middlesbrough
Ellerington, W. (2) 1948/9 Southampton
Elliott, W. H. (5) 1951/2 Burnley

Fantham, J. (1) 1961/2 Sheffield W
Fashanu, J. (2) 1988/9 Wimbledon
Fenwick, T. (20) 1983/4 QPR, Tottenham H
Ferdinand, L. (17) 1992/3 QPR, Newcastle U, Tottenham H
Ferdinand, R. G. (33) 1997/8 West Ham U, Leeds U, Manchester U
Finney, T. (76) 1946/7 Preston NE
Flowers, R. (49) 1954/5 Wolverhampton W
Flowers, T. (11) 1992/3 Southampton, Blackburn R
Foster, S. (3) 1981/2 Brighton
Foulkes, W. (1) 1954/5 Manchester U
Fowler, R. B. (26) 1995/6 Liverpool, Leeds U
Francis, G. (12) 1974/5 QPR
Francis, T. (52) 1976/7 Birmingham C, Nottingham F, Manchester C, Sampdoria
Franklin, N. (27) 1946/7 Stoke C
Froggatt, J. (13) 1949/50 Portsmouth
Froggatt, R. (4) 1952/3 Sheffield W

Gardner, A. (1) 2003/04 Tottenham H
Garrett, T. (3) 1951/2 Blackpool
Gascoigne, P. J. (57) 1988/9 Tottenham H, Lazio, Rangers, Middlesbrough
Gates, E. (2) 1980/1 Ipswich T
George, F. C. (1) 1976/7 Derby Co
Gerrard, S. G. (28) 1999/00 Liverpool
Gidman, J. (1) 1976/7 Aston Villa
Gillard, I. (3) 1974/5 QPR
Goddard, P. (1) 1981/2 West Ham U

Grainger, C. (7) 1955/6 Sheffield U, Sunderland
Gray, A. A. (1) 1991/2 Crystal P
Gray, M. (3) 1998/9 Sunderland
Greaves, J. (57) 1958/9 Chelsea, Tottenham H
Greenhoff, B. (18) 1975/6 Manchester U
Gregory, J. (6) 1982/3 QPR
Guppy, S. (1) 1999/00 Leicester C

Hagan, J. (1) 1948/9 Sheffield U
Haines, J. (1) 1948/9 WBA
Hall, J. (17) 1955/6 Birmingham C
Hancocks, J. (3) 1948/9 Wolverhampton W
Hardwick, G. (13) 1946/7 Middlesbrough
Harford, M. G. (2) 1987/8 Luton T
Hargreaves, O. (22) 2001/02 Bayern Munich
Harris, G. (1) 1965/6 Burnley
Harris, P. (2) 1949/50 Portsmouth
Harvey, C. (1) 1970/1 Everton
Hassall, H. (5) 1950/1 Huddersfield T, Bolton W
Hateley, M. (32) 1983/4 Portsmouth, AC Milan, Monaco, Rangers
Haynes, J. (56) 1954/5 Fulham
Hector, K. (2) 1973/4 Derby Co
Hellawell, M. (2) 1962/3 Birmingham C
Hendrie, L. A. (1) 1998/9 Aston Villa
Henry, R. (1) 1962/3 Tottenham H
Heskey, E. W. (43) 1998/9 Leicester C, Liverpool, Birmingham C
Hill, F. (2) 1962/3 Bolton W
Hill, G. (6) 1975/6 Manchester U
Hill, R. (3) 1982/3 Luton T
Hinchcliffe, A. G. (7) 1996/7 Everton, Sheffield W
Hinton, A. (3) 1962/3 Wolverhampton W, Nottingham F
Hirst, D. E. (3) 1990/1 Sheffield W
Hitchens, G. (7) 1960/1 Aston Villa, Internazionale
Hoddle, G. (53) 1979/80 Tottenham H, Monaco
Hodge, S. B. (24) 1985/6 Aston Villa, Tottenham H, Nottingham F
Hodgkinson, A. (5) 1956/7 Sheffield U
Holden, D. (5) 1958/9 Bolton W
Holliday, E. (3) 1959/60 Middlesbrough
Hollins, J. (1) 1966/7 Chelsea
Hopkinson, E. (14) 1957/8 Bolton W
Howe, D. (23) 1957/8 WBA
Howe, J. (3) 1947/8 Derby Co
Howey, S. N. (4) 1994/5 Newcastle U
Hudson, A. (2) 1974/5 Stoke C

Hughes, E. (62) 1969/70 Liverpool, Wolverhampton W
Hughes, L. (3) 1949/50 Liverpool
Hunt, R. (34) 1961/2 Liverpool
Hunt, S. (2) 1983/4 WBA
Hunter, N. (28) 1965/6 Leeds U
Hurst, G. (49) 1965/6 West Ham U

Ince, P. (53) 1992/3 Manchester U, Internazionale, Liverpool, Middlesbrough

James, D. B. (28) 1996/7 Liverpool, Aston Villa, West Ham U, Manchester C
Jeffers, F. (1) 2002/03 Arsenal
Jenas, J. A. (6) 2002/03 Newcastle U
Jezzard, B. (2) 1953/4 Fulham
Johnson, D. (8) 1974/5 Ipswich T, Liverpool
Johnson, G. M. C. (1) 2003/04 Chelsea
Johnson, S. A. M. (1) 2000/01 Derby Co
Johnston, H. (10) 1946/7 Blackpool
Jones, M. (3) 1964/5 Sheffield U, Leeds U
Jones, R. (8) 1991/2 Liverpool
Jones, W. H. (2) 1949/50 Liverpool

Kay, A. (1) 1962/3 Everton
Keegan, K. (63) 1972/3 Liverpool, SV Hamburg, Southampton
Kennedy, A. (2) 1983/4 Liverpool
Kennedy, R. (17) 1975/6 Liverpool
Keown, M. R. (43) 1991/2 Everton, Arsenal
Kevan, D. (14) 1956/7 WBA
Kidd, B. (2) 1969/70 Manchester U
King, L. B. (7) 2001/02 Tottenham H
Knowles, C. (4) 1967/8 Tottenham H
Konchesky, P. M. (1) 2002/03 Charlton Ath

Labone, B. (26) 1962/3 Everton
Lampard, F. J. (23) 1999/00 West Ham U, Chelsea
Lampard, F. R. G. (2) 1972/3 West Ham U
Langley, J. (3) 1957/8 Fulham
Langton, R. (11) 1946/7 Blackburn R, Preston NE, Bolton W
Latchford, R. (12) 1977/8 Everton
Lawler, C. (4) 1970/1 Liverpool
Lawton, T. (15) 1946/7 Chelsea, Notts Co
Lee, F. (27) 1968/9 Manchester C
Lee, J. (1) 1950/1 Derby C
Lee, R. M. (21) 1994/5 Newcastle U
Lee, S. (14) 1982/3 Liverpool
Le Saux, G. P. (36) 1993/4 Blackburn R, Chelsea

282

Le Tissier, M. P. (8) 1993/4 Southampton
Lindsay, A. (4) 1973/4 Liverpool
Lineker, G. (80) 1983/4 Leicester C, Everton, Barcelona, Tottenham H
Little, B. (1) 1974/5 Aston Villa
Lloyd, L. (4) 1970/1 Liverpool, Nottingham F
Lofthouse, N. (33) 1950/1 Bolton W
Lowe, E. (3) 1946/7 Aston Villa

Mabbutt, G. (16) 1982/3 Tottenham H
Macdonald, M. (14) 1971/2 Newcastle U, Arsenal
Madeley, P. (24) 1970/1 Leeds U
Mannion, W. (26) 1946/7 Middlesbrough
Mariner, P. (35) 1976/7 Ipswich T, Arsenal
Marsh, R. (9) 1971/2 QPR, Manchester C
Martin, A. (17) 1980/1 West Ham U
Martyn, A. N. (23) 1991/2 Crystal P, Leeds U
Marwood, B. (1) 1988/9 Arsenal
Matthews, R. (5) 1955/6 Coventry C
Matthews, S. (37) 1946/7 Stoke C, Blackpool
McCann, G. P. (1) 2000/01 Sunderland
McDermott, T. (25) 1977/8 Liverpool
McDonald, C. (8) 1957/8 Burnley
McFarland, R. (28) 1970/1 Derby C
McGarry, W. (4) 1953/4 Huddersfield T
McGuinness, W. (2) 1958/9 Manchester U
McMahon, S. (17) 1987/8 Liverpool
McManaman, S. (37) 1994/5 Liverpool, Real Madrid
McNab, R. (4) 1968/9 Arsenal
McNeil, M. (9) 1960/1 Middlesbrough
Meadows, J. (1) 1954/5 Manchester C
Medley, L. 1950/1 Tottenham H
Melia, J. (2) 1962/3 Liverpool
Merrick, G. (23) 1951/2 Birmingham C
Merson, P. C. (21) 1991/2 Arsenal, Middlesbrough, Aston Villa
Metcalfe, V. (2) 1950/1 Huddersfield T
Milburn, J. (13) 1948/9 Newcastle U
Miller, B. (1) 1960/1 Burnley
Mills, D. J. (19) 2000/01 Leeds U
Mills, M. (42) 1972/3 Ipswich T
Milne, G. (14) 1962/3 Liverpool
Milton, C. A. (1) 1951/2 Arsenal
Moore, B. (108) 1961/2 West Ham U
Morley, A. (6) 1981/2 Aston Villa
Morris, J. (3) 1948/9 Derby Co
Mortensen, S. (25) 1946/7 Blackpool
Mozley, B. (3) 1949/50 Derby Co
Mullen, J. (12) 1946/7 Wolverhampton W

Mullery, A. (35) 1964/5 Tottenham H
Murphy, D. B. (9) 2001/02 Liverpool

Neal, P. (50) 1975/6 Liverpool
Neville, G. A. (67) 1994/5 Manchester U
Neville, P. J. (50) 1995/6 Manchester U
Newton, K. (27) 1965/6 Blackburn R, Everton
Nicholls, J. (2) 1953/4 WBA
Nicholson, W. (1) 1950/1 Tottenham H
Nish, D. (5) 1972/3 Derby Co
Norman, M. (23) 1961/2 Tottenham H

O'Grady, M. (2) 1962/3 Huddersfield T, Leeds U
Osgood, P. (4) 1969/70 Chelsea
Osman, R. (11) 1979/80 Ipswich T
Owen, M. J. (60) 1997/8 Liverpool
Owen, S. (3) 1953/4 Luton T

Paine, T. (19) 1962/3 Southampton
Pallister, G. (22) 1987/8 Middlesbrough, Manchester U
Palmer, C. L. (18) 1991/2 Sheffield W
Parker, P. A. (19) 1988/9 QPR, Manchester U
Parker, S. M. (2) 2003/04 Charlton Ath, Chelsea
Parkes, P. (1) 1973/4 QPR
Parlour, R. (10) 1998/9 Arsenal
Parry, R. (2) 1959/60 Bolton W
Peacock, A. (6) 1961/2 Middlesbrough, Leeds U
Pearce, S. (78) 1986/7 Nottingham F, West Ham U
Pearson, Stan (8) 1947/8 Manchester U
Pearson, Stuart (15) 1975/6 Manchester U
Pegg, D. (1) 1956/7 Manchester U
Pejic, M. (4) 1973/4 Stoke C
Perry, W. (3) 1955/6 Blackpool
Perryman, S. (1) 1981/2 Tottenham H
Peters, M. (67) 1965/6 West Ham U, Tottenham H
Phelan, M. C. (1) 1989/90 Manchester U
Phillips, K. (8) 1998/9 Sunderland
Phillips, L. (3) 1951/2 Portsmouth
Pickering, F. (3) 1963/4 Everton
Pickering, N. (1) 1982/3 Sunderland
Pilkington, B. (1) 1954/5 Burnley
Platt, D. (62) 1989/90 Aston Villa, Bari, Juventus, Sampdoria, Arsenal
Pointer, R. (3) 1961/2 Burnley
Powell, C. G. (5) 2000/01 Charlton Ath
Pye, J. (1) 1949/50 Wolverhampton W

Quixall, A. (5) 1953/4 Sheffield W

283

Radford, J. (2) 1968/9 Arsenal
Ramsey, A. (32) 1948/9 Southampton, Tottenham H
Reaney, P. (3) 1968/9 Leeds U
Redknapp, J. F. (17) 1995/6 Liverpool
Reeves, K. (2) 1979/80 Norwich C
Regis, C. (5) 1981/2 WBA, Coventry C
Reid, P. (13) 1984/5 Everton
Revie, D. (6) 1954/5 Manchester C
Richards, J. (1) 1972/3 Wolverhampton W
Richardson, K. (1) 1993/4 Aston Villa
Rickaby, S. (1) 1953/4 WBA
Ricketts, M. B. (1) 2001/02 Bolton W
Rimmer, J. (1) 1975/6 Arsenal
Ripley, S. E. (2) 1993/4 Blackburn R
Rix, G. (17) 1980/1 Arsenal
Robb, G. (1) 1953/4 Tottenham H
Roberts, G. (6) 1982/3 Tottenham H
Robinson, P. W. (5) 2002/03 Leeds U, Tottenham H
Robson, B. (90) 1979/80 WBA, Manchester U
Robson, R. (20) 1957/8 WBA
Rocastle, D. (14) 1988/9 Arsenal
Rooney, W. (17) 2002/03 Everton
Rowley, J. (6) 1948/9 Manchester U
Royle, J. (6) 1970/1 Everton, Manchester C
Ruddock, N. (1) 1994/5 Liverpool

Sadler, D. (4) 1967/8 Manchester U
Salako, J. A. (5) 1990/1 Crystal P
Sansom, K. (86) 1978/9 Crystal P, Arsenal
Scales, J. R. (3) 1994/5 Liverpool
Scholes, P. (66) 1996/7 Manchester U
Scott, L. (17) 1946/7 Arsenal
Seaman, D. A. (75) 1988/9 QPR, Arsenal
Sewell, J. (6) 1951/2 Sheffield W
Shackleton, L. (5) 1948/9 Sunderland
Sharpe, L. S. (8) 1990/1 Manchester U
Shaw, G. (5) 1958/9 Sheffield U
Shearer, A. (63) 1991/2 Southampton, Blackburn R, Newcastle U
Shellito, K. (1) 1962/3 Chelsea
Sheringham, E. (51) 1992/3 Tottenham H, Manchester U, Tottenham H
Sherwood, T. A. (3) 1998/9 Tottenham H
Shilton, P. (125) 1970/1 Leicester C, Stoke C, Nottingham F, Southampton, Derby Co
Shimwell, E. (1) 1948/9 Blackpool
Sillett, P. (3) 1954/5 Chelsea
Sinclair, T. (12) 2001/02 West Ham U, Manchester C
Sinton, A. (12) 1991/2 QPR, Sheffield W

Slater, W. (12) 1954/5 Wolverhampton W
Smith, A. (8) 2000/01 Leeds U
Smith, A. M. (13) 1988/9 Arsenal
Smith, L. (6) 1950/1 Arsenal
Smith, R. (15) 1960/1 Tottenham H
Smith, Tom (1) 1970/1 Liverpool
Smith, Trevor (2) 1959/60 Birmingham C
Southgate, G. (57) 1995/6 Aston Villa, Middlesbrough
Spink, N. (1) 1982/3 Aston Villa
Springett, R. (33) 1959/60 Sheffield W
Staniforth, R. (8) 1953/4 Huddersfield T
Statham, D. (3) 1982/3 WBA
Stein, B. (1) 1983/4 Luton T
Stepney, A. (1) 1967/8 Manchester U
Sterland, M. (1) 1988/9 Sheffield W
Steven, T. M. (36) 1984/5 Everton, Rangers, Marseille
Stevens, G. A. (7) 1984/5 Tottenham H
Stevens, M. G. (46) 1984/5 Everton, Rangers
Stewart, P. A. (3) 1991/2 Tottenham H
Stiles, N. (28) 1964/5 Manchester U
Stone, S. B. (9) 1995/6 Nottingham F
Storey-Moore, I. (1) 1969/70 Nottingham F
Storey, P. (19) 1970/1 Arsenal
Streten, B. (1) 1949/50 Luton T
Summerbee, M. (8) 1967/8 Manchester C
Sunderland, A. (1) 1979/80 Arsenal
Sutton, C. R. (1) 1997/8 Blackburn R
Swan, P. (19) 1959/60 Sheffield W
Swift, F. (19) 1946/7 Manchester C

Talbot, B. (6) 1976/7 Ipswich T
Tambling, R. (3) 1962/3 Chelsea
Taylor, E. (1) 1953/4 Blackpool
Taylor, J. (2) 1950/1 Fulham
Taylor, P. H. (3) 1947/8 Liverpool
Taylor, P. J. (4) 1975/6 Crystal P
Taylor, T. (19) 1952/3 Manchester U
Temple, D. (1) 1964/5 Everton
Terry, J. G. (11) 2002/03 Chelsea
Thomas, Danny (2) 1982/3 Coventry C
Thomas, Dave (8) 1974/5 QPR
Thomas, G. R. (9) 1990/1 Crystal P
Thomas, M. L. (2) 1988/9 Arsenal
Thompson, A. (1) 2003/04 Celtic
Thompson, P. (16) 1963/4 Liverpool
Thompson, P. B. (42) 1975/6 Liverpool
Thompson, T. (2) 1951/2 Aston Villa, Preston NE
Thomson, R. (8) 1963/4 Wolverhampton W
Todd, C. (27) 1974/5 Derby Co
Towers, T. (3) 1975/6 Sunderland
Tueart, D. (6) 1974/5 Manchester C

Ufton, D. (1) 1953/4 Charlton Ath
Unsworth, D. G. (1) 1994/5 Everton
Upson, M. J. (6) 2002/03 Birmingham C

Vassell, D. (22) 2001/02 Aston Villa
Venables, T. (2) 1964/5 Chelsea
Venison, B. (2) 1994/5 Newcastle U
Viljoen, C. (2) 1974/5 Ipswich T
Viollet, D. (2) 1959/60 Manchester U

Waddle, C. R. (62) 1984/5 Newcastle U, Tottenham H, Marseille
Waiters, A. (5) 1963/4 Blackpool
Walker, D. S. (59) 1988/9 Nottingham F, Sampdoria, Sheffield W
Walker, I. M. (4) 1995/6 Tottenham H, Leicester C
Wallace, D. L. (1) 1985/6 Southampton
Walsh, P. (5) 1982/3 Luton T
Walters, K. M. (1) 1990/1 Rangers
Ward, P. (1) 1979/80 Brighton
Ward, T. (2) 1947/8 Derby C
Watson, D. (12) 1983/4 Norwich C, Everton
Watson, D. V. (65) 1973/4 Sunderland, Manchester C, Southampton, Werder Bremen, Southampton, Stoke C
Watson, W. (4) 1949/50 Sunderland
Webb, N. (26) 1987/8 Nottingham F, Manchester U
Weller, K. (4) 1973/4 Leicester C
West, G. (3) 1968/9 Everton
Wheeler, J. (1) 1954/5 Bolton W
White, D. (1) 1992/3 Manchester C
Whitworth, S. (7) 1974/5 Leicester C

Whymark, T. (1) 1977/8 Ipswich T
Wignall, F. (2) 1964/5 Nottingham F
Wilcox, J. M. (3) 1995/6 Blackburn R, Leeds U
Wilkins, R. (84) 1975/6 Chelsea, Manchester U, AC Milan
Williams, B. (24) 1948/9 Wolverhampton W
Williams, S. (6) 1982/3 Southampton
Willis, A. (1) 1951/2 Tottenham H
Wilshaw, D. (12) 1953/4 Wolverhampton W
Wilson, R. (63) 1959/60 Huddersfield T, Everton
Winterburn, N. (2) 1989/90 Arsenal
Wise, D. F. (21) 1990/1 Chelsea
Withe, P. (11) 1980/1 Aston Villa
Wood, R. (3) 1954/5 Manchester U
Woodcock, A. (42) 1977/8 Nottingham F, FC Cologne, Arsenal
Woodgate, J. S. (5) 1998/9 Leeds U, Newcastle U
Woods, C. C. E. (43) 1984/5 Norwich C, Rangers, Sheffield W
Worthington, F. (8) 1973/4 Leicester C
Wright, I. E. (33) 1990/1 Crystal P, Arsenal, West Ham U
Wright, M. (45) 1983/4 Southampton, Derby C, Liverpool
Wright, R. I. (2) 1999/00 Ipswich T, Arsenal
Wright, T. (11) 1967/8 Everton
Wright, W. (105) 1946/7 Wolverhampton W

Young, G. (1) 1964/5 Sheffield W

NORTHERN IRELAND

Aherne, T. (4) 1946/7 Belfast Celtic, Luton T
Anderson, T. (22) 1972/3 Manchester U, Swindon T, Peterborough U
Armstrong, G. (63) 1976/7 Tottenham H, Watford, Real Mallorca, WBA, Chesterfield

Baird, C. P. (11) 2002/03 Southampton
Barr, H. (3) 1961/2 Linfield, Coventry C
Best, G. (37) 1963/4 Manchester U, Fulham
Bingham, W. (56) 1950/1 Sunderland, Luton T, Everton, Port Vale
Black, K. (30) 1987/8 Luton T, Nottingham F
Blair, R. (5) 1974/5 Oldham Ath
Blanchflower, D. (54) 1949/50 Barnsley, Aston Villa, Tottenham H

Blanchflower, J. (12) 1953/4 Manchester U
Bowler, G. (3) 1949/50 Hull C
Braithwaite, R. (10) 1961/2 Linfield, Middlesbrough
Brennan, R. (5) 1948/9 Luton T, Birmingham C, Fulham
Briggs, R. (2) 1961/2 Manchester U, Swansea
Brotherston, N. (27) 1979/80 Blackburn R
Bruce, W. (2) 1960/1 Glentoran

Campbell, A. (2) 1962/3 Crusaders
Campbell, D. A. (10) 1985/6 Nottingham F, Charlton Ath
Campbell, J. (2) 1950/1 Fulham
Campbell, R. M. (2) 1981/2 Bradford C
Campbell, W. (6) 1967/8 Dundee

Capaldi, A. C. (5) 2003/04 Plymouth Arg

Carey, J. (7) 1946/7 Manchester U

Carroll, R. E. (14) 1996/7 Wigan Ath, Manchester U

Casey, T. (12) 1954/5 Newcastle U, Portsmouth

Caskey, A. (7) 1978/9 Derby C, Tulsa Roughnecks

Cassidy, T. (24) 1970/1 Newcastle U, Burnley

Caughey, M. (2) 1985/6 Linfield

Clarke, C. J. (38) 1985/6 Bournemouth, Southampton, Portsmouth

Cleary, J. (5) 1981/2 Glentoran

Clements, D. (48) 1964/5 Coventry C, Sheffield W, Everton, New York Cosmos

Cochrane, D. (10) 1946/7 Leeds U

Cochrane, T. (26) 1975/6 Coleraine, Burnley, Middlesbrough, Gillingham

Coote, A. (6) 1998/9 Norwich C

Cowan, J. (1) 1969/70 Newcastle U

Coyle, F. (4) 1955/6 Coleraine, Nottingham F

Coyle, L. (1) 1988/9 Derry C

Coyle, R. (5) 1972/3 Sheffield W

Craig, D. (25) 1966/7 Newcastle U

Craigan, S. (8) 2002/03 Partick T, Motherwell

Crossan, E. (3) 1949/50 Blackburn R

Crossan, J. (23) 1959/60 Sparta Rotterdam, Sunderland, Manchester C, Middlesbrough

Cunningham, W. (30) 1950/1 St Mirren, Leicester C, Dunfermline Ath

Cush, W. (26) 1950/1 Glentoran, Leeds U, Portadown

D'Arcy, S. (5) 1951/2 Chelsea, Brentford

Davison, A. J. (3) 1995/6 Bolton W, Bradford C, Grimsby T

Dennison, R. (18) 1987/8 Wolverhampton W

Devine, J. (1) 1989/90 Glentoran

Dickson, D. (4) 1969/70 Coleraine

Dickson, T. (1) 1956/7 Linfield

Dickson, W. (12) 1950/1 Chelsea, Arsenal

Doherty, L. (2) 1984/5 Linfield

Doherty, P. (6) 1946/7 Derby Co, Huddersfield T, Doncaster R

Doherty, T. E. (5) 2002/03 Bristol C

Donaghy, M. (91) 1979/80 Luton T, Manchester U, Chelsea

Dougan, D. (43) 1957/8 Portsmouth, Blackburn R, Aston Villa, Leicester C, Wolverhampton W

Douglas, J. P. (1) 1946/7 Belfast Celtic

Dowd, H. (3) 1972/3 Glentoran, Sheffield W

Dowie, I. (59) 1989/90 Luton T, Southampton, Crystal P, West Ham, QPR

Duff, M. J. (3) 2001/02 Cheltenham T

Dunlop, G. (4) 1984/5 Linfield

Eglington, T. (6) 1946/7 Everton

Elder, A. (40) 1959/60 Burnley, Stoke C

Elliott, S. (20) 2000/01 Motherwell, Hull C

Farrell, P. (7) 1946/7 Everton

Feeney, J. (2) 1946/7 Linfield, Swansea C

Feeney, W. (1) 1975/6 Glentoran

Feeney, W. J. (3) 2001/02 Bournemouth

Ferguson, G. (5) 1998/9 Linfield

Ferguson, W. (2) 1965/6 Linfield

Ferris, R. (3) 1949/50 Birmingham C

Fettis, A. (25) 1991/2 Hull C, Nottingham F, Blackburn R

Finney, T. (14) 1974/5 Sunderland, Cambridge U

Fleming, J. G. (31) 1986/7 Nottingham F, Manchester C, Barnsley

Forde, T. (4) 1958/9 Ards

Gallogly, C. (2) 1950/1 Huddersfield T

Garton, R. (1) 1968/9 Oxford U

Gillespie, K. R. (55) 1994/5 Manchester U, Newcastle U, Blackburn R, Leicester C

Gorman, W. (4) 1946/7 Brentford

Graham, W. (14) 1950/1 Doncaster R

Gray, P. (26) 1992/3 Luton T, Sunderland, Nancy, Luton T, Burnley, Oxford U

Gregg, H. (25) 1953/4 Doncaster R, Manchester U

Griffin, D. J. (29) 1995/6 St Johnstone, Dundee U, Stockport Co

Hamill, R. (1) 1998/9 Glentoran

Hamilton, B. (50) 1968/9 Linfield, Ipswich T, Everton, Millwall, Swindon T

Hamilton, G. (4) 2002/03 Portadown

Hamilton, W. (41) 1977/8 QPR, Burnley, Oxford U

Harkin, T. (5) 1967/8 Southport, Shrewsbury T

Harvey, M. (34) 1960/1 Sunderland

Hatton, S. (2) 1962/3 Linfield

Healy, D. J. (35) 1999/00 Manchester U, Preston NE

286

Healy, P. J. (4) 1981/2 Coleraine, Glentoran
Hegan, D. (7) 1969/70 WBA, Wolverhampton W
Hill, C. F. (27) 1989/90 Sheffield U, Leicester C, Trelleborg, Northampton T
Hill, J. (7) 1958/9 Norwich C, Everton
Hinton, E. (7) 1946/7 Fulham, Millwall
Holmes, S. P. (1) 2001/02 Wrexham
Horlock, K. (32) 1994/5 Swindon T, Manchester C
Hughes, A. W. (35) 1997/8 Newcastle U
Hughes, M. E. (69) 1991/2 Manchester C, Strasbourg, West Ham U, Wimbledon, Crystal Palace
Hughes, P. (3) 1986/7 Bury
Hughes, W. (1) 1950/1 Bolton W
Humphries, W. (14) 1961/2 Ards, Coventry C, Swansea T
Hunter, A. (53) 1969/70 Blackburn R, Ipswich T
Hunter, B. V. (15) 1994/5 Wrexham, Reading

Irvine, R. (8) 1961/2 Linfield, Stoke C
Irvine, W. (23) 1962/3 Burnley, Preston NE, Brighton & HA

Jackson, T. (35) 1968/9 Everton, Nottingham F, Manchester U
Jamison, A. (1) 1975/6 Glentoran
Jenkins, I. (6) 1996/7 Chester C, Dundee U
Jennings, P. (119) 1963/4 Watford, Tottenham H, Arsenal, Tottenham H, Everton, Tottenham H
Johnson, D. M. (30) 1998/9 Blackburn R, Birmingham C
Johnston, W. (1) 1961/2 Glentoran, Oldham Ath
Jones, J. (3) 1955/6 Glenavon
Jones, S. G. (11) 2002/03 Crewe Alex

Keane, T. (1) 1948/9 Swansea T
Kee, P. V. (9) 1989/90 Oxford U, Ards
Keith, R. (23) 1957/8 Newcastle U
Kelly, H. (4) 1949/50 Fulham, Southampton
Kelly, P. (1) 1949/50 Barnsley
Kennedy, P. H. (20) 1998/9 Watford, Wigan Ath
Kirk, A. (5) 1999/00 Heart of Midlothian

Lawther, I. (4) 1959/60 Sunderland, Blackburn R
Lennon, N. F. (40) 1993/4 Crewe Alex, Leicester C, Celtic

Lockhart, N. (8) 1946/7 Linfield, Coventry C, Aston Villa
Lomas, S. M. (45) 1993/4 Manchester C, West Ham U
Lutton, B. (6) 1969/70 Wolverhampton W, West Ham U

Magill, E. (26) 1961/2 Arsenal, Brighton & HA
Magilton, J. (52) 1990/1 Oxford U, Southampton, Sheffield W, Ipswich T
Mannus, A. (1) 2003/04 Linfield
Martin, C. (6) 1946/7 Glentoran, Leeds U, Aston Villa
McAdams, W. (15) 1953/4 Manchester C, Bolton W, Leeds U
McAlinden, J. (2) 1946/7 Portsmouth, Southend U
McBride, S. (4) 1990/1 Glenavon
McCabe, J. (6) 1948/9 Leeds U
McCann, G. S. (9) 2001/02 West Ham U, Cheltenham T
McCarthy, J. D. (18) 1995/6 Port Vale, Birmingham C
McCartney, G. (16) 2001/02 Sunderland
McCavana, T. (3) 1954/5 Coleraine
McCleary, J. W. (1) 1954/5 Cliftonville
McClelland, J. (6) 1960/1 Arsenal, Fulham
McClelland, J. (53) 1979/80 Mansfield T, Rangers, Watford, Leeds U
McCourt, F. (6) 1951/2 Manchester C
McCourt, P. J. (1) 2001/02 Rochdale
McCoy, R. (1) 1986/7 Coleraine
McCreery, D. (67) 1975/6 Manchester U, QPR, Tulsa Roughnecks, Newcastle U, Heart of Midlothian
McCrory, S. (1) 1957/8 Southend U
McCullough, W. (10) 1960/1 Arsenal, Millwall
McCurdy, C. (1) 1979/80 Linfield
McDonald, A. (52) 1985/6 QPR
McElhinney, G. (6) 1983/4 Bolton W
McEvilly, L. R. (1) 2001/02 Rochdale
McFaul, I. (6) 1966/7 Linfield, Newcastle U
McGarry, J. K. (3) 1950/1 Cliftonville
McGaughey, M. (1) 1984/5 Linfield
McGibbon, P. C. G. (7) 1994/5 Manchester U, Wigan Ath
McGrath, R. (21) 1973/4 Tottenham H, Manchester U
McIlroy, J. (55) 1951/2 Burnley, Stoke C
McIlroy, S. B. (88) 1971/2 Manchester U, Stoke C, Manchester C
McKeag, W. (2) 1967/8 Glentoran
McKenna, J. (7) 1949/50 Huddersfield T

McKenzie, R. (1) 1966/7 Airdrieonians

McKinney, W. (1) 1965/6 Falkirk

McKnight, A. (10) 1987/8 Celtic, West Ham U

McLaughlin, J. (12) 1961/2 Shrewsbury T, Swansea T

McMahon, G. J. (17) 1994/5 Tottenham H, Stoke C

McMichael, A. (39) 1949/50 Newcastle U

McMillan, S. (2) 1962/3 Manchester U

McMordie, E. (21) 1968/9 Middlesbrough

McMorran, E. (15) 1946/7 Belfast Celtic, Barnsley, Doncaster R

McNally, B. A. (5) 1985/6 Shrewsbury T

McParland, P. (34) 1953/4 Aston Villa, Wolverhampton W

McVeigh, P. (16) 1998/9 Tottenham H, Norwich C

Montgomery, F. J. (1) 1954/5 Coleraine

Moore, C. (1) 1948/9 Glentoran

Moreland, V. (6) 1978/9 Derby Co

Morgan, S. (18) 1971/2 Port Vale, Aston Villa, Brighton & HA, Sparta Rotterdam

Morrow, S. J. (39) 1989/90 Arsenal, QPR

Mullan, G. (4) 1982/3 Glentoran

Mulryne, P. P. (25) 1996/7 Manchester U, Norwich C

Murdock, C. J. (21) 1999/00 Preston NE, Hibernian

Napier, R. (1) 1965/6 Bolton W

Neill, T. (59) 1960/1 Arsenal, Hull C

Nelson, S. (51) 1969/70 Arsenal, Brighton & HA

Nicholl, C. (51) 1974/5 Aston Villa, Southampton, Grimsby T

Nicholl, J. M. (73) 1975/6 Manchester U, Toronto Blizzard, Sunderland, Rangers, WBA

Nicholson, J. (41) 1960/1 Manchester U, Huddersfield T

Nolan, I. R. (18) 1996/7 Sheffield W, Bradford C, Wigan Ath

O'Boyle, G. (13) 1993/4 Dunfermline Ath, St Johnstone

O'Doherty, A. (2) 1969/70 Coleraine

O'Driscoll, J. (3) 1948/9 Swansea T

O'Kane, L. (20) 1969/70 Nottingham F

O'Neill, C. (3) 1988/9 Motherwell

O'Neill, H. M. (64) 1971/2 Distillery, Nottingham F, Norwich C, Manchester C, Norwich C, Notts Co

O'Neill, J. (1) 1961/2 Sunderland

O'Neill, J. (39) 1979/80 Leicester C

O'Neill, M. A. (31) 1987/8 Newcastle U, Dundee U, Hibernian, Coventry C

Parke, J. (13) 1963/4 Linfield, Hibernian, Sunderland

Patterson, D. J. (17) 1993/4 Crystal P, Luton T, Dundee U

Peacock, R. (31) 1951/2 Celtic, Coleraine

Penney, S. (17) 1984/5 Brighton & HA

Platt, J. A. (23) 1975/6 Middlesbrough, Ballymena U, Coleraine

Quinn, J. M. (46) 1984/5 Blackburn R, Leicester, Bradford C, West Ham U, Bournemouth, Reading

Quinn, S. J. (32) 1995/6 Blackpool, WBA, Willem II

Rafferty, P. (1) 1979/80 Linfield

Ramsey, P. (14) 1983/4 Leicester C

Rice, P. (49) 1968/9 Arsenal

Robinson, S. (5) 1996/7 Bournemouth

Rogan, A. (18) 1987/8 Celtic, Sunderland, Millwall

Ross, E. (1) 1968/9 Newcastle U

Rowland, K. (19) 1994/5 West Ham U

Russell, A. (1) 1946/7 Linfield

Ryan, R. (1) 1949/50 WBA

Sanchez, L. P. (3) 1986/7 Wimbledon

Scott, J. (2) 1957/8 Grimsby T

Scott, P. (10) 1974/5 Everton, York C, Aldershot

Sharkey, P. (1) 1975/6 Ipswich T

Shields, J. (1) 1956/7 Southampton

Simpson, W. (12) 1950/1 Rangers

Sloan, D. (2) 1968/9 Oxford

Sloan, T. (3) 1978/9 Manchester U

Sloan, W. (1) 1946/7 Arsenal

Smith, A. W. (11) 2002/03 Glentoran

Smyth, S. (9) 1947/8 Wolverhampton W, Stoke C

Smyth, W. (4) 1948/9 Distillery

Sonner, D. J. (12) 1997/8 Ipswich T, Sheffield W, Birmingham C, Nottingham F

Spence, D. (29) 1974/5 Bury, Blackpool, Southend U

Stevenson, A. (3) 1946/7 Everton

Stewart, A. (7) 1966/7 Glentoran, Derby

Stewart, D. (1) 1977/8 Hull C

Stewart, I. (31) 1981/2 QPR, Newcastle U

Stewart, T. (1) 1960/1 Linfield

Taggart, G. P. (51) 1989/90 Barnsley, Bolton W, Leicester C

Taylor, M. S. (38) 1998/9 Fulham, Birmingham C
Todd, S. (11) 1965/6 Burnley, Sheffield W
Toner, C. (2) 2002/03 Leyton Orient
Trainor, D. (1) 1966/7 Crusaders
Tully, C. (10) 1948/9 Celtic

Uprichard, N. (18) 1951/2 Swindon T, Portsmouth

Vernon, J. (17) 1946/7 Belfast Celtic, WBA
Walker, J. (1) 1954/5 Doncaster R
Walsh, D. (9) 1946/7 WBA
Walsh, W. (5) 1947/8 Manchester C
Watson, P. (1) 1970/1 Distillery
Welsh, S. (4) 1965/6 Carlisle U
Whiteside, N. (38) 1981/2 Manchester U, Everton

Whitley, Jeff (12) 1996/7 Manchester C, Sunderland
Whitley, Jim (3) 1997/8 Manchester C
Williams, M. S. (30) 1998/9 Chesterfield, Watford, Wimbledon, Stoke C, Wimbledon
Williams, P. (1) 1990/1 WBA
Wilson, D. J. (24) 1986/7 Brighton & HA, Luton, Sheffield W
Wilson, K. J. (42) 1986/7 Ipswich T, Chelsea, Notts C, Walsall
Wilson, S. (12) 1961/2 Glenavon, Falkirk, Dundee
Wood, T. J. (1) 1995/6 Walsall
Worthington, N. (66) 1983/4 Sheffield W, Leeds U, Stoke C
Wright, T. J. (31) 1988/9 Newcastle U, Nottingham F, Manchester C

SCOTLAND

Aird, J. (4) 1953/4 Burnley
Aitken, G. G. (8) 1948/9 East Fife, Sunderland
Aitken, R. (57) 1979/80 Celtic, Newcastle U, St Mirren
Albiston, A. (14) 1981/2 Manchester U
Alexander, G. (14) 2001/02 Preston NE
Allan, T. (2) 1973/4 Dundee
Anderson, J. (1) 1953/4 Leicester C
Anderson, R. (4) 2002/03 Aberdeen
Archibald, S. (27) 1979/80 Aberdeen, Tottenham H, Barcelona
Auld, B. (3) 1958/9 Celtic

Baird, H. (1) 1955/6 Airdrieonians
Baird, S. (7) 1956/7 Rangers
Bannon, E. (11) 1979/80 Dundee U
Bauld, W. (3) 1949/50 Heart of Midlothian
Baxter, J. (34) 1960/1 Rangers, Sunderland
Bell, W. (2) 1965/6 Leeds U
Bernard, P. R. (2) 1994/5 Oldham Ath
Bett, J. (25) 1981/2 Rangers, Lokeren, Aberdeen
Black, E. (2) 1987/8 Metz
Black, I. (1) 1947/8 Southampton
Blacklaw, A. (3) 1962/3 Burnley
Blackley, J. (7) 1973/4 Hibernian
Blair, J. (1) 1946/7 Blackpool
Blyth, J. (2) 1977/8 Coventry C
Bone, J. (2) 1971/2 Norwich C
Booth, S. (21) 1992/3 Aberdeen, Borussia Dortmund, Twente
Bowman, D. (6) 1991/2 Dundee U

Boyd, T. (72) 1990/1 Motherwell, Chelsea, Celtic
Brand, R. (8) 1960/1 Rangers
Brazil, A. (13) 1979/80 Ipswich T, Tottenham H
Bremner, D. (1) 1975/6 Hibernian
Bremner, W. (54) 1964/5 Leeds U
Brennan, F. (7) 1946/7 Newcastle U
Brogan, J. (4) 1970/1 Celtic
Brown, A. (14) 1949/50 East Fife, Blackpool
Brown, H. (3) 1946/7 Partick Thistle
Brown, J. (1) 1974/5 Sheffield U
Brown, R. (3) 1946/7 Rangers
Brown, W. (28) 1957/8 Dundee, Tottenham H
Brownlie, J. (7) 1970/1 Hibernian
Buchan, M. (34) 1971/2 Aberdeen, Manchester U
Buckley, P. (3) 1953/4 Aberdeen
Burchill, M. J. (6) 1999/00 Celtic
Burley, C. W. (46) 1994/5 Chelsea, Celtic, Derby Co
Burley, G. (11) 1978/9 Ipswich T
Burns, F. (1) 1969/70 Manchester U
Burns, K. (20) 1973/4 Birmingham C, Nottingham F
Burns, T. (8) 1980/1 Celtic

Calderwood, C. (36) 1994/5 Tottenham H, Aston Villa
Caldow, E. (40) 1956/7 Rangers
Caldwell, G. (8) 2001/02 Newcastle U, Hibernian
Caldwell, S. (4) 2000/01 Newcastle U
Callaghan, W. (2) 1969/70 Dunfermline

Cameron, C. (26) 1998/9 Heart of Midlothian, Wolverhampton W
Campbell, R. (5) 1946/7 Falkirk, Chelsea
Campbell, W. (5) 1946/7 Morton
Canero, P. (1) 2003/04 Leicester C
Carr, W. (6) 1969/70 Coventry C
Chalmers, S. (5) 1964/5 Celtic
Clark, J. (4) 1965/6 Celtic
Clark, R. (17) 1967/8 Aberdeen
Clarke, S. (6) 1987/8 Chelsea
Collins, J. (58) 1987/8 Hibernian, Celtic, Monaco, Everton
Collins, R. (31) 1950/1 Celtic, Everton, Leeds U
Colquhoun, E. (9) 1971/2 Sheffield U
Colquhoun, J. (1) 1987/8 Heart of Midlothian
Combe, R. (3) 1947/8 Hibernian
Conn, A. (1) 1955/6 Heart of Midlothian
Conn, A. (2) 1974/5 Tottenham H
Connachan, E. (2) 1961/2 Dunfermline Ath
Connelly, G. (2) 1973/4 Celtic
Connolly, J. (1) 1972/3 Everton
Connor, R. (4) 1985/6 Dundee, Aberdeen
Cooke, C. (16) 1965/6 Dundee, Chelsea
Cooper, D. (22) 1979/80 Rangers, Motherwell
Cormack, P. (9) 1965/6 Hibernian, Nottingham F
Cowan, J. (25) 1947/8 Morton, Motherwell
Cowie, D. (20) 1952/3 Dundee
Cox, C. (1) 1947/8 Heart of Midlothian
Cox, S. (24) 1947/8 Rangers
Craig, J. (1) 1976/7 Celtic
Craig, J. P. (1) 1967/8 Celtic
Craig, T. (1) 1975/6 Newcastle U
Crainey, S. (6) 2001/02 Celtic, Southampton
Crawford, S. (20) 1994/5 Raith R, Dunfermline Ath
Crerand, P. (16) 1960/1 Celtic, Manchester U
Cropley, A. (2) 1971/2 Hibernian
Cruickshank, J. (6) 1963/4 Heart of Midlothian
Cullen, M. (1) 1955/6 Luton T
Cumming, J. (9) 1954/5 Heart of Midlothian
Cummings. W. (1) 2001/02 Chelsea
Cunningham, W. (8) 1953/4 Preston NE
Curran, H. (5) 1969/70 Wolverhampton W

Dailly, C. (53) 1996/7 Derby Co, Blackburn R, West Ham U
Dalglish, K. (102) 1971/2 Celtic, Liverpool
Davidson, C. I. (17) 1998/9 Blackburn R, Leicester C
Davidson, J. (8) 1953/4 Partick Thistle
Dawson, A. (5) 1979/80 Rangers
Deans, D. (2) 1974/5 Celtic
Delaney, J. (4) 1946/7 Manchester U
Devlin, P. J. (10) 2002/03 Birmingham C
Dick, J. (1) 1958/9 West Ham U
Dickov, P. (8) 2000/01 Mancheser C, Leicester C
Dickson, W. (5) 1969/70 Kilmarnock
Docherty, T. (25) 1951/2 Preston NE, Arsenal
Dobie, R. S. (6) 2001/02 WBA
Dodds, D. (2) 1983/4 Dundee U
Dodds, W. (26) 1996/7 Aberdeen, Dundee U, Rangers
Donachie, W. (35) 1971/2 Manchester C
Donnelly, S. (10) 1996/7 Celtic
Dougall, C. (1) 1946/7 Birmingham C
Dougan, R. (1) 1949/50 Heart of Midlothian
Douglas, R. (17) 2001/02 Celtic
Doyle, J. (1) 1975/6 Ayr U
Duncan, A. (6) 1974/5 Hibernian
Duncan, D. (3) 1947/8 East Fife
Duncanson, J. (1) 1946/7 Rangers
Durie, G. S. (43) 1987/8 Chelsea, Tottenham H, Rangers
Durrant, I. (20) 1987/8 Rangers, Kilmarnock

Elliott, M. S. (18) 1997/8 Leicester C
Evans, A. (4) 1981/2 Aston Villa
Evans, R. (48) 1948/9 Celtic, Chelsea
Ewing, T. (2) 1957/8 Partick Thistle

Farm, G. (10) 1952/3 Blackpool
Ferguson, B. (21) 1998/9 Rangers, Blackburn R
Ferguson, Derek (2) 1987/8 Rangers
Ferguson, Duncan (7) 1991/2 Dundee U, Everton
Ferguson, I. (9) 1988/9 Rangers
Ferguson, R. (7) 1965/6 Kilmarnock
Fernie, W. (12) 1953/4 Celtic
Flavell, R. (2) 1946/7 Airdrieonians
Fleck, R. (4) 1989/90 Norwich C
Fleming, C. (1) 1953/4 East Fife
Fletcher, D. B. (8) 2003/04 Manchester U
Forbes, A. (14) 1946/7 Sheffield U, Arsenal
Ford, D. (3) 1973/4 Heart of Midlothian

Forrest, J. (1) 1957/8 Motherwell
Forrest, J. (5) 1965/6 Rangers,
  Aberdeen
Forsyth, A. (10) 1971/2 Partick Thistle,
  Manchester U
Forsyth, C. (4) 1963/4 Kilmarnock
Forsyth, T. (22) 1970/1 Motherwell,
  Rangers
Fraser, D. (2) 1967/8 WBA
Fraser, W. (2) 1954/5 Sunderland
Freedman, D. A. (2) 2001/02 Crystal P

Gabriel, J. (2) 1960/1 Everton
Gallacher, K. W. (53) 1987/8 Dundee
  U, Coventry C, Blackburn R,
  Newcastle U
Gallacher, P. (8) 2001/02 Dundee U
Gallagher, P. (1) 2003/04 Blackburn R
Galloway, M. (1) 1991/2 Celtic
Gardiner, W. (1) 1957/8 Motherwell
Gemmell, T. (2) 1954/5 St Mirren
Gemmell, T. (18) 1965/6 Celtic
Gemmill, A. (43) 1970/1 Derby Co,
  Nottingham F, Birmingham C
Gemmill, S. (26) 1994/5 Nottingham F,
  Everton
Gibson, D. (7) 1962/3 Leicester C
Gillespie, G. T. (13) 1987/8 Liverpool,
  Celtic
Gilzean, A. (22) 1963/4 Dundee,
  Tottenham H
Glass, S. (1) 1998/9 Newcastle U
Glavin, R. (1) 1976/7 Celtic
Glen, A. (2) 1955/6 Aberdeen
Goram, A. L. (43) 1985/6 Oldham Ath,
  Hibernian, Rangers
Gordon, C. S. (1) 2003/04 Heart of
  Midlothian
Gough, C. R. (61) 1982/3 Dundee U,
  Tottenham H, Rangers
Gould, J. (2) 1999/00 Celtic
Govan, J. (6) 1947/8 Hibernian
Graham, A. (10) 1977/8 Leeds U
Graham, G. (12) 1971/2 Arsenal,
  Manchester U
Grant, J. (2) 1958/9 Hibernian
Grant, P. (2) 1988/9 Celtic
Gray, A. (20) 1975/6 Aston Villa,
  Wolverhampton W, Everton
Gray, A. D. (2) 2002/03 Bradford C
Gray, E. (12) 1968/9 Leeds U
Gray F. (32) 1975/6 Leeds U,
  Nottingham F, Leeds U
Green, A. (6) 1970/1 Blackpool,
  Newcastle U
Greig, J. (44) 1963/4 Rangers
Gunn, B. (6) 1989/90 Norwich C

Haddock, H. (6) 1954/5 Clyde
Haffey, F. (2) 1959/60 Celtic
Hamilton, A. (24) 1961/2 Dundee

Hamilton, G. (5) 1946/7 Aberdeen
Hamilton, W. (1) 1964/5 Hibernian
Hansen, A. (26) 1978/9 Liverpool
Hansen, J. (2) 1971/2 Partick Thistle
Harper, J. (4) 1972/3 Aberdeen
Hartford, A. (50) 1971/2 WBA,
  Manchester C, Everton, Manchester
  C
Harvey, D. (16) 1972/3 Leeds U
Haughney, M. (1) 1953/4 Celtic
Hay, D. (27) 1969/70 Celtic
Hegarty, P. (8) 1978/9 Dundee U
Henderson, J. (7) 1952/3 Portsmouth,
  Arsenal
Henderson, W. (29) 1962/3 Rangers
Hendry, E. C. J. (51) 1992/3 Blackburn
  R, Rangers, Coventry C, Bolton W
Herd, D. (5) 1958/9 Arsenal
Herd, G. (5) 1957/8 Clyde
Herriot, J. (8) 1968/9 Birmingham C
Hewie, J. (19) 1955/6 Charlton Ath
Holt, D. D. (5) 1962/3 Heart of
  Midlothian
Holt, G. J. (6) 2000/01 Kilmarnock,
  Norwich C
Holton, J. (15) 1972/3 Manchester U
Hope, R. (2) 1967/8 WBA
Hopkin, D. (7) 1996/7 Crystal P, Leeds
  U
Houliston, W. (3) 1948/9 Queen of the
  South
Houston, S. (1) 1975/6 Manchester U
Howie, H. (1) 1948/9 Hibernian
Hughes, J. (8) 1964/5 Celtic
Hughes, R. D. (2) 2003/04 Portsmouth
Hughes, W. (1) 1974/5 Sunderland
Humphries, W. (1) 1951/2 Motherwell
Hunter, A. (4) 1971/2 Kilmarnock,
  Celtic
Hunter, W. (3) 1959/60 Motherwell
Husband, J. (1) 1946/7 Partick Thistle
Hutchison, D. (26) 1998/9 Everton,
  Sunderland, West Ham U
Hutchison, T. (17) 1973/4 Coventry C

Imlach, S. (4) 1957/8 Nottingham F
Irvine, B. (9) 1990/1 Aberdeen

Jackson, C. (8) 1974/5 Rangers
Jackson, D. (28) 1994/5 Hibernian,
  Celtic
Jardine, A. (38) 1970/1 Rangers
Jarvie, A. (3) 1970/1 Airdrieonians
Jess, E. (18) 1992/3 Aberdeen,
  Coventry C, Aberdeen
Johnston, A. (18) 1998/9 Sunderland,
  Rangers, Middlesbrough
Johnston, M. (38) 1983/4 Watford,
  Celtic, Nantes, Rangers
Johnston, W. (22) 1965/6 Rangers,
  WBA

291

Johnstone, D. (14) 1972/3 Rangers
Johnstone, J. (23) 1964/5 Celtic
Johnstone, L. (2) 1947/8 Clyde
Johnstone, R. (17) 1950/1 Hibernian,
  Manchester C
Jordan, J. (52) 1972/3 Leeds U,
  Manchester U, AC Milan

Kelly, H. (1) 1951/2 Blackpool
Kelly, J. (2) 1948/9 Barnsley
Kennedy, J. (6) 1963/4 Celtic
Kennedy, J. (1) 2003/04 Celtic
Kennedy, S. (5) 1974/5 Rangers
Kennedy, S. (8) 1977/8 Aberdeen
Kerr, A. (2) 1954/5 Partick Thistle
Kerr, B. (2) 2002/03 Newcastle U
Kyle, K. (9) 2001/02 Sunderland

Lambert, P. (40) 1994/5 Motherwell,
  Borussia Dortmund, Celtic
Law, D. (55) 1958/9 Huddersfield T,
  Manchester C, Torino, Manchester
  U, Manchester C
Lawrence, T. (3) 1962/3 Liverpool
Leggat, G. (18) 1955/6 Aberdeen,
  Fulham
Leighton, J. (91) 1982/3 Aberdeen,
  Manchester U, Hibernian,
  Aberdeen
Lennox, R. (10) 1966/7 Celtic
Leslie, L. (5) 1960/1 Airdrieonians
Levein, C. (16) 1989/90 Heart of
  Midlothian
Liddell, W. (28) 1946/7 Liverpool
Linwood, A. (1) 1949/50 Clyde
Little, A. (1) 1952/3 Rangers
Logie, J. (1) 1952/3 Arsenal
Long, H. (1) 1946/7 Clyde
Lorimer, P. (21) 1969/70 Leeds U

Macari, L. (24) 1971/2 Celtic,
  Manchester U
Macaulay, A. (7) 1946/7 Brentford,
  Arsenal
MacDougall, E. (7) 1974/5 Norwich C
Mackay, D. (22) 1956/7 Heart of
  Midlothian, Tottenham H
Mackay, G. (4) 1987/8 Heart of
  Midlothian
Mackay, M. (3) 2003/04 Norwich C
Malpas, M. (55) 1983/4 Dundee U
Marshall, G. (1) 1991/2 Celtic
Martin, B. (2) 1994/5 Motherwell
Martin, F. (6) 1953/4 Aberdeen
Martin, N. (3) 1964/5 Hibernian,
  Sunderland
Martis, J. (1) 1960/1 Motherwell
Mason, J. (7) 1948/9 Third Lanark
Masson, D. (17) 1975/6 QPR, Derby C
Mathers, D. (1) 1953/4 Partick Thistle
Matteo, D. (6) 2000/01 Leeds U

McAllister, B. (3) 1996/7 Wimbledon
McAllister, G. (57) 1989/90 Leicester
  C, Leeds U, Coventry C
McAllister, J. R. (1) 2003/04
  Livingston
McAvennie, F. (5) 1985/6 West Ham
  U, Celtic
McBride, J. (2) 1966/7 Celtic
McCall, S. M. (40) 1989/90 Everton,
  Rangers
McCalliog, J. (5) 1966/7 Sheffield W,
  Wolverhampton W
McCann, N. D. (22) 1998/9 Heart of
  Midlothian, Rangers, Southampton
McCann, R. (5) 1958/9 Motherwell
McClair, B. (30) 1986/7 Celtic,
  Manchester U
McCloy, P. (4) 1972/3 Rangers
McCoist, A. (61) 1985/6 Rangers,
  Kilmarnock
McColl, I. (14) 1949/50 Rangers
McCreadie, E. (23) 1964/5 Chelsea
MacDonald, A. (1) 1975/6 Rangers
MacDonald, J. (2) 1955/6 Sunderland
McFadden, J. (14) 2001/02
  Motherwell, Everton
McFarlane, W. (1) 1946/7 Heart of
  Midlothian
McGarr, E. (2) 1969/70 Aberdeen
McGarvey, F. (7) 1978/9 Liverpool,
  Celtic
McGhee, M. (4) 1982/3 Aberdeen
McGinlay, J. (13) 1993/4 Bolton W
McGrain, D. (62) 1972/3 Celtic
McGrory, J. (3) 1964/5 Kilmarnock
McInally, A. (8) 1988/9 Aston Villa,
  Bayern Munich
McInally, J. (10) 1986/7 Dundee U
McInnes, D. (2) 2002/03 WBA
McKay, D. (14) 1958/9 Celtic
McKean, R. (1) 1975/6 Rangers
McKenzie, J. (9) 1953/4 Partick Thistle
McKimmie, S. (40) 1988/9 Aberdeen
McKinlay, T. (22) 1995/6 Celtic
McKinlay, W. (29) 1993/4 Dundee U,
  Blackburn R
McKinnon, R. (28) 1965/6 Rangers
McKinnon, R. (3) 1993/4 Motherwell
McLaren, A. (4) 1946/7 Preston NE
McLaren, A. (24) 1991/2 Heart of
  Midlothian, Rangers
McLaren, A. (1) 2000/01 Kilmarnock
McLean, G. (1) 1967/8 Dundee
McLean, T. (6) 1968/9 Kilmarnock
McLeish, A. (77) 1979/80 Aberdeen
McLeod, J. (4) 1960/1 Hibernian
MacLeod, M. (20) 1984/5 Celtic,
  Borussia Dortmund, Hibernian
McLintock, F. (9) 1962/3 Leicester C,
  Arsenal

McMillan, I. (6) 1951/2 Airdrieonians, Rangers
McNamara, J. (25) 1996/7 Celtic
McNamee, D. (2) 2003/04 Livingston
McNaught, W. (5) 1950/1 Raith R
McNaughton, K. (2) 2001/02 Aberdeen
McNeill, W. (29) 1960/1 Celtic
McPhail, J. (5) 1949/50 Celtic
McPherson, D. (27) 1988/9 Heart of Midlothian, Rangers
McQueen, G. (30) 1973/4 Leeds U, Manchester U
McStay, P. (76) 1983/4 Celtic
McSwegan, G. (2) 1999/00 Heart of Midlothian
Millar, J. (2) 1962/3 Rangers
Miller, C. (1) 2000/01 Dundee U
Miller, K. (12) 2000/01 Rangers, Wolverhampton W
Miller, W. (6) 1946/7 Celtic
Miller, W. (65) 1974/5 Aberdeen
Mitchell, R. (2) 1950/1 Newcastle U
Mochan, N. (3) 1953/4 Celtic
Moir, W. (1) 1949/50 Bolton W
Moncur, R. (16) 1967/8 Newcastle U
Morgan, W. (21) 1967/8 Burnley, Manchester U
Morris, H. (1) 1949/50 East Fife
Mudie, J. (17) 1956/7 Blackpool
Mulhall, G. (3) 1959/60 Aberdeen, Sunderland
Munro, F. (9) 1970/1 Wolverhampton W
Munro, I. (7) 1978/9 St Mirren
Murdoch, R. (12) 1965/6 Celtic
Murray, I. (1) 2002/03 Hibernian
Murray, J. (5) 1957/8 Heart of Midlothian
Murray, S. (1) 1971/2 Aberdeen
Murty, G. S. (1) 2003/04 Reading

Narey, D. (35) 1976/7 Dundee U
Naysmith, G. A. (22) 1999/00 Heart of Midlothian, Everton
Nevin, P. K. F. (28) 1985/6 Chelsea, Everton, Tranmere R
Nicholas, C. (20) 1982/3 Celtic, Arsenal, Aberdeen
Nicholson, B. (2) 2000/01 Dunfermline Ath
Nicol, S. (27) 1984/5 Liverpool

O'Connor, G. (3) 2001/02 Hibernian
O'Donnell, P. (1) 1993/4 Motherwell
O'Hare, J. (13) 1969/70 Derby Co
O'Neil, B. (6) 1995/6 Celtic, Wolfsburg, Derby Co
O'Neil, J. (1) 2000/01 Hibernian
Ormond, W. (6) 1953/4 Hibernian
Orr, T. (2) 1951/2 Morton

Parker, A. (15) 1954/5 Falkirk
Parlane, D. (12) 1972/3 Rangers
Paton, A. (2) 1951/2 Motherwell
Pearson, S. P. (2) 2003/04 Motherwell, Celtic
Pearson, T. (2) 1946/7 Newcastle U
Penman, A. (1) 1965/6 Dundee
Pettigrew, W. (5) 1975/6 Motherwell
Plenderleith, J. (1) 1960/1 Manchester C
Pressley, S. J. (19) 1999/00 Heart of Midlothian
Provan, D. (5) 1963/4 Rangers
Provan, D. (10) 1979/80 Celtic

Quashie, N. F. (2) 2003/04 Portsmouth
Quinn, P. (4) 1960/1 Motherwell

Rae, G. (9) 2000/01 Dundee, Rangers
Redpath, W. (9) 1948/9 Motherwell
Reilly, L. (38) 1948/9 Hibernian
Ring, T. (12) 1952/3 Clydebank
Rioch, B. (24) 1974/5 Derby Co, Everton, Derby Co
Ritchie, P. S. (7) 1998/9 Heart of Midlothian, Bolton W, Walsall
Robb, D. (5) 1970/1 Aberdeen
Robertson, A. (5) 1954/5 Clyde
Robertson, D. (3) 1991/2 Rangers
Robertson, H. (1) 1961/2 Dundee
Robertson, J. (16) 1990/1 Heart of Midlothian
Robertson, J. G. (1) 1964/5 Tottenham H
Robertson, J. N. (28) 1977/8 Nottingham F, Derby Co
Robinson, B. (4) 1973/4 Dundee
Ross, M. (13) 2001/02 Rangers
Rough, A. (53) 1975/6 Partick Thistle, Hibernian
Rougvie, D. (1) 1983/4 Aberdeen
Rutherford, E. (1) 1947/8 Rangers

St John, I. (21) 1958/9 Motherwell, Liverpool
Schaedler, E. (1) 1973/4 Hibernian
Scott, A. (16) 1956/7 Rangers, Everton
Scott, J. (1) 1965/6 Hibernian
Scott, J. (2) 1970/1 Dundee
Scoular, J. (9) 1950/1 Portsmouth
Severin, S. (8) 2001/02 Heart of Midlothian
Sharp, G. M. (12) 1984/5 Everton
Shaw, D. (8) 1946/7 Hibernian
Shaw, J. (4) 1946/7 Rangers
Shearer, D. (7) 1993/4 Aberdeen
Shearer, R. (4) 1960/1 Rangers
Simpson, N. (4) 1982/3 Aberdeen
Simpson, R. (5) 1966/7 Celtic
Sinclair, J. (1) 1965/6 Leicester C

293

Smith, D. (2) 1965/6 Aberdeen, Rangers
Smith, E. (2) 1958/9 Celtic
Smith, G. (18) 1946/7 Hibernian
Smith, H. G. (3) 1987/8 Heart of Midlothian
Smith, J. (4) 1967/8 Aberdeen, Newcastle U
Smith, J. (2) 2002/03 Celtic
Souness, G. (54) 1974/5 Middlesbrough, Liverpool, Sampdoria
Speedie, D. R. (10) 1984/5 Chelsea, Coventry C
Spencer, J. (14) 1994/5 Chelsea, QPR
Stanton, P. (16) 1965/6 Hibernian
Steel, W. (30) 1946/7 Morton, Derby C, Dundee
Stein, C. (21) 1968/9 Rangers, Coventry C
Stephen, J. (2) 1946/7 Bradford C
Stewart, D. (1) 1977/8 Leeds U
Stewart, J. (2) 1976/7 Kilmarnock, Middlesbrough
Stewart, M. J. (3) 2001/02 Manchester U
Stewart, R. (10) 1980/1 West Ham U
Stockdale, R. K. (5) 2001/02 Middlesbrough
Strachan, G. (50) 1979/80 Aberdeen, Manchester U, Leeds U
Sturrock, P. (20) 1980/1 Dundee U
Sullivan, N. (28) 1996/7 Wimbledon, Tottenham H

Telfer, P. N. (1) 1999/00 Coventry C
Telfer, W. (1) 1953/4 St Mirren
Thompson, S. (13) 2001/02 Dundee U, Rangers
Thomson, W. (7) 1979/80 St Mirren
Thornton, W. (7) 1946/7 Rangers
Toner, W. (2) 1958/9 Kilmarnock
Turnbull, E. (8) 1947/8 Hibernian

Ure, I. (11) 1961/2 Dundee, Arsenal

Waddell, W. (17) 1946/7 Rangers

WALES

Aizlewood, M. (39) 1985/6 Charlton Ath, Leeds U, Bradford C, Bristol C, Cardiff C
Allchurch, I. (68) 1950/1 Swansea T, Newcastle U, Cardiff C, Swansea T
Allchurch, L. (11) 1954/5 Swansea T, Sheffield U
Allen, B. (2) 1950/1 Coventry C
Allen, M. (14) 1985/6 Watford, Norwich C, Millwall, Newcastle U

Walker, A. (3) 1987/8 Celtic
Walker, J. N. (2) 1992/3 Heart of Midlothian, Partick Thistle
Wallace, L. A. (3) 1977/8 Coventry C
Wallace, W. S. B. (7) 1964/5 Heart of Midlothian, Celtic
Wardhaugh, J. (2) 1954/5 Heart of Midlothian
Wark, J. (29) 1978/9 Ipswich T, Liverpool
Watson, J. (2) 1947/8 Motherwell, Huddersfield T
Watson, R. (1) 1970/1 Motherwell
Webster, A. (8) 2002/03 Heart of Midlothian
Weir, A. (6) 1958/9 Motherwell
Weir, D. G. (37) 1996/7 Heart of Midlothian, Everton
Weir, P. (6) 1979/80 St Mirren, Aberdeen
White, J. (22) 1958/9 Falkirk, Tottenham H
Whyte, D. (12) 1987/8 Celtic, Middlesbrough, Aberdeen
Wilkie, L. (11) 2001/02 Dundee
Williams, G. (5) 2001/02 Nottingham F
Wilson, A. (1) 1953/4 Portsmouth
Wilson, D. (22) 1960/1 Rangers
Wilson, I. A. (5) 1986/7 Leicester C, Everton
Wilson, P. (1) 1974/5 Celtic
Wilson, R. (2) 1971/2 Arsenal
Winters, R. (1) 1998/9 Aberdeen
Wood, G. (4) 1978/9 Everton, Arsenal
Woodburn, W. (24) 1946/7 Rangers
Wright, K. (1) 1991/2 Hibernian
Wright, S. (2) 1992/3 Aberdeen
Wright, T. (3) 1952/3 Sunderland

Yeats, R. (2) 1964/5 Liverpool
Yorston, H. (1) 1954/5 Aberdeen
Young, A. (9) 1959/60 Heart of Midlothian, Everton
Young, G. (53) 1946/7 Rangers
Younger, T. (24) 1954/5 Hibernian, Liverpool

Baker, C. (7) 1957/8 Cardiff C
Baker, W. (1) 1947/8 Cardiff C
Barnard, D. S. (22) 1997/8 Barnsley, Grimsby T
Barnes, W. (22) 1947/8 Arsenal
Bellamy, C. D. (25) 1997/8 Norwich C, Coventry C, Newcastle U
Berry, G. (5) 1978/9 Wolverhampton W, Stoke C

Blackmore, C. G. (39) 1984/5 Manchester U, Middlesbrough
Blake, N. (29) 1993/4 Sheffield U, Bolton W, Blackburn R, Wolverhampton W
Bodin, P. J. (23) 1989/90 Swindon T, Crystal P, Swindon T
Bowen, D. (19) 1954/5 Arsenal
Bowen, J. P. (2) 1993/4 Swansea C, Birmingham C
Bowen, M. R. (41) 1985/6 Tottenham H, Norwich C, West Ham U
Boyle, T. (2) 1980/1 Crystal P
Browning, M. T. (5) 1995/6 Bristol R, Huddersfield T
Burgess, R. (32) 1946/7 Tottenham H
Burton, O. (9) 1962/3 Norwich C, Newcastle U

Cartwright, L. (7) 1973/4 Coventry C, Wrexham
Charles, J. (38) 1949/50 Leeds U, Juventus, Leeds U, Cardiff C
Charles, J. M. (19) 1980/1 Swansea C, QPR, Oxford U
Charles, M. (31) 1954/5 Swansea T, Arsenal, Cardiff C
Clarke, R. (22) 1948/9 Manchester C
Coleman, C. (32) 1991/2 Crystal P, Blackburn R, Fulham
Collins, J. M. (2) 2003/04 Cardiff C
Cornforth, J. M. (2) 1994/5 Swansea C
Coyne, D. (5) 1995/6 Tranmere R, Grimsby T, Leicester C
Crossley, M. G. (7) 1996/7 Nottingham F, Middlesbrough, Fulham
Crowe, V. (16) 1958/9 Aston Villa
Curtis, A. (35) 1975/6 Swansea C, Southampton, Cardiff C

Daniel, R. (21) 1950/1 Arsenal, Sunderland
Davies, A. (13) 1982/3 Manchester U, Newcastle U, Swansea C, Bradford C
Davies, D. (52) 1974/5 Everton, Wrexham, Swansea C
Davies, G. (16) 1979/80 Fulham, Chelsea, Manchester C
Davies, R. Wyn (34) 1963/4 Bolton W, Newcastle U, Manchester C, Manchester U, Blackpool
Davies, Reg (6) 1952/3 Newcastle U
Davies, Ron (29) 1963/4 Norwich C, Southampton, Portsmouth
Davies, S. (19) 2000/01 Tottenham H
Davies, S. I. (1) 1995/6 Manchester U
Davis, C. (1) 1971/2 Charlton Ath
Davis, G. (4) 1977/8 Wrexham
Deacy, N. (11) 1976/7 PSV Eindhoven, Beringen

Delaney, M. A. (26) 1999/00 Aston Villa
Derrett, S. (4) 1968/9 Cardiff C
Dibble, A. (3) 1985/6 Luton T, Manchester C
Durban, A. (27) 1965/6 Derby C
Dwyer, P. (10) 1977/8 Cardiff C

Earnshaw, R. (13) 2001/02 Cardiff C
Edwards, C. N. H. (1) 1995/6 Swansea C
Edwards, G. (12) 1946/7 Birmingham C, Cardiff C
Edwards, I. (4) 1977/8 Chester
Edwards, R. O. (6) 2002/03 Aston Villa
Edwards, R. W. (4) 1997/8 Bristol C
Edwards, T. (2) 1956/7 Charlton Ath
Emanuel, J. (2) 1972/3 Bristol C
England, M. (44) 1961/2 Blackburn R, Tottenham H
Evans, B. (7) 1971/2 Swansea C, Hereford U
Evans, I. (13) 1975/6 Crystal P
Evans, P. S. (2) 2001/02 Brentford, Bradford C
Evans, R. (1) 1963/4 Swansea T

Felgate, D. (1) 1983/4 Lincoln C
Fletcher, C. N. (4) 2003/04 Bournemouth
Flynn, B. (66) 1974/5 Burnley, Leeds U, Burnley
Ford, T. (38) 1946/7 Swansea T, Aston Villa, Sunderland, Cardiff C
Foulkes, W. (11) 1951/2 Newcastle U
Freestone, R. (1) 1999/00 Swansea C

Gabbidon, D. L. (12) 2001/02 Cardiff C
Giggs, R. J. (48) 1991/2 Manchester U
Giles, D. (12) 1979/80 Swansea C, Crystal P
Godfrey, B. (3) 1963/4 Preston NE
Goss, J. (9) 1990/1 Norwich C
Green, C. (15) 1964/5 Birmingham C
Green, R. M. (2) 1997/8 Wolverhampton W
Griffiths, A. (17) 1970/1 Wrexham
Griffiths, H. (1) 1952/3 Swansea T
Griffiths, M. (11) 1946/7 Leicester C

Hall, G. D. (9) 1987/8 Chelsea
Harrington, A. (11) 1955/6 Cardiff C
Harris, C. (24) 1975/6 Leeds U
Harris, W. (6) 1953/4 Middlesbrough
Hartson, J. (40) 1994/5 Arsenal, West Ham U, Wimbledon, Coventry C, Celtic
Haworth, S. O. (5) 1996/7 Cardiff C, Coventry C

Hennessey, T. (39) 1961/2 Birmingham
C, Nottingham F, Derby Co
Hewitt, R. (5) 1957/8 Cardiff C
Hill, M. (2) 1971/2 Ipswich T
Hockey, T. (9) 1971/2 Sheffield U,
Norwich C, Aston Villa
Hodges, G. (18) 1983/4 Wimbledon,
Newcastle U, Watford, Sheffield U
Holden, A. (1) 1983/4 Chester C
Hole, B. (30) 1962/3 Cardiff C,
Blackburn R, Aston Villa, Swansea
T
Hollins, D. (11) 1961/2 Newcastle U
Hopkins, J. (16) 1982/3 Fulham,
Crystal P
Hopkins, M. (34) 1955/6 Tottenham H
Horne, B. (59) 1987/8 Portsmouth,
Southampton, Everton, Birmingham
C
Howells, R. (2) 1953/4 Cardiff C
Hughes, C. M. (8) 1991/2 Luton T,
Wimbledon
Hughes, I. (4) 1950/1 Luton T
Hughes, L. M. (72) 1983/4 Manchester
U, Barcelona, Manchester U,
Chelsea, Southampton
Hughes, W. (3) 1946/7 Birmingham C
Hughes, W. A. (5) 1948/9 Blackburn R
Humphreys, J. (1) 1946/7 Everton

Jackett, K. (31) 1982/3 Watford
James, G. (9) 1965/6 Blackpool
James, L. (54) 1971/2 Burnley, Derby
C, QPR, Burnley, Swansea C,
Sunderland
James, R. M. (47) 1978/9 Swansea C,
Stoke C, QPR, Leicester C, Swansea
C
Jarvis, A. (3) 1966/7 Hull C
Jenkins, S. R. (16) 1995/6 Swansea C,
Huddersfield T
Johnson, A. J. (14) 1998/9 Nottingham
F, WBA
Johnson, M. (1) 1963/4 Swansea T
Jones, A. (6) 1986/7 Port Vale,
Charlton Ath
Jones, Barrie (15) 1962/3 Swansea T,
Plymouth Argyle, Cardiff C
Jones, Bryn (4) 1946/7 Arsenal
Jones, C. (59) 1953/4 Swansea T,
Tottenham H, Fulham
Jones, D. (8) 1975/6 Norwich C
Jones, E. (4) 1947/8 Swansea T,
Tottenham H
Jones, J. (72) 1975/6 Liverpool,
Wrexham, Chelsea, Huddersfield T
Jones, K. (1) 1949/50 Aston Villa
Jones, M. G. (13) 1999/00 Leeds U,
Leicester C
Jones, P. L. (2) 1996/7 Liverpool,
Tranmere R

Jones, P. S. (38) 1996/7 Stockport Co,
Southampton, Wolverhampton W
Jones, R. (1) 1993/4 Sheffield W
Jones, T. G. (13) 1946/7 Everton
Jones, V. P. (9) 1994/5 Wimbledon
Jones, W. (1) 1970/1 Bristol C

Kelsey, J. (41) 1953/4 Arsenal
King, J. (1) 1954/5 Swansea T
Kinsey, N. (7) 1950/1 Norwich C,
Birmingham C
Knill, A. R. (1) 1988/9 Swansea C
Koumas, J. (9) 2000/01 Tranmere R,
WBA
Krzywicki, R. 1969/70 WBA,
Huddersfield T

Lambert, R. (5) 1946/7 Liverpool
Law, B. J. (1) 1989/90 QPR
Lea, C. (2) 1964/5 Ipswich T
Leek, C. (13) 1960/1 Leicester C,
Newcastle U, Birmingham C
Legg, A. (6) 1995/6 Birmingham C,
Cardiff C
Lever, A. (1) 1952/3 Leicester C
Lewis, D. (1) 1982/3 Swansea C
Llewellyn, C. M. (4) 1997/8 Norwich C,
Wrexham
Lloyd, B. (3) 1975/6 Wrexham
Lovell, S. (6) 1981/2 Crystal P, Millwall
Lowndes, S. (10) 1982/3 Newport Co,
Millwall, Barnsley
Lowrie, G. (4) 1947/8 Coventry C,
Newcastle U
Lucas, M. (4) 1961/2 Leyton Orient
Lucas, W. (7) 1948/9 Swansea T

Maguire, G. T. (7) 1989/90 Portsmouth
Mahoney, J. (51) 1967/8 Stoke C,
Middlesbrough, Swansea C
Mardon, P. J. (1) 1995/6 WBA
Margetson, M. W. (1) 2003/04 Cardiff
C
Marriott, A. (5) 1995/6 Wrexham
Marustik, C. (6) 1981/2 Swansea C
Medwin, T. (30) 1952/3 Swansea T,
Tottenham H
Melville, A. K. (63) 1989/90 Swansea
C, Oxford U, Sunderland, Fulham,
West Ham U
Mielczarek, R. (1) 1970/1 Rotherham
U
Millington, A. (21) 1962/3 WBA,
Crystal P, Peterborough U, Swansea
C
Moore, G. (21) 1959/60 Cardiff C,
Chelsea, Manchester U,
Northampton T, Charlton Ath
Morris, W. (5) 1946/7 Burnley

Nardiello, D. (2) 1977/8 Coventry C

Neilson, A. B. (5) 1991/2 Newcastle U, Southampton
Nicholas, P. (73) 1978/9 Crystal P, Arsenal, Crystal P, Luton T, Aberdeen, Chelsea, Watford
Niedzwiecki, E. A. (2) 1984/5 Chelsea
Nogan, L. M. (2) 1991/2 Watford, Reading
Nurse, E. A. (2) 1984/5 Chelsea
Norman, A. J. (5) 1985/6 Hull C
Nurse, M. (12) 1959/60 Swansea T, Middlesbrough

O'Sullivan, P. (3) 1972/3 Brighton & HA
Oster, J. M. (11) 1997/8 Everton, Sunderland

Page, M. (28) 1970/1 Birmingham C
Page, R. J. (33) 1996/7 Watford, Sheffield U
Palmer, D. (3) 1956/7 Swansea T
Parry, J. (1) 1950/1 Swansea T
Parry, P. I. (3) 2003/04 Cardiff C
Pascoe, C. (10) 1983/4 Swansea C, Sunderland
Paul, R. (33) 1948/9 Swansea T, Manchester C
Pembridge, M. A. (51) 1991/2 Luton T, Derby C, Sheffield W, Benfica, Everton, Fulham
Perry, J. (1) 1993/4 Cardiff C
Phillips, D. (62) 1983/4 Plymouth Argyle, Manchester C, Coventry C, Norwich C, Nottingham F
Phillips, J. (4) 1972/3 Chelsea
Phillips, L. (58) 1970/1 Cardff C, Aston Villa, Swansea C, Charlton Ath
Pipe, D. R. (1) 2002/03 Coventry C
Pontin, K. (2) 1979/80 Cardiff C
Powell, A. (8) 1946/7 Leeds U, Everton, Birmingham C
Powell, D. (11) 1967/8 Wrexham, Sheffield U
Powell, I. (8) 1946/7 QPR, Aston Villa
Price, P. (25) 1979/80 Luton T, Tottenham H
Pring, K. (3) 1965/6 Rotherham U
Pritchard, H. K. (1) 1984/5 Bristol C

Rankmore, F. (l) 1965/6 Peterborough U
Ratcliffe, K. (59) 1980/1 Everton, Cardiff C
Ready, K. (5) 1996/7 QPR
Reece, G. (29) 1965/6 Sheffield U, Cardiff C
Reed, W. (2) 1954/5 Ipswich T
Rees, A. (1) 1983/4 Birmingham C
Rees, J. M. (1) 1991/2 Luton T

Rees, R. (39) 1964/5 Coventry C, WBA, Nottingham F
Rees, W. (4) 1948/9 Cardiff C, Tottenham H
Richards, S. (1) 1946/7 Cardiff C
Roberts, A. M. (2) 1992/3 QPR
Roberts, D. (17) 1972/3 Oxford U, Hull C
Roberts, G. W. (6) 1999/00 Tranmere R
Roberts, I. W. (15) 1989/90 Watford, Huddersfield T, Leicester C, Norwich C
Roberts, J. G. (22) 1970/1 Arsenal, Birmingham C
Roberts, J. H. (1) 1948/9 Bolton W
Roberts, N. W. (3) 1999/00 Wrexham, Wigan Ath
Roberts, P. (4) 1973/4 Portsmouth
Robinson, C. P. (17) 1999/00 Wolverhampton W, Portsmouth
Robinson, J. R. C. (30) 1995/6 Charlton Ath
Rodrigues, P. (40) 1964/5 Cardiff C, Leicester C, Sheffield W
Rouse, V. (1) 1958/9 Crystal P
Rowley, T. (1) 1958/9 Tranmere R
Rush, I. (73) 1979/80 Liverpool, Juventus, Liverpool

Saunders, D. (75) 1985/6 Brighton & HA, Oxford U, Derby C, Liverpool, Aston Villa, Galatasaray, Nottingham F, Sheffield U, Benfica, Bradford C
Savage, R. W. (35) 1995/6 Crewe Alexandra, Leicester C, Birmingham C
Sayer, P. (7) 1976/7 Cardiff C
Scrine, F. (2) 1949/50 Swansea T
Sear, C. (1) 1962/3 Manchester C
Sherwood, A. (41) 1946/7 Cardiff C, Newport C
Shortt, W. (12) 1946/7 Plymouth Argyle
Showers, D. (2) 1974/5 Cardiff C
Sidlow, C. (7) 1946/7 Liverpool
Slatter, N. (22) 1982/3 Bristol R, Oxford U
Smallman, D. (7) 1973/4 Wrexham, Everton
Southall, N. (92) 1981/2 Everton
Speed, G. A. (80) 1989/90 Leeds U, Everton, Newcastle U
Sprake, G. (37) 1963/4 Leeds U, Birmingham C
Stansfield, F. (1) 1948/9 Cardiff C
Stevenson, B. (15) 1977/8 Leeds U, Birmingham C
Stevenson, N. (4) 1981/2 Swansea C
Stitfall, R. (2) 1952/3 Cardiff C

297

Sullivan, D. (17) 1952/3 Cardiff C
Symons, C. J. (37) 1991/2 Portsmouth, Manchester C, Fulham, Crystal P

Tapscott, D. (14) 1953/4 Arsenal, Cardiff C
Taylor, G. K. (14) 1995/6 Crystal P, Sheffield U, Burnley, Nottingham F
Thatcher, B. D. (3) 2003/04 Leicester C
Thomas, D. (2) 1956/7 Swansea T
Thomas, M. (51) 1976/7 Wrexham, Manchester U, Everton, Brighton & HA, Stoke C, Chelsea, WBA
Thomas, M. R. (1) 1986/7 Newcastle U
Thomas, R. (50) 1966/7 Swindon T, Derby C, Cardiff C
Thomas, S. (4) 1947/8 Fulham
Toshack, J. (40) 1968/9 Cardiff C, Liverpool, Swansea C
Trollope, P. J. (9) 1996/7 Derby Co, Fulham, Coventry C, Northampton T

Van Den Hauwe, P. W. R. (13) 1984/5 Everton
Vaughan, D. O. (2) 2002/03 Crewe Alex
Vaughan, N. (10) 1982/3 Newport Co, Cardiff C
Vearncombe, G. (2) 1957/8 Cardiff C
Vernon, R. (32) 1956/7 Blackburn R, Everton, Stoke C
Villars, A. (3) 1973/4 Cardiff C

Walley, T. (1) 1970/1 Watford

Walsh, I. (18) 1979/80 Crystal P, Swansea C
Ward, D. (2) 1958/9 Bristol R, Cardiff C
Ward, D. (5) 1999/00 Notts Co, Nottingham F
Webster, C. (4) 1956/7 Manchester U
Weston, R. D. (6) 1999/00 Arsenal, Cardiff C
Williams, A. (13) 1993/4 Reading, Wolverhampton W, Reading
Williams, A. P. (2) 1997/8 Southampton
Williams, D. G. 1987/8 13, Derby Co, Ipswich T
Williams, D. M. (5) 1985/6 Norwich C
Williams, G. (1) 1950/1 Cardiff C
Williams, G. E. (26) 1959/60 WBA
Williams, G. G. (5) 1960/1 Swansea T
Williams, H. (4) 1948/9 Newport Co, Leeds U
Williams, Herbert (3) 1964/5 Swansea T
Williams, S. (43) 1953/4 WBA, Southampton
Witcomb, D. (3) 1946/7 WBA, Sheffield W
Woosnam, P. (17) 1958/9 Leyton Orient, West Ham U, Aston Villa

Yorath, T. (59) 1969/70 Leeds U, Coventry C, Tottenham H, Vancouver Whitecaps
Young, E. (21) 1989/90 Wimbledon, Crystal P, Wolverhampton W

EIRE

Aherne, T. (16) 1945/6 Belfast Celtic, Luton T
Aldridge, J. W. (69) 1985/6 Oxford U, Liverpool, Real Sociedad, Tranmere R
Ambrose, P. (5) 1954/5 Shamrock R
Anderson, J. (16) 1979/80 Preston NE, Newcastle U
Babb, P. (35) 1993/4 Coventry C, Liverpool, Sunderland
Bailham, E. (1) 1963/4 Shamrock R
Barber, E. (2) 1965/6 Shelbourne, Birmingham C
Barrett, G. (5) 2002/03 Arsenal, Coventry C
Beglin, J. (15) 1983/4 Liverpool
Bonner, P. (80) 1980/1 Celtic
Braddish, S. (1) 1977/8 Dundalk
Brady, T. R. (6) 1963/4 QPR
Brady, W. L. (72) 1974/5 Arsenal,

Juventus, Sampdoria, Internazionale, Ascoli, West Ham U
Branagan, K. G. (1) 1996/7 Bolton W
Breen, G. (60) 1995/6 Birmingham C, Coventry C, West Ham U, Sunderland
Breen, T. (3) 1946/7 Shamrock R
Brennan, F. (1) 1964/5 Drumcondra
Brennan, S. A. (19) 1964/5 Manchester U, Waterford
Browne, W. (3) 1963/4 Bohemians
Buckley, L. (2) 1983/4 Shamrock R, Waregem
Burke, F. (1) 1951/2 Cork Ath
Butler, P. J. (1) 1999/00 Sunderland
Butler, T. (2) 2002/03 Sunderland
Byrne, A. B. (14) 1969/70 Southampton
Byrne, J. (23) 1984/5 QPR, Le Havre, Brighton & HA, Sunderland, Millwall

Byrne, J. (1) 2003/04 Shelbourne
Byrne, P. (8) 1983/4 Shamrock R

Campbell, A. (3) 1984/5 Santander
Campbell, N. (11) 1970/1 St Patrick's Ath, Fortuna Cologne
Cantwell, N. (36) 1953/4 West Ham U, Manchester U
Carey, B. P. (3) 1991/2 Manchester U, Leicester C
Carey, J. J. (21) 1945/6 Manchester U
Carolan, J. (2) 1959/60 Manchester U
Carr, S. (30) 1998/9 Tottenham H
Carroll, B. (2) 1948/9 Shelbourne
Carroll, T. R. (17) 1967/8 Ipswich T, Birmingham C
Carsley, L. K. (29) 1997/8 Derby Co, Blackburn R, Coventry C, Everton
Cascarino, A. G. (88) 1985/6 Gillingham, Millwall, Aston Villa, Celtic, Chelsea, Marseille, Nancy
Chandler, J. (2) 1979/80 Leeds U
Clarke, C. R. (2) 2003/04 Stoke C
Clarke, J. (1) 1977/8 Drogheda U
Clarke, K. (2) 1947/8 Drumcondra
Clarke, M. (1) 1949/50 Shamrock R
Clinton, T. J. (3) 1950/1 Everton
Coad, P. (11) 1946/7 Shamrock R
Coffey, T. (1) 1949/50 Drumcondra
Colfer, M. D. (2) 1949/50 Shelbourne
Colgan, N, (8) 2001/02 Hibernian
Conmy, O. M. (5) 1964/5 Peterborough U
Connolly, D. J. (40) 1995/6 Watford, Feyenoord, Wolverhampton W, Excelsior, Wimbledon, West Ham U
Conroy, G. A. (27) 1969/70 Stoke C
Conway, J. P. (20) 1966/7 Fulham, Manchester C
Corr, P. J. (4) 1948/9 Everton
Courtney, E. (1) 1945/6 Cork U
Coyle, O. (1) 1993/4 Bolton W
Coyne, T. (22) 1991/2 Celtic, Tranmere R, Motherwell
Crowe, G. (2) 2002/03 Bohemians
Cummins, G. P. (19) 1953/4 Luton T
Cuneen, T. (1) 1950/1 Limerick
Cunningham, K. (57) 1995/6 Wimbledon, Birmingham C
Curtis, D. P. (17) 1956/7 Shelbourne, Bristol C, Ipswich T, Exeter C
Cusack, S. (1) 1952/3 Limerick

Daish, L. S. (5) 1991/2 Cambridge U, Coventry C
Daly, G. A. (48) 1972/3 Manchester U, Derby C, Coventry C, Birmingham C, Shrewsbury T
Daly, M. (2) 1977/8 Wolverhampton W
Daly, P. (1) 1949/50 Shamrock R

Delap, R. J. (11) 1997/8 Derby Co, Southampton
De Mange, K. J. P. P. (2) 1986/7 Liverpool, Hull C
Deacy, E. (4) 1981/2 Aston Villa
Dempsey, J. T. (19) 1966/7 Fulham, Chelsea
Dennehy, J. (11) 1971/2 Cork Hibernian, Nottingham F, Walsall
Desmond, P. (4) 1949/50 Middlesbrough
Devine, J. (12) 1979/80 Arsenal, Norwich C
Doherty, G. M. T. (26) 1999/00 Luton T, Tottenham H
Donovan, D. C. (5) 1954/5 Everton
Donovan, T. (1) 1979/80 Aston Villa
Douglas, J. (2) 2003/04 Blackburn R
Doyle, C. (1) 1958/9 Shelbourne
Doyle, M. P. (1) 2003/04 Coventry C
Duff, D. A. (43) 1997/8 Blackburn R, Chelsea
Duffy, B. (1) 1949/50 Shamrock R
Dunne, A. P. (33) 1961/2 Manchester U, Bolton W
Dunne, J. C. (1) 1970/1 Fulham
Dunne, P. A. J. (5) 1964/5 Manchester U
Dunne, R. P. (20) 1999/00 Everton, Manchester C
Dunne, S. (15) 1952/3 Luton T
Dunne, T. (3) 1955/6 St Patrick's Ath
Dunning, P. (2) 1970/1 Shelbourne
Dunphy, E. M. (23) 1965/6 York C, Millwall
Dwyer, N. M. (14) 1959/60 West Ham U, Swansea T

Eccles, P. (1) 1985/6 Shamrock R
Eglington, T. J. (24) 1945/6 Shamrock R, Everton
Evans, M. J. (1) 1997/8 Southampton

Fagan, E. (1) 1972/3 Shamrock R
Fagan, F. (8) 1954/5 Manchester C, Derby C
Fairclough, M. (2) 1981/2 Dundalk
Fallon, S. (8) 1950/1 Celtic
Farrell, P. D. (28) 1945/6 Shamrock R, Everton
Farrelly, G. (6) 1995/6 Aston Villa, Everton, Bolton W
Finnan, S. (28) 1999/00 Fulham, Liverpool
Finucane, A. (11) 1966/7 Limerick
Fitzgerald, F. J. (2) 1954/5 Waterford
Fitzgerald, P. J. (5) 1960/1 Leeds U, Chester
Fitzpatrick, K. (1) 1969/70 Limerick
Fitzsimons, A. G. (26) 1949/50 Middlesbrough, Lincoln C

299

Fleming, C. (10) 1995/6 Middlesbrough
Fogarty, A. (11) 1959/60 Sunderland, Hartlepool U
Foley, D. J. (6) 1999/00 Watford
Foley, T. C. (9) 1963/4 Northampton T
Fullam, J. 1960/1 Preston NE, Shamrock R

Gallagher, C. (2) 1966/7 Celtic
Gallagher, M. (1) 1953/4 Hibernian
Galvin, A. (29) 1982/3 Tottenham H, Sheffield W
Gannon, E. (14) 1948/9 Notts Co, Sheffield W, Shelbourne K
Gannon, M. (1) 1971/2 Shelbourne
Gavin, J. T. (7) 1949/50 Norwich C, Tottenham H, Norwich C
Gibbons, A. (4) 1951/2 St Patrick's Ath
Gilbert, R. (1) 1965/6 Shamrock R
Giles, C. (1) 1950/1 Doncaster R
Giles, M. J. (59) 1959/60 Manchester U, Leeds U, WBA, Shamrock R
Given, S. J. J. (60) 1995/6 Blackburn R, Newcastle U
Givens, D. J. (56) 1968/9 Manchester U, Luton T, QPR, Birmingham C, Neuchatel Xamax
Glynn, D. (2) 1951/2 Drumcondra
Godwin, T. F. (13) 1948/9 Shamrock R, Leicester C, Bournemouth
Goodman, J. (4) 1996/7 Wimbledon
Goodwin, J. (1) 2002/03 Stockport Co
Gorman, W. C. (2) 1946/7 Brentford
Grealish, A. (44) 1975/6 Orient, Luton T, Brighton & HA, WBA
Gregg, E. (8) 1977/8 Bohemians
Grimes, A. A. (17) 1977/8 Manchester U, Coventry C, Luton T

Hale, A. (13) 1961/2 Aston Villa, Doncaster R, Waterford
Hamilton, T. (2) 1958/9 Shamrock R
Hand, E. K. (20) 1968/9 Portsmouth
Harte, I. P. (56) 1995/6 Leeds U
Hartnett, J. B. (2) 1948/9 Middlesbrough
Haverty, J. (32) 1955/6 Arsenal, Blackburn R, Millwall, Celtic, Bristol R, Shelbourne
Hayes, A. W. P. (1) 1978/9 Southampton
Hayes, W. E. (2) 1946/7 Huddersfield T
Hayes, W. J. (1) 1948/9 Limerick
Healey, R. (2) 1976/7 Cardiff C
Healy, C. (13) 2001/02 Celtic, Sunderland
Heighway, S. D. (34) 1970/1 Liverpool, Minnesota Kicks
Henderson, B. (2) 1947/8 Drumcondra

Hennessy, J. (5) 1955/6 Shelbourne, St Patrick's Ath
Herrick, J. (3) 1971/2 Cork Hibernians, Shamrock R
Higgins, J. (1) 1950/1 Birmingham C
Holland, M. R. (43) 1999/00 Ipswich T, Charlton Ath
Holmes, J. 1970/1 Coventry C, Tottenham H, Vancouver Whitecaps
Houghton, R. J. (73) 1985/6 Oxford U, Liverpool, Aston Villa, Crystal P, Reading
Howlett, G. (1) 1983/4 Brighton & HA
Hughton, C. (53) 1979/80 Tottenham H, West Ham U
Hurley, C. J. (40) 1956/7 Millwall, Sunderland, Bolton W

Irwin, D. J. (56) 1990/1 Manchester U

Kavanagh, G. A. (5) 1997/8 Stoke C, Cardiff C
Keane, R. D. (52) 1997/8 Wolverhampton W, Coventry C, Internazionale, Leeds U, Tottenham H
Keane, R. M. (59) 1990/1 Nottingham F, Manchester U
Keane, T. R. (4) 1948/9 Swansea T
Kearin, M. (1) 1971/2 Shamrock R
Kearns, F. T. (1) 1953/4 West Ham U
Kearns, M. (18) 1969/70 Oxford U, Walsall, Wolverhampton W
Kelly, A. T. (34) 1992/3 Sheffield U, Blackburn R
Kelly, D. T. (26) 1987/8 Walsall, West Ham U, Leicester C, Newcastle U, Wolverhampton W, Sunderland, Tranmere R
Kelly, G. (52) 1993/4 Leeds U
Kelly, J. A. (48) 1956/7 Drumcondra, Preston NE
Kelly, J. P. V. (5) 1960/1 Wolverhampton W
Kelly, M. J. (4) 1987/8 Portsmouth
Kelly, N. (1) 1953/4 Nottingham F
Kenna, J. J. (27) 1994/5 Blackburn R
Kennedy, M. (34) 1995/6 Liverpool, Wimbledon, Manchester C, Wolverhampton W
Kennedy, M. F. (2) 1985/6 Portsmouth
Kenny, P. (2) 2003/04 Sheffield U
Keogh, J. (1) 1965/6 Shamrock R
Keogh, S. (1) 1958/9 Shamrock R
Kernaghan, A. N. (22) 1992/3 Middlesbrough, Manchester C
Kiely, D. L. (8) 1999/00 Charlton Ath
Kiernan, F. W. (5) 1950/1 Shamrock R, Southampton
Kilbane, K. D. (53) 1997/8 WBA, Sunderland, Everton

Kinnear, J. P. (26) 1966/7 Tottenham H, Brighton & HA

Kinsella, M. A. (48) 1997/8 Charlton Ath, Aston Villa, WBA

Langan, D. (25) 1977/8 Derby Co, Birmingham C, Oxford U

Lawler, J. F. (8) 1952/3 Fulham

Lawlor, J. C. (3) 1948/9 Drumcondra, Doncaster R

Lawlor, M. (5) 1970/1 Shamrock R

Lawrenson, M. (39) 1976/7 Preston NE, Brighton & HA, Liverpool

Lee, A. L. (7) 2002/03 Rotherham U, Cardiff C

Leech, M. (8) 1968/9 Shamrock R

Lowry, D. (1) 1961/2 St Patrick's Ath

McAlinden, J. (2) 1945/6 Portsmouth

McAteer, J. W. (52) 1993/4 Bolton W, Liverpool, Blackburn R, Sunderland

McCann, J. (1) 1956/7 Shamrock R

McCarthy, M. (57) 1983/4 Manchester C, Celtic, Lyon, Millwall

McConville, T. (6) 1971/2 Dundalk, Waterford

McDonagh, J. (24) 1980/1 Everton, Bolton W, Notts C

McDonagh, Joe (3) 1983/4 Shamrock R

McEvoy, M. A. (17) 1960/1 Blackburn R

McGeady, A. (1) 2003/04 Celtic

McGee, P. (15) 1977/8 QPR, Preston NE

McGoldrick, E. J. (15) 1991/2 Crystal P, Arsenal

McGowan, D. (3) 1948/9 West Ham U

McGowan, J. (1) 1946/7 Cork U

McGrath, M. (22) 1957/8 Blackburn R, Bradford Park Avenue

McGrath, P. (83) 1984/5 Manchester U, Aston Villa, Derby C

Macken, A. (1) 1976/7 Derby Co

Mackey, G. (3) 1956/7 Shamrock R

McLoughlin, A. F. (42) 1989/90 Swindon T, Southampton, Portsmouth

McMillan, W. (2) 1945/6 Belfast Celtic

McNally, J. B. (3) 1958/9 Luton T

McPhail, S. (10) 1999/00 Leeds U

Mahon, A. J. (2) 1999/00 Tranmere R

Malone, G. (1) 1948/9 Shelbourne

Mancini, T. J. (5) 1973/4 QPR, Arsenal

Martin, C. J. (30) 1945/6 Glentoran, Leeds U, Aston Villa

Martin, M. P. (51) 1971/2 Bohemians, Manchester U, WBA, Newcastle U

Maybury, A. (8) 1997/8 Leeds U, Heart of Midlothian

Meagan, M. K. (17) 1960/1 Everton, Huddersfield T, Drogheda

Miller, L. W. P. (4) 2003/04 Celtic

Milligan, M. J. (1) 1991/2 Oldham Ath

Mooney, J. (2) 1964/5 Shamrock R

Moore, A. (8) 1995/6 Middlesbrough

Moran, K. (70) 1979/80 Manchester U, Sporting Gijon, Blackburn R

Moroney, T. (12) 1947/8 West Ham U

Morris, C. B. (35) 1987/8 Celtic, Middlesbrough

Morrison, C. H. (21) 2001/02 Crystal P, Birmingham C

Moulson, G. B. (3) 1947/8 Lincoln C

Mucklan, C. (1) 1977/8 Drogheda

Mulligan, P. M. (50) 1968/9 Shamrock R, Chelsea, Crystal P, WBA, Shamrock R

Munroe, L. (1) 1953/4 Shamrock R

Murphy, A. (1) 1955/6 Clyde

Murphy, B. (1) 1985/6 Bohemians

Murphy, J. (1) 1979/80 Crystal P

Murphy, J. (1) 2003/04 WBA

Murray, T. (1) 1949/50 Dundalk

Newman, W. (1) 1968/9 Shelbourne

Nolan, R. (10) 1956/7 Shamrock R

O'Brien, A. J. (13) 2000/01 Newcastle U

O'Brien, F. (4) 1979/80 Philadelphia Fury

O'Brien, L. (16) 1985/6 Shamrock R, Manchester U, Newcastle U, Tranmere R

O'Brien, R. (4) 1975/6 Notts Co

O'Byrne, L. B. (1) 1948/9 Shamrock R

O'Callaghan, B. R. (6) 1978/9 Stoke C

O'Callaghan, K. (20) 1980/1 Ipswich T, Portsmouth

O'Connell, A. (2) 1966/7 Dundalk, Bohemians

O'Connor, T. (4) 1949/50 Shamrock R

O'Connor, T. (7) 1967/8 Fulham, Dundalk, Bohemians

O'Driscoll, J. F. (3) 1948/9 Swansea T

O'Driscoll, S. (3) 1981/2 Fulham

O'Farrell, F. (9) 1951/2 West Ham U, Preston NE

O'Flanagan, K. P. (3) 1946/7 Arsenal

O'Flanagan, M. (1) 1946/7 Bohemians

O'Hanlon, K. G. (1) 1987/8 Rotherham U

O'Keefe, E. (5) 1980/1 Everton, Port Vale

O'Leary, D. (68) 1976/7 Arsenal

O'Leary, P. (7) 1979/80 Shamrock R

O'Neill, F. S. (20) 1961/2 Shamrock R

O'Neill, J. (17) 1951/2 Everton

O'Neill, J. (1) 1960/1 Preston NE

301

O'Neill, K. P. (13) 1995/6 Norwich C, Middlesbrough
O'Regan, K. (4) 1983/4 Brighton & HA
O'Reilly, J. (2) 1945/6 Cork U
O'Shea, J. F. (14) 2001/02 Manchester U

Peyton, G. (33) 1976/7 Fulham, Bournemouth, Everton
Peyton, N. (6) 1956/7 Shamrock R, Leeds U
Phelan, T. (42) 1991/2 Wimbledon, Manchester C, Chelsea, Everton, Fulham

Quinn, A. (4) 2002/03 Sheffield W
Quinn, B. S. (4) 1999/00 Coventry C
Quinn, N. J. (91) 1985/6 Arsenal, Manchester C, Sunderland

Reid, A. M. (7) 2003/04 Nottingham F
Reid, S. J. (13) 2001/02 Millwall, Blackburn R
Richardson, D. J. (3) 1971/2 Shamrock R, Gillingham
Ringstead, A. (20) 1950/1 Sheffield U
Robinson, M. (23) 1980/1 Brighton & HA, Liverpool, QPR
Roche, P. J. (8) 1971/2 Shelbourne, Manchester U
Rogers, E. (19) 1967/8 Blackburn R, Charlton Ath
Rowlands, M. C. (3) 2003/04 QPR
Ryan, G. (16) 1977/8 Derby Co, Brighton & HA
Ryan, R. A. (16) 1949/50 WBA, Derby C

Sadlier, R. T. (1) 2001/02 Millwall
Savage, D. P. T. (5) 1995/6 Millwall
Saward, P. (18) 1953/4 Millwall, Aston Villa, Huddersfield T
Scannell, T. (1) 1953/4 Southend U
Scully, P. J. (1) 1988/9 Arsenal
Sheedy, K. (45) 1983/4 Everton, Newcastle U

Sheridan, J. J. (34) 1987/8 Leeds U, Sheffield W
Slaven, B. (7) 1989/90 Middlesbrough
Sloan, J. W. (2) 1945/6 Arsenal
Smyth, M. (1) 1968/9 Shamrock R
Stapleton, F. (70) 1976/7 Arsenal, Manchester U, Ajax, Derby Co, Le Havre, Blackburn R
Staunton, S. (102) 1988/9 Liverpool, Aston Villa, Liverpool, Aston Villa
Stevenson, A. E. (6) 1946/7 Everton
Strahan, F. (5) 1963/4 Shelbourne
Swan, M. M. G. (1) 1959/60 Drumcondra
Synott, N. (3) 1977/8 Shamrock R

Thomas, P. (2) 1973/4 Waterford
Thompson, J. (1) 2003/04 Nottingham F
Townsend, A. D. (70) 1988/9 Norwich C, Chelsea, Aston Villa, Middlesbrough
Traynor, T. J. (8) 1953/4 Southampton
Treacy, R. C. P. (42) 1965/6 WBA, Charlton Ath, Swindon T, Preston NE, WBA, Shamrock R
Tuohy, L. (8) 1955/6 Shamrock R, Newcastle U, Shamrock R
Turner, P. (2) 1962/3 Celtic

Vernon, J. (2) 1945/6 Belfast Celtic

Waddock, G. (20) 1979/80 QPR, Millwall
Walsh, D. J. (20) 1945/6 WBA, Aston Villa
Walsh, J. (1) 1981/2 Limerick
Walsh, M. (21) 1975/6 Blackpool, Everton, QPR, Porto
Walsh, M. (4) 1981/2 Everton, Norwich C
Walsh, W. (9) 1946/7 Manchester C
Waters, J. (2) 1976/7 Grimsby T
Whelan, R. (2) 1963/4 St Patrick's Ath
Whelan, R. (53) 1980/1 Liverpool, Southend U
Whelan, W. (4) 1955/6 Manchester U
Whittaker, R. (1) 1958/9 Chelsea

Name		Name		Name	
Robson, B.	26	Bone, J.	1	Graham, G.	3
Robson, R.	4	Booth, S.	6	Gray, A.	5
Rooney, W.	9	Boyd, T.	1	Gray, E.	3
Rowley, J.F.	6	Brand, R.	8	Gray, F.	1
Royle, J.	2	Brazil, A.	1	Greig, J.	3
		Bremner, W.J.	3		
Sansom, K.	1	Brown, A.D.	6	Hamilton, G.	4
Scholes, P.	14	Buckley, P.	1	Harper, J.M.	2
Sewell, J.	3	Burley, C.W.	3	Hartford, R.A.	4
Shackleton, L.F.	1	Burns, K.	1	Henderson, J.G.	1
Shearer, A.	30			Henderson, W.	5
Sheringham, E.P.	11	Caldwell, G.	1	Hendry, E.C.J.	3
Smith, A.	1	Calderwood, C.	1	Herd, D.G.	3
Smith, A.M.	2	Caldow, E.	4	Herd, G.	1
Smith, R.	13	Cameron, C.	2	Hewie, J.D.	2
Southgate, G.	2	Campbell, R.	1	Holt, G.J.	1
Steven, T.M.	4	Chalmers, S.	3	Holton, J.A.	2
Stiles, N.P.	1	Collins, J.	12	Hopkin, D.	2
Stone, S.B.	2	Collins, R.V.	10	Houliston, W.	2
Summerbee, M.G.	1	Combe, J.R.	1	Howie, H.	1
		Conn, A.	1	Hughes, J.	1
Tambling, R.V.	1-	Cooper, D.	6	Hunter, W.	1
Taylor, P.J.	2	Craig, J.	1	Hutchison, D.	6
Taylor, T.	16	Crawford, S.	4	Hutchison, T.	1
Thompson, P.B.	1	Curran, H.P.	1		
Tueart, D.	2			Jackson, C.	1
		Dailly, C.	4	Jackson, D.	4
Vassell, D.	6	Dalglish, K.	30	Jardine, A.	1
Viollet, D.S.	1	Davidson, J.A.	1	Jess, E.	2
		Dickov, P.	1	Johnston, A.	2
Waddle, C.R.	6	Dobie, R. S.	1	Johnston, L.H.	1
Wallace, D.L.	1	Docherty, T.H.	1	Johnston, M.	14
Walsh, P.	1	Dodds, D.	1	Johnstone, D.	2
Watson, D.V.	4	Dodds, W.	7	Johnstone, J.	4
Webb, N.	4	Duncan, D.M.	1	Johnstone, R.	9
Weller, K.	1	Durie, G.S.	7	Jordan, J.	11
Wignall, F.	2				
Wilkins, R.G.	3	Elliott, M.S.	1	Kyle, K.	1
Wilshaw, D.J.	10				
Wise, D.F.	1	Ferguson, B.	2	Lambert, P.	1
Withe, P.	1	Fernie, W.	1	Law, D.	30
Woodcock, T.	16	Flavell, R.	2	Leggat, G.	8
Worthington, F.S.	2	Fleming, C.	2	Lennox, R.	3
Wright, I.E.	9	Fletcher, D.	2	Liddell, W.	6
Wright, M.	1	Freedman, D.A.	1	Linwood, A.B.	1
Wright, W.A.	3			Lorimer, P.	4
		Gallacher, K.W.	9		

SCOTLAND

Name		Name		Name	
Aitken, R.	1	Gemmell, T.K (St Mirren)	1	Macari, L.	5
Archibald, S.	4	Gemmell, T.K (Celtic)	1	McAllister, G.	5
		Gemmill, A.	8	MacDougall, E.J.	3
Baird, S.	2	Gemmill, S.	1	MacKay, D.C.	4
Bannon, E.	1	Gibson, D.W.	3	Mackay, G.	1
Bauld, W.	2	Gilzean, A.J.	12	MacKenzie, J.A.	1
Baxter, J.C.	3	Gough, C.R.	6	MacLeod, M.	1
Bett, J.	1	Graham, A.	2	McAvennie, F.	1
				McCall, S.M.	1
				McCalliog, J.	1

McCann, N.	3	St John, I.	9	Edwards, G.	2
McClair, B.	2	Scott, A.S.	5	Edwards, R.I.	4
McCoist, A.	19	Sharp, G.	1	England, H.M.	4
McFadden, J.	4	Shearer, D.	2	Evans, I.	1
McGhee, M.	2	Smith, G.	4		
McGinlay, J.	3	Souness, G.J.	4	Flynn, B.	7
McInally, A.	3	Steel, W.	12	Ford, T.	23
McKimmie, S.I.	1	Stein, C.	10	Foulkes, W.J.	1
McKinlay, W.	4	Stewart, R.	1		
McKinnon, R.	1	Strachan, G.	5	Giggs, R.J.	8
McLaren, A.	4	Sturrock, P.	3	Giles, D.	2
McLean, T.	1			Godfrey, B.C.	2
McLintock, F.	1	Thompson, S.	2	Griffiths, A.T.	6
McMillan, I.L.	2	Thornton, W.	1	Griffiths, M.W.	2
McNeill, W.	3				
McPhail, J.	3	Waddell, W.	6	Harris, C.S.	1
McQueen, G.	5	Wallace, I.A.	1	Hartson, J.	11
McStay, P.	9	Wark, J.	7	Hewitt, R.	1
McSwegan, G.J.	1	Weir, A.	1	Hockey, T.	1
Mason, J.	4	Weir, D.	1	Hodges, G.	2
Masson, D.S.	5	White, J.A.	3	Horne, B.	2
Miller, K.	2	Wilkie, L.	1	Hughes, L.M.	16
Miller, W.	1	Wilson, D.	9		
Mitchell, R.C.	1			James, L.	10
Morgan, W.	1	Young, A.	2	James, R.	7
Morris, H.	3			Jones, A.	1
Mudie, J.K.	9	**WALES**		Jones, B.S.	2
Mulhall, G.	1	Allchurch, I.J.	23	Jones, Cliff	16
Murdoch, R.	5	Allen, M.	3	Jones, D.E.	1
Murray, J.	1			Jones, J.P.	1
		Barnes, W.	1		
Narey, D.	1	Bellamy, C.D.	6	Koumas, J.	1
Naysmith, G.A.	1	Blackmore, C.G.	1	Kryzwicki, R.I.	1
Nevin, P.K.F.	5	Blake, N.A.	4		
Nicholas, C.	5	Bodin, P.J.	3	Leek, K.	5
		Bowen, D.I.	3	Lovell, S.	1
O'Hare, J.	5	Bowen, M.	2	Lowrie, G.	2
Ormond, W.E.	1	Boyle, T.	1		
Orr, T.	1	Burgess, W.A.R.	1	Mahoney, J.F.	1
Own goals	9			Medwin, T.C.	6
		Charles, J.	1	Melville, A.K.	3
Parlane, D.	1	Charles, M.	6	Moore, G.	1
Pettigrew, W.	2	Charles, W.J.	15		
Provan, D.	1	Clarke, R.J.	5	Nicholas, P.	2
		Coleman, C.	4		
Quashie, N.F.	1	Curtis, A.	6	O'Sullivan, P.A.	1
Quinn, J.	7			Own goals	5
Quinn, P.	1	Davies, G.	2		
		Davies, R.T.	9	Palmer, D.	1
Reilly, L.	22	Davies, R.W.	6	Parry, P.I.	1
Ring, T.	2	Davies, Simon	4	Paul, R.	1
Rioch, B.D.	6	Deacy, N.	4	Pembridge, M.A.	6
Ritchie, P.S.	1	Durban, A.	2	Phillips, D.	2
Robertson, A.	2	Dwyer, P.	2	Powell, A.	1
Robertson, J.	2			Powell, D.	1
Robertson, J.N.	9	Earnshaw, R.	7	Price, P.	1

Reece, G.I.	2	
Rees, R.R.	3	
Roberts, P.S.	1	
Robinson, J.R.C.	3	
Rush, I.	28	
Saunders, D.	22	
Savage R.W.	2	
Slatter, N.	2	
Smallman, D.P.	1	
Speed, G.A.	6	
Symons, C.J.	2	
Tapscott, D.R.	4	
Taylor, G.J.	1	
Thomas, M.	4	
Toshack, J.B.	12	
Vernon, T.R.	8	
Walsh, I.	7	
Williams, A.	1	
Williams, G.E.	1	
Williams, G.G.	1	
Woosnam, A.P.	3	
Yorath, T.C.	2	
Young, E.	1	

NORTHERN IRELAND

Anderson, T.	4
Armstrong, G.	12
Barr, H.H.	1
Best, G.	9
Bingham, W.L.	10
Black, K.	1
Blanchflower, D.	2
Blanchflower, J.	1
Brennan, R.A.	1
Brotherston, N.	3
Campbell, W.G.	1
Casey, T.	2
Caskey, W.	1
Cassidy, T.	1
Clarke, C.J.	13
Clements, D.	2
Cochrane, T.	1
Crossan, E.	1
Crossan, J.A.	10
Cush, W.W.	5
D'Arcy, S.D.	1
Doherty, I.	1
Doherty, P.D.	2

Dougan, A.D.	8
Dowie, I.	12
Elder, A.R.	1
Elliott, S.	2
Ferguson, W.	1
Ferris, R.O.	1
Finney, T.	2
Gillespie, K.R.	1
Gray, P.	6
Griffin, D.J.	1
Hamilton, B.	4
Hamilton, W.	5
Harkin, J.T.	2
Harvey, M.	3
Healy, D.J.	14
Hill, C.F.	1
Humphries, W.	1
Hughes, M.E.	5
Hunter, A.	1
Hunter, B.V.	1
Irvine, W.J.	8
Johnston, W.C.	1
Jones, J.	1
Jones, S.	1
Lennon, N.F.	2
Lockhart, N.	3
Lomas, S.M.	3
Magilton, J.	5
McAdams, W.J.	7
McCartney, G.	1
McClelland, J.	1
McCrory, S.	1
McCurdy, C.	1
McDonald, A.	3
McGarry, J.K.	1
McGrath, R.C.	4
McIlroy, J.	10
McIlroy, S.B.	5
McLaughlin, J.C.	6
McMahon, G.J.	2
McMordie, A.S.	3
McMorran, E.J.	4
McParland, P.J.	10
Moreland, V.	1
Morgan, S.	3
Morrow, S.J.	1
Mulryne, P.P.	3
Neill, W.J.T.	2

Nelson, S.	1
Nicholl, C.J.	3
Nicholl, J.M.	1
Nicholson, J.J.	6
O'Boyle, G.	1
O'Kane, W.J.	1
O'Neill, J.	2
O'Neill, M.A.	4
O'Neill, M.H.	8
Own goals	5
Patterson, D.J.	1
Peacock, R.	2
Penney, S.	2
Quinn, J.M.	12
Quinn, S.J.	4
Rowland, K.	1
Simpson, W.J.	5
Smyth, S.	5
Spence, D.W.	3
Stewart, I.	2
Taggart, G.P.	7
Tully, C.P.	3
Walker, J.	1
Walsh, D.J.	5
Welsh, E.	1
Whiteside, N.	9
Whitley, Jeff	1
Williams, M.S.	1
Wilson, D.J.	1
Wilson, K.J.	6
Wilson, S.J.	7

EIRE

Aldridge, J.	19
Ambrose, P.	1
Anderson, J.	1
Barrett, G.	2
Brady, L.	9
Breen, G.	6
Byrne, J. (QPR)	4
Cantwell, J.	14
Carey, J.	3
Carroll, T.	1
Cascarino, A.	19
Coad, P.	3
Connolly, D.J.	9
Conroy, T.	2
Conway, J.	3

Name		Name		Name	
Coyne, T.	6	Holland, M.R.	5	O'Callaghan, K.	1
Cummings, G.	5	Holmes, J.	1	O'Connor, T.	2
Curtis, D.	8	Houghton, R.	6	O'Farrell, F.	2
		Hughton, C.	1	O'Keefe, E.	1
Daly, G.	13	Hurley, C.	2	O'Leary, D.A.	1
Dempsey, J.	1			O'Neill, F.	1
Dennehy, M.	2	Irwin, D.	4	O'Neill, K.P.	4
Doherty, G.M.T.	4			O'Reilly, J.	1
Duff, D.A.	6	Kavanagh, G.A.	1	O'Shea, J.F.	1
Duffy, B.	1	Keane, R.D.	20	Own goals	10
Dunne, R.P.	4	Keane, R.M.	9		
		Kelly, D.	9	Quinn, N.	21
Eglinton, T.	2	Kelly, G.	2		
		Kennedy, M.	3	Reid, S.J.	2
Fagan, F.	5	Kernaghan, A.	1	Ringstead, A.	7
Fallon, S.	2	Kilbane, K.D.	4	Robinson, M.	4
Farrell, P.	3	Kinsella, M.A.	3	Rogers, E.	5
Finnan, S.	1			Ryan, G.	1
Fitzgerald, J.	1	Lawrenson, M.	5	Ryan, R.	3
Fitzgerald, P.	2	Leech, M.	2		
Fitzsimons, A.	7			Sheedy, K.	9
Fogarty, A.	3	McAteer, J.W.	3	Sheridan, J.	5
Foley, D.	2	McCann, J.	1	Slaven, B.	1
Fullam, J.	1	McCarthy, M.	2	Sloan, W.	1
		McEvoy, A.	6	Stapleton, F.	20
Galvin, A.	1	McGee, P.	4	Staunton, S.	7
Gavin, J.	2	McGrath, P.	8	Strahan, F.	1
Giles, J.	5	McLoughlin, A.	2		
Givens, D.	19	McPhail, S.	1	Townsend, A.D.	7
Glynn, D.	1	Mancini, T.	1	Treacy, R.	5
Grealish, T.	8	Martin, C.	6	Tuohy, L.	4
Grimes, A.A.	1	Martin, M.	4		
		Mooney, J.	1	Waddock, G.	3
Hale, A.	2	Moran, K.	6	Walsh, D.	5
Hand, E.	2	Moroney, T.	1	Walsh, M.	3
Harte, I.P.	9	Morrison, C.H.	5	Waters, J.	1
Haverty, J.	3	Mulligan, P.	1	Whelan, R.	3
Healy, C.	1				

UEFA UNDER-21 CHAMPIONSHIP 2004

GROUP 1
Slovenia 1, Malta 0
Cyprus 0, France 1
Malta 0, Israel 1
France 1, Slovenia 0
Malta 0, France 3
Cyprus 2, Malta 0
Cyprus 2, Israel 0
France 2, Malta 0
Israel 0, France 3
Slovenia 2, Cyprus 0
Malta 0, Slovenia 0
Israel 0, Cyprus 3
Israel 0, Slovenia 0
Malta 0, Cyprus 1
Slovenia 1, Israel 2
France 2, Cyprus 0
Israel 3, Malta 0
Slovenia 0, France 0
France 2, Israel 0
Cyprus 4, Slovenia 0

GROUP 2
Norway 3, Denmark 0
Bosnia 2, Romania 1
Denmark 9, Luxembourg 0
Romania 0, Norway 1
Norway 0, Bosnia 0
Luxembourg 0, Romania 2
Bosnia 1, Luxembourg 0
Romania 0, Denmark 1
Denmark 3, Bosnia 0
Luxembourg 0, Norway 5
Romania 0, Bosnia 1
Denmark 2, Norway 0
Norway 2, Romania 1
Luxembourg 0, Denmark 6
Bosnia 1, Norway 3
Romania 2, Luxembourg 0
Denmark 0, Romania 0
Luxembourg 0, Bosnia 1
Norway 5, Luxembourg 0
Bosnia 0, Denmark 3

GROUP 3
Holland 0, Belarus 1
Austria 1, Moldova 0
Belarus 0, Austria 1
Moldova 0, Czech Republic 2
Austria 1, Holland 1
Czech Republic 3, Belarus 0
Holland 0, Czech Republic 3
Belarus 3, Moldova 1
Czech Republic 3, Austria 1
Moldova 2, Holland 2
Belarus 2, Holland 1
Moldova 0, Austria 1
Czech Republic 3, Moldova 0
Austria 0, Belarus 2
Belarus 1, Czech Republic 0
Holland 0, Austria 0
Czech Republic 1, Holland 2
Moldova 0, Belarus 2
Austria 0, Czech Republic 2
Holland 0, Moldova 0

GROUP 4
Latvia 0, Sweden 4
San Marino 1, Poland 5
Poland 3, Latvia 0
Sweden 1, Hungary 0
Hungary 4, San Marino 1
San Marino 0, Latvia 2
Poland 3, Hungary 2
Poland 7, San Marino 0
Hungary 5, Sweden 2
Latvia 4, San Marino 0
Hungary 3, Latvia 1
San Marino 1, Sweden 5
Sweden 1, Poland 1
San Marino 1, Hungary 2
Latvia 0, Poland 2
Sweden 0, San Marino 3
Poland 1, Sweden 1
Latvia 2, Hungary 0
Sweden 3, Latvia 2
Hungary 1, Poland 2

GROUP 5
Lithuania 1, Germany 4
Iceland 0, Scotland 2
Iceland 1, Lithuania 2
Scotland 1, Iceland 0
Germany 1, Lithuania 0
Lithuania 2, Scotland 1
Scotland 2, Germany 2
Lithuania 3, Iceland 0
Iceland 1, Germany 3
Germany 0, Scotland 1
Scotland 3, Lithuania 2
Germany 1, Iceland 0

GROUP 6
Armenia 1, Ukraine 1
Greece 1, Spain 0
Ukraine 1, Greece 1
Spain 1, Northern Ireland 0
Northern Ireland 1, Ukraine 1
Greece 2, Armenia 1
Armenia 2, Northern Ireland 0
Ukraine 0, Spain 0
Northern Ireland 2, Greece 6
Spain 5, Armenia 0
Ukraine 4, Armenia 0
Spain 2, Greece 0
Northern Ireland 1, Spain 4
Greece 0, Ukraine 0
Ukraine 1, Northern Ireland 0
Armenia 0, Greece 0
Northern Ireland 3, Armenia 1
Spain 2, Ukraine 0
Armenia 0, Spain 2
Greece 0, Northern Ireland 1

GROUP 7
Turkey 2, Slovakia 1
Portugal 1, Macedonia 0
Macedonia 0, Turkey 4
Slovakia 0, England 4
Turkey 4, Portugal 2
England 3, Macedonia 1

Portugal 4, England 2
Macedonia 0, Slovakia 2
Slovakia 0, Portugal 2
England 1, Turkey 1
Slovakia 0, Turkey 1
Macedonia 1, Portugal 4
Turkey 3, Macedonia 0
England 2, Slovakia 0
Macedonia 1, England 1
Portugal 1, Turkey 0
England 1, Portugal 2
Slovakia 5, Macedonia 1
Turkey 1, England 0
Portugal 4, Slovakia 1

GROUP 8
Croatia 3, Estonia 1
Belgium 3, Bulgaria 1
Bulgaria 1, Croatia 3
Estonia 0, Belgium 1
Croatia 1, Belgium 1
Estonia 1, Bulgaria 1
Bulgaria 2, Belgium 1
Estonia 0, Croatia 0
Bulgaria 1, Estonia 0
Belgium 0, Croatia 2
Croatia 0, Bulgaria 1
Belgium 4, Estonia 2

GROUP 9
Finland 2, Wales 1
Azerbaijan 0, Italy 3
Finland 3, Azerbaijan 0
Italy 4, Serbia-Montenegro 1
Serbia-Montenegro 3, Finland 3
Wales 1, Italy 2
Azerbaijan 0, Wales 1
Serbia-Montenegro 3, Azerbaijan 0
Wales 1, Azerbaijan 0
Italy 1, Finland 0
Finland 1, Serbia-Montenegro 2
Finland 1, Italy 2
Azerbaijan 0, Serbia-Montenegro 2
Serbia-Montenegro 3, Wales 0
Italy 8, Wales 1
Azerbaijan 0, Finland 1
Wales 0, Finland 0
Serbia-Montenegro 1, Italy 0
Wales 0, Serbia-Montenegro 1
Italy 6, Azerbaijan 0

GROUP 10
Russia 2, Republic of Ireland 0
Switzerland 2, Georgia 0
Albania 0, Switzerland 0
Georgia 0, Russia 3
Republic of Ireland 2, Switzerland 3
Russia 1, Albania 0
Georgia 1, Republic of Ireland 1
Albania 1, Russia 4
Albania 1, Republic of Ireland 0
Georgia 0, Switzerland 2
Switzerland 1, Russia 0
Republic of Ireland 0, Albania 3
Switzerland 2, Albania 1
Republic of Ireland 1, Georgia 1
Republic of Ireland 2, Russia 0

Georgia 3, Albania 1
Albania 3, Georgia 0
Russia 1, Switzerland 2
Switzerland 0, Republic of Ireland 0
Russia 3, Georgia 2

PLAY-OFFS FIRST LEG
Serbia-Montenegro 5, Norway 1
Germany 1, Turkey 0
Portugal 1, France 2
Denmark 1, Italy 1
Belarus 1, Poland 1
Sweden 2, Spain 0
Switzerland 1, Czech Republic 2
Croatia 2, Scotland 0

PLAY-OFFS SECOND LEG
Norway 3, Serbia-Montenegro 0
Turkey 1, Germany 1
France 1, Portugal 2
Portugal won 4-1 on penalties.
Italy 0, Denmark 0
Poland 0, Belarus 4
Spain 1, Sweden 1
Czech Republic 1, Switzerland 2
Switzerland won 4-3 on penalties.
Scotland 1, Croatia 0

FINALS IN GERMANY

GROUP A
Serbia-Montenegro 3, Croatia 2
Italy 1, Belarus 2
Belarus 1, Croatia 1
Italy 2, Serbia-Montenegro 1
Italy 1, Croatia 0
Belarus 1, Serbia-Montenegro 2

GROUP B
Germany 2, Switzerland 1
Sweden 3, Portugal 1
Germany 1, Sweden 2
Switzerland 2, Portugal 2
Germany 1, Portugal 2
Switzerland 1, Sweden 3

SEMI-FINALS
Sweden 1, Serbia-Montenegro 1
Serbia-Montenegro won 6-5 on penalties.
Italy 3, Portugal 1

MATCH FOR 3RD PLACE
Sweden 2, Portugal 3

FINAL
Italy 3, Serbia-Montenegro 0
*Italy, Serbia-Montenegro and Portugal
qualified for the Olympics.*

PREVIOUS WINNERS
1978 Yugoslavia	1992 Italy
1980 USSR	1994 Italy
1982 England	1996 Italy
1984 England	1998 Spain
1986 Spain	2000 Italy
1988 France	2002 Czech Republic
1990 USSR	

NATIONWIDE FOOTBALL CONFERENCE 2003–2004

			Home					Away					Total					
		P	W	D	L	F	A	W	D	L	F	A	W	D	L	F	A	Gd	Pts
1	Chester C	42	16	4	1	45	18	11	7	3	40	16	27	11	4	85	34	51	92
2	Hereford U	42	14	3	4	42	20	14	4	3	61	24	28	7	7	103	44	59	91
3	Shrewsbury T	42	13	6	2	38	14	7	8	6	29	28	20	14	8	67	42	25	74
4	Barnet	42	11	6	4	30	17	8	8	5	30	29	19	14	9	60	46	14	71
5	Aldershot T	42	12	6	3	40	24	8	4	9	40	43	20	10	12	80	67	13	70
6	Exeter C	42	10	7	4	33	24	9	5	7	38	33	19	12	11	71	57	14	69
7	Morecambe	42	14	4	3	43	25	6	3	12	23	41	20	7	15	66	66	0	67
8	Stevenage B	42	10	5	6	29	22	8	4	9	29	30	18	9	15	58	52	6	63
9	Woking	42	10	9	2	40	23	5	7	9	25	29	15	16	11	65	52	13	61
10	Accrington S	42	13	3	5	46	31	2	10	9	22	30	15	13	14	68	61	7	58
11	Gravesend & N	42	7	6	8	34	35	7	9	5	35	31	14	15	13	69	66	3	57
12	Telford U	42	10	3	8	28	28	5	7	9	21	23	15	10	17	49	51	-2	55
13	Dagenham & R	42	8	3	10	30	34	7	6	8	29	30	15	9	18	59	64	-5	54
14	Burton Alb	42	7	4	10	30	29	8	3	10	27	30	15	7	20	57	59	-2	52
15	Scarborough	42	8	9	4	32	25	4	6	11	19	29	12	15	15	51	54	-3	51
16	Margate	42	8	2	11	30	32	6	7	8	26	32	14	9	19	56	64	-8	51
17	Tamworth	42	9	6	6	32	30	4	4	13	17	38	13	10	19	49	68	-19	49
18	Forest Green R	42	6	8	7	32	36	6	4	11	26	44	12	12	18	58	80	-22	48
19	Halifax T	42	9	4	8	28	26	3	4	14	15	39	12	8	22	43	65	-22	44
20	Farnborough T	42	7	6	8	31	34	3	3	15	22	40	10	9	23	53	74	-21	39
21	Leigh RMI	42	4	6	11	26	44	3	2	16	20	53	7	8	27	46	97	-51	29
22	Northwich Vic	42	2	8	11	15	38	2	3	16	15	42	4	11	27	30	80	-50	23

Leading Goalscorers 2003–04

	League	P-offs	FA Cup	LDV	Trophy	Total
Daryl Clare (Chester C)	29	0	1	0	0	30
Steve Guinan (Hereford U)	25	0	3	1	0	29
David McNiven (Leigh RMI)	25	0	0	0	1	26
Giuliano Grazioli (Barnet)	24	0	2	0	0	26
Roscoe D'Sane (Aldershot T)	21	1	2	0	3	27
Sean Devine (Exeter C)	20	0	2	0	3	25
Paul Mullin (Accrington S)	20	0	3	0	1	24
Darryn Stamp (Chester C)	20	0	0	0	0	20
Tim Sills (Aldershot T)	18	0	1	0	2	21
Anthony Elding (Stevenage B)	17	0	2	0	0	19
Lutel James (Accrington S)	17	0	1	0	0	18
Danny Carlton (Morecambe)	17	0	0	0	0	17
Mark Cooper (Tamworth)	15	0	0	0	0	15
David Brown (Hereford U)	14	1	0	2	0	17
Mark Quayle (Scarborough)	14	0	1	0	0	15

NATIONWIDE FOOTBALL CONFERENCE RESULTS 2003–2004

	Accrington S	Aldershot T	Barnet	Burton Alb	Chester C	Dagenham & R	Exeter C	Farnborough T	Forest Green R	Gravesend & N	Halifax T	Hereford U	Leigh RMI	Margate	Morecambe	Northwich Vic	Scarborough	Shrewsbury T	Stevenage B	Tamworth	Telford U	Woking
Accrington S	—	4-2	2-0	3-1	1-1	3-2	1-2	3-1	3-1	3-3	2-1	2-1	4-1	3-2	1-0	2-1	1-2	1-1	2-0	3-0	1-5	3-3
Aldershot T	2-1	—	1-1	3-1	1-1	2-1	2-3	1-0	3-0	2-2	3-1	1-2	2-0	0-2	1-0	4-3	2-1	1-1	2-0	1-1	3-1	1-1
Barnet	1-4	2-3	—	2-4	1-1	2-3	2-3	0-2	5-0	3-2	3-1	1-1	2-0	2-1	2-1	2-1	1-2	1-2	1-2	1-1	3-1	3-0
Burton Alb	3-3	4-2	—	—	1-2	0-2	3-4	1-0	2-3	3-0	2-2	4-1	3-2	3-0	2-1	0-1	2-0	2-1	1-2	0-1	0-0	2-0
Chester C	0-1	2-3	1-1	0-2	—	1-2	3-4	3-2	1-0	2-2	4-1	0-9	3-2	3-0	2-1	0-1	1-0	5-0	1-2	0-0	0-0	2-1
Dagenham & R	3-2	2-1	1-1	2-0	0-2	—	1-2	0-2	5-2	0-4	0-1	0-5	1-2	1-1	1-3	2-0	1-2	3-2	1-2	3-2	0-3	2-1
Exeter C	1-1	3-1	4-0	1-0	1-1	1-2	—	0-2	1-0	2-0	1-0	1-7	3-1	1-1	2-4	2-0	4-0	3-3	2-0	3-2	0-3	1-0
Farnborough T	1-1	3-1	1-1	2-0	1-1	1-2	1-1	—	0-1	1-2	1-2	0-5	2-5	1-1	6-0	2-1	4-0	1-0	2-3	2-1	0-2	1-0
Forest Green R	0-0	4-0	1-3	1-1	1-2	0-4	1-2	1-1	—	1-0	1-2	2-5	2-1	2-1	1-2	0-1	2-1	0-0	1-0	2-1	0-0	2-2
Gravesend & N	1-0	1-3	3-0	2-0	1-1	3-0	1-1	2-0	5-1	—	2-0	2-5	3-1	4-2	6-0	0-2	3-0	2-0	1-2	2-1	1-0	2-2
Halifax T	1-0	1-2	1-1	1-1	3-0	1-1	1-1	2-0	1-1	1-0	—	2-0	0-1	1-1	3-0	5-3	2-1	5-1	2-0	3-2	1-3	0-1
Hereford U	4-3	1-2	1-2	1-2	1-1	2-0	0-1	0-1	0-1	0-1	7-1	—	0-1	4-2	1-1	3-0	1-0	3-0	1-2	3-2	2-1	1-2
Leigh RMI	1-2	2-2	1-4	0-1	2-6	1-1	0-2	3-0	0-1	1-2	1-0	0-5	—	3-3	1-0	3-1	2-1	1-1	1-4	3-2	1-0	2-1
Margate	3-1	1-4	0-1	1-2	0-1	3-3	0-3	3-0	2-0	1-3	2-0	1-0	1-0	—	3-1	1-0	0-2	1-2	1-2	3-2	1-0	2-1
Morecambe	1-0	2-0	1-3	0-1	2-4	3-2	0-3	2-0	3-2	2-0	1-1	0-5	3-0	0-3	—	3-0	2-1	2-2	1-4	3-2	1-1	1-4
Northwich Vic	3-3	1-1	1-1	1-2	2-2	0-0	2-3	1-1	4-0	1-1	2-0	4-1	2-0	0-1	3-1	—	4-1	1-1	2-2	0-1	1-1	2-2
Scarborough	2-1	1-1	2-0	0-0	2-2	2-2	2-0	1-0	2-0	1-3	1-0	2-0	1-0	2-1	1-1	1-0	—	2-0	1-0	3-1	2-1	2-0
Shrewsbury T	0-0	1-2	0-1	2-2	2-2	2-2	2-2	2-4	1-1	1-3	2-0	4-1	4-0	2-1	2-3	3-1	1-1	—	3-1	2-0	1-0	1-1
Stevenage B	2-1	3-3	1-1	1-0	1-5	0-2	2-2	2-0	1-3	0-1	2-1	4-3	4-0	2-1	2-3	0-0	4-1	2-0	—	2-0	2-1	1-2
Tamworth	1-0	2-5	1-0	2-2	1-0	1-0	2-4	2-2	0-2	0-3	2-1	0-3	4-2	1-1	2-3	3-1	0-0	1-1	1-2	—	2-0	1-0
Telford U	1-0	2-5	0-2	1-0	1-5	1-0	2-0	2-4	0-2	5-0	1-1	0-3	5-0	1-1	5-0	0-1	2-1	3-3	1-2	2-0	—	3-1
Woking	2-2	2-2	2-2	1-0	1-2	0-0	1-0	3-2	3-2	4-1	2-2	0-1	2-0	0-0	4-1	3-0	2-1	3-3	1-1	4-0	3-1	—

APPEARANCES AND GOALSCORERS 2003–2004

ACCRINGTON STANLEY
Goals: *League (68):* Mullin 20, James 17 (4 pens), Prendergast 6, Gouck 5, Durnin 4, Cavanagh 2, Flitcroft 2, Howarth 2, McEvilly 2, Proctor 2, Brannan 1, Calcutt 1, Cook 1, Hollis 1, Kempson 1, own goal 1.
FA Cup (4): Mullin 3, James 1.
Trophy (2): Howarth 1, Mullin 1.
League Appearances: Armstrong, 4+9; Brannan, 19+1; Calcutt, 6+14; Cavanagh, 35+1; Cook, 28+6; Durnin, 4+12; Fitzgerald, 7; Flitcroft, 13+11; Gouck, 20+6; Halford, 24+2; Hindle, 1; Hollis, 27+2; Howarth, 15+2; Jackson, 0+2; James, 40+1; Kempson, 9+2; Kennedy, 32+1; Madden, 0+2; McEvilly, 3+3; Mullin, 41; Prendergast, 36+2; Proctor, 36+3; Smith, 18+4; Speare, 10+1; Waine, 0+1; Welch, 1+1; Williams, 33.

ALDERSHOT TOWN
Goals: *League (80):* D'Sane 21 (8 pens), Sills 18, Challinor 12, Charles L 7, McLean 6, Miller 5, Warburton 2, Chewins 1, Gosling 1, Manuella 1, Mumford 1, Taylor 1, Thomas 1, own goals 3.
FA Cup (5): D'Sane 2 (1 pen), McLean 1, Sills 1, Warburton 1.
Trophy (12): D'Sane 3 (1 pen), McLean 2, Miller 2, Sills 2, Charles 1, Nutter 1, Warburton 1.
Play-Offs (2): D'Sane 1 (pen), McLean 1.
League Appearances: Antwi, 13; Barnard, 18+3; Bull, 24; Challinor, 36; Charles, L., 20+10; Chewins, 26+9; D'Sane, 39+1; Downer, 8; Gedling, 1+6; Giles, 4+1; Gosling, 7+1; Hammond, 7; Harper, 0+12; Hooper, 29; Johnson, 1+5; Lovett, 1; Manuella, 8; McLean, 24+13; Miller, 23+1; Mumford, 4; Nutter, 10+11; Rees, 7; Roddis, 9+1; Rodwell, 11+2; Shields, 12+1; Sills, 39; Smith, 2+1; Sterling, 33+5; Tanfield, 1+5; Taylor, 0+3; Thomas, 5; Warburton, 40; Westell, 0+1.

BARNET
Goals: *League (60):* Grazioli 24 (2 pens), Strevens 9, Hendon 6 (4 pens), Hatch 4, Beadle 3, Plummer 3, Yakubu 2, Clist 1, Gamble 1, Hogg 1, Pearson 1, Pitcher 1, Redmile 1, Taggart 1, own goals 2.
FA Cup (8): Beadle 2, Gamble 2, Grazioli 2, Hatch 2.
LDV Vans Trophy (3): Hatch 1, Henry 1 (pen), Lopez 1.
Trophy (3): Pitcher 2, Roach 1.
Play-Offs (2): Clist 1, Strevens 1 (pen).
League Appearances: Bankole, 8; Beadle, 10+3; Campion, 0+1; Clist, 13+2; Forde, 7; Gamble, 40; Gore, 19; Grazioli, 38; Hatch, 17+6; Hendon, 37+1; Henry, 0+3; Hogg, 11+5; King, 33+2; Lopez, 15+10; Maddix, 32; McNamee, 2+3; Millard, 1; Naisbitt, 7;

Pearson, 2+8; Pitcher, 5; Pluck, 0+1; Plummer, 34; Redmile, 12; Roach, 0+1; Rooney, 23+6; Saunders, 0+1; Scully, 1; Silk, 1; Solomon, 0+1; Strevens, 35+4; Sylla, 0+4; Taggart, 8+14; Williams, 19+15; Yakubu, 32+7.

BURTON ALBION
Goals: *League (57):* Talbot 11, Anderson 7, Webster 7 (5 pens), Howard 4, Kirkwood 4, Stride 4, Moore 3, Ducros 2, Williams 2, Wright 2, Chettle 1, Colkin 1, Corbett 1, Dudley 1, Gill 1, Henshaw 1, Sinton 1, Twigg 1, White 1, own goals 2.
FA Cup (8): Anderson 3, Talbot 2, Webster 2, own goal 1.
Trophy (6): Webster 3, Anderson 1, Howard 1, Stride 1.
League Appearances: Anderson, 26+11; Baptiste, 3; Chettle, 22+2; Clough, 15+12; Colkin, 12+2; Corbett, 10+15; Crosby, 0+2; Ducros, 20+6; Dudley, 23+4; Duke, 42; Gill, 4+1; Gummer, 0+1; Henshaw, 29+2; Howard, 30+6; Hoyle, 12+4; Kirkwood, 19+6; McMahon, 12+3; Moore, 4+3; Murray, 2; Shilton, 15; Sinton, 2+3; Stride, 28+2; Sugden, 2+2; Talbot, 28+9; Twigg, 3+1; Wassall, 27+3; Webster, 31+3; White, 3; Williams, 13+5; Willis, 6; Wright, 15+4.

CHESTER CITY
Goals: *League (85):* Clare 29 (6 pens), Stamp 20, Twiss 7, Davies 5, Bolland 4, Smith 4, Collins 3, Foster 2 (1 pen), Guyett 2, Rapley 2, Ruffer 2, Brady 1, Carden 1, Hatswell 1, McIntyre 1, own goal 1.
FA Cup (1): Clare 1.
Trophy (1): Bolland 1.
League Appearances: Beesley, 0+3; Bolland, 30+5; Brady, 15; Brodie, 0+2; Brown, 16+1; Carden, 33+2; Carey, 21+1; Clare, 27+3; Collins, 41; Davies, 26+9; Elam, 1+3; Foster, 10+10; Gill, 3+1; Guyett, 24+3; Harris, 10+4; Hatswell, 8; Heard, 24+1; Lane, 1+3; McCaldon, 13; McIntyre, 40; Rapley, 9+17; Regan, 4; Ruffer, 23+1; Smith, 20; Stamp, 35+3; Turner, 12; Twiss, 10+20; Williams, 5; Woods, 1+1.

DAGENHAM & REDBRIDGE
Goals: *League (59):* Moore 10, Bentley 6, Braithwaite 5, Cole 5, Shipp 5, Stein 5, Piper C 4 (2 pens), Watts 3, Bruce 2, Goodwin 2, Janney 2, Meechan 2, Beckwith 1, Hill 1, Jackson J 1, Jackson K 1, Mustafa 1, Pacquette 1, Vickers 1, own goal 1.
FA Cup (1): Shipp 1.
LDV Vans Trophy (5): Bentley 2, Scully 2, Braithwaite 1.
Trophy (3): Jackson K 2, Braithwaite 1.
League Appearances: Beckwith, 4; Bentley, 23+2; Braithwaite, 20+14; Bruce, 30+6;

312

Cole, 29; Eaton, 0+2; Gill, 5; Goodwin, 15+5; Hill, 16+8; Hoyle, 1; Jackson, J., 17+2; Jackson, K., 4; Janney, 22+15; Kimble, 19+3; Matthews, 15+1; McGowan, 0+3; Meechan, 6+10; Moore, 19+1; Mustafa, 35+1; Naisbitt, 7; Pacquette, 3; Perfect, 1+5; Piper, C., 29+5; Piper, L., 6+8; Pullen, 9; Rees, 1; Roberts, 26; Scully, 13; Shipp, 29+6; Smith, 5; Stein, 6; Terry, 2; Venus, 5; Vickers, 30+1; Watts, 7+7; Whitman, 3+1.

EXETER CITY

Goals: *League (71):* Devine 20 (2 pens), Coppinger 8 (2 pens), Sheldon 8, Flack 6, Canham 5, Cronin 5, Gaia 4, Lee 3, Afful 2, Jeannin 2, McConnell 2 (1 pen), Moor 2, Moxey 2, Todd 2, own goal 1.
FA Cup (3): Devine 2, Lee 1.
Trophy (10): Devine 3, Flack 3, Sheldon 3, Coppinger 1.
League Appearances: Afful, 17+13; Ampadu, 29+10; Bittner, 37; Canham, 10+11; Cheeseman, 0+2; Coppinger, 36+3; Cronin, 40; Devine, 24+9; Flack, 24+13; Gaia, 39; Hiley, 42; Jeannin, 39; Lee, 18+3; McConnell, 13+7; Moor, 7+5; Moxey, 9+8; Reed, 0+1; Rice, 5+2; Sheldon, 30+4; Taylor, 0+7; Thomas, 5+6; Todd, 38+1.

FARNBOROUGH TOWN

League (53): Hodgson 9 (2 pens), Burton 8, Fashanu 5 (1 pen), Chaaban 4, Harkness 4, Charlery 3, Forington 3 (1 pen), Hayes 2, Semple 2, Weatherstone 2, Beall 1, Belgrave 1, Charles 1, Doudou 1, Griffiths 1 (pen), Iffufo 1, Manuella 1, Mulhern 1, own goals 3.
FA Cup (2): Clarke 1, Hayes 1.
League Appearances: Allen-Page, 3+1; Ashwood, 1; Beall, 31+3; Belgrave, 12+12; Burton, 30; Chaaban, 18+5; Charlery, 12+11; Charles, 16; Christou, 1+2; Clarke, 6+3; Deacons, 2+1; Donovan, 7; Doudou, 5+3; Fashanu, 7+6; Forington, 21+4; Green, 1+1; Griffiths, 15+13; Harkness, 27+7; Hodgson, 32+1; Howell, 2+2; Hutchings, 20; Iffufo, 2+8; Ifura, 5+1; Lavin, 1; Lovett, 3+6; Manuella, 9+5; Martin, 3+2; Mendonca, 0+1; Moussali, 1+1; Mulhern, 6; Neil, 5; Oli, 4; Opinel, 35; Osborn, 39; Packham, 2; Pardesi, 0+1; Pattison, 8+10; Peters, 2+1; Pitcher, 3; Reece, 1+1; Sappleton, 7; Semple, 9; Sombili Jalo, 1; Stanley, 0+1; Theo, 3+2; Thompson, 16+5; Toms, 4; Weatherstone, 19+2.

FOREST GREEN ROVERS

Goals: *League (58):* Grayson 9 (1 pen), Rogers 9, Cowe 6, Meechan 6, Searle 4 (3 pens), Bowen 3, Brodie 3, Foster 3, Sykes 3, Ingram 2 (1 pen), Moralee 2, Phillips 2, Cant 1, Kennedy 1, Langan 1, Moore 1, Owers 1, own goal 1.
FA Cup (1): Cowe 1.

Trophy (7): Grayson 4, Foster 1, Ingram 1 (pen), Rogers 1.
League Appearances: Adams, 0+4; Aubrey, 2+6; Bowen, 7; Brodie, 7; Cant, 4+7; Cook, 0+1; Cowe, 21+13; Fitzpatrick, 4+1; Foster, 42; Gilroy, 2+3; Grayson, 24+1; Green, 5; Ingram, 32; Jenkins, 10+1; Jones, D., 10; Jones, J., 3+2; Jones, L., 0+9; Jones, S., 11; Jordan, 5; Kennedy, 11+2; Langan, 11+5; McAuley, 6+7; Meechan, 22; Moore, 4+2; Moralee, 6+4; Morgan, 7; Owers, 14; Perrin, 42; Phillips, 19+2; Richardson, 33; Rogers, 27+12; Russell, 3+1; Searle, 31; Simpson, 2+1; Stoker, 24; Sykes, 16+8.

GRAVESEND & NORTHFLEET

Goals: *League (69):* Essandoh 10, Drury 9 (3 pens), Pinnock 9, Moore 7, Abbey 6, Haworth 6, Perkins 6, Gradley 2, Omoyinmi 2, Owen 2, Walshe 2, Duku 1, Evans 1, Lee 1, McKimm 1, Miller 1, Shearer 1, Sidibe 1, Strouts 1.
FA Cup (5): Abbey 1, Haworth 1, Moore 1, Perkins 1, Skinner 1 (pen).
Trophy (2): Abbey 1, Haworth 1.
League Appearances: Abbey, 11+12; Battersby, 0+1; Daly, 0+1; Drury, 25+6; Duku, 17+2; Essandoh, 14; Evans, 1+6; Finn, 0+1; Gibbs, 2; Gledhill, 12+1; Goodwin, 0+2; Gradley, 12+1; Haworth, 21+1; Huggins, 2; Kwashi, 1+1; Lee, 25+4; McClements, 12+1; McKimm, 36+2; Miller, 4; Mitten, 5; Moore, 33; O'Reilly, 10+1; Oli, 5; Omoyinmi, 4+3; Owen, 30+3; Pennock, 4; Perkins, 30+7; Pinnock, 22+8; Protheroe, 10; Rouse, 1+1; Shearer, 26+3; Sidibe, 5+7; Skinner, 26; Strouts, 4+7; Surey, 7+1; Trott, 1+1; Walshe, 17+6; Wilkerson, 27+1.

HALIFAX TOWN

Goals: *League (43):* Midgley 11 (7 pens), Killeen 7, Lee 5, Bushell 3, Mallon 3, Elam 2, Farrell 2, Little 2 (1 pen), Allan 1, Cameron 1, McCombe 1, Monington 1, Owen 1, Quinn 1, Sagare 1, Sandwith 1.
LDV Vans Trophy (6): Killeen 1, Mallon 1, Midgley 1 (pen), Owen 1, Quinn 1, Sandwith 1.
Trophy (6): Farrell 3 (1 pen), Killeen 1, Quinn 1, own goal 1.
League Appearances: Allan, 9+5; Bushell, 37+1; Cameron, 6+3; Carney, 2+1; Cartwright, 32; Colley, 6+1; Cullen, 7; Davies, 8; Donaldson, 2+2; Dudgeon, 9+1; Elam, 14+1; Farrell, 6+12; Garnett, 11; Golden, 16+1; Hockenhull, 27+4; Hoyle, 0+1; Hudson, 21+7; Ingram, 6; Killeen, 29+3; Lee, 17+9; Little, 8; Lowe, 2; Mallon, 29+8; May, 2+1; McAuley, 11+4; McCombe, 7; Midgley, 28+10; Monington, 26+2; Naylor, 0+1; Owen, 15+2; Parke, 0+5; Parry, 2; Price, 5; Quinn, 21+4; Sagare, 11+14; Sandwith, 31; Senior, 0+4; Stoneman, 0+1; Thornley, 1+2; Tozer, 2+1; Yates, 12.

HEREFORD UNITED

Goals: *League (103):* Guinan 25, Brown 14, Smith 13, James 9 (9 pens), Parry 9, Purdey 8, Williams 5, Carey-Bertram 3, Beesley 2, Pitman 2, Rose 2, Tretton 2, U'ddin 2, Willis 2, Green 1, Mkandawire 1, Teesdale 1, Travis 1, own goal 1.
FA Cup (6): Guinan 3, Smith 1, Carey-Bertram 1, Smith 1.
LDV Vans Trophy (3): Brown 2, Guinan 1.
Trophy (2): Carey-Bertram 1, Purdey 1.
Play-Offs (1): Brown 1.

League Appearances: Baker, 42; Beesley, 4+8; Betts, 3+2; Brown, 25+13; Carey-Bertram, 2+18; Cozic, 0+2; Craven, 5+6; Green, 38; Guinan, 34+2; James, 42; King, 1+1; Mkandawire, 14; Palmer, 3; Parry, 25; Pitman, 39; Purdey, 34+2; Rose, 37+1; Sawyers, 0+1; Smith, 35; Teesdale, 4+8; Travis, 0+1; Tretton, 22; U'ddin, 9; Williams, 31+6; Willis, 8.

LEIGH RMI

Goals: *League (46):* McNiven 25 (4 pens), Brodie 4, Maden 4, Daniel 3, Barrowclough 2, Peyton 2, Durkin 1, Lancaster 1, Redmond 1, Robinson 1, Roscoe 1, Shepherd 1.
Trophy (1): McNiven 1.

League Appearances: Alford, 1; Ashmole, 0+1; Barrowclough, 12+3; Brodie, 5; Coburn, 10; Courtney, 0+5; Coyne, 1+1; Daniel, 10+6; Downey, 0+4; Durkin, 37; Ellison, 4; Fitzpatrick, 2; Forrest, 6; Gunby, 8+2; Hallows, 0+7; Hardy, 1; Harris, 1+2; Harrison, 2+6; Heald, 3; Hill, 9+1; Holmes, 11+1; Kelly, 14; Kielty, 7+3; Lancaster, 32+1; Lane, 2; Maden, 23+4; Martin, 16; McGrath, 2+1; McHale, 5+2; McNiven, 41; Milligan, 1; Monk, 14+7; Orr, 1+6; Pendlebury, 0+1; Peyton, 27+7; Price, 1+2; Redmond, 22+4; Rezai, 16+4; Rickers, 3; Robinson, 9; Roscoe, 30+3; Salisbury, 2; Shepherd, 25+4; Smith, 1+2; Starbuck, 5+3; Tench, 1+2; Tickle, 2+2; Whitehead, 0+11; Whitman, 7+1; Williams, 3.

MARGATE

Goals: *League (56):* Watson 6, Baptiste 5, Clarke 5 (1 pen), Omoyinmi 5, Porter 4, Saunders 4, Sigere 4, Stadhart 4, Piper 3, Leberl 2, McFlynn 2, Sodje 2, Annon 1, Baltazar 1, Keister 1, Oates 1, Patmore 1, Pullman 1, own goals 4.
FA Cup (6): Saunders 2, Clarke 1 (pen), Patmore 1, Porter 1, Watson 1.
Trophy (6): Clarke 2, Saunders 2, Keister 1, Sodje 1.

League Appearances: Abbott, 0+6; Annon, 38+3; Baltazar, 1+1; Baptiste, 12; Beard, 1+1; Clarke, 27+8; Edwards, 27+5; Hankin, 3; Jjunju, 0+2; Keister, 26+5; Kwashi, 0+3; Leberl, 39; McFlynn, 10+2; Mitten, 0+1; Murphy, 12; O'Connell, 4+3; Oates, 36; Omoyinmi, 13+1; Patmore, 6; Piper, 7+1; Porter, 35+3; Pullman, 2+9; Saunders, 36;

Sigere, 18+13; Smith, 42; Sodje, 28+1; Stadhart, 19+16; Watson, 9+13; Whitby, 0+1; Zorisich, 11.

MORECAMBE

Goals: *League (66):* Carlton 17 (1 pen), Curtis 8 (2 pens), Sugden 6, Thompson 6, Drummond 5 (1 pen), Bentley 4, Rogan 4, Howell 3, McFlynn 3, Rigoglioso 3 (2 pens), Walmsley 2, Collins 1, Lane 1, Murphy 1, Stringfellow 1, own goal 1.
FA Cup (2): Collins 1, Sugden 1.
LDV Vans Trophy (1): own goal 1.

League Appearances: Bentley, 36; Black, 0+4; Blackburn, 4+1; Carlton, 28+10; Collins, 10+2; Curtis, 18+5; Dodgson, 0+3; Drummond, 31; Dunbavin, 3; Garnett, 12; Howell, 24+6; Hunter, 8+7; Lane, 15+1; Mawson, 39+1; McFlynn, 16+3; McKearney, 26+8; Murphy, 22+5; Osborne, 6+2; Perkins, 39; Rigoglioso, 13; Rogan, 3+21; Stringfellow, 26+3; Sugden, 13+20; Swan, 14+5; Thompson, 29+6; Walmsley, 27.

NORTHWICH VICTORIA

Goals: *League (30):* Ward 6, Garvey 5 (1 pen), Wright 4, Devlin 3, Thompson 3, Allan 2, Foran 2, Nicholas 1, Norris 1, Potts 1, Ross 1, own goal 1.
FA Cup (2): Thompson 2.

League Appearances: Allan, 15+1; Barnard, 8; Bennett, 0+1; Black, 2+4; Blackburn, 25+3; Brazier, 34+2; Briscoe, 1+5; Brough, 3+2; Brown, 6; Butterworth, 1+4; Came, 13+2; Charnock, 21+6; Connett, 10; Devlin, 35; Foran, 36+3; Garvey, 30+5; Hankin, 1; McAuley, 0+1; McCoy, 0+2; McGuire, 9+3; Mitchell, 3; Murray, 3; Nicholas, 12; Norris, 10+17; Owen, 8+5; Potts, 10+1; Ralph, 9; Rioch, 7; Ross, 3; Royle, 30+3; Sawtell, 2; Teale, 5+1; Thompson, 18+9; Tolley, 5; Ward, 15+10; Willis, 4; Woods, 23; Woodyatt, 19+7; Wright, 20+2; Young, 6+3.

SCARBOROUGH

Goals: *League (51):* Quayle 14 (5 pens), Senior 6, Marcelle 4, Rose 4, Gilroy 3 (1 pen), Hackworth 3, Redmile 3, Kelly 2 (1 pen), Sestanovic 2, Blackman 1, Cryan 1, Downey G 1, Gill 1, Henry 1, Ketchanke 1, Nicholson 1, Price 1, Williams 1, own goal 1.
FA Cup (7): Kerr 3, Lyth 1, Quayle 1, Rose 1, Sestanovich 1.
LDV Vans Trophy (2): Kelly 1, Senior 1.
Trophy (1): Senior 1.

League Appearances: Bachelor, 0+1; Baker, 18+1; Blackman, 5+1; Brownrigg, 2+1; Burt, 1; Capper, 18+2; Cryan, 10; Davidson, 2; Donaldson, 2; Downey, G., 14+1; Dudgeon, 0+1; Gill, 28+7; Gilroy, 5+7; Graydon, 1+1; Hackworth, 11; Henry, 8; Hotte, 37+1; Kelly, 30; Kerr, 36+1; Ketchanke, 5; Lyth, 22+5; Marcelle, 26+3;

McSweeney, 0+3; Nesovic, 0+1; Nicholson, 13; O'Neill, 1; Price, 12+4; Quayle, 35+1; Raw, 7+4; Redmile, 22; Robinson, 2; Rose, 23+4; Senior, 7+33; Sestanovic, 7; Sherlock, 1+6; Sollitt, 7+2; Walker, 35; Whitman, 4+2; Williams, 6+6.

SHREWSBURY TOWN

Goals: *League (67):* Rodgers 13 (1 pen), Cramb 12 (1 pen), Darby 10, Lowe 9, Quinn 4, Tolley J 3, Banim 2, Lawrence 2, O'Connor 2, Ridler 2, Sedgemore 2 (1 pen), Street 2, Jagielka 1, Tinson 1, Watts 1, own goal 1.
FA Cup (5): Lowe 2, Quinn 2, Aiston 1.
LDV Vans Trophy (1): Lowe 1.
Trophy (6): Cramb 2 (1 pen), Aiston 1, Lowe 1, Moss 1, Street 1.
Play-Offs (2): Rodgers 2 (2 pens), Darby 1.
League Appearances: Aiston, 30+2; Banim, 7+9; Bell, 1+2; Challis, 7+1; Cramb, 24+10; Darby, 20+4; Drysdale, 1; Dunbavin, 3; Edwards, 7+9; Fitzpatrick, 3+4; Hart, 2; Howie, 37+1; Jagielka, 8+3; Lawrence, 6+1; Lowe, 20+14; Moss, 37+1; Murray, 4+2; O'Connor, 35+1; Potter, 4+1; Quinn, 8+8; Ridler, 39; Rioch, 18+2; Rodgers, 26+8; Sedgemore, 27+8; Stevens, 0+1; Street, 20+8; Tinson, 38+1; Tolley, J., 26+2; Watts, 4+4.

STEVENAGE BOROUGH

Goals: *League (58):* Elding 17, Maamria 3 (3 pens), Baptiste 4, Richards 4, Battersby 3 (1 pen), Holloway 3, Brennan 2, Brough 2, Wormull 2, Barnard 1, Boyd 1, Bunce 1, Carroll 1, Cook 1, Costello 1, Flack 1, Goodliffe 1, Gould 1, Rogers 1, Travis 1, own goal 1.
FA Cup (6): Maamria 3, Elding 2, Watson 1.
Trophy (3): Brady 1, Maamria 1, Richards 1.
League Appearances: Abbey, 6; Baptiste, 9+11; Barnard, 2+2; Battersby, 10+4; Boyd, 4+7; Brady, 13+7; Brennan, 13+4; Brough, 11; Bunce, 0+4; Camara, 0+1; Carroll, 15+5; Cook, 15+11; Costello, 8+4; Cracknell, 0+1; Elding, 33+3; Flack, 0+1; Flynn, 22; Goodliffe, 9; Gould, 26+1; Hodgson, 3+3; Holloway, 13+11; Laker, 35; Langston, 1+1; Maamria, 25; Marcelle, 0+3; Perez, 2; Pitcher, 4+1; Richards, 9+16; Rogers, 4; Scott, 2+4; Smith, 12+2; Travis, 20+2; Warner, 30+5; Watson, 26+1; Weatherstone, 2+2; Westhead, 9+1; Williams, 0+1; Wormull, 20+1.

TAMWORTH

Goals: *League (49):* Cooper 15 (3 pens), Barnes 4, Sylla 4, Follett 3, Rickards 3 (1 pen), Robinson 3, Whitman 3, Dryden 2, Setchell 2 (1 pen), Smith N 2, Watson 2, Blunt 1, Brooks 1, Ebdon 1, Powell 1, Scully 1, own goal 1.

FA Cup (5): Fisher 2, Jordan 2, Setchell 1 (pen).
Trophy (6): Barnes 2, Blunt 1, Ebdon 1, Quailey 1, Warner 1.
League Appearances: Ayres, 23; Baptiste, 4; Barnard, 3+3; Barnes, 17+1; Blunt, 26+1; Brooks, 1; Brush, 10; Colkin, 9; Collins, 4+2; Cooper, 35+3; Darby, 13+13; Dryden, 22; Ebdon, 13+1; Fisher, 14+1; Follett, 27+5; Fox, 0+1; Goodwin, 2+2; Hannie, 0+2; Henderson, 3; Johnson, 6+5; Jordan, 17+2; Langmead, 2; Lindley, 6; McGregor, 4+3; Noon, 5+2; One, 4; Powell, 5; Price, 8; Quailey, 14+3; Rickards, 13+6; Robinson, 24+1; Rodwell, 6; Scott, 4; Scully, 1; Setchell, 17; Smith, A., 3+1; Smith, N., 6+5; Stanford, 6+1; Sylla, 12+13; Taylor, 5+1; Trainer, 5+1; Turner, 3+5; Warner, 34+5; Watson, 6+1; Whitehead, 15; Whitman, 5+2; Wilson, 0+1.

TELFORD UNITED

Goals: *League (49):* Naylor 11, Mills 9, Murphy 7, Grant 6, Ricketts 4, Blackwood 3, Green 3, Hulbert 1, Lavery 1, Moore P 1, Stanley 1, Whitehead 1, Williams 1.
FA Cup (13): Moore 4 (1 pen), Murphy 3, Mills 2, Blackwood 1, Green 1 (pen), Lavery 1, Ricketts 1.
LDV Vans Trophy (1): Mills 1.
Trophy (12): Grant 4, Naylor 3, Blackwood 2, Clarke 1, Green 1, Ricketts 1.
League Appearances: Blackwood, 25+11; Challis, 33; Clarke, 29+5; Daniels, 0+1; Eustace, 6; Grant, 20+15; Green, 16+4; Howarth, 26; Hulbert, 21+1; Lavery, 23+8; MacKenzie, 39; Mills, 26; Moore, C., 0+1; Moore, P., 18+12; Murphy, 15+9; Naylor, 16+5; Ricketts, 39+2; Rowe, 2+6; Rushbury, 8+2; Simpson, 28+3; Stanley, 11+1; Taylor, 3; Uddin, 6; Whitehead, 36+1; Wilkinson, 8; Williams, 8+5.

WOKING

Goals: *League (65):* Foyewa 10, Ferguson 9, Selley 8 (5 pens), Nade 6, Louis 5 (1 pen), Sharpling 5, Haule 4, Cornwall 3, Smith 3 (1 pen), Canham 2, Harris 2, Sharp 2, Boardman 1, Johnson 1, Murray 1, Noble 1, own goals 2.
FA Cup (6): Ferguson 2, Selley 2 (1 pen), Haule 1, Sharpling 1.
League Appearances: Ajoge, 7+1; Allum, 0+1; Basoo, 3; Bayes, 35; Bevan, 4; Boardman, 37; Campbell, 3+1; Canham, 33+4; Cockerill, 20+3; Cornwall, 5+2; Ferguson, 32+7; Foyewa, 20+14; Giles, 6; Harlisha, 0+1; Harris, 7; Haule, 5+19; Johnson, 9+8; Louis, 8; MacDonald, 32; McNab, 0+1; Murray, 13; Nade, 34+3; Narada, 8; Noble, 5; Oliver, 1+1; Parsons, 0+3; Pitcher, 3; Selley, 30; Sharp, 23+1; Sharpling, 11+11; Simpemba, 5; Smith, 30+4; Townsend, 33+5.

NATIONWIDE CONFERENCE PLAY-OFFS 2003–2004

SEMI-FINALS FIRST LEG

Thursday, 29 April 2004
Aldershot T (1) 1 *(D'Sane 45 (pen))*
Hereford U (1) 1 *(Brown 7)*   6379
Aldershot T: Bull; Downer (McLean 80), Sterling, Antwi (Chewins 76), Warburton, Giles, Gosling, Challinor, Sills, D'Sane (Nutter 90), Charles.
Hereford U: Baker; Green, Travis, James, Tretton, Smith, Pitman, Brown, Carey-Bertram (Beesley 68), Rose, Purdie (Betts 90).

Barnet (1) 2 *(Strevens 13 (pen), Clist 90)*
Shrewsbury T (1) 1 *(Rodgers 43 (pen))*   4171
Barnet: Gore; Hendon, King, Lopez (Clist 65), Plummer, Maddix, Strevens, Gamble, Grazioli, Hatch, Yakubu.
Shrewsbury T: Howie; Moss, Challis (Lawrence 76), O'Connor, Tinson (Sedgemore 46), Ridler, Lowe, Tolley, Rodgers (Quinn 85), Darby, Aiston.

SEMI-FINAL SECOND LEG

Monday, 3 May 2004
Hereford U (0) 0
Aldershot T (0) 0   7044
Hereford U: Baker; Green, Travis (Betts 84), Smith, Tretton*, James, Pitman, Rose, Guinan (Beesley 73), Brown, Williams (Cozic 109).
Aldershot T: Bull; Downer (Chewins 60), Charles (D'Sane 70), Giles, Warburton, Sterling, Gosling, Antwi, Sills, McLean (Nutter 84), Challinor.
aet; Aldershot T won 4-2 on penalties:- D'Sane (hit bar), Brown (saved), Gosling (scored), Beesley (saved), Giles (scored), James (scored), Sills (scored), Smith (scored), Antwi (scored).

ATTENDANCES BY CLUB 2003–2004

Shrewsbury T (1) 1 *(Rodgers 44 (pen))*
Barnet (0) 0   7012
Shrewsbury T: Howie; Moss, Challis, O'Connor (Edwards 46), Tinson, Ridler, Lowe, Tolley, Rodgers, Darby (Cramb 105), Aiston (Sedgemore 113).
Barnet: Gore; Hendon, King, Lopez (Clist 55), Plummer, Maddix (Redmile 59), Strevens, Gamble, Grazioli, Hatch, Yakubu.
aet; Shrewsbury T won 5-3 on penalties:- Sedgemore (scored), Strevens (scored), Tolley (scored), Grazioli (scored), Rodgers (scored), Yakubu (scored), Cramb (scored), Clist (saved), Moss (scored).

CONFERENCE FINAL (AT BRITANNIA STADIUM)

Sunday, 16 May 2004
Shrewsbury T (1) 1 *(Darby 43)*
Aldershot T (1) 1 *(McLean 35)*   19,216
Shrewsbury T: Howie; Sedgemore, Challis, O'Connor (Street), Tinson (Lawrence), Ridler, Lowe, Tolley, Rodgers, Darby (Cramb), Aiston.
Aldershot T: Bull; Downer (Hooper), Sterling, Antwi, Warburton, Giles, Gosling, Challinor, McLean (Sills), D'Sane (Charles), Miller.
aet; Shrewsbury T won 3-0 on penalties:- Rodgers (missed), Sills (saved), Tolley (scored), Giles (saved), Sedgemore (scored), Gosling (saved), Challis (scored).
Referee: K. Stroud (Bournemouth).

	Aggregate 2003–04	Average 2003–04	Highest Attendance 2002–03
Shrewsbury Town	84,150	4,007	6,738 v Telford United
Hereford United	77,784	3,704	7,240 v Chester City
Exeter City	76,957	3,665	8,256 v Accrington Stanley
Aldershot Town	69,164	3,294	4,637 v Woking
Chester City	64,362	3,065	5,987 v Scarborough
Woking	48,746	2,321	4,158 v Aldershot Town
Telford United	43,634	2,078	4,337 v Shrewsbury Town
Stevenage Borough	42,044	2,002	3,019 v Barnet
Barnet	38,436	1,830	2,988 v Leigh RMI
Accrington Stanley	37,731	1,797	3,143 v Shrewsbury Town
Morecambe	37,393	1,781	3,084 v Accrington Stanley
Burton Albion	35,326	1,682	3,203 v Shrewsbury Town
Halifax Town	31,617	1,506	2,160 v Morecambe
Dagenham & Redbridge	30,302	1,443	1,948 v Stevenage Borough
Scarborough	28,028	1,335	2,503 v Woking
Tamworth	28,036	1,335	2,535 v Burton Albion
Gravesend & Northfleet	24,746	1,178	1,725 v Margate
Farnborough Town	19,847	945	3,233 v Aldershot Town
Forest Green Rovers	18,949	902	1,576 v Hereford United
Northwich Victoria	17,875	851	3,268 v Shrewsbury Town
Margate	11,905	567	1,030 v Gravesend & N
Leigh RMI	11,881	566	2,002 v Chester City

DR MARTENS LEAGUE 2003–2004

Premier Division

			Home					Away					Total					
	P	W	D	L	F	A	W	D	L	F	A	W	D	L	F	A	Gd	Pts
1 Crawley Town	42	13	4	4	45	23	12	5	4	32	20	25	9	8	77	43	34	84
2 Weymouth	42	10	6	5	37	18	10	6	5	39	29	20	12	10	76	47	29	72
3 Stafford Rangers	42	12	3	6	34	21	7	8	6	21	22	19	11	12	55	43	12	68
4 Nuneaton Borough	42	11	6	4	34	19	6	9	6	31	30	17	15	10	65	49	16	66
5 Worcester City	42	12	3	6	42	19	6	9	6	29	31	18	9	15	71	50	21	63
6 Hinckley United	42	7	8	6	28	21	8	6	7	27	25	15	14	13	55	46	9	59
7 Newport County	42	6	9	6	23	30	9	5	7	29	20	15	14	13	52	50	2	59
8 Cambridge City	42	6	8	7	28	32	8	7	6	26	21	14	15	13	54	53	1	57
9 Welling United	42	10	2	9	32	29	6	6	9	24	29	16	8	18	56	58	-2	56
10 Weston Super Mare	42	10	5	6	31	24	4	8	9	21	28	14	13	15	52	52	0	55
11 Eastbourne Bor	42	7	9	5	25	23	7	4	10	23	33	14	13	15	48	56	-8	55
12 Havant & W	42	8	5	8	35	38	7	5	9	24	32	15	10	17	59	70	-11	55
13 Moor Green	42	7	6	8	21	24	7	6	8	21	30	14	12	16	42	54	-12	54
14 Merthyr Tydfil	42	7	7	7	28	31	6	7	8	32	35	13	14	15	60	66	-6	53
15 Tiverton Town	42	7	11	3	35	24	5	4	12	28	40	12	15	15	63	64	-1	51
16 Bath City	42	10	4	7	27	20	3	8	10	22	37	13	12	17	49	57	-8	51
17 Dorchester Town	42	9	5	7	30	23	5	4	12	26	46	14	9	19	56	69	-13	51
18 Chelmsford City	42	5	9	7	22	27	6	7	8	24	26	11	16	15	46	53	-7	49
19 Dover Athletic	42	9	7	5	33	26	3	6	12	17	33	12	13	17	50	59	-9	49
20 Hednesford Town	42	7	7	7	35	28	5	5	11	21	41	12	12	18	56	69	-13	48
21 Chippenham Town	42	4	9	8	23	31	6	8	7	28	32	10	17	15	51	63	-12	47
22 Grantham Town	42	7	6	8	26	33	3	9	9	19	34	10	15	17	45	67	-22	45

LEADING GOALSCORERS 2003–04

Premier Division

Allan Tait (Crawley Town)	22
20 scored for Folkestone Invicta	
Daniel Bloomfield (Cambridge City)	20
Steve Claridge (Weymouth)	20
Scott Partridge (Bath City)	20
Lee Phillips (Weymouth)	20
Daniel Davidson (Stafford Rangers)	19
Chukkie Eribenne (Havant & Waterlooville)	19
Charlie MacDonald (Crawley Town)	19
Scott Ramsay (Eastbourne Borough)	18
Cortez Belle (Merthyr Tydfil)	17
Darren Edwards (Tiverton Town)	17
13 scored for Mangotsfield United	
Charles Griffin (Chippenham Town)	17
Gerald Murphy (Nuneaton Borough)	17
Craig Wilkins (Dover Athletic)	17
Paul Booth (Welling United)	16
Mark Danks (Hednesford Town)	16
Leon Kelly (Worcester City)	16
Neil Davis (Moor Green)	13
James Mudge (Tiverton Town)	13
James Constable (Chippenham Town)	12
Kevin Wilkin (Nuneaton Borough)	12

ATTENDANCES

Premier Division

Premier Average   673
Division Highest: 4522   Crawley Town v Weymouth (6/3/2004)

DR MARTEN'S LEAGUE – PREMIER DIVISION RESULTS 2003–2004

	Bath City	Cambridge City	Chelmsford City	Chippenham Town	Crawley Town	Dorchester Town	Dover Athletic	Eastbourne Borough	Grantham Town	Havant & Waterlooville	Hednesford Town	Hinckley United	Merthyr Tydfil	Moor Green	Newport County	Nuneaton Borough	Stafford Rangers	Tiverton Town	Welling United	Weston super Mare	Weymouth	Worcester City
Bath City	—	1-2	0-1	0-3	0-0	2-0	1-0	1-1	1-1	2-0	2-0	0-2	0-2	0-1	0-2	1-3	1-0	2-1	2-0	3-1	0-2	1-1
Cambridge City	0-0	—	2-0	2-2	2-5	0-4	2-1	2-3	1-1	2-3	2-0	2-2	2-2	1-1	0-2	1-0	1-0	6-4	0-3	1-1	1-0	0-0
Chelmsford City	0-0	1-0	—	1-3	0-4	3-0	1-2	0-1	1-0	2-0	2-0	0-3	3-1	1-1	1-1	1-1	2-0	3-3	0-1	0-0	1-3	2-2
Chippenham Town	1-1	1-3	0-0	—	0-1	1-6	2-3	0-2	2-2	3-0	2-0	2-1	3-3	4-0	2-1	0-3	2-3	3-1	0-2	1-1	1-3	1-2
Crawley Town	2-0	3-2	4-1	3-2	—	3-4	0-2	2-0	4-2	3-1	6-1	1-1	1-0	2-1	1-0	0-0	0-1	1-0	2-0	2-0	2-1	4-0
Dorchester Town	1-0	4-1	1-1	3-1	2-0	—	0-2	1-0	3-1	3-4	3-1	0-3	0-1	0-1	1-2	0-2	0-0	2-1	2-1	0-2	2-3	3-0
Dover Athletic	3-3	1-1	2-2	0-2	1-2	2-0	—	1-0	2-2	0-2	0-2	1-1	1-0	0-1	2-1	0-5	1-0	2-1	1-1	2-0	2-3	2-1
Eastbourne Borough	1-1	2-1	1-1	2-4	1-0	1-0	1-0	—	1-0	2-0	2-2	0-2	0-1	0-1	0-1	0-5	0-2	2-1	2-0	1-0	2-3	1-3
Grantham Town	1-1	2-3	1-3	0-2	1-3	1-0	4-0	4-1	—	2-2	2-2	2-0	4-2	0-2	2-2	0-5	0-2	3-2	2-2	1-0	2-0	4-3
Havant & Waterlooville	4-0	0-2	1-2	4-1	0-0	2-4	0-1	1-0	1-0	—	1-0	2-0	0-4	4-4	5-1	1-2	0-0	3-1	1-0	0-1	3-2	0-5
Hednesford Town	1-2	2-0	2-0	1-0	4-0	1-0	2-4	1-0	1-0	2-0	—	1-1	0-0	1-2	0-3	0-2	3-1	2-0	0-2	2-2	0-0	3-1
Hinckley United	0-3	1-3	1-3	3-2	2-1	1-3	0-1	0-1	2-1	0-2	2-1	—	1-2	0-0	1-1	0-1	0-0	2-1	2-0	0-1	0-2	0-2
Merthyr Tydfil	2-1	1-2	1-0	4-1	1-0	2-4	0-1	1-0	4-0	1-0	4-0	0-3	—	1-2	2-1	2-2	1-1	2-1	2-1	1-2	0-2	0-2
Moor Green	2-1	0-0	1-3	3-1	2-1	1-0	1-0	2-1	3-1	1-0	2-1	0-0	1-1	—	2-0	1-0	0-0	3-1	2-0	1-0	0-2	0-2
Newport County	2-0	1-0	1-3	2-2	1-2	2-0	3-0	1-0	2-0	1-2	2-1	0-2	3-0	2-0	—	1-2	0-3	2-1	1-4	2-1	0-1	1-4
Nuneaton Borough	1-1	1-1	1-1	0-1	0-0	2-1	2-1	2-1	1-0	0-0	2-1	1-1	0-0	0-1	3-1	—	0-3	1-2	2-2	2-1	2-2	2-1
Stafford Rangers	2-1	1-1	2-1	3-0	3-0	3-0	2-3	3-0	0-0	2-0	3-0	2-0	1-1	2-1	1-0	0-3	—	1-2	3-2	1-1	2-2	2-0
Tiverton Town	1-0	3-3	3-3	1-1	0-1	2-3	1-1	1-1	3-2	2-0	3-0	2-0	3-1	2-1	1-2	2-1	1-2	—	3-2	2-2	2-0	1-1
Welling United	2-1	0-1	0-1	1-3	6-1	6-1	1-1	1-0	5-1	0-1	3-0	2-0	3-2	2-3	0-2	3-0	0-2	4-0	—	2-1	1-2	0-0
Weston super Mare	1-0	1-0	1-0	1-2	0-1	0-1	3-0	1-0	1-0	0-1	3-0	2-2	2-3	2-0	2-1	1-1	1-1	1-3	1-2	—	0-0	1-2
Weymouth	3-3	2-2	2-0	0-1	0-1	3-0	5-1	0-0	1-1	4-1	2-0	2-0	3-0	3-0	1-1	4-0	0-1	1-2	3-1	3-0	—	3-1
Worcester City	7-0	1-0	2-2	0-0	4-0	3-0	2-1	1-3	4-3	0-5	3-1	0-2	0-2	0-2	0-2	1-1	0-0	1-2	1-1	2-2	2-2	—

318

DR MARTENS LEAGUE CUP 2003–04

FIRST ROUND
Banbury 1, Kings Lynn 1
(Kings Lynn won 3-2 on penalties).
Bashley 1, Fleet Town 2
Erith & Belvedere 3, Ashford Town 1
Gloucester City 1, Solihull Borough 4
Gresley Rovers 4, Shepshed Dynamo 1
Hastings United 2, Folkestone Invicta 6
Mangotsfield United 1,
    Cinderford Town 2
Rugby United 2, Ilkeston Town 1
Sittingbourne 1, Chatham Town 2
Stamford 1, Corby Town 1
Stourport Swifts 1, Redditch United 1
(Stourport Swifts won 4-2 on penalties).
Sutton Coldfield Town 3,
    Evesham United 2
Tonbridge Angels 0, Fisher Athletic 3
Yate Town 0, Clevedon Town 3
Dartford 0, Burgess Hill Town 3
Eastleigh 3, Burnham 1
Swindon Supermarine 0,
    Taunton Town 3
Newport (IW) 3, Salisbury City 2
Bromsgrove Rovers 2,
    Halesowen Town 1
Rothwell Town 0, Histon 1
Team Bath 2, Cirencester Town 3

SECOND ROUND
Bedworth United 4, Solihull Borough 2
Cambridge City 4, Stamford 1
Cirencester Town 3, Clevedon Town 0
Erith & Belvedere 0, Fleet Town 2
Folkestone Invicta 3, Fisher Athletic 2
Gresley Rovers 3, Stourport Swifts 2
Kings Lynn 1, Histon 2
Sutton Coldfield Town 2,
    Rugby United 1
Weymouth 3, Taunton Town 1
Eastleigh 2, Newport (IW) 1
Chatham Town 1, Burgess Hill Town 0
Cinderford Town 3,
    Bromsgrove Rovers 3
Replay: Bromsgrove Rovers 3,
    Cinderford Town 1

THIRD ROUND
Worcester City 1,
    Sutton Coldfield Town 1
(Worcester City won 5-4 on penalties).

Bath City 3, Cirencester Town 0
Dover Athletic 4, Chatham Town 1
Dorchester Town 2,
    Weston-Super-Mare 0
Granthan Town 0, Cambridge City 2
Hednesford Town 3,
    Bedworth United 3
(Hednesford Town won 4-2 on penalties).
Folkestone Invicta 4, Chelmsford City 3
Hinckley United 3, Histon 0
Moor Green 5, Stafford Rangers 0
Weymouth 4, Merthyr Tydfil 2
Nuneaton Borough 1, Gresley Rovers 0
Havant & Waterlooville 2,
    Crawley Town 3
Eastleigh 4, Fleet Town 1
Newport County 0,
    Chippenham Town 4
Welling United 2,
    Eastbourne Borough 1
(After match abandoned 0-0: fog).
Tiverton Town 3, Bromsgrove Rovers 0

FOURTH ROUND
Crawley Town 1, Welling United 0
Hinckley United 0, Hednesford Town 1
Tiverton Town 1, Chippenham Town 4
Weymouth 2, Bath City 0
Cambridge City 2, Nuneaton Borough 1
Dorchester Town 1, Eastleigh 2
Dover Athletic 2, Folkestone Invicta 0
Worcester City 0, Moor Green 2

FIFTH ROUND
Eastleigh 5, Weymouth 2
Cambridge City 1, Hednesford Town 0
Crawley Town 1, Dover Athletic 0
Moor Green 3, Chippenham Town 1

SEMI-FINALS
Crawley Town 2, Eastleigh 0
Moor Green 3, Cambridge City 0

FINAL FIRST LEG
Moor Green 1, Crawley Town 2

FINAL SECOND LEG
Crawley Town 2, Moor Green 0

UNIBOND LEAGUE 2003–2004

Premier Division		Home					Away					Total					
	P	W	D	L	F	A	W	D	L	F	A	W	D	L	F	A	Gd	Pts
1 Hucknall Town	44	15	5	2	38	14	14	3	5	45	24	29	8	7	83	38	45	95
2 Droylsden	44	15	4	3	51	29	11	4	7	45	35	26	8	10	96	64	32	86
3 Barrow	44	14	4	4	41	20	8	10	4	41	32	22	14	8	82	52	30	80
4 Alfreton Town	44	14	5	3	45	18	9	4	9	28	25	23	9	12	73	43	30	78
5 Harrogate Town	44	15	2	5	44	26	9	3	10	35	37	24	5	15	79	63	16	77
6 Southport	44	10	7	5	36	25	10	3	9	35	27	20	10	14	71	52	19	70
7 Worksop Town	44	10	6	6	34	22	9	7	6	35	28	19	13	12	69	50	19	70
8 Lancaster City	44	12	4	6	40	25	8	5	9	22	24	20	9	15	62	49	13	69
9 Vauxhall Motors	44	12	5	4	44	32	7	5	10	34	43	19	10	15	78	75	3	67
10 Gainsborough Trinity	44	12	5	5	46	25	5	8	9	24	27	17	13	14	70	52	18	64
11 Stalybridge Celtic	44	8	6	8	35	33	10	4	8	37	33	18	10	16	72	66	6	64
12 Altrincham	44	9	8	5	36	24	7	7	8	30	27	16	15	13	66	51	15	63
13 Runcorn FC Halton	44	5	9	8	32	32	11	4	7	35	31	16	13	15	67	63	4	61
14 Ashton United	44	7	5	10	34	44	10	3	9	25	35	17	8	19	59	79	–20	59
15 Whitby Town	44	9	3	10	24	34	5	8	9	31	36	14	11	19	55	70	–15	53
16 Marine	44	8	5	9	32	31	5	7	10	30	43	13	12	19	62	74	–12	51
17 Bradford Park Av	44	2	9	11	23	32	10	5	7	25	30	12	14	18	48	62	–14	50
18 Spennymoor United	44	8	2	12	30	51	6	4	12	25	42	14	6	24	55	93	–38	48
19 Burscough	44	6	8	8	27	30	4	7	11	20	37	10	15	19	47	67	–20	45
20 Radcliffe Borough	44	9	1	12	39	46	3	5	14	35	53	12	6	26	74	99	–25	42
21 Blyth Spartans	44	5	7	10	30	40	5	3	14	24	34	10	10	24	54	74	–20	40
22 Frickley Athletic	44	8	4	10	29	32	3	16	22	51	11	7	26	51	83	–32	40	
23 Wakefield & Emley	44	4	2	16	18	45	4	4	14	27	54	8	6	30	45	99	–54	30

LEADING GOALSCORERS

(In order of League Goals)

Premier Division

	Lge	Cup	Total
Fearns (Vauxhall Motors)	35	2	37
Hughes (Lancaster City)	22	9	31
Cumiskey (Vauxhall Motors)	22	8	30
Ricketts (Hucknall Town)	22	5	27
Byrne (Droylsden)	21	6	27
Morris (Frickley Athletic)	18	6	24
Hayward (Stalybridge Celtic)	20	3	23
Bacon (Hucknall Town)	19	4	23
Banim (Radcliffe Borough)	18	4	22
(now Shrewsbury T)			
Godber (Alfreton Town)	18	4	22
Rendell (Runcorn FC Halton)	11	11	22

ATTENDANCES

Premier Division
Highest Average Attendance: 1159 Barrow
Highest Attendances: 1750 Barrow v Lancaster City
                        1451 Barrow v Alfreton Town
                        1416 Barrow v Hucknall Town

UNIBOND LEAGUE – PREMIER DIVISION RESULTS 2003–2004

	Alfreton Town	Altrincham	Ashton United	Barrow	Blyth Spartans	Bradford Park Avenue	Burscough	Droylsden	Frickley Athletic	Gainsborough Trinity	Harrogate Town	Hucknall Town	Lancaster City	Marine	Radcliffe Borough	Runcorn FC Halton	Southport	Spennymoor United	Stalybridge Celtic	Vauxhall Motors	Wakefield & Emley	Whitby Town	Worksop Town
Alfreton Town	—	0-0	1-1	1-0	1-0	0-1	4-1	2-1	0-3	2-4	1-0	3-3	0-1	0-1	1-0	2-2	1-0	1-0	2-2	1-0	2-0	0-3	2-1
Altrincham	0-1	—	0-2	2-1	1-2	1-0	1-1	1-1	1-4	2-3	3-1	2-3	3-1	3-3	1-0	0-2	1-1	1-1	1-3	0-1	1-1	4-0	2-1
Ashton United	1-1	1-3	—	2-0	2-2	3-0	0-2	2-1	1-2	3-0	0-0	1-6	0-2	4-3	3-3	4-2	2-1	2-1	0-2	0-1	2-3	1-3	0-3
Barrow	1-2	1-2	3-0	—	2-0	4-0	0-0	1-1	3-1	0-1	3-4	1-2	4-3	1-1	3-3	4-2	2-1	2-1	3-0	2-4	2-5	1-3	0-2
Blyth Spartans	1-0	2-0	2-0	0-2	—	0-0	2-0	1-3	3-1	1-0	2-0	1-2	0-2	1-1	1-1	1-3	1-0	4-0	1-0	0-1	1-2	1-0	3-3
Bradford Park Avenue	0-1	2-2	0-1	4-0	0-0	—	1-1	2-0	0-1	3-0	3-3	0-1	1-0	0-0	1-3	0-1	2-1	2-4	2-0	1-0	2-1	1-2	1-1
Burscough	4-1	1-2	0-0	0-1	1-5	1-0	—	2-0	2-0	3-1	4-4	1-0	1-0	4-0	1-0	1-0	0-2	3-2	1-0	0-1	2-2	1-1	0-0
Droylsden	2-1	1-4	2-1	1-1	1-2	1-3	0-3	—	1-0	0-3	4-4	1-2	2-3	0-1	1-1	2-1	3-2	1-3	0-2	0-2	0-1	2-1	2-2
Frickley Athletic	0-3	1-2	3-1	1-3	1-3	2-1	4-0	4-0	—	2-0	3-0	0-0	4-0	2-0	2-0	6-2	0-2	4-2	1-1	0-1	0-1	1-3	1-1
Gainsborough Trinity	2-4	2-3	1-2	3-0	0-1	3-3	4-1	0-1	3-0	—	2-0	0-0	4-3	2-1	6-2	1-0	3-2	3-1	2-1	1-0	3-0	2-0	2-1
Harrogate Town	1-0	3-0	1-0	0-1	1-0	3-3	1-0	2-4	0-0	2-0	—	2-0	0-1	3-0	0-2	1-2	3-1	3-1	4-3	3-2	3-0	1-0	2-1
Hucknall Town	3-3	2-1	0-3	2-1	1-1	0-1	1-0	1-1	0-3	2-1	1-4	—	3-0	1-1	4-2	0-1	1-3	1-3	3-0	1-1	1-3	1-0	0-2
Lancaster City	0-1	1-1	0-2	3-1	0-2	1-0	0-3	3-1	0-2	1-2	0-1	3-0	—	3-0	0-1	1-2	4-0	6-0	2-0	2-1	2-0	0-1	3-0
Marine	0-1	0-1	1-0	1-1	1-3	0-0	4-0	1-3	2-0	1-4	1-1	1-2	3-1	—	3-1	2-2	1-1	1-2	4-1	3-1	1-2	1-2	0-2
Radcliffe Borough	1-0	0-1	1-1	3-3	1-1	1-3	1-0	3-6	5-4	6-2	4-2	1-1	4-2	3-2	—	3-2	1-3	1-3	0-2	3-1	0-5	4-1	4-1
Runcorn FC Halton	2-2	1-3	4-2	4-2	2-1	0-1	3-3	1-3	1-2	0-1	0-1	0-1	1-2	3-1	1-1	—	1-1	6-0	3-5	0-5	1-0	1-0	2-3
Southport	1-0	0-1	2-1	2-1	1-4	0-3	1-0	3-2	2-0	1-1	1-3	1-1	4-0	1-1	1-1	1-1	—	2-2	2-1	0-2	0-5	1-0	1-0
Spennymoor United	3-0	2-2	1-0	2-0	0-2	0-4	1-1	3-2	3-2	3-1	3-1	1-2	6-0	1-3	1-2	2-3	2-3	—	4-2	1-0	1-0	4-0	1-1
Stalybridge Celtic	2-0	1-0	3-3	0-2	0-1	0-0	1-2	0-0	1-2	0-2	1-0	4-3	1-3	0-2	3-2	3-0	3-0	1-3	—	1-1	1-3	2-1	0-3
Vauxhall Motors	3-1	5-1	6-2	0-1	3-6	6-2	3-1	0-2	0-2	0-2	2-0	3-2	0-0	4-3	0-0	3-2	3-2	3-1	2-1	—	3-4	0-1	4-3
Wakefield & Emley	2-1	1-1	2-3	1-2	1-0	1-2	1-2	3-2	3-1	3-1	3-0	3-1	0-1	3-0	5-0	4-1	5-3	3-3	1-0	1-0	—	2-1	4-0
Whitby Town	3-0	4-0	1-3	0-3	1-1	2-3	0-2	2-0	3-1	2-2	1-0	2-0	1-0	4-3	0-5	1-1	2-0	1-3	0-3	2-1	0-3	—	1-1
Worksop Town	0-0	0-0	3-0	2-4	1-0	1-2	1-3	1-3	3-0	0-0	0-3	0-3	1-2	1-2	4-1	0-1	1-0	4-0	2-1	4-3	4-0	1-1	—

UNIBOND LEAGUE CHALLENGE CUP 2003–04

FIRST ROUND
Ashton United 1, Leek Town 1
aet; Ashton United won 6-5 on penalties.
Bamber Bridge 1, Lancaster City 2
Bishop Auckland 2, Blyth Spartans 0
Burscough 5, Colwyn Bay 0
Guiseley 4, Wakefield & Emley 1
Hyde United 0, Altrincham 1
Kidsgrove Athletic 0, Matlock Town 2
Lincoln United 2, Gainsborough Trinity 1
Marine 2, Runcorn FC Halton 1
Ossett Town 3, Farsley Celtic 1
Rossendale United 4, Kendal Town 1
Stocksbridge Park Steels 1, Frickley Athletic 3
Workington 2, Gateshead 1

SECOND ROUND
Ashton United 1, Southport 3
Bradford Park Avenue 1, Bishop Auckland 6
Droylsden 4, Chorley 1
Frickley Athletic 4, Hucknall Town 5
Guiseley 2, Harrogate Town 1
Lancaster City 1, Radcliffe Borough 2
Lincoln United 2, Alfreton Town 1
Marine 1, Burscough 2
Matlock Town 1, Belper Town 0
Spennymoor United 4, Ossett Town 2
Stalybridge Celtic 1, Prescot Cables 2
Vauxhall Motors 3, Rossendale United 0
Whitby Town 2, Bridlington Town 1
Witton Albion 4, Barrow 1
Workington 0, Altrincham 0
aet; Altrincham won 3-1 on penalties.
Worksop Town 3, North Ferriby United 4

THIRD ROUND
Altrincham 1, Vauxhall Motors 2
Bishop Auckland 4, Prescot Cables 0
Burscough 4, Spennymoor United 2
Hucknall Town 2, Lincoln United 1
Matlock Town 2, North Ferriby United 1
Southport 2, Guiseley 3
Whitby Town 6, Radcliffe Borough 2
Witton Albion 0, Droylsden 1

FOURTH ROUND
Bishop Auckland 2, Burscough 1 *aet*
Matlock Town 1, Guiseley 0
Vauxhall Motors 0, Hucknall Town 1
Whitby Town 1, Droylsden 2

SEMI-FINALS
Droylsden 3, Bishop Auckland 2
Hucknall Town 2, Matlock Town 1

FINAL
Droylsden 2, 2, Hucknall Town 0, 1

RYMAN LEAGUE 2003–2004

		Home					Away					Total						
		P	W	D	L	F	A	W	D	L	F	A	W	D	L	F	A	Gd	Pts
1	Canvey Island	46	17	4	2	62	23	15	4	4	44	19	32	8	6	106	42	64	104
2	Sutton United	46	11	6	6	46	30	14	4	5	48	26	25	10	11	94	56	38	85
3	Thurrock	46	12	5	6	43	18	12	6	5	44	27	24	11	11	87	45	42	83
4	Hendon	46	11	6	6	33	24	14	2	7	35	23	25	8	13	68	47	21	83
5	Hornchurch*	46	16	3	4	34	12	8	8	7	29	23	24	11	11	63	35	28	82
6	Grays Athletic	46	13	10	0	51	16	9	5	9	31	23	22	15	9	82	39	43	81
7	Carshalton Athletic	46	12	5	6	36	31	12	4	7	30	24	24	9	13	66	55	11	81
8	Hayes	46	11	8	4	29	15	10	3	10	27	31	21	11	14	56	46	10	74
9	Kettering Town	46	10	6	7	34	34	10	5	8	29	29	20	11	15	63	63	0	71
10	Bognor Regis Town	46	13	3	7	45	25	7	7	9	24	42	20	10	16	69	67	2	70
11	Bishop's Stortford	46	11	6	6	45	26	9	3	11	33	35	20	9	17	78	61	17	69
12	Maidenhead United	46	10	4	9	31	36	8	5	10	29	32	18	9	19	60	68	-8	63
13	Ford United	46	11	6	6	42	26	5	8	10	27	37	16	14	16	69	63	6	62
14	Basingstoke Town	46	7	3	13	24	37	10	6	7	34	27	17	9	20	58	64	-6	60
15	Bedford Town	46	11	3	9	41	34	3	10	10	21	29	14	13	19	62	63	-1	55
16	Heybridge Swifts	46	7	5	11	31	37	7	6	10	26	41	14	11	21	57	78	-21	53
17	Harrow Borough	46	5	8	10	21	28	7	6	10	26	35	12	14	20	47	63	-16	50
18	Kingstonian	46	5	10	8	21	22	7	3	13	19	34	12	13	21	40	56	-16	49
19	St Albans City	46	5	2	16	24	36	7	10	6	31	47	12	12	22	55	83	-28	48
20	Hitchin Town	46	6	6	11	29	42	7	2	14	26	47	13	8	25	55	89	-34	47
21	Northwood	46	6	4	13	34	45	6	5	12	31	50	12	9	25	65	95	-30	45
22	Billericay Town	46	6	5	12	20	31	5	6	12	31	35	11	11	24	51	66	-15	44
23	Braintree Town	46	3	4	16	19	48	7	5	11	22	40	10	9	27	41	88	-47	39
24	Aylesbury United	46	3	6	14	17	45	2	8	13	24	56	5	14	27	41	101	-60	29

*1 point deducted for fielding an ineligible player.

LEADING GOALSCORERS

(In order of League Goals)

Premier Division

			Lge	BC
42	Lee Boylan	Canvey Island	42	
32	Tresor Kandol	Thurrock	27	5
30	Freddie Eastwood	Grays Athletic	29	1
27	Drew Roberts	Bedford Town	24	
	Includes 3 play-off goals			
26	Cliff Akurang	Thurrock	25	1
22	Danny Hockton	Billericay Town	22	
22	Craig McAllister	Basingstoke Town	21	
	Includes 1 play-off goal			
21	Eugene Ofori	Hendon	19	2
20	Nick Bailey	Sutton United	19	1

Lge, League; BC, Bryco Cup.

ATTENDANCES

Premier Division

Highest Attendances

1260	Kettering Town v Bedford Town (12/4/2004)
1213	Sutton United v Carshalton Athletic (27/12/2003)
1174	Bedford Town v Kettering Town (26/12/2003)

RYMAN LEAGUE – PREMIER DIVISION RESULTS 2003–2004

	Aylesbury United	Basingstoke Town	Bedford Town	Billericay Town	Bishop's Stortford	Bognor Regis Town	Braintree Town	Canvey Island	Carshalton Athletic	Ford United	Grays Athletic	Harrow Borough	Hayes	Hendon	Heybridge Swifts	Hitchin Town	Hornchurch	Kettering Town	Kingstonian	Maidenhead United	Northwood	St Albans City	Sutton United	Thurrock
Aylesbury United	—	0-3	3-3	3-2	2-0	1-0	0-0	1-0	3-2	1-2	0-3	0-1	0-1	1-1	1-4	0-4	0-2	2-2	2-0	1-3	2-0	0-2	0-6	2-4
Basingstoke Town	2-0	—	2-0	0-1	3-1	3-1	2-0	0-2	2-1	2-1	2-1	1-1	1-0	1-4	2-3	2-3	0-3	2-2	2-0	2-1	1-0	1-0	0-5	0-3
Bedford Town	4-1	0-0	—	1-0	0-0	8-0	3-0	1-0	2-1	1-0	3-1	1-1	0-2	2-0	1-1	2-1	2-1	3-1	1-2	2-1	1-4	1-1	0-0	0-0
Billericay Town	2-2	3-0	0-0	—	3-0	1-0	2-3	0-3	4-1	1-1	1-1	1-1	1-2	2-0	1-2	3-0	2-0	4-1	2-1	0-1	2-0	1-1	1-1	1-1
Bishop's Stortford	4-4	2-0	1-0	1-0	—	1-1	4-1	1-0	1-1	0-2	1-0	2-0	0-0	1-1	3-0	2-0	2-1	1-0	2-0	0-1	1-4	2-2	1-1	1-3
Bognor Regis Town	4-0	0-2	0-3	1-1	0-1	—	0-1	0-3	0-3	3-1	1-2	0-1	3-2	0-2	1-0	2-0	3-0	1-0	2-1	1-2	4-0	2-4	0-2	6-1
Braintree Town	4-0	2-0	1-0	2-3	4-1	0-3	—	3-0	1-1	1-3	1-1	1-1	2-0	1-0	2-0	4-0	2-1	3-2	0-1	1-2	3-2	2-4	1-1	1-0
Canvey Island	4-0	2-0	4-1	0-3	0-1	3-0	2-4	—	3-0	0-3	0-1	2-2	0-2	1-3	1-3	4-0	0-0	2-0	0-1	3-2	2-0	0-1	1-3	4-3
Carshalton Athletic	4-1	3-1	1-0	1-1	4-0	3-0	1-0	1-0	—	1-1	0-2	2-1	2-0	1-1	4-0	3-0	3-2	3-2	6-1	3-2	2-2	2-4	4-3	2-3
Ford United	3-1	1-1	1-1	1-1	3-2	6-0	1-0	0-2	2-0	—	2-0	0-0	0-1	1-3	4-0	3-2	2-0	0-1	1-1	0-1	1-1	3-1	2-3	1-1
Grays Athletic	2-1	2-1	3-0	0-1	0-2	0-2	1-1	1-2	0-2	2-0	—	1-1	0-0	1-1	0-0	2-0	0-1	0-0	1-1	2-1	3-2	0-0	3-4	2-3
Harrow Borough	2-1	1-1	0-0	1-1	0-2	0-1	3-1	2-2	2-1	0-0	1-1	—	1-2	1-2	0-2	0-0	1-0	0-2	1-0	3-2	1-1	2-2	1-2	1-2
Hayes	3-0	1-0	2-0	2-0	0-1	2-1	2-1	1-1	2-0	0-1	1-0	0-0	—	1-0	0-1	0-0	0-2	1-2	2-0	2-0	1-1	1-0	3-1	1-1
Hendon	1-1	1-0	1-1	2-0	2-0	2-0	2-0	1-0	1-0	0-1	3-1	0-2	3-1	—	3-1	5-1	4-0	0-0	1-1	1-0	2-0	2-0	0-1	2-0
Heybridge Swifts	1-2	2-2	1-1	3-1	2-0	1-0	1-0	1-3	4-0	0-1	2-0	4-0	4-0	3-1	—	4-1	0-2	0-1	1-1	3-1	1-1	0-1	0-2	2-0
Hitchin Town	2-2	2-2	1-0	4-2	2-5	1-2	2-1	4-0	4-0	0-0	3-0	2-3	0-0	1-0	5-1	—	4-0	2-0	0-2	3-1	3-2	1-0	2-4	2-0
Hornchurch	1-0	1-3	1-1	0-1	2-1	3-0	1-0	1-3	3-2	0-3	0-1	2-0	1-1	0-0	4-2	1-1	—	1-0	0-1	0-1	3-0	1-2	1-0	1-0
Kettering Town	0-0	2-0	1-0	3-1	3-0	1-0	1-2	2-0	2-0	0-2	1-1	1-2	1-0	1-1	1-1	1-1	3-2	—	1-0	3-1	0-1	1-2	1-2	2-0
Kingstonian	0-0	2-0	2-1	1-2	3-1	0-1	4-0	2-0	2-0	2-1	1-4	0-2	1-0	1-1	2-0	1-0	0-1	1-0	—	0-1	1-1	3-4	1-1	2-1
Maidenhead United	4-2	2-0	1-1	0-1	2-0	3-0	2-1	1-2	3-2	0-1	2-3	2-3	0-1	0-1	0-0	1-0	3-1	3-1	3-1	—	3-0	3-1	1-0	2-0
Northwood	1-1	0-0	1-3	1-4	0-1	4-1	2-1	3-0	0-4	3-1	0-3	0-0	3-4	0-1	0-4	1-0	3-1	1-2	0-4	3-1	—	1-0	1-2	2-0
St Albans City	3-1	0-3	0-3	1-1	2-2	1-0	1-0	2-4	2-4	1-3	0-0	1-0	2-1	0-4	0-5	1-0	0-1	2-1	1-2	1-2	0-1	—	4-1	1-3
Sutton United	2-2	2-2	0-5	1-1	1-1	1-2	2-1	1-1	4-3	2-3	3-4	1-2	3-1	0-1	0-5	2-4	1-0	1-2	1-1	1-0	1-2	2-0	—	0-3
Thurrock	5-0	0-0	0-3	4-1	1-3	4-1	1-0	6-1	4-3	1-1	2-3	1-2	1-1	2-0	1-1	2-0	1-0	2-0	2-1	3-1	2-0	2-0	0-1	—

THE BRYCO CUP 2003–2004

FIRST ROUND
Arlesey Town 3, Abingdon Town 0
Chalfont St Peter 5, Ware 1
Clapton *v* Bracknell Town
(Bracknell T walkover – Clapton withdrew)
Dorking 0, Worthing 1
Dunstable Town 7, Wivenhoe Town 1
East Thurrock United 2, Croydon 1
Epsom & Ewell 0, Waltham Forest 1
Flackwell Heath 1, Egham Town 5
Great Wakering Rovers 2, Barton Rovers 1
Harlow Town 2, Hertford Town 0
Kingsbury Town 0, Wealdstone 8
Leatherhead 1, Croydon Athletic 4
Leighton Town 0, Ashford Town (Mx) 2
Marlow 2, Barking & East Ham United 2
(Marlow won 5-4 on penalties).
Metropolitan Police 2, Corinthian Casuals 1
Molesey 3, Windsor & Eton 1
Oxford City 1, Cheshunt 3
Staines Town 4, Witham Town 4
(Witham Town won 5-4 on penalties).
Tooting & Mitcham United 1, Leyton 2
Wembley 0, Camberley Town 1
Wingate & Finchley 2, Chertsey Town 0
Wokingham Town 2, Tilbury 4
Yeading 5, Edgware Town 1

SECOND ROUND
Arlesey Town 0, Hornchurch 2
Basingstoke Town 2, Aylesbury United 0
Bedford Town 1, Bognor Regis Town 0
Berkhamsted Town 0, Ashford Town (Mx) 2
Billericay Town 1, East Thurrock United 2
Bracknell Town 5, Chalfont St Peter 0
Braintree Town 1, Thurrock 2
Camberley Town 0, Northwood 1
Canvey Island 0, Hendon 3
Carshalton Athletic 0, Harlow Town 1
Chesham United 1, Lewes 0
Dulwich Hamlet 3, Hampton & Richmond Borough 3
(H&RB won 4-3 on penalties).
Egham Town 4, Tilbury 2
Ford United 2, Bishop's Stortford 1
Great Wakering Rovers 2, Banstead Athletic 1
Harrow Borough 2, Bromley 0
Heybridge Swifts 3, St Albans City 1
Horsham 2, Witham Town 1
Kingstonian 2, Croydon Athletic 0
Leyton 4, Enfield 1
Maidenhead United 3, Hayes 2
Marlow 3, Boreham Wood 2
Molesey 0, Walton & Hersham 0
(Molesey won 4-3 on penalties).
Slough Town 1, Cheshunt 4
Sutton United 2, Metropolitan Police 0

Thame United 1, Hitchin Town 2
Uxbridge 1, Dunstable Town 2
Waltham Forest 0, Aveley 2
Whyteleafe 0, Grays Athletic 2
Wingate & Finchley 2, Wealdstone 0
Worthing 1, Kettering Town 0
Yeading 2, Hemel Hempstead Town 1

THIRD ROUND
Aveley 0, Hornchurch 5
Basingstoke Town 0, Ashford Town (Mx) 0
(Ashford Town (Mx) won 3-2 on penalties).
Bracknell Town 4, Hendon 3
Chesham United 6, Molesey 1
East Thurrock United 1, Wingate & Finchley 2
Egham Town 0, Grays Athletic 1
Ford United 0, Northwood 1
Harlow Town 3, Great Wakering Rovers 1
Heybridge Swifts 3, Harrow Borough 2
Hitchin Town 1, Marlow 3
Horsham 0, Bedford Town 3
Leyton 1, Hampton & Richmond Borough 2
Sutton United 2, Dunstable Town 3
Thurrock 1, Kingstonian 0
Worthing 2, Maidenhead United 0
Yeading 4, Cheshunt 4
(Cheshunt won 9-8 on penalties).

FOURTH ROUND
Bracknell Town 2, Worthing 1
Chesham United 2, Ashford Town (Mx) 0
Dunstable Town 1, Grays Athletic 0
Hampton & Richmond Borough 4, Wingate & Finchley 2
Heybridge Swifts 3, Cheshunt 4
Hornchurch 0, Harlow Town 0
(Harlow Town won 4-2 on penalties).
Marlow 2, Northwood 0
Thurrock 4, Bedford Town 1

FIFTH ROUND
Thurrock 2, Chesham United 1
Bracknell Town 1, Hampton & Richmond Borough 2
Dunstable Town 4, Harlow Town 1
Marlow 1, Cheshunt 2

SEMI-FINALS FIRST LEG
Cheshunt 0, Thurrock 2
Dunstable Town 2, Hampton & Richmond Borough 1

SEMI-FINALS SECOND LEG
Hampton & Richmond Borough 1, Dunstable Town 3
Thurrock 1, Cheshunt 2

FINAL
Final due to be played on 3 May was postponed. New date for final still to be arranged.

PONTINS HOLIDAY LEAGUE

PREMIER DIVISION

	P	W	D	L	F	A	GD	Pts
Stoke C	22	13	4	5	45	31	+14	43
Tranmere R	22	13	3	6	42	32	+10	42
Walsall	22	12	5	5	38	18	+20	41
Sheffield U	22	11	4	7	28	26	+2	37
Hull C	22	9	6	7	39	32	+7	33
Bradford C	22	6	9	7	30	28	+2	27
Sheffield W	22	8	3	11	32	33	−1	27
Preston NE	22	6	7	9	39	34	+5	25
Barnsley	22	6	7	9	31	37	−6	25
Rotherham U	22	7	4	11	35	56	−21	25
Huddersfield T*	22	6	6	10	28	34	−6	24
Burnley*	22	4	4	14	26	52	−26	16

DIVISION ONE WEST

	P	W	D	L	F	A	GD	Pts
Wigan Ath	18	11	3	4	43	25	+18	36
Stockport Co	18	10	3	5	31	23	+8	33
Carlisle U	18	10	2	6	38	35	+3	32
Blackpool	18	7	5	6	29	25	+4	26
Oldham Ath	18	7	5	6	24	24	0	26
Bury	18	7	3	8	22	25	−3	24
Shrewsbury T	18	6	2	10	36	31	+5	20
Macclesfield T	18	4	8	6	20	27	−7	20
Wrexham	18	5	4	9	36	46	−10	19
Rochdale	18	5	1	12	25	43	−18	16

DIVISION ONE EAST

	P	W	D	L	F	A	GD	Pts
Hartlepool U	18	12	4	2	41	18	+23	40
Newcastle U	18	9	3	6	38	28	+10	30
Scunthorpe U	18	7	8	3	22	22	0	29
Boston U	18	8	0	10	34	33	+1	24
Grimsby T	18	5	7	6	28	27	+1	22
Notts Co	18	6	4	8	25	26	−1	22
Darlington	18	6	4	8	29	35	−5	22
Doncaster R	18	4	8	6	20	25	−5	20
York C	18	4	7	7	24	34	−10	19
Lincoln C	18	3	7	8	23	37	−14	16

*Relegated teams.

PONTINS HOLIDAY COMBINATION

CENTRAL AND EAST DIVISION

	P	W	D	L	F	A	GD	Pts
Reading	14	12	1	1	48	11	+37	37
Gillingham	14	10	2	2	27	9	+18	32
Northampton T	14	8	3	3	33	25	+8	27
Millwall	14	8	3	3	31	25	+6	27
Cambridge U	14	7	2	5	29	24	+5	23
Crystal Palace	14	6	3	5	25	18	+7	21
Brighton & HA	14	6	2	6	34	24	+10	20
QPR	14	6	2	6	16	22	−6	20
Peterborough U	14	4	7	3	31	25	+6	19
Colchester U	14	5	2	7	15	13	+2	17
Norwich C	14	5	2	7	21	23	−2	17
Wycombe W	14	3	4	7	14	22	−8	13
Brentford	14	1	7	6	22	33	−11	10
Aldershot T	14	2	1	11	16	66	−50	7
Southend U	14	1	1	12	7	29	−22	4

Southend U awarded 1-0 win v Aldershot T following late postponement.

WALES AND WEST DIVISION

	P	W	D	L	F	A	GD	Pts
Cardiff C	18	11	3	4	35	20	+15	36
Plymouth Arg	18	11	2	5	49	21	+28	35
Yeovil T	18	9	5	4	53	34	+19	32
Bristol C	18	6	7	5	37	27	+10	25
Bournemouth	18	5	7	6	22	34	−12	22
Bristol R	18	6	3	9	33	37	−4	21
Swansea C	18	5	5	8	24	36	−12	20
Swindon T	18	4	7	7	25	34	−9	19
Cheltenham T	18	4	6	8	30	36	−6	18
Oxford U	18	5	3	10	31	60	−29	18

Swansea C awarded 1-0 win v Bristol C following late postponement.

FA ACADEMY UNDER-19 LEAGUE

Group A	P	W	D	L	F	A	GD	Pts
Manchester C	26	20	2	4	58	24	+34	62
Blackburn R	26	13	7	6	42	25	+17	46
Liverpool	26	12	9	5	46	36	+10	45
Crewe Alex	26	10	9	7	40	36	+4	39
Everton	26	10	8	8	36	37	–1	38
Manchester U	26	10	7	9	38	36	+2	37
Wolverhampton W	26	9	8	9	38	32	+6	35
Bolton W	26	8	4	14	39	52	–13	28
Stoke C	26	4	7	15	37	63	–26	19
Sheffield W	26	4	6	16	31	50	–19	18

Group B	P	W	D	L	F	A	GD	Pts
Sheffield U	26	16	5	5	52	29	+23	53
Middlesbrough	26	15	3	8	54	36	+18	48
Leeds U	26	12	5	9	36	27	+9	41
Newcastle U	26	13	2	11	49	45	+4	41
Sunderland	26	12	5	9	46	42	+4	41
Nottingham F	26	11	3	12	41	38	+3	36
Huddersfield T	26	7	5	14	35	45	–10	26
Derby Co	26	6	8	12	38	52	–14	26
Barnsley	26	6	5	15	34	59	–25	23

Group C	P	W	D	L	F	A	GD	Pts
Arsenal	26	16	4	6	58	29	+29	52
Chelsea	26	12	3	11	40	33	+7	39
Aston Villa	26	12	2	12	54	48	+6	38
Birmingham C	26	10	7	9	30	24	+6	37
Leicester C	26	10	5	11	40	43	–3	35
Watford	26	10	5	11	38	51	–13	35
Reading	26	9	4	13	36	40	–4	31
Fulham	26	4	7	15	22	52	–30	19
Bristol C	26	3	5	18	37	64	–27	14

Group D	P	W	D	L	F	A	GD	Pts
Southampton	26	20	5	1	58	22	+36	65
Charlton Ath	26	16	3	7	44	34	+10	51
West Ham U	26	13	5	8	51	36	+15	44
Millwall	26	9	8	9	48	44	+4	35
Tottenham H	26	10	3	13	27	38	–11	33
Norwich C	26	9	4	13	46	55	–9	31
Wimbledon	26	9	3	14	23	40	–17	30
Ipswich T	26	7	8	11	34	43	–9	29
Crystal Palace	26	7	5	14	27	43	–16	26

FA ACADEMY UNDER-17 LEAGUE

Group A	P	W	D	L	F	A	GD	Pts
Everton	26	17	5	4	52	24	+28	56
Blackburn R	26	16	4	6	80	38	+42	52
Manchester U	26	14	7	5	50	36	+14	49
Liverpool	26	11	7	8	53	43	+10	40
Manchester C	26	12	2	12	48	55	−7	38
Crewe Alex	26	6	7	13	46	58	−12	25

Group B	P	W	D	L	F	A	GD	Pts
Leeds U	26	12	7	7	45	30	+15	43
Sheffield U	26	10	8	8	46	47	−1	38
Nottingham F	26	9	6	11	42	41	+1	33
Middlesbrough	26	8	6	12	45	52	−7	30
Wolverhampton W	26	6	5	15	28	64	−36	23
Derby Co	26	4	7	15	36	58	−22	19

Group C	P	W	D	L	F	A	GD	Pts
Aston Villa	26	16	5	5	90	41	+49	53
Leicester C	26	14	5	7	59	54	+5	47
Coventry C	26	12	6	8	55	46	+9	42
Arsenal	26	12	6	8	39	40	−1	42
Birmingham C	26	11	7	8	52	47	+5	40
Bristol C	26	9	3	14	55	62	−7	30
Fulham	26	7	6	13	37	56	−19	27
Watford	26	5	5	16	38	71	−33	20

Group D	P	W	D	L	F	A	GD	Pts
Southampton	26	17	6	3	79	43	+36	57
Tottenham H	26	13	6	7	59	44	+15	45
West Ham U	26	13	5	8	57	38	+19	44
Charlton Ath	26	10	6	10	48	48	0	36
Millwall	26	10	5	11	44	48	−4	35
Crystal Palace	26	5	4	17	26	64	−38	19
Reading	26	5	3	18	34	69	−35	18
Wimbledon	26	3	5	18	29	55	−26	14

WOMEN'S FOOTBALL 2003–2004

National Division	P	W	D	L	F	A	GD	Pts
1 Arsenal	18	15	2	1	65	11	54	47
2 Charlton Ath	18	15	1	2	52	17	35	46
3 Fulham	18	14	2	2	60	20	40	44
4 Leeds U	18	8	4	6	32	28	4	28
5 Doncaster Belles	18	8	3	7	41	40	1	27
6 Everton	18	6	2	10	21	36	−15	20
7 Birmingham C	18	4	5	9	17	31	−14	17
8 Bristol R	18	3	3	12	27	37	−10	12
9 Aston Villa*	18	1	4	13	18	63	−45	7
10 Tranmere R*	18	1	4	13	13	63	−50	7

THE FA WOMEN'S CUP FINAL 2003–2004

(at Loftus Road)

Monday, 3 May 2003

Arsenal (2) 3 *(Fleeting 23, 25, 83)*

Charlton Athletic (0) 0   12,244

Arsenal: Byrne; Pealling, Wheatley, White, Asante, Champ, Ludlow, Maggs (Lorton 90), Sanderson (Potter 73), Fleeting (Scott 90), Grant.
Charlton Athletic: Cope; Murphy, Fletcher (Coss 70), Smith (Hunn 81), Stoney, Mills, Williams, Broadhurst, Barr, Walker, Heatherson (Aluko 70).
Referee: A. Rayner (Leicestershire & Rutland).

FA PREMIER RESERVE LEAGUES

NORTH SECTION

	P	W	D	L	F	A	GD	Pts
Aston Villa	26	17	5	4	55	31	+24	56
Liverpool	26	14	8	4	41	21	+20	50
Manchester U	26	13	8	5	55	39	+16	47
Newcastle U	26	13	4	9	50	42	+8	43
Manchester C	26	11	8	7	34	24	+10	41
Blackburn R	26	11	6	9	49	45	+4	39
Everton	26	10	8	8	37	33	+4	38
Leeds U	26	10	7	9	40	40	0	37
Middlesbrough	26	8	10	8	33	33	0	34
Sunderland	26	8	7	11	37	46	−9	31
WBA	26	8	6	12	36	48	−12	30
Birmingham C	26	6	5	15	28	42	−14	23
Wolverhampton W	26	4	6	16	27	49	−22	18
Bolton W	26	3	4	19	22	51	−29	13

Leading Goalscorers

Simon Johnson (Leeds U)	15	Elliott (Manchester C)	8
Proctor (Sunderland)	13	Wright-Phillips, B (Manchester C)	8
Mellor (Liverpool)	10	Brown (WBA)	8
Johnson (Blackburn R)	9	Moore S (Aston Villa)	7
Nardiello (Manchester U)	9	Figueroa (Birmingham C)	7
Chopra (Newcastle U)	9	Osman (Liverpool)	7
Moore L (Aston Villa)	8	Guy (Newcastle U)	7
Chadwick (Everton)	8		

SOUTH SECTION

	P	W	D	L	F	A	GD	Pts
Charlton Ath	28	17	6	5	46	19	+27	57
Derby Co	28	13	10	5	46	31	+15	49
Southampton	28	14	6	8	43	28	+15	48
West Ham U	28	12	8	8	37	35	+2	44
Tottenham H	28	11	9	8	42	35	+7	42
Arsenal	28	10	9	9	41	35	+6	39
Chelsea	28	11	6	11	37	33	+4	39
Leicester C	28	9	11	8	34	40	−6	38
Coventry C	28	9	10	9	38	40	−2	37
Wimbledon	28	9	5	14	35	47	−12	32
Watford	28	6	12	10	32	40	−8	30
Portsmouth	28	6	11	11	36	39	−3	29
Nottingham F	28	6	11	11	33	41	−8	29
Ipswich T	28	8	4	16	34	44	−10	28
Fulham	28	6	8	14	27	54	−27	26

Leading Goalscorers

Kneissl (Chelsea)	12	Junior (Derby Co)	6
Bowditch (Ipswich T)	9	McLeod (Derby Co)	6
Aliadiere (Arsenal)	8	Sava (Fulham)	6
Labarthe (Derby Co)	8	Armstrong (Ipswich T)	6
Davies (Southampton)	8	Westcarr (Nottingham F)	6
Jephott (Coventry C)	7	Barnard (Tottenham H)	6
Blackstock (Southampton)	7	Pearson (West Ham U)	6
Griffit (Southampton)	7		

THE FA TROPHY 2003–2004

FINAL (at Villa Park) – Sunday, 23 May 2004

Hednesford Town (1) 3 *(Maguire 27, Hines 53, Brindley 86)*

Canvey Island (0) 2 *(Boylan 46, Brindley 47 (og))*   6635

Hednesford Town: Young; Simkin, Hines, Brindley, Ryder (Barrow), Palmer, Maguire, King, Anthrobus, Danks (Piearce), Charie (Evans S).
Canvey Island: Potter; Kennedy, Midgley (Berquez), Chenery, Ward, Cowan, Gooden (Dobinson), Minton, Gregory (McDougald), Boylan, Duffy.
Referee: M. Dean (Wirral).

THE FA VASE 2003–2004

FINAL (at St Andrews, Birmingham) – Sunday, 16 May 2004

AFC Sudbury (0) 0

Winchester City (1) 2 *(Forbes 18, Dyke 77 (pen))*   5080

AFC Sudbury: Greygoose; Head, Betson (Francis 85), Girling, Tracey, Wardley, Hyde (Calver 56), Norfolk, Bennett, Claydon, Owen (Banya 62).
Winchester City: Arthur; Dyke (Tate 84), Bicknell, Blake, Redwood, Goss, Smith, Webber, Mancey, Forbes (Rogers 70), Green.
Referee: P. Crossley (Kent).

THE FA YOUTH CUP 2003–2004

FINAL (First Leg) – Thursday, 15 April 2004

Aston Villa (0) 0

Middlesbrough (0) 3 *(Wheater 47, Morrison 52, 78 (pen))*   6551

Aston Villa: Olejnik; Ward, Green (Grant 72), Gardner, Troest, Cahill, Kabeya (Paul 68), Foley, Agbonlahor, Moore L, Nix.
Middlesbrough: Knight; McMahon, Masters, Kennedy, Bates, Wheater, Morrison (Johnson 90), Liddle, Craddock, Taylor, Peacock.
Referee: A. D'Urso (Essex).

FINAL (Second Leg) – Monday, 19 April 2004

Middlesbrough (0) 1 *(Kennedy 47)*

Aston Villa (0) 0   16,321

Middlesbrough: Knight; McMahon, Masters, Kennedy (Johnson 76), Bates, Wheater, Morrison, Liddle, Craddock (Reed 82), Taylor, Peacock.
Aston Villa: Olejnik; Ward (Kabeya 58), Green, Gardner, Troest, Cahill, Paul (Morgan 79), Foley, Agbonlahor, Moore L, Nix.
Referee: A. D'Urso (Essex).

THE FA SUNDAY CUP 2003–2004

FINAL (at Liverpool FC)

Nicosia (1) 3 *(Olu 25 (og), Gibiliru 50, Madin 88)*

UK Flooring (0) 1 *(Pritchard 90)*   1526

THE FA COUNTY YOUTH CUP 2003–2004

FINAL

North Riding v Durham   0-4   att: 902

SOUTH AMERICAN CHAMPIONSHIP

(Copa America)

1916	Uruguay	1939	Peru	1967	Uruguay
1917	Uruguay	1941	Argentina	1975	Peru
1919	Brazil	1942	Uruguay	1979	Paraguay
1920	Uruguay	1945	Argentina	1983	Uruguay
1921	Argentina	1946	Argentina	1987	Uruguay
1922	Brazil	1947	Argentina	1989	Brazil
1923	Uruguay	1949	Brazil	1991	Argentina
1924	Uruguay	1953	Paraguay	1993	Argentina
1925	Argentina	1955	Argentina	1995	Uruguay
1926	Uruguay	1956	Uruguay	1997	Brazil
1927	Argentina	1957	Argentina	1999	Brazil
1929	Argentina	1959	Argentina	2001	Colombia
1935	Uruguay	1959	Uruguay		
1937	Argentina	1963	Bolivia		

SOUTH AMERICAN CUP

(Copa Libertadores)

1960	Penarol (Uruguay)	1983	Gremio Porto Alegre (Brazil)
1961	Penarol	1984	Independiente
1962	Santos (Brazil)	1985	Argentinos Juniors (Argentina)
1963	Santos	1986	River Plate (Argentina)
1964	Independiente (Argentina)	1987	Penarol
1965	Independiente	1988	Nacional (Uruguay)
1966	Penarol	1989	Nacional (Colombia)
1967	Racing Club (Argentina)	1990	Olimpia
1968	Estudiantes (Argentina)	1991	Colo Colo (Chile)
1969	Estudiantes	1992	São Paulo (Brazil)
1970	Estudiantes	1993	São Paulo
1971	Nacional (Uruguay)	1994	Velez Sarsfield (Argentina)
1972	Independiente	1995	Gremio Porto Alegre
1973	Independiente	1996	River Plate
1974	Independiente	1997	Cruzeiro
1975	Independiente	1998	Vasco da Gama
1976	Cruzeiro (Brazil)	1999	Palmeiras
1977	Boca Juniors (Argentina)	2000	Boca Juniors
1978	Boca Juniors	2001	Boca Juniors
1979	Olimpia (Paraguay)	2002	Olimpia
1980	Nacional	2003	Boca Juniors
1981	Flamengo (Brazil)	2004	Once Caldas
1982	Penarol		

NATIONAL LIST OF REFEREES FOR SEASON 2003–2004

*Indicates Select Group Referees

Armstrong, P (Paul) Berkshire
Atkinson, M (Martin) W. Yorkshire
Barry, NS (Neale) N. Lincolnshire*
Bates, A (Tony) Staffordshire
Beeby, RJ (Richard) Northamptonshire
Bennett, SG (Steve) Kent*
Booth, RJ (Russell) Nottinghamshire
Boyeson, C (Carl) E. Yorkshire
Cable, LE (Lee) Surrey
Clattenburg, M (Mark) Tyne & Wear*
Cowburn, MG (Mark) Lancashire
Crossley, PT (Phil) Kent
Curson, B (Brian) Leicestershire
Danson, PS (Paul) Leicestershire
Dean, ML (Mike) Wirral*
Dowd, P (Phil) Staffordshire*
Drysdale, D (Darren) Lincolnshire
Dunn, SW (Steve) Gloucestershire*
D'Urso, AP (Andy) Essex*
Evans, EM (Eddie) Greater Manchester
Fletcher, M (Mick) Worcestershire
Foy, CJ (Chris) Merseyside*
Friend, KA (Kevin) Leicestershire
Gallagher, DJ (Dermot) Oxfordshire*
Graham, F (Fred) Essex
Hall, AR (Andy) W. Midlands
Halsey, MR (Mark) Lancashire*
Hegley, GK (Grant) Hertfordshire
Hill, KD (Keith) Hertfordshire
Ilderton, EL (Eddie) Tyne & Wear
Jones, MJ (Michael) Cheshire
Joslin, PJ (Phil) Nottinghamshire
Kaye, A (Alan) W. Yorkshire
Kettle, TM (Trevor) Berkshire
Knight, B (Barry) Kent*
Laws, G (Graham) Tyne & Wear
Leake, AR (Tony) Lancashire
Lewis, GJ (Gary) Haddenham,
  Cambridgeshire

Marriner, AM (Andre) W. Midlands
Mason, LS (Lee) Lancashire
Mathieson, SW (Scott) Cheshire
Melin, PW (Paul) Surrey
Messias, MD (Matt) W. Yorkshire*
Miller, NS (Nigel) Co. Durham
Oliver, CW (Clive) Northumberland
Olivier, RJ (Ray) W. Midlands
Parkes, TA (Trevor) W. Midlands
Penn, AM (Andy) W. Midlands
Penton, C (Clive) Sussex
Pike, MS (Mike) Cumbria
Poll, G (Graham) Hertfordshire*
Probert, LW (Lee) Gloucestershire
Prosser, PJ (Phil) W. Yorkshire
Rennie, UD (Uriah) S. Yorkshire*
Riley, MA (Mike) W. Yorkshire*
Robinson, JP (Paul) E. Yorkshire
Ross, JJ (Joe) London
Russell, MP (Mike) Hertfordshire
Ryan, M (Michael) Lancashire
Salisbury, G (Graham) Lancashire
Singh, J (Jarnall) Middlesex
Stroud, KP (Keith) Dorset
Styles, R (Rob) Hampshire*
Tanner, SJ (Steve) Somerset
Taylor, P (Paul) Hertfordshire
Thorpe, M (Mike) Suffolk
Tomlin, SG (Steve) E. Sussex
Walton, P (Peter) Northamptonshire*
Warren, MR (Mark) W. Midlands
Webb, HM (Howard) S. Yorkshire*
Webster, CH (Colin) Tyne & Wear
Wiley, AG (Alan) Staffordshire*
Williamson, IG (Iain) Berkshire
Woolmer, KA (Andy)
  Northamptonshire
Wright, KK (Kevin) Cambridgeshire

USEFUL ADDRESSES

The Football Association: The Secretary, 25 Soho Square, London W1D 4FA. *0207 745 4545*

Scotland: D. Taylor, Hampden Park, Glasgow G42 9AY. *0141 616 6000*

Northern Ireland (Irish FA): D. I. Bowen, 20 Windsor Avenue, Belfast BT9 6EG. *028 9066 9458*

Wales: D. Collins, 3 Westgate Street, Cardiff, South Glamorgan CF10 1DP. *029 2037 2325*

Republic of Ireland (FA of Ireland): B. Menton, 80 Merrion Square South, Dublin 2. *00353 16766864*

International Federation (FIFA): Secretary, PO Box 85 8030 Zurich, Switzerland. *00 411 384 9595. Fax: 00 411 384 9696*

Union of European Football Associations: Secretary, Route de Geneve 46, Case Postale, CH-1260 Nyon, Switzerland. *0041 22 994 4444. Fax: 0041 22 994 4488*

The Premier League: M. Foster, 11 Connaught Place, London W2 2ET. *0207 298 1600*

The Football League: Secretary, The Football League, Unit 5, Edward VII Quay, Navigation Way, Preston, Lancashire PR2 2YF. *01772 325800. Fax 01772 325801*

Scottish Premier League: R. Mitchell, Hampden Park, Somerville Drive, Glasgow G42 9BA. *0141 646 6962*

The Scottish League: The Secretary, Hampden Park, Glasgow G42 9AY. *0141 616 6000*

The Irish League: H. Wallace, 96 University Street, Belfast BT7 1HE. *028 9024 2888*

Football League of Ireland: D. Crowther, 80 Merrion Square, Dublin 2. *00353 167 65120*

Conference National: Riverside House, 14b High Street, Crayford DA1 4HG. *01322 411021*

Northern Premier: R. D. Bayley, 22 Woburn Drive, Hale, Altrincham, Cheshire WA15 8LZ. *0161 980 7007*

Isthmian League: Triumph House, Station Approach, Sanderstead Road, South Croydon, Surrey CR2 0PL. *020 8409 1978. Fax 020 7639 5726*

English Schools FA: J. Read, 1/2 Eastgate Street, Stafford ST16 2NG. *01785 251142*

Southern League: D. J. Strudwick, PO Box 90, Worcester WR3 8XR. *01905 757509*

The Football Supporters Federation: Chairman: Ian D. Todd MBE, 8 Wyke Close, Wyke Gardens, Isleworth, Middlesex TW7 5PE. *020 8847 2905 (and fax)*. *Mobile: 0961 558908.* National Secretary: Mark Agate, 'The Stadium', 14 Coombe Close, Lordswood, Chatham, Kent ME5 8NU. *01634 319461 (and fax)*

Professional Footballers' Association: G. Taylor, 2 Oxford Court, Bishopsgate, Off Lower Mosley Street, Manchester M2 3WQ. *0161 236 0575*

Referees' Association: A. Smith, 1 Westhill Road, Coundon, Coventry CV6 2AD. *024 7660 1701*

Women's Football Alliance: The Football Association, 25 Soho Square, London W1D 4FA. *0207 745 4545*

The Football Programme Directory: David Stacey, 'The Beeches', 66 Southend Road, Wickford, Essex SS11 8EN. *01268 732041 (and fax)*

England Football Supporters Association: Publicity Officer, David Stacey, 66 Southend Road, Wickford, Essex SS11 8EN. *01268 732041 (and fax)*

World Cup (1966) Association: as above.

The Football Foundation Ltd: 25 Soho Square, London W1D 4FF. *0207 534 4210. Fax 0207 287 0459*

ENGLISH LEAGUE FIXTURES 2004–2005

*Sky Sports; †Prem Plus pay per view

Saturday, 7 August 2004
Coca-Cola Football League
Championship
Burnley v Sheffield U
Coventry C v Sunderland* (5:15)
Crewe Alex v Cardiff C
Ipswich T v Gillingham
Leeds U v Derby Co* (12:15)
Leicester C v West Ham U
Plymouth Arg v Millwall
Preston NE v Watford
QPR v Rotherham U
Reading v Brighton & HA
Wigan Ath v Nottingham F

Coca-Cola Football League One
Bristol C v Torquay U
Chesterfield v Brentford
Doncaster R v Blackpool
Hartlepool U v Bradford C
Hull C v Bournemouth
Luton T v Oldham Ath
Milton Keynes Dons v Barnsley
Peterborough U v Tranmere R
Sheffield W v Colchester U
Stockport Co v Huddersfield T
Walsall v Port Vale
Wrexham v Swindon T

Coca-Cola Football League Two
Boston U v Oxford U
Bury v Yeovil T
Darlington v Grimsby T
Leyton Orient v Macclesfield T
Mansfield T v Bristol R
Notts Co v Chester
Rushden & D'monds v
    Kidderminster H
Scunthorpe U v Rochdale
Shrewsbury v Lincoln C
Southend U v Cheltenham T
Swansea C v Northampton T
Wycombe W v Cambridge U

Sunday, 8 August 2004
Coca-Cola Football League
Championship
Stoke C v Wolverhampton W*

Monday, 9 August 2004
Coca-Cola Football League
Championship
Watford v QPR* (7:45)

Tuesday, 10 August 2004
Coca-Cola Football League
Championship
Brighton & HA v Plymouth Arg
Cardiff C v Coventry C
Gillingham v Leeds U
Millwall v Wigan Ath
Rotherham U v Burnley
Sheffield U v Stoke C
Sunderland v Crewe Alex
West Ham U v Reading* (8:00)
Wolverhampton W v Preston NE

Coca-Cola Football League One
Barnsley v Bristol C
Blackpool v Sheffield W
Bournemouth v Walsall
Bradford C v Peterborough U
Brentford v Doncaster R
Colchester U v Stockport Co
Huddersfield T v Chesterfield
Oldham Ath v Wrexham
Port Vale v Milton Keynes Dons
Torquay U v Hull C
Tranmere R v Hartlepool U

Coca-Cola Football League Two
Bristol R v Bury
Cambridge U v Leyton Orient
Cheltenham T v Scunthorpe U
Chester v Wycombe W
Grimsby T v Boston U
Kidderminster H v Notts Co
Lincoln C v Southend U

Macclesfield T v Shrewsbury
Northampton T v Rushden & D'monds
Rochdale v Swansea C
Yeovil T v Darlington

Wednesday, 11 August 2004
Coca-Cola Football League Championship
Derby Co v Leicester C
Nottingham F v Ipswich T

Coca-Cola Football League One
Swindon T v Luton T

Coca-Cola Football League Two
Oxford U v Mansfield T

Saturday, 14 August 2004
Barclays Premiership
Aston Villa v Southampton
Blackburn R v WBA
Bolton W v Charlton Ath
Manchester C v Fulham
Middlesbrough v Newcastle U† (5:15)
Norwich C v Crystal Palace
Portsmouth v Bimingham C
Tottenham H v Liverpool† (12:45)

Coca-Cola Football League Championship
Brighton & HA v Coventry C
Cardiff C v Plymouth Arg
Derby Co v Ipswich T
Gillingham v Preston NE
Millwall v Leicester C
Nottingham F v Crewe Alex
Rotherham U v Stoke C
Sheffield U v Reading
Sunderland v QPR
Watford v Burnley
West Ham U v Wigan Ath
Wolverhampton W v Leeds U

Coca-Cola Football League One
Barnsley v Luton T
Blackpool v Stockport Co
Bournemouth v Bristol C
Bradford C v Doncaster R
Brentford v Wrexham
Colchester U v Peterborough U
Huddersfield T v Hartlepool U
Oldham Ath v Walsall
Port Vale v Hull C
Swindon T v Milton Keynes Dons
Torquay U v Sheffield W
Tranmere R v Chesterfield

Coca-Cola Football League Two
Bristol R v Notts Co
Cambridge U v Shrewsbury
Cheltenham T v Leyton Orient
Chester v Mansfield T
Grimsby T v Bury
Kidderminster H v Darlington
Lincoln C v Rushden & D'monds
Macclesfield T v Swansea C
Northampton T v Wycombe W
Oxford U v Scunthorpe U
Rochdale v Southend U
Yeovil T v Boston U

Nationwide Conference
Accrington Stanley v Burton Alb
Aldershot T v York C
Barnet v Forest Green R
Carlisle U v Canvey Island
Dagenham & Red v Stevenage B
Exeter C v Morecambe
Gravesend & N v Northwich Vic
Hereford U v Farnborough T
Leigh RMI v Crawley T
Scarborough v Woking
Tamworth v Halifax T

Sunday, 15 August 2004
Barclays Premiership
Chelsea v Manchester U* (4:05)
Everton v Arsenal* (2:00)

Tuesday, 17 August 2004
Nationwide Conference
Burton Alb v Leigh RMI
Canvey Island v Gravesend & N
Crawley T v Hereford U
Farnborough T v Barnet
Forest Green R v Dagenham & Red
Halifax T v Scarborough
Morecambe v Accrington Stanley
Northwich Vic v Carlisle U
Stevenage B v Aldershot T
Woking v Exeter C
York C v Tamworth

Saturday, 21 August 2004
Barclays Premiership
Bimingham C v Chelsea
Charlton Ath v Portsmouth
Crystal Palace v Everton
Fulham v Bolton W
Liverpool v Manchester C
Manchester U v Norwich C
Newcastle U v Tottenham H
Southampton v Blackburn R† (12:45)

Coca-Cola Football League Championship
Burnley v Wolverhampton W
Coventry C v Millwall
Crewe Alex v West Ham U
Ipswich T v Cardiff C
Leeds U v Nottingham F
Leicester C v Watford
Plymouth Arg v Sunderland
Preston NE v Sheffield U
QPR v Derby Co
Reading v Rotherham U
Stoke C v Gillingham
Wigan Ath v Brighton & HA

Coca-Cola Football League One
Bristol C v Swindon T
Chesterfield v Colchester U
Doncaster R v Tranmere R
Hartlepool U v Blackpool
Hull C v Oldham Ath
Luton T v Torquay U
Milton Keynes Dons v Bournemouth
Peterborough U v Brentford
Sheffield W v Huddersfield T
Stockport Co v Bradford C
Walsall v Barnsley
Wrexham v Port Vale

Coca-Cola Football League Two
Boston U v Macclesfield T
Bury v Chester
Darlington v Bristol R
Leyton Orient v Oxford U
Mansfield T v Kidderminster H
Notts Co v Yeovil T
Rushden & D'monds v Grimsby T
Scunthorpe U v Lincoln C
Shrewsbury v Northampton T
Southend U v Cambridge U
Swansea C v Cheltenham T
Wycombe W v Rochdale

Nationwide Conference
Burton Alb v Dagenham & Red
Canvey Island v Tamworth
Crawley T v Aldershot T
Farnborough T v Scarborough
Forest Green R v Carlisle U
Halifax T v Barnet
Morecambe v Gravesend & N
Northwich Vic v Exeter C
Stevenage B v Accrington Stanley
Woking v Leigh RMI
York C v Hereford U

Sunday, 22 August 2004
Barclays Premiership
Arsenal v Middlesbrough* (4:05)
WBA v Aston Villa* (1:00)

Tuesday, 24 August 2004
Barclays Premiership
Arsenal v Blackburn R
Bimingham C v Manchester C
Charlton Ath v Aston Villa
Crystal Palace v Chelsea* (8:00)
WBA v Tottenham H

Wednesday, 25 August 2004
Barclays Premiership
Fulham v Middlesbrough
Liverpool v Portsmouth
Manchester U v Everton
Newcastle U v Norwich C* (8:00)
Southampton v Bolton W

Saturday, 28 August 2004
Aston Villa v Newcastle U
Blackburn R v Manchester U† (12:45)
Chelsea v Southampton
Everton v WBA
Manchester C v Charlton Ath
Middlesbrough v Crystal Palace
Norwich C v Arsenal† (5:15)
Tottenham H v Bimingham C

Coca-Cola Football League Championship
Brighton & HA v Preston NE
Cardiff C v Stoke C
Derby Co v Crewe Alex
Gillingham v QPR
Millwall v Reading
Nottingham F v Coventry C
Rotherham U v Ipswich T
Sheffield U v Leeds U
Sunderland v Wigan Ath
Watford v Plymouth Arg
West Ham U v Burnley
Wolverhampton W v Leicester C

Coca-Cola Football League One
Barnsley v Hull C
Blackpool v Luton T
Bournemouth v Wrexham
Bradford C v Chesterfield
Brentford v Stockport Co
Colchester U v Doncaster R
Huddersfield T v Peterborough U
Oldham Ath v Milton Keynes Dons

337

Port Vale v Bristol C
Swindon T v Hartlepool U
Torquay U v Walsall
Tranmere R v Sheffield W

Coca-Cola Football League Two
Bristol R v Southend U
Cambridge U v Swansea C
Cheltenham T v Boston U
Chester v Darlington
Grimsby T v Mansfield T
Kidderminster H v Wycombe W
Lincoln C v Notts Co
Macclesfield T v Scunthorpe U
Northampton T v Leyton Orient
Oxford U v Shrewsbury
Rochdale v Bury
Yeovil T v Rushden & D'monds

Nationwide Conference
Accrington Stanley v Crawley T
Aldershot T v Burton Alb
Barnet v Northwich Vic
Carlisle U v Farnborough T
Dagenham & Red v Woking
Exeter C v Canvey Island
Gravesend & N v York C
Hereford U v Stevenage B
Leigh RMI v Halifax T
Scarborough v Morecambe
Tamworth v Forest Green R

Sunday, 29 August 2004
Barclays Premiership
Bolton W v Liverpool* (4:05)

Monday, 30 August 2004
Barclays Premiership
Portsmouth v Fulham* (8:00)

Coca-Cola Football League
Championship
Burnley v Gillingham
Coventry C v West Ham U
Crewe Alex v Millwall
Ipswich T v Wolverhampton W
Leeds U v Watford
Leicester C v Brighton & HA
Plymouth Arg v Nottingham F
Preston NE v Rotherham U
QPR v Sheffield U
Reading v Sunderland
Stoke C v Derby Co
Wigan Ath v Cardiff C

Coca-Cola Football League One
Bristol C v Brentford
Chesterfield v Port Vale
Doncaster R v Huddersfield T
Hartlepool U v Colchester U
Hull C v Bradford C
Luton T v Bournemouth
Milton Keynes Dons v Torquay U
Peterborough U v Blackpool
Sheffield W v Oldham Ath
Stockport Co v Tranmere R
Walsall v Swindon T
Wrexham v Barnsley

Coca-Cola Football League Two
Boston U v Chester
Bury v Kidderminster H
Darlington v Cambridge U
Leyton Orient v Rochdale
Mansfield T v Yeovil T
Notts Co v Oxford U
Rushden & D'monds v Bristol R
Scunthorpe U v Northampton T
Shrewsbury v Cheltenham T
Southend U v Macclesfield T
Swansea C v Lincoln C
Wycombe W v Grimsby T

Nationwide Conference
Burton Alb v Scarborough
Canvey Island v Barnet
Crawley T v Dagenham & Red
Farnborough T v Exeter C
Forest Green R v Gravesend & N
Halifax T v Carlisle U
Morecambe v Leigh RMI
Northwich Vic v Hereford U
Stevenage B v Tamworth
Woking v Aldershot T
York C v Accrington Stanley

Saturday, 4 September 2004
Coca-Cola Football League One
Blackpool v Wrexham
Bradford C v Port Vale
Brentford v Bournemouth
Chesterfield v Milton Keynes Dons
Colchester U v Swindon T
Doncaster R v Walsall
Hartlepool U v Barnsley
Huddersfield T v Hull C
Peterborough U v Bristol C
Sheffield W v Luton T
Stockport Co v Torquay U
Tranmere R v Oldham Ath

Coca-Cola Football League Two
Boston U v Cambridge U
Bristol R v Shrewsbury
Bury v Lincoln C
Chester v Macclesfield T
Darlington v Scunthorpe U
Grimsby T v Rochdale
Kidderminster H v Leyton Orient
Mansfield T v Northampton T
Notts Co v Cheltenham T
Rushden & D'monds v Southend U
Wycombe W v Oxford U
Yeovil T v Swansea C

Nationwide Conference
Accrington Stanley v Woking
Aldershot T v Northwich Vic
Barnet v Morecambe
Carlisle U v Burton Alb
Dagenham & Red v York C
Exeter C v Crawley T
Gravesend & N v Stevenage B
Hereford U v Halifax T
Leigh RMI v Forest Green R
Scarborough v Canvey Island
Tamworth v Farnborough T

Saturday, 11 September 2004
Barclays Premiership
Aston Villa v Chelsea† (12:45)
Bolton W v Manchester U
Fulham v Arsenal
Liverpool v WBA
Manchester C v Everton
Middlesbrough v Birmingham C
Newcastle U v Blackburn R
Portsmouth v Crystal Palace* (5:15)

Coca-Cola Football League Championship
Burnley v Crewe Alex
Derby Co v Reading
Gillingham v Sunderland
Ipswich T v Millwall
Leeds U v Coventry C
Nottingham F v Cardiff C
Preston NE v Stoke C
QPR v Plymouth Arg
Rotherham U v Leicester C
Sheffield U v West Ham U
Watford v Brighton & HA
Wolverhampton W v Wigan Ath

Coca-Cola Football League One
Barnsley v Tranmere R
Bournemouth v Colchester U

Bristol C v Stockport Co
Hull C v Blackpool
Luton T v Chesterfield
Milton Keynes Dons v Doncaster R
Oldham Ath v Hartlepool U
Port Vale v Huddersfield T
Swindon T v Peterborough U
Torquay U v Brentford
Walsall v Sheffield W
Wrexham v Bradford C

Coca-Cola Football League Two
Cambridge U v Mansfield T
Cheltenham T v Yeovil T
Leyton Orient v Bristol R
Lincoln C v Boston U
Macclesfield T v Grimsby T
Northampton T v Notts Co
Oxford U v Rushden & D'monds
Rochdale v Darlington
Scunthorpe U v Chester
Shrewsbury v Bury
Southend U v Wycombe W
Swansea C v Kidderminster H

Nationwide Conference
Crawley T v York C
Dagenham & Red v Accrington Stanley
Farnborough T v Canvey Island
Gravesend & N v Hereford U
Halifax T v Forest Green R
Leigh RMI v Aldershot T
Northwich Vic v Morecambe
Scarborough v Exeter C
Stevenage B v Burton Alb
Tamworth v Barnet
Woking v Carlisle U

Sunday, 12 September 2004
Barclays Premiership
Tottenham H v Norwich C* (4:05)

Monday, 13 September 2004
Barclays Premiership
Charlton Ath v Southampton* (8:00)

Tuesday, 14 September 2004
Coca-Cola Football League Championship
Brighton & HA v Wolverhampton W
Cardiff C v Watford
Crewe Alex v QPR
Leicester C v Sheffield U
Millwall v Derby Co
Plymouth Arg v Leeds U

Reading v Preston NE
Stoke C v Ipswich T
Sunderland v Nottingham F
West Ham U v Rotherham U
Wigan Ath v Burnley

Wednesday, 15 September 2004
Coca-Cola Football League
Championship
Coventry C v Gillingham

Saturday, 18 September 2004
Barclays Premiership
Arsenal v Bolton W† (12:45)
Bimingham C v Charlton Ath
Blackburn R v Portsmouth
Crystal Palace v Manchester C
Everton v Middlesbrough
Norwich C v Aston Villa
WBA v Fulham

Coca-Cola Football League
Championship
Brighton & HA v QPR
Cardiff C v Derby Co
Coventry C v Rotherham U
Crewe Alex v Leeds U
Leicester C v Burnley
Millwall v Watford
Plymouth Arg v Wolverhampton W
Reading v Gillingham
Stoke C v Nottingham F
Sunderland v Preston NE
West Ham U v Ipswich T
Wigan Ath v Sheffield U

Coca-Cola Football League One
Blackpool v Swindon T
Bradford C v Bristol C
Brentford v Port Vale
Chesterfield v Walsall
Colchester U v Milton Keynes Dons
Doncaster R v Oldham Ath
Hartlepool U v Torquay U
Huddersfield T v Barnsley
Peterborough U v Hull C
Sheffield W v Bournemouth
Stockport Co v Luton T
Tranmere R v Wrexham

Coca-Cola Football League Two
Boston U v Shrewsbury
Bristol R v Lincoln C
Bury v Scunthorpe U
Chester v Cambridge U

Darlington v Northampton T
Grimsby T v Leyton Orient
Kidderminster H v Macclesfield T
Mansfield T v Rochdale
Notts Co v Southend U
Rushden & D'monds v Cheltenham T
Wycombe W v Swansea C
Yeovil T v Oxford U

Nationwide Conference
Accrington Stanley v Leigh RMI
Aldershot T v Dagenham & Red
Barnet v Gravesend & N
Burton Alb v Crawley T
Canvey Island v Halifax T
Carlisle U v Tamworth
Exeter C v Stevenage B
Forest Green R v Farnborough T
Hereford U v Scarborough
Morecambe v Woking
York C v Northwich Vic

Sunday, 19 September 2004
Barclays Premiership
Chelsea v Tottenham H* (4:05)
Southampton v Newcastle U* (2:00)

Monday, 20 September 2004
Barclays Premiership
Manchester U v Liverpool* (8:00)

Tuesday, 21 September 2004
Nationwide Conference
Barnet v Burton Alb
Canvey Island v Crawley T
Carlisle U v Scarborough
Farnborough T v Stevenage B
Forest Green R v Exeter C
Gravesend & N v Dagenham & Red
Halifax T v Morecambe
Hereford U v Aldershot T
Northwich Vic v Accrington Stanley
Tamworth v Woking
York C v Leigh RMI

Saturday, 25 September 2004
Barclays Premiership
Aston Villa v Crystal Palace
Bolton W v Bimingham C
Fulham v Southampton
Liverpool v Norwich C
Manchester C v Arsenal
Middlesbrough v Chelsea† (12:45)
Newcastle U v WBA
Tottenham H v Manchester U

340

Coca-Cola Football League Championship
Burnley v Stoke C
Derby Co v Wigan Ath
Gillingham v Brighton & HA
Ipswich T v Plymouth Arg
Leeds U v Sunderland
Nottingham F v West Ham U
Preston NE v Crewe Alex
QPR v Leicester C
Rotherham U v Millwall
Sheffield U v Coventry C
Watford v Reading
Wolverhampton W v Cardiff C

Coca-Cola Football League One
Barnsley v Chesterfield
Bournemouth v Doncaster R
Bristol C v Huddersfield T
Hull C v Stockport Co
Luton T v Peterborough U
Milton Keynes Dons v Hartlepool U
Oldham Ath v Colchester U
Port Vale v Blackpool
Swindon T v Bradford C
Torquay U v Tranmere R
Walsall v Brentford
Wrexham v Sheffield W

Coca-Cola Football League Two
Cambridge U v Grimsby T
Cheltenham T v Wycombe W
Leyton Orient v Boston U
Lincoln C v Chester
Macclesfield T v Darlington
Northampton T v Bristol R
Oxford U v Bury
Rochdale v Notts Co
Scunthorpe U v Mansfield T
Shrewsbury v Yeovil T
Southend U v Kidderminster H
Swansea C v Rushden & D'monds

Nationwide Conference
Accrington Stanley v Gravesend & N
Aldershot T v Carlisle U
Burton Alb v York C
Crawley T v Forest Green R
Dagenham & Red v Halifax T
Exeter C v Tamworth
Leigh RMI v Hereford U
Morecambe v Farnborough T
Scarborough v Barnet
Stevenage B v Northwich Vic
Woking v Canvey Island

Sunday, 26 September 2004
Barclays Premiership
Portsmouth v Everton* (4:05)

Monday, 27 September 2004
Barclays Premiership
Charlton Ath v Blackburn R* (8:00)

Tuesday, 28 September 2004
Coca-Cola Football League Championship
Burnley v Cardiff C
Gillingham v Leicester C
Ipswich T v Reading
Leeds U v Stoke C
Preston NE v Plymouth Arg
QPR v Coventry C
Rotherham U v Crewe Alex
Sheffield U v Sunderland
Watford v Wigan Ath
Wolverhampton W v Millwall

Wednesday, 29 September 2004
Coca-Cola Football League Championship
Derby Co v West Ham U
Nottingham F v Brighton & HA

Saturday, 2 October 2004
Barclays Premiership
Arsenal v Charlton Ath
Blackburn R v Aston Villa
Everton v Tottenham H
Manchester U v Middlesbrough
Norwich C v Portsmouth
Southampton v Manchester C† (12:45)
WBA v Bolton W† (5:15)

Coca-Cola Football League Championship
Brighton & HA v Sheffield U
Cardiff C v Leeds U
Coventry C v Ipswich T
Crewe Alex v Watford
Leicester C v Preston NE
Millwall v Nottingham F
Plymouth Arg v Gillingham
Reading v Burnley
Stoke C v QPR
Sunderland v Derby Co
West Ham U v Wolverhampton W
Wigan Ath v Rotherham U

Coca-Cola Football League One
Blackpool v Bournemouth

Bradford C v Barnsley
Brentford v Oldham Ath
Chesterfield v Bristol C
Colchester U v Port Vale
Doncaster R v Wrexham
Hartlepool U v Hull C
Huddersfield T v Walsall
Peterborough U v Torquay U
Sheffield W v Milton Keynes Dons
Stockport Co v Swindon T
Tranmere R v Luton T

Coca-Cola Football League Two
Boston U v Scunthorpe U
Bristol R v Oxford U
Bury v Macclesfield T
Chester v Swansea C
Darlington v Southend U
Grimsby T v Cheltenham T
Kidderminster H v Cambridge U
Mansfield T v Lincoln C
Notts Co v Leyton Orient
Rushden & D'monds v Rochdale
Wycombe W v Shrewsbury
Yeovil T v Northampton T

Nationwide Conference
Barnet v Woking
Canvey Island v Morecambe
Carlisle U v Crawley T
Farnborough T v Accrington Stanley
Forest Green R v Scarborough
Gravesend & N v Leigh RMI
Halifax T v Exeter C
Hereford U v Burton Alb
Northwich Vic v Dagenham & Red
Tamworth v Aldershot T
York C v Stevenage B

Sunday, 3 October 2004
Barclays Premiership
Bimingham C v Newcastle U (3:00)
Chelsea v Liverpool* (4:05)

Monday, 4 October 2004
Barclays Premiership
Crystal Palace v Fulham* (8:00)

Tuesday, 5 October 2004
Nationwide Conference
Accrington Stanley v Tamworth
Aldershot T v Gravesend & N
Burton Alb v Halifax T
Crawley T v Farnborough T

Dagenham & Red v Hereford U
Exeter C v Barnet
Leigh RMI v Carlisle U
Morecambe v York C
Scarborough v Northwich Vic
Stevenage B v Canvey Island
Woking v Forest Green R

Saturday, 9 October 2004
Coca-Cola Football League One
Barnsley v Brentford
Bournemouth v Stockport Co
Bristol C v Tranmere R
Hull C v Chesterfield
Luton T v Hartlepool U
Milton Keynes Dons v Bradford C
Oldham Ath v Blackpool
Port Vale v Doncaster R
Swindon T v Sheffield W
Torquay U v Huddersfield T
Walsall v Colchester U
Wrexham v Peterborough U

Coca-Cola Football League Two
Cambridge U v Bristol R
Cheltenham T v Chester
Leyton Orient v Bury
Lincoln C v Kidderminster H
Macclesfield T v Notts Co
Northampton T v Grimsby T
Oxford U v Darlington
Rochdale v Yeovil T
Scunthorpe U v Wycombe W
Shrewsbury v Rushden & D'monds
Southend U v Boston U
Swansea C v Mansfield T

Nationwide Conference
Accrington Stanley v Hereford U
Barnet v Dagenham & Red
Burton Alb v Gravesend & N
Canvey Island v Forest Green R
Crawley T v Northwich Vic
Exeter C v Carlisle U
Farnborough T v York C
Leigh RMI v Stevenage B
Morecambe v Tamworth
Scarborough v Aldershot T
Woking v Halifax T

Saturday, 16 October 2004
Barclays Premiership
Arsenal v Aston Villa
Bimingham C v Manchester U† (12:45)
Blackburn R v Middlesbrough

Bolton W v Crystal Palace
Everton v Southampton
Fulham v Liverpool
Manchester C v Chelsea
WBA v Norwich C

Coca-Cola Football League Championship
Cardiff C v Rotherham U
Coventry C v Leicester C
Crewe Alex v Brighton & HA
Derby Co v Watford
Gillingham v Sheffield U
Ipswich T v Burnley
Leeds U v Preston NE
Nottingham F v Wolverhampton W
Plymouth Arg v Wigan Ath
QPR v West Ham U
Stoke C v Reading
Sunderland v Millwall

Coca-Cola Football League One
Blackpool v Colchester U
Bournemouth v Port Vale
Bristol C v Hull C
Doncaster R v Torquay U
Hartlepool U v Chesterfield
Luton T v Huddersfield T
Milton Keynes Dons v Brentford
Sheffield W v Barnsley
Stockport Co v Peterborough U
Swindon T v Oldham Ath
Tranmere R v Bradford C
Wrexham v Walsall

Coca-Cola Football League Two
Boston U v Wycombe W
Cambridge U v Northampton T
Darlington v Bury
Grimsby T v Bristol R
Kidderminster H v Scunthorpe U
Leyton Orient v Shrewsbury
Mansfield T v Notts Co
Oxford U v Lincoln C
Rochdale v Cheltenham T
Rushden & D'monds v Chester
Southend U v Swansea C
Yeovil T v Macclesfield T

Nationwide Conference
Aldershot T v Accrington Stanley
Carlisle U v Barnet
Dagenham & Red v Leigh RMI
Forest Green R v Morecambe
Gravesend & N v Exeter C
Halifax T v Farnborough T

Hereford U v Woking
Northwich Vic v Burton Alb
Stevenage B v Crawley T
Tamworth v Scarborough
York C v Canvey Island

Sunday, 17 October 2004
Barclays Premiership
Charlton Ath v Newcastle U* (4:05)

Monday, 18 October 2004
Barclays Premiership
Portsmouth v Tottenham H* (8:00)

Tuesday, 19 October 2004
Coca-Cola Football League Championship
Brighton & HA v Cardiff C
Burnley v Coventry C
Leicester C v Ipswich T
Millwall v Gillingham
Preston NE v QPR
Reading v Leeds U
Rotherham U v Plymouth Arg
Sheffield U v Nottingham F
Watford v Sunderland
West Ham U v Stoke C
Wigan Ath v Crewe Alex
Wolverhampton W v Derby Co

Coca-Cola Football League One
Barnsley v Doncaster R
Bradford C v Blackpool
Brentford v Hartlepool U
Colchester U v Wrexham
Huddersfield T v Tranmere R
Hull C v Milton Keynes Dons
Oldham Ath v Bristol C
Peterborough U v Sheffield W
Port Vale v Swindon T
Torquay U v Bournemouth
Walsall v Luton T

Coca-Cola Football League Two
Bristol R v Yeovil T
Bury v Boston U
Cheltenham T v Mansfield T
Chester v Kidderminster H
Lincoln C v Rochdale
Macclesfield T v Cambridge U
Northampton T v Oxford U
Notts Co v Darlington
Scunthorpe U v Southend U
Shrewsbury v Grimsby T

Swansea C v Leyton Orient
Wycombe W v Rushden & D'monds

Wednesday, 20 October 2004
Coca-Cola Football League One
Chesterfield v Stockport Co

Saturday, 23 October 2004
Barclays Premiership
Aston Villa v Fulham
Chelsea v Blackburn R
Crystal Palace v WBA
Liverpool v Charlton Ath* (5:15)
Middlesbrough v Portsmouth
Newcastle U v Manchester C
Norwich C v Everton† (12:45)
Tottenham H v Bolton W

Coca-Cola Football League Championship
Brighton & HA v Leeds U
Burnley v Derby Co
Leicester C v Stoke C
Millwall v Cardiff C
Preston NE v Nottingham F
Reading v Crewe Alex
Rotherham U v Sunderland
Sheffield U v Plymouth Arg
Watford v Ipswich T
West Ham U v Gillingham
Wigan Ath v Coventry C
Wolverhampton W v QPR

Coca-Cola Football League One
Barnsley v Swindon T
Bradford C v Sheffield W
Brentford v Blackpool
Chesterfield v Doncaster R
Colchester U v Tranmere R
Huddersfield T v Milton Keynes Dons
Hull C v Luton T
Oldham Ath v Bournemouth
Peterborough U v Hartlepool U
Port Vale v Stockport Co
Torquay U v Wrexham
Walsall v Bristol C

Coca-Cola Football League Two
Bristol R v Kidderminster H
Bury v Rushden & D'monds
Cheltenham T v Cambridge U
Chester v Grimsby T
Lincoln C v Leyton Orient
Macclesfield T v Oxford U
Northampton T v Rochdale

Notts Co v Boston U
Scunthorpe U v Yeovil T
Shrewsbury v Southend U
Swansea C v Darlington
Wycombe W v Mansfield T

Nationwide Conference
Barnet v York C
Canvey Island v Leigh RMI
Carlisle U v Hereford U
Exeter C v Aldershot T
Farnborough T v Dagenham & Red
Forest Green R v Northwich Vic
Halifax T v Gravesend & N
Morecambe v Stevenage B
Scarborough v Accrington Stanley
Tamworth v Crawley T
Woking v Burton Alb

Sunday, 24 October 2004
Barclays Premiership
Manchester U v Arsenal* (4:05)
Southampton v Bimingham C* (2:00)

Saturday, 30 October 2004
Barclays Premiership
Arsenal v Southampton
Bimingham C v Crystal Palace† (12:45)
Blackburn R v Liverpool† (5:15)
Charlton Ath v Middlesbrough
Everton v Aston Villa
Fulham v Tottenham H
Portsmouth v Manchester U
WBA v Chelsea

Coca-Cola Football League Championship
Cardiff C v Leicester C
Coventry C v Reading
Crewe Alex v Sheffield U
Derby Co v Rotherham U
Gillingham v Wolverhampton W
Ipswich T v Preston NE
Leeds U v Wigan Ath
Nottingham F v Watford
Plymouth Arg v West Ham U
QPR v Burnley
Stoke C v Millwall
Sunderland v Brighton & HA

Coca-Cola Football League One
Blackpool v Huddersfield T
Bournemouth v Barnsley
Bristol C v Colchester U
Doncaster R v Peterborough U

Hartlepool U v Port Vale
Luton T v Bradford C
Milton Keynes Dons v Walsall
Sheffield W v Chesterfield
Stockport Co v Oldham Ath
Swindon T v Torquay U
Tranmere R v Brentford
Wrexham v Hull C

Coca-Cola Football League Two
Boston U v Bristol R
Cambridge U v Lincoln C
Darlington v Wycombe W
Grimsby T v Swansea C
Kidderminster H v Shrewsbury
Leyton Orient v Scunthorpe U
Mansfield T v Bury
Oxford U v Cheltenham T
Rochdale v Macclesfield T
Rushden & D'monds v Notts Co
Southend U v Northampton T
Yeovil T v Chester

Sunday, 31 October 2004
Barclays Premiership
Bolton W v Newcastle U* (4:05)

Monday, 1 November 2004
Barclays Premiership
Manchester C v Norwich C* (8:00)

Tuesday, 2 November 2004
Coca-Cola Football League
Championship
Cardiff C v West Ham U
Crewe Alex v Leicester C
Gillingham v Watford
Ipswich T v Sheffield U
Leeds U v Burnley
Plymouth Arg v Reading
QPR v Millwall
Stoke C v Wigan Ath
Sunderland v Wolverhampton W

Wednesday, 3 November 2004
Coca-Cola Football League
Championship
Coventry C v Preston NE
Derby Co v Brighton & HA
Nottingham F v Rotherham U

Saturday, 6 November 2004
Barclays Premiership
Aston Villa v Portsmouth† (12:45)
Chelsea v Everton

Crystal Palace v Arsenal* (5:15)
Liverpool v Bimingham C
Newcastle U v Fulham
Norwich C v Blackburn R
Southampton v WBA
Tottenham H v Charlton Ath

Coca-Cola Football League
Championship
Brighton & HA v Crewe Alex
Burnley v Ipswich T
Leicester C v Coventry C
Millwall v Sunderland
Preston NE v Leeds U
Reading v Stoke C
Rotherham U v Cardiff C
Sheffield U v Gillingham
Watford v Derby Co
West Ham U v QPR
Wigan Ath v Plymouth Arg
Wolverhampton W v Nottingham F

Coca-Cola Football League One
Barnsley v Port Vale
Bradford C v Colchester U
Bristol C v Milton Keynes Dons
Chesterfield v Blackpool
Hartlepool U v Doncaster R
Huddersfield T v Brentford
Hull C v Walsall
Luton T v Wrexham
Peterborough U v Bournemouth
Stockport Co v Sheffield W
Torquay U v Oldham Ath
Tranmere R v Swindon T

Coca-Cola Football League Two
Cheltenham T v Bury
Chester v Leyton Orient
Kidderminster H v Boston U
Lincoln C v Northampton T
Mansfield T v Macclesfield T
Notts Co v Shrewsbury
Rochdale v Cambridge U
Rushden & D'monds v Darlington
Scunthorpe U v Grimsby T
Southend U v Oxford U
Swansea C v Bristol R
Wycombe W v Yeovil T

Nationwide Conference
Accrington Stanley v Exeter C
Aldershot T v Morecambe
Burton Alb v Farnborough T
Crawley T v Woking
Dagenham & Red v Scarborough

345

Gravesend & N v Carlisle U
Hereford U v Barnet
Leigh RMI v Tamworth
Northwich Vic v Canvey Island
Stevenage B v Halifax T
York C v Forest Green R

Sunday, 7 November 2004
Barclays Premiership
Manchester U v Manchester C* (4:05)
Middlesbrough v Bolton W* (2:00)

Saturday, 13 November 2004
Barclays Premiership
Bimingham C v Everton† (5:15)
Bolton W v Aston Villa
Charlton Ath v Norwich C
Fulham v Chelsea
Liverpool v Crystal Palace
Manchester C v Blackburn R
Southampton v Portsmouth
Tottenham H v Arsenal* (12:00)

Coca-Cola Football League
Championship
Burnley v Nottingham F
Coventry C v Plymouth Arg
Gillingham v Derby Co
Ipswich T v Leeds U
Leicester C v Sunderland
Preston NE v Millwall
QPR v Wigan Ath
Reading v Cardiff C
Rotherham U v Wolverhampton W
Sheffield U v Watford
Stoke C v Crewe Alex
West Ham U v Brighton & HA

Sunday, 14 November 2004
Barclays Premiership
Newcastle U v Manchester U* (4:05)
WBA v Middlesbrough* (2:00)

Saturday, 20 November 2004
Barclays Premiership
Arsenal v WBA
Chelsea v Bolton W
Crystal Palace v Newcastle U
Everton v Fulham
Manchester U v Charlton Ath† (12:45)
Middlesbrough v Liverpool
Norwich C v Southampton
Portsmouth v Manchester C* (5:15)

Coca-Cola Football League
Championship
Brighton & HA v Burnley
Cardiff C v Preston NE
Crewe Alex v Gillingham
Derby Co v Sheffield U
Leeds U v QPR
Millwall v West Ham U
Nottingham F v Reading
Plymouth Arg v Stoke C
Sunderland v Ipswich T
Watford v Rotherham U
Wigan Ath v Leicester C
Wolverhampton W v Coventry C

Coca-Cola Football League One
Blackpool v Tranmere R
Bournemouth v Chesterfield
Brentford v Bradford C
Colchester U v Huddersfield T
Doncaster R v Stockport Co
Milton Keynes Dons v Luton T
Oldham Ath v Barnsley
Port Vale v Torquay U
Sheffield W v Hartlepool U
Swindon T v Hull C
Walsall v Peterborough U
Wrexham v Bristol C

Coca-Cola Football League Two
Boston U v Mansfield T
Bristol R v Scunthorpe U
Bury v Notts Co
Cambridge U v Rushden & D'monds
Darlington v Lincoln C
Grimsby T v Kidderminster H
Leyton Orient v Wycombe W
Macclesfield T v Cheltenham T
Northampton T v Chester
Oxford U v Rochdale
Shrewsbury v Swansea C
Yeovil T v Southend U

Nationwide Conference
Barnet v Accrington Stanley
Canvey Island v Hereford U
Carlisle U v Dagenham & Red
Exeter C v Leigh RMI
Farnborough T v Northwich Vic
Forest Green R v Burton Alb
Halifax T v Aldershot T
Morecambe v Crawley T
Scarborough v Stevenage B
Tamworth v Gravesend & N
Woking v York C

Sunday, 21 November 2004
Barclays Premiership
Blackburn R v Bimingham C* (4:05)

Monday, 22 November 2004
Barclays Premiership
Aston Villa v Tottenham H* (8:00)

Saturday, 27 November 2004
Barclays Premiership
Bimingham C v Norwich C
Bolton W v Portsmouth
Charlton Ath v Chelsea
Fulham v Blackburn R† (12:45)
Manchester C v Aston Villa
Southampton v Crystal Palace
Tottenham H v Middlesbrough
WBA v Manchester U

Coca-Cola Football League
Championship
Burnley v Millwall
Coventry C v Crewe Alex
Gillingham v Nottingham F
Ipswich T v Brighton & HA
Leicester C v Plymouth Arg
Preston NE v Derby Co
QPR v Cardiff C
Reading v Wigan Ath
Rotherham U v Leeds U
Sheffield U v Wolverhampton W
Stoke C v Sunderland
West Ham U v Watford

Coca-Cola Football League One
Barnsley v Blackpool
Bradford C v Oldham Ath
Bristol C v Sheffield W
Chesterfield v Swindon T
Hartlepool U v Bournemouth
Huddersfield T v Wrexham
Hull C v Brentford
Luton T v Doncaster R
Peterborough U v Port Vale
Stockport Co v Walsall
Torquay U v Colchester U
Tranmere R v Milton Keynes Dons

Coca-Cola Football League Two
Cheltenham T v Darlington
Chester v Oxford U
Kidderminster H v Northampton T
Lincoln C v Yeovil T
Mansfield T v Leyton Orient
Notts Co v Cambridge U

Rochdale v Boston U
Rushden & D'monds v Macclesfield T
Scunthorpe U v Shrewsbury
Southend U v Grimsby T
Swansea C v Bury
Wycombe W v Bristol R

Nationwide Conference
Accrington Stanley v Canvey Island
Aldershot T v Barnet
Burton Alb v Exeter C
Crawley T v Scarborough
Dagenham & Red v Morecambe
Gravesend & N v Woking
Hereford U v Tamworth
Leigh RMI v Farnborough T
Northwich Vic v Halifax T
Stevenage B v Forest Green R
York C v Carlisle U

Sunday, 28 November 2004
Barclays Premiership
Liverpool v Arsenal* (4:05)
Newcastle U v Everton* (2:00)

Saturday, 4 December 2004
Barclays Premiership
Arsenal v Bimingham C
Aston Villa v Liverpool
Blackburn R v Tottenham H* (5:15)
Chelsea v Newcastle U† (12:45)
Everton v Bolton W
Manchester U v Southampton
Norwich C v Fulham
Portsmouth v WBA

Coca-Cola Football League
Championship
Brighton & HA v Rotherham U
Cardiff C v Gillingham
Crewe Alex v Ipswich T
Derby Co v Coventry C
Leeds U v Leicester C
Millwall v Sheffield U
Nottingham F v QPR
Plymouth Arg v Burnley
Sunderland v West Ham U
Watford v Stoke C
Wigan Ath v Preston NE
Wolverhampton W v Reading

Nationwide Conference
Barnet v Leigh RMI
Canvey Island v Burton Alb
Carlisle U v Stevenage B

Exeter C v York C
Farnborough T v Aldershot T
Forest Green R v Accrington Stanley
Halifax T v Crawley T
Morecambe v Hereford U
Scarborough v Gravesend & N
Tamworth v Dagenham & Red
Woking v Northwich Vic

Sunday, 5 December 2004
Barclays Premiership
Crystal Palace v Charlton Ath* (4:05)

Monday, 6 December 2004
Barclays Premiership
Middlesbrough v Manchester C* (8:00)

Tuesday, 7 December 2004
Coca-Cola Football League One
Blackpool v Torquay U
Bournemouth v Bradford C
Brentford v Luton T
Colchester U v Barnsley
Doncaster R v Bristol C
Milton Keynes Dons v Peterborough U
Oldham Ath v Chesterfield
Port Vale v Tranmere R
Walsall v Hartlepool U
Wrexham v Stockport Co

Coca-Cola Football League Two
Bristol R v Chester
Bury v Wycombe W
Cambridge U v Scunthorpe U
Darlington v Mansfield T
Grimsby T v Notts Co
Leyton Orient v Southend U
Macclesfield T v Lincoln C
Northampton T v Cheltenham T
Shrewsbury v Rochdale
Yeovil T v Kidderminster H

Nationwide Conference
Accrington Stanley v Carlisle U
Aldershot T v Canvey Island
Burton Alb v Morecambe
Crawley T v Barnet
Dagenham & Red v Exeter C
Gravesend & N v Farnborough T
Hereford U v Forest Green R
Leigh RMI v Scarborough
Northwich Vic v Tamworth
Stevenage B v Woking
York C v Halifax T

Wednesday, 8 December 2004
Coca-Cola Football League One
Sheffield W v Hull C
Swindon T v Huddersfield T

Coca-Cola Football League Two
Boston U v Rushden & D'monds
Oxford U v Swansea C

Saturday, 11 December 2004
Barclays Premiership
Crystal Palace v Blackburn R
Everton v Liverpool† (12:45)
Manchester C v Tottenham H
Newcastle U v Portsmouth
Norwich C v Bolton W
Southampton v Middlesbrough
WBA v Charlton Ath

Coca-Cola Football League Championship
Burnley v Preston NE
Cardiff C v Sunderland
Crewe Alex v Plymouth Arg
Derby Co v Nottingham F
Leicester C v Reading
Millwall v Brighton & HA
QPR v Ipswich T
Rotherham U v Sheffield U
Stoke C v Coventry C
Watford v Wolverhampton W
West Ham U v Leeds U
Wigan Ath v Gillingham

Coca-Cola Football League One
Blackpool v Bristol C
Bradford C v Walsall
Colchester U v Hull C
Hartlepool U v Stockport Co
Luton T v Port Vale
Milton Keynes Dons v Wrexham
Oldham Ath v Huddersfield T
Peterborough U v Chesterfield
Sheffield W v Brentford
Swindon T v Doncaster R
Torquay U v Barnsley
Tranmere R v Bournemouth

Coca-Cola Football League Two
Bristol R v Macclesfield T
Bury v Southend U
Chester v Shrewsbury
Darlington v Leyton Orient
Kidderminster H v Rochdale
Lincoln C v Cheltenham T

Mansfield T v Rushden & D'monds
Northampton T v Boston U
Notts Co v Wycombe W
Oxford U v Cambridge U
Scunthorpe U v Swansea C
Yeovil T v Grimsby T

Nationwide Conference
Crawley T v Burton Alb
Dagenham & Red v Aldershot T
Farnborough T v Forest Green R
Gravesend & N v Barnet
Halifax T v Canvey Island
Leigh RMI v Accrington Stanley
Northwich Vic v York C
Scarborough v Hereford U
Stevenage B v Exeter C
Tamworth v Carlisle U
Woking v Morecambe

Sunday, 12 December 2004
Barclays Premiership
Arsenal v Chelsea* (4:05)
Aston Villa v Bimingham C* (1:00)

Monday, 13 December 2004
Barclays Premiership
Fulham v Manchester U* (8:00)

Saturday, 18 December 2004
Barclays Premiership
Bimingham C v WBA
Blackburn R v Everton
Bolton W v Manchester C
Chelsea v Norwich C
Liverpool v Newcastle U† (12:45)
Manchester U v Crystal Palace
Middlesbrough v Aston Villa
Tottenham H v Southampton

Coca-Cola Football League
Championship
Brighton & HA v Stoke C
Coventry C v Watford
Gillingham v Rotherham U
Ipswich T v Wigan Ath
Leeds U v Millwall
Nottingham F v Leicester C
Plymouth Arg v Derby Co
Preston NE v West Ham U
Reading v QPR
Sheffield U v Cardiff C
Sunderland v Burnley
Wolverhampton W v Crewe Alex

Coca-Cola Football League One
Barnsley v Peterborough U
Bournemouth v Swindon T
Brentford v Colchester U
Bristol C v Luton T
Chesterfield v Torquay U
Doncaster R v Sheffield W
Huddersfield T v Bradford C
Hull C v Tranmere R
Port Vale v Oldham Ath
Stockport Co v Milton Keynes Dons
Walsall v Blackpool
Wrexham v Hartlepool U

Coca-Cola Football League Two
Boston U v Darlington
Cambridge U v Bury
Cheltenham T v Kidderminster H
Grimsby T v Oxford U
Leyton Orient v Yeovil T
Macclesfield T v Northampton T
Rochdale v Bristol R
Rushden & D'monds v Scunthorpe U
Shrewsbury v Mansfield T
Southend U v Chester
Swansea C v Notts Co
Wycombe W v Lincoln C

Nationwide Conference
Accrington Stanley v Dagenham & Red
Aldershot T v Leigh RMI
Barnet v Tamworth
Burton Alb v Stevenage B
Canvey Island v Farnborough T
Carlisle U v Woking
Exeter C v Scarborough
Forest Green R v Halifax T
Hereford U v Gravesend & N
Morecambe v Northwich Vic
York C v Crawley T

Sunday, 19 December 2004
Barclays Premiership
Portsmouth v Arsenal* (4:05)

Monday, 20 December 2004
Barclays Premiership
Charlton Ath v Fulham* (8:00)

Sunday, 26 December 2004
Barclays Premiership
Arsenal v Fulham
Bimingham C v Middlesbrough* (3:30)
Blackburn R v Newcastle U
Chelsea v Aston Villa† (1:00)

Crystal Palace v Portsmouth
Everton v Manchester C
Manchester U v Bolton W
Norwich C v Tottenham H
Southampton v Charlton Ath
WBA v Liverpool* (6:00)

**Coca-Cola Football League
Championship**
Brighton & HA v Gillingham
Cardiff C v Wolverhampton W
Coventry C v Sheffield U
Crewe Alex v Burnley
Leicester C v Rotherham U
Millwall v Ipswich T
Plymouth Arg v QPR
Reading v Watford
Stoke C v Preston NE
Sunderland v Leeds U
West Ham U v Nottingham F
Wigan Ath v Derby Co

Coca-Cola Football League One
Blackpool v Hull C
Bradford C v Wrexham
Brentford v Torquay U
Chesterfield v Luton T
Colchester U v Bournemouth
Doncaster R v Milton Keynes Dons
Hartlepool U v Oldham Ath
Huddersfield T v Port Vale
Peterborough U v Swindon T
Sheffield W v Walsall
Stockport Co v Bristol C
Tranmere R v Barnsley

Coca-Cola Football League Two
Boston U v Lincoln C
Bristol R v Leyton Orient
Bury v Shrewsbury
Chester v Scunthorpe U
Darlington v Rochdale
Grimsby T v Macclesfield T
Kidderminster H v Swansea C
Mansfield T v Cambridge U
Notts Co v Northampton T
Rushden & D'monds v Oxford U
Wycombe W v Southend U
Yeovil T v Cheltenham T

Nationwide Conference
Accrington Stanley v Halifax T
Aldershot T v Forest Green R
Burton Alb v Tamworth
Crawley T v Gravesend & N
Dagenham & Red v Canvey Island

Exeter C v Hereford U
Leigh RMI v Northwich Vic
Morecambe v Carlisle U
Scarborough v York C
Stevenage B v Barnet
Woking v Farnborough T

**Tuesday, 28 December 2004
Barclays Premiership**
Aston Villa v Manchester U* (8:00)
Bolton W v Blackburn R
Charlton Ath v Everton
Fulham v Bimingham C
Liverpool v Southampton* (4:30)
Manchester C v WBA
Middlesbrough v Norwich C
Portsmouth v Chelsea
Tottenham H v Crystal Palace

**Coca-Cola Football League
Championship**
Burnley v Wigan Ath
Derby Co v Millwall
Gillingham v Coventry C
Ipswich T v Stoke C
Leeds U v Plymouth Arg
Nottingham F v Sunderland
Preston NE v Reading
QPR v Crewe Alex
Rotherham U v West Ham U
Sheffield U v Leicester C
Watford v Cardiff C
Wolverhampton W v Brighton & HA

Coca-Cola Football League One
Barnsley v Stockport Co
Bournemouth v Huddersfield T
Bristol C v Hartlepool U
Hull C v Doncaster R
Luton T v Colchester U
Milton Keynes Dons v Blackpool
Oldham Ath v Peterborough U
Port Vale v Sheffield W
Swindon T v Brentford
Torquay U v Bradford C
Walsall v Tranmere R
Wrexham v Chesterfield

Coca-Cola Football League Two
Cambridge U v Yeovil T
Cheltenham T v Bristol R
Leyton Orient v Rushden & D'monds
Lincoln C v Grimsby T
Macclesfield T v Wycombe W
Northampton T v Bury
Oxford U v Kidderminster H

Rochdale v Chester
Scunthorpe U v Notts Co
Shrewsbury v Darlington
Southend U v Mansfield T
Swansea C v Boston U

Nationwide Conference
Barnet v Scarborough
Canvey Island v Woking
Carlisle U v Aldershot T
Farnborough T v Morecambe
Forest Green R v Crawley T
Gravesend & N v Accrington Stanley
Halifax T v Dagenham & Red
Hereford U v Leigh RMI
Northwich Vic v Stevenage B
Tamworth v Exeter C
York C v Burton Alb

Wednesday, 29 December 2004
Barclays Premiership
Newcastle U v Arsenal* (8:00)

Saturday, 1 January 2005
Barclays Premiership
Aston Villa v Blackburn R
Bolton W v WBA
Charlton Ath v Arsenal
Fulham v Crystal Palace
Liverpool v Chelsea
Manchester C v Southampton
Middlesbrough v Manchester U
Newcastle U v Bimingham C
Portsmouth v Norwich C
Tottenham H v Everton

Coca-Cola Football League
Championship
Burnley v Leicester C
Derby Co v Cardiff C
Gillingham v Reading
Ipswich T v West Ham U
Leeds U v Crewe Alex
Nottingham F v Stoke C
Preston NE v Sunderland
QPR v Brighton & HA
Rotherham U v Coventry C
Sheffield U v Wigan Ath
Watford v Millwall
Wolverhampton W v Plymouth Arg

Coca-Cola Football League One
Barnsley v Hartlepool U
Bournemouth v Brentford
Bristol C v Peterborough U

Hull C v Huddersfield T
Luton T v Sheffield W
Milton Keynes Dons v Chesterfield
Oldham Ath v Tranmere R
Port Vale v Bradford C
Swindon T v Colchester U
Torquay U v Stockport Co
Walsall v Doncaster R
Wrexham v Blackpool

Coca-Cola Football League Two
Cambridge U v Boston U
Cheltenham T v Notts Co
Leyton Orient v Kidderminster H
Lincoln C v Bury
Macclesfield T v Chester
Northampton T v Mansfield T
Oxford U v Wycombe W
Rochdale v Grimsby T
Scunthorpe U v Darlington
Shrewsbury v Bristol R
Southend U v Rushden & D'monds
Swansea C v Yeovil T

Nationwide Conference
Barnet v Stevenage B
Canvey Island v Dagenham & Red
Carlisle U v Morecambe
Farnborough T v Woking
Forest Green R v Aldershot T
Gravesend & N v Crawley T
Halifax T v Accrington Stanley
Hereford U v Exeter C
Northwich Vic v Leigh RMI
Tamworth v Burton Alb
York C v Scarborough

Monday, 3 January 2005
Barclays Premiership
Arsenal v Manchester C
Bimingham C v Bolton W
Blackburn R v Charlton Ath
Chelsea v Middlesbrough
Crystal Palace v Aston Villa
Everton v Portsmouth
Manchester U v Tottenham H
Norwich C v Liverpool
Southampton v Fulham
WBA v Newcastle U

Coca-Cola Football League
Championship
Brighton & HA v Watford
Cardiff C v Nottingham F
Coventry C v Leeds U
Crewe Alex v Preston NE

Leicester C v QPR
Millwall v Rotherham U
Plymouth Arg v Ipswich T
Reading v Derby Co
Stoke C v Burnley
Sunderland v Gillingham
West Ham U v Sheffield U
Wigan Ath v Wolverhampton W

Coca-Cola Football League One
Blackpool v Port Vale
Bradford C v Swindon T
Brentford v Walsall
Chesterfield v Barnsley
Colchester U v Oldham Ath
Doncaster R v Bournemouth
Hartlepool U v Milton Keynes Dons
Huddersfield T v Bristol C
Peterborough U v Luton T
Sheffield W v Wrexham
Stockport Co v Hull C
Tranmere R v Torquay U

Coca-Cola Football League Two
Boston U v Leyton Orient
Bristol R v Northampton T
Bury v Oxford U
Chester v Lincoln C
Darlington v Macclesfield T
Grimsby T v Cambridge U
Kidderminster H v Southend U
Mansfield T v Scunthorpe U
Notts Co v Rochdale
Rushden & D'monds v Swansea C
Wycombe W v Cheltenham T
Yeovil T v Shrewsbury

Saturday, 8 January 2005
Coca-Cola Football League One
Blackpool v Oldham Ath
Bradford C v Milton Keynes Dons
Brentford v Barnsley
Chesterfield v Hull C
Colchester U v Walsall
Doncaster R v Port Vale
Hartlepool U v Luton T
Huddersfield T v Torquay U
Peterborough U v Wrexham
Sheffield W v Swindon T
Stockport Co v Bournemouth
Tranmere R v Bristol C

Coca-Cola Football League Two
Boston U v Southend U
Bristol R v Cambridge U
Bury v Leyton Orient

Chester v Cheltenham T
Darlington v Oxford U
Grimsby T v Northampton T
Kidderminster H v Lincoln C
Mansfield T v Swansea C
Notts Co v Macclesfield T
Rushden & D'monds v Shrewsbury
Wycombe W v Scunthorpe U
Yeovil T v Rochdale

Nationwide Conference
Accrington Stanley v Farnborough T
Aldershot T v Tamworth
Burton Alb v Hereford U
Crawley T v Carlisle U
Dagenham & Red v Northwich Vic
Exeter C v Halifax T
Leigh RMI v Gravesend & N
Morecambe v Canvey Island
Scarborough v Forest Green R
Stevenage B v York C
Woking v Barnet

Saturday, 15 January 2005
Barclays Premiership
Aston Villa v Norwich C
Bolton W v Arsenal
Charlton Ath v Bimingham C
Fulham v WBA
Liverpool v Manchester U
Manchester C v Crystal Palace
Middlesbrough v Everton
Newcastle U v Southampton
Portsmouth v Blackburn R
Tottenham H v Chelsea

Coca-Cola Football League Championship
Burnley v Reading
Derby Co v Sunderland
Gillingham v Plymouth Arg
Ipswich T v Coventry C
Leeds U v Cardiff C
Nottingham F v Millwall
Preston NE v Leicester C
QPR v Stoke C
Rotherham U v Wigan Ath
Sheffield U v Brighton & HA
Watford v Crewe Alex
Wolverhampton W v West Ham U

Coca-Cola Football League One
Barnsley v Huddersfield T
Bournemouth v Sheffield W
Bristol C v Bradford C
Hull C v Peterborough U

352

Luton T v Stockport Co
Milton Keynes Dons v Colchester U
Oldham Ath v Doncaster R
Port Vale v Brentford
Swindon T v Blackpool
Torquay U v Hartlepool U
Walsall v Chesterfield
Wrexham v Tranmere R

Colchester U v Luton T
Doncaster R v Hull C
Hartlepool U v Bristol C
Huddersfield T v Bournemouth
Peterborough U v Oldham Ath
Sheffield W v Port Vale
Stockport Co v Barnsley
Tranmere R v Walsall

Coca-Cola Football League Two
Cambridge U v Chester
Cheltenham T v Rushden & D'monds
Leyton Orient v Grimsby T
Lincoln C v Bristol R
Macclesfield T v Kidderminster H
Northampton T v Darlington
Oxford U v Yeovil T
Rochdale v Mansfield T
Scunthorpe U v Bury
Shrewsbury v Boston U
Southend U v Notts Co
Swansea C v Wycombe W

Coca-Cola Football League Two
Boston U v Swansea C
Bristol R v Cheltenham T
Bury v Northampton T
Chester v Rochdale
Darlington v Shrewsbury
Grimsby T v Lincoln C
Kidderminster H v Oxford U
Mansfield T v Southend U
Notts Co v Scunthorpe U
Rushden & D'monds v Leyton Orient
Wycombe W v Macclesfield T
Yeovil T v Cambridge U

Saturday, 22 January 2005
Barclays Premiership
Arsenal v Newcastle U
Bimingham C v Fulham
Blackburn R v Bolton W
Chelsea v Portsmouth
Crystal Palace v Tottenham H
Everton v Charlton Ath
Manchester U v Aston Villa
Norwich C v Middlesbrough
Southampton v Liverpool
WBA v Manchester C

Nationwide Conference
Barnet v Exeter C
Canvey Island v Stevenage B
Carlisle U v Leigh RMI
Farnborough T v Crawley T
Forest Green R v Woking
Gravesend & N v Aldershot T
Halifax T v Burton Alb
Hereford U v Dagenham & Red
Northwich Vic v Scarborough
Tamworth v Accrington Stanley
York C v Morecambe

Coca-Cola Football League Championship
Brighton & HA v Nottingham F
Cardiff C v Burnley
Coventry C v QPR
Crewe Alex v Rotherham U
Leicester C v Gillingham
Millwall v Wolverhampton W
Plymouth Arg v Preston NE
Reading v Ipswich T
Stoke C v Leeds U
Sunderland v Sheffield U
West Ham U v Derby Co
Wigan Ath v Watford

Saturday, 29 January 2005
Coca-Cola Football League One
Barnsley v Bradford C
Bournemouth v Blackpool
Bristol C v Chesterfield
Hull C v Hartlepool U
Luton T v Tranmere R
Milton Keynes Dons v Sheffield W
Oldham Ath v Brentford
Port Vale v Colchester U
Swindon T v Stockport Co
Torquay U v Peterborough U
Walsall v Huddersfield T
Wrexham v Doncaster R

Coca-Cola Football League One
Blackpool v Milton Keynes Dons
Bradford C v Torquay U
Brentford v Swindon T
Chesterfield v Wrexham

Coca-Cola Football League Two
Cambridge U v Kidderminster H
Cheltenham T v Grimsby T
Leyton Orient v Notts Co
Lincoln C v Mansfield T

Macclesfield T v Bury
Northampton T v Yeovil T
Oxford U v Bristol R
Rochdale v Rushden & D'monds
Scunthorpe U v Boston U
Shrewsbury v Wycombe W
Southend U v Darlington
Swansea C v Chester

Nationwide Conference
Accrington Stanley v Northwich Vic
Aldershot T v Hereford U
Burton Alb v Barnet
Crawley T v Canvey Island
Dagenham & Red v Gravesend & N
Exeter C v Forest Green R
Leigh RMI v York C
Morecambe v Halifax T
Scarborough v Carlisle U
Stevenage B v Farnborough T
Woking v Tamworth

Tuesday, 1 February 2005
Barclays Premiership
Arsenal v Manchester U
Bimingham C v Southampton
Bolton W v Tottenham H
Charlton Ath v Liverpool
Portsmouth v Middlesbrough
WBA v Crystal Palace

Wednesday, 2 February 2005
Barclays Premiership
Blackburn R v Chelsea
Everton v Norwich C
Fulham v Aston Villa
Manchester C v Newcastle U

Saturday, 5 February 2005
Barclays Premiership
Aston Villa v Arsenal
Chelsea v Manchester C
Crystal Palace v Bolton W
Liverpool v Fulham
Manchester U v Bimingham C
Middlesbrough v Blackburn R
Newcastle U v Charlton Ath
Norwich C v WBA
Southampton v Everton
Tottenham H v Portsmouth

Coca-Cola Football League
Championship
Brighton & HA v Derby Co
Burnley v Leeds U

Leicester C v Crewe Alex
Millwall v QPR
Preston NE v Coventry C
Reading v Plymouth Arg
Rotherham U v Nottingham F
Sheffield U v Ipswich T
Watford v Gillingham
West Ham U v Cardiff C
Wigan Ath v Stoke C
Wolverhampton W v Sunderland

Coca-Cola Football League One
Barnsley v Sheffield W
Bradford C v Tranmere R
Brentford v Milton Keynes Dons
Chesterfield v Hartlepool U
Colchester U v Blackpool
Huddersfield T v Luton T
Hull C v Bristol C
Oldham Ath v Swindon T
Peterborough U v Stockport Co
Port Vale v Bournemouth
Torquay U v Doncaster R
Walsall v Wrexham

Coca-Cola Football League Two
Bristol R v Grimsby T
Bury v Darlington
Cheltenham T v Rochdale
Chester v Rushden & D'monds
Lincoln C v Oxford U
Macclesfield T v Yeovil T
Northampton T v Cambridge U
Notts Co v Mansfield T
Scunthorpe U v Kidderminster H
Shrewsbury v Leyton Orient
Swansea C v Southend U
Wycombe W v Boston U

Nationwide Conference
Accrington Stanley v Scarborough
Aldershot T v Exeter C
Burton Alb v Woking
Crawley T v Tamworth
Dagenham & Red v Farnborough T
Gravesend & N v Halifax T
Hereford U v Carlisle U
Leigh RMI v Canvey Island
Northwich Vic v Forest Green R
Stevenage B v Morecambe
York C v Barnet

Saturday, 12 February 2005
Barclays Premiership
Arsenal v Crystal Palace
Bimingham C v Liverpool

354

Blackburn R v Norwich C
Bolton W v Middlesbrough
Charlton Ath v Tottenham H
Everton v Chelsea
Fulham v Newcastle U
Manchester C v Manchester U
Portsmouth v Aston Villa
WBA v Southampton

**Coca-Cola Football League
Championship**
Cardiff C v Brighton & HA
Coventry C v Burnley
Crewe Alex v Wigan Ath
Derby Co v Wolverhampton W
Gillingham v Millwall
Ipswich T v Leicester C
Leeds U v Reading
Nottingham F v Sheffield U
Plymouth Arg v Rotherham U
QPR v Preston NE
Stoke C v West Ham U
Sunderland v Watford

Coca-Cola Football League One
Blackpool v Brentford
Bournemouth v Oldham Ath
Bristol C v Walsall
Doncaster R v Chesterfield
Hartlepool U v Peterborough U
Luton T v Hull C
Milton Keynes Dons v Huddersfield T
Sheffield W v Bradford C
Stockport Co v Port Vale
Swindon T v Barnsley
Tranmere R v Colchester U
Wrexham v Torquay U

Coca-Cola Football League Two
Boston U v Bury
Cambridge U v Macclesfield T
Darlington v Notts Co
Grimsby T v Shrewsbury
Kidderminster H v Chester
Leyton Orient v Swansea C
Mansfield T v Cheltenham T
Oxford U v Northampton T
Rochdale v Lincoln C
Rushden & D'monds v Wycombe W
Southend U v Scunthorpe U
Yeovil T v Bristol R

Nationwide Conference
Barnet v Hereford U
Canvey Island v Northwich Vic
Carlisle U v Gravesend & N

Exeter C v Accrington Stanley
Farnborough T v Burton Alb
Forest Green R v York C
Halifax T v Stevenage B
Morecambe v Aldershot T
Scarborough v Dagenham & Red
Tamworth v Leigh RMI
Woking v Crawley T

Saturday, 19 February 2005
**Coca-Cola Football League
Championship**
Brighton & HA v Sunderland
Burnley v QPR
Leicester C v Cardiff C
Millwall v Stoke C
Preston NE v Ipswich T
Reading v Coventry C
Rotherham U v Derby Co
Sheffield U v Crewe Alex
Watford v Nottingham F
West Ham U v Plymouth Arg
Wigan Ath v Leeds U
Wolverhampton W v Gillingham

Coca-Cola Football League One
Barnsley v Bournemouth
Bradford C v Luton T
Brentford v Tranmere R
Chesterfield v Sheffield W
Colchester U v Bristol C
Huddersfield T v Blackpool
Hull C v Wrexham
Oldham Ath v Stockport Co
Peterborough U v Doncaster R
Port Vale v Hartlepool U
Torquay U v Swindon T
Walsall v Milton Keynes Dons

Coca-Cola Football League Two
Bristol R v Boston U
Bury v Mansfield T
Cheltenham T v Oxford U
Chester v Yeovil T
Lincoln C v Cambridge U
Macclesfield T v Rochdale
Northampton T v Southend U
Notts Co v Rushden & D'monds
Scunthorpe U v Leyton Orient
Shrewsbury v Kidderminster H
Swansea C v Grimsby T
Wycombe W v Darlington

Nationwide Conference
Accrington Stanley v Barnet
Aldershot T v Halifax T

Burton Alb v Forest Green R
Crawley T v Morecambe
Dagenham & Red v Carlisle U
Gravesend & N v Tamworth
Hereford U v Canvey Island
Leigh RMI v Exeter C
Northwich Vic v Farnborough T
Stevenage B v Scarborough
York C v Woking

Tuesday, 22 February 2005
Coca-Cola Football League
Championship
Cardiff C v Millwall
Crewe Alex v Reading
Gillingham v West Ham U
Ipswich T v Watford
Leeds U v Brighton & HA
Plymouth Arg v Sheffield U
QPR v Wolverhampton W
Stoke C v Leicester C
Sunderland v Rotherham U

Coca-Cola Football League One
Blackpool v Bradford C
Bournemouth v Torquay U
Bristol C v Oldham Ath
Doncaster R v Barnsley
Hartlepool U v Brentford
Luton T v Walsall
Milton Keynes Dons v Hull C
Stockport Co v Chesterfield
Tranmere R v Huddersfield T
Wrexham v Colchester U

Coca-Cola Football League Two
Cambridge U v Cheltenham T
Darlington v Swansea C
Grimsby T v Chester
Kidderminster H v Bristol R
Leyton Orient v Lincoln C
Mansfield T v Wycombe W
Rochdale v Northampton T
Rushden & D'monds v Bury
Southend U v Shrewsbury
Yeovil T v Scunthorpe U

Wednesday, 23 February 2005
Coca-Cola Football League
Championship
Coventry C v Wigan Ath
Derby Co v Burnley
Nottingham F v Preston NE

Coca-Cola Football League One
Sheffield W v Peterborough U
Swindon T v Port Vale

Coca-Cola Football League Two
Boston U v Notts Co
Oxford U v Macclesfield T

Saturday, 26 February 2005
Barclays Premiership
Aston Villa v Everton
Chelsea v WBA
Crystal Palace v Bimingham C
Liverpool v Blackburn R
Manchester U v Portsmouth
Middlesbrough v Charlton Ath
Newcastle U v Bolton W
Norwich C v Manchester C
Southampton v Arsenal
Tottenham H v Fulham

Coca-Cola Football League
Championship
Brighton & HA v Millwall
Coventry C v Stoke C
Gillingham v Wigan Ath
Ipswich T v QPR
Leeds U v West Ham U
Nottingham F v Derby Co
Plymouth Arg v Crewe Alex
Preston NE v Burnley
Reading v Leicester C
Sheffield U v Rotherham U
Sunderland v Cardiff C
Wolverhampton W v Watford

Coca-Cola Football League One
Barnsley v Torquay U
Bournemouth v Tranmere R
Brentford v Sheffield W
Bristol C v Blackpool
Chesterfield v Peterborough U
Doncaster R v Swindon T
Huddersfield T v Oldham Ath
Hull C v Colchester U
Port Vale v Luton T
Stockport Co v Hartlepool U
Walsall v Bradford C
Wrexham v Milton Keynes Dons

Coca-Cola Football League Two
Boston U v Northampton T
Cambridge U v Oxford U
Cheltenham T v Lincoln C
Grimsby T v Yeovil T
Leyton Orient v Darlington

356

Macclesfield T v Bristol R
Rochdale v Kidderminster H
Rushden & D'monds v Mansfield T
Shrewsbury v Chester
Southend U v Bury
Swansea C v Scunthorpe U
Wycombe W v Notts Co

Nationwide Conference
Barnet v Aldershot T
Canvey Island v Accrington Stanley
Carlisle U v York C
Exeter C v Burton Alb
Farnborough T v Leigh RMI
Forest Green R v Stevenage B
Halifax T v Northwich Vic
Morecambe v Dagenham & Red
Scarborough v Crawley T
Tamworth v Hereford U
Woking v Gravesend & N

Saturday, 5 March 2005
Barclays Premiership
Arsenal v Portsmouth
Aston Villa v Middlesbrough
Crystal Palace v Manchester U
Everton v Blackburn R
Fulham v Charlton Ath
Manchester C v Bolton W
Newcastle U v Liverpool
Norwich C v Chelsea
Southampton v Tottenham H
WBA v Birmingham C

Coca-Cola Football League
Championship
Burnley v Sunderland
Cardiff C v Sheffield U
Crewe Alex v Wolverhampton W
Derby Co v Plymouth Arg
Leicester C v Nottingham F
Millwall v Leeds U
QPR v Reading
Rotherham U v Gillingham
Stoke C v Brighton & HA
Watford v Coventry C
West Ham U v Preston NE
Wigan Ath v Ipswich T

Coca-Cola Football League One
Blackpool v Walsall
Bradford C v Huddersfield T
Colchester U v Brentford
Hartlepool U v Wrexham
Luton T v Bristol C
Milton Keynes Dons v Stockport Co

Oldham Ath v Port Vale
Peterborough U v Barnsley
Sheffield W v Doncaster R
Swindon T v Bournemouth
Torquay U v Chesterfield
Tranmere R v Hull C

Coca-Cola Football League Two
Bristol R v Rochdale
Bury v Cambridge U
Chester v Southend U
Darlington v Boston U
Kidderminster H v Cheltenham T
Lincoln C v Wycombe W
Mansfield T v Shrewsbury
Northampton T v Macclesfield T
Notts Co v Swansea C
Oxford U v Grimsby T
Scunthorpe U v Rushden & D'monds
Yeovil T v Leyton Orient

Nationwide Conference
Accrington Stanley v Forest Green R
Aldershot T v Farnborough T
Burton Alb v Canvey Island
Crawley T v Halifax T
Dagenham & Red v Tamworth
Gravesend & N v Scarborough
Hereford U v Morecambe
Leigh RMI v Barnet
Northwich Vic v Woking
Stevenage B v Carlisle U
York C v Exeter C

Saturday, 12 March 2005
Coca-Cola Football League
Championship
Burnley v Rotherham U
Coventry C v Cardiff C
Crewe Alex v Sunderland
Ipswich T v Nottingham F
Leeds U v Gillingham
Leicester C v Derby Co
Plymouth Arg v Brighton & HA
Preston NE v Wolverhampton W
QPR v Watford
Reading v West Ham U
Stoke C v Sheffield U
Wigan Ath v Millwall

Coca-Cola Football League One
Bristol C v Barnsley
Chesterfield v Huddersfield T
Doncaster R v Brentford
Hartlepool U v Tranmere R
Hull C v Torquay U

Luton T v Swindon T
Milton Keynes Dons v Port Vale
Peterborough U v Bradford C
Sheffield W v Blackpool
Stockport Co v Colchester U
Walsall v Bournemouth
Wrexham v Oldham Ath

Coca-Cola Football League Two
Boston U v Grimsby T
Bury v Bristol R
Darlington v Yeovil T
Leyton Orient v Cambridge U
Mansfield T v Oxford U
Notts Co v Kidderminster H
Rushden & D'monds v Northampton T
Scunthorpe U v Cheltenham T
Shrewsbury v Macclesfield T
Southend U v Lincoln C
Swansea C v Rochdale
Wycombe W v Chester

Nationwide Conference
Barnet v Crawley T
Canvey Island v Aldershot T
Carlisle U v Accrington Stanley
Exeter C v Dagenham & Red
Farnborough T v Gravesend & N
Forest Green R v Hereford U
Halifax T v York C
Morecambe v Burton Alb
Scarborough v Leigh RMI
Tamworth v Northwich Vic
Woking v Stevenage B

Tuesday, 15 March 2005
Coca-Cola Football League
Championship
Brighton & HA v Wigan Ath
Cardiff C v Ipswich T
Gillingham v Stoke C
Millwall v Coventry C
Rotherham U v Reading
Sheffield U v Preston NE
Sunderland v Plymouth Arg
Watford v Leicester C
West Ham U v Crewe Alex
Wolverhampton W v Burnley

Wednesday, 16 March 2005
Coca-Cola Football League
Championship
Derby Co v QPR
Nottingham F v Leeds U

Saturday, 19 March 2005
Barclays Premiership
Bimingham C v Aston Villa
Blackburn R v Arsenal
Bolton W v Norwich C
Charlton Ath v WBA
Chelsea v Crystal Palace
Liverpool v Everton
Manchester U v Fulham
Middlesbrough v Southampton
Portsmouth v Newcastle U
Tottenham H v Manchester C

Coca-Cola Football League
Championship
Brighton & HA v Reading
Cardiff C v Crewe Alex
Derby Co v Leeds U
Gillingham v Ipswich T
Millwall v Plymouth Arg
Nottingham F v Wigan Ath
Rotherham U v QPR
Sheffield U v Burnley
Sunderland v Coventry C
Watford v Preston NE
West Ham U v Leicester C
Wolverhampton W v Stoke C

Coca-Cola Football League One
Barnsley v Milton Keynes Dons
Blackpool v Doncaster R
Bournemouth v Hull C
Bradford C v Hartlepool U
Brentford v Chesterfield
Colchester U v Sheffield W
Huddersfield T v Stockport Co
Oldham Ath v Luton T
Port Vale v Walsall
Swindon T v Wrexham
Torquay U v Bristol C
Tranmere R v Peterborough U

Coca-Cola Football League Two
Bristol R v Mansfield T
Cambridge U v Wycombe W
Cheltenham T v Southend U
Chester v Notts Co
Grimsby T v Darlington
Kidderminster H v Rushden &
    D'monds
Lincoln C v Shrewsbury
Macclesfield T v Leyton Orient
Northampton T v Swansea C
Oxford U v Boston U

Rochdale v Scunthorpe U
Yeovil T v Bury

Nationwide Conference
Accrington Stanley v Morecambe
Aldershot T v Stevenage B
Barnet v Farnborough T
Carlisle U v Northwich Vic
Dagenham & Red v Forest Green R
Exeter C v Woking
Gravesend & N v Canvey Island
Hereford U v Crawley T
Leigh RMI v Burton Alb
Scarborough v Halifax T
Tamworth v York C

Friday, 25 March 2005
Nationwide Conference
Burton Alb v Accrington Stanley
Canvey Island v Carlisle U
Crawley T v Leigh RMI
Farnborough T v Hereford U
Forest Green R v Barnet
Halifax T v Tamworth
Morecambe v Exeter C
Northwich Vic v Gravesend & N
Stevenage B v Dagenham & Red
Woking v Scarborough
York C v Aldershot T

Saturday, 26 March 2005
Coca-Cola Football League One
Bristol C v Bournemouth
Chesterfield v Tranmere R
Doncaster R v Bradford C
Hartlepool U v Huddersfield T
Hull C v Port Vale
Luton T v Barnsley
Milton Keynes Dons v Swindon T
Peterborough U v Colchester U
Sheffield W v Torquay U
Stockport Co v Blackpool
Walsall v Oldham Ath
Wrexham v Brentford

Coca-Cola Football League Two
Boston U v Yeovil T
Bury v Grimsby T
Darlington v Kidderminster H
Leyton Orient v Cheltenham T
Mansfield T v Chester
Notts Co v Bristol R
Rushden & D'monds v Lincoln C
Scunthorpe U v Oxford U
Shrewsbury v Cambridge U

Southend U v Rochdale
Swansea C v Macclesfield T
Wycombe W v Northampton T

Monday, 28 March 2005
Coca-Cola Football League One
Barnsley v Walsall
Blackpool v Hartlepool U
Bournemouth v Milton Keynes Dons
Bradford C v Stockport Co
Brentford v Peterborough U
Colchester U v Chesterfield
Huddersfield T v Sheffield W
Oldham Ath v Hull C
Port Vale v Wrexham
Swindon T v Bristol C
Torquay U v Luton T
Tranmere R v Doncaster R

Coca-Cola Football League Two
Bristol R v Darlington
Cambridge U v Southend U
Cheltenham T v Swansea C
Chester v Bury
Grimsby T v Rushden & D'monds
Kidderminster H v Mansfield T
Lincoln C v Scunthorpe U
Macclesfield T v Boston U
Northampton T v Shrewsbury
Oxford U v Leyton Orient
Rochdale v Wycombe W
Yeovil T v Notts Co

Nationwide Conference
Accrington Stanley v York C
Aldershot T v Woking
Barnet v Canvey Island
Carlisle U v Halifax T
Dagenham & Red v Crawley T
Exeter C v Farnborough T
Gravesend & N v Forest Green R
Hereford U v Northwich Vic
Leigh RMI v Morecambe
Scarborough v Burton Alb
Tamworth v Stevenage B

Saturday, 2 April 2005
Barclays Premiership
Arsenal v Norwich C
Bimingham C v Tottenham H
Charlton Ath v Manchester C
Crystal Palace v Middlesbrough
Fulham v Portsmouth
Liverpool v Bolton W
Manchester U v Blackburn R

Newcastle U v Aston Villa
Southampton v Chelsea
WBA v Everton

**Coca-Cola Football League
Championship**
Burnley v Watford
Coventry C v Brighton & HA
Crewe Alex v Nottingham F
Ipswich T v Derby Co
Leeds U v Wolverhampton W
Leicester C v Millwall
Plymouth Arg v Cardiff C
Preston NE v Gillingham
QPR v Sunderland
Reading v Sheffield U
Stoke C v Rotherham U
Wigan Ath v West Ham U

Coca-Cola Football League One
Bristol C v Port Vale
Chesterfield v Bradford C
Doncaster R v Colchester U
Hartlepool U v Swindon T
Hull C v Barnsley
Luton T v Blackpool
Milton Keynes Dons v Oldham Ath
Peterborough U v Huddersfield T
Sheffield W v Tranmere R
Stockport Co v Brentford
Walsall v Torquay U
Wrexham v Bournemouth

Coca-Cola Football League Two
Boston U v Cheltenham T
Bury v Rochdale
Darlington v Chester
Leyton Orient v Northampton T
Mansfield T v Grimsby T
Notts Co v Lincoln C
Rushden & D'monds v Yeovil T
Scunthorpe U v Macclesfield T
Shrewsbury v Oxford U
Southend U v Bristol R
Swansea C v Cambridge U
Wycombe W v Kidderminster H

Nationwide Conference
Burton Alb v Aldershot T
Canvey Island v Exeter C
Crawley T v Accrington Stanley
Farnborough T v Carlisle U
Forest Green R v Tamworth
Halifax T v Leigh RMI
Morecambe v Scarborough
Northwich Vic v Barnet

Stevenage B v Hereford U
Woking v Dagenham & Red
York C v Gravesend & N

Tuesday, 5 April 2005
**Coca-Cola Football League
Championship**
Burnley v West Ham U
Crewe Alex v Derby Co
Ipswich T v Rotherham U
Leeds U v Sheffield U
Leicester C v Wolverhampton W
Plymouth Arg v Watford
Preston NE v Brighton & HA
QPR v Gillingham
Reading v Millwall
Stoke C v Cardiff C
Wigan Ath v Sunderland

Wednesday, 6 April 2005
**Coca-Cola Football League
Championship**
Coventry C v Nottingham F

Saturday, 9 April 2005
Barclays Premiership
Aston Villa v WBA
Blackburn R v Southampton
Bolton W v Fulham
Chelsea v Bimingham C
Everton v Crystal Palace
Manchester C v Liverpool
Middlesbrough v Arsenal
Norwich C v Manchester U
Portsmouth v Charlton Ath
Tottenham H v Newcastle U

**Coca-Cola Football League
Championship**
Brighton & HA v Leicester C
Cardiff C v Wigan Ath
Derby Co v Stoke C
Gillingham v Burnley
Millwall v Crewe Alex
Nottingham F v Plymouth Arg
Rotherham U v Preston NE
Sheffield U v QPR
Sunderland v Reading
Watford v Leeds U
West Ham U v Coventry C
Wolverhampton W v Ipswich T

Coca-Cola Football League One
Barnsley v Wrexham
Blackpool v Peterborough U

Bournemouth v Luton T
Bradford C v Hull C
Brentford v Bristol C
Colchester U v Hartlepool U
Huddersfield T v Doncaster R
Oldham Ath v Sheffield W
Port Vale v Chesterfield
Swindon T v Walsall
Torquay U v Milton Keynes Dons
Tranmere R v Stockport Co

Coca-Cola Football League Two
Bristol R v Rushden & D'monds
Cambridge U v Darlington
Cheltenham T v Shrewsbury
Chester v Boston U
Grimsby T v Wycombe W
Kidderminster H v Bury
Lincoln C v Swansea C
Macclesfield T v Southend U
Northampton T v Scunthorpe U
Oxford U v Notts Co
Rochdale v Leyton Orient
Yeovil T v Mansfield T

Nationwide Conference
Accrington Stanley v Stevenage B
Aldershot T v Crawley T
Barnet v Halifax T
Carlisle U v Forest Green R
Dagenham & Red v Burton Alb
Exeter C v Northwich Vic
Gravesend & N v Morecambe
Hereford U v York C
Leigh RMI v Woking
Scarborough v Farnborough T
Tamworth v Canvey Island

Saturday, 16 April 2005
Barclays Premiership
Arsenal v Everton
Bimingham C v Portsmouth
Charlton Ath v Bolton W
Crystal Palace v Norwich C
Fulham v Manchester C
Liverpool v Tottenham H
Manchester U v Chelsea
Newcastle U v Middlesbrough
Southampton v Aston Villa
WBA v Blackburn R

Coca-Cola Football League Championship
Burnley v Brighton & HA
Coventry C v Wolverhampton W
Gillingham v Crewe Alex

Ipswich T v Sunderland
Leicester C v Wigan Ath
Preston NE v Cardiff C
QPR v Leeds U
Reading v Nottingham F
Rotherham U v Watford
Sheffield U v Derby Co
Stoke C v Plymouth Arg
West Ham U v Millwall

Coca-Cola Football League One
Barnsley v Oldham Ath
Bradford C v Brentford
Bristol C v Wrexham
Chesterfield v Bournemouth
Hartlepool U v Sheffield W
Huddersfield T v Colchester U
Hull C v Swindon T
Luton T v Milton Keynes Dons
Peterborough U v Walsall
Stockport Co v Doncaster R
Torquay U v Port Vale
Tranmere R v Blackpool

Coca-Cola Football League Two
Cheltenham T v Northampton T
Chester v Bristol R
Kidderminster H v Yeovil T
Lincoln C v Macclesfield T
Mansfield T v Darlington
Notts Co v Grimsby T
Rochdale v Shrewsbury
Rushden & D'monds v Boston U
Scunthorpe U v Cambridge U
Southend U v Leyton Orient
Swansea C v Oxford U
Wycombe W v Bury

Nationwide Conference
Burton Alb v Carlisle U
Canvey Island v Scarborough
Crawley T v Exeter C
Farnborough T v Tamworth
Forest Green R v Leigh RMI
Halifax T v Hereford U
Morecambe v Barnet
Northwich Vic v Aldershot T
Stevenage B v Gravesend & N
Woking v Accrington Stanley
York C v Dagenham & Red

Tuesday, 19 April 2005
Barclays Premiership
Bolton W v Southampton
Middlesbrough v Fulham

Norwich C v Newcastle U
Portsmouth v Liverpool

Wednesday, 20 April 2005
Barclays Premiership
Aston Villa v Charlton Ath
Blackburn R v Crystal Palace
Chelsea v Arsenal
Everton v Manchester U
Manchester C v Bimingham C
Tottenham H v WBA

Saturday, 23 April 2005
Barclays Premiership
Arsenal v Tottenham H
Aston Villa v Bolton W
Blackburn R v Manchester C
Chelsea v Fulham
Crystal Palace v Liverpool
Everton v Bimingham C
Manchester U v Newcastle U
Middlesbrough v WBA
Norwich C v Charlton Ath
Portsmouth v Southampton

Coca-Cola Football League
Championship
Brighton & HA v West Ham U
Cardiff C v Reading
Crewe Alex v Stoke C
Derby Co v Gillingham
Leeds U v Ipswich T
Millwall v Preston NE
Nottingham F v Burnley
Plymouth Arg v Coventry C
Sunderland v Leicester C
Watford v Sheffield U
Wigan Ath v QPR
Wolverhampton W v Rotherham U

Coca-Cola Football League One
Blackpool v Chesterfield
Bournemouth v Peterborough U
Brentford v Huddersfield T
Colchester U v Bradford C
Doncaster R v Hartlepool U
Milton Keynes Dons v Bristol C
Oldham Ath v Torquay U
Port Vale v Barnsley
Sheffield W v Stockport Co
Swindon T v Tranmere R
Walsall v Hull C
Wrexham v Luton T

Coca-Cola Football League Two
Boston U v Kidderminster H
Bristol R v Swansea C
Bury v Cheltenham T
Cambridge U v Rochdale
Darlington v Rushden & D'monds
Grimsby T v Scunthorpe U
Leyton Orient v Chester
Macclesfield T v Mansfield T
Northampton T v Lincoln C
Oxford U v Southend U
Shrewsbury v Notts Co
Yeovil T v Wycombe W

Nationwide Conference
Aldershot T v Scarborough
Carlisle U v Exeter C
Dagenham & Red v Barnet
Forest Green R v Canvey Island
Gravesend & N v Burton Alb
Halifax T v Woking
Hereford U v Accrington Stanley
Northwich Vic v Crawley T
Stevenage B v Leigh RMI
Tamworth v Morecambe
York C v Farnborough T

Saturday, 30 April 2005
Barclays Premiership
Bimingham C v Blackburn R
Bolton W v Chelsea
Charlton Ath v Manchester U
Fulham v Everton
Liverpool v Middlesbrough
Manchester C v Portsmouth
Newcastle U v Crystal Palace
Southampton v Norwich C
Tottenham H v Aston Villa
WBA v Arsenal

Coca-Cola Football League
Championship
Burnley v Plymouth Arg
Coventry C v Derby Co
Gillingham v Cardiff C
Ipswich T v Crewe Alex
Leicester C v Leeds U
Preston NE v Wigan Ath
QPR v Nottingham F
Reading v Wolverhampton W
Rotherham U v Brighton & HA
Sheffield U v Millwall
Stoke C v Watford
West Ham U v Sunderland

Coca-Cola Football League One
Barnsley v Colchester U
Bradford C v Bournemouth
Bristol C v Doncaster R
Chesterfield v Oldham Ath
Hartlepool U v Walsall
Huddersfield T v Swindon T
Hull C v Sheffield W
Luton T v Brentford
Peterborough U v Milton Keynes Dons
Stockport Co v Wrexham
Torquay U v Blackpool
Tranmere R v Port Vale

Coca-Cola Football League Two
Cheltenham T v Macclesfield T
Chester v Northampton T
Kidderminster H v Grimsby T
Lincoln C v Darlington
Mansfield T v Boston U
Notts Co v Bury
Rochdale v Oxford U
Rushden & D'monds v Cambridge U
Scunthorpe U v Bristol R
Southend U v Yeovil T
Swansea C v Shrewsbury
Wycombe W v Leyton Orient

Nationwide Conference
Accrington Stanley v Aldershot T
Barnet v Carlisle U
Burton Alb v Northwich Vic
Canvey Island v York C
Crawley T v Stevenage B
Exeter C v Gravesend & N
Farnborough T v Halifax T
Leigh RMI v Dagenham & Red
Morecambe v Forest Green R
Scarborough v Tamworth
Woking v Hereford U

Saturday, 7 May 2005
Barclays Premiership
Arsenal v Liverpool
Aston Villa v Manchester C
Blackburn R v Fulham
Chelsea v Charlton Ath
Crystal Palace v Southampton
Everton v Newcastle U
Manchester U v WBA
Middlesbrough v Tottenham H
Norwich C v Bimingham C
Portsmouth v Bolton W

Coca-Cola Football League One
Blackpool v Barnsley

Bournemouth v Hartlepool U
Brentford v Hull C
Colchester U v Torquay U
Doncaster R v Luton T
Milton Keynes Dons v Tranmere R
Oldham Ath v Bradford C
Port Vale v Peterborough U
Sheffield W v Bristol C
Swindon T v Chesterfield
Walsall v Stockport Co
Wrexham v Huddersfield T

Coca-Cola Football League Two
Boston U v Rochdale
Bristol R v Wycombe W
Bury v Swansea C
Cambridge U v Notts Co
Darlington v Cheltenham T
Grimsby T v Southend U
Leyton Orient v Mansfield T
Macclesfield T v Rushden & D'monds
Northampton T v Kidderminster H
Oxford U v Chester
Shrewsbury v Scunthorpe U
Yeovil T v Lincoln C

Sunday, 8 May 2005
Coca-Cola Football League Championship
Brighton & HA v Ipswich T
Cardiff C v QPR
Crewe Alex v Coventry C
Derby Co v Preston NE
Leeds U v Rotherham U
Millwall v Burnley
Nottingham F v Gillingham
Plymouth Arg v Leicester C
Sunderland v Stoke C
Watford v West Ham U
Wigan Ath v Reading
Wolverhampton W v Sheffield U

Saturday, 14 May 2005
Barclays Premiership
Bimingham C v Arsenal
Bolton W v Everton
Charlton Ath v Crystal Palace
Fulham v Norwich C
Liverpool v Aston Villa
Manchester C v Middlesbrough
Newcastle U v Chelsea
Southampton v Manchester U
Tottenham H v Blackburn R
WBA v Portsmouth

OTHER FIXTURES — SEASON 2004–2005

July 2004

1 Thur UEFA Championship Finals –
Semi Final 2
3 Sat UEFA Intertoto Cup 2 (1)
4 Sun UEFA Intertoto Cup 2 (1)
UEFA Euro 2004 Champi-
onship Final
Luz Stadium, Lisbon – 8.45pm
(local time)
7 Wed
10 Sat UEFA Intertoto Cup 2 (2)
11 Sun UEFA Intertoto Cup 2 (2)
14 Wed UEFA Champions League 1Q
(1)
15 Thur UEFA Cup 1Q (1)
17 Sat UEFA Intertoto Cup 3 (1)
18 Sun UEFA Intertoto Cup 3 (1)
21 Wed UEFA Champions League 1Q
(2)
24 Sat UEFA Intertoto Cup 3 (2)
28 Wed UEFA Champions League 2Q
(1)
UEFA Intertoto Cup SF (1)
29 Thur UEFA Cup 1Q (2)
31 Sat

August 2004

4 Wed UEFA Champions League 2Q
(2)
UEFA Intertoto Cup SF (2)
7 Sat Start of Football League
8 Sun FA Community Shield
10 Tues UEFA Champions League 3Q
(1)
UEFA Intertoto Cup Final (1)
11 Wed UEFA Champions League 3Q
(1)
12 Thur UEFA Cup 2Q (1)
14 Sat Start of FA Premier League
18 Wed International (Friendly)
21 Sat
24 Tues UEFA Champions League 3Q
(2)
UEFA Intertoto Cup Final (2)
25 Wed UEFA Champions League 3Q
(2)
FL Carling Cup 1

26 Thur UEFA Cup 2Q (2)
27 Fri UEFA Super Cup
28 Sat FA Cup EP
30 Mon Bank Holiday

September 2004

1 Wed
4 Sat FA Cup P
FIFA World Cup – Austria v
England
5 Sun FA Women's Cup 1Q
8 Wed FIFA World Cup – Poland v
England
11 Sat FA Vase 1Q
13 Mon FA Youth Cup P**
14 Tues UEFA Champions League
Match Day 1
15 Wed UEFA Champions League
Match Day 1
16 Thur UEFA Cup (1)
18 Sat FA Cup 1Q
22 Wed FL Carling Cup 2
25 Sat FA Vase 2Q
26 Sun FA Women's Cup 2Q
27 Mon FA Youth Cup 1Q**
28 Tues UEFA Champions League
Match Day 2
29 Wed UEFA Champions League
Match Day 2
FL LDV Trophy 1
30 Thur UEFA Cup 1 (2)

October 2004

2 Sat FA Cup 2Q
6 Wed
9 Sat FA Trophy P
FIFA World Cup – England v
Wales
FA County Youth Cup 1*
10 Sun FA Sunday Cup 1
11 Mon FA Youth Cup 2Q**
13 Wed FIFA World Cup – Azerbaijan
v England
16 Sat FA Cup 3Q
19 Tues UEFA Champions League
Match Day 3

20 Wed UEFA Champions League
        Match Day 3
        FL LDV Trophy 2
21 Thur UEFA Cup Match Day 1
23 Sat FA Vase 1P
24 Sun FA Women's Cup 1P
25 Mon FA Youth Cup 3Q**
27 Wed FL Carling Cup 3
30 Sat FA Cup 4Q

November 2004

 2 Tues UEFA Champions League
        Match Day 4
 3 Wed UEFA Champions League
        Match Day 4
 4 Thur UEFA Cup Match Day 2
 6 Sat FA Trophy 1
        FA County Youth Cup 2*
10 Wed FL Carling Cup 4
13 Sat FA Cup 1P
        FA Youth Cup 1P**
14 Sun FA Women's Cup 2P
17 Wed International (Friendly)
20 Sat FA Vase 2P
21 Sun FA Sunday Cup 2
23 Tues UEFA Champions League
        Match Day 5
24 Wed UEFA Champions League
        Match Day 5
        FA Cup 1P (replays)
25 Thur UEFA Cup Match Day 3
27 Sat FA Trophy 2
        FA Youth Cup 2P*

December 2004

 1 Wed UEFA Cup Match Day 4
        FL Carling Cup 5
        FL LDV Trophy AQF
 2 Thur UEFA Cup Match Day 4
 4 Sat FA Cup 2P
 5 Sun FA Women's Cup 3P
 7 Tues UEFA Champions League
        Match Day 6
 8 Wed UEFA Champions League
        Match Day 6
11 Sat FA Vase 3P
        FA County Youth Cup 3*
12 Sun FA Sunday Cup 3
15 Wed UEFA Cup Match Day 5
        FA Cup 2P (replays)

16 Thur UEFA Cup Match Day 5
18 Sat FA Youth Cup 3P**
22 Wed
25 Sat Christmas Day
26 Sun Boxing Day
27 Mon Bank Holiday
28 Tues Bank Holiday

January 2005

 1 Sat New Year's Day
 3 Mon Bank Holiday
 5 Wed
 8 Sat FA Cup 3P
 9 Sun FA Sunday Cup 4P
12 Wed FL Carling Cup SF (1)
15 Sat FA Trophy 3
19 Wed FA Cup 3P (replays)
22 Sat FA Vase 4P
        FA Youth Cup 4P*
23 Sun FA Sunday Cup 4
26 Wed FL Carling Cup SF (2)
        FL LDV Trophy ASF
29 Sat FA Cup 4P
        FA County Youth Cup 4*
30 Sun FA Women's Cup 5P

February 2005

 5 Sat FA Trophy 4
 9 Wed International Friendly
        FA Cup 4P (replays)
12 Sat FA Vase 5P
13 Sun FA Sunday Cup 5
        FA Women's Cup 6P
16 Wed UEFA Cup 32 (1)
        FL LDV Trophy AF1
17 Thur UEFA Cup 32 (1)
19 Sat FA Cup 5P
        FA Youth Cup 5P*
22 Tues UEFA Champions League 16
        (1)
23 Wed UEFA Champions League 16
        (1)
24 Thur UEFA Cup 32 (2)
26 Sat FA Trophy 5
27 Sun FL Carling Cup Final

March 2005

 2 Wed FA Cup 5P (replays)
 5 Sat FA Vase 6P
        FA County Youth Cup SF*

8 Tues UEFA Champions League 16 (2)
9 Wed UEFA Champions League 16 (2)
FL LDV Trophy AF2
10 Thur UEFA Cup 16 (1)
12 Sat FA Cup 6P
FA Trophy 6
13 Sun FA Women's Cup SF
16 Wed UEFA Cup 16 (2)
17 Thur UEFA Cup 16 (2)
19 Sat FA Vase SF (1)
FA Youth Cup 6P*
20 Sun FA Sunday Cup SF
22 Tues FA Cup 6P (replays)
25 Fri Good Friday
26 Sat FIFA World Cup – England v
Northern Ireland
FA Vase SF (2)
28 Mon Easter Monday
30 Wed FIFA World Cup – England v
Azerbaijan

April 2005
2 Sat FA Trophy SF (1)
5 Tues UEFA Champions League QF (1)
6 Wed UEFA Champions League QF (1)
7 Thur UEFA Cup QF (1)
9 Sat FA Trophy SF (2)
FA Youth Cup SF (1)*
10 Sun FL LDV Trophy Final
12 Tues UEFA Champions League QF (2)
13 Wed UEFA Champions League QF (2)
14 Thur UEFA Cup QF (2)
16 Sat FA Cup SF
20 Wed
23 Sat FA Youth Cup SF (2)*

*Closing date of round
**Ties to be played week commencing

24 Sun FA Sunday Cup Final (prov)
26 Tues UEFA Champions League SF (1)
27 Wed UEFA Champions League SF (1)
28 Thur UEFA Cup SF (1)
30 Sat

May 2005
2 Mon Bank Holiday
FA Women's Cup Final
3 Tues UEFA Champions League SF (2)
4 Wed UEFA Champions League SF (2)
5 Thur UEFA Cup SF (2)
7 Sat End of Football League
11 Wed
14 Sat FA Vase Final
End of FA Premier League
FL Play Off SF (1)
18 Wed UEFA Cup Final
FL Play Off SF (2)
21 Sat FA Cup Final
22 Sun FA Trophy Final
25 Wed UEFA Champions League Final
28 Sat FL Division 3 Play Off Final
29 Sun FL Division 2 Play Off Final
30 Mon Bank Holiday
FL Division 1 Play Off Final

June 2005
4 Sat FIFA World Cup – No England Fixture
8 Wed FIFA World Cup – No England Fixture

To be decided
FA Youth Cup Final
FA County Youth Cup Final

CLUB AND OTHER RECORDS DURING 2003–2004

Arsenal
40 unbeaten Premier League matches.
Youngest goalscorer: Francesc Fabregas, 16 years 212 days.

Celtic
25 consecutive wins; 33 unbeaten games; 31 wins.

Doncaster Rovers
Most points: 92, Division Three.

Gillingham
Most capped player: Mamady Sidibe 7, Mali.

Grimsby Town
Most League appearances: John McDermott, 553.

Hartlepool United
Youngest League player: David Foley, 16 years 105 days.

Leeds United
Youngest Premier League appearance: Aaron Lennon, 16 years 129 days.

Liverpool
1226 wins; the highest for an English League club in history.

Manchester United
Ruud Van Nistelrooy scoring 15 goals in ten consecutive Premier League matches; Highest Premier League attendance: 67,758 v Southampton.

Newcastle United
Alan Shearer, 250th League career goal; Gary Speed, 400 Premier League appearances.

Norwich City
Most points: 94, Division One.

Notts County
4296 matches; the highest for an English League club in history.
Season's youngest League player: David McGoldrick, 16 years 56 days.

Rushden & Diamonds
Most capped player: Onandi Lowe 9, Jamaica.

Stranraer
Most League goals: 87.

Torquay United
Most points: 81, Division Three.

Wigan Athletic
Most League goals: Andy Liddell, 70.

Wycombe Wanderers
Most League appearances: Steve Brown, 371.

Champions League
Highest score: Juventus 7, Olympiakos 0;
Highest aggregate: Monaco 8, Deportivo La Coruna 3.

European Cups
Most appearances in European competitions:
Paolo Maldini, AC Milan 130.

England
Youngest goalscorer: Wayne Rooney, 17 years 317 days.

Football League
Most clubs played for in one season: Mickael Antoine-Curier, six: Oldham Ath, Kidderminster H, Rochdale, Sheffield W, Notts Co and Grimsby T.

FA Cup
Youngest finalist: Curtis Weston, Millwall, 17 years 119 days.

Now you can buy any of these other bestselling sports titles from your bookshop or *direct from the publisher*.

FREE P&P AND UK DELIVERY
(Overseas and Ireland £3.50 per book)

Sky Sports Football Yearbook 2004–2005	Glenda Rollin and Jack Rollin	£19.99
1966 and All That	Geoff Hurst	£6.99
Psycho	Stuart Pearce	£6.99
King John	John Charles	£7.99
The Autobiography	Gareth Edwards	£7.99
Vinnie	Vinnie Jones	£6.99
My Autobiography	Tom Finney	£7.99
A Lot of Hard Yakka	Simon Hughes	£7.99
Left Foot Forward	Garry Nelson	£6.99
The Way It Was	Stanley Matthews	£7.99
The Autobiography	Niall Quinn	£7.99
Fathers, Sons and Football	Colin Shindler	£6.99
Cloughie	Brian Clough	£7.99
My Autobiography	Garry Sobers	£6.99
Lions and Falcons	Jonny Wilkinson	£6.99
Taking Fresh Guard	Tony Lewis	£7.99
Menace	Dennis Lillee	£7.99

TO ORDER SIMPLY CALL THIS NUMBER

01235 400 414

or visit our website:
www.madaboutbooks.com

Prices and availability subject to change without notice.